BROADCAST/CABLE PROGRAMMING

Wadsworth Series in Mass Communication

Rebecca Hayden, Senior Editor

General

The New Communications by Frederick Williams

Mediamerica: Form, Content, and Consequence of Mass Communication, 3d, by Edward Jay Whetmore

The Interplay of Influence: Mass Media & Their Publics in News, Advertising, Politics by Kathleen Hall Jamieson and Karlyn Kohrs Campbell

Mass Communication and Everyday Life: A Perspective on Theory and Effects by Dennis K. Davis and Stanley J. Baran

Mass Media Research: An Introduction by Roger D. Wimmer and Joseph R. Dominick

The Internship Experience by Lynne Schafer Gross

Telecommunications

Stay Tuned: A Concise History of American Broadcasting by Christopher H. Sterling and John M. Kittross

Writing for Television and Radio, 4th, by Robert L. Hilliard

Communicating Effectively on Television by Evan Blythin and Larry A. Samovar

World Broadcasting Systems by Sydney W. Head

Broadcast/Cable Programming: Strategies and Practices, 2d, by Susan Tyler Eastman, Sydney W. Head and Lewis Klein

Advertising in the Broadcast and Cable Media, 2d, by Elizabeth J. Heighton and Don R. Cunningham

Strategies in Broadcast and Cable Promotion by Susan Tyler Eastman and Robert A. Klein

Modern Radio Station Practices, 2d, by Joseph S. Johnson and Kenneth K. Jones

The Magic Medium: An Introduction to Radio in America by Edward Jay Whetmore

Audio in Media by Stanley R. Alten

Television Production Handbook, 4th, by Herbert Zettl

Sight-Sound-Motion: Applied Media Aesthetics by Herbert Zettl

Electronic Cinematography: Achieving Photographic Control over the Video Image by Harry Mathias and Richard Patterson

Journalism

Media Writing: News for the Mass Media by Doug Newsom and James A. Wollert

Excellence in College Journalism by Wayne Overbeck and Thomas M. Pasqua, Jr.

When Words Collide: A Journalist's Guide to Grammar & Style by Lauren Kessler and Duncan McDonald

News Editing in the '80s: Text and Exercises by William L. Rivers

Reporting Public Affairs: Problems and Solutions by Ronald P. Lovell

Newswriting for the Electronic Media: Principles, Examples, Applications by Daniel E. Garvey and William L. Rivers

Free-Lancer and Staff Writer: Newspaper Features and Magazine Articles, 3d, by William L. Rivers and Shelley Smolkin

Magazine Editing in the '80s: Text and Exercises by William L. Rivers

This is PR: The Realities of Public Relations, 3d, by Doug Newsom and Alan Scott

Writing in Public Relations Practice: Form and Style by Doug Newsom and Tom Siegfried

Creative Strategy in Advertising, 2d, by A. Jerome Jewler

BROADCAST/CABLE PROGRAMMING

Strategies and Practices

Second Edition

Susan Tyler Eastman
Indiana University

Sydney W. Head
University of Miami

Lewis Klein
Temple University
Gateway Communications, Inc.

Wadsworth Publishing Company
Belmont, California
A Division of Wadsworth, Inc.

Senior Editor: Rebecca Hayden
Production Editor: Robin Lockwood
Designer: Hal Lockwood
Copy Editor: Stephen McElroy
Technical Illustrator: Terri Brand
Cover: Hal Lockwood

Printed in the United States of America

4 5 6 7 8 9 10—89 88 87

ISBN 0-534-03353-9

Library of Congress Cataloging in Publication Data

Eastman, Susan Tyler.
  Broadcast/cable programming.

  (Wadsworth series in mass communication)
  Rev. ed. of: Broadcast programming, strategies for winning
  television and radio audiences. c1981.
  Bibliography: p.
  Includes indexes.
  1. Television programs—Planning. 2. Radio programs—
Planning. I. Head, Sydney W. II. Klein, Lewis
III. Eastman, Susan Tyler. Broadcast programming,
strategies for winning television and radio audiences.
IV. Title. V. Series.
PN1992.55.E18 1984   791.44'0973   84-13172

Preface

In the short time since the original edition of this book in 1981, the subject matter has evolved considerably. Cable television has expanded and developed new forms; satellite relays have stimulated radio networking and format syndication; public broadcasting has reorganized; and the process of broadcast deregulation has advanced. We therefore made the following changes in addition to updating industry strategies and specific program examples:

- We now devote a separate part of this book to *cable television*, adding entirely new chapters on the programming of cable systems, basic cable networks, premium services and local origination.
- We *regrouped the chapters*, placing together television chapters, cable chapters, radio chapters and public broadcasting chapters. This regrouping closely fits the structure of many programming courses and permits teachers to conveniently reorder whole parts.
- Deregulation rendered moot most of the material on regulation in the previous edition, leading us to *recast the entire introductory part* of this edition. We reduced three chapters to one which directly introduces the rest of the chapters.
- We added a *chapter on program and audience research* covering the procedures and vocabulary of ratings analysis for broadcasting and cable. It includes reproduced pages from a variety of ratings books.
- We added a *chapter on radio networks and format syndicators* to lead the section on radio programming, indicating the revitalized role of nationwide radio programming.
- We expanded the *group-ownership chapter into radio and cable* to show the role that multiple-system owners are now having on cable programming.
- The dramatic alterations in *national public radio and public television* led to a complete reworking of these chapters and the addition of two new contributors.

Despite these changes, we believe our fundamental approach to the subject of programming proved viable and so have retained much of the first edition. As we said in the preface to that edition, only on the most generalized level can one make statements about programmers and their functions that apply equally to all sorts of programming situations. We start with such generalizations because all types of broadcasting and cable ultimately share certain common attributes, no matter how diverse the surrounding circumstances. But the heart of our book is the testimony of actual practitioners in varied programming situations.

One caveat should be made at the outset: We do not attempt to evaluate programming except in the pragmatic sense that progammers themselves use—

its ability to attract targeted audiences. This approach does not mean that we discount the importance of program quality or absolve broadcasters from responsibility for taking quality into consideration. We feel, however, that there is sufficient critical literature available. Our task was to examine objectively how programming decisions are actually made, whatever the wider artistic or social implications of those decisions might be.

ORGANIZING PRINCIPLES

One of the more perplexing problems we faced at the start was the decision as to what we meant by programming and hence what types of program decision makers we should include. It was tempting, for example, to think in terms of program genres and therefore to seek out experts in such specializations as sports, news and feature film programming. We were also tempted to call upon specialists in the making of programs, such as the package producers responsible for fashioning most of the network television entertainment programming.

We needed some defining principle that would impose limits and logical coherence on the selection of authors and the subjects of the chapters. In the end, we decided that we should confine the book to situations in which program executives are responsible not only for choosing and shaping individual programs or program segments but also for organizing such separate program items into coherent program services. It is universally recognized that an important—in some situations even the most important—part of the broadcast programmer's job is *scheduling*. Significant though producing organizations are in the creative aspects of program making, such organizations have no responsibility for designing entire program services. Instead, they focus their energies on turning out specific program series, leaving it to broadcast and cable programmers to decide if, when and how to use these programs in designing the continuous sequences that constitute broadcast or cable services. We therefore selected authors that had responsibility for the design of entire network, station or cable services.

We divided the job of the programmer into three arenas—*evaluation, selection and scheduling*—and structured each chapter to take account of current strategies and practices in each arena. Therefore, although selection and scheduling strategies are introduced in Chapter 1, and ratings are covered in detail in Chapter 2, each following chapter shows how selection and scheduling strategies and ratings are used in its programming situations. These three content topics guide the organization of the individual chapters in Parts 2, 3, 4 and 5.

STRUCTURE OF THE BOOK

The book divides into five major sections: Part 1 introduces the concepts and vocabulary for understanding the contexts of the remaining chapters; Parts 2, 3, 4 and 5 look at programming strategy for television, cable, radio and public broadcasting from the authors' perspectives as industry programming experts.

- Each *part* begins with a brief *overview,* relating the set of chapters to each other and the rest of the book.
- Each *chapter* is preceded by an *outline* of its headings and subheadings to provide a handy guide to its contents.
- A *summary* concludes each chapter, followed by *footnotes* and *selected reference sources.* The readings cite books, reports and trade publications that expand, support, complement or contrast with the subject of each chapter. These sources are annotated in the bibliography at the end of the book.
- An *afterword* closes the text—projecting some of the influences new technologies may have on the programming strategies in this book.
- A list of *abbreviations and acronyms* appears near the end of the book.
- Concepts and vocabulary pertaining to programming appear in the *glossary.*
- An *annotated bibliography* of books, articles, reports, guides, theses and dissertations on programming follows the glossary. References appearing in the footnotes are not repeated in the bibliography if they are highly topical or do not relate mainly to programming. For items on specific topics, readers should consult the *selected sources, chapter notes* and the *bibliography.*
- The *general index* at the end of the book is preceded by an *index of the movies and television and radio program titles* mentioned in the text.

ACKNOWLEDGMENTS

We want to thank warmly the individuals and organizations that assisted us: Bruce Austin, Rochester Institute of Technology; Joel Chaseman of Post-Newsweek Stations; Roger Jon Desmond of the University of Hartford; James Fiorito and Robert Libel of Warner Amex Cable; Robert Klein of Klein &; Timothy Meyer of the University of Wisconsin, Green Bay; James Miller of Showtime Entertainment; Herbert Seltz of Indiana University; Mitchell Shapiro of the University of Miami; James R. Smith of the State University of New York at New Paltz; Jacob J. Wakshlag of Indiana University; and Andy Yocom of WTTW in Chicago (who was also a first-edition author). All made useful suggestions that aided in the formation or refinement of specific chapters.

Rebecca Hayden of Wadsworth warmly supported and counseled us through both editions. Christopher Sterling of George Washington University assisted substantively with the first edition's bibliography. Charles R. Bantz of the University of Minnesota, David Eshelman of Central Missouri State University, Donald G. Godfrey of the University of Washington, Daniel E. Gold of Comcast, Ralph L. Smith of Illinois State University, Jacob J. Wakshlag of Indiana University and Robert D. West of Kent State University commented beneficially on the first edition manuscript in draft.

Most especially we thank Norman Marcus of Boston University, Timothy Meyer of the University of Wisconsin, Green Bay, and Mitchell Shapiro of the University of Miami who reviewed the second edition manuscript in painstaking detail and made many invaluable suggestions; and we thank John Lee Jellicorse of the University of North Carolina at Greenboro for his suggestions based on using the first edition. Our Production Editor, Robin Lockwood, handled the numerous last-minute changes with patience and good humor, and the copy editor, Steve McElroy, aided substantially with the writing's flow.

We are grateful to all these people for their help, to the National Association of Television Program Executives for sustaining a survey of its members and to the Department of Telecommunications at Indiana University for its support.

Susan Tyler Eastman
Sydney W. Head
Lewis Klein

Contents

PART ONE

*Programming
Principles, Methods,
Resources and Constraints*

Part I has a dual purpose. Chapters 1 and 2 provide concepts and vocabulary used in the rest of the book. Chapters 3 and 4 introduce broad perspectives that span the contents of two or more subsequent parts.

*Chapter 1 introduces the major concepts and vocabulary of programming strategy, providing a **framework** for the individual chapters that follow. It lays the groundwork for conceptualizing the essential nature of the programming function. Despite the tremendous variety of programming situations that occurs in broadcasting and cable, all programmers face similar problems and approach them with similar strategies. Common principles, then, underlie programming behaviors that can be understood by examining the programmer's options. Some of the constraints operating on programming situations are beyond the programmer's immediate control. Others leave latitude for the exercise of the programmer's skills. This chapter spells out the wide range of skills a programmer needs and reports what programmers have said about the characteristics of the job of programming.*

*Chapter 2 introduces the major concepts of program and audience **research** crucial to understanding many of the strategies in the remainder of the book. Subsequent authors in this book draw on these concepts, assuming that the reader is familiar with them. This chapter describes the qualitative and quantitative research tools of broadcasting and cable, explains how they can be put to use and assesses their programming value. The author focuses on national and local market ratings because they are the industry's primary method of program evaluation, providing the major measures of success and failure and the means for setting advertising rates. Authors in the rest of the book, especially in Chapters 3, 5, 9 and 13, supplement the measurement tools introduced in this chapter by discussing more specialized data collection methods and by reviewing highly specialized research and ratings reports. Chapter 2, then, supplies the reader with a basic understanding of how the industry evaluates programs and audiences.*

*Chapter 3 introduces the role of the station representative. A **rep programmer** works for one of about a half-dozen major station representative firms and brings a nationwide perspective to programming. Reps advise station and cable system programmers rather than program a station or service themselves. Of about two dozen national rep firms, only the largest have rep programmers. The firms help their clients because stations in dominant market positions are easy to sell to advertisers, the primary job of the rep firm. Rep programmers ensure that client stations' program schedules are salable, and they find national advertisers for some of the nationally distributed cable networks. In Chapter 3, the author also discusses many of the research reports that reps interpret and relay to their clients. Rep programmers concentrate on television station programming; they are less involved in radio programming, a more local activity. In the cable industry, group owners generally advise their owned systems on programming from a national perspective.*

*Chapter 4 covers **group ownership** of broadcasting stations and cable systems. Its content encompasses Parts II, III and IV on television, radio and cable. Group ownership refers to common ownership of two or more broadcasting stations or cable systems. There are over 150 group owners of television stations, averaging three stations each and including half of all television stations. Most of the nearly 10,000 commercial radio stations in the United States are owned by individuals or companies that own more than one radio station; many of them also own television stations or cable systems. And over 300 group owners of cable systems control from a few to hundreds of individual cable franchises, and often they also have interests in broadcasting. The author of Chapter 4 discusses the influence group ownership has on station and system programming.*

The four chapters making up Part I, then, discuss programming strategies from broad perspectives. The authors of these chapters supply an overview of programming strategies and the tools to interpret the more specialized chapters in the rest of the book.

CHAPTER ONE

A Framework for Programming Strategies

Sydney W. Head

A QUICK GUIDE TO CHAPTER ONE

SYDNEY W. HEAD *brings to this book a lifetime of experience with broadcasting, both as a practitioner and as an academic. After working as technical director of the university theater at the University of Colorado, he founded and administered as full professor and chairman the Department of Radio-Television-Film at the University of Miami (Florida). Later, he headed teams advising the governments of the Sudan and Ethiopia on radio broadcasting development. Between 1970 and 1980, he served as a senior faculty member at Temple University in Philadelphia. In 1980 he retired from Temple University only to be recalled to revise the curriculum of the department he had started at the University of Miami. During his teaching career, he wrote and produced many radio and television programs and, in addition to numerous journal articles, is author of* Broadcasting in America: A Survey of Television and Radio *(Houghton-Mifflin, 1982, fourth edition) and editor of* Broadcasting in Africa: A Continental Survey *(Temple University Press, 1974). He is presently working on a book on comparative broadcasting. His awards include a 1952 Kaltenborn Fellowship, an Academy of Television Arts and Sciences Fellowship in 1960, a Fulbright senior lectureship at the University of Ghana in 1976–77, and the 1983 Broadcast Education Association Service Award. His books have won Broadcast Preceptor Awards from San Francisco State University, including the first edition of this book.*

WHAT IS PROGRAMMING?

The program you see or hear on your receiving set arrived there at that moment and at that place on the dial or channel selector as the end result of two types of creative activity: *production* and *programming*. The two activities differ fundamentally. This book is about programming, not production, and because discussions of programming often get sidetracked into discussions about production, we want to draw the line between the two very explicitly at the outset.

Strategy vs. Tactics

We find it helpful to make the programming–production distinction in terms of *strategy* versus *tactics*. Strategy refers to the planning and directing of large-scale operations—in this case, entire schedules of broadcast stations and cable systems, and of broadcasting and cable networks. Tactics refers to the methods and techniques used to reach the goals that strategy has defined. Strategic considerations say that Hill No. 25 must be stormed and occupied; tactical operations carry out the assignment. It is no accident that terms associated with warfare fittingly describe the programmer's mission. Programmers work in a highly combative environment, besieged on all sides by rival programmers and competing media. The successful practitioner surveys the terrain, deploys the troops and goes on the attack. John Haldi concludes his chapter in this book on network affiliate strategies with the words, "Programming is war. You are a general. The object is to win!"

Programming generalship starts with searching out and selecting programming materials appropriate to a particular market and a predefined target audience. After negotiating to get the selected materials on the best possible terms, the programmer organizes the items into a coherent program service designed to appeal to the target audience. Finally, the programmer assesses results in terms of ratings reports, learning from mistakes, and returning to the fray with new insights. Boiling it down to a brief job description one can say:

> The programmer uses appropriate strategies in searching out and acquiring program materials designed to attract a defined audience in a specific market, and in scheduling program items so as to create a coherent program service.

The last point should not be overlooked: A program service adds up to more than the sum of its parts. Decisions about how to combine programs (or program elements) into an effective whole are just as important as decisions about which program items to accept or reject. Programming is not merely collecting so many bricks and throwing them into a pile; the bricks must be put in place, one by one, according to a rational plan. In the end, they form a structure, not just a meaningless jumble. The art of the schedule builder, like that of the architect, lends meaning to an otherwise meaningless assembly of parts.

This definition suggests that programmers must be skilled in at least seven areas of operation. They must (1) define an appropriate target audience for a given medium in a given market, (2) evaluate the potential of available programs and services, (3) know where to find programs, (4) negotiate program acquisition, (5) select from available program materials items best suited to a specific audience, (6) combine the selected materials into an identifiable program service and (7) participate in marketing that service to the public. Reduced to their simplest terms, these skills involve *evaluation, selection* and *scheduling*—concepts that will be encountered again and again in the following chapters.

In practice, programmers rarely have the luxury of starting up a brand-new program service. Usually they have to deal with an already existing set of programs, goals, assumptions and viewpoints. Therefore, the programmer's most likely first task will be to evaluate the strengths and weaknesses of an existing program schedule. Changes may have to be delayed while the new programmer straightens out the mess a predecessor left behind—at least that is the way it often seems to the newcomer.

Later in this chapter I will discuss each of the seven areas of programmer expertise in detail. First, however, let us survey the field of programming. Can we identify a general framework of programming strategies?

Diversity of Programming Environments

Programming takes place under circumstances so varied that many people question whether they share any common principles. Picture a small-town radio station in a one-station market. A husband and wife team own the station and do most of the work. They have only a limited range of programming decisions to make because the entire day unrolls according to a music formula. Under the formula, the DJs have a good deal of personal input. Therefore, hiring a new DJ to cover an important daypart becomes not just a personnel decision but a major programming decision as well.

The husband and wife can barely see one another across desks piled high with stacks of unanswered mail, promotional pieces, equipment catalogs, give-away discs, tapes, cartridges, old commercial copy, and trade journals. They sip coffee from battered mugs as they go over the pros and cons of hiring a new DJ. At last they decide to hire the best of a dozen applicants they have already interviewed to take over the 10 A.M. to 3 P.M. daypart.

The cable television equivalent of this minimal programming situation might be a small-town system with 1,500 subscribers. Nine of its twelve channels deliver television station signals. The remaining three supply a pay channel, a local origination channel and a superstation. Programming decisions for this system might consist of ordering a new alphanumeric service for the local origination channel, promoting a documentary on the superstation or (a more weighty decision!) changing to a different pay program supplier.

At the other extreme is the situation of a television prime-time network programmer. We can imagine him (we'll say it's a man because relatively few women as yet operate at this level in network hierarchies) in a luxuriously decorated executive office high above Manhattan's midtown traffic. Expensively tailored, he lounges at a marble-topped table that takes the place of a desk. He confers with several equally well turned out colleagues. Many weeks of close study and earnest debate have preceded this showdown meeting. Like the husband and wife team at the radio station, they are about to arrive at a momentous decision. One of their sit-coms, now scheduled at 8:30 Thursday nights, will be shifted to 8:00 Saturday nights!

This one decision will affect the viewing habits of millions of viewers. Millions of dollars in gross revenue are at stake. Some 200 television stations will feel the repercussions. Thousands of stockholders of affiliated stations as well as the network's own stockholders may eventually sense the shock waves. Prime-time network programmers make the most highly specialized, exacting and consequential decisions in the programming field. Their work has no parallel in other broadcasting or cable settings. Even the programming options and decisions of the country's largest cable system, Cox Cable, or those of Tele-Communications Inc., one of the largest multiple system operators, or of the nation's largest pay-television supplier, HBO, are not on the scale of network television programmers' decisions.

Between these extremes exist many other programming situations, each presenting its own special problems and opportunities—programming by group-owned television stations, for example, by community groups on access channels, by the public broadcasting system network, by over-the-air subscription television stations and so on. Because of this diversity, we thought it best to go to specialized programmers for information about the strategies used in various programming settings.

COMMON ATTRIBUTES

All of these programming environments, so different in size, scope and importance, share a number of attributes that have important implications for both production tactics and programming strategies. For present purposes, five of these shared qualities seem especially relevant: (1) the *ease* with which radio and television *deliver* materials to consumers, (2) the continuous, day-and-night *availability* of program services, (3) the ease of consumer *access*, (4) the capacity for *realism* and (5) their potential for exerting *social effects*. Note that this book uses the term *radio and television* to mean programs delivered either directly from broadcasting stations or through the intermediary of cable systems, many of which carry radio stations as well as television stations. When used alone, the words *broadcasting* and *cable* distinguish explicitly between the two methods of delivery.

Ease of Delivery

The attribute of *wirelessness* sets broadcasting apart from other communications media. Because of it, broadcasting can reach larger numbers of people simultaneously than any other medium. Moreover, unlike other media within a given area, it costs a television or radio station no more to reach a million people than to reach only one person.

To take advantage of this potential, programmers must motivate people to buy, to maintain and to use receiving sets. Audience members will make this investment of time and money only if they find programs worthwhile by their own standards—not by the standards of other people or those of some ideal goal. Cable television relies on the same free-will investment in receivers as does broadcasting; indeed, in most cases, broadcasting alone motivated the initial receiver purchase. By definition, however, cable is not wireless; therefore, it becomes cost ineffective if its customers are too widely dispersed. Nevertheless, like broadcasting, it delivers programs directly to the home receiver; and, once the cable installation has been made, the consumer accepts both broadcast and cable signals on equal terms.

The fact that both broadcasting and cable deliver their services directly to the home with minimum effort on the part of its occupants has important consequences for programmers. Television remains essentially a home-centered activity. Studies of how people use their leisure time put television (whether broadcast or cable) at the top of the list as the primary leisure-time activity in the home, ahead of reading, music and yes—even ahead of sex. This attribute, home-centeredness, limits what programmers can safely schedule without raising a storm of protest about "undermining the family," but it also permits programmers to schedule programs to fit into the typical pattern of home activities.

The jury is still out on whether or not cable will in the long run be less constrained by its use in the home environment than broadcasting has been. At present, some cable programmers offer pornographic channels, arguing that broadcasting precedents against pornography do not necessarily apply to cable, which comes into the home only by invitation and upon payment of a subscription fee. Moreover, cable uses private means of delivery, namely the coaxial cable network installed by the cable company, not the public airwaves. Long, drawn-out legal battles can be expected before the legal status of the two media are resolved.

In view of the changing nature of the family, we might also ask whether the traditional view of broadcasting as home-centered remains valid. Certainly programmers must take into account current trends toward single-person households and single-parent families. In single-parent households, the child has even greater control over television viewing and the choice of channels than when two adults are present; in the after-school hours, "latchkey" children use all the home-centered media without supervision, a programming situation requiring great variety in entertainment and information to hold their attention. Working adults comprising single-person homes find their time at a premium and spend it with television only when they feel they are getting adequate value. Adults not bound by child-centered activities insist on scheduling patterns that suit their convenience; television becomes a disposable medium, automatically recorded, edited and replayed (or not) at the user's whim. Using the past as a guide to programming strategies becomes increasingly problematic as living styles change.

Continuous Availability

Both cable and broadcasting are continuously available, making compatibility strategies possible. Whereas books, newspapers, magazines or movies deliver discrete items of content, radio and television have a continuously unfolding nature. They are always *there*, but also always *imminent*. The most routine program might be interrupted for an unscheduled and possibly vitally important message. This quality of incipience creates suspense and gives television and radio a special usefulness unique to them alone.

Their continuous availability also means radio and television consume program material relentlessly, compelling conservation of resources—typically by using the same program over and over again in many different markets and countries. Chief among conservation mechanisms are *networking* and *syndication,* the primary means of reducing programming costs to manageable proportions by sharing them among many users, on an international as well as national scale.

Ease of Access

Broadcast and cable audiences need no preparation to become audience members. People need not learn to read, buy a ticket, get dressed or assemble at a special place outside the home. Thus these media reach a wider, more varied group of consumers than any other medium. Broadcasting, more than cable, can surmount geographic and economic barriers to reach rich and poor, old and young, rural and urban dwellers, the educated and the dropouts, the shut-ins and travelers, blue-collar workers and professionals, minorities and majorities. For economic reasons, cable will probably never be as accessible as broadcasting. Fees for cable services keep some people out of its audience, and the need for installing expensive connecting links to each individual home makes it uneconomical to install cable in rural areas.

The heterogeneity of people within reach of broadcasting and cable has important implications for programmers. It means the creation of larger audiences than ever before possible, creating the need for a new type of program material. Prime-time broadcasting presents a challenging situation to programmers—how to interest and entertain audiences of unprecedented size and dissimilarity on a daily basis, year in and year out. Of course, most programmers aim at much smaller, more localized audiences than do those responsible for prime-time network television. But always they face the challenge of *maximizing and maintaining audience size*, even for the most narrowly defined subcategory of the population.

Capacity for Realism

Among the most memorable and highest rated of radio and television achievements have been their coverage of actual news and sports events—the burning of the zeppelin Hindenburg, the Kennedy funeral, the Apollo moon landing, the Superbowl and World Cup games—real-life events picked up as they actually transpired. That the media deliver the sights and sounds of real events even as they take place compels our attention.

Cable has exploited this potential to good effect. The all-news cable services, lacking the time constraints of broadcast television newscasts, present extended live coverage of events. Cable-Satellite Public Affairs Network, C-SPAN, sponsored primarily by the cable industry, provides a unique service with its live, gavel-to-gavel coverage of House of Representatives' sessions and other events in Washington, D.C. Entertainment as well as news, public affairs and sports programs make use of the media's capacity for relaying real events in real time.

Potential for Social Impact

Though described separately for purposes of analysis, in practice the four previously mentioned attributes work together, giving radio and television unique power among the media to affect audiences, to reflect and shape social change. This impact comes from the combined weight of their ability to enter directly into the home, from their continuous and almost universal availability, from their easy accessibility, from their realism. Government regulation, industry self-regulation and audience response constantly remind programmers that they must keep in mind the social consequences of their decisions.

COMMON STRATEGIES

Given that radio and television have the attributes just described, what programming strategies do they imply? What can programmers learn from studying and reflecting on the media's characteristics? Five principles emerge from the experts who wrote the specialist chapters in this book that they regard as major sources of the strategies they employ—though they do not necessarily use the same terminology in describing them. The five principles, briefly character-ized, consist of: (1) compatibility, (2) habit formation, (3) control of audience flow, (4) conservation of program resources and (5) mass appeal.

Compatibility Principle

Scheduling strategies take advantage of the fact that programs can be timed to coincide with what people do throughout the daily cycle of their lives. The continuous unfolding nature of radio and television allows programmers to schedule different kinds of program material, or similar program materials in different ways, in the various dayparts. They strive to make their programming *compatible* with the day's round of what most people do—getting up in the morning and preparing for the day, driving to work, doing the morning household chores, the luncheon period, the afternoon lull, the ingathering of children in the late afternoon, the reaccelerated tempo of home activities as the day draws to a close, the relaxed atmosphere of early prime time, the more exclusively adult interests of later prime time, late fringe hours and the small hours of the morning before the whole cycle begins again. And, of course, the compatibility principle calls for adaptation to the changed schedule of Saturday and Sunday activities.

Compatibility strategies affect not only scheduling, but also the choice of program types and subject matters. The programmer must consider both who the audience is in each daypart and what the available audience members are most likely to be doing at the time. To apply the compatibility principle, the programmer studies the *lifestyles* of listeners and viewers. For this reason and for many others, programmers must know the community for which they design their program schedules. As a concrete example, in his chapter on radio music programming, Edd Routt advises programmers to "observe lifestyles by visiting restaurants, shopping centers, gas stations, discotheques, bars, taverns and other places where people let their hair down."

Subsequent chapters will describe compatibility strategies in specific pro-gramming environments. These strategies are spoken of in terms of *dayparting,* the scheduling of different types of programs to match parts of the day known by such terms as *drive time, fringe time* and *prime time.* Even in the rigid format of all-news radio, as Brewer and Eastman point out, the format must be subtly adjusted to suit the needs of different dayparts.

Cable television's approach to compatibility differs from broadcasting's approach. Because each broadcast station or network has only a single channel at its disposal, broadcast programmers must plan compatibility strategies for the "typical" lifestyle in its target audience. But cable can devote entire channels to atypical audiences. It can cater to the night-shift worker by scheduling football at 6 A.M., to the single-person household with movies at 6 P.M., to the teenager with round-the-clock musical performance shorts (**videos**) using separate deliv-ery channels.

Time-zone differences work both for and against compatibility goals, as Sid Pike details in his chapter on superstation strategies. A children's program on superstation WTBS-TV in Atlanta at 7 A.M. would turn up on cable systems in California at 4 A.M.—hardly a compatible hour. On the other hand, an evening sports event in Atlanta kicking off at 5 or 6 P.M. on cable in the West might be welcomed by sports enthusiasts having no interest in watching the sit-coms or news that most local stations probably carry at those hours. In her chapter on programming for cable systems, Susan Eastman lists a dozen specialized services, about half of which are unique to cable, such as the all-weather and all-games channels. Such *dedicated* cable channels (in the sense that they devote themselves to single subjects) will always be compatible with some of the people some of the time. Cable operators need not worry about the majority of subscribers not interested in weather at any particular moment because they can still serve those subscribers with other channels.

Habit Formation

The compatibility principle acquires even more power because audience members form listening and watching *habits*. Scheduling programs for strict predictability (along with promotional efforts to make people aware of both the service as a whole and of individual programs) establishes tuning habits that eventually become automatic. Indeed, some people will go to extraordinary lengths to avoid missing the next episode in a favorite series. Programmers discovered this principle in the early days of radio when the *Amos 'n' Andy* habit became so strong that movie theaters in the 1930s shut down their pictures temporarily and hooked radios into their sound systems at 7:15 P.M. when *Amos 'n' Andy* came on. About that time the fanatic loyalty of soap-opera fans to their favorite series also became apparent, a loyalty still cultivated by today's televised serial dramas.

Ideally, habit formation calls for **stripping** programs—scheduling them Monday through Friday at the same time each day. To strip prime-time programs, however, would require building up a backlog of these expensive shows, which would tie up far too much capital. Moreover, networks want maximum latitude for strategic maneuvers in the all-important prime-time schedule. If a broadcast network stripped its three prime-time hours with the same six half-hour shows each night, it would be left with only six pawns to move around in the scheduling chess game, instead of the twenty or so pawns that weekly scheduling of programs of varying length makes possible.

However, when weekly prime-time network shows go into **syndication**, stations and cable systems schedule them daily, a strategy requiring a large number of episodes. According to Ed Aiken in his chapter on independent television station programming strategies, a prime-time series must have been on the network at least five years to accumulate enough for a year's stripping in syndication (including a substantial number of reruns). Since few weekly shows survive five years of prime-time competition, the industry faces a nagging shortage of quality, off-network programs suitable for syndication.

Like all programming rules, those concerning habit formation are subject to selective violation. The most brilliant of the early television strategists, Sylvester "Pat" Weaver, president of NBC, recognized that too much predictability can beget boredom. In the 1950s he invented the *spectacular* (nowadays called the *special*). Although at the time it seemed like a potentially destructive maneuver, Weaver boldly broke the established pattern of routine scheduling in prime time with one-time, blockbuster programs, usually much longer than the normal series episodes they displaced. The interruption itself attracted attention, furnishing a peg on which to hang special promotional campaigns.

In the 1970s, the number of specials increased greatly, spurred on by the discovery that audience members with the most purchasing power, the ones advertisers especially covet, tolerated schedule irregularities and found the specials attractive. The more habit-bound viewers, in both younger and older age ranges, interested advertisers less than the ones that favored change.

More recently, research data on people's feelings about television (as compared with simple tuning data) suggest that the increased variety of programs and schedule options made possible by cable television and home video recording may be weakening viewing habits. One survey found that fewer than half of a sample of viewers chose *in advance* the programs they watched. Furthermore, channel switching occurred more often in cable homes than in broadcast-only homes.[1] But even so, one can hypothesize that some people may prefer to have only a limited number of choices. They may find it confusing and wearying to sift through scores of options before settling on a program. Broadcast scheduling, as a result of compatibility strategies, preselects a varied sequence of listening and viewing experiences, skillfully adapted to the desires and needs of a target audience. People choose an entire service—an overall pattern (or "sound" in the case of radio)—rather than individual programs.

No definitive research has settled the question of whether audiences find themselves more comfortable with the structured, compatible, predictable scheduling of traditional broadcasting than with a multitude of programming choices. However, researchers have often observed that when dozens or scores of options are available to listeners and viewers, most tune in to only a very few of the possible sources. For example, a 1983 A.C. Nielsen survey of homes with access to 20 or more television channels found that viewers watched only 8 of the 20 for more than an hour per week; other studies show viewers tuning an average of 10 channels. The most successful of the cable network programming services come from superstations, which supply broadcast-oriented program schedules (though, as noted earlier, distribution of superstation programs through several time zones undermines compatibility). As Eastman points out in discussing cable programming strategies, some of the leading cable satellite channels have turned to dayparting for compatibility in the manner of broadcasting networks. She refers to such operations as "full-service" cable networks, citing USA Network as an example.

Control of Audience Flow

The assumption that audiences welcome, or a least tolerate, preselection of their programs most of the time accounts for strategies arising from the notion of **audience flow**. To explain, at scheduling breaks, when one program comes to an end and another begins, programmers visualize audience members as flowing from one program to the next. They try to maximize the number that flow *through* to the next program on their own channel and the number that flow *in* from rival channels, at the same time minimizing the number that flow *away* to competing channels. Many strategies at all programming levels, described by

authors in subsequent chapters, hinge on this concept. Audience flow considerations dominate the strategies of the commercial networks and affiliates, as well
as of their rivals, the cable networks and independent television stations. Aiken,
for example, stresses the role of *counterprogramming* (simultaneously scheduling programs with different appeal) in the strategies of independent television
stations seeking to direct the flow away from competing network affiliates.

Controlling audience flow becomes problematical, however, because listeners and viewers now have an unprecedented *freedom of choice.* Unlike the
consumer faced with the limited decision of whether or not to buy a book,
subscribe to a newspaper or attend a movie, broadcasting and cable consumers
can choose instantaneously and repeatedly by switching back and forth among
programs at will. Hence, the programmer cannot count on even the slight self-
constraint that keeps a book buyer reading a book or a ticket buyer watching a
movie so as not to waste the immediate investment. And, obviously, the polite
social restraint that keeps a bored lecture audience seated, does not inhibit radio
and television audiences. Programmers have the job of holding the attention of
a very tenuously committed audience. Its members take flight at the smallest
provocation. Boredom or unintelligibility acts like a sudden shot into a flock
of birds.

Fortunately for programmers, audiences are afflicted by *tuning inertia.* People
tend to leave the dial or switch pad alone unless stimulated into action by some
forceful reason for change. For example, programmers believe that children can
be used as a kind of stalking horse: Adults will tend to leave the set tuned to
whatever channel the children chose for an earlier program.

But some evidence suggests that the increased options cable provides may
encourage *channel hopping;* and remote control keypads make channel switching easy for even the most passive viewer. So far, however, programmers continue
to assume that tuning inertia prevails in the absence of compelling reasons for
change. Formats such as all-news radio and weather cable channels are, of course,
exceptions. They aim not at keeping audiences continuously tuned in but constantly coming back. As a widely used all-news station slogan goes, "Give us
twenty-two minutes, and we will give you the world."

In any case, the overall strategic lesson taught by the freedom-of-choice
factor is that programming must always please, entertain and be easily understood. Much criticism of the program quality arises simply because programmers
must deal realistically with the democratic nature of the medium. And for their
common sense, they are often accused of catering to the lowest common denominator among the audience.

Conservation of Program Resources

Radio and television notoriously burn up program materials faster than other
media—an inevitable consequence of their continuousness. That fact makes
program resource conservation an essential programming strategy. Although the
satellite cable networks actively compete for channel space on cable systems,
suggesting an excess of programs, the reverse holds. A high percentage of the
programming on cable networks consists of reruns of the same items. Moreover,
there is a good deal of repetitious programming among the broadcast networks

themselves. Some cable networks are losing propositions, and their numbers will eventually dwindle. Pay cable has stimulated the production of new programs and discovery of new types of program material, but on the whole, cable heightens program scarcity rather than alleviating it. Cable makes parsimonious use of resources all the more essential.

A popular fallacy holds that innumerable workable new program ideas and countless usable new scripts by embryonic writers await discovery and that only the perversity or shortsightedness of program executives keeps this treasure trove of new material off the air. But one can hardly blame programmers and their employers for being unwilling to risk huge production costs on untried talents and untested ideas. Even if they were willing, however, the results would not be much different as long as mass entertainment remains the goal. A national talent pool, even in a country the size of the United States (and even for superficial, imitative programming), is not infinitely large. It takes a certain unusual gift to create programs capable of holding the attention of millions of people hour by hour, day by day, week after week.

Anyone doubting the difficulty of appealing to mass audiences need only consider the experience of the older media. In a recent year, of 27,000 new books printed, only 33 sold 100,000 or more copies; of 13,000 records copyrighted, only 185 singles went gold; of 205 feature film releases, only 11 grossed the $20 million reckoned as the minimum to qualify as a hit. And yet audiences for these media are small compared to the nightly prime-time television audience.[2]

Sometimes audience demands and conservation happily coincide, as when the appetite for a new hit song demands endless replays and innumerable rearrangements. Eventually, however, obsolescence sets in, and the song becomes old hat. Radio and television are perhaps the most obvious indices of our throwaway society. Even the most massively popular and brilliantly successful program series eventually lose their freshness. Then they go into the limbo of the umpteenth rerun circuit.

Frugality must be practiced at every level and in every aspect of programming. Consider how often you see or hear "the best of so-and-so," a compilation of bits and pieces from previous programs; news actualities broken into many segments and parceled out over a period of several hours or days; the annual return of past year's special-occasion programs; the documentaries patched together out of stock footage; the weather report broken down into separate little packets labeled "marine forecasts," "shuttle-city weather," "long-term forecast," "weather update," "aviation weather" and so on.

The enormous increase in demand for program materials created by the growth of cable television would be impossible to satisfy were it not that the multichannel medium lends itself to repeating programs much more liberally than does broadcasting. A pay cable channel operates full-time by scheduling only 40 or so new programs a month, largely movies. As Jeffrey Reiss points out in his chapter on premium cable networks, each one runs four to six times. Furthermore, films first scheduled the previous month turn up again the following month in still more reruns, which pay-cable programmers euphemistically call "encores."

A major aspect of the programmer's job consists, then, in devising ingenious ways to get the maximum mileage out of each program item, to develop formats that require as little new material as possible for the next episode or program in the series, to invent clever excuses for repeating old programs over and over again. The first programming coup of Fred Silverman, at one time or another a programming executive for each of the three national television networks, consisted simply of inventing a new framework for presenting overused theatrical films. Soon after getting his master's degree from Ohio State University, Silverman found a job in the program department of WGN-TV in Chicago. His simple but effective stratagem for reviving the old films in WGN's library incorporated them into a series under a high-sounding name, *Family Classics*. He hired an attractive presenter to introduce them in an impressive looking library setting. This window-dressing gave the old turkeys a new lease on life.

The first question a programmer asks about any proposed series has to do with its staying power. William Paley, who, as president and later chairman of CBS Incorporated from 1928 to 1983, had more top-level programming experience than any other broadcaster, made the point in his autobiography: " 'What are you going to do for the next ten shows?' we might ask a writer. . . . What we really want to find out is how well the writer can handle his material over the long run."[3] Any tyro could design a winning schedule for a single week; a professional has to plan for the attrition that inevitably sets in as weeks stretch into the indefinite future.

Breadth of Appeal

Stations and cable systems recoup their high capital investment and operating costs only by appealing to a wide range of audience interests. This statement might seem self-evident, yet initially some public broadcasters made a virtue out of ignoring "the numbers game," leaving the race for ratings to commercial broadcasters. But as John Fuller explains in his chapter on national public television programming, this fundamentally unrealistic viewpoint has given way to the strategy of aiming for a high *cumulative* number of viewers rather than for high ratings for each individual program. This strategy coincides with that of cable television that, because of its many channels, programs to small audiences on some channels, counting on the cumulative appeal of all its channels to bring in sufficient subscriptions to make a profit.

The difference between the two goals has been expressed in terms of *broadcasting* vs. *narrowcasting*. Gene Jankowski, president of the CBS/Broadcast Group, uses the term *aggregation* and *disaggregation*, pointing out that the former deals with shared feelings and interests while the latter with highly personalized tastes and needs. Jankowski's terms take into account our complementary needs for belonging to the group while at the same time retaining our personal individualities.[4]

To *broadcast* originally meant to sow seed by hand, throwing it at random upon cultivated fields. Broadcasters began by throwing signals across the land, signals that blossomed by chance wherever receivers happened to be located. But as the medium developed, stations began to define audiences in demographic terms, adjusting the appeals of their programs accordingly. Now, cable goes beyond the broad vs. narrow dichotomy. Nevertheless, a broad-appeal service can have a narrowly defined clientele, as in the case of the Spanish International Network

(SIN), a hybrid broadcast–cable network having broad appeal but only for Spanish-speaking audiences. On the other hand, a narrow-appeal service (also called vertical-appeal) can have a broadly defined clientele, as in the case of Lifetime (once Cable Health Network), which though focused on the subject of health, ranges broadly within that subject to appeal to a wide range of viewers. Such vertical appeal contrasts with that of Music Television (MTV), the cable music network, whose narrowly defined music limits its appeal to a particular segment of the total population.

Only the national television broadcasting networks continue to "cast" their programs across the land from coast to coast with the aim of filling the entire landscape. Of course, no network expects to capture *all* the available viewers. A top-rated prime-time television broadcast taken individually generally captures only 20 to 25 percent of the potential audience. But extraordinary programs get up to three times that many viewers. Nostalgic viewers tuned in three-quarters of all the sets in use in the nation to the last episode of *M*A*S*H* in 1983, an estimated 60+ percent of the total population.

By any standard, audiences for prime-time, broadcast television networks are enormous. A single prime-time program can draw an audience so large that it could fill a Broadway theater every night for a century. Such size is achieved only by cutting across demographic lines and appealing to composite aggregations of people. Broadcasting surmounts differences of age, sex, education and lifestyle that would ordinarily segregate people into many separate audiences.

Alex Haley's 1977 dramatization of his search for his African ancestors illustrates this point. The remarkably successful miniseries *Roots* held obvious fascination for blacks because they identified profoundly with Haley's search for family origins. Had the appeal of the story stopped short at that level, however, it would never have broken any ratings records. But minority groups everywhere seek recognition of their distinctive heritages. The underlying appeal of *Roots* therefore touched all minorities (and everyone belongs to a minority in the final analysis). Non-blacks saw in the black yearning for ancient roots a paradigm of their own desires. The tremendous odds against Haley's ever being able to reconstruct his family history heightened the drama of the search. Many other elements increased the heterogeneity (and hence the size) of the audience: large dollops of sex and violence (legitimized by the serious nature of the story); the titillating sense of historic guilt; the very length of the series, representing a disruption of normal scheduling unprecedented in times other than national emergencies; and the extraordinary skill of the production staff and performers. *Roots* plugged into a contemporary social movement at just the right stage and in just the right way.

TYPES OF AUDIENCE APPEAL

Programmers must be aware of such movements and sensitive to their implications for programming strategies. Market researcher Daniel Yankelovich has made the point that a good marketer—and a program executive is after all a marketer of programs—combines research findings on social trends with a "reading of tea leaves."[5] Most of the social trends he listed in a 1974 article continue in evidence: emphasis on creativity, meaningful work, mysticism, return to nature, ethnicity, liberalized attitudes toward sex, use of stimulants and drugs, tolerance for disorder, challenge to authority, female careerism, reaction against the complexity of modern life. Yankelovich warned, however, against merely jumping on the bandwagon of perceived trends (as the unimaginative programmer does). The skillful marketer sorts out deep-seated trends from short-term fads generated by splinter groups. Similarly, a good programmer anticipates the graduation of a trend from the status of an innovation among a few dedicated adherents to a genuine mass movement.

Programmers of the 1980s need the background that Yankelovich's article supplies, but they also must be aware that the pendulum has begun its swing in the opposite direction. New trends are emerging—the Protestant work ethnic is on the rise again, and a renewed emphasis on basic education, reactions against the drug culture, the return of dress codes, more disciplined treatment of children, harsher penalties for criminals. Are these genuine social trends, or merely rip tides in the social-political waters? Programmers must assess such questions and place their bets on what the future will bring. Programmers should, in fact, be classified as futurists. By combining logic, research and tea leaves, a good programmer foresees changes in public tastes, the rise and fall of fashions, the emergence of trends, the decline of current fads and preoccupations.

Considering social trends has to do with *program appeals,* to which most discussions of programming devote a good deal of time. Detailed consideration of appeals properly belongs in the study of program writing and production— areas that we make no attempt to cover in this book, as was explained at the outset. In any case, most station programmers deal with ready-made programs from networks, syndication sources and independent production firms. They rarely have any say in the writing and production of the programs they use. They rely more on the past record of programs in the marketplace than on subjective judgments about what sorts of appeals a candidate program has and how well the writers and producers have developed those appeals.

Nevertheless, programmers must grasp the notion of program appeals if they are to make informed choices among programs destined to serve particular demographic groups. Selecting among program proposals, scripts and pilots is a major portion of the network programmer's job. That winnowing process involves appeals assessment as well as economic, scheduling and competitive considerations. And, occasionally, station and cable programmers also oversee the production of local programming.

To deduce which appeals have the most universal effect, the programmer would do well to study programming on a cross-national basis. For the most part, the appeals of American prime-time network broadcast programs seem universal. Seen in syndication all over the world, they seem to work as well in Singapore as in San Francisco. They evidently arouse universal human interest. A second class of programming that circulates worldwide, news, also draws universal attention.

What appeals do these programs have in common? No doubt they could be defined in various ways, but I suggest the following: (1) conflict, (2) ego-involvement, (3) sex, (4) self-preservation, (5) recognition, (6) curiosity and (7) escape. These appeals are not tightly compartmentalized; any such classifications will inevitably break down under close scrutiny.

Conflict

Every drama, game show, and comedy, and most news stories contain elements of conflict. In explaining why television drama tends toward violence, a professional scriptwriter pointed out that dramatic plots evolve out of conflicts between man and nature, man and God, man against himself and man against man. The first three, he said, are generally too difficult to develop within the narrow confines of television drama formats, so that most scriptwriters resort to man-against-man conflicts, which tend to result in violent confrontations before the plot finally works itself out.[6] Perhaps conflict could be better characterized in terms of suspense. We want to know who is going to win—or, if the winner is foreordained, how the conflict will be resolved. The skillful writer, seconded by skillful producers and performers, wrings the maximum amount of suspense out of the situation before revealing the answer.

Ego-Involvement

I use the term *ego-involvement* to refer to any kind of personal identification the listener–viewer makes with what goes on in the program. Thus, dramas succeed best when members of the audience identify with protagonists and begin to live their experiences vicariously. So too, in a similar manner, news grabs attention when it has some perceived implications for the audience member— the sense of danger conveyed by reports of disasters and crimes, the sense of pleasure in reports that touch the sympathies, the sense of triumph in reports that show enemies put down and friends rewarded and so on. Ego-involvement also occurs when people who belong to the same organization or interest-group, or who have the same profession or hobby as we appear in dramas or the news. Music triggers ego-involvement when the listener nostalgically associates particular songs or melodies with past experiences. One of the fascinations of phone-in talk shows is the ego-involvement that callers unconsciously betray.

Sex

It hardly needs saying that sex and sex-related emotions constitute powerful appeals that radio and television exploit in many ways, but mainly, of course, through featuring sexy stars in love songs and love stories. Top-rated newscasters generally possess a great deal of sex appeal as do many radio DJs.

Self-Preservation

Programs devoted to self-improvement and therapy are obvious examples of the self-preservation appeal, which hinges on concerns for safety, health and well-being. Weather and traffic reports are other examples. The news, especially local news, as indicated earlier, appeals to our sense of self-preservation. Ego-involved appeals often contain an element of self-preservation.

Recognition

What makes an interview with a movie star appealing when the same interview with a nonentity would be utterly boring? It may be that there is a certain appeal in simply recognizing "important" figures on the screen. Recognition gives a feeling of being in the know because one is "acquainted" with the personality being interviewed. Recognizing someone the viewer knows in a newscast can be exciting and rewarding.[7] Recognition seems to be an element in the appeal of music: One's mind races forward, anticipating with pleasure the phrases, both musical and verbal, a few bars ahead.

Curiosity

Wondering what next, how things are going to turn out, what other people and places are like—these kinds of appeals I classify as curiosity. They are related, perhaps, to the penchant for gossip and the appeal of the human interest story. Certainly all types of conflict involve an element of suspense; we want to know who will win in the end. So perhaps mere curiosity could be categorized as a lower order of suspense. One can be curious to know how a quiz show will turn out, but the suspense is less gripping than that of a murder mystery or a closely fought sporting event.

Escape

Finally, programmers must constantly keep in mind the viewer's desire to "escape." More than anything else, people seem to want from radio and television simply escape from the problems, the stresses and strains, of everyday existence. In a study of audience satisfactions, respondents most often gave as their reason for liking programs simply this notion: "They offer a pleasant way to pass the time."[8]

People have always experienced problems in the workplace, in their living arrangements and in their interpersonal relations. But modern society has added a new problem, formerly the bane of only the "idle rich": boredom. Industrialized society has freed most of us from the need to work incessantly just to keep alive, but many find that ample leisure time and discretionary purchasing power are mixed blessings. Many find life intolerably boring unless it is relieved by hobbies, drugs (including work addiction!) and—entertainment. Far from being mere frivolity, entertainment qualifies as a serious matter. Everybody connected with radio and television programming—writer, producer, performer, programmer—does well to keep in mind the essentially therapeutic role they play in saving vast numbers of people from the intolerable state of being bored.

THE PROGRAMMER'S BASIC SKILLS

The definition of programming given earlier calls for expertise in eight areas: schedule evaluation, program evaluation, audience targeting, program acquisition, negotiating skills, program selecting, scheduling and marketing. This section discusses each of these basic job skills.

Evaluating Programs and Targeting Audiences

Programmers spend a great deal of time and effort studying their markets, their competition, their coverage and their prospective advertisers. Their goal is to define specific salable targets within the total population reachable by their programs. Merely striving to reach the *largest* possible audience can be self-defeating since programs inevitably have a push–pull effect. What attracts one listener or viewer may repel another. Programmers have to decide which audience members to attract, which to sacrifice. This process reaches its highest degree of precision in the field of radio music programming. In his chapter on that subject, Edd Routt devotes a section to showing how to find a definable audience subgroup not already adequately served by existing music radio stations. Cable systems also pose an interesting (and intricate) targeting problem because their multiple channels permit appeals to many audiences.

Essentially, targeting is a matter of applying knowledge of demographics. Programmers acquire this knowledge and the skills for targeting their audiences from the study and practice of audience research. Mastering the basics of this somewhat technical field is an absolutely essential qualification for a well-rounded programmer. Programmers must be able to read, intepret and understand the limitations of standard audience rating reports, and analyze those reports to get information specific to their own stations. They must also know how to conduct additional local research, either in-house or on contract to a nearby university or research firm. Because of its fundamental importance, a chapter on the subject of audience research introduces the chapters on specific programming situations.

Broadcast audience research has evolved out of half a century of experience; corresponding research on cable audiences still has a long way to go. The sheer size of the broadcasting industry and its massive amount of advertising justify spending large sums on research—to make regular, detailed audience measurements and to conduct methodological research to improve accuracy. Cable still had not generated sufficient advertising support by 1984 to justify comparable research investments.

Nevertheless, the major audience rating firms include cable audience estimates in their broadcast audience reports and conduct research on the problems of cable-use measurement. However, the fragmentation of the cable audience among many channels creates difficult measurement problems, especially because cable subscribers apparently switch channels more often than broadcast-only users. Methodological research indicates that viewing diaries, upon which much broadcasting audience measurement depends, underestimate viewing in cable homes. This conclusion comes as no surprise, considering the prevalence of channel hopping in cable homes and the consequently large number of channels that would have to be "diarized." Then, too, advertisers want comparable measurements of broadcasting vs. cable audiences in the same market; but broadcast television ratings aim at estimating the *one-time-only* audience for programs, while cable audience measurements aim at estimating the *cumulative* audiences for programs repeated many times in various dayparts.

Cable research moves toward *qualitative* measurements to supplement the audience size-and-composition measures traditional in broadcasting. Research has long since established that audience size measurements can differ markedly from appreciation measurements. In dealing with advertisers, cable companies may find it advantageous to show that their audiences, though relatively small in absolute numbers, have strongly favorable attitudes toward a given channel or program. Moreover, cable programmers need to know all they can about audience attitudes to develop strategies for combating *churn*, that debilitating turnover among subscribers undermining cable's credibility and costing money to combat.

Copyright Constraints

Now we turn to the development of negotiating skills and program acquisition, skills essential to the programmer when dealing with copyrighted materials. Except for news and most public affairs programs and most local productions, all programs entail the payment of royalties to copyright owners. Programmers must understand how the copyright system works, how users of copyrighted material negotiate licenses to use them and the limitations on program use that the copyright law entails.

Broadcast stations and networks usually obtain blanket licenses for music from copyright licensing organizations, which give licensees the right to unlimited plays of all the music in their catalogs. For the rights to individual programs and films, users usually obtain licenses authorizing a limited number of performances ("plays") over a stipulated time period. One of the programmer's arts is to schedule the repeat plays at strategic intervals to get the best mileage possible out of the product.

Cable television systems introduced a new and exceedingly controversial element into copyright licensing. Stations and networks obtain licenses for the materials they broadcast, with fees calculated on the basis of a station's usual over-the-air coverage areas. The problem lurked in the background while cable systems merely improved broadcast signals in areas of weak coverage, but came to the forefront when cable companies began picking up distant television stations relayed to them by satellite. That stretched the original single-market license to include hundreds of unrelated markets all across the country, to the obvious detriment of copyright owners.

The copyright law of 1976 (effective in 1978) tried to solve this problem. It introduced *mandatory licensing* of cable companies that retransmit television station signals. It provided retransmission compensation to the copyright owners in the form of a percentage of cable companies' revenues. The law also created a Copyright Royalty Tribunal that sets the percentage cable companies must pay for retransmission rights, collects the money and distributes it to the copyright owners on a group basis. For example, the Motion Picture Association of America receives and redistributes transmission royalties to the owners of feature films;

Broadcast Music Incorporated and the other music performing rights societies redistribute music royalties to individual composers and lyricists. Sidney Pike discusses the details of this complex operation, still highly controversial because of disagreements about the amounts of payment, in his chapter on superstations.

Owners of the rights to sporting and other public events negotiate permission to broadcast these events with networks and individual stations or cable interests. Again, when cable systems retransmit such events, copyright owners are entitled to added compensation from users, through the tribunal mechanism. Broadcast networks and stations themselves receive some retransmission compensation for the relatively few programs to which they own the copyrights.

Program Acquisition

Would-be program suppliers are abundant, but they never have enough programs of just the right type to fit the target audience, to fit into the schedule and to fit the user's pocketbook. Programmers must therefore know the program market. Speaking of a particular class of users, Ed Aiken says in his chapter on independent stations, "Effective communication with program suppliers is the lifeblood of the independent programmer."

Three basic program sources exist: broadcast **network** programs, **syndicated** programs (including feature films) and **locally** produced programs. These compartments, however, are by no means watertight. Locally produced shows sometimes develop into hybrid blends of local production and syndication, as in the case of *PM Magazine* described by Lew Klein in his chapter on group-owned television stations. Network entertainment programs "go into syndication" to affiliated stations after their initial plays on the national network. Networks produce "made-for-television" feature films. Pay television suppliers produce made-for-pay-TV feature films and entertainment specials—on-location taping of live performances at concerts, nightclubs and in theaters. Live sports events crop up in both cable and broadcasting network services and also as local productions.

1. *Network Programs.* The national, full-service, interconnected network is broadcasting's distinctive contribution toward conservation of program resources (of course, newspapers had developed the principle of syndication before broadcasting even began). The three national television networks supply the bulk of all broadcast television programming, filling about 60 percent of their affiliates' schedules. About 75 percent of all commercial television stations have network affiliations. Cable satellite networks similarly furnish the bulk of cable system programming.

Aside from news and news-related public affairs materials, the broadcast networks buy their programs from independent production firms. In their discussion of prime-time broadcast programming, Lewine, Eastman and Adams describe the tortuous route from program idea to finished, on-the-air network series. Each year, network programmers sift through five or six *thousand* initial proposals, shepherding them through successive levels of screening, ending up in the fall with twenty-odd programs for their actual schedules. Outside authors write the scripts, and production houses do the rest of the creative work.

Until 1983, a Federal Communications Commission regulation forbade networks to acquire the resale rights to any programs they had not produced on their own. Thus outside production companies that created the programs retained copyright ownership and merely licensed the networks to use programs for a stipulated number of plays; thereafter, rights reverted to the original owners who could resell them to other users. The FCC was reconsidering this rule at the time this book was written, and the Commission appeared likely to approve partial syndication rights for the three commercial networks.[9]

Cable networks differ in major respects from television broadcast networks. In technical delivery, they are similar: In both cases a central headquarters assembles programs and distributes them nationwide, using common carrier relay facilities to reach individual broadcast stations or cable systems. But the financial and working relationships between broadcasting affiliates and their networks and between cable affiliates and their networks differ fundamentally. Cable systems depend almost totally on network-distributed programming to fill their channels, and because they have many channels, they deal with many networks. The symbiotic relationship between broadcast networks and their affiliates does not exist in the cable field. Eastman in her chapter on cable system programming points out that less than 1 percent of cable programming originates locally, whereas television stations average about 10 percent (and many broadcast a great deal more locally produced material than that).[10] Retransmitted broadcast programs constitute three-quarters of cable scheduling, with over 50 national cable networks (many in decidedly shaky financial condition) supplying the remaining programming. Cable network programmers have less input into the creative aspect of programming than their broadcasting counterparts.

In radio, networks now resemble syndicators. They supply features or program inserts such as newscasts and no longer meet the traditional definition of networks. In their chapter, Johnson and McLaughlin illustrate the blending of networking and syndicating in the radio industry.

Public broadcasting network programmers face still a different situation, as John Fuller explains in his chapter on PBS. Designed as an alternative to the commercial system, PBS programming comes ready-made from member stations specializing in production for the network, from small independent producers, and from foreign sources, notably the British Broadcasting Corporation. Foreign sources supply more elaborate productions than PBS can generally afford to commission, costing PBS about one-tenth of what a similar program would if produced in the United States.

A small amount of crossover usage occurs in the varying programming situations. *The Paper Chase* examplifies such commercial–noncommercial exchange. It began as a feature theatrical film in 1973. In 1978–79, CBS spun it off into a critically acclaimed but unsuccessful prime-time commercial network series. After CBS dropped the series, PBS picked up the rights in 1981. Still later, the cable satellite network Showtime obtained rights to the 22 original episodes, producing further episodes on its own. Another example of crossover usage is the PBS movie review program originated by the public broadcasting station in Chicago, *Sneak Previews*, featuring Chicago-newspaper critics Roger Ebert and Gene Siskel. When the stars failed to agree with the noncommercial station on contract renewal, they accepted an offer from a commercial syndicator and retained the same format under a new title, *At the Movies*.

   2. *Syndicated Programs and Feature Films.*   Local broadcast programmers come into their own when they address the task of selecting syndicated
programs. They may use: (1) **off-network series** (programs controlled by copyright
owners after the network has used up its contracted number of plays), (2) **independently packaged programs** such as game shows and wildlife series and (3)
feature films made originally for theatrical exhibition. Syndicators put their wares
on display nationally and internationally at a number of annual meetings and
trade shows. They rely primarily on the conventions of the National Association
of Television Programming Executives and the National Cable Television Association, held each spring. At the 1983 NATPE convention, over 200 syndication
firms fought for the attention of programming executives. To give an idea of the
variety of companies and the range of their offerings, here is a selection of syndicators present at the 1983 NATPE convention and some of their programs:[11]

Alfred Haber	35 episodes of *Barbara Mandrell and the Mandrell Sisters*
ARP Films	26 episodes of *New Spiderman*
Blair Video Enterprises	*NFL Great Moments*
CBN Syndicaton	*700 Club*
Columbia Pictures International	*Hart to Hart*
DFS Program Exchange	166 episodes of *The Flintstones*
Embassy Telecommunications	133 episodes of *Sanford and Son*
Excel Video International	*Ronald Reagan—Truth About Communism*
Four Star Entertainment	145 episodes of *Zane Grey Theater*
Golden West Productions	*Scared Straight*
Group W Productions	*PM Magazine*
Independent News	*IN Evening News*
King Features Entertainment	220 episodes of *Popeye*
Lionheart Television	14 episodes of *Civilization*
National Telefilm Associates	30 *John Wayne Classic Westerns*
OPT/TPE	*Entertainment Tonight*
Pearson International	122 *Encyclopaedia Britannica* films
Pro Sports Entertainment	22 episodes of *NFL Week in Review*
D. L. Taffner	75 episodes of *Benny Hill Show*
Turner Program Services	26 episodes of *World Championship Wrestling*
TV Global Network of Brazil	20 episodes of *Quem Ama Nao Mata*
Twentieth Century-Fox Television	255 episodes of *M*A*S*H*
Warner Brothers Television	61 episodes of *Wonder Woman*
Worldvision Enterprises	150 episodes of *Love Boat*

   Programmers also may use the following information sources: sales staffs
of the syndicators (though according to Pike in his chapter on superstations, they
do not visit the smaller markets); special reports on all shows currently in syndication published by the major ratings services (Wimmer and Popowski describe
these reports in their chapter on audience research); station sales representatives
(Bompane discusses their programming role in a special chapter); and the trade
press, which devotes much editorial and advertising space to syndicators and
their products.

Trade press annuals print directories of syndicators and program suppliers for both broadcasting and cable. The 1983 issue of the *Broadcasting-Cablecasting Yearbook* lists the following directories of interest to programmers:

Some 900 producers, distributors and production service companies.

About 100 program suppliers for cable systems using satellite distribution.

About 50 "basic cable services" (that is, the cable networks such as ESPN, MTV, Nickelodeon, USA Network and the superstations).

Over 20 pay cable services (such as HBO and Showtime).

3. *Local Production.* As the chapters on television station programming will show, local news programs play an important role in broadcast station program strategies (even these programs, though locally produced, often contain a great deal of syndicated material as inserts). But aside from news, locally produced material plays only a minor role as a program source. True, all-news and all-talk radio stations depend almost entirely on local production, but those formats cost so much to run and have such a specialized appeal that they remain few in number. Stations simply find syndicated material cheaper to obtain and easier to sell to advertisers. This pattern may change, however. Many observers think that when satellite-to-home distribution of centrally produced entertainment and news becomes common, broadcasting stations will find locally produced programs much in demand. Indeed, some forecasters predict that broadcasters will eventually abandon mass entertainment to cable and direct broadcasting (DBS) and devote their time and effort to producing programs locally. Already, according to Lewis Klein in his chapter on group-owned stations, some leading broadcasting groups have begun to develop resources for local production efforts.

DBS could eventually drive cable toward local production as well, but at present cable systems lack experience and adequate facilities for competing effectively in this field. Some cable systems do make a stab at local news production but do not invest the kind of money in facilities and staff required for an effective news department. As Agostino and Eastman point out, even though metropolitan cable franchises usually mandate one or more access channels for use by the general public, municipal agencies and education, these sources account for only a tiny fraction of cable system programming. Local origination channels, used by cable systems for their own programming and syndicated material such as electronic text, likewise contribute only minimally in most cases to the total program service supplied by cable systems.

Negotiating Skills

The preceding section should have made it clear that programmers must be skilled negotiators. They deal constantly with outside suppliers—networks, syndicators, production houses—and the business relationships between stations or cable systems and their suppliers have few hard-and-fast rules. Bargaining and bartering characterize practically every deal. For example, because they purchase programs or services for several markets in a single transaction, group-owned stations and multiple system cable operators have a bargaining advantage. They can demand discounts because they're big spenders; small, individual stations cannot. Similarly, syndicators give discounts to network owned-and-operated broadcast stations because they reach such a large and desirable percentage of the total national market, and the syndicators want exposure on prestigious stations within those bellwether markets, according to Klein's chapter on group-owned stations.

Clearly, single-outlet operators must bargain all the harder to obtain advantages. Eastman notes that even if a program supplier sticks to a fixed price for proffered cable services, a cable system's management can bargain for advantages other than discounts, such as advertising in *TV Guide* or local-level promotional assistance. Also, since purveyors of premium programming to cable systems split subscriber fees for such programming with their affiliated systems, an able negotiator may be able to increase the percentage of the fee the system retains.

Negotiating skills aid programmers within their own shops as well. Management regards programming as too important to leave solely to programmers; major programming decisions therefore reflect the input of several top executives, and programmers must be able to present their own views persuasively to the rest of the team (a point I will develop more fully later in this chapter in discussing the constraints under which programmers operate).

Program Selection

Having pegged out a suitable target audience, defined in terms of market, facilities and competition, and having identified program sources, the programmer next faces the task of program selection. One might expect an approach to the problem in the spirit of the critic, asking, "Which of the affordable programs has the highest quality?" As a matter of fact this sort of question is rarely asked. Instead, programmers and other executives ask about demographics, past performance, lead-in and lead-out, counterprogramming strategies and the like.

This point was forcefully made in a decision-making simulation staged by the International Radio and Television Society at one of its annual seminars for college teachers of broadcasting. College professors in the seminar assumed the roles of programmer–sales manager–general manager teams. Industry participants played their own real-life roles as representatives of syndication firms and advertising time-buyers. The teams had to choose a series for their "stations." They had to fill a specific early-evening time slot with a replacement series in which three advertisers would be willing to buy spots. They could opt to produce a local series or to buy a syndicated series selected from the actual catalogs of distribution firms. Most teams opted for a syndicated package, but one chose to place its bets on a local news program. The simulation imposed the following rules:

1. A program series had to be either produced within a prescribed budget or bought competively from offerings in the syndicators' catalogs.

2. The stations had to consider their respective network affiliations, coverage areas, existing audiences and program schedules, production resources and competitors.

3. The stations had to strive to make a profit on the program series; that is, they could not pay an exhorbitant price for a "loss leader" program series.

The management teams could:

1. Select a program series from the available sources, including the option of local production.
2. Manipulate the existing schedule, if the team so desired, to enhance the attractiveness of the new program with a strong lead-in and the like.
3. Negotiate with representatives of the syndication companies and compete with the other stations in the market to get the best possible programs at the lowest possible price (including the option of negotiating a discount by offering to buy other syndicated programs as part of a package).
4. Try to persuade prospective advertisers that the proposed series offered the best advertising vehicle available in the market.

Among their tools, the teams had the use of standard audience rating reports for the market and the Nielsen *Report on Syndicated Program Audiences.* The latter aided in predicting the probable success of the programs they chose.

This exercise pointed up four significant aspects of program decision making in a commercial setting: (1) programming decisions are based on monetary considerations, (2) the content and quality of the programs as such are treated neutrally as "product," (3) programmers rely heavily on a limited range of research data and (4) negotiating skills play a prominent role in program selection.

Channel Selection

In choosing programs for cable at the system level, entire programming services (channels) rather than individual programs must be considered, and as a result, extraneous technical and legal considerations intrude in the decision-making process. For example, in her chapter on cable systems, Eastman mentions the need for matching program choices to the engineering parameters of the system, for example, the number of channels available vs. the number of must-carry and franchise-mandated channels. A cable programmer could be prevented from scheduling a desirable new satellite network if it came via a satellite other than the one relaying the rest of the system's programs since picking up the new program might require the installation of a new receiving dish—an expense many systems cannot afford.

Scheduling

Of all the programmer's basic skills, perhaps scheduling comes closest to qualifying as uniquely a radio and television specialty. One critic has referred to broadcast television scheduling as an "arcane, crafty, and indeed, crucial" operation; another has said that "half a [network] program director's job is coming up with new shows. The other half, some would say the other 90 percent, is in knowing how to design a weekly schedule, in knowing where to put shows to attract maximum audience."[12]

Scheduling a station, cable system or network is a singularly difficult process. Editing functions in other media bear little resemblance to it. Scheduling draws upon many other programming skills—utilizing the principles of compatibility, habit formation, flow control and resource conservation. It demands an understanding of the coverage patterns of one's own and one's competitors' delivery systems (stations, cable systems, broadcast or cable satellite networks), one's market, one's audience and its demographics.

Each of the specialist chapters later in the book deals with the strategies of scheduling within a particular programming environment. Each has its own strategies, yet all of them rest on fundamental programming principles. To give an idea of the range of scheduling considerations, here is a sampling from the ensuing chapters:

1. Prime-time broadcast network television programmers are experts in fine-tuning their schedules. They have even had to invent names for special strategies, such as "stunting," "hammocking" and "tent-poling."

2. Nonprime-time network television programmers must be particularly conscious of daypart demographics because their programs must appeal to a disparate audience ranging from children on Saturday morning to adults in the after-midnight hours.

3. Broadcast network affiliate programmers have the luxury of being able to concentrate most of their energies on filling the 40 percent of their hours when the network is not feeding them programs. Attention here focuses particularly on the prime-time access period strategies, early fringe and local evening news.

4. Independents can take advantage of their greater scheduling flexibility in competing with affiliates in their markets by using counterprogramming strategies.

5. Radio station formula programming requires precision scheduling, sometimes calling for split-second timing. The all-news and music radio chapters illustrate the use of scheduling "clocks" that break an hour's programming into precisely defined short segments.

6. Cable television and cable radio use all the previously developed broadcast scheduling strategies and introduce many of their own. Though blessed with the scheduling latitude that many channels confer, cable programmers find themselves constrained by mandatorily scheduled channels. They think of scheduling in terms of deploying entire program services, while the broadcast programmer thinks in terms of deploying individual programs or program series.

7. Though some of its leaders at first thought that public broadcasting should and could ignore commercial strategies, programmers have increasingly adopted the familiar ploys of commercial stations, such as counterprogramming and bridging. Network programmers in public broadcasting have relatively little choice in program selection, as Fuller explains in his chapter on national public television programming. Their strategies necessarily center on scheduling.

WHAT PROGRAMMERS SAY

How does the foregoing description of the programmer's role jibe with the self-perception of people on the job? Some surveys of working programmers give an inkling. J. David Lewis conducted interviews with working programmers asking them to identify what influenced their programming decisions.[13] On the basis of the answers he received, Lewis identified 45 influences. He then sent questionnaires to 521 stations, asking programmers to rate each influence on an 11-point scale, running from "unimportant" to "important." He received 301 usable replies, a statistically satisfactory rate of return for the type of questionnaire he used. Analyzing the responses, Lewis found that they clustered in the following way (not listed in order of importance):

Direct feedback—various types of personal audience response, notably viewers' phone calls and letters.

Regulatory constraints—including station policy, FCC rules and industry self-regulation.

Inferential feedback—formal audience research plus input from syndicated program salespersons (which ranked high as an influence).

Conditional feedback—opinions of friends, family, critics and the trade press.

Staff feedback—opinions of fellow professionals at the station, including the news director, whose influence ranked highest.

Personal judgment—including instinct, common sense, knowledge of the community, personal experience and the general manager's opinions.

Financial constraints—the sales manager's opinions, costs, advertiser opinions.

Tactical considerations—scheduling, viewing trends.

Michael Fisher sent questionnaires to 400 members of the National Association of Television Program Executives (NATPE), getting a 40 percent response.[14] Replying to a question about what influenced their program decisions, the executives listed in order of importance:

1. Total potential audience.
2. Management policies.
3. Specific audiences sought for particular programs, sales potential and FCC regulations (three-way tie).
4. The program executive's personal judgments.

The Arbitron research company published a guide for program directors of music stations containing 21 factors that influence decision making, as shown in Figure 1-1. The factors divide about evenly between those external to the station and those internal to the station.

There is substantial agreement between the influences cited in these three studies and the skill and knowledge requirements mentioned in this chapter's earlier discussion, though different terminology may be used. The one area not discussed was what the working programmers identified as "instinct" or "personal judgment," an important attribute for any successful programmer. But instinct and personal judgment are terms that defy logical analysis. They're talents or gifts, not learnable skills. They have to do with an instinctive feel for what will "catch on" with large numbers of people at a given moment. All great programmers have that instinct. One commentator, describing that quality in William

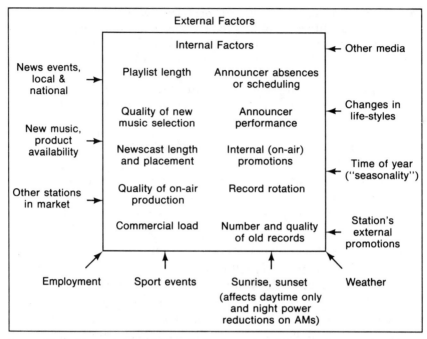

Source: Used with permission of Arbitron Radio, *Research Guidelines for Programming Decision Makers, 1977.* Beltsville, Md.; Arbitron Co.

FIGURE 1-1. Factors That Influence Radio Music Programmers

S. Paley, said Paley had "a sixth sense about a program, whether or not it would work. At programming meetings he was always most alert, genuinely listening, never underestimating (or overestimating) any ideas."[15] Other than this elusive qualification, there seems to be no innate characteristic that makes some individuals successful programmers and others less successful. The rest of a programmer's skills are acquired, developed, experiential.

REGULATORY CONSTRAINTS

Radio and television, more than most businesses (including other media), must live within constraints imposed by national, state and local statutes and administrative boards. Moreover, public opinion imposes its own limitations, even in the absence of government regulation. But even so, the hybrid nature of most of the newer communication technologies has created novel regulatory problems. Reflecting traditional distinctions, the Communications Act in 1983 covers common carriers in its Title II and broadcasting in Title III. Today commentators sometimes refer to "Title II-1/2," referring to the regulatory no-man's land between broadcasting and common carriers occupied by such systems as cable television and multipoint distribution services (MDS).

Regulation is thus in a transitional state, made even more confusin deregulatory frenzy that has overtaken Washington lawmakers and bure While the FCC busies itself erasing old rules, Congress intervenes with ments to the Communications Act of 1934, as well as with new statutes, such as the proposals for cable television under consideration as this text was written. Under the circumstances, one cannot cite existing regulations with any certainty that they will still be on the books a few months later. Fortunately for programmers, responsibility for compliance with the law devolves upon top management, guided by legal counsel. Programmers should be kept informed by their colleagues of changes in the laws, but in any event, relatively few regulations directly affect their day-to-day work since First Amendment freedom of the press limits government interference. Nevertheless, "ignorance of the law is no excuse," so programmers should be aware of possible violations within their jurisdiction. Following is a checklist of the chief regulatory constraints with which programmers should be familiar.[16]

Fairness

Both broadcast and local cable-originated programming must observe the fairness principles embodied in the Fairness Doctrine, the equal time rules governing candidates for political office, rules on station editorials about political candidates, and the right to reply to personal attacks that occur during discussion of controversial issues. Day-to-day enforcement of these regulations devolves largely upon the production staff in the course of operations, but programmers might set policies and stipulate compliance methods. Fairness looms large in talk radio, as indicated in Bruce Marr's chapter, because it frequently deals in controversial topics. Equal Employment Opportunities compliance might also be considered an aspect of the fairness issue since EEO rules apply both to broadcasting and to cable operations employing five or more persons.

Monopoly

Various rules limit concentrations of media ownership, all of them aimed at ensuring diversity of information sources, in keeping with implicit First Amendment goals. Group owners of broadcast stations are particularly sensitive to regulatory compliance in this area. They have a high financial stake in compliance and of course are conspicuous targets, susceptible to monopoly charges. This sensitivity affects programming policies. Whether or not cable franchising agencies may grant monopolies within certain geographic areas remains a subject of legal dispute. In a way cable franchises may be regarded as "natural monopolies," for it would seem uneconomic to duplicate cable installations. But if monopoly is construed as denial of freedom of speech, then perhaps even the "natural monopolies" cable franchises create may violate the First Amendment.

The **network financial interest and prime-time access rules** seek to prevent networks from monopolizing prime-time entertainment programming. The prime-time access rule directly bears on programmers because it creates a lively market for so-called "access programming," a primary concern of program directors at network-affiliated stations.

Localism

Several FCC rules, such as the so-called *ascertainment* requirement, combined with the commission's interest in encouraging locally produced programs, news and public affairs, the airing of controversial issues and a preference for local ownership and owner participation in management, nudge broadcasters toward a modicum of **localism** in their program mix. Management's desire to "please" the FCC (or, to put it more generously, management's desire to fulfill its public service obligations as defined by the FCC) pressures programmers to pay some attention to local programming. Deregulatory moves have lessened this pressure somewhat, but so far the Communication Act's goal of serving the public interest has not been explicitly abandoned.

Cable operators have no such federal mandate; hence, a major difference exists between the programming outlooks of broadcasting and cable. True, municipal franchise agreements usually require cable operators to furnish local access channels, but furnishing channels in no way compares with broadcasting's affirmative public service obligations.

Copyright

I discussed copyright constraints and the actions of the Copyright Royalty Tribunal in the previous section. As Sidney Pike makes clear in Chapter 13 on superstations, cable companies, bitterly opposed to the tribunal's royalty levy on distant signals, lobby vigorously for changes.

Must-Carry Rules

One of the most controversial of the FCC regulations affecting cable, the **must-carry rules**, obligates cable systems to allot channels for broadcast television stations with substantial numbers of viewers within cable coverage areas. These rules aim at preventing cable companies from discriminating against stations by excluding them from their channels and then undercutting them by importing stations with the same network affiliations from other markets. However, the obligation to carry an arbitrary number of local stations constrains the cable programmer's freedom of action, especially in those cable systems located between two large television markets. In mid-1983, a small Washington State cable company located between Spokane and Seattle brought suit against the FCC for forcing it to carry stations from both adjacent markets. The company claimed that in fining it for failing to comply with must-carry rules, the FCC violated its freedom of speech and took its property without just compensation.[17]

Lotteries, Fraud, Obscenity

Federal laws forbid lottery, fraud and obscenity by wire or radio and apply to locally originated cable as well as to broadcast programs. Programmers also need to be aware of special Communications Act provisions regarding fraudulent contests, **plugola** and **payola**.

Cable Franchise Constraints

When municipalities issue cable franchises, they incorporate a variety of stipulations about content that affect a programmer's freedom of action. Mandatory access channels and obscenity clauses were two examples noted earlier. Furthermore, Congress will probably usurp some local control by imposing federal controls.

PROGRAMMING AS TEAMWORK

You may have noticed that I have avoided the term *program director*, using instead *programmer*. I chose this less precise title because in most cases management teams, not just a program director, make programming decisions of any consequence. Indeed, most cable operations do not even employ an executive with a programming title.

Programmers work in a highly charged atmosphere, full of pressures and counterpressures. In a speech before the International Radio and Television Society, Frederick S. Pierce, then president of ABC Television, summarized some of these pressures as they appear to a broadcasting network executive:

> Programming decisions are made only after the "votes" are in. And the "votes" take many forms and come from many directions. Input comes from ratings and research, from thousands of letters from viewers and from countless phone calls. It comes from advertisers, who aren't shy, believe me, about communication of their views; and it comes from the creative community.
>
> We also measure reactions from our affiliates, who are important in measuring response in over 200 separate communities. And we pay attention to polls, surveys, and to special interest groups, who are very vocal and visible.[18]

He might have added that the programmer must also be concerned about a morass of constantly changing laws and regulations at the federal, state and municipal levels. Programmers do not enjoy the luxury of autonomous decision making. In arriving at decisions, often sales or corporate image-making motives outweigh programming considerations. Programming may be an art, but it is not a fine art. Creativity in radio and television organizations is buried under layers of bureaucracy—more so than in other of the media. Radio and television are set apart by unique technology, their special legal status and the fact that so much of the creative work of program making takes place outside the walls of stations, cable systems and networks. This separation of functions explains why leading writers and producers like Norman Lear (what Pierce refers to as "the creative community" in the statement above) complain so bitterly about the frustrations of creating television entertainment.[19] When Lear first offered *All in the Family*, network executives looked upon its innovative realism and satirical bite as far too risky for television. It survived only because Lear had far more clout with executives than do most producers. As Les Brown put it, television is an "executive's medium."[20]

When television programmers formed their own professional organization in 1962, they called themselves the National Association of Television Program *Executives*—tacitly acknowledging that membership would be dominated by general managers and other executives who play more important programming roles than those specifically designated as programmers. The programming team is usually made up of the general manager, sales manager and program manager. In cable organizations, the executive in charge of marketing plays a key management role and may be the one with the most influence on programming decisions:

> Small independent systems often have the general manager making program decisions. At the MSOs (Multiple System Operators), the task may be spread among several departments and supervised by the marketing vice-president. Other MSOs may divide programming into several distinct areas such as program development, satellite programming and public access/local programming.[21]

If salary is any measure of perceived job importance (and it usually is), television station program executives rank a distant third behind general managers and sales managers, according to an annual study released at the NATPE conventions. The 1983 study also indicated that 77 percent of the television station general managers surveyed and 61 percent of the sales managers earned $50,000 or more annually, but only 11 percent of the program executives earned that much.[22] In the same year a *Cable Marketing* survey (the first of its kind) reported that cable program executives earn even less than those in broadcasting. Of those working for MSOs, 50 percent earned no more than $20,000.[23]

Program executives play an information-processing role. Paul Virts, in the course of his doctoral research, interviewed a group of television station executives in the Midwest. He concluded that briefing the other members of the programming team constituted one of the programmer's basic roles. The program managers he interviewed said they assembled the pertinent data on audience, scheduling, program availabilities and costs, then presented their findings to the sales manager and general manager.[24] The programmer defines the constraints within which the decision must be made from the programming point of view, the sales manager defines them from the advertiser's point of view, and the general manager defines them from the policy point of view. How much attention the others pay to the programmer's recommendations varies with the make up of the team. If the sales manager happens to be aggressive and the general manager sales-minded, the programmer's viewpoint tends to get submerged. To cite a practical example at the most basic level, Bill Drake of Drake-Chenault Enterprises—one of the most influential figures in modern radio programming—recalled in an interview his start as a small-town Georgia disc jockey:

> Stations would sell everything they could, because most General Managers were sales oriented. . . . A lot of commercials would be recorded by the owners and the Sales Manager, who were tight with the account (i.e., advertiser) and the account wanted them to do the commercials. As it turned out, you'd have what were supposed to be one minute commercials and by the time they got through ad-libbing and recording the damned things, they were two minutes and fifteen seconds, which I guess was why the accounts loved them.[25]

Drake attributes much of his later success to his insistence on separating radio programming from sales. As he put it, Cadillac dealers sell the product; they do not spend their time calling Detroit to tell General Motors how to design Caddies. The programmer's role is to persuade sales-minded executives to concentrate on selling, leaving program design to programmers. The best general managers referee the warfare between sales and programming fairly, encouraging the best efforts of both without giving too much firepower to either.

Few U.S. cable systems have executives with the word *program* in their title. This fact does not mean, of course, that programming functions are not performed, but that they take less time than in broadcasting organizations and so can be treated as a part-time responsibility of the general manager or other primary executive. In the *Cable Marketing* survey mentioned above, 60 percent of the responding MSOs and 47 percent of the independents said they treated programming as a separately organized function, but only one-third of the multiple system operators and 27 percent of the independent cable systems replying to the questionnaire reported full-time managers. Eastman discusses these results in more depth in a section in Chapter 13 on "The Job of the Cable System Programmer."

The previous section included the ability to negotiate effectively with program suppliers as one of the programmer's basic skills. Equally important, programmers must negotiate effectively within the management team. When Michael Fisher asked professional programmers what qualities lead to success in the field, most mentioned, among other things, the ability to work well with all kinds of people.[26] Fisher's survey also revealed the following programmer characteristics:

Education: Sixty-five percent of the program executives surveyed had a college degree, most of them from a department of broadcasting or a related field such as journalism.

Prior Experience: The great majority had experience in television production before becoming program managers.

Whom does the program manager consult?   In addition to the general manager and sales manager, program executives mentioned consulting their film buyers, news directors, corporate officers, network scheduling coordinators, treasurers, corporate attorneys, business managers and comptrollers.

Fisher summarized the personal characteristics of the program executives represented in his survey. He found they tended to be

male, relatively young, likely to be college educated—especially those in the top markets and at the largest stations; have considerable experience in broadcasting—both in terms of longevity and in terms of variety of jobs held; believe that a person should start his or her career in a station where he or she can perform many different tasks, but also believe that it is not so much the possession of particular skills that will lead to success as it is the possession of an appropriate attitude. The program managers in this sample watch a lot of television as part of their job and at home, and they perceive themselves as having something less than complete freedom in decision-making, subject always to the scrutiny of the station manager.[27]

About 60 percent of the respondents to the *Cable Marketing* survey previously cited had college degrees, and one-fourth had done graduate work. Their prior experience included work in radio and television broadcast programming, film production, program syndication and distribution and in satellite networks. The survey concludes, "As much as cable systems need top notch specialists, they must employ them very often as generalists—with the ability to understand activities outside their prime area of responsibility and to make meaningful contributions wherever they must focus their attention."[28]

SUMMARY

Programming can be defined as the strategic use of programs arranged in schedules designed to attract carefully defined target audiences. Programmers need the knowledge and skills to define such audiences and to select, acquire and schedule programs that will attract them. In carrying out their tasks, programmers use strategies based on the inherent characteristics of radio and television (whether delivered by broadcast signals, cable or other electronic means). Some of these strategies are termed compatibility, habit formation, audience flow control, program conservation and breadth of appeal. In carrying out their work, programmers must have the ability to negotiate effectively and an understanding of audience research principles and techniques. They obtain programs from broadcast and cable network and syndicators or produce them locally. They consider program appeals, licensing costs, targeting goals as well as copyright constraints and fees, must-carry rules, franchise and broadcast license renewal; and they schedule programs in repetitive cycles, across-the-week or once-a-week or in targeted rotations, depending on their medium and the particular strategy they adopt. Programmers are not autonomous; they work within a certain framework that limits their freedom of action. They are constrained by the nature of their markets and their facilities and by government regulations. As only part of a management team, programmers must often defer to the other team members, usually the general manager and the sales or marketing manager. Programmers are usually college educated, persuasive, able to get along well with other people, capable of assimilating and retaining large amounts of detailed information and equipped with prior experience in broadcasting, film or cable production.

Notes

[1] *The Audience Rates Television* (Cambridge, Massachusetts: Television Audience Assessment, Inc., 1983).

[2] Figures quoted by Gene F. Jankowski, President of CBS/Broadcast Group, in "Choices and Needs: The Meaning of the New Technologies," address to Connecticut Broadcasters Association, Hartford, 20 October 1982.

[3] William S. Paley, *As It Happened: A Memoir* (New York: Doubleday, 1979), p. 260.

[4] Jankowski.

[5] Daniel Yankelovich, "What New Life Styles Mean to Market Planners," *Marketing/Communications*, June 1971, pp. 38–45.

[6]This analysis came from an anonymous scriptwriter who was responding to queries by researchers analyzing violence in television, cited in Thomas F. Baldwin and Colby Lewis, "Violence in Television: The Industry Looks at Itself," in George Comstock and E. Rubenstein, *Television and Social Behavior: Media Content and Control, I* (Washington, D.C.: Government Printing Office, 1972), pp. 290–365.

[7]Some commentators classify this appeal as "importance," but one has to recognize importance in the first instance.

[8]*Audience Rates Television*, p. 20.

[9]The rule forbidding full network participation in the syndication market may be rescinded in the course of deregulation.

[10]The 10 percent local origination average figure dates from 1978. Recent data are unavailable because, as part of an economy drive, the FCC stopped issuing annual programming reports.

[11]The trade press carries lists of exhibitors and their offerings at the time of the NATPE conventions. The examples shown were drawn from "What's on Parade in the Market Place," *Broadcasting*, 21 March 1983, pp. 88–126.

[12]William H. Read, *America's Mass Media Merchants* (Baltimore: Johns Hopkins University Press, 1976), p. 72; Thomas Thompson, "The Crapshoot for Half a Billion: Fred Silverman Rolls the Dice for CBS," *Life*, 10 December 1971, pp. 46–58.

[13]J. David Lewis, "Programmer's Choice: Eight Factors in Program Decision-Making," *Journal of Broadcasting* 14, Winter 1969–70, pp. 71–82.

[14]Michael G. Fisher, "A Survey of Selected Television Station Program Managers: Their Backgrounds and Perceptions of Role" (M.A. thesis, Temple University, 1978), p. 110.

[15]David Halberstam, *The Powers That Be* (New York: Alfred A. Knopf, 1979), p. 131.

[16]A convenient source for details on these regulations is the annual *Broadcasting-Telecasting Yearbook*, supplemented for more recent developments by "Where Things Stand," a quarterly update in the weekly trade journal *Broadcasting*.

[17]For background, see Quincy Cable TV, Inc., 51 *Radio Regulation* 2d 701 (1982), 32 FCC 2d 1484.

[18]Fredrick S. Pierce, remarks before the International Radio and Television Society, New York City, 6 November 1978.

[19]"Hollywood Fights Back," *TV Guide*, 27 August 1977, pp. 4–18 (reprinted in part in Barry Cole, ed., *Television Today* (New York: Oxford University Press, 1981), pp. 331–36.

[20]Les Brown, "Is Silverman Worth It?" *New York Times*, 1 January 1978, p. 26.

[21]Alan Radding, "Who Is the Cable System Program Director and What Does He Really Do?" *Cable Marketing*, March 1982, p. 30.

[22]"1982 Salary Levels," *Facts, Figures, Film*, March 1983, p. 70.

[23]"Cable Marketing Survey: Not Many Full Time Program Directors But Their Value to the Management Team Increases," *Cable Marketing*, March 1982, pp. 14–17. According to another trade journal survey, television broadcast station program directors' salaries averaged as follows: $51,400 at large stations; $39,800 at mid-sized stations; and $26,400 at small stations ("Program Directors Feel Concern by Syndicators over PTAR Inhibits Development of New Shows," *Television/Radio Age*, 14 March 1983, p. 150).

[24]Paul H. Virts, "Television Entertainment Gatekeeping: A Study of Local Television Director's Decision Making" (Ph.D. diss., University of Iowa, 1979), p. 104.

[25]Quoted in "The Top-40 Story: Bill Drake," *Radio & Records*, September 1977, p. 30.

[26]Fisher.

[27]*Ibid.*, pp. 171–72.

[28]*Cable Marketing*, "Cable Marketing Survey," p. 17.

Selected Sources

Gross, Lynne Schafer. *The New Television Technologies.* Dubuque, Iowa: Wm. C. Brown Co., 1983.

Head, Sydney W., and Sterling, Christopher H. *Broadcasting in America: A Survey of Television, Radio, and New Technologies.* 4th ed. Boston, Massachusetts: Houghton Mifflin, 1982.

Howard, Herbert H., and Kievman, Michael S. *Radio and TV Programming.* Columbus, Ohio: Grid Publishing, 1983.

New Technologies Affecting Radio and Television Broadcasting. Washington, D.C.: National Association of Broadcasters, 1982.

Smith, V. Jackson. *Programming for Radio and Television.* Washington, D.C.: University Press of America, 1980.

CHAPTER TWO

Program and Audience Research

Roger D. Wimmer and Martha L. Popowski

A QUICK GUIDE TO CHAPTER TWO

ROGER D. WIMMER *is the senior research analyst for Cox Communications, Inc., in Atlanta, Georgia, with responsibility for radio and television research, market analysis and corporate business analysis. Prior to joining Cox in 1982, he was an associate professor of communications at the University of Georgia and for four years prior to that, an assistant professor at the University of Mississippi. He received his Ph.D. in Radio-Television-Film from Bowling Green State University in 1976. He is senior author of* Mass Media Research: An Introduction *(Wadsworth Publishing Company, 1983), author of other books published by the National Association of Broadcasters and has published scholarly articles in the* Journal of Broadcasting, Journal of Advertising Research *and* Journalism Quarterly.

MARTHA L. POPOWSKI *is a junior research analyst for Cox Communications, Inc. She received her master's degree at the University of Georgia in Media Management and was the 1981 recipient of the George Foster Peabody Fellowship in Broadcast Management. She worked as a paralegal dealing with FCC matters at the Washington, D.C. law firm of Fisher, Wayland, Cooper and Leader from 1978 to 1980. Since coming to Cox Communications in 1982, she has worked on a variety of radio and television research projects.*

DECISION-MAKING INFORMATION FOR PROGRAMMERS

This book focuses on the strategies broadcast and cable programmers use to program the electronic media. Most programmers are striving for the same goal: to reach the largest available audience. Program and audience research and ratings guide the process of selecting and scheduling programs to attract the desired audience and provide feedback on programming decisions.

The broadcast and cable industries use many research approaches to evaluate programs and audiences, most of which fall into one of three groupings: (1) qualitative and quantitative measures of the programs themselves, (2) qualitative and quantitative measures of audiences and (3) quantitative measures of audience size. Qualitative research tries to explain WHY people make specific program choices; quantitative data, in the form of ratings or surveys, report WHAT programs people are listening to or watching. Programmers use qualitative information on programs to select and improve programs and to understand program content; qualitative audience data explain people's reactions to programs. Quantitative audience data, on the other hand, generally provide measures of the size and demographic composition of sets of viewers, listeners or subscribers. Of all these findings, however, **ratings** are the major form of program evaluation and they most influence the other concerns of this book, program selection and scheduling. This chapter examines the industry's current program research practices and qualitative audience measurement techniques and then, because of their special position in industry economics, explains and interprets audience ratings.

Effects vs. Industry Research

Research on how media programs affect individuals is rarely used in selecting or scheduling programs for television, cable or radio. Although the major commercial networks analyze program content and how it might influence people (especially children), the impetus for this research comes from outside the broadcasting industry, not within, and its findings have little effect on programming.

From an industry perspective, the problem with all effects research, from the first *Surgeon General's Report* on the effects of violence on television onward, is that the research hinges on differences in methods and manner of interpretation of results. Research on the effects of television violence is probably the most heavily analyzed, yet at the same time least understood, aspect of U.S. broadcasting. Of course, programmers must keep current on the issues and methods of scholarly research on media effects, but at the same time must remember that in the 20-year analysis of violence on television, no one has yet come close to fully explaining the problem—or, indeed, to incontrovertably proving that a problem exists. Some scholarly research develops methods for approaching some problems, methods that transfer readily to industry research practices, but generally the two arenas are guided by different goals and different values. This chapter focuses on the research the industry actually uses to evaluate programming.

PROGRAM TESTING

The enormous expense of producing television programs necessitates program testing before and during the actual production of a show. In addition, promotional announcements that advertise programs (**promos**) are usually tested to gauge their effectiveness and ability to communicate the intended message.

Concept, Pilot and Program Testing

Concept testing is asking audiences whether or not they like the ideas for proposed programs. Producers generally conduct it before the program has been offered to a broadcast or cable network. *Pilot testing* occurs when a network is considering the purchase of a new series, and audiences are asked to react to the pilot episode. This process is described in detail in Chapter 5 on network prime-time programming. *Program testing* happens when a series is under way and, very rarely, when the edited form of a special entertainment program does not live up to expectations. Plot lines, the relative visibility of minor and major characters, the appeal of the settings and so on can be tested to determine current audience preferences.

ASI Market Research, based in Los Angeles, is one of the best known of the companies conducting program tests (and tests of commercials). Typically, ASI researchers invite people into a testing theater to watch a television program, a film or a commercial, asking them to rate it by pushing "positive" and "negative" buttons attached to their seats. Generally participants are paid, often in products rather than cash, for taking part in the test. Computers monitor individual responses, producing a graph of the viewer's "votes" over time. These data are correlated with demographic and other information (**psychographics**) obtained from each participant. ASI research has been criticized for its unrepresentative audience samples, yet it remains a major contributor to network and movie studio program testing in America.

Frequently prime-time series that have slipped in the ratings are tested with live audiences to determine which aspects of the program, if any, can be manipulated to improve series popularity. The testing instruments range from simple levers and buttons, such as used in ASI theaters, to more controversial methods such as galvanic skin response meters measuring respiration and perspiration. Programmers seek aids in understanding the weaknesses and strengths of a series performing below expectations. Sometimes the research suggests a change of characters or setting that revitalizes a program.

Concept and pilot testing stress general plot lines and main characters, seeking to find out if they are understood and appeal to a variety of people. Ongoing program testing seeks subtler evaluations of the voices, manners, style and interactions of all characters. In fact, different actors and plot lines are sometimes used for separate screening to find out which cast and plot audiences prefer. Postproduction research can discover a poor program opening or difficulty in understanding the main theme of an episode. Unfortunately, the theater environment cannot reflect at-home viewing conditions and is thus a less than ideal research method. It does, however, supply detailed data that can be matched to screen actions, adding fodder for programming decisions.

Promotion Testing

Competition for audiences requires that most programmers continually produce effective promotional materials. Promotional spots advertise particular episodes of a series, special shows, movies, newscasts or unique aspects of a station's or service's programming. These promos can be tested before they are aired to find out whether they communicated what was intended. Testing firms generally conduct tests in shopping centers, intercepting people at random to invite them to view promos in return for cash or merchandise. Demographic data are gathered and other questions are asked and associated with participants' opinions. In the past few years, promo-copy testing has become a standard practice in the industry.

QUALITATIVE AUDIENCE RESEARCH

In addition to program testing, which applies mostly to television programs and movies, stations use qualitative research to get audience reactions to program materials, personalities and station or system image. Using focus groups is one such research method. Radio stations also use call-out research to test their programming, and network television and major market stations make use of TvQs. All of this research is grouped under the heading "Qualitative Audience Research," its most common title in the industry.

Focus Groups

One method used to gather information from a group of people is to conduct focus groups.[1] A **focus group** is a set of ten or twelve people involved in a controlled discussion. A moderator leads a conversation on a predetermined topic, such as a music format or television newscast, and structures the discussion with a set of questions. Predetermined criteria guide group recruitment: Station management may want people who listen to country music or women aged 25 to 34 for example. Finding people who fit the predetermined criteria (**screening**) can be costly: More qualifications result in a greater turn-down rate, increasing the price for screening. Assembling a typical focus group generally costs between $1,500 and $2,000, including the fee paid to each participant ($20 is the standard fee, although it is sometimes as high as $100 for individuals difficult to recruit such as physicians and other professionals).

Focus group research provides preliminary information about a topic or provides questions that will be used later in field surveys of a large sample of people. It generates informal information about whether a station has enough news, how people react to the newscasters, whether music is too soft or loud, whether personalities are perceived as interesting, friendly and so on. One advantage of focus groups is that visual materials (videotapes, newspaper ads) and recordings can be evaluated in the session, providing immediate stimuli and avoiding confused recall.

Due to the small size of focus groups, research results cannot be generalized. However, focused discussions can elicit unusual perceptions that would be overlooked by techniques such as survey questionnaires used with larger groups of people. Focus groups are especially suited to answering programmers' WHY questions in depth.

Music Research

Radio programmers want to know their audiences' opinions of different songs and different types of music. They need to know which songs are well liked and which ones no longer have audience approval (which songs are "burned out"). **Call-out research** is one popular, although controversial, method for discovering what listeners think about music selection.[2]

Programmers conduct call-out research by selecting 5- to 15-second "hooks" from well-established songs and play them for respondents over the telephone. A **hook** is a brief segment or musical phrase that captures the song's essence, frequently its theme or title. Programmers ask randomly selected respondents to rate 15 or 20 song-hooks on a predetermined scale. Often a scale of 1 to 10 is used, where 1 represents "don't like" and 10 represents "like a lot." If stations perform call-out research frequently (and some use it every day), a track record for each song develops, and based on it, the music programmer can decide whether to leave the song in the station's rotation or drop it. Chapter 15 describes a particular form of this research in detail and shows how it can be applied to programming decisions.

Call-out research indicates listeners' musical tastes at a given moment. When tied to the same songs for some time, it indicates their popularity but does not tell the programmer how often a particular song should be played. That remains the programmer's decision.

Another popular method of testing music is the **auditorium music test**. Programmers invite 75 to 150 people to a location where they jointly listen to and rate a variety of songs. Instead of rating just 15 or 20 hooks as in telephone research, auditorium tests involve from 200 to 400 hooks. Like call-out research, the method tells which songs are liked and disliked at the moment but not how often they should be aired.

Music testing is expensive. Call-out research requires an investment in employees to make the calls as well as computer time (if desired) to analyze the results. Auditorium tests involve recruiting costs and "co-op" money for participants (usually $20–$35). Those stations lacking facilities and personnel for testing can hire commercial firms specializing in such work.

TvQs

TvQ (Television Quotient) data are used by many programmers to supplement Nielsen and Arbitron ratings.[3] The latter two services provide information on how many people watched a program; TvQs measure the popularity and familiarity of a program. Programmers use TvQs as indicators of a show's potential success. If a show has become "one of my favorites" among the people who have seen it, it may eventually perform better on the networks or at least perform well in syndication. Some research companies own computer programs that use TvQs to project the eventual success of a network program in syndication. The models consider how the people who watched felt about a show, but not how many watched.

PROGRAMMING, SALES AND RATINGS

The rest of this chapter focuses on how programmers use and interpret ratings data. Ratings exert a powerful influence on the industry. This phenomenon is powerfully illustrated in Chapter 3, on the role of station representatives in programming, and in chapters 5 and 6 on network television programming. Radio programmers also use ratings information to evaluate their market positions and convince advertisers to buy time, as discussed in Chapter 15 in relation to other evaluation techniques. Ratings are also used in cable and public broadcasting in specialized ways as analyzed in chapters 9 and 18. In fact, all programmers use ratings as part of their program decision making.

Using audience ratings is not restricted to programming applications, however. In fact, ratings were originally intended to provide information for advertisers curious about audience size. But once ratings data were on "solid" statistical ground, programmers used them to gauge the success of their decisions. As competition among networks and stations increased, ratings became the most important decision-making data in commercial broadcasting. Broadcast revenues, programs, stations and individual careers depend on audience ratings. For insofar as it is a business, broadcasting is usually a very simple business: High ratings result in profits (and continuing careers). Chapter 5 examines many of the factors that influence ratings and looks at other considerations, such as license costs, that affect programming decisions at the network and station level. Of course broadcasting also has public service obligations and other aspirations and commitments. On the purely economic side, however, a network or station will eliminate a program that receives low "numbers" if other options are available.

Cable and broadcast ratings cannot be compared directly because cable's potential audience is only about 40 percent that of the commercial networks (as of the mid-1980s), and its programs are scheduled in rotating rather than one-time-only patterns. Therefore, cable programmers analyze ratings to determine **audience reach**—how many people over a period of time viewed a program or channel, much as public television programmers use ratings.[4] But the absence of cable ratings comparable to those of broadcast television results in conservative advertising purchases and has contributed to the unprofitability and subsequent demise of several advertiser-supported cable networks.[5]

Articulating the power of audience ratings may sound crass to those who consider broadcasting an art form, but the reality is that ratings are the most important measure of commercial success. The efforts of most people involved in commercial broadcasting focus on achieving the highest possible numbers. Targeting more precisely defined audiences such as women 18–49 is a fall-back position for stations that cannot immediately achieve a number one position in the adults 18+ category. In the case of the final episode of *M*A*S*H* (February 28, 1983), the combined efforts of writers, programmers, promotion and advertising personnel and individual performers, produced the most-watched series episode in television history—and a great deal of advertising revenue for CBS.[6] *M*A*S*H* gained a Nielsen rating of 60.3 and a 77 percent share of the viewing audience.

Ratings affect television and radio programming and sales at stations and at networks; they affect independent producers, Hollywood studios, distributing companies and advertisers and their agencies. Understanding the basics of the all-powerful numbers is essential in all of these businesses. And because nearly all basic cable networks are advertiser-supported, they also need ratings information to convince advertising agencies to purchase time. The premium cable services, such as HBO, use their national ratings to convince local cable systems that their programs are watched and important to promoting the local system. High ratings, demonstrating television's widespread household penetration, also carry clout with Congress. Legislators generally use television to get elected and reelected and tend to pay attention to their local broadcasters and the three national networks because they can reach such enormous numbers of people.

Three companies in the United States produce most of the nationally syndicated audience measurements for broadcasting and cable: A.C. Nielsen, The Arbitron Ratings Company and Birch Radio. Other companies, such as RADAR and TvQ conduct audience measurements but have a more limited use. Station programmers may use local ratings to evaluate specific stations, but Nielsen, Arbitron and Birch cover the whole country so programmers can use their reports to cross-compare markets in widely different places and at different times. Subsequent chapters in this book discuss how these ratings are used in a specific set of circumstances.

A.C. Nielsen Company

A.C. Nielsen Company, headquartered in Northbrook, Illinois, gathers and interprets data on a wide range of consumer products and services and on television. Nielsen collects audience estimates for local market television and generates the only estimates for network television. Nielsen *local market* estimates, known as the **Nielsen Station Index (NSI)**, are reported in local ratings books and in a form called *Viewers in Profile*. The most important television surveys

Nielsen conducts are the four sweeps in November, February, May and July, during which all 210± television markets are measured. Data for NSI reports are gathered from diaries sent to randomly selected households in each market.

The **Nielsen Television Index** (NTI) for *network* television is produced from two samples: (1) approximately 1,700 households whose television sets are attached to electronic recording devices called **audimeters** and (2) about 2,000 households that are mailed diaries. The diaries actually returned in usable form make up the **in-tab** sample from which results are calculated. The meter and diary samples are combined to produce twice-annual reports called NTIs that estimate audiences for the three broadcast networks.

Nielsen also uses audimeters in seven cities throughout the United States to produce overnight ratings. **Overnights**, because of the smaller samples used, are only indicators of what the network ratings will probably be when the six-month NTI reports are issued. A handy short-form of NTI data from metered homes is incorporated in the biweekly "pocketpieces" discussed in Chapter 5.

Nielsen began measuring cable television in 1981, including cable households in its NSI reports. Now it issues biannual reports on cable audiences. To be included in NSI reports, 3 percent of the viewer diaries must record viewing of a cable television network. Nielsen also uses metered homes to collect data for reports on cable viewing, but like Arbitron, finds it difficult to devise reliable data collection and analysis methods.

The Arbitron Ratings Company

Arbitron, a subsidiary of Control Data Corporation, is based in Laurel, Maryland. It rates both television and radio audience size, using electronic meters and diaries for television estimates and diaries alone for radio estimates. Arbitron, however, provides only *local* ratings. Its metered homes generate local, overnight ratings in nine cities, allowing station programmers to track the daily performance of television programs in those urban markets. The company issues the same number of television reports as Nielsen.

Few differences exist between Arbitron and Nielsen—except in the numbers they report. Sampling error (and possibly other measurement practices) may produce varying numbers for the same program. Crafty programmers always use the service reporting the highest numbers for their programs.

The *quantity* of demographic detail in local television and radio market reports steadily increased in the late 1970s and early 1980s because of increased competition between Nielsen and Arbitron and pressure from programmers and advertisers for more information about an increasingly fragmented audience. The advent of cable and the increased audience share commanded by independent television stations created demand for an even more precise picture of audience viewing habits. Thus, in local market reports, the ratings companies broke demographic information into smaller units (such as by 10-year jumps for radio) and into more useful categories for different groups of advertisers (both women 18–34 and women 25–49 are now included, for example). In addition to local and national ratings reports, Nielsen and Arbitron customize reports covering smaller audience segments (women 18–49 only, for example) and specialized programming, such as analyses of syndicated program ratings, that are particularly useful to stations making program purchases. Bompane and Aiken, in chapters 3 and 8, make a special point of the importance of the syndicated program reports, which are covered in detail later in this chapter.

Birch Radio

Birch Radio, founded in 1978 as the Birch Report and based in Florida, is Arbitron's chief competitor in radio audience measurements. As of the mid-1980s, Birch is still working hard to gain acceptance in the field. In 1982, the company absorbed both Mediastat and Mediatrend and expanded into branch offices in several cities. As of 1983, the company was just shy of reaching all of the top 50 markets. The service is being used in about three-quarters of the top 100 radio markets, having subscribers in over 150 markets overall. The company has yet to apply, however, for accreditation by the Electronic Media Ratings Council— an important step in gaining acceptance from some ratings users.

Birch uses **aided-recall** telephone surveys (giving lists of station call letters) rather than diaries to gather its listening data. It surveys only one person in a household in daily telephone interviews.[7] In contrast, Arbitron uses seven-day written diaries and asks respondents to report on the listening habits of an entire household. Birch Radio issues twelve "Standard Reports" each covering one month's survey and comparing it to the previous month's report (using **rolling averages**). Quarterly, it summarizes ratings and presents qualitative information on product usage. However, the industry perceives Birch's product numbers as unreliable, as having insufficient stability to guide major time purchases.

Stations and advertising agencies can purchase the Birch Radio service for around $1,000 per month (in the top 10 markets), the price decreasing as a station's market size decreases. These rates are about one-tenth the cost of Arbitron reports for comparable markets.

RADAR Reports

RADAR (Radio's All Dimension Audience Research), produced by Statistical Research, Inc., Westfield, New Jersey, reports on the performance of the national radio services. Called the "network radio report," it is published twice annually, fall and spring, and is based on analyses of 32 weeks of continuous measurement beginning at the end of August and running through the end of April. Statistical Research, Inc., collects the data by telephone. The report covers the size and demographic composition of the major services, including ABC's six radio networks, CBS radio, NBC radio, RKO radio, Mutual, Sheridan, National Black Network and others.

RATINGS TERMINOLOGY AND MEASUREMENT COMPUTATIONS

Arbitron and Nielsen collect audience estimates by randomly selecting listeners and viewers from about 210± U.S. broadcast markets. The number of markets varies slightly from year to year but has remained at just over 200 for several years. In technical terms, Arbitron calls the markets **Areas of Dominant Influence (ADI)**, and Nielsen uses the term **Designated Market Areas (DMA)**.

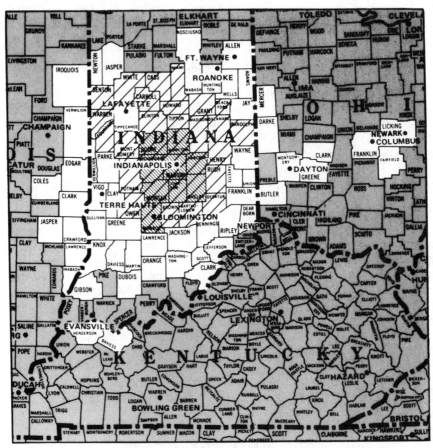

Copyright American Map Co., New York, License No. 14092 ▲ City of License of Satellite Station

The "Total Survey Area" of this market is shown in white on the accompanying map. Where appropriate, the "Area of Dominant Influence" is indicated by coarse cross-hatching and the Arbitron "Metro (or Home County) Rating Area" by fine cross-hatching.

SOURCE: Reproduced with the permission of the American Map Corporation. Further reproduction prohibited.

FIGURE 2-1. Map of a Television Market Survey Area

Survey Areas

However, Arbitron and Nielsen collect ratings data from more than ADIs/ DMAs, as shown in Figure 2-1. In the illustration, the smallest measurement unit is the Metro Area (also called Metro Rating Area, Metro Survey Area and Metro Sampling Area by Arbitron); next largest is the ADI/DMA; the largest unit is the Total Survey Area (TSA), called NSI Area by Nielsen.

1. *TSA/NSI Area.* The TSA or NSI Area includes all counties measured in an Arbitron or Nielsen survey. The rating service includes counties outside the ADI/DMA when substantial viewing of stations inside the ADI/DMA occurs

in them—viewership usually attributable to the presence of cable systems. Rarely used by commercial television programmers, TSA/NSI Area figures show a station's total estimated reach or circulation. As indicated earlier, **reach** tells how many people have viewed or listened to a station in the past, and therefore suggests how many could view or listen in the future. In cable, reach tells how many households subscribe to basic cable service. Reach is an important measure for radio, public television and cable. Another name for reach is **cumulative audience**, or **cume**.

2. *ADI/DMA.* Each county in the United States is assigned to only one ADI or DMA. Occasionally, Arbitron's ADIs and Nielsen's DMAs differ in size because each company independently decides which counties belong to the particular market. Generally, an ADI/DMA centers on a single city, such as Indianapolis or Denver or New York, but in some cases two or even three cities are linked as in the Dallas–Ft. Worth and Springfield-Decatur-Champaign markets. All stations in these multiple markets reach most viewers, making the cities one television viewing market. Arbitron and Nielsen rank each ADI/DMA according to the estimated number of television households within its counties.

As of 1984, the top ADIs/DMAs were:

ADI		DMA	
Rank	*Market*	*Rank*	*Market*
1	New York	1	New York
2	Los Angeles	2	Los Angeles–Palm Springs
3	Chicago	3	Chicago
4	Philadelphia	4	Philadelphia
5	San Francisco	5	San Francisco–Oakland

The bottom five ADIs/DMAs were:

ADI		DMA	
Rank	*Market*	*Rank*	*Market*
205	Helena	201	Bend
206	Selma	202	Fairbanks
207	North Platte	203	North Platte
208	Alpena	204	Alpena
209	Glendive	205	Glendive

These lists indicate overall agreement between Arbitron's and Nielsen's major market surveys, but show differences at the small-market end. Nielsen rates fewer total markets (only 205 in 1984) because it collapses more cities into double markets.

3. *Metro Areas.* The third geographical area, the Metro Survey Area (MSA) in radio and Metro Rating Area (MRA) or simply "Metro," is the smallest of the three survey areas and is the one most frequently used for radio programming. The Metro includes only a small number of counties closest to the home city of

the ADI/DMA, and consists of only a single, large county in some parts of the United States—especially in the West. Since competing big-city radio signals generally blanket the Metro, urban radio programmers use it to determine the success or failure of programming decisions. (Coverage patterns in outlying areas may vary too widely to compare.) The Metro represents the majority of the urban listeners, the bulk of office and store listening, and a large part of in-car listening. Radio stations on the fringe of the Metro area are more likely to refer to TSA/NSI Area measures. Television programmers rarely use Metro ratings because no demographic breakouts are available.

But to use any of these ratings services for programming decisions, programmers must understand how the estimates are produced. Using ratings without this knowledge is like trying to play chess without ever learning the rules; pieces can be moved, but winning the game is unlikely. The following subsections, therefore, provide an overview of the basics of audience computations.

Ratings/Shares/HUTS

A **rating** is an estimate of the *percentage of the total* number of people or households in a population *tuned* to a specific station or network during a specific time period (daypart). A **share** is an estimate of the percentage of people or households actually *using* radio or television and who *are tuned* to a specific station or network during a specific daypart. Ratings depend on a count of all receivers; shares on a count of all users. Shares are always bigger percentages than ratings for the same program or station because some people who *could* watch television (or listen to radio) are always NOT watching (they are sleeping or playing or working).

Ratings are always an estimate of an entire population whether the population refers to all households in the country or all people age 25–54 or all adults 12+ or all women 18–49 and so on. A share is always a percentage of those households or people in that population *using* the particular medium at a specific time. To repeat, *shares always appear larger than ratings* because they are based on a smaller sample of people; fewer people use television (or radio or cable) than *could* use it if all were at home, awake and choosing television above other activities. Both estimates are always percentages of an entire group—although the percent designation (%) is often omitted.

Sales staffs use ratings to set ad rates; *shares are used most typically in decisions about programming because they show how well a program does against its competition.* Broadcast networks and stations and cable services typically refer to their shares of an actual audience, not their percentage of all households having receivers (or cable service).

The combined ratings of all stations or networks during a particular daypart provide an estimate of the number of homes using television (HUT) or the persons using radio (PUR). HUTs and PURs are used to compute the shares for each station or network.

To illustrate these concepts, assume only three television options in the United States. Also assume that Nielsen's 1,700 metered households indicate the following data:

Network	Household Viewing*
ABC	374
CBS	326
NBC	291
Not Watching	709
	1700

*Empirical data from meters.

The HUT level is .583 or 58.3% (991/1700); calculated by adding households watching television and dividing by the total number of households with television (374 + 326 + 291 ÷ 1700 = .583). The answer is changed from a decimal to a percentage by multiplying by 100. A HUT of 58.3 means an estimated 58% of all households had a television set on at the time of the measurement.

The individual ratings and shares for the three networks can now be calculated.

Network	Ratings	Share
ABC	$\frac{374}{1700} = .22$ or 22%	$\frac{374}{991} = .377$ or 37.7%
CBS	$\frac{326}{1700} = .192$ or 19.2%	$\frac{326}{991} = .329$ or 32.9%
NBC	$\frac{291}{1700} = .171$ or 17.1%	$\frac{291}{991} = .294$ or 29.4%

To calculate a rating, the number of households watching a network was *divided by the total number of households having receivers* (e.g., for ABC, 374 ÷ 1700 = .22). To calculate shares, the number of households watching ABC, for example, was *divided by the total number of households watching television* (374 ÷ 991 = .377).

Network programmers primarily use rating and share estimates to compare program audiences, but often they also will be interested in the specific number of households (HH) or persons in that audience. Ratings can be used to project to a particular population. For example, using the data above produces these estimates for the entire United States (having a total population of about 83.3 million households).

Network	Rating	×	Population	=	Pop. HH Estimate
ABC	.220	×	83.3 million	=	18,326,000
CBS	.192	×	83.3 million	=	15,993,600
NBC	.171	×	83.3 million	=	14,244,300
	.583				48,563,900

The number 18,326,000 represents the 18+ million people estimated to be watching ABC (at this specific time). These calculations can be verified by mul-

TABLE 2-1.
Arbitron Local Market Report, Atlanta Market, November 1982

ATLANTA, GA

DAYPART / TIME (ETZ) / STATION	METRO HH	DMA HH SHARE TREND							
	RTG SHR	R T G	S H R	JUL '82	MAY '82	FEB '82	NOV '81		

MON.-FRI.

7.00AM-9.00AM

Station						
WAGA 5 C	2 10	2 10	11	8	10	7	7
WANX 46 I	2 12	2 12	10	10	14	8	8
WATL 36 I	<<	<<	NR	NR	NR	NR	NR
WGTV 8 P				NR			
WSB 2 A	7 40	7 42	33	39	37	37	37
WTBS 17 I	2 11	2 11	13	11	12	15	15
WXIA 11 N	4 23	3 19	25	23	21	29	29
HUT/PUT/TOTALS *	18		15	17	18	16	16

9.00AM-NOON

WAGA 5 C	6 32	6 30	32	31	34	33	33
WANX 46 I	1 6	1 5	1		4	4	4
WATL 36 I	<<	<<	NR	NR	NR	NR	NR
WGTV 8 P					NR		
WSB 2 A	4 23	4 22	29	30	27	31	31
WTBS 17 I	2 10	2 9	7	7	8	8	8
WXIA 11 N	5 25	4 22	20	21	15	16	16
HUT/PUT/TOTALS *	19		15	21	16	16	16

NOON-4.30PM

WAGA 5 C	6 23	7 26	31	24	27	24	24
WANX 46 I	2 9	2 8	9	6	6	9	9
WATL 36 I	<<	<<	NR	NR	NR	NR	NR
WGTV 8 P				NR			
WSB 2 A	8 32	8 29	28	36	30	36	36
WTBS 17 I	2 6	1 6	6	5	7	6	6
WXIA 11 N	7 26	6 22	18	21	21	26	26
HUT/PUT/TOTALS *	25	26	26	23	29	26	26

3.00PM-5.00PM

WAGA 5 C	6 22	6 22	29	25	26	22	22
WANX 46 I	4 15	4 14	11	9	11	9	9
WATL 36 I	1 1	1 1	3	2	NR	NR	NR
WGTV 8 P	1 3	1 3		2	NR	2	2
WSB 2 A	9 34	9 31	27	33	27	34	34
WTBS 17 I	2 7	2 7	12	7	12	8	8
WXIA 11 N	4 16	4 14	14	13	20	18	18
HUT/PUT/TOTALS *	27	28	26	26	26	32	29

SOURCE: A.C. Nielsen Company (1982), used with permission.

tiplying the HUT, 58.3, by the total number of households: .583 × 83.3 million = 48,563,900, the total figure for the three networks.

Using a page from the November 1982 Atlanta Nielsen book, we can see how ratings and shares were computed for WTBS, WAGA and WANX.

To calculate the rating and share for WTBS, in this example, Nielsen first analyzed diaries from a sample of households (HH) in the Atlanta DMA. It then projected the sample returns to the DMA household population. Approximately 2 percent of the total diaries were tuned to WTBS from 7 A.M. to 9 A.M.. If one assumes that 2 percent of the diaries reflects 2 percent of the total households, the number of homes watching WTBS can then be calculated. An estimated 1,117,400 households in the Atlanta DMA produces a 2 rating for WTBS (22,000/ 1,117,400 = .02 or 2 percent). The share for WTBS was computed by using the HUT (see the HUT/PUT/TOTALS), which was 17 or 17 percent. Seventeen percent of 1,117,400 yields 189,958 HH, and when that figure is divided into WTBS's 22,000 HH, a share of 11 results.

Arbitron and Nielsen always round rating and share figures to the nearest whole number, making numbers easier to read, but creating some interpretive problems. If you refer again to the 7 A.M.–9 A.M. time period on the Nielsen report, you will see that WAGA, WANX and WTBS all have "2" ratings, but each station's share is different. We can compute more accurate ratings by manipulating the basic formula, usually written as:

$$\frac{\text{Rating}}{\text{HUT}} \times 100 = \text{Share}$$

The calculated value is multiplied by 100 to create whole numbers instead of decimals for shares and ratings. If we transpose to:

$$\text{Rating} = \frac{\text{Share} \times \text{HUT}}{100}$$

we can rate more accurately.

$$\text{WAGA Rating} = \frac{10 \times 17}{100} = 1.7$$
$$\text{WANX Rating} = \frac{12 \times 17}{100} = 2.04$$
$$\text{WTBS Rating} = \frac{11 \times 17}{100} = 1.87$$

Keep in mind that all ratings and shares are percentages and must include decimal points for all calculations although to make their reports easy to read ratings companies do not print the decimals.

One final point concerning the 7 A.M.–9 A.M. example is that the HUT/PUT/ TOTAL line is 17, but if we add all of the stations, the total rating is actually 16. The uncounted rating point means that 1 percent of the households in the ADI/ DMA were using their television sets for other things—viewing cable stations from other markets, playing video games or displaying for a computer.

PUTS/PURS

Also remember that ratings and shares for television generally represent households, but occasionally refer to specific demographic groups such as women 18–49. Radio ratings always represent individuals or persons, and therefore, the term *persons-using-radio* (PUR) is used. *Persons-using-television* (PUT) is appropriate when calculations of individuals are made. Sales staffs and time buyers tend to be more interested in these calculations than programmers.

AQH/Cume

Programmers use two very important computations in calculating ratings: average quarter-hour audiences (**AQH**) and cumulative audience estimates (**Cume**). Program audiences are typically measured in 15-minute intervals, hence "quarter-hour audience." Meters can, in fact, measure one-minute audiences, but a person or household is counted in a quarter-hour if the television was turned on for a minimum of five minutes during the measurement period.

Although radio and television diaries also measure audience size in 15-minute intervals, programmers utilize these data in much larger units—by whole program or daypart. Quarter-hours are the particular concern of those who try to count fickle radio listeners.

Cumulative audience measures, on the other hand, are appropriate for *small audiences* that would not show up in rating/share measures. Cume measurements indicate the number of different people tuned in during a 15-minute (or longer) time period. *Cume figures are always larger than AQH figures.*

The basic difference between AQH and cume is that in the average quarter-hour calculation persons can be counted more than once. For instance, a person could tune to a station for five minutes, switch stations or tune-out, and then tune back into the original station during a later quarter-hour. This viewer would be counted twice in an AQH calculation, but not in a cume calculation since it counts only the number of different persons listening. *Cume* is considered the *reach* of a station because it tells you *how many different persons* were in the audience during a time period or daypart. It also reflects the growth or decay of an audience over time.

Cable and public television audiences are often too small for accurate measurement within one quarter-hour, but cumulative ratings may reflect more substantial audiences. Cumes can also be calculated for a program over several airings, a common pattern in cable and public television scheduling, permitting programmers to estimate the total number of people who watched a program. Commercial broadcasting with its special interest in the number of people watching one commercial spot generally uses AQH ratings.

Reach and Frequency Analysis

Sales people most often use the concepts of *reach* and *frequency*. As we said earlier, reach refers to circulation, or the net size of the audience; **frequency** indicates the number of times a person was exposed to a particular advertising message (or program in the case of pay cable). A high frequency means exposure to a message several times and indicates the "holding power" of a station, network or program. Programmers usually schedule several interesting programs in succession, trying to create audience flow and achieve a high frequency for advertisers.

TELEVISION MARKET REPORTS

Market reports (or "books") are divided into sections to allow programmers, sales people and advertisers to examine an audience from many perspectives. In television, the major sections are: Daypart Audiences, Network Dayparts, Time Period Averages, and Program Audience. (The section names vary slightly between Nielsen and Arbitron—and their order differs.)

Daypart Audience

The Daypart Audience section divides viewing into roughly 21 dayparts, a highly useful format for analyzing a station's performance in specific time blocks. For instance, early fringe (4:30 P.M.–6:00 P.M. EST) provides a quick summary of the ratings and shares for all stations during this daypart (refer to Table 2-2, a page from an Arbitron book).

Arbitron uses 21 demographic categories. Nielsen divides the viewers into 19 age and sex classifications for both the DMA and the TSA. For just one station, then, 399 ratings cells are required to fill out all 19 Nielsen people categories and 21 daypart categories for TSA ratings only. A ratings book page contains an immense amount of data.

A look at Table 2-2 shows that WSB-TV dominated the market in the early fringe daypart, with a commanding 14 rating/35 share in the ADI and 15/39 in the Metro. It was very strong with persons 18–34, women 18–49 and men 18–49. No doubt this station's programmer was delighted since these demographics are very easy to sell to advertisers.

Programmers normally compare the most current numbers to previous performances. **Tracking** a daypart shows how the station or program is doing over time. It is also important in selecting syndicated programs, as explained in Chapter 8 on independent station programming. Rarely will program decisions be based on only one book unless the numbers are very low and very credible, and no hope for improvement is in sight.

Network Daypart

The Network Daypart section provides broad time-segment information for network programming (ABC, CBS, NBC). Arbitron and Nielsen divide data on dayparts and demographic groups for the networks just as they do for stations in each market's report. An example is not included here since the layout of the Network Daypart section is similar to that of Table 2-2. This ratings book section shows how network programming performed on the local station—which on occasion is very different from national averages.

TABLE 2-2. Arbitron Local Market Report, Daypart Audience Section

Daypart Audience Estimates Summary

Persons, Women, Men and Teens figures are for Total Survey Area, in thousands (000's).

DAYPART AND STATION	ADI RTG	ADI SHR	JUL '82	MAY '82	FEB '82	NOV '81	METRO RTG	METRO SHR	TV HH	P TOT 2+	P 18+	P 18-49	P 12-24	P 12-34	P 18-34	W TOT 18+	W 18-49	W 12-24	W 18-34	W 25-49	W 25-54	WKG WMN 18+	M TOT 18+	M 18-49	M 18-34	M 25-49	M 25-54	T 12-17
(col) 5	6	58	59	60	61	8	9	11	12	13	14	15	16	17	18	19	20	21	22	23	24	25	26	27	28	29	30
MON-FRI 7:00A-9:00A																												
WSB	6	33	35	42	34	38	6	33	71	90	86	44	8	21	19	52	27	4	12	25	29	12	34	17	7	13	15	2
WAGA	2	11	10	11	8	8	2	11	22	27	27	14	3	6	5	16	9	1	2	8	9	4	11	5	3	4	5	1
WXIA	4	23	24	24	25	25	5	24	47	62	59	27	5	11	10	35	16	3	6	14	15	9	24	10	4	9	11	1
WTBS	2	11	8	14	14	8	2	11	51	82	42	35	20	33	23	30	25	11	16	18	20	9	12	10	7	7	8	0
WATL									3	4	4	2				3	1			1	1	1	2	1				
WANX	3	15	13	7	11	15	3	16	3	5	11	9	3	9	7	6	6		5	4	4		5	3	3	2	4	6
WGTV									2	2	1	1	1	1		1	1		1	1	1	1	1	1		1	1	1
WETV									1	1	1	1											1					
HUT/TOT	18		13	15	15	16	18		229	318	230	131	45	85	64	142	84	23	41	70	78	35	87	45	24	35	43	20
9:00A-4:30P																												
WSB	7	29	30	30	30	32	8	33	83	124	104	70	35	59	49	74	51	23	35	32	35	11	30	20	14	12	14	10
WAGA	6	25	27	30	31	27	6	24	73	105	90	47	18	33	27	60	31	13	18	22	25	7	30	16	9	12	15	6
WXIA	6	23	21	19	19	21	6	25	66	92	79	43	17	32	27	57	32	12	21	20	26	8	22	12	6	9	11	5
WTBS	1	5	6	8	8	7	1	6	31	43	30	22	11	18	15	17	12	6	9	13	10	4	13	9	6	6	7	4
WATL									5	5	4	2	1	1	1	2	2	1	1	1	1	1	2	1	1	1	1	1
WANX	1		6	5	6	4	1		6	25	9	4	1	3	2	6	4	1	2	2	4	1	3	2	1	1	1	3
WGTV									2	3	3	3	1	1	1	1	1	1	1	1	1		1	1	1			
WETV									1	1	1	1											1					
HUT/TOT	24		24	20	23	22	23		276	398	317	194	88	155	126	216	133	58	88	90	101	31	99	61	38	41	49	29
9:00A-NOON																												
WSB	4	23	26	29	28	33	5	25	53	77	63	38	18	30	24	43	27	11	17	18	20	7	20	11	7	7	8	6
WAGA	5	28	30	37	35	26	5	27	63	93	77	41	16	29	25	51	29	11	18	20	25	5	26	13	7	14	11	4
WXIA	5	26	24	17	16	23	5	28	60	84	70	40	16	29	24	50	29	11	19	20	26	9	20	12	5	9	11	5
WTBS	1	8	7	8	10	6	2	9	34	44	36	28	10	20	17	23	19	7	12	13	14	5	13	9	5	6	8	2
WATL									4	6	3	3	1	1	1	3	2	1	1	1	1		3	2	1	1	1	1
WANX	1						1		2	35	7	10	1	2	2	5	4	1	1	2	2	1	2	4	3	1	2	
WGTV									3	3	1	1	1	1		1	1		1	1	1		1					
WETV									1	1													2	1				
HUT/TOT	19		20	15	17	15	19		225	316	256	153	62	111	93	175	108	40	68	74	83	26	82	45	25	33	39	17
NOON-4:30P																												
WSB	9	32	32	31	33	28	10	38	103	155	131	92	47	77	65	94	67	31	47	42	44	13	37	26	19	16	18	12
WAGA	7	25	30	27	26	22	8	22	80	113	98	51	19	35	29	67	33	14	19	24	28	8	32	18	10	14	17	7
WXIA	6	22	20	20	23	23	6	23	70	98	86	46	18	29	24	62	33	13	19	20	28	7	24	12	7	9	11	5
WTBS	1	5	6	8	7	6	1	5	29	44	27	18	12	18	13	13	8	6	12	13	7	3	13	9	6	6	6	5
WATL									4	6	3	3	1	1	1	2	2	1	1	1	1		2	2	1	1	1	1
WANX	2		7	6	7	5	2	7	2	35	11	10	9	13	8	7	4	4	5	6	7	1	4	4	3	1	2	5
WGTV									1	3	1	1	1	1		1	1		1	1	1		3	2		1		1
WETV									1	1	1												4	4		2		
HUT/TOT	28		26	23	26	26	26		311	455	358	221	107	192	147	265	148	69	100	100	113	32	113	71	46	49	55	35

3.00P–6.00P																						
WSB	12	34	30	33	29	31	13	38	139	225	172	124	71	117	86	107	76	43	54	51	54	29
WAGA	8	23	26	26	28	25	22	22	95	153	116	65	36	56	37	75	41	25	25	29	33	12
WXIA	6	16	18	14	18	15	16	16	67	107	86	46	31	40	29	52	27	13	17	19	24	12
WTBS	2	7	8	17	11	10	6	6	56	94	45	38	31	43	28	23	19	19	14	11	22	7
WATL	1	2	10	10	9	8	5	3	10	17	12	10		11	7	23	4	2	2	3	2	1
WANX						1	2	1	46	79	19	18	5	26	15	13	12	8	10	8	10	3
WGTV	4	10	3		2	4	4	1	6	10	1	1	1	1		1	1					1
WETV							1	1	1	2												
HUT/TOT	35		29	30	34	32	34		420	687	451	302	184	294	202	275	180	110	122	122	135	64
4.30P–6.00P																						
WSB	14	35	27	35	29	30	15	39	168	277	210	156	85	145	105	113	82	47	57	58	61	39
WAGA	9	23	27	28	27	26	23	23	109	189	135	79	50	74	48	85	51	34	32	34	38	17
WXIA	6	16	18	17	14	15	9	15	76	124	104	50	22	41	30	60	27	12	16	21	27	16
WTBS	3	7	8	18	18	18	6	6	63	107	56	47	36	51	34	30	25	23	18	14	16	10
WATL	1	3	9	9	8		2	4	12	21	15	14	6	13	9	5	4	2	3	4	4	1
WANX	4			8	9	12	4	1	51	89	24	22	19	30	19	16	15	9	13	9	9	3
WGTV	1	4	2	2	2	5	1	1	9	14	2	1	1	1		1	1				1	
WETV	2	10					2		2	3	1		1		9	1	1		3		1	3
HUT/TOT	40		31	34	39	35	39		490	824	546	369	219	355	245	310	205	127	139	141	156	86
4.30P–7.30P																						
WSB	16	32	28	33	30	30	17	35	190	324	268	175	73	136	105	141	91	39	54	68	76	46
WAGA	12	24	25	25	26	25	12	24	140	238	194	107	43	75	55	112	60	26	32	46	53	29
WXIA	9	18	19	17	14	17	12	17	107	176	158	69	20	44	36	85	34	10	18	28	35	25
WTBS	4	11	11	14	18	12	11	9	84	148	95	78	46	78	57	54	44	29	33	29	31	22
WATL	2	4	9	9	12	11	4	4	20	37	25	23	13	25	17	10	9	5	7	8	8	3
WANX	4	9	2	10	8	10	2	5	56	104	40	36	25	42	28	24	21	16	17	14	15	7
WGTV				1		2		1	9	10	3	2	1	1		2	1	1		1	1	
WETV					1					2	1	1		1		2		2	1		1	
HUT/TOT	49		39	41	49	46	48		605	1039	784	491	221	402	298	428	260	121	161	194	219	132
WSB	31	73	64	51	85	128	46	76	68	39	54											
WAGA	20	47	38	23	47	83	29	53	46	26	32											
WXIA	8	35	30	18	35	73	25	35	28	10	18											
WTBS	21	26	24	24	34	40	22	31	29	29	33											
WATL	8	11	10	10	14	15	3	8	8	5	7											
WANX	14	11	10	11	15	16	7	15	14	12	17											
WGTV	1	1			1	1		1														
HUT/TOT	103	204	177	137	231	356	132	219	194	121	161											

NOVEMBER 1982 DAYPART SUMMARY

* ESTIMATES EXCLUDE QTR-HRS STATION WAS NOT ON AIR
.. SHARE/HUT TRENDS NOT AVAILABLE
+ COMBINED PARENT/SATELLITE

DPS-1

ATLANTA

SOURCE: Arbitron Ratings Co. (1982), used with permission.

Time Period Averages

Television programmers are interested not only in broad dayparts, but in quarter-hour or half-hour segments within them. This information, found in the Time Period Averages section of ratings books, is useful in determining a program's strength against the competition for a specific quarter-hour or half-hour. Managers of affiliates look here, for example, to see how their local newscast stacks up against its competitors. It also has an overview of access time and early fringe competition and shows lead-in and lead-out effects. Programmers use it to analyze broad *time* segments.

Monday–Friday time averages are also published in the Time Period Averages section. It includes most prime-time network programming since it varies from night to night. These figures show performance during a daypart or time period when all days are averaged together, useful data when a programmer is looking at stripped programming in early fringe and prime-time access (7:30 P.M.–8 P.M. EST).

Program Audience

The last major section of a television ratings book, one television programmers often use, is the Program Audience section. Rather than lumping a program into a daypart, this section breaks each daypart and program into 15- or 30-minute segments—to isolate individual programs on different days of the sweep weeks. The Program Audience section is considered the "pure programming" section since each program is analyzed individually. It shows scheduling variations from night to night and allows programmers to examine ratings for their local news, say, night by night, and to eliminate the odd night when a sporting event, for example, cut into the news time.

Look at the Arbitron Program Audience data for WXIA-TV at 4:30 P.M. in Table 2-3. Notice that *Three's Company* is rated only for the first three weeks of the survey period. What happened? Look at the top of the column under WXIA-TV at 4:00 P.M. The station ran *NBC Pro Football* the fourth week of the survey, and it ran into the *Three's Company* time slot, as well as into *Live Eleven News* at 5:00 P.M. The Time Period Averages rating for 4:30 P.M. would include both *Three's Company* and *NBC Pro Football*; a hand calculation will quickly show how *Three's Company* rated for the three weeks it was on and how *NBC Pro Football* did at 4:30 P.M. This section permits analysis of individual programs without interference from ratings for other programs.

In summary, then, the sections of a television book provide programmers with at least four different ways to evaluate station performance. Daypart Audience examines broad time periods without regard to specific programs; Network Daypart includes only network programming; Time Period Averages provide programming data by quarter-hours and half-hours on a daily basis and are useful in analyzing competitive performance. Finally, Program Audience information isolates the "pure program" data. Each section answers different questions, and television programmers use every section as their questions shift.

TABLE 2-3.
Arbitron Local Market Report, Program Audience Section

Weekly Program Estimates / Program Audience Estimates

TIME AND STATION — DAY	PROGRAM	TELE-CASTS # OF WKS	# OF QTR-HRS	WK1 11/3	WK2 11/10	WK3 11/17	WK4 11/24	ADI TV HH RTG	ADI SHR	ADI HUT	METRO RTG	METRO SHR	METRO HUT	TV HH	PERSONS TOT 2+	18+	18-49	12-24	12-34	18-34	WOMEN TOT 18+	18-49	12-24	18-34	25-49	25-54	WKG WMN 18+
RELATIVE STD-ERR THRESHOLDS (1σ) 25%														12	28	18	15	19	18	17	14	13	18	15	12	12	13
50%														3	7	4	3	4	4	4	3	3	4	3	3	3	3
4:00P WXIA																											
THU	NBC PRO FTBL	1	13	6	6	6	7	13	32	40	13	31	42	153	348	310	205	41	127	114	109	71	15	50	59	67	28
FRI	WKRP IN CNN	3	6		4			5	16	32	5	15	30	62	102	74	51	37	50	33	46	30	22	22	17	18	10
FRI	WKRP IN CNN	4	7	7	5	5		6	19	31	6	20	30	71	116	75	59	42	68	48	46	35	22	27	22	29	15
SAT	SPORTSWORLD	4	22	8				1	5	30	1	5	30	18	26	26	14	7	7	9	11	6	3	6	5	5	1
SUN	NBC PRO FTBL	2	24		10	10	16	13	31	41	13	34	38	149	262	218	163	53	125	100	75	60	9	41	49	51	35
AVG	NBC PRO FTBL	2	37		10	10	14	13	32	39	13	34	39	150	292	250	178	48	126	105	87	64	17	44	53	56	33
AVG	WKRP IN CNN	4	38	6	5		5	5	18	30	5	18	29	66	107	71	46	38	56	35	42	25	18	19	16	20	10
WTBS																											
MON	MUNSTERS	4	8	2	2	3	3	2	8	28	2	8	27	52	85	43	35	27	37	26	23	18	16	13	9	11	6
TUE	MUNSTERS	4	8	2	2	3	6	3	12	27	3	12	25	64	99	54	47	34	49	39	23	20	17	16	11	11	4
WED	MUNSTERS	4	8	2	1	4	1	3	9	34	2	7	31	67	120	55	47	45	57	35	26	22	26	19	12	14	6
THU	MUNSTERS	4	8	2	2	5		2	6	32	2	9	31	59	110	54	45	36	54	33	28	23	23	14	13	15	6
FRI	MOVIE SPC	1	6	1			2	2	6	36	1	7	32	45	75	46	22	23	35	17	18	11	6	8	5	7	2
AVG	MUNSTERS	4	38	2	2	3	3	3	9	30	2	8	29	59	101	51	42	34	47	31	26	21	20	16	12	13	6
WATL																											
MON	STRSKY-HUTCH	4	16	1	1		1	1	3	29	1	2	28	5	12	8	8	2	7	4	2	2		1	2	2	1
TUE	STRSKY-HUTCH	4	16	1	1	1		1	3	27	1	2	25	8	13	9	8	5	10	6	5	5	1	1	3	3	
WED	STRSKY-HUTCH	4	16	1	1	1	1	1	3	35	1	2	34	6	11	10	7	1	3	4	1	1		3	3	3	1
THU	STRSKY-HUTCH	4	16	1	1	1		1	3	32	1	2	30	9	13	13	11	3	6	3	2	2	2	1	3	3	
FRI	STRSKY-HUTCH	4	16	1	1	1	1	1	3	30	1	2	31	7	16	11	7	3	8	6	5	3	3	5	3	3	
SAT	36 JUKBX SA2	4	16	1	2	1	1	1	3	33	1	5	31	10	16	8	8	3	8	7	6	6	3	1	3	4	4
SUN	FAMILY MOVIE	4	32	2	2	1	1	1	2	31	1	3	30	16	27	19	15	7	15	13	9	8	3	5	6	6	6
AVG	STRSKY-HUTCH	4	80	1	1	1		1	3	31	1	3	30	7	12	10	8	2	6	4	2	2	1	1	2	2	1
WANX																											
MON	TOM-JERY WDY	4	16	2	4	4	4	4	14	29	4	15	28	52	86	18	18	19	29	15	12	12	11	11	7	7	3
TUE	TOM-JERY WDY	4	16	6	6	1	4	4	14	27	4	15	30	50	84	18	13	26	30	10	10	10	13	9	5	5	
WED	TOM-JERY WDY	4	16	5	5	8	3	4	14	35	5	15	34	64	117	32	30	29	44	27	22	20	13	19	12	12	4
THU	TOM-JERY WDY	4	16	3	6	8	2	5	15	34	5	15	31	57	95	25	24	27	39	20	18	18	12	14	10	11	4
FRI	TOM-JERY WDY	4	16	3	3	8	1	5	15	32	5	16	30	57	95	24	22	20	31	19	17	17	10	14	9	9	7
SAT	BIG VALLE SA	4	16	3	2	2	1	2	5	33	2	7	31	28	54	30	17	10	19	13	24	12	2	7	10	10	9
SUN	MILLN $ MV	4	32	2	1	1	1	2	5	33	4	15	31	24	36	30	23	5	16	13	15	13		14	12	12	9
AVG	TOM-JERY WDY	4	80	5	5	7	7	4	14	31	4	15	30	56	96	22	21	24	34	18	16	15	12	14	9	9	3
4:30P WXIA																											
MON	ATHREES CMPNY	4	8	5	7	6	6	6	21	30	6	20	28	78	124	81	47	41	60	38	47	26	20	21	14	17	8
TUE	ATHREES CMPNY	4	8	5	8	6	4	5	18	28	5	18	26	67	118	81	42	41	53	30	48	22	21	14	15	20	12
WED	ATHREES CMPNY	4	8	8	8	8	4	7	20	36	7	17	35	91	144	90	59	57	77	40	59	34	30	23	24	28	11
THU	ATHREES CMPNY	3	6	8	8	4	3	6	20	33	6	17	31	80	130	92	59	43	59	39	58	34	26	27	24	23	10
FRI	ATHREES CMPNY	4	8	7	8	6	1	6	20	31	6	18	31	77	137	90	59	48	68	44	59	37	21	24	31	31	17
AVG	THREES CMPNY	4	38	7	7	6	7	6	20	31	6	18	30	79	130	87	53	46	64	38	54	31	24	21	20	24	12

SOURCE: Arbitron Ratings Co. (1982), used with permission.

OTHER ANALYSES AND COMPUTATIONAL
AIDS FOR PROGRAMMERS

Ratings companies issue reports on specific demographic groups or types of programs or station market sizes in easy-to-use formats, and stations, reps and ad agencies rely heavily on them. They also depend on other companies to re-analyze Arbitron's and Nielsen's ratings data and to supplement them with other research. Of all these additional services, programmers find analyses of syndicated television programs the most valuable.

Syndicated Program Reports

Affiliates and independents rely on off-network and first-run syndicated programming to fill parts of their broadcast days. But because syndicated programs are expensive, station decision makers want to know about a program's past performance. Will a program perform well in their market? Will its ratings justify its cost? Reps and program consultants especially want this information since they advise station programmers. Projecting or estimating ratings success for a first-run product is an involved process that, finally, comes down to an educated guess. The potentials of off-network programs are somewhat easier to evaluate, but even here no hard-and-fast guidelines exist. Lead-in programs, local competition and audience fads always influence ratings. Even the most successful network program may fail in syndication or perform below its network numbers at a given time or in a given market.

In making decisions about syndicated programs, Arbitron's *Syndicated Program Analysis* (Nielsen's publication is called the *Report on Syndicated Programs*) is helpful. The major television rep firms also provide similar analyses in less bulky and unwieldy formats. A page from the Arbitron analysis for *Barney Miller* is shown in Table 2-4. At the top of the page, the program, program type and overall ADI rating and share for all markets where the program is currently broadcast are specified. The number of markets carrying the program and the number of previous syndicated program analyses (SPAs) reporting on that program also appear.

The second section provides overall ratings and share data by daypart and by market size. For example, in prime-time access, *Barney Miller* had a 10 rating and 17 share in 14 markets with 4 or more stations. This section indicates the dayparts and market sizes where the program has played most effectively, quite useful information for programmers. Demographic data by daypart fill out the rest of this section.

The third section of the page shows a market breakout of specific stations carrying the syndicated *Barney Miller*. For example, in Albany, Ga., *Barney Miller* ran on WALB-TV during prime-time access in November 1982. The program had a 32 ADI rating and a 51 ADI share. This strong showing overpowered the competition—*The Jeffersons* on WTSG-TV and various programs on WVGA-TV. Other programmers, then, use this information either to purchase the show or to schedule it during a daypart where it seems to be most successful.

This third section also provides ADI demographic ratings and shares for a program in key demographic groups. In Albany, for example, *Barney Miller's* strength was with men and women 18+. Further analysis shows that since it

TABLE 2-4.
Syndicated Program Analysis, Arbitron 1982

III INDIVIDUAL PROGRAM SUMMARY III

BARNEY MILLER

BARNEY MILLER

129	MARKETS TELECASTING		PROGRAM TYPE: SITUATION COMEDY	DISTRIBUTOR: COLUMBIA PICTURES TV
129	STATIONS TELECASTING		PROGRAM DURATION: 30 MINUTES	
7	PREVIOUS SPA'S		TVHH IN ADI MKTS: 69,757,800	ADI TVHH RATING: 8.8
NOV 80 FIRST SPA			ADI MKTS % U.S. 83 58	ADI TVHH SHARE: 18.8

AGGREGATE TSA PROGRAM TOTALS FOR HOME STATIONS IN THOUSANDS (000)

DAYPARTS IN WHICH TELECASTS BEGAN	4+ STA. NO. TVHH MKTS R SH	3 STA. NO. TVHH MKTS R SH	2 STA. NO. TVHH MKTS R SH	1 STA. NO. TVHH MKTS R SH	ALL STA. NO. TVHH MKTS R SH	NO. OF STNS BY DAY-PART	TOTAL TVHH	WOMEN 18+	18-49	MEN 18+	18-49	TEENS 12-17	CHILD 2-11
M-F MORNING	1 3 16				1 3 16	1	28	19	11	12	12	1	4
M-F AFTERNOON	1 7 17				1 7 17	1	295	217	111	171	171	35	20
M-F TOTAL DAYTIME	2 6 17				2 6 17	2	323	236	122	183	183	36	24
M-F EARLY FRINGE	33 8 16				57 8 17	57	3698	2635	1469	2370	1464	548	710
MN-SA PRIME ACCESS	14 10 17	19 10 23	5 8 16		32 12 19	32	1837	1426	807	1336	825	242	303
SU-SA PRIME	3 13 24	2 13 25	1 19 32		6 13 25	6	240	183	90	163	92	31	40
M-F LATE NIGHT	12 7 22	9 7 24	1 12 36	3 12 24	23 7 23	23	757	583	359	490	334	53	32
SAT MORNING				1 8 37									
SU-SA SGN/ON-SGN/OFF	70 8 18	42 11 25	13 11 24	4 10 27	129 9 19	TOTAL PRGM 129	7188	5307	2977	4771	2938	944	1146

MARKET NAME SGN-ON/SGN-OFF SH DAY/TIME/TELECASTS TSA (000) COMPETING PROGRAMS	CALL LETTER	TV HH HH RTG RT IDX	HH SH SH IDX	WOMEN 18+ R SH	18-49 R SH	MEN 18+ R SH	18-49 R SH	TEENS 12-17 RTG	CHILD 2-11 RTG	LEAD-IN HALF HOUR PROGRAM NAME	TV HH R SH	WOMEN 18+ R SH	18-49 R SH	MEN 18+ R SH	18-49 R SH	TEENS 12-17 RTG	CHILD 2-11 RTG	LEADOUT ADI TV HH R SH
		(000)		(000)	(000)	(000)	(000)	(000)	(000)		(000)	(000)	(000)	(000)	(000)	(000)	(000)	(000)
ALBANY, GA M-F 7:30P 20T/C TSA (000) THE JEFERSNS VARIOUS	WALB WTSG* WVGA*	55S/S 32 367 51 271 68 10 1 16 1		23 48 53 9 20 1	17 39 25 12 26 1	26 53 51 7 14 2	19 44 26 8 18 1	17 10 15 1	12 13 1	NBC NGHT NWS TSA (000) SANFORD-SON VARIOUS	39 58 71 9 13 1	28 58 59 7 15 1	20 48 25 9 21 1	32 62 55 6 11 2	22 51 26 7 17 1	12 6 15 1	7 12 1	35 51 71 4 5 3 4
ALBNY-SCHDY-TROY M-F 5:00P 19T/C TSA (000) MASH-S HR HPY DAYS AGN	WNYT WTEN+ WRGB	20S/S 8 86 18 96 38 13 32 8 18		6 22 30 5 18	4 17 14 9 36 5 20	5 20 22 10 39 4 15	3 14 10 9 40 4 17	2 4 13 11	3 6 6 9	THE JEFERSNS TSA (000) CHIPS-S LITTLE HOUSE	6 18 38 8 23 8 25	4 20 21 4 23 6 33	4 20 13 4 21 6 32	3 20 21 4 29 3 18	2 16 6 3 25 3 19	7 11 9 6	4 6 9 10	8 17 39 15 34 9 21
ALBNY-SCHDY-TROY AVG 5:00P> 23T/C TSA (000) VARIOUS	WNYT WTEN+	20S/S 8 91 19 101 39 12 30		6 23 32 9 33	4 17 14 9 34	5 19 23 9 36	3 14 10 9 37	3 5 11	3 6 6	THE JEFERS> TSA (000) CHIPS-S >	7 20 41 8 22	5 23 26 4 21	4 20 13 4 21	4 20 23 5 26	3 17 8 4 24	6 9 8	3 6 8	8 18 41 14 30

SOURCE: Arbitron Ratings Co. (1982), used with permission.

did less well with women and men 18–49 (only 17 and 19 ratings), it appeals strongly to the older audience (50+) in this market. The data in the market section show how a syndicated program has performed against specific competition.

Before purchasing a syndicated program, station programmers typically choose markets that are similar to their own in size and regional characteristics and chart the performance of that program to determine its best daypart, its strength and weaknesses against specific competing programs and its demographic appeal. The *Syndicated Program Analysis* enables programmers to estimate the likely performance of a syndicated program and then to schedule it effectively in their line-up. If a program proves unsuitable (demographically or in terms of ratings projections), the analysis is helpful in targeting another program to meet a station's programming needs.

The *Syndicated Program Analysis* is limited since it contains program data only about syndicated programs already on the air, and quite often stations must decide whether or not to purchase a program *before* it is released in syndication (or even produced). This is particularly the case with **first-run syndicated** programs (never on a network) and popular off-network programs (often purchased before any station has tried them out). (The subject of purchasing **futures** on programs is covered in chapters 7 and 8.) In the case of off-network programming, national and local data from the program network performance can be projected to the local market—though many markets differ substantially from the national market. However, airing programs in first-run syndication is riskier since they lack both network and station track records.

A ratings book represents only a fraction of the data available from Arbitron and Nielsen. The books exclude each diarist's age, county of residence, zip code and specific viewing and listening patterns. A diary also tells what the diarist was watching at 5:45 P.M. before he/she began watching the 6:00 P.M. news, but Arbitron and Nielsen store this raw diary information on computer tapes that stations can examine for a substantial fee, by means of a computer terminal. Arbitron's terminal system is called *AID* (Arbitron Information on Demand); Nielsen call theirs *Data Command*. The information on these computer tapes allows programmers to analyze nonstandard dayparts, specific groups of zip codes, nonstandard demographics, county-by-county viewing and audience flow patterns. In addition, sales staffs use the terminals to compute audience reach and frequency.

Other Computer Analysis Services

Several other companies provide ratings data-analysis services to stations and advertising agencies. Two of them, Marketron in radio and Telmar in television, have copyrighted software that analyzes Arbitron data. They use the local Arbitron market reports on computer tape. Because they have access only to published ratings reports and not raw diary data, these companies cannot provide customized demographic or daypart analyses. However, Marketron's and Telmar's analyses have many features that Arbitron and Nielsen reports lack. For example, they rank stations in a market and give audience distribution information.

Diary Analysis

The management of any station, network or cable service subscribing to either Arbitron or Nielsen can personally review viewer and listener diaries. Arbitron stores its diaries in Laurel, Maryland, and Nielsen in Dunedin, Florida. Naturally, companies specializing in diary reanalysis for stations have grown up within commuting distance of these warehouses.

The main reason for inspecting diaries is to search for unexpected entries—such as how viewers or listeners recorded the station's or service's name or call letters (or slogan or air personalities). Sometimes diarists name things differently than stations expect them to. A station can remedy incorrect attributions in subsequent ratings periods by submitting a limited number of different "nicknames" to Arbitron or Nielsen (or by changing a slogan if it is easily confused with the competition's).

Before computerized systems became available, reviewing diaries was standard procedure after each ratings book was published. This procedure declined with the arrival of computer tape, and now the information can be examined anywhere with the appropriate software.

Customized Television News and Radio Research

Most professionally managed stations continually conduct research for their station and about their market. They try to understand problems and interpret trends that may affect programming *before* they affect ratings. Many large-market stations spend hundreds of thousands of dollars each year to find out:

- how programming is perceived
- which on-air personalities are liked and disliked
- how other competing stations/channels are perceived
- how we can improve our station image

Programmers use this research to head off problems before they become serious.

Microcomputers and Ratings

As of the early 1980s, broadcast stations and cable services of all sizes routinely used microcomputers in all their operations, including programming. By early 1984, a limited amount of Arbitron radio data was available on disks in the IBM-PC format, an option called Arbitrend. Arbitrend reflects only the continuously measured markets and contains only a few demographics. In the era of the "electronic ratings book," programmers (and sales executives) need only insert the appropriate disk in a portable computer to call up specific dayparts and demographics. Television ratings and syndicated program reports should be available on disk (in several formats) by the middle of the decade.

Programmers for music radio stations can also purchase (or write) software to accomplish most of the tedious work involved in developing a station's music playlist. Edd Routt covers the process of creating music wheels in Chapter 15. Even now, one software program on the market accounts for up to 50 different position and rotation characteristics of songs.

Using microcomputers in broadcasting and cable may be the most important single programming development since the invention of magnetic recording tape. Present practices barely hint at the ways microcomputers will affect program evaluation, purchase and scheduling over the coming decades. Clearly, those planning to enter the fields of broadcasting and cable will need microcomputer experience.

RADIO REPORTS

Audiences for radio stations are more fragmented than broadcast television audiences (although the introduction of cable is altering that condition for television). The largest radio markets such as Los Angeles have more than 80 stations, dividing the audience into tiny slivers per station. In general, radio stations compare their share of the audience and their cumulative audience to that of other stations with similar formats in the same market. The most popular stations use shares and the least popular use cumulative audiences—although formats lending themselves to tuning in and out (such as all-news) use cumulative audience ratings even when they are popular. This subject is examined in Part IV in detail. The top 100 radio markets correspond closely to television ADI/DMAs, but because some areas of the United States have radio but no television (largely in the West and South), the total number of radio markets is larger than the 210± television ADI/DMAs. As of 1983, Arbitron measured 275 radio markets.

Ratings books for radio are organized differently from those for television. An Arbitron radio ratings book contains Share Trends, followed by Demographic Breakouts, Daypart Averages, Cume Estimates, Hour by Hour Estimates and a few smaller sections. The age and sex categories used in radio differ from those used for television because radio stations target their programming to more precisely defined demographic groups. Thus, age ranges for radio are smaller than those used in television, typically just ten years, as in 25 to 34. Most classification groups end in "4" for radio (24, 34, 44, 54); the "9" groups used for television (18–49, 25–49) are broader, reflecting the more heterogeneous nature of television audiences and thus television advertising sales.

Share Trend

The Share Trend section reports a station's shares for five ratings books—the current survey and the previous four surveys, covering, altogether, a period of about a year. These data show a station's share pattern (its "trend") over time. An example for the demographic category of total persons 12 + is shown in Table 2-5. A programmer can get a very quick overview of all stations' performances in the market from the Share Trend section.

For example, consider WNCI-AM in Table 2-5, Mon.–Sun. 6 A.M.–MID. From the fall of 1980 to fall 1982 shown as O/N on Table 2-5, the stations 12 + share has shown a steady decline from 11.1 to 6.1. The drop is consistent and should greatly concern the station's management. However, WLVQ-AM, though it has gone up and down, is basically stable and leads the market. These data tell WLVQ's program director that its music probably needs some fine tuning in the

TABLE 2-5.
Arbitron Radio Market Report, Share Trends

Average Share Trends - Metro Survey Area

TOTAL PERSONS 12+

MON-SUN 6:00AM-MID

STATION CALL LETTERS	O/N 80	SPRG 81	FALL 81	SPRG 82	FALL 82
WBBY	1.8	1.6	.8	1.4	2.0
WBNS	5.5	6.3	6.7	6.7	5.8
WBNS FM	9.1	7.8	6.7	7.4	6.9
WCOL	5.2	7.9	7.2	6.6	5.5
WHOK	3.7	4.6	3.7	3.3	4.1
+WLOH	1.5	1.1	1.4	.9	.7
WLVQ	14.0	15.9	12.6	11.0	12.6
WMNI	6.1	6.7	6.2	5.1	6.5
WNCI	11.1	10.0	8.6	8.5	6.1
WNRE	..	.1	.2	.1	
WNRE FM	.7	.7	.3	.8	.7
WRFD	1.0	.4	.8	.5	1.8
WRMZ	2.9	3.4	2.6	3.0	1.8
+WSNY	2.2	3.4	4.7	7.1	8.3
WSYX	..	..	..	..	.3
WTVN	12.3	7.3	13.0	9.3	11.2
WVKO	3.7	2.2	3.1	4.5	7.0
WXGT	9.1	10.8	10.9	10.9	8.6
WLW	.8	1.1	1.0	1.5	.6
METRO TOTALS	15.3	15.7	14.0	16.2	16.6

MON-FRI 6:00 AM-10:00 AM

STATION CALL LETTERS	O/N 80	SPRG 81	FALL 81	SPRG 82	FALL 82
WBBY	1.3	1.1	.2	.7	1.0
WBNS	6.8	9.1	9.9	10.1	9.5
WBNS FM	7.7	6.7	4.6	5.9	5.4
WCOL	6.0	7.5	8.3	6.5	6.8
WHOK	4.9	4.9	4.4	2.9	3.6
+WLOH	1.5	.8	1.5	.4	.8
WLVQ	11.7	12.2	9.6	8.8	11.2
WMNI	9.7	9.6	7.5	6.3	9.1
WNCI	11.4	9.3	8.6	9.8	6.5
WNRE	..	.1	.2	.2	
WNRE FM	1.0	1.2	.8	1.5	1.4
WRFD	1.0	.4	.5	.3	1.4
WRMZ	1.4	3.0	1.7	2.6	1.3
+WSNY	2.4	3.5	4.6	5.6	7.6
WSYX	..	..	..	..	.4
WTVN	15.3	11.5	17.0	13.8	15.1
WVKO	2.2	1.5	2.1	3.9	3.2
WXGT	7.5	9.6	8.8	10.1	7.3
WLW	.5	.7	.8	.8	.6
METRO TOTALS	21.7	22.2	19.6	22.2	22.9

MON-FRI 10:00 AM-3:00 PM

STATION CALL LETTERS	O/N 80	SPRG 81	FALL 81	SPRG 82	FALL 82
WBBY	1.6	.6	.6	1.8	1.5
WBNS	5.4	6.1	6.3	7.1	5.6
WBNS FM	13.1	11.0	8.7	10.9	9.4
WCOL	5.7	9.2	9.5	7.9	6.5
WHOK	4.4	5.7	3.7	4.3	5.2
+WLOH	1.3	1.2	1.0	1.1	.2
WLVQ	14.4	14.5	11.8	10.8	13.3
WMNI	5.9	6.0	7.9	4.9	6.2
WNCI	11.2	10.1	9.5	8.1	6.2
WNRE	..	.2	.2	.2	
WNRE FM	.8	.6	.4	.4	.4
WRFD	1.3	.4	1.1	.2	1.6
WRMZ	4.1	5.0	3.7	3.6	3.0
+WSNY	1.1	1.8	2.3	3.3	9.9
WSYX	..	..	..	..	.3
WTVN	9.9	7.3	11.3	9.1	7.8
WVKO	3.0	1.6	2.6	3.8	5.6
WXGT	7.5	7.9	8.3	9.3	6.5
WLW	.5	.6	.9	1.1	.3
METRO TOTALS	18.3	19.1	15.6	18.9	19.4

MON-FRI 3:00 PM-7:00 PM

STATION CALL LETTERS	O/N 80	SPRG 81	FALL 81	SPRG 82	FALL 82
WBBY	2.0	1.4	1.0	1.4	2.3
WBNS	4.6	6.3	5.2	6.5	5.1
WBNS FM	10.0	8.7	8.3	8.3	8.0
WCOL	5.6	9.4	8.3	9.1	6.2
WHOK	3.0	4.3	2.7	2.8	3.9
+WLOH	1.2	.4	.6	.6	.4
WLVQ	14.7	17.4	15.4	11.7	13.3
WMNI	5.1	5.9	6.1	4.8	6.0
WNCI	11.7	10.6	8.5	8.1	5.8
WNRE	..	..	.1		
WNRE FM	.5	.5	.2	.5	.1
WRFD	1.2	.5	.7	.9	2.0
WRMZ	3.9	3.7	3.5	3.0	2.0
+WSNY	2.5	3.1	4.6	7.0	9.7
WSYX	..	..	..	..	.2
WTVN	9.1	6.3	10.1	8.5	8.2
WVKO	3.3	1.5	1.2	3.1	7.2
WXGT	10.9	10.7	12.0	10.8	9.3
WLW	.9	1.1	1.0	1.2	.4
METRO TOTALS	16.0	17.4	15.4	17.2	18.2

MON-FRI 7:00 PM-MID

STATION CALL LETTERS	O/N 80	SPRG 81	FALL 81	SPRG 82	FALL 82
WBBY	4.3	1.8	1.9	2.1	3.6
WBNS	5.6	3.4	5.7	4.9	5.0
WBNS FM	8.1	6.6	6.4	5.1	5.9
WCOL	5.6	5.6	3.8	3.7	2.8
WHOK	1.8	3.3	3.9	2.8	4.2
+WLOH					
WLVQ	18.9	20.4	18.1	14.5	16.9
WMNI	3.0	5.4	4.6	4.6	5.8
WNCI	10.8	9.0	7.8	7.2	6.7
WNRE					
WNRE FM	.8	.5	.1	.6	.8
WRFD					
WRMZ	3.2	2.8	3.3	2.1	1.9
+WSNY	4.3	5.4	9.7	13.8	8.6
WSYX	..	..	..	..	.4
WTVN	8.8	3.9	7.7	7.8	11.4
WVKO					
WXGT	12.3	14.4	14.2	13.4	12.0
WLW	2.6	3.8	1.4	3.8	1.9
METRO TOTALS	8.0	9.9	9.4	10.5	9.0

Trends may not always reflect actual changes over time due to changes in methodology, etc. See paragraph 39 n, page ii.
Footnote Symbols: (**) Station not reported this survey. (+) Station reported with different call letters - see page 5B.

SOURCE: Arbitron Ratings Co. (1982), used with permission.

TABLE 2-6.
Arbitron Radio Market Report, Demographic Breakouts

Average Quarter-Hour Listening Estimates

DAYTON FALL 1982

AVERAGE PERSONS — TOTAL SURVEY AREA, IN HUNDREDS

STATION CALL LETTERS	TOT PERS 12-	MEN 18-24	MEN 25-34	MEN 35-44	MEN 45-54	MEN 55-64	WOMEN 18-24	WOMEN 25-34	WOMEN 35-44	WOMEN 45-54	WOMEN 55-64	TNS 12-17
*WAVI	66	1	2	6	1	4		4	3	3	16	16
WBZI	29	2	3	2	2	1	3	3	2	4	5	1
WDAO	82	5	16	3	3	4	7	12	8	8	3	11
WDJX	55	3	6	1	4	1	9	11	8	1		16
*WELX	11		1	1	1		1	1	1		2	
WFCJ	24	3	1	5	3			3	1	4	6	
WHIO	137	4	5	4	15		1	8	9	13	16	2
WHIO FM	301	1	14	31	14	11	1	18	33	29	49	1
WING	86	3	12	12	3	26	9	17	15	5	4	1
WJAI	66	1	3	6	8	4	5	1	6	6	7	1
WONE	152	4	12	18	18	8	7	14	22	16	6	6
*WPTW	8				6				1			
*WPTW FM	10					6				2	2	
WTUE	202	54	31	1	2		33	16	2	2	1	60
WVUD	55	10	15	1		2	14	9	2			3
WBLZ	77	5	5	2		1	13	11	5	1		33
WEBN	34	12	4	1			6	4				6
WKRQ	63	9	2	3			13	5	3			27
WLW	76	2	13	7	6	8	2	9	3	5	6	1
WPBF	28		6	4	1		4	7	3	2		1
WPFB	14			4	1	1			2			
WSKS	24	11	3	1			3	2	1	3	3	3
WYYS	63	6	13	2		2	12	15	3	3	2	5

AVERAGE PERSONS — METRO SURVEY AREA, IN HUNDREDS

STATION CALL LETTERS	TOT PERS 12+	MEN 18-24	MEN 25-34	MEN 35-44	MEN 45-54	MEN 55-64	WOMEN 18-24	WOMEN 25-34	WOMEN 35-44	WOMEN 45-54	WOMEN 55-64	TNS 12-17
*WAVI	60	1		6		4		4	3	3	11	
WBZI	22		3	2	2	2	2	3	3		3	1
WDAO	67	5	16	3	3	3	4	10	7	5	5	8
WDJX	51	3	6	1	1	1	9	9	7		1	15
*WELX	7			3			1	1			2	
WFCJ	5						1	1		1	1	
WHIO	123	4	5	4	14	9	1	8	8	13	12	1
WHIO FM	170	1	12	9	10	10	3	13	24	16	31	1
WING	78	2	12	11	3	4	5	15	13	3	3	1
WJAI	44	1	1	3	4	7		1	1	5	5	1
WONE	82	2	9	5	12	5	5	4	17	9	5	4
*WPTW	5					6			1		6	
*WPTW FM	8				6		8					
WTUE	150	37	24	1	1	1	28	12	2	2	1	44
WVUD	44	9	11	1		1	14	5	2			2
WBLZ	52	4	1	2			12	10	1	1	1	20
WEBN	6	3	1	1								1
WKRQ	7	1										6
WLW	20		2	4	1	3	2	6	1			1
WPBF	18		2	3					3	1		1
WPFB	5			3					2			
WSKS	10	5	2				1	2	1		1	2
WYYS	16	2	4	1		2	3	2	1	2	2	2
TOTAL LISTENING IN METRO SURVEY AREA	1128	88	122	71	52	59	94	114	104	72	83	111

SHARES — METRO SURVEY AREA

STATION CALL LETTERS	TOT PERS 12+ %	MEN 18-24 %	MEN 25-34 %	MEN 35-44 %	MEN 45-54 %	MEN 55-64 %	WOMEN 18-24 %	WOMEN 25-34 %	WOMEN 35-44 %	WOMEN 45-54 %	WOMEN 55-64 %	TNS 12-17 %
*WAVI	5.3	1.1		8.5		6.8		3.5	2.9	4.2	13.3	
WBZI	2.0		2.5	2.8	3.8		2.1	2.6	1.9	4.2	4.8	
WDAO	5.9	5.7	13.1	4.2	3.8	5.1	4.3	8.8	6.7	6.9	2.4	7.2
WDJX	4.5	3.4	4.9	1.4		1.7	9.6	7.9	6.7			13.5
*WELX	.6		.8	4.2				.9		1.4	2.4	
WFCJ	.4							.9			1.2	
WHIO	10.9	4.5	4.1	5.6	26.9	15.3	1.1	7.0	7.7	18.1	14.5	.9
WHIO FM	15.1	1.1	9.8	12.7	19.2	16.9	3.2	11.4	23.1	22.1	37.3	.9
WING	6.9	2.3	9.8	15.5	5.8	6.8	5.3	13.2	12.5	5.6	3.6	.9
WJAI	3.9	1.1	1.1	4.2	7.7	11.9		2.9	2.9	6.9	6.0	
WONE	7.3	2.3	7.4	7.0	23.1	8.5	5.3	3.5	16.3	12.5	6.0	3.6
*WPTW	.7					10.2			1.0			
*WPTW FM						1.7				2.8	1.2	
WTUE	13.3	42.0	19.7	1.4		1.7	29.8	10.5	1.9	1.4		39.6
WVUD	3.9	10.2	9.0	1.4			14.9	4.4	1.9			1.8
WBLZ	4.6	4.5	8	2.8			12.8	8.8	1.0	1.4		18.0
WEBN	5	3.4	8	1.4								.9
WKRQ	6	1.1										5.4
WLW	1.8		1.6	5.6	1.9	5.1	2.1	1.8	1.0	1.4		.9
WPBF	1.6		1.6	4.2				5.3	2.9	1.4		.9
WPFB	.4			4.2					1.9			
WSKS	.9	5.7	1.6				1.1				2.4	1.8
WYYS	1.4	2.3	3.3				3.2	1.8	1.0	2.8		1.8

Mon.–Sun. 6 A.M.–10 A.M. slot where the numbers are weaker than in any other of the major dayparts reported on this page. WLVQ's programmer needs to examine additional pages in the book, however, before making any major decision.

Demographic Breakouts

A page from Arbitron's radio Demographics Breakouts section, Average Quarter-Hour and Cume Listening Estimates, is shown in Table 2-6. An Arbitron radio book is broken down into four major groups: men, women, adults and teens. The first three groups are further sudivided into six age categories and various dayparts. Teen numbers are given for various dayparts, but in only one age category, 12–17. All demographics include average quarter-hour persons and cume persons for both the TSA and metro areas. Station shares are included for the Metro area. Programmers use this section to analyze the station's performance in a specific demographic group for all dayparts, such as women, ages 25 to 49, Monday to Friday 6 A.M.to 10 A.M. (commonly written "W25–49, M–F 6a–10a").

The Daypart Averages and Cume section (see Table 2-7, Average Quarter-Hour and Cume Listening Estimates) is similar to the Demographics section except that the organization is different, and additional demographic categories appear for further breakouts.

Hour-by-Hour Estimates

Arbitron also reports an hour-by-hour analysis that includes 16 demographic groups by AQH for the TSA and Metro areas. A programmer can track a station's performance hour-by-hour from 6 A.M. to 1 A.M. to isolate particularly strong or weak hours during the broadcast day. Other sections of the Arbitron radio book include Away-from-Home-Listening and ADI data by demographics and daypart, both of which help radio programmers understand how listeners use radio.

TSL

Programmers are rarely content with the bare facts reported by Arbitron (or Nielsen in the case of television), and so they use all these various ratings to make many different computations. For example, radio programmers generally want to know how long their audience listens to their station, known as *time-spent-listening* (**TSL**). TSL is computed by dividing the product of the number of quarter-hours in a daypart times the rating by the cumulative audience.

To illustrate, assume we have the Los Angeles *Arbitron Radio Market Report* and want to compute the 18 + TSL for KABC-AM. We can pull the AQH and cume from the book to produce the TSL. The TSL for adults 18 + for this station, Mon.–Sun., 6 A.M.–MID., is calculated using the following formula:

$$TSL = \frac{AQH \text{ in Time Period} \times AQH \text{ Audience}}{Cume \text{ Audience}}$$

TABLE 2-7. Arbitron Radio Market Report, AQH and Cume Section

Average Quarter-Hour and Cume Listening Estimates

STATION CALL LETTERS	ADULTS 18 +						ADULTS 18-34						ADULTS 18-49					
	TOTAL AREA		METRO SURVEY AREA				TOTAL AREA		METRO SURVEY AREA				TOTAL AREA		METRO SURVEY AREA			
	AVG. PERS (00)	CUME PERS (00)	AVG. PERS (00)	CUME PERS (00)	AVG. PERS RTG.	AVG. PERS SHR.	AVG. PERS (00)	CUME PERS (00)	AVG. PERS (00)	CUME PERS (00)	AVG. PERS RTG.	AVG. PERS SHR.	AVG. PERS (00)	CUME PERS (00)	AVG. PERS (00)	CUME PERS (00)	AVG. PERS RTG.	AVG. PERS SHR.
*WAVI	66	464	60	440	1.0	5.9	7	43	6	37	.2	1.4	18	172	17	160	.4	2.6
WBZI	28	425	22	291	.4	2.2	11	134	8	91	.3	1.9	16	289	13	208	.3	2.0
WDAO	71	782	59	666	1.0	5.8	40	422	35	365	1.4	8.4	57	614	48	517	1.2	7.4
WDJX	39	812	36	741	.6	3.5	29	549	27	510	1.1	6.5	38	753	35	682	.9	5.4
*WELX	11	115	7	82	.1	.7	2	22	2	15	.1	.5	9	71	5	38	.1	.8
WFCJ	24	341	5	157	.1	.5	7	103	1	51		.2	9	182	1	102		.2
WHIO	135	1991	122	1656	2.0	12.0	18	385	18	343	.7	4.3	44	876	42	785	1.1	6.4
WHIO FM	300	3016	169	1685	2.8	16.6	42	491	29	334	1.2	6.9	128	1372	75	852	1.9	11.5
WING	85	1683	77	1406	1.3	7.6	37	767	34	665	1.4	8.1	69	1289	62	1060	1.6	9.5
WJAI	65	712	44	446	.7	4.3	5	90	2	58	.1	.5	21	310	10	179	.3	1.5
WONE	146	1870	78	1031	1.3	7.7	37	517	20	279	.8	4.8	95	1198	53	687	1.3	8.1
*WPTW	8	100	8	95	.1	.8		23		23			1	35	1	35		.2
*WPTW FM	10	237	5	126	.1	.5		38		19			2	90	2	59	.1	.3
WTUE	142	1694	106	1073	1.8	10.4	134	1420	101	865	4.1	24.2	139	1590	105	1001	2.7	16.1
WVUD	52	934	42	677	.7	4.1	48	785	39	556	1.6	9.3	52	894	42	642	1.1	6.4
WBLZ	44	712	32	445	.5	3.1	34	539	27	329	1.1	6.5	42	652	31	414	.8	4.8
WEBN	28	466	5	76	.1	.5	26	406	4	55	.2	1.0	27	438	5	76	.1	.8
WKRQ	36	623	1	118		.1	29	480	1	86		.2	35	586	1	114		.2
WLW	75	1778	19	593	.3	1.9	26	595	4	169	.2	1.0	41	1051	11	347	.3	1.7
WPBF	27	513	17	325	.3	1.7	17	323	10	198	.4	2.4	25	466	16	303	.4	2.5
WPFB	14	428	5	89	.1	.5		40		10			6	145	5	63	.1	.8
WSKS	21	528	8	197	.1	.8	19	473	8	176	.3	1.9	21	504	8	193	.2	1.2
WYYS	58	749	14	247	.2	1.4	46	553	11	197	.5	2.6	52	648	12	230	.3	1.8
METRO TOTALS			1017	5704	16.9				418	2353	17.1				652	3807	16.5	

Footnote Symbols: (*) means audience estimates adjusted for actual broadcast schedule

STATION CALL LETTERS	ADULTS 25-49 TOTAL AREA AVG PERS (00)	CUME PERS (00)	METRO SURVEY AREA AVG PERS (00)	CUME PERS (00)	AVG PERS RTG.	AVG PERS SHR.	ADULTS 25-54 TOTAL AREA AVG PERS (00)	CUME PERS (00)	METRO SURVEY AREA AVG PERS (00)	CUME PERS (00)	AVG PERS RTG.	AVG PERS SHR.	ADULTS 35-64 TOTAL AREA AVG PERS (00)	CUME PERS (00)	METRO SURVEY AREA AVG PERS (00)	CUME PERS (00)	AVG PERS RTG.	AVG PERS SHR.
*WAVI	17	155	16	143	.5	3.4	19	176	18	164	.5	3.4	33	259	28	241	1.0	6.3
WBZI	11	233	11	177	.4	2.3	16	266	15	204	.4	2.8	16	252	13	176	.5	2.9
WDAO	45	413	39	352	1.3	8.3	51	467	43	398	1.3	8.0	29	302	22	243	.8	5.0
WDJX	26	480	23	417	.8	4.9	26	492	23	429	.7	4.3	10	263	9	231	.3	2.0
*WELX	9	71	5	38	.2	1.1	9	88	5	55	.1	.9	9	78	5	52	.2	1.1
WFCJ	5	118	1	76		.2	9	155	2	93	.1	.4	15	197	2	92	.1	.5
WHIO	39	735	37	665	1.3	7.9	54	939	52	847	1.6	9.7	68	1118	60	936	2.2	13.6
WHIO FM	118	1256	71	797	2.4	15.1	139	1510	84	949	2.5	15.7	182	1794	100	1012	3.6	22.7
WING	61	1055	55	870	1.9	11.7	64	1115	58	930	1.7	10.8	43	757	38	605	1.4	8.6
WJAI	20	284	9	153	.3	1.9	30	370	16	215	.5	3.0	41	477	27	307	1.0	6.1
WONE	84	939	46	535	1.6	9.8	100	1105	56	637	1.7	10.5	88	1085	53	645	1.9	12.0
*WPTW	1	25	1	25		.2	1	30	1	30		.2	7	54	7	49	.3	1.6
*WPTW FM	2	69	2	51	.1	.4	2	80	2	56	.1	.4	5	124	4	78	.1	.9
WTUE	52	759	40	494	1.4	8.5	52	785	40	514	1.2	7.5	8	268	5	202	.2	1.1
WVUD	28	580	19	369	.7	4.0	28	596	19	385	.6	3.6	4	143	3	115	.1	.7
WBLZ	24	358	15	236	.5	3.2	24	370	15	248	.4	2.8	9	167	4	110	.1	.9
WEBN	9	178	2	43	.1	.4	9	178	2	43	.1	.4	2	52	1	21		.2
WKRQ	13	291		79			13	308		83			6	135		32		
WLW	37	925	11	311	.4	2.3	43	1079	11	339	.3	2.1	35	863	12	313	.4	2.7
WPBF	21	350	14	237	.5	3.0	23	366	15	245	.4	2.8	10	181	7	127	.3	1.6
WPFB	6	116	5	57	.2	1.1	7	166	5	57	.1	.9	9	262	5	62	.2	1.1
WSKS	7	157	2	75	.1	.4	7	161	2	79	.1	.4	2	41		21		
WYYS	34	423	7	134	.2	1.5	36	450	9	142	.3	1.7	10	149	3	50	.1	.7
METRO TOTALS			470	2826	16.1				535	3232	16.0				441	2604	16.1	

SOURCE: Arbitron Ratings Co. (1982), used with permission.

Therefore, the TSL for KABC-AM is:

$$\text{AQH in Time Period} = 504^*$$

$$\text{AQH Audience} = 872 \ (00)^{**}$$

$$\text{Cume Audience} = 9,875 \ (00)$$

$$\text{TSL} = \frac{504 \times 872}{9875} = 39.9$$

Therefore, the programmer concludes that the average length of listening to KABC for an adult 18+ is 39.9 quarter-hours during a given week, 6 A.M.–MID. A high TSL indicates that people (who listen) are listening for long periods of time, not that a lot of listening goes on. TSL refers only to the amount of listening by those who do listen. Television programmers also calculate time-spent-viewing using the same formula.

Turnover

Another calculation, **turnover**, indexes the rate at which an audience changes, or turns over, during a time period. Turnover is calculated by dividing the cumulative audience by a quarter-hour rating:

$$\text{Turnover} = \frac{\text{Cume Households or Persons}}{\text{AQH} + \text{Households or Persons}}$$

A low turnover rate indicates a loyal audience, and high turnover means a station lacks "holding power." Television stations, on the other hand, *expect* more turnover than radio stations and go after greater *reach*. Turnover is calculated for public broadcasting and cable as well as commercial radio and television. Tracking the amount of turnover over time and graphing it provide a quick clue to changes in audience listening or viewing patterns for an individual station.

CABLE RATINGS

Arbitron and Nielsen currently provide only limited national data for cable and pay cable services. Both companies supply audience estimates for premium services and some of the larger basic cable networks; local origination would also be included in Nielsen's *Monthly Cable TV Status Report* if and when it achieved a 3 percent audience share (this figure has yet to be reached).

Nielsen gathers and interprets national ratings for cable services exactly as it does for broadcast television and radio. Its 1700 metered television homes, of which about one-third have cable, provide the national data. Nielsen issues monthly cable reports based on NTI data.

---

*There are 504 quarter-hours from 6 A.M.–MID., Mon.–Sun.

**Zeros indicate that these numbers are in thousands, i.e., 87,200.

On the local market level, both Arbitron and Nielsen measure cable service audiences along with broadcast station audiences in the all-market sweeps (using diaries). Cable ratings are not stable, however. To qualify for inclusion in the standard television sweep reports, a cable service must hit 20 percent of net weekly circulation. In the first year of cable reporting (1982) only HBO, WTBS-TV (the superstation), Showtime and ESPN qualified. By the end of 1983, WTBS qualified in 92 Arbitron markets, WOR in 11, WGN in 24, HBO in 32, CBN in 12, CNN in 2, USA in 2 and Showtime in 1. A cable service is included if 20 percent of TV households in the market view it for at least 5 minutes during a survey week.

Arbitron and Nielsen are testing methods to measure cable audiences independently from broadcast audiences, but to date these methods have proved unreliable. It was hoped that the Cabletelevision Advertising Bureau's 1983 Cable Audience Methodology Study (CAMS) would clean up some of these methodological problems, but the preliminary results demonstrated the inadequacies of *all* current methods of measuring cable audiences and suggested no new format for better measurement.[8] The A.C. Nielsen Company conducted the CAMS study for the CAB, testing six different measurement methods for both broadcast and cable audiences on data collected in 44,000 diaries and 82,00 telephone calls. No one method was equally successful in measuring both cable and broadcasting audiences. Cable measurement is in its infancy and much more research will be needed.[9] Accurate measurement may await a large number of interactively wired homes.

Premium Services

The pay cable services, called premium networks in this book, have special measurement problems. Movies, the largest element in their programming, are scheduled in repeating and rotating patterns, to attract large cumulative audiences for each feature. This method contrasts with the broadcast television pattern of scheduling a movie or series episode only once in prime time (typically) and seeking the largest possible audience for that one showing.

Indeed, viewers shift the times they watch pay cable so much more than they do broadcast television by changing channels back and forth, recording movies on home recorders and so forth that it becomes problematic to use the same measurement criteria. And the greater number of cable television networks fragment the ratings much as radio stations do in major markets. Cable programmers, however, use available ratings information to judge individual program popularity and channel popularity, but as yet cable networks rarely win particular time periods. Occasionally, however, the cumulative audiences in all showings for a topnotch movie on HBO equal the size of a television network's audience.

Table 2-8 is a sample page from Nielsen's *Pay Cable Report.* Its terminology differs from that of broadcast ratings books. For example, MAFF refers to the combined ratings of stations with more than one affiliation ("multi-affiliates"). DIST refers to distant independent stations not transmitted by satellite, whereas SSS refers to satellite transmitted independents ("superstations"). CBLE refers to all cable-originated programming except pay networks, including basic cable networks transmitted by satellite and local origination channels. Table 2-9 shows

TABLE 2-8.
Nielsen Ratings for HBO, April 1983

SOURCE: A. C. Nielsen Co., used with permission.

DAY / TIME / STATION — PROGRAM NAME	HH RTG	HH SHR	ADL 18+	WOM 18+	WOM 18-24	WOM 18-34	WOM 18-49	WOM 25-54	WOM 50+	MEN 18+	MEN 18-24	MEN 18-34	MEN 18-49	MEN 25-54	MEN 50+	TNS 12-17	CHD 2-11
WEDNESDAY NOV 23																	
7.15PM																	
HBO MEN GYMNASSP	2	4	1	1	2	1	1	1		1	1	1	1	1		2	
ABC ABC 3	10	21	7	8	6	6	6	7	12	6	2	4	5	6	11	2	1
CBS CBS 3	10	20	7	7	3	4	5	7	13	6	2	3	5	6	13	3	3
NBC NBC 3	9	18	6	7	3	4	5	6	12	6	3	3	5	6	10	3	3
MAFF MAFF 3	<v																2
IND IND 3	9	18	5	5	8	6	5	5	5	5	3	5	4	5	6	8	7
DIST DIST 3	3	5	2	2	3	2	2	2	1	2	1	1	2	2	1	2	2
SSS SSS 3	3	6	2	2	1	2	2	2	2	2		2	2	2	2	2	2
CBLE CBLE 3	4	8	2	2		2	2		3		3	1	1	1	1	2	2
PBS PBS 3	1	2	1	1	3			1		1					1		
HUT & PUT *	50		33	34	28	28	29	31	50	32	17	23	27	31	48	25	23
7.30PM																	
HBO MEN GYMNASSP	2	4	1	1	2	2	2	1		1	1	1	1	1		2	
ABC ABC 3	11	22	8	9	9	8	8	8	12	7	3	5	6	7	10	4	1
CBS CBS 3	11	20	7	8	6	6	6	7	12	7	4	5	5	6	12	4	6
NBC NBC 3	10	19	7	8	5	6	6	7	13	7	4	5	6	6	10	4	3
MAFF MAFF 3	<v																5
IND IND 3	8	15	4	5	5	4	5	5	5	4	2	3	3	4	7	7	7
DIST DIST 3	2	4	1	1	2	1	1	1	1	1		2	2	2	1	1	1
SSS SSS 3	3	5	2	2	1	2	1	2	2	2		2	2	2	3	2	2
CBLE CBLE 3	4	8	2	2		2	2		3		3	1	1	1	2	2	1
PBS PBS 3	1	2	1	1	3			2	2	3							
HUT & PUT *	51		35	36	33	31	32	33	52	33	22	26	28	32	49	26	23
8.00PM																	
HBO BUDDYBUDDY E12	6	11	4	4		4	4	4	5	4		4	4	5			
ABC FALL GUY	15	26	11	12	12	13	12	12	13	10	9	10	10	10	10	10	2
CBS WHIZ KIDS	8	13	4	5	4	4	5	5	4	4	3	3	3	4	4	7	11
NBC BOB HOPE	14	24	10	11	9	9	9	9	18	10	6	7	8	8	16	9	8
MAFF MAFF 3	<v																5
IND IND 3	5	9	3	3	3	2	3	3	4	4	2	3	3	4	4	4	3
DIST DIST 3	2	3	1	1	1	1	1	1	2	1	1	1	1	1	1	3	1
SSS SSS 3	3	4	1	1	1	1	1	1		2		2	2	2	3	1	
CBLE CBLE 3	3	6	2	2	1	1	2	1	3	2	2	2	2	3	3	2	2
PBS PBS 3		5	2														
HUT & PUT *	59		42	43	37	37	40	41	56	41	30	36	38	41	52	38	36
8.30PM																	
HBO BUDDYBUDDY E12	6	11	4	4	4	4	4	4	5	4		3	4	5	5	4	2
ABC FALL GUY	16	26	12	13	14	13	13	13	13	10	10	11	10	10	10	10	11
CBS WHIZ KIDS	14	13	4	5	4	4	5	5	4	4	3	4	4	4	4	6	8
NBC BOB HOPE	14	23	10	11	9	9	9	9	18	9	6	7	8	8	16	9	5
MAFF MAFF 3	<v																3
IND IND 3	6	9	3	3	3	3	3	3	5	4	2	3	4	4	5	3	
DIST DIST 3	2	3	1	1	1	1	1	1	1	1	1	1	1	2	1	1	1
SSS SSS 3	2	4	2	2	2	1	1	1	3	2		2	2	2	3	1	1
CBLE CBLE 3	3	5	2	2	1	1	2	3	3	2	2	2	2	2	3	2	2
PBS PBS 3	3	6	2	2	1	1	2				1						
HUT & PUT *	59		43	44	38	38	41	42	56	42	30	37	39	42	52	38	35

TABLE 2-9.
Directions for Reading the Daypart Section of Nielsen's Pay Cable Report

HOW TO READ THE DAYPART SECTION

DAY TIME STATION CH	NETWORK	HH RTG	HH SHR	CUM %	ADL 18+	
SUN-SAT						An estimated 10 percent of HBO households were tuned to ABC during the average quarter hour Sun-Sat 8:00PM-11:00PM.
8:00PM-11:00PM						
HBO		12	25	64	8	
ABC	A	10	21	67	6	
CBS	C	10	21	64	6	
NBC	N	8	17	61	5	An estimated 17 percent of HBO households using television were tuned to NBC during the average quarter hour Sun-Sat 8:00PM-11:00PM.
MAFF	A-C-N	<<				
IND	I	3	6	25	2	
DIST		2	4	16	1	
SSS		2	4	21	2	
CBLE		2	4	22	1	
PBS	P	1	2	17	1	
HUT & PUT	*	47			33	
8:00PM-11:00PM MON-SAT & 7:00PM-11:00PM	SUN					
HBO		11	24	65	8	An estimated 33 percent of all adults 18 years or older in HBO households viewed their television during the average quarter hour Mon-Sat 8:00PM-11:00PM & Sun 7:00PM-11:00PM.
ABC	A	10	22	67	6	
CBS	C	10	22	66	7	
NBC	N	8	17	61	5	
MAFF	A-C-N	<<				
IND	I	3	6	26	2	
DIST		2	4	16	1	
SSS		2	4	22	2	
CBLE		2	4	22	1	
PBS	P	1	2	17	1	
HUT & PUT	*	47			33	
11:00PM-11:30PM						An estimated 37 percent of HBO households viewed one quarter hour or more of HBO Sun-Sat 11:00PM-11:30PM.
HBO		8	21	37	5	
ABC	A	9	23	33	7	
CBS	C	8	21	28	6	
NBC	N	7	18	25	5	
MAFF	A-C-N	<<				
IND	I	3	8	12	2	
DIST		2	5	7	1	
SSS		1	3	7	1	
CBLE		2	5	9	1	An estimated 39 percent of HBO households were using their television during the average quarter hour Sun-Sat 11:00PM-11:30PM.
PBS	P	1	3	3		
HUT & PUT	*	39			28	
9:00AM-12:00MD						
HBO		5	16	74	3	
ABC	A	7	23	82	4	
CBS	C	6	20	82	4	
NBC	N	5	16	79	3	
MAFF	A-C-N	<<				
IND	I	3	10	44	1	An estimated 4 percent of all adults 18 years or older in HBO households viewed CBS during the average quarter hour Sun-Sat 9:00AM-12:00MIDNIGHT.
DIST		2	7	32	1	
SSS		2	7	43	1	
CBLE		2	7	38	1	
PBS	P	1	3	31	1	
HUT & PUT	*	31			18	

SOURCE: A.C. Nielsen Co., used with permission.

TABLE 2-10.

	Source (Date of Estimate)			
	A.C. Nielsen Company (February 1984)	Arbitron Television (February 1984)	ICR, Titsch Communications (March 1984)	Paul Kagan Associates (December 31)
Basic Cable Subscribers	34.740 million	32.547 million	30.700 million	31.36 million
U.S. Television Households	83.8 million	83.97 million	83.775 million	84.0 million
Cable Penetration of U.S. Television Households	41.2%	38.8%	36.7%	37.3%
Homes Passed by Cable			54.500 million	55.9 million
Cable Penetration of Homes			56.4%	56.1%
Pay Cable Subscribers			18.300 million	
Pay Cable Units				26.42 million
Pay Penetration of Basic Cable			59.1% (Subscriber Penetration)	84.2% (Unit Penetration)
Headends	8,171			
Systems			5,865 (February 1984)	5,546

Reprinted with permission of NCTA Research and Policy Analysis Department.

how to read the Daypart section of the report. This information is the current equivalent of national broadcast television ratings (NTIs). Notice that specific program titles appearing on the broadcast network affiliates are omitted.

Cable Penetration Measures

Using figures supplied by the cable systems themselves, the industry updates cable statistics monthly, reporting how many households have access to cable wires at the present time—called **homes passed** or HP (see Tables 2-10 and 2-11). They show that 51–55 million homes were passed by cable. Basic cable subscribers are a percentage of the total number of television households in the United States (TVHH), which is the measure of **cable penetration.** In Table 2-11, cable penetration is 35.7 percent, with 56.7 percent of homes passed shown as subscribing to cable. The number of pay cable subscribers appears both as a percentage of total television households and as a percentage of basic cable subscribers. Thus, 32.9 percent of U.S. households subscribed to pay cable in May 1983, and 58.1 percent of basic cable subscribers took one or more pay channels.

Churn or Turnover

In cable, turnover is the ratio of disconnecting subcribers to newly connecting cable subscribers. When applied to cable, the number of disconnects divided by the number of new subscribers yields turnover. The common industry

TABLE 2-11.
CableVision's Cable Barometer

Cable barometer	
Television households (TVHH)	83,900,000
Homes passed by cable (HP)	51,019,700
Percent of TVHH passed by cable	60.8%
Basic cable subscribers	28,933,300
Percent of TVHH with basic cable	35.7%
Percent of HP with basic cable	56.7%
Pay cable subs	16,800,000
Percent of TVHH with pay cable	20.2%
Percent of HP with pay cable	32.9%
Percent of basic subs with pay cable	58.1%

Figures are as of May 31, 1983

term for turnover is **churn**. The problems associated with churn are described in detail in Chapter 9.

The audiences for most advertiser-supported cable networks are too small (at any one time) to show up in Arbitron and Nielsen ratings books (although ESPN and WTBS-TV are included in Nielsen's NTI reports). Most basic cable networks estimate their audiences on the basis of customized research. The importance of cable ratings will increase once there is general agreement on a single approach to data collection and analysis. As of the mid-1980s, for cable networks other than the very largest, cable reports are restricted to estimates of network penetration and turnover.

RATINGS LIMITATIONS

Although many broadcast programmers are aware of the limitations of ratings, in practice these limitations are rarely considered. This result is not one of ignorance or carelessness so much as of the pressure to do daily business using some yardstick. Programmers, sales staff, station reps and advertising agencies all deal with the same numbers. In any one market, all participants—those buying programs, those selling time and those buying time—refer to the same sets of numbers (Arbitron and/or Nielsen reports); and they have done so for decades. The "numbers" for any single market usually show a consistent pattern that makes sense in general to those who know local history (such as changes in power, formats and ownership). Although broadcasters and the ratings companies know the "numbers"are imperfect, they remain the industry standard. In practice the numbers are perceived as "facts," not estimates.

Occasionally, a gross error will require a ratings company to reissue a book, but, for the most part, small statistical inequities are simply overlooked. To eliminate as much error as possible, Nielsen and Arbitron use advisory boards that suggest how to improve the ratings estimates. However, a change in ratings methodology always means additional costs passed on to broadcasters—a fact destined to create a conservative rate of change.

The major ratings limitations can be briefly summarized. Readers interested in further information should consult the references listed at the end of this chapter. The following five factors limit the validity, reliability, significance and generalizability of ratings data:

1. *Sample size.* Although each company tries to reach a sample that represents the population distribution geographically (by age, by sex, by income, etc.), occasionally a short-fall occurs in every market. In these instances, certain demographic groups have to be weighted to adjust for the lack of people in the sample (such as too few men aged 25 to 49). Weighting by large amounts makes the estimates less reliable. In this case, the responses of too few individuals represent too many other people/households.

2. *Lack of representation.* Both ratings companies refuse to sample from group living-quarters such as college dormitories. The problem with measuring viewing in group quarters is that the number of individuals viewing one television set cannot be estimated; in addition, choosing diary keepers is difficult.

(For the in-home sample, each diary is considered to represent an average number of people based on the in-tab sample.) Away-from-home-viewing (such as in hotels, motels, resorts) is also excluded for similar reasons.

3. *Ethnic underrepresentation.*　Estimates for ethnic groups are the most hotly debated aspect of broadcast audience estimates. Arbitron and Nielsen identify markets with large ethnic populations and offer a larger premium to minority group members for completing diaries. The usual payment is 50 cents for filling out a diary, but in high-density ethnic areas, black persons and Hispanics are offered from $3 to $5 each to complete a diary. Many critics feel this procedure produces inflated, inaccurate numbers. Telephoning individual homes (minority only) to stimulate the return of completed diaries has also been tried. Arbitron calls its version of this method "differential survey treatment." It is argued this method biases returns because those responding to it are probably not randomly representative of all blacks (or Hispanics); those diary keepers responding only to earn the money probably differ (in tuning habits) from the general distribution of minority groups. Ethnic procedures are continually discussed at industry meetings, and neither ratings company has yet developed a plan in which the majority of broadcasters and the Electronic Media Ratings Council concur.

4. *Differences in metered cities.*　Data from electronic meters frequently differ from diary data, and many analysts claim, with subtantiation, that metered cities show a decline in shares for independent stations. At least in the cities presently metered, viewing spreads to different services such as the national cable networks and home video recorders and computer games.

5. *Complexity of signal.*　Television and radio programming are now distributed by many means—over-the-air signals, MDS, DBS, basic cable television, premium cable services, cable music channels, digital electronic stock and bond reporting services and so on—all competing for audience attention. Current ratings methodology has not quite caught up with changes in consumer reception technologies. Both Arbitron and Nielsen are developing methods to measure multiple entertainment and information channels, but so far methodologies are weak. Often the cost of measuring viewing or listening outstrips the value of the data. Broadcasters, cablecasters and advertisers have yet to perceive enough need for the information to pay the cost of obtaining it.

Standard Error

The concept of standard error is not a ratings limitation, but rather a mathematical model whose use can eliminate some of the problems associated with ratings procedures. In practice, however, very few people using audience ratings ever take standard error into consideration. The "numbers" are seen as factual; sampling errors and other errors or weaknesses in research methodology are not considered in any way.

In essence, using the standard error model compensates for the fact that ratings are produced from a sample of people, not a complete count of an entire population. For whenever researchers project sample findings into the general population from which the sample was drawn, some error necessarily occurs. A standard error figure establishes the range around a given estimate within which the actual number probably falls. The range suggests how high or how low the actual number may be. The formula for standard error is:

$$SE = \sqrt{\frac{p(100-p)}{n}}$$

where SE = standard error

p = audience estimate expressed as a rating

n = sample size

For example, suppose that a random sample of 1,200 households produces a rating of 20. The standard error associated with this rating is computed as:

$$SE = \sqrt{\frac{20(100-20)}{1200}}$$

$$= \sqrt{\frac{20(80)}{1200}}$$

$$\sqrt{1.33}$$

$$= 1.15$$

A rating of 20 therefore has a standard error of plus or minus 1.15 points—meaning that the actual rating could be anywhere from a low of 18.8 to a high of 21.1. Another difficulty in calculating error is determining how confident we want to be of the results. It is possible to be very confident (with, say, a 95 percent probability of being right) or somewhat confident (with only a 65 percent probability of being right). Nielsen and Arbitron ratings are generally calculated to the lesser standard. Most social science research uses the higher standard. Both Arbitron and Nielsen include standard error formulas in all their rating books for those wishing to calculate error in specific ratings and shares, but of course printing the range for each rating/share would make rating books unusable. Nonetheless, the range is the most accurate version of each rating or share, given its data base—which may itself introduce a great deal more error.

SUMMARY

Program and audience research splits into qualitative investigations of audience reactions and preferences and into quantitative ratings information on audience size, age and sex. Television, cable and radio programmers in nearly all markets need a thorough understanding of ratings. The data provided by Nielsen and Arbitron are the "thermometers" for judging the success of programming decisions. The two widely recognized estimates of viewing are ratings and shares, and both figures can be calculated for a whole network, for a particular station, for a whole daypart, for a specific program, for a wide geographic area, for a metropolitan area, for a whole demographic group, for a subset of women and men and so on.

In addition to ratings and shares, the other major measurement tools television programmers use are homes-using-television (HUTs) and person-using-television or radio (PUTs and PURs). Television programmers use syndicated program reports, AID and other specialized analyses to select and schedule programs. Radio programmers often use computer software to help them analyze their demographics and schedule their music. Radio programmers look at computations of average quarter-hour persons (AQH), cumulative audience (cumes), time-spent-listening (TSL) and turnover. Reach and frequency are tools for radio, cable and public television. All rating or share numbers are only estimates of viewing and listening. They contain significant amounts of error because they are based on samples of the total audience. Unfortunately, for a variety of reasons, ratings data are treated as more reliable then they are. Qualitative research methods interpret ratings information; they tell programmers what ratings information means. Focus groups and microcomputers are changing the program decision-making process.

Notes

[1]James E. Fletcher and Roger D. Wimmer, *Focus Group Interviews in Radio Research* (Washington, D.C.: National Association of Broadcasters, 1981). See also Dennis S. Howard, "Don't Believe Everything You Hear on Focus Groups; Follow These Guidelines in Evaluating the Sessions," *Marketing News*, 28 January 1977, pp. 20–21.

[2]James E. Fletcher and Roger D. Wimmer, *Call-Out Research in Managing Radio Stations* (Washington, D.C.: National Association of Broadcasters, 1982). See also "Use of Call-Out Research for Radio Expanding as Stations Employ More Sophisticated Techniques," *Television/Radio Age*, 31 May 1982, pp. 40–41.

[3]James P. Forkan, "TvQs Complement Prime Time Ratings," *Electronic Media*, 16 June 1983, p. 10ff.

[4]Thomas F. Baldwin and D. Stevens McVoy, *Cable Communication* (Englewood Cliffs, New Jersey: Prentice-Hall, 1983), pp. 254–258.

[5]Hugh M. Bellville, Jr., "Cable Ratings Methodology Must Employ Common Parameters to Those Used by Broadcast Television," *Television/Radio Age*, 17 January 1983, pp. 70–73.

[6]The final two-hour episode of $M*A*S*H$ garnered 77 percent of the audience using television on the night of February 28, 1983. That rating exceeds by seven points the previous all-time high rating for the "Who Shot J.R.?" episode of *Dallas*. "News Update; $M*A*S*H$ Sets Ratings Record," *TV Guide*, 12 March 1983, p. A-2.

[7]"A Ratings Infant Makes Marked Progress," *Broadcasting*, 20 September 1982, pp. 63–64.

[8]Karen Bloom, "CAMS: Great Expectations on Hold," *View*, April 1983, pp. 56–57.

[9]Gale D. Metzger, "Cable Television Audiences: Learning from the Past and the Present," *Journal of Advertising Research* 23, August/September 1983, pp. 41–47. See also George Swisshelm, "Need Seen for Expanded Meters, Different Diaries to Measure Cable," *Television/Radio Age*, 28 March 1983, pp. 37–39.

Selected Sources

Description of Methodology: Arbitron Radio Market Reports. Laurel, Maryland: Arbitron Radio, 1983.

Description of Methodology: Arbitron Television Market Reports. Laurel, Maryland: Arbitron Television, October 1982.

Fletcher, James E. *Handbook of Radio and TV Broadcasting: Research Procedures in Audience, Programs and Revenues.* New York: Van Nostrand Reinhold Company, 1981.

Inside: Nielsen Station Index, 1982–83. New York: A.C. Nielsen Company, 1982.

Radio & Records, *R&R Ratings Report.* Los Angeles, California: Radio & Records, Inc., semiannual special reports.

Research Guidelines for Programming Decision Makers: A Programmer's Guide to the Dynamics of Radio. Laurel, Maryland: Arbitron Radio, 1977.

Webster, James. *Audience Research.* Washington, D.C.: National Association of Broadcasters, 1983.

Webster, James. *The Impact of Cable and Pay Cable Television on Local Station Audiences.* Washington, D.C.: National Association of Broadcasters, October 1982.

Wimmer, Robert D., and Dominick, Joseph R. *Mass Media Research: An Introduction.* Belmont, California: Wadsworth Publishing Co., 1983.

CHAPTER THREE

Station Representatives' Role in Programming

Richard A. Bompane

A QUICK GUIDE TO CHAPTER THREE

RICHARD A. BOMPANE, *as vice-president of research and programming at Avery-Knodel Television, collected, analyzed and applied programming research to station strategy. Avery-Knodel is one of New York's largest representative firms, with clients primarily in midsized markets. Before joining Avery-Knodel Television in 1974, Mr. Bompane was a research manager for Harrington, Righter & Parsons. Since 1961 he has held the positions of director of research and sales promotion for WCBS-TV in New York, director of research for WTOP-TV in Washington, D.C., research manager for H-R Television in New York, assistant director of research and sales promotion for Storer Television Sales, Inc., in New York, and research analyst for RKO General Broadcasting in the National Sales Division. He is presently vice-president for programming for Sandy Frank Associates, handling program syndication to rep programmers and stations.*

THE EMERGENCE OF THE PROGRAMMING REPRESENTATIVE

One of the significant changes in the television industry since 1970 has been the greater influence of national sales representatives in programming at the local station level. Because of changes in key sources of revenue, in regulation, in program supply and in competition, program strategies changed, which in turn created a new role for station representatives. Reps now advise stations on newscasts and on-air scheduling as part of a package of research, promotion and full-marketing services. Such programming services are offered only by major station rep firms. (Generally firms specialize in network-affiliated stations or independent stations in similar-sized markets.) This chapter examines the difference between the job of the rep programmer and the local station programmer. It spells out the sensitive relationship between syndicators and rep programmers and covers the kinds of research and program recommendations reps supply to their affiliates. In the 1970s a new role was created for national sales reps.

Program Depletion

As network-affiliated station revenues shifted from dependence on network compensation to local and national spot advertising in the 1970s, competition among the stations in a market increased in vigor. Many station managers felt unprepared to program their stations successfully and sought professional advice. Several segments of the industry responded to this need, among them television news and radio program consultants and sales representatives.

In the early 1970s, the Federal Communications Commission's prime-time access rule (PTAR) further complicated this situation. It opened up six half-hours of prime time each week for local station programming, leading to an even greater need for syndicated off-network situation comedies, westerns, drama series and cartoons to fill the half-hour access slots in large markets and the whole hour preceding prime time in markets smaller than the top 50. By the mid-1970s fewer series survived the five-year prime-time run necessary to generate enough episodes for effective stripping, and the supply of off-network reruns dwindled. (Stripping is covered in detail in chapters 7 and 8 because it is crucial to television station program strategy.) Since affiliates in the top 50 markets are prohibited from using off-network programs and so must rely on sources of first-run programming, the need for accurate information on which to base program purchase decisions became even more crucial.

One final complication in this program depletion scenario was that feature films—the television mainstay in the 1950s and early 1960s—became increasingly scarce in the 1970s. All three major networks expanded the number of movie nights in their prime-time and late-night schedules. As a result, stations faced higher costs for the movie packages remaining after network purchases. Then the pay cable movie services further depleted the supply of feature films by saturation scheduling. Since the networks and the pay services licensed the best titles, the local stations chose among movies of less promotional value.

Increased Competition

In addition to the program shortage, increased competition from independent stations in the major markets and from the growth of cable nationwide further stimulated the prices for desirable programs. A growing sophistication in the use of demographics and computerized coverage data by national (and some local) advertising agencies also altered the local competitive television programming situation. The combination of all of these factors created an interest in local station programming on the part of national sales representatives. The urgent need for professionalism in program purchases, newscasts and program scheduling resulted in an increased role for reps in local station programming.

The mutual interests of both representatives and stations are served by programming support from national reps, and station managers now rely on their reps for specific recommendations on program purchases and scheduling. In local programming, however, national reps remain in an advisory capacity. The rep simply does not have, and should not have, decision-making responsibility or control over a station's programming policies. The station, as a licensed trustee of the public airwaves, has ultimate responsibility for everything it broadcasts. Experienced station managers consider their rep's advice before committing funds to a particular program or deciding on a specific schedule, but they also consult local program and promotional departments, local and network sales management advisers and, occasionally, local community representatives.

REP PROGRAMMERS VS. STATION PROGRAM DEPARTMENTS

One might ask what sets the rep programmer apart from the station programmer. The differences, of course, lie in their backgrounds, in the information available to each and in their differing approaches to the same problems, particularly in the smaller markets.

The Local Program Director

Local program directors, with some exceptions in the largest markets, are generally graduates of a station's production staff. Their major responsibilities lie in producing and directing local programs, commercials, newscasts, sports and other special-event telecasts. They seldom have experience with national sales representatives, agencies or national advertisers. However, they do know about station budgets and facilities, the local market, the nature of the competition and the socioeconomic, religious, ethnic and cultural backgrounds of their audience. They also are aware of their stations' obligations and commitments to locally produced programming and public service.

In medium- and small-sized markets, program directors' primary responsibilities remain in on-air production. They have other program-related functions too, such as issuing the station's program schedules, maintaining liaison with network program sources and coordinating the arrival, telecasting and bicycling of program tapes. Although large-market program directors have considerable experience in program purchase and scheduling, only rarely do medium- and small-market program directors have a background in these areas. Consequently, national rep program departments deal infrequently with local station program directors; their main contact is the station manager in midsized and small-market stations.

The Rep Program Director

Programmers for national rep firms typically have some local station experience, generally in programming and probably in combination with research experience. They also frequently have experience in sales and promotion. Rep program directors know about local and national ratings service data, audience flow, duplication of viewing, demographics and psychographics. Rep program directors deal with several different television markets, attuning them to a greater variety of programming situations than local programmers or station managers see.

Rep program departments also have sources of information unavailable to their local counterparts either because of the expense of major research reports or the specialized interpretation some require or the failure of program syndicators to disseminate their information effectively to all stations in a reasonable time. National sales representative firms maintain daily contacts with stations in several markets that yield information on program trends and new techniques, and they usually purchase all of the audience-research information published by the Arbitron and Nielsen rating services. This information includes all reports published in every television market in the country, performance reports on all programs on network television and in syndication on a market-by-market basis, cable penetration information and special analyses such as TvQ data.

Rep programmers are also in constant communication with all three national television networks, independent groups, syndicators and producers, news and program consultants outside the firm and the various trade organizations, including the National Association of Television Program Executives (NATPE), the Television Programmers' Conference (TVPC), the Independent Television Station Association (INTV) and the National Cable Television Association (NCTA). Daily contacts among national sales representatives, advertising agencies and major advertisers also add to the information available to rep programmers.

The Rep–Station Program Team

Because of their very differences, rep programmers complement local station program directors. Their relationship involves a two-way flow of information—from the station manager (who in turn is informed by the local program department) to the national representative firm and from the rep programmers back to local management. More extensive and higher quality data for all parties result from this kind of teamwork. For the station, the desired outcome is a more competitive position in its market; for the representative firm, the goal is a station with higher ratings whose time is more valuable to sell. Higher profits are the underlying motive for both parties.

REP PROGRAMMERS' RELATIONSHIPS WITH SYNDICATORS

Rep programmers offer syndicators the opportunity to screen programs at a central location for individuals or groups of people who inform and influence a large number of prospective buyers. If a syndicator can convince the rep programmers that a series will produce high ratings for some or all of their stations, the syndicator gains their support for the series in several markets throughout the country without the added expense of travel to each market to make a presentation—an especially important consideration in medium- and small-market sales in which travel expenses greatly reduce potential return to the syndicator. Reps inform their clients of all presentations and recommend programs to individual stations as warranted. Even when the rep programmers do not believe in a program's appeal for a mass audience, they inform client stations of the existence of all shows, giving syndicators free publicity, if not open support.

Although syndicators maintain direct contact with stations, most tell rep programmers of their activities. Syndicators arrange periodic screenings of new and old program availabilities, discuss plans for producing new series and keep reps aware of contacts with their client stations. If syndicators feel sure their programs are viable, they will frequently suggest that local program directors or station managers contact their rep program department for its evaluation. Syndicators sometimes contact reps to get their opinions on the possibility of placing a show in a particular market and to discuss pricing before they approach specific stations.

Because rep programmers are indirect agents of their client stations, they must constantly be aware of their responsibilities to them and be cautious in dealing with syndicators. Certain unwritten rules apply to the relationship between rep programmers and syndicators. Rep program departments almost never give blanket recommendations for any program or series. No program will have equal appeal in every market, and each must be considered on a market-by-market basis. Rep programmers do not supply information to syndicators to aid them in negotiations with stations. This stance precludes any indication of prices paid by a given station for other programs, contract expiration dates, recent program purchases, future plans and speculation on which other programs a station is considering.

National sales representatives have no control over the prices charged for programming or what clients or other stations in a market actually pay. Rep program directors are occasionally involved in negotiating with syndicators, but instances in which the rep has the authority not only to negotiate but also to purchase programming on the station's behalf are rare. One main job of the rep programmers is to keep track of prices for major syndicated properties throughout the country, particularly in light of escalating program costs, so they can tell a station what a program's asking price is in its market and in other markets.

SERVICES PROVIDED BY REP PROGRAMMERS
TO STATIONS

A national representative's program department offers its clients extremely diversified programming services. Much of the information the rep program department disseminates is of a general nature covering networks, syndication, barter, specials, program performance, movies, trends and pilots in production or in planning stages. (These subjects are covered in other chapters, especially 3, 5, and 8, and definitions of many of the terms appear in the Glossary.) National reps also send local station sales staffs as well as sales departments reports on the overall ratings performances of new series and specials.

Network Program Information

The rep programmer located in New York has access to key programming sources at each of the three networks, at independent groups and from trade press publications. Until the end of the 1970s, an adversary relationship existed between reps and the networks. Obtaining any information from a network regarding program changes, specials or sports was extraordinarily difficult for a rep program department. Consequently, reps turned to other sources of information and frequently uncovered data not yet sent to one or more network affiliates. Occasionally, the reps' lists of the networks' upcoming specials, for instance, included twice as many programs as the lists the networks sent to some of their affiliates. This discrepancy pointed to a serious problem: Some network affiliates received program information sooner than others. The networks denied this situation existed, but on one occasion, reps found one client affiliate had been told of 30 upcoming specials and another client was aware of fewer than a dozen.

NBC was the first of the three networks to try to end the adversary relationship with national sales representatives. In 1978, it invited all firms to a preview presentation of its 1978–79 schedule. NBC also appointed a staff member in its Affiliate Relations Department as a rep contact for information on NBC programming. The timing of this decision may have been related to NBC's third place in the ratings and to its loss of several key affiliates to ABC. Although NBC's conciliatory gesture may have been self-serving, it solved one-third of the reps' problems in gathering network program information. In 1979 both ABC and CBS followed NBC's lead and held similar presentations of their 1979–80 schedules. As of the mid-1980s, the networks routinely supplied large amounts of information to reps.

Consequently, rep program departments are able to issue information on all three networks' program schedules. Rep program departments generally provide network information as follows:

Prime-time network schedules (monthly)

Daytime network schedules (quarterly)

Sports schedules (quarterly)

Specials (quarterly)

Movies (monthly)

Changes announced by the networks in any of these areas are sent out to the rep's client stations as addenda to monthly or quarterly reports. Because of the frequency of network program changes and new announcements about specials, rep program departments usually issue night-by-night prime-time schedules covering a one-month period.

Syndicated Program Information

Rep programmers also notify clients of new developments in syndicated programming. They report on (1) off-network programs released for syndicated rerun—as well as keeping track of those yet to be offered, (2) new programs produced especially for syndication, (3) barter programs, (4) specials, (5) sports series and (6) mini-network ventures such as Operation Prime Time (OPT).

When rep programmers screen a pilot or an episode of a new series, they issue program bulletins to client stations indicating their reaction to the show's content, production values, possible demographic appeals and proposed time periods. These reactions typically are stated in very general terms. Although rep programmers practically never give blanket recommendations to new series, even more rarely do they suggest that none of their client stations consider a particular series. However, in the late 1970s, few reps could resist high praise for *The Muppet Show* and this after seeing only a demo-tape, not even a full pilot.

The rep program department issues similar program bulletins to stations when it learns of a network television series to be offered in syndicated rerun. Traditionally, these series became available after network cancelation. However, beginning in the late 1970s, currently scheduled network series were offered several years prior to their release dates, generally with a guaranteed availability date. (The role of *futures* in program licensing is explained in chapters 7 and 8.) This situation sometimes led to stations airing a series of reruns while the first-run episodes of the same program were aired by the network in prime time. In these circumstances, network contracts usually require syndicators to change the on-air title of the reruns until the first-run show is canceled by the network.

For example, *Bonanza* reruns were called *Ponderosa* in syndication; *Marcus Welby, M.D.* became *Family Doctor; Emergency* became *Emergency One;* and *Happy Days* was *Happy Days Again.* CBS's *M*A*S*H* was an exception: It carried the same title in syndication as on the network.

Unlike bulletins about new programs, bulletins about off-network series or specials usually include some audience information relative to network performance in prime time plus daytime or late-night rerun track records. The syndicator generally supplies this information, but rep program departments may also gather such data.

Program Research Sources

Rep program departments provide client stations with the ratings and demographics for syndicated programs and feature films, along with data on developments in audience research. To do so, rep program departments invest several hundred thousand dollars each year in a variety of audience-research data from Arbitron, Nielsen and other sources. The Nielsen Television Index, for example, is so expensive, it is purchased solely by the networks for their exclusive use. However, networks supply much of the NTI information to trade publications, and so weekly reports become available to rep programmers. The overnight reports for the metered markets are also extremely expensive, but a few major-market sales reps do purchase them. Other representative organizations purchase the ratings service's weekly reports based on these overnight samplings. These weekly reports contain valuable information about the performance of new network programs—particularly important at the start of a new television season—and also include data on audiences for syndicated programs carried on stations in the metered markets.

Most reps subscribe to either Arbitron's or Nielsen's "rep package," which includes a copy of every ratings report published for every television market. These reports help reps keep track of program performance under all possible circumstances: how particular programs perform on weak stations (or small-market UHFs), on strong stations, in various dayparts, in particular regions of the country, in small markets and large markets and against every conceivable type of competition. They are also used to measure a program's potential in an untried market. If a client station is considering scheduling a new show in prime-time access, rep programmers can report on how the program did in any number of similar circumstances including daypart, competition, cable influence and other relevant factors.

As described in Chapter 2, following each major sweep period (November, February, May of each year) the ratings services publish compendiums of the performance of all major syndicated programs, called *Syndicated Program Analysis* by Arbitron and *Report on Syndicated Programs* by Nielsen. These reports are among the rep programmer's most valuable tools. Although they are published at least a full month after the usual ratings reports for the sweep, the syndicated-program reports list all the markets in which a program ran in an easy-to-use format. When rep programmers look for a group of programs to recommend to a particular client, these syndicated-program reports are generally the first source to which they refer—after finding out what the client station requires and what programs are available in its market. Rep programmers also use the information in syndicated-program reports to back up their estimates of anticipated audience levels for a recommended program.

Most rep firms also purchase Arbitron's and Nielsen's triyearly analyses of network programming. These reports (which Arbitron calls *The Network Program Analysis* and Nielsen calls *Network Programs by DMA*) list ratings levels achieved in every market in the country by every network program telecast during a ratings period. They lack the detail of their syndicated programming counterparts because they show only ratings in each market, not shares; they do include an index comparing each program's rating to its national average. Overall, however, these reports have little value for program decision making at stations.

Syndicators often have their own research and promotion departments issue information on the performance of the programs they distribute. This material is sent to all prospective purchasers and to national sales representatives. Rep program departments check the accuracy of these data and inform the syndicator and their client stations if the material is erroneous. If rep programmers use research information supplied by syndicators, they do so with the full knowledge that it is promotional. Occasionally, the syndicator of a new program retains a nationally known audience-testing firm for special research similar to network pilot testing. These test results are made available to reps and stations. However, such audience-reaction testing is done rarely because it is expensive for a series produced especially for syndication.

Computerized Research Analyses

Arbitron's Information on Demand (AID) and Nielsen's NSI-Plus are computerized research programs allowing subscribers to solicit more specific viewing information from the diary samples than is available in the standard printed research reports. Rep programmers use these research programs to interpret audience flow, duplication of audience and county-by-county coverage.

Audience flow analyses show what the audience does between programs. They show if a program held onto the audience that viewed the preceding program. They show if a program provides a good lead-in to a more important show. For instance, a stripped, syndicated series leading into the local news at 6 P.M., may generate a high audience share and therefore appear to be a success. However, if at the end of the series' episodes, a large percentage of its audience turns to the competition's nonnews programming or turns the set off, the series harms the station's local news: It is not supplying a strong flow of viewers to that newscast. If a large portion of the lead-in program's audience stays tuned for the news, then the show is a success in that it not only performs well but also builds the audience for the succeeding program. In another scenario, the lead-in series' viewers watch the *competition's* local news at six o'clock, leading to the conclusion that the first station's local news is weak. This type of analysis is one of the primary jobs of the rep programmer.

Duplication of audience studies are also audience-flow studies, but the programs being compared do not run adjacent to one another. Rep programmers use a duplication of audience study to determine if a station's news viewers tend to watch both the early and late local newscasts or to see which of several programs in one genre (such as sit-coms or adult adventure dramas) should be placed in a station's schedule and in what order.

Using computerized research or the *county-by-county coverage studies* published annually by the two ratings services, a programmer or news consultant can determine the weak areas in a station's coverage or in the performance of local news in any particular county or group of counties. If some counties are not watching a newscast to the same extent as "the average county," rep programmers may recommend that a station produce and promote news features of interest to the residents of that area.

Programming is a chess game in which the station strives to achieve the highest ADI and DMA share (CHECK) combined with a dominance in key demographics (MATE). All national advertisers and a growing number of local advertisers concentrate their advertising on particular demographic categories. The most requested demographic in the 1970s was women viewers between 18 and 49 years of age. The station that reached that audience had a strong advantage when soliciting advertising. However, because of changes in population growth, buying-power shifts and myriad other factors, as they entered the 1980s, many major television advertisers changed their key target audience to women aged 25 to 54. Such trends are monitored by rep programmers, and information of this nature is passed on to the stations.

THE PRIME REP SERVICE: PROGRAM RECOMMENDATIONS

The individual program recommendation is the most important rep service provided to client stations and the one demonstrating the rep programmer's real effectiveness and expertise. The station program department or station manager assumes responsibility for successfully programming one station, but rep programmers must successfully recommend programming to all the stations their companies represent. Of course, rep programmers cannot improve every station's audience in every time period, but their recommendations are expected to bring improvement in most cases. Consequently, rep programmers rely heavily on quantitative audience-research data. They also scrutinize all client stations to locate pending problems—inroads made by competitors, downtrends in shares or demographics and unusual program availabilities in any market (such as network programs that were not cleared)—so they can recommend changes without waiting for client stations to ask for them.

Station—Market History

The most recent ratings book tells programmers only that a problem exists; it ignores the extent and source of the problem. To become familar with long-term trends in a market, rep programmers study the programming posture of each client station over a period of as much as five years. This process means (1) tracking the programs aired successfully in the past in those markets, (2) determining whether problems are with individual programs, related to overall station problems or due to an increase in the competitiveness of other stations in the markets and (3) locating other program areas needing improvement. If a problem extends beyond a single half-hour of programming, it will not be visible in one ratings period; a long-term analysis is needed to bring it into perspective.

Counterprogramming

Once a programming problem is located and a clear understanding of the market's program preferences is determined, the rep's next step is to study the weaknesses and strengths of the client station's competitors. One key question is always whether the client station should try to draw audiences away from the competitors with similar-appeal programs or should build its own image with a different viewer group.

The station offering viewers a strong alternative to the types of shows available on other stations in the market will maximize its audience potential and inevitably draw some viewers from its competitors. This strategy is particularly effective when all competing stations are vying for similar demographics, often women 18 + years. For example, in a market in which two of the three stations are scheduling talk shows in early fringe (*Merv Griffin* against *John Davidson*), the third station will maximize its potential by programming a very different type of fare (for example, a series of half-hour situation comedies). This strategy should assure the station of higher shares and younger demographics (such as women 18–34)than either of its competitors because talk shows appeal to older adults and sit-coms generate 18–34 audiences. (Children and teens also tend to favor situation comedies over talk shows.)

In most markets, however, finding the right counterprogramming formula is not quite so easy. Consider a hypothetical three-station market in which all stations seek the same demographics, women 18–49. If one station carries strong sit-coms and another schedules a popular western series, the third station may program a talk show, although it would not normally do well among the 18–49 demographic group. A movie is a better choice, but stations must purchase the broadcast rights to several hundred features to develop a strong film library for stripping. Some stations have tried stripping a block of first-run syndicated game shows in early fringe—a practice that has met with limited success. The answer to this particular problem is not counterprogramming with specific programs but developing a stronger overall program line-up than either competitor.

Access is the time period that the networks cannot fill (other than with their regularly scheduled newscasts and a few other exceptions). In consequence, other counterprogramming factors enter the picture. Affiliates in the 50 largest television markets must air first-run syndicated series between 7:30 P.M. and 8 P.M. (EST). This restriction has led to programs specifically made for the access slot, mostly in the game show genre. Although most access shows were produced originally as once-a-week half-hours, the trend is toward strip programming, that is, five episodes per week.

Stripped programs generate more viewer loyalty (and are much easier to promote) than a series of five different shows each week (**checkerboarding**). Since 1976 the success of such stripped game shows as *Newlywed Game, Tic Tac Dough, Joker's Wild, Crosswits* and *Liars Club* has led several stations to abandon diversification in access-time programming. It is not unusual to see three or four stations in major markets vying for viewers with game shows in access. The independents in these markets, however, are not subject to the same restrictions as the network affiliates and compete very effectively in access with syndicated sit-coms previously run on network television in prime time (*Happy Days, All in the Family, M*A*S*H, Mary Tyler Moore*, to name a few). Chapter 7 makes detailed recommendations on affiliate strategies for access and other dayparts; Chapter 8 spells out independent strategies.

A new factor in programming comes from the cable networks and superstations choosing portions of their programming from the same restricted pool (Christian Broadcasting Network and WTBS, for example, purchase older off-network series and some first-run syndicated programs). In heavily cabled markets, then, the options for station programmers are reduced and competition fueled. Increasingly, rep programmers are used to interpret the effects of cable programming on broadcast stations and to locate the remaining scheduling options.

Creating an Audience Flow

To develop a strong schedule for a station, the rep programmer and local program staff must look beyond individual half-hours. Ideally, each program feeds viewers to the next show, creating audience flow. Special computerized research studies indicate how to group programs to create the strongest audience flow. If, for instance, a station wants to build a large young-adult following, it should begin by loading its early fringe schedule with a strong, kid-oriented cartoon series. This show, at about 4 P.M. (EST), will shift control of the television set from adults to children and effectively counterprogram the competition. To entice more adults into watching, the next half-hour should contain a sit-com having strong nonadult appeal (to hold the kids and teens from the lead-in) and yet also attract the 18–34 adults, especially women (**kiddult** programming). The third half-hour should contain an even more adult-oriented sit-com appealing also to men to continue building up the news block at 5:30 P.M. or 6 P.M. This strategy is called "growing your demographics" or "aging your demos."

However, some programs do not need a strong, or even compatible, lead-in to generate large audiences. At certain times of the day the available audience changes so much that it is not wise to rely on a lead-in strategy. Although factors vary by market, the strategies just outlined work well in early fringe and following the evening news. The time local schools let out—taking into account travel time—suggests the most appropriate time to begin scheduling for a nonadult audience. Generally 4 P.M. in Eastern time zone markets offers the best opportunity for switching from an adult-oriented network daytime schedule to kids' shows. Following the local or network newscasts, which lean toward older adult demographics, many stations draw more young adults using a highly popular comedy or a stripped game show.

Choosing the Right Program

To determine the best program choice for a client station, rep programmers list all available programs within the desired category, then rank them based on the average share performance of each show according to the syndicated ratings reports. Programs having a low share value or having undesirable demographic appeals are eliminated. The remaining programs are then examined for performance on similar stations, in markets in the same geographic area. Reps also consider how well they compete against the types of programs the client station's opposition schedules. Potential lead-in strength is also considered.

The rep programmer then presents the client with a list of first, second and third program choices, research data, projected audience levels for each show and the rationale behind the recommendations. Occasionally, a list of eliminated programs is prepared with brief statements explaining why each was dropped.

The Sales Factor

Each rep organization approaches the relationship between its sales and programming departments differently. Some firms allow the sales department to override the decisions of the program director. Others have group meetings, allowing programming, sales, promotion and other personnel to voice their opinions. A few firms give total program responsibility to their program departments.

Most program directors do not report to sales departments, but rather to corporate management. The rep programmer's function is to help stations develop the strongest, most salable schedule possible, while remaining aware of other important factors: FCC commitments, pricing, local pressures, station image, long-term planning and—something that should never enter into decisions but often does—the personal viewing tastes of the key decision maker, usually the local station manager. Although obviously important, sales value should not be the overriding factor in program recommendations because of the host of other considerations, especially station image and local pressure, that play a part in programming strategy.

NEWS CONSULTING

The Katz Agency formed the first formal rep news department in 1974. In 1975 Avery-Knodel Television entered into an exclusive agreement with an outside news consulting firm to conduct news analyses for its client stations and by 1977 had organized its own news consulting department. As of 1979 these two firms were the only national ones having formal news departments, but other rep firms are expected to enter the field in the mid-1980s.

Although station representative firms generally do not charge their clients more than the sales commission rate for programming services, news consulting is an exception. Both the Katz Agency and Avery-Knodel Television charge about $10,000 a year plus travel expenses for this extra service. These fees do not nearly cover the cost of operations, but if the client stations deliver higher news ratings using the news service, the rep firms can sell the news at higher advertising rates and make up their losses.

The first step in news consulting is to review videotapes of the client station's news programs and those of its competitors. An initial evaluation of the client's news—based on set design, camera work, news anchors' talents, content, and use of electronic news gathering (ENG) equipment and special effects techniques—is made. In a follow-up visit to the station the news consultant's preliminary evaluation is discussed in detail with station management, news directors, producers and on-air personalities. (Attitudinal research is used sometimes in rep news consulting but requires an independent research study, which is usually quite expensive.)

On every station visit, the news consultant studies the station's on-air news broadcast in depth, as well as the behind-the-scenes operations so important to a newscast. The production and assignment desks are given a critical inspection, as is the role played by the news director. The rep programmer suggests ways for these departments and individuals to improve their work. The news consultant also trains news anchors during these station visits to help them improve their camera presence, voice and delivery.

All of this work is intended to improve the quality of the client station's news and ratings. To this end, priorities, deadlines, training and personnel responsibilities are clearly assigned in a written evaluation covering every possible area of news broadcasting, including the following:

News set design

On-air talent (performance and training)

Format (newsroom, eyewitness, magazine, action)

Graphics

News administration (structure and control)

News director (role evaluation)

Assignment desk (library, news sources, story assignment)

Production desk (strategy, techniques, control)

Special projects

Staff training

Special series and features (minidocumentary series)

Electronic newsgathering (ENG)

Reporting (roles, story coverage, investigative)

Writing

Photography and editing

Promotion

The comments and evaluations of a station's *own* rep firm on news programs often are seen as less threatening to the station's talent and staff than those originating with an outside consulting firm. Sales reps have long-term relationships with client stations and are part of their ongoing activities. Station staffs see improving the news as in the best interests of all concerned.

THE FUTURE ROLE OF THE REP

The programming arena of the late 1980s will be even more competitive than it is at present, and the role of the rep programmer even more significant.

More television stations on the air, cable penetration of between 30 and 50 percent in most major markets and more superstations—combined with home videorecording, videodiscs and direct broadcasting (DBS)—all will be vying for more and more of the viewers' leisure time. By the late 1980s, an affiliated station will not be tied to one choice for its prime-time schedule but will be able to pick and choose from a variety of satellite-relayed programs. More option means a larger role for rep programmers: Television stations will need *more input* to make decisions more quickly. Because of the need for *more programming*, in the early 1980s several rep firms entered the field of production for syndication.

Clearly, the rep programmer's role will be magnified by increasing competition in all markets, but the question remains: Is the television industry ready to face the challenges ahead? In 1971, Les Brown, then television editor for *Variety*, wrote:[1]

> The system seems to change but never really does; there are only modifications and changes in style. The president of a network can buy shows and set operating policies, but he is powerless to alter the machinery of his industry. Whatever their capabilities, however forceful they may be as leaders, the men in television are lashed to the system. But the public is not lashed to it, and hope for the medium survives in that implicit freedom. The freedom of the public, in fact, is the time bomb in television.

SUMMARY

This chapter reviewed how the rep role changed as a result of the decreasing program supply and increased competition. The major rep firms now function as programmers, drawing on their nationwide experience in analyzing client stations. Nowadays, reps must have a background in research and programming. Reps usually understand multiple markets better than local station programmers. They generally deal with station managers rather than station programmers, but draw on the local market knowledge of both. Reps have access to a large amount of specialized ratings information such as network and syndicated program ratings; they analyze this information for their client stations. They also use three special ratings analyses—audience flow, audience duplication and county-by-county studies—to help client stations make program purchases and scheduling decisions. The largest rep firms also consult on local news. However, the primary concern of rep programmers remains the specific program recommendation that takes into account such strategies as counterprogramming, creating flow, targeting key demographics and sales appeal. The rep firm's programming role is likely to increase further in the face of cable and DBS competition.

Note

[1] Les Brown, *Television: The Business Behind the Box* (New York: Harcourt Brace Jovanovich, 1971), p. 365.

Selected Sources

"Cable Interconnects: Making Big Ones Out of Little Ones." *Broadcasting* (1 March 1982): 59–61.

Heighton, Elizabeth J., and Cunningham, Don R. *Advertising in the Broadcast and Cable Media*, 2d ed. Belmont, California: Wadsworth Publishing Company, 1983.

"The Radio Rep: Down in Number But Up in Ambition." *Broadcasting* (2 July 1979): 39–63.

"The Skyrocketing World of TV Reps." *Broadcasting* (4 June 1979): 37–62.

The Station Representative: His Role in National Broadcast Advertising. New York: Station Representatives Association, September 1980.

CHAPTER FOUR

The Influence of Group Ownership on Programming

Lewis Klein

A QUICK GUIDE TO CHAPTER FOUR

Lewis Klein *is president of Gateway Communications, Inc., a group owner of four television stations: WBNG, Binghamton, New York; WTAJ, Altoona-Johnstown, Pennsylvania; WLYH, Lancaster-Lebanon, Pennsylvania; and WOWK, Huntington-Charleston, West Virginia. Gateway Communications is a wholly owned subsidiary of the Bergen Evening Record Corporation. Before Gateway was formed, Klein was the director of television programming for Triangle publications from 1967 to 1972, supervising the program activities of Triangle's six stations and serving WFIL in Philadelphia from 1950 to 1972 in various program department functions. He was executive producer of the award-winning* Frontiers of Knowledge *series as well as* American Bandstand *and* College News Conference. *He served on the faculty of the University of Pennsylvania and is an adjunct professor of Radio-Television-Film at Temple University in Philadelphia, having taught there for 30 years. Mr. Klein is past president of the National Association of Television Program Executives, the Television and Radio Advertising Club of Philadelphia and the Delaware Valley Chapter of the Broadcast Pioneers; and he became president of the NATPE Educational Foundation in 1979. In 1982 he received the NATPE President's Award and in 1983 was made the Broadcast Pioneers' Man of the Year.*

TYPES OF GROUP OWNERSHIP

The largest percentage of broadcast stations and cable systems are owned by companies and corporations that own several other stations and/or systems. In broadcasting, the owner of several stations is called a **group owner,** the owner of several cable systems, a **multiple system operator** or **MSO.** Group ownership provides an edge in resources and clout over individual ownership but has some acknowledged limitations as well. This chapter examines the varied patterns of controls existing among group owners and MSOs, their operating methods, and the economic advantages and disadvantages of shared research, resources and recruiting among group-owned entities. The chapter's final section contains the projections of some broadcast television group presidents on programming strategies for the 1980s, collected especially for this book by Joel Chaseman, president of Post-Newsweek Stations, Inc.

Group-Owned Stations

Group stations are a broad class of stations. They can be owned by a network or by a nonmedia corporation; they can be network-affiliated or independent, UHF or VHF and located in the nation's largest markets (New York, Los Angeles, Chicago) or smallest markets (Tuscaloosa, Alabama; Binghamton, New York;

Austin, Minnesota; Waterloo, Iowa). More than 70 percent of the television stations in the top 100 markets and more than half of *all* television stations are group owned. More than three-quarters of all radio stations are group owned as are the majority of cable systems. Corporations buy stations because of their tremendous profitability. The average pretax profit for VHF television stations in the top 10 markets was about 40 percent of gross revenues in 1983. The profits on radio stations are much lower, but substantial in the top 100 markets.[1] Cable system ownership remains a shaky proposition, but the lure of large profits in the coming decades attracted many nonmedia corporations into cable in the 1970s.

The FCC imposes rules aimed at preventing undue concentration of media control. Chief among these is the "rule of seven" limiting a single owner to control of no more than seven stations in each class (AM, FM and television, with no more than five of the television stations in the VHF band). Many FCC observers expect the commission to revise the "rule of seven" in the mid-1980s so that groups can become larger. Neither Congress nor the FCC has yet imposed similar restrictions on group owners of cable systems. The proliferation of broadcast signals in cabled markets reduced government concern about ownership concentration of broadcasting stations; at the same time, cable consolidations in the late 1970s gave rise to questions about concentration in cable system ownership.[2]

The most prominent group-owned stations are the network-owned WNBC, WABC and WCBS in New York. The nine network **O&Os** (owned and operated stations) in the top three markets—the New York stations plus the Los Angeles stations (KABC, KNXT, KNBC) and the Chicago stations (WLS, WBBM, WMAQ)— garner the greatest gross dollars of all groups of stations. Most of the 15 network-owned stations are located in top 10 markets, are highly profitable and quite frequently lead their markets in ratings.

The remainder of group-owned stations are controlled largely by giant corporations, many of which also own radio stations, newspapers and cable systems. In addition to the ABC, CBS and NBC groups, about 135 of the nation's 165 television group owners are multiple-station owners, controlling valuable stations in more than one midsized or large market.

Table 4-1 shows the top ten groups plus ABC, CBS and NBC, listing them by rank and showing their circulation among U.S. television households as of January 1983. Each of the top three groups (CBS, ABC and Metromedia) reaches about 19 percent of U.S. homes.

As of 1983, Metromedia's coverage exceeds that of NBC's stations because Metromedia owns stations (largely independents) in more of the top ten markets. Metromedia became a major programming syndicator to other stations and cable systems in the 1980s.[3]

Although the issue of cross-media ownership remains thorny in many markets, overall, group ownership is one of the more positive trends in American broadcasting of the last 20 years. However, an enormous power gap separates the individual station and the national network, but fortunately many groups are of an appropriate size and strength to form an intermediate force between these extremes.

TABLE 4-1.
Top 13 Television Group Owners

Group Owner	Number of Stations Owned	1980 Rank	Percentage of TVHH
CBS	5	1	18.9
ABC	5	2	18.8
Metromedia	7	3	18.5
NBC	5	4	17.8
Tribune Co.	3	5	12.2
Group W	6	6	10.7
RKO General	3	7	9.7
Storer	7	8	8.8
Field	5	9	8.7
Gaylord	7	10	7.3
Cox	6	11	7.3
Capital Cities	6	12	7.2
Taft	7	13	7.1

SOURCE: January 1983 data from Herbert H. Howard, *Group and Cross-Media Ownership of Television Stations in 1983*, prepared for the National Association of Broadcasters, 1983, p.14.

Cable MSOs

Five group owners, MSOs, dominate the cable industry, owning nearly 1,500 local cable systems out of a total of over 5,000. In cable, as in broadcasting, the total number of subscribers is actually more important than the number of systems. Systems in urban locations have far greater concentrations of homes and larger subscriber rolls, just as broadcast stations in major markets have greater reach than rural stations. The very largest MSOs are Tele-Communications, Inc. (TCI), ATC (owned by Time, Inc.) and Group W; Cox and Warner Amex own fewer sytems but also have large numbers of subscribers because their systems are in desirable locations. Table 4-2 shows the top ten group owners in cable, many of whom also have broadcast interests.

PATTERNS OF CONTROL

Group owners exercise control of their stations and/or systems in a variety of styles. Most employ an executive headquarters programmer and staff to oversee and coordinate the programming functions for all their stations or systems. Some headquarters closely supervise local program budgets and programming-related decisions. Cox Broadcasting, Storer Broadcasting, Meredith and Group W are examples of this type of broadcast group owner. They require home office approval before an individual station may proceed with a major program purchase. Typically, the headquarters staff does not instigate purchases but does retain final approval. However, Combined Communications, another group owner, tends to purchase programs jointly for all of its stations and thereby centers virtually all program strategy within the home office.

TABLE 4-2.
Ten Largest Cable System Operators

		No. of Subscribers July 31, 1983	No. of Franchises Dec. 31, 1983
1.	TeleCommunications	2,297,000	428
2.	Time Inc.	2,267,000	119
3.	Westinghouse	1,872,000	140
4.	Cox Cable	1,379,000	58
5.	Warner Amex	1,340,000	146
6.	Storer Communications	1,291,000	122
7.	Times Mirror	858,000	67
8.	Rogers/Rogers UA	776,000	22*
9.	Newhouse	742,000	64
10.	Continental	686,000	66

* Includes only U.S. franchises

SOURCE: *Cable TV Investor Newsletter*, 1983, used with permission.

Other groups restrict themselves to veto power over the plans of the stations they own. Still others serve in an unstructured, advisory role. The stations Capital Cities Communications owns are autonomous in the area of program determinations. The three sets of network O&Os and Group W stations, however, have very close program ties to their headquarters. In groups in which program autonomy is encouraged, such as in Capital Cities, the headquarters uses detailed financial reports to track the profit picture of individual programs. Most group owners rely on local program directors to assume day-to-day program responsibility including scheduling, but the headquarters staffs play vital roles in major program-purchase decisions, key personnel hiring, program syndication and program department budgeting.

In cable, programming can be even more tightly centralized because cable does not operate under regulations requiring local responsibility (such as public service programming). TCI, for example, controls all programming decisions for its over 435 local systems in 43 states, reaching more than 2.4 million subscribers.[4] The local system manager and programmer act only as buffers for the headquarters staff, collecting local information and complaints and relaying them to headquarters. Local managers for TCI-owned systems lack the authority to make programming changes—or even wire uncabled areas. Cox Communications specifically prohibits program suppliers from communicating directly with its local cable systems. ATC, on the other hand, individualizes the array of channels on each of its cable systems and gives local programmers considerable authority over local scheduling.[5] In all cases the MSO negotiates contracts to license national cable networks. The pattern of control, then, varies widely from owner to owner, reflecting a fluid industry with large numbers of program decision makers.

ADVANTAGES OF GROUP OWNERSHIP

The overriding programming advantage of group ownership is that group *buying* cuts programming costs—although groups also *produce* programs for less because they can be used on several stations. Group ownership often means a station has first crack at syndicated programming and perhaps a lower cost per episode; cable group licensing also has definite impact on pricing. Program distributors often sell syndicated programs to group-station operators for less than if the programs were sold in the same markets on a station-by-station basis. This reduction in cost is, of course, a great financial advantage to the individual stations of the group. In program sales, distributor overhead is less when sales are to groups because travel and time is reduced. This savings permits stations and systems to carry programming they might not otherwise afford. Group stations also often share the use of film prints and videotapes, further reducing program costs.

Broadcasting Advantages

Group broadcasters often have the financial strength to buy desirable new programs that otherwise might be snapped up by their competition. The largest group owners can afford to purchase series and films with broad appeal to keep them from superstation competitors and local broadcast stations (known as **warehousing**). Group owners also have an edge with sydicators who call on headquarters programmers first because group program sales are more profitable than making market-by-market offerings. Sometimes programs are sold to group-owned stations even before competing stations are aware they are available. Often producers of a proposed new series delay production until at least one of the major station groups has contracted for the series. Many prime-time access program proposals languish on the drawing boards because no group of stations has made an advance commitment to purchase.

Aside from finances and programming, group program staffs help member stations in their day-to-day operations—overseeing everything from commercial copy, contests, staffing, government affairs and budgets to set design. Even program personnel are temporarily exchanged when illnesses or special productions create problems for group members. Most contacts between a local program director and the group program director are channeled through the headquarters, but occasionally exchanges occur directly between program directors within the group. Some groups hold periodic training sessions or idea-exchange meetings for their program directors and production managers. Some routinely exchange videocassettes, program activity reports and station visits. Program directors for group-owned stations can strive for promotion within the group stations without giving up tenure—a boon to both employee and group owner.

Cable Advantages

Group-owned cable systems also have certain advantages. As a rule, cable systems license networks of cable programming, both pay and nonpay, rather than individual programs. This subject is discussed in depth in chapters 9, 10,

11 and 12 in Part III. Group ownership of a very large number of cable systems, such as occurs with TCI, ATC and Group W, gives each of these groups enormous leverage over the cable program suppliers. Contracting to place a cable network on its 300 to 450 systems gives the group owner significant leverage in price negotiations: Often a cable network's survival depends on such a contract. Local systems then place the cable networks the MSO contracts on the local system in an array the system programmer designs.

MSOs, like group broadcasters, plan regular meetings for their local system programmers. As of the 1980s, these meetings focus more on technical and marketing problems than on programming strategy, but a gradual evolution of the industry is occurring. As the engineering problems of the 1970s were solved, managerial attention shifted in the early 1980s to marketing concerns such as churn. In the last half of the 1980s, system programming is expected to dominate managerial efforts as cable networks merge and fold. Chapters 9 and 12 deal with this subject in detail.

DISADVANTAGES OF GROUP OWNERSHIP

The nongroup program director is generally a more independent, more aggressive and faster-moving executive than the group programmer in broadcasting or cable. Groups usually employ experienced programmers along with extensive staffs, but consequently, group-owned stations and systems are often hampered by the committee-type decisions that ensue.[6] Groups tend to be slow to arrive at programming decisions and often breed several layers of inert program management. Nongroup programmers must make program decisions more quickly.

Group-owned or not, a station's and a cable system's programming strategies should be geared to specific local market factors. A small-market programmer may find that a group-acquired program or basic cable channel selected to suit the large-market stations or systems in the group is not useful in the smaller market.

Groups that force purchases on unenthusiastic stations and systems may reduce profits. When formats are too regimented for local origination and fixed numbers of entertainers and personnel required, such as with *PM Magazine*, individual stations may suffer. Inflexibility often afflicts group-owned systems. For example, TCI's centralization of cable programming has been a definite local marketing disadvantage. The standardized package of cable networks delivered to nearly all of its 450 systems fits poorly in some cases, creates local marketing headaches and increases costs because of subscriber cancelations. Group ownership is most alluring when it accommodates specific market needs and tastes.

THE SPECIAL CASE OF NETWORK O&O GROUPS

Network-owned stations in the top three markets have extraordinary collective power as members of groups. Since each group reaches about 19 percent of the total U.S. households with television sets, their purchase of a syndicated program often makes the crucial difference between the property's success or failure. These few group-owned stations can set programming trends for the entire syndicated-program market.

Although network O&Os are not directly controlled by their networks, they naturally share many common goals and interests with their networks. For example, an ordinary network affiliate does not necessarily give high-priority consideration to its prime-time access programs' lead-in effect on the 8 P.M. network programs. A network O&O, however, is extremely conscious of lead-in effects since the parent company's success depends in part on the audience delivered by the stations it owns and affiliates.

O&Os are also more concerned with group image. They *worry* more about it—especially in New York where they live next door to company headquarters—than stations in markets with less visibility. In the seven-station New York market, image determines certain viewing habits. For instance, on weekend afternoons when NBC programs sports, WNBC-TV often programs sports in its local time. This imitative practice may seem like overkill, but it maintains a consistent image with viewers and advertisers.

Network-owned stations use their networks' logos on the air and in their overall promotion; many nonowned affiliates do the same. WNBC-TV begins local news with the NBC chimes; WCBS-TV opens local public affairs programs with the CBS-eye design. As a result of such practices; viewers seldom distinguish between network programming and the owned station's local programming despite station-identity campaigns. Often, in consequence, owned stations must spend large amounts of time and money conveying station identity in the market—generally by more and better community programs, extensive on-air support of community projects and activities and occasional station-image campaigns like "your community-minded station." Despite these efforts, the average viewer does not yet differentiate between the television network and the local network-owned station, but educational efforts continue.

The 15 network-owned and operated stations produce tremendous profits for their corporate owners. At times the O&Os have made even more money than their networks. O&Os are also valuable to their networks because they assure **clearance** of all network programs in the top markets, setting a precedent for the rest of the country. Inability to clear programs in major markets can damage a network's schedule. Capital Cities, for example, owns stations affiliated with ABC that contribute almost 10 percent of ABC's national coverage. If Capital Cities decided not to carry a given program on its group of stations, ABC's program would be in considerable ratings difficulty. The remaining affiliates clearing the program would not only have a smaller collective audience, they would lack several major markets crucial to advertising buys. Understandably, network O&Os play an important role in ensuring clearance in major markets.

Some syndicators offer special inducements to get exposure for their wares in the prestigious prime-time access slots in the top O&O markets. These inducements may take the form of syndicated barter buys or outright cash discounts.[7] The latter, known as **compensation incentive**, is a common practice in New York because, as the premiere market in the country, New York coverage is critically important to advertisers. Beyond the very top markets, however, barter with compensation is rarely used in broadcasting. An equivalent practice exists in cable whereby premium network suppliers accept a smaller per-subscriber return to assure carriage, and basic cable networks discount their licensing price to especially desirable MSOs.

COMMUNITY RESPONSIVENESS

Programmers of group-owned stations have to be more sensitive than non-group-owned station programmers to pressures from government regulators. The high visibility of broadcast groups and the factor of absentee ownership also make them an easy target for consumer groups. The feeling of vulnerability induces a corresponding sense of local responsibility among group-owned managers. The result is that group-owned stations make strenuous efforts to demonstrate sensitivity to political and consumer interests in their communities and to serve local needs with extensive local programming efforts. Many single-owner stations also do considerable public affairs programming, but, of necessity, group-owned stations tend to be even more public-affairs oriented. The O&Os also have to be particularly sensitive to such programming needs.

Although the need for community responsiveness has not yet become a political issue in cable programming, cable management sees it as a tool for reducing subscriber turnover (churn), one of the industry's major economic problems. The cable MSOs are less vulnerable than group broadcasters simply because they are not licensed by the FCC. On the other hand, cable **franchise renewal** time at the local level stimulates similar attacks of local programming consciousness. Just as the FCC is impressed by a commitment to local programming, so local franchise authorities look for local commitment on the part of cable operators. The period of time between franchise renewals is much longer than broadcast license renewal periods, however, and the penalties for not fulfilling franchise promises less well established.

TRADE ASSOCIATIONS WITH A PROGRAMMING ROLE

More than a dozen trade associations represent broadcasters and cablecasters to the federal government and other industry groups. Some of these organizations actively represent programmers, and most get involved in matters affecting programming on occasion. The largest number of trade groups, and the most powerful, focus on television broadcasting.

Organizations in Television Programming

Because the participants in trade associations are as diverse as their stations, continuing conflicts arise about the proper role of some of the organizations discussed below. The major television trade associations shift their positions on programming issues in response to political and economic pressures.

In addition to its many other activities, the oldest and largest broadcast trade association, the National Association of Broadcasters (NAB), conducts annual programming seminars attended by industry executives. Generally, the NAB confines these programming seminars to the sensitive political issues of the moment—children's programming in the late 1960s, overcommercialization in the early 1970s and excessive violence in the mid-1970s. In the early 1980s, the NAB shifted its focus to the economic impact of new technologies such as MDS (multipoint distribution service) and DBS (direct broadcast satellites), outlining both the risks and the opportunities for broadcast investment. In addition to its major annual trade convention in April, the NAB also conducts an annual fall radio programming conference, lobbies for broadcast interests, and supplies member stations with statistical information on the industry, research reports and analyses of FCC activities. Many group owners of television stations, expressing the opinion that the NAB had not effectively represented them to Congress and the FCC, formed ad hoc associations in the mid-1980s to improve relations with government officials and elected representatives.[8] Having to speak for all of the television and radio stations in the United States hampers the NAB's ability to support some of its constituencies.

The National Association of Television Program Executives (NATPE), founded by local station program directors in 1962, has grown into the largest program-oriented organization in the industry, and its members tend to be top-level management at stations and groups. It is primarily a forum for the sale of syndicated television programs at its annual spring convention. Group-owned stations are the prime prospects for these programs, and executives commit many millions of dollars during the few days of the annual convention. NATPE also supports an annual faculty internship program, arranging summer positions at major stations for award winners.

As the impact of independent television stations grew in the late 1970s, so did the visibility of its trade association, the Association of Independent Television Stations (INTV). INTV serves the nonaffiliated television stations by lobbying in their interests and supplying sales and program information. It conducts an annual meeting attended by syndicators offering their programs to independent stations. At the same convention, group programmers of independents meet to discuss mutual problems and joint programming efforts.

The Television Programmers' Conference (TVPC), an informal organization with much less structure than the NAB, NATPE or INTV, was formed in the mid-1970s to educate its members on day-to-day programming practices. Although supported by some of the larger group owners, it consists primarily of single-station and small-market operators, and practicing programmers rather than high-level executives attend its annual July meeting. The conference is small, serving a few hundred attendees, and more concerned with television production than with syndicated buys. Local news occupies many of the annual sessions because of its crucial role in creating a station's image.

Another industry organization, the Television Bureau of Advertising (TvB), coordinates interests in television advertising and sales. Based in New York, its primary function is supplying sales promotion materials comparing the value of television spots over other media. It also generates product information to aid station sales efforts, conducts surveys and holds regional sales seminars.

In addition to the associations described above, the Radio-Television News Directors Association (RTNDA), the International Radio-Television Society (IRTS), the Station Representatives Association (SRA) and, to a lesser extent, the Society of Motion Picture and Television Engineers (SMPTE) and the Association of

Advertising Agencies (AAA) play a role in programming. Such organizations conduct occasional seminars on programming questions and lobby for specialized programming regulations.

Organizations in Cable Programming

The primary representative of the cable industry, the National Cable Television Association (NCTA), occupies an increasingly important position in programming. Its annual June convention has become the second most important sales opportunity for off-network series, movie and short-program syndicators looking to sell to local origination channel programmers and to MSOs programming entire networks. The major business of the convention, the coming together of cable system and network program executives, continues to expand as new cable services form and others merge and change direction. Like the NAB, the NCTA also functions as the major lobbying organization for cable interests and supplies its members with research reports, industry statistics and analyses of the actions of Congress and the FCC.

The cable industry supports three additional organizations involved in programming, the Cable Television Administration and Marketing Society (CTAM), the National Federation of Local Cable Programmers (NFLCP) and the Cable-television Advertising Bureau (CAB). CTAM's annual August conference focuses on marketing and management issues, interweaving programming concerns generally from a marketing perspective. Typically, group and MSO cable executives make up the bulk of conference attendees.

The NFLCP concerns itself with local origination and access programming. Its annual conference has sessions on production problems and the buying of syndicated feature films and shorts to be used as **interstitial programming** (between odd-length programs). This conference is attended primarily by local system programmers handling local origination programming.

Like the TvB, the CAB provides statistics and advice on cable advertising, including records on regionally syndicated programs with small circulations and access programming. As with the trade organizations peripheral to broadcast programming, these associations often lobby on issues affecting cable.

Organizations in Radio Programming

The two major organizations in radio merged their annual conferences in 1984. The annual Radio Programming Conference (RPC) conducted by the NAB will be held in September jointly with the conference sponsored by the National Radio Broadcasters Association (NRBA). The two organizations co-chair the meeting that focuses on programming and regulatory and sales considerations. In the past, two separate conferences held overlapping sessions, and the primary difference was who attended: Radio programmers generally attended the RPC while station managers and sales managers attended the NRBA. Representatives of the major format and feature syndicators and the radio networks attended both meetings to make contact with independent and affiliated stations. To save on costs and consolidate their impact, the NAB and NRBA joined forces in 1984 to conduct one annual radio meeting. Both organizations continue to lobby independently on regulatory issues and supply their own members with industry statistics and specialized research reports.

The Radio Advertising Bureau (RAB) provides statistics and reports on advertising revenues and practices within the industry. Its role is similar to that of the TvB and CAB in television and cable since it focuses on sales and is oriented toward station management. The RAB holds numerous regional seminars for sales managers and executives and has its annual conference in February, often in Dallas, Texas, for sales managers and station managers. Because of considerable overlap in functions and goals, the RAB has been urged to merge or hold its annual meeting with one of the other radio organizations (NAB, NRBA).

All of the organizations described above provide opportunities for the exchange of program ideas and joint program efforts among many stations. Their increasingly visible programming activites reflect the more influential position of the programmer as a result of higher program costs, greater competition and deregulation. Group owners in both broadcasting and cable, including ABC, CBS and NBC, tend to occupy the most powerful positions within, and direct the activities of, these trade associations.

PRODUCTION BY GROUP OWNERS AND MSOs

Increasingly, broadcast groups and cable MSOs enter the production business. Several groups syndicate their locally produced programming beyond the stations they own. Metromedia has, in fact, signed up so many "affiliates" for several of its series, it is close to becoming a fourth commercial television network.[9] Several group-owned radio stations have moved into program syndication, and many cable MSOs have developed program-producing arms as well as system-operating divisions. And some owners produce for both broadcasting and cable.

Local Broadcast Production

Television programming sources are the same for every affiliate in the country. About 65 percent of the network-affiliated or network-owned station's schedule originates at ABC, CBS or NBC. These programs are seldom preempted and rarely rescheduled from their original-feed time period. (See Chapter 6 for more detail on this subject.) The remaining 35 percent of the affiliate's schedule is programmed locally. About 15 percent is actually produced locally; the remaining 20 percent comes from syndicators distributing programs on a national basis produced by a variety of sources.

Of late, group owners have been assuming the syndicator's role, producing programs not only for use by other stations within their groups but also for regional and even national syndication. Escalating costs for off-network, syndicated programs encourage these efforts. The success of several pioneering group-produced programs in the 1970s accelerated this trend. Of course, when a program is produced for use by more than one station, additional expenses accrue such as increased talent fees, union fees and music royalty payments. Nonetheless, multiple use of good program ideas can be a money-saving programming strategy in the long run.

Group W's *PM Magazine* is one such program series. This magazine-format series originated at Group W's San Francisco station, KPIX-TV as *Evening Mag-*

azine in the early 1970s. Later it was shared by all five Group W stations and ultimately distributed to over 100 stations. Other group-owned national syndications are Multimedia's *Phil Donahue* and Metromedia's *Golden Circle.*[10] As a result of this trend, some group program directors are becoming increasingly active in local programming.

In radio program production the Bonneville group has taken the lead by moving from regional to national syndication (or networking) via satellite. It began distributing a 24-hour beautiful music format to affiliates in the early 1980s, and other radio groups are likely to follow suit as they define formats and programs suitable for syndication. Other radio groups, especially ABC, CBS and Mutual, syndicate features and specials to large numbers of radio stations. This growing trend is described in Chapter 14 on broadcast radio networks and syndicators.

Cable Production

Group W is typical of a corporation owning television and radio stations as well as cable systems; it is, at the same time, a major syndicator of both broadcast and cable programming. *PM Magazine,* as described above, is one of its television programs. It also owns HTN Plus, a pay-cable movie network, and introduced a pay-cable sports network in 1984.

Like Group W, ABC produces cable programming in a big way. In fact, it participated with Group W in the jointly owned Satellite News Channel, later sold to Ted Turner. It co-owns the Hearst/ABC Sports Network. In addition, ABC creates cultural programming for ARTS. Eventually, because of program scarcity, many of the same events and programs will probably be rerun or even **prerun** on cable after or before broadcast airing.

Warner Amex Cable Communications, one of the top five MSOs, has led the industry in development of two-way **interactive cable** technology and, through its subsidiary WASEC, created MTV, Nickelodeon and the Movie Channel. The group owner's commitment to building large metropolitan cable systems undermined its overall profitability in the first half of the 1980s, but its programming arm supplies some of the truly original cable formats.[11]

MSOs have expanded their group programming efforts to amortize costs over large numbers of cable subscribers and to concentrate programming budgets. Many local system programming efforts were unfavorably compared to local broadcast programming in the 1970s, resulting in pressure to syndicate better-quality programs among group members. An increased potential for local advertising sales also resulted in increases in the amount of local cable programming. This subject is covered in Chapter 12.

Selling advertising and inserting commercial announcements into the program schedule are simpler tasks when handled at the MSO headquarters level than when individual systems duplicate insertions at the local level, and they are jointly accomplished for a group of systems at much less cost and with much less error (whether on a "same time" or "staggered" schedule for multiple time zones). Group programming of cable systems also makes selling advertising easier, just as it does for broadcast networks. Advertising interconnections for cable systems are discussed in Chapter 9.

THE 1976 WATERSHED IN TELEVISION PROGRAMMING

Television revenues took a significant upward surge in 1976, a watershed year in television programming. The quadrennial combination of the national elections and the Olympic games contributed to the burgeoning profit picture by limiting television program inventory, thereby raising prices. In addition, the number of UHF receivers increased, and the independent UHF stations took advantage of their new prosperity by buying off-network programs at prices they could not have afforded in previous years. The consequent shortage of syndicated programs led to higher price levels throughout the industry. The other event of significance in 1976 was the formation of Home Box Office, the premium cable network.

With these events in mind, Joel Chaseman, president of Post-Newsweek Stations, Inc., questioned representatives of 10 group-broadcasting firms on post–1976 television programming strategies.[12] In written interviews, he asked three questions: (1) Has your group programming strategy changed since 1976? If so, in what way? (2) Do you believe that the new technologies such as cable will affect your fundamental programming strategies? If so, can you outline what the effects will be? (3) Do you anticipate less dependence on existing broadcast networks? If so, how will you fill the programming gap? In the following sections, representative responses illustrate the trends in group television programming for the 1980s.

Program Strategy

Most of the correspondents agreed that 1976 was a watershed year in their programming strategies, calling for increased emphasis on local news and information programs:

> Our program strategy has changed since 1976 with greater emphasis now placed on local program productions which include magazines, documentaries, children's shows, public affairs programs and weeks devoted to special interests and projects within each of our communities.
> —Richard B. Belkin, Vice-President-Broadcasting, Lee Enterprises, Inc.

> We are developing systems and methods to provide for greater independence of the network services. Our objectives include greater local origination (i.e., entertainment, news and public service) through ENG and remote equipment.
> —Ancil H. Payne, President, King Broadcasting Company

Influences of New Technology

There is no question among group broadcasters that this increased emphasis on news and informational programming ties in with the advent of new technology. ENG (electronic news gathering) has increased local news staff mobility, reduced transmission and production costs, created opportunities to produce local programs and stimulated the imaginations of program strategists. The following response suggests the impact of this new technology on broadcast television:

Smaller, high-quality electronic cameras permit us to do a better job of news coverage, and, for the first time, permit us to seek out local programming that is not confined to in-the-studio, talking-heads programs. Satellite–earth stations will permit greater diversity of program choices to stations, particularly for the independents, by reducing the cost of transmission of sports, entertainment and news programming.
—Crawford P. Rice, Executive Vice-President, Gaylord Broadcasting Company

Many of the group-broadcasting leaders responding to Chaseman's survey mentioned the influence of satellites, the possibility of a fourth network and the growth of syndication services. Although the influence of satellite programming relay will surely grow in broadcast television, so far its major effects have been felt in cable, commercial radio and public television and radio. Each of these subjects is discussed in detail in later chapters. For broadcast stations and groups, the expansion of cable networks has made new programming sources available to stations that once considered the broadcast networks and their syndicated reruns the sole source of viable programming.

The Challenge to Network Hegemony

The ultimate effect of new delivery technology and news capability will be less dependence on network programming and the syndicated reruns derived from it. Broadcast stations now tend toward ever more specialized programming, reflecting the segmented lifestyles increasingly evident in society. George Koehler described the economic underpinning of this strategic thinking:

> Our group programming strategy has not changed since 1976 in any really apparent way, except that we are more interested now than we were then in local specials and some of the off-network series like *Roots*. What has changed is the way local stations now are forced to buy successful network series substantially in advance of their network termination periods of use, eight to ten years from the date of the original commitment. No longer is it possible to assess one's program needs accurately and to fill those needs through purchases in the marketplace. The game has become a gamble of frightening proportions.
>
> It seems to me that this is rather the reverse of the broadcast networks' gamble. The networks put a lot of money into development, winnow the development product, come up with new programs for insertion into their schedules and hope to get two or three hits every season. When those hits start to miss— in three months or three years or ten years—the networks simply terminate their commitment.
>
> Stations now are being asked to risk millions of dollars on the prospect that a *Happy Days* is not just faddish, that it will not have worn out its acceptance in six or eight network showings, that it will appeal to viewers in 1986 as it has appealed to viewers in 1976. The number of runs dictates that the series will last three or four years in stripping; the price commitment dictates that the station must use most of the runs to make the series pay out.
>
> Our small group of four stations has committed over $6.5 million on a long-range bet that says *Happy Days, Laverne & Shirley, Little House on the Prairie*

and *Eight Is Enough* will retain their popularity for six to eight years. That amount of money programs just three hours a day, five days a week. And just now there is no way of telling how many stations will be feeding these same programs into our medium and small markets via cable. In 1982 that conduit of culture, *The Odd Couple*, could be seen six times each day in Altoona.

While reruns are not original programming, it is true, they are a vital part of programming a station, and in this respect programming has changed mightily in the last several years. The risks have become enormous.

—George A. Koehler, President, Gateway Communications, Inc.

In organizations like Operation Prime Time (OPT) and Program Development Group (PDG), broadcast groups such as Golden West, Cox and Gaylord put aside their rivalry to contribute prorated financial support to major programming ventures. These ventures, ranging from novel dramatizations to game shows, were much too big for individual groups to finance. Since they compete with network-financed programs and with the best feature films on the premium cable channels, these efforts must be mounted stylishly. Metromedia, Embassy, Chris Craft and Paramount began creating ad hoc networks comprised of independent television stations and some affiliates in 1983, banding together to present first-run programming in prime time.[13] Generally, the organizations can support only quarterly or monthly first-run programming, often movies, but the expansion of non-network program sources continues.

Al Masini of Cox's television sales representation firm (TeleRep) conceived the idea of Operation Prime Time and sold it simultaneously to several group broadcasters, a producing organization (MCA/Universal) and certain national advertisers. In the words of Joel Chaseman, "His foresightedness and perseverance—and the courage of the independents and groups and stations involved—were rewarded with acceptable production quality and ratings." In the process, of course, network prime time was preempted on 73 network-affiliated stations in addition to 22 independent stations, and a precedent was created for ventures similar to Masini's pioneering success, *Testimony of Two Men*.[14]

Where group operators have a limited resource base, it may be possible for them to form consortiums. The next ten years will be really exciting, and program developments will take their place in the forefront of the business.

—Robert L. Glaser, President, RKO General Television

On the other hand, another respondent reminds us of the enduring mutuality of network and affiliate:

As we get into the changing technology of the 1980s, I believe the $2 billion per year that the three networks in combination spend on programming will be critical to the continuation of broadcasting as we know it. I certainly believe the broadcaster's localism, his commitment to his community, is what sets us apart from a national programming service and gives us the right to expect continued development of our business in the future.

—Wilson Wearn, President, Multimedia, Inc.

PROGRAMMING CHANGES IN THE 1980s

What emerges from these informal statements is a picture of the television industry already radically changed during the late 1970s. Aided by technology and challenged by a new awareness among the consuming public, group-owned television stations have moved toward more local production, more factual production, more mobile production. The economics have at one and the same time lessened station dependence on off-network production and created a marketplace for new programs in competition with network and off-network programming.

Many groups, including Time, Cox, Group W, Viacom and Storer, already owning a large number of television stations simultaneously have large stakes in the cable programming and cable system ownership arenas. All indications are that broadcast groups will continue to purchase more and more cable systems. Radio group owners are also syndicating features and formats as satellite distribution becomes inexpensive for audio signals. Like television broadcasters, radio groups have the technical knowledge, creative talent and fianancial resources to operate cable systems competitively. The late 1980s will see increasing numbers of cable, DBS and broadcast entities owned and programmed by divisions of the same parent corporation. One key to the economic success of such partnerships will be shared program production through ad hoc networks.

The simultaneous trends toward consolidation and merger among cable programming services reflects the tight economic conditions of the first half of the decade and the less than financially cautious entry of cable networks into the marketplace in the early 1980s. Cable MSOs will react to overextension in the industry by selling some of their less profitable acquisitions, and use their muscle in negotiating favorable contracts with national cable networks. The second half of the 1980s will see the demise of several cable program services and competition from DBS, accompanied by a revived power position for the major cable group owners. Group production of entertainment programming will expand enormously in broadcast television. Ad hoc networks, formed of major group owners, will be the program innovators in the coming years.

SUMMARY

Group ownership characterizes both the broadcasting and cable industries. Group-owned broadcast stations divide into those owned by networks and those owned by others; most are affiliates rather than independents. Group owners frequently own other media such as newspapers and cable systems, which may create conflicts of interest even as it encourages advanced, highly beneficial, group management practices. Group ownership has particular economic advantages such as in group program purchases and the availability of experienced management. Group ownership in television often is accompanied by pronounced community responsiveness. On the other hand, centralization of control and rigid operational formats generate problems for both local stations and local cable systems. These problems affect television and cable more than radio since it remains a more local phenomenon.

Trade associations representing programming interests increasingly lobby for their constituent groups and act as informational conduits for their members. The 1980s will be a period of slowly increasing local and nonnetwork production for both broadcasting and cable, reflecting growing profitability of syndication and strongly influenced by savings from inexpensive satellite relays. Increasingly, broadcasting and cable will not have to rely on traditional program sources. The role of the broadcast network is diminishing in the face of new programming options for affiliates, but for the 1980s at least, it will remain mutually advantageous for both affiliates and networks. The growing participation of broadcast group owners in the cable and DBS industries signals newly evolving programming relationships and common interests.

Notes

[1] See annual reports on radio profitability in trade publications, including "Radio 1980: Gross Up, Net Down," *Broadcasting*, 8 February 1982, pp. 45–78; "Radio Profitability on the Rise in 1982," *Radio/TV Highlights*, newsletter of the National Association of Broadcasters, 12 September 1983, p. 2.

[2] See extensive discussion of cross-media ownership in Benjamin M. Compaine, ed., *Who Owns the Media? Concentration of Ownership in the Mass Communications Industry* (New York: Crown/Harmony, 1979), especially Chapter 3 by Christopher H. Sterling, "Television and Radio Broadcast," pp. 92–96.

[3] *Golden Circle* is Metromedia's first-run syndication vehicle, producing and distributing four major multipart dramas per year. *Golden Circle* is licensed to individual stations for cash; barter and time-banking arrangements are not used. Peter Warner, "Metromedia Productions Broadening Base with 'Wild Times,'" *The Hollywood Reporter*, 19 September 1979, p. 4.

[4] "Update: TCI's Nationwide Network," *View*, May 1983, pp. 38–42; "TCI's No. 1 Cable Strategy," *New York Times*, 19 October 1983, pp. 29ff.

[5] "The ABC's of ATC," *Broadcasting*, 8 November 1982, pp. 48–58.

[6] "The Programmers Speak," *View*, March 1983, pp. 53–58.

[7] **Syndication barter** is a practice in which advertisers (rather than stations) purchase the rights to use syndicated programs. After incorporating its own advertising into some of the program's commercial breaks, the advertiser markets the program to stations. A station makes its profit on the program by selling the unfilled commercial breaks. The advertiser and the station usually split the commercial spots 50-50 in barter deals, but the advertiser may offer the station more than half as an incentive to accept the deal.

[8] "MMTC: New Set of Initials to Reckon with in Washington," *Broadcasting*, 11 July 1983, p. 28; "The Groups Plant a Flag of Their Own," *Broadcasting*, 13 June 1983, pp. 39–40.

[9] "How Network Delivery Varies by Market," *Broadcasting/Cablecasting Yearbook 1982*, pp. B-80–83.

[10] "Metromedia's New Notions," *Broadcasting*, 31 January 1983, p. 58; "The 'Can Do' Style of Robert Bennett," *Broadcasting*, 11 April 1983, pp. 134–43.

[11] "Warner Amex: Life on the Media Front Line," *Broadcasting*, 13 June 1983, pp. 114ff.

[12] Joel Chaseman is president of Post-Newsweek Stations, Inc., which consists of WFSB-TV, Hartford; WPLG-TV, Miami; WJXT-TV, Jacksonville; and WDIV-TV,

Detroit. The broadcasting company is a subsidiary of the Washington Post Company, publisher of the *Washington Post, Newsweek,* and the *Everett Herald* (Washington State) and part owner of the *International Herald Tribune.*

[13] "Broadcasters Band Together to Form Movie Network," *Broadcasting,* 14 February 1983, pp. 36–37; "The New Ad-Hoc Networks, *View,* June 1983, pp. 38–42.

[14] *Testimony of Two Men* carried 6 minutes of advertising in each of its 6 hours. OPT's second vehicle, *The Bastards,* was telecast by 68 affiliates and 25 independents, including 49 of the top 50 stations, and carried no advertising. More recent ad hoc productions tend to carry advertising and come as barter arrangements.

Selected Sources

Broadcast Management/Engineering. Trade magazine with technical production focus; 1965 to date. Starting in the late 1970s, it carried scattered articles called "TV Programming & Production for Profit" reporting on the programming of major television groups such as Post-Newsweek (1977, 1978) and Capital Cities (1979).

"Company Profile: RKO, Fighting the FCC and Expanding TV." *View* (September 1983): 49–50.

DiSante, Evelyn. "Who Will Survive?" *Multichannel News* (19 July 1982): 9ff.

Howard, Herbert H. "Cox Broadcasting Corporation: A Group-Ownership Case Study." *Journal of Broadcasting* 20 (Spring 1976): 209–31.

New Technologies Affecting Radio & Television Broadcasting. Washington, D.C.: National Association of Broadcasters, November 1981.

Regulatory Trends in the 1980's: More Owners—More Stations. New York: Station Representatives Association, Inc., 1980.

"Special Reports: Media Corporations." *Broadcasting* (4 January 1982): 39–47; (8 February 1982): 45–56; and (9 May 1983): 37–43.

PART TWO

Television Strategies for Commercial Broadcasting

Part II has four chapters addressing television programming in the commercial broadcasting industry. The first two chapters look at **network** programming and the second two at **station** practices. The television chapters were placed ahead of commercial radio and cable and noncommercial broadcasting because broadcast television dominates the audience's and industry's thinking about programming. Because of the huge sums of money involved in television programming decisions, the commercial television networks and major market stations set the patterns for the rest of the industry. In the 1950s, broadcast television forced radio out of its leading media position; eventually, radio found more specialized programming niches. Now, cable copies many of broadcast television's strategies, applying them in a different set of circumstances. Each television chapter looks at the evaluation, selection and scheduling of television programs, the components of programming strategy.

As the programming strategies of the three commercial broadcast television networks—ABC, CBS and NBC—differ more by time of day than they do from network to network, the first two chapters in Part II subdivide programming by daypart rather than by network.

The first chapter in Part II, Chapter 5, examines the high-visibility entertainment programming of **network prime time.** These programs generate a network's image in the public eye, and their ratings define a network's commercial importance in the minds of advertisers. Insofar as affiliated-station images and revenues tie to network programming, they reflect prime-time programming successes. Chapter 5 therefore has special importance. It covers the competitive strategies the three national networks use in prime-time entertainment programming.

Chapter 6 deals with **nonprime-time** programming. It examines early-morning, daytime, late-night and weekend programs. The author analyzes the constraints operating on magazine shows, soap operas, game shows, children's programming, talk shows and weekend sports and public affairs programming for all three broadcast networks and describes the role of program development for each format. Chapter 6 provides an insider's perspective on commercial network television programming for the nonprime-time dayparts.

Chapters 7 and 8 examine television strategies from a station's perspective—in one chapter when the station affiliates with a television network and in the other when the station operates independently. The special case of the strategies of superstation independents appears in Part III on cable programming since local delivery by hundreds or even thousands of cable systems determines much of their strategy.

Affiliates dominate television station programming. Of approximately 800 commercial television stations, more than 600 are network affiliates, and they typify television to the general public. Of more than 1,000 television stations in the United States, 212 are affiliated with ABC, 198 with CBS and 197 with NBC (as of 1983). Individual stations often associate more closely in viewers' minds with the network names than with the station call letters, in part because affiliates air between 10 and 20 hours per day of network programming, leaving very few hours in which to develop unique local images. Chapter 7 introduces the professional programming language commercial station management and programmers use. The author writes from the viewpoint of major and midsized market **affiliates,** and spells out the competitive options for the station programmer for each daypart. The chapter analyzes the specific decisions an affiliate programmer must make in each time period and examines ratings strategies for an affiliate competing with two rival affiliates and an independent station.

Chapter 8 looks at station programming strategy primarily from the vantage of **independents** competing with network affiliates. The three-affiliate/one-independent situation is typical of the top 150 markets as of the mid-1980s, though this competitive picture will change by the 1990s as distant independent station signals, cable networks, DBS and low-power television stations are introduced. Only in the 1970s did independents become truly competitive—upsetting two decades of three-way market division by affiliates. Even with major inroads, independents still settle for a smaller portion of the audience and advertising revenues. Nevertheless, the independent station, not the affiliate, has the full range of television programming options and fills an entire schedule with syndicated or locally produced programming. On the whole, independents have become profitable by counterprogramming their affiliate competitors. The options the author describes apply to small- and large-market UHF and VHF independents including such giants as superstation WGN-TV. From behind the smorgasbord of options available to the independent programmer, whatever the station size, however, stands the unappetizing question of costs.

Part II, then, covers commercial broadcast television programming. Cable television follows in the next section, radio after that and noncommercial broadcasting at the end of the book. Part II focuses on the evaluation, selection and scheduling of programs from the separate perspectives of networks and television stations.

CHAPTER FIVE

Prime-Time Network Television Programming

Robert F. Lewine, Susan Tyler Eastman and William J. Adams

A QUICK GUIDE TO CHAPTER FIVE

ROBERT F. LEWINE *is president of the Academy of Television Arts and Sciences Foundation, an office he assumed in 1964. He has the distinction of having served as a vice-president of programming at all three networks—ABC and NBC in New York and CBS in Hollywood—and as vice-president of television at Warner Brothers. His background includes commercial production, program research, advertising and program production. In addition to founding* Television Quarterly, *Mr. Lewine has been actively involved in the development of the Emmy awards since their inception and the establishment of the ATAS/UCLA television archival library in Los Angeles. He often teaches at the University of California at Los Angeles, the University of Southern California, Columbia College and California State University at Northridge while serving as trustee of Columbia College and of the American Women in Radio and Television Foundation. Columbia College awarded him an honorary doctorate of Humane Letters in 1982.*

SUSAN TYLER EASTMAN, *editor and author of other chapters, supplied sections on program evaluation, seasonal strategies and recent trends in network scheduling and program cancelation.*

WILLIAM J. ADAMS, *a doctoral student in the Department of Telecommunications at Indiana University, contributed historical data on program cancelations and renewals, accompanied by an analysis of network stunting and format changes. Together, the three authors delineate the procedures the three broadcast networks use for selecting, evaluating and scheduling prime-time programs.*

NETWORK AUDIENCES

Network television's visibility makes it an inviting target for critics. Its national popularity focuses public attention on its strengths and weaknesses. Of the almost 15,000 hours the three commercial networks program each year, about one-fifth is singled out for special critical attention—the weekly 22 hours of prime-time programming. That figure multiplied by 52 weeks and again multiplied by three networks equals 3,432 hours of prime-time network programs a year.

The 32 weeks from September to May form the main viewing year. The remaining 20 weeks are filled largely with reruns, unused pilots and tryouts for potential series. In the early 1980s, the networks began using the summer for testing new program ideas in short runs. This practice accelerated partly to counteract the loss of audiences to independent stations and cable television, and partly to satisfy affiliated stations worried about the extreme ratings drop occurring during the May and July sweeps. Also, summer tryouts give the networks first-run programs to promote to audiences (as opposed to the traditional summer reruns) and an extended period for testing audience reaction to these proposed fall shows. But the period from September to May still has the largest audiences and therefore warrants the networks' most strenuous programming efforts.

Audience ratings throughout the day are important to the networks, of course, but high ratings in the 22 prime-time hours are absolutely vital. A failure in prime-time programming may take years to remedy. NBC's ten years in third place is a case in point. Low ratings affect viewer and affiliate loyalty and public image as well as advertising revenue. The prime-time hours—from 8 P.M. to 11 P.M. six days each week and from 7 P.M. to 11 P.M. on Sundays—constitute the center ring, the arena in which each network's mettle is tested. Prime-time programs are the most vulnerable to cancelation because they are the most viewed and the most costly to advertisers. Both advertisers and networks expect the highest return from prime-time hours.

Demographic Targets

Some advertisers are interested mainly in **tonnage**—the sheer, raw size of an audience. This scattershot approach best suits advertisers of soaps, foods and over-the-counter drug products. Other sponsors prefer a rifled approach, aiming at particular audiences most likely to buy their services or products. Consequently, the demographics of each network's prime-time audience influence advertising sales. Broadcasters generally agree with advertisers that most consumer purchasing power rests in the hands of young marrieds in their twenties and thirties. However, the prime-time hours are programmed to attract an even younger audience, ranging from 18 to 34, and in certain time periods, reaching down as low as 16 or 17 years of age. (The lower end of the group seems to find programs like *Mork & Mindy, Charlie's Angels* and *Happy Days* most satisfactory.)

A close look at ABC's overall schedule in the late 1970s shows it sought a very youthful viewer. But as a *Los Angeles Times* television critic wrote recently, "You can't sell bubble gum to ballet fans or Xerox copiers to teenagers."[1] ABC's appeal to a very young audience throughout the prime-time schedule in the 1970s ran contrary to its advertisers' interests. By the 1980s, all three networks were aiming their programs at the 25–44 age group, the group having the bulk of the U.S. population and the discretionary income most advertisers seek. Of the three networks, ABC, however, continues to target somewhat younger viewers.

In the late 1970s, ABC and CBS were hot competitors, but NBC had slipped far back in the ratings race. Then CBS slowly pulled ahead and by 1983 was entering its fifth consecutive year in first place. NBC, clearly behind for almost a decade, appointed a new network president, Grant Tinker, in 1982, and its position in the ratings and with the critics began to improve. But by the early 1980s, cable penetration had dramatically reduced the three networks' overall audience share by almost 20 percent. As a result, by the mid-1980s no network had a commanding lead over its competition.

The demographic picture has also changed. In the 1950s and 1960s, the two decades in which CBS commanded the highest prime-time ratings, its overall audience demographics slowly aged. NBC found itself in a similar position as it entered the 1970s. In response, both networks canceled a large number of entertainment programs because they appealed to a predominantly older demographic group, not because they lacked sizable audiences. The networks canceled about half of the 30 top-rated programs in 1970 and 1971, replacing them with prime-time series aimed at the younger adult audience.[2] ABC took the lead in this new demographic targeting. CBS and NBC followed along but tried to retain some of the older people as well.

Despite this overall appeal to younger audiences, the age demographics for a particular program or night may be more crucial than a network's overall age demographics. Programs appealing to an older audience (25 to 54) may draw advertisers who want that particular demographic breakdown rather than the demographic average for all of a network's programming. In the early 1980s, *Seven Brides for Seven Brothers* and *The Mississippi* were two programs skewed toward older viewers.

Unfortunately, the quality of the programming, aside from its ability to generate numbers, has rarely been of serious concern to most advertisers—at least not enough to affect their practices. Of course, there are exceptions. A select circle of sponsors (Firestone, Hallmark, IBM, Xerox and AT&T, for example) insist on quality programs as vehicles for their advertisements and therefore tend to sponsor entire special programs (rather than buying participating spots). In contrast, *most* advertisers look only for programs reaching appropriate markets for their products.

Audience Flow

Aside from a program's demographics, the networks look for its flow—does its audience flow-through to the next program? As explained in Chapter 1, each network hopes to capture and hold the largest possible (young) audience, especially from 8 P.M. until midnight or later. Network strategies are usually directed at achieving flow-through in prime-time programs. Network analysis shows that, on average, for every ten points in a lead-in program's ratings, four points will "flow through" to the succeeding program.

Is it any wonder, given demographics and flow-through considerations, that the selection of ideas to be developed and entered into program line-ups seems as risky as the turn of a roulette wheel? (Roulette, however, in recent years would pay off more often!) What may appear to be a relatively simple operation—programming—is, in fact, an involved complex of strategies. Recent estimates of the costs of program development for the three networks in a given year range from $250 million to $300 million. Not included in this staggering sum are the overhead costs of maintaining the departments and individuals who make these decisions. The salaries of top programmers reach the six- to seven-figure level, reflecting the substantial rewards for picking a winning schedule. The entire process of prime-time programming breaks down into three major phases: deciding to keep or cancel already scheduled series, developing and choosing new programs from the ideas proposed for the coming season and scheduling the entire group.

NETWORK SEASONS

During the 1950s and 1960s, the network season lasted a minimum of 39 weeks each year. By the mid-1970s, high per-episode costs had reduced the total number of episodes usually licensed to 32. But further cost increases combined with a high program mortality rate put an end to this pattern, and by the mid-1980s, the networks typically licensed just 11 episodes with one or two intended for repetition, and contracts said "cancelable any time." To fill out the 32 weeks of the main season, a program may be renewed and another 11 new episodes ordered, or another program may be substituted. The fierce competition among the three networks has greatly altered the concept of the television season.

Fall Premieres

Traditionally, the networks premiered their new series during a much-publicized week in late September. However, during the late 1970s, the traditional September premiere week slowly vanished. In the fall of 1982, it took fully seven weeks to get the season started. Program premieres began during the week of September 11–17 with *The Powers of Matthew Star* and ended during the week of October 23–29 with the first episodes of *The New Odd Couple, Newhart, Gavilon* and *St. Elsewhere.* The remaining 20 new series were premiered in scattershot fashion throughout this period.

The final disappearance of a uniformly recognizable network "premiere week" can be linked to the actors' and writers' strikes of 1980 and 1981. In those years, the networks were forced to delay series premieres until the strikes were settled and production on individual programs could resume. No strike occurred in 1982, yet the fall introductions still stretched for seven weeks. In 1983, NBC jumped the gun on its competition by premiering several programs in early September. Clearly, the networks have learned a new strategy: As the numbers of new fall premieres rose in the late 1970s, some programs were getting lost in the clutter of the crowded, fall promotional bang. When it was forced on them by the strikes, the networks rapidly recognized the value of a long premiere period. They now spread the fall introductions to give each program some room. The length of time used for premieres, however, fluctuates from year to year as the three giants jockey for best starting position. Even with all of this program juggling, the success rate of new programs has not improved and the decline in network audience shares continues.

Second Season

Although many new series and new episodes of returning programs still start in September, by the 1960s, some new programs began their runs in January or February, thus creating a **second season**. By the late fall the fate of most prime-time programs already on the air was clear. Holiday specials usually preempted those destined for cancelation or restructuring, so that by January or February, the networks were ready to launch their second season—with almost the same amount of promotion and ballyhoo as was accorded the new season in September.

Continuous Season

A warning of the future breakdown of the two-season system, however, occurred in 1974–75. In that year, the number of new entertainment series introduced other than at the start of either season (during the September/October or January/February starting periods) jumped from three to eight. In 1975–76 odd-month introductions rose to 9 and in 1976–77 leaped to 16. The number of such introductions continued to climb until, by 1983, they equalled the number of new series offered in September. See Table 5-2 later in the chapter to trace this pattern. Odd-month starts are now almost double the number of new series begun in January/February. As a strategy, this approach is called the **continuous season**.

Summer Schedules

Traditionally, the summer has been exempt from the ratings race. It has been an arena for reruns (often of weak series episodes), tryouts of questionable new series intended for the next fall, and leftover pilots and episodes of never-scheduled or canceled series. The networks ignored the summers, and so those months became goldmines for the pay cable movie networks and independent television stations. By the early 1980s, cable and independent stations had captured a substantial share of the summer audience.

Although there are fewer viewers in the summer, an overall decline in their collective audience share has forced ABC, CBS and NBC to begin budgeting millions of dollars for new programming to be aired in time slots once set aside for summer reruns.[3] ABC started the trend in the summer of 1983, and NBC rapidly followed suit. CBS has been slow to take full advantage of the summer season. With the advent of summer schedules, the July ratings book has begun to take on increased importance as a measure of network or pay-service audience pull and as a vehicle for prefall testing of programs. In the summer, networks can air several episodes of a new series and gauge audience reactions over a period of weeks.

FALL LINEUPS

To attract and hold young viewers in large numbers, the networks introduce nearly four dozen new programs into their prime-time schedules each year. Discounting movies and specials, the 1982–83 year had 46 new programs, added to the 44 established ones returning to the air. Which new entries will beat the odds and survive this critical sweepstakes is the key question. On the average, more than 60 percent and often as much as 75 percent of new series bite the dust along the way. Some are pulled within a few weeks; others may last until early spring if a network believes that too few viewers sampled them in the fall; some are kept on the schedule until their replacements are readied.

Cancelation History

From January 1974 to December 1978, the three networks canceled more than 100 series. This figure does not include temporary substitutes used during the year nor does it disclose how many series struggled for only a few months and how many made it through the year. From 1979 to 1982, 155 series were canceled, 103 of them—more than a two-to-one ratio—were one-hour programs. These figures reflect the fact that since 1964 one-hour series have greatly out-numbered other formats. For example, in the fall of 1982, 46 series were 60 minutes long while only 28 series were 30 minutes in length.

New Program Deaths

New programs have a higher cancelation rate than programs overall—since the latter reflects the few hits that go on from year to year. The total number of failures for all three networks is sometimes much higher than 60 percent, but rarely lower. The network enjoying the highest overall ratings naturally cuts the fewest programs and conversely. What the network in the middle does will vary from year to year. Consider Table 5-1 that lists just the numbers of *NEW* programs canceled after the seasons had begun.

In the fall of 1974, for example, the ABC network scheduled 12 new pro-grams—seven 1-hour dramas or adventure shows, one 1-hour musical variety, and four half-hour comedies. Of these, 11 failed to finish the year or were not renewed for another year. CBS fared much better, having scheduled only seven new programs in the fall and two in the spring. But eight of these nine failed to return the following year—four 1-hour and four half-hour comedies. Only one

TABLE 5-1.
New Programs Canceled (Fall and Spring Seasons Combined)

	ABC		*CBS*		*NBC*		*Total*
1970–71	12	75%	7	78%	7	64%	26
1971–72	8	73%	7	58%	7	47%	22
1972–73	7	58%	4	36%	9	64%	20
1973–74	9	75%	6	60%	12	86%	27
1974–75	11	61%	8	73%	8	50%	27
1975–76	10	50%	9	53%	15	79%	34
1976–77	13	65%	12	71%	12	60%	37
1977–78	11	61%	17	81%	14	70%	42
1978–79	9	60%	14	70%	22	79%	45
1979–80	13	72%	11	58%	14	70%	38
1980–81	6	55%	9	69%	9	50%	24
1981–82	13	72%	8	67%	13	65%	34
1982–83	13	87%	13	81%	8	50%	34
Aver. % canceled:		66%		66%		64%	

These figures are for new series tried between September and May. They show the actual number of new series canceled and the percentage of all new series canceled. The apparent decline in the total since 1979 is misleading since the three networks also increased March introductions dramatically during that year, and many of these shows, though not canceled during that spring, were gone by November of the following year; *The Ropers* is an example. These programs did not survive for long but are counted as survivors for their first season.

SOURCE: Annual *Variety* listings, compiled for this book by William J. Adams.

half-hour comedy, *Rhoda,* survived. Nevertheless, considering the average failure rate, in the aggregate CBS enjoyed a good fall season.

NBC presented ten new shows in the fall of 1974–75, and their record was the best by far: Of their seven new one-hour series, only three failed, and only one of their two half-hour comedies was canceled; of the ten new NBC programs (one a movie), six survived—an exceptional percentage. In the spring, however, four additional failures brought NBC's yearly total also to eight. It should be remembered that on four nights NBC offered movies, which, because of their length, reduced the number of new programs needed and lessened the number of potential failures.

Totals from Table 5-1 and Figure 5-1 show cancelations of new programs peaked in 1979, forcing changes in network policy. Since 1979, the networks have given some programs a slightly longer tryout, which explains the drop to 24 cancelations in 1980–81.

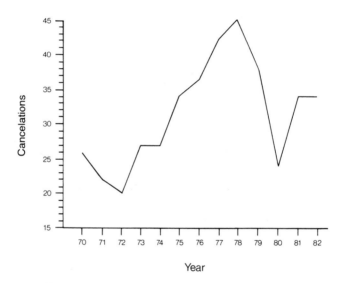

FIGURE 5-1. New Program Cancelations, 1970–1982

Promotion's Role

All three networks use on-air promotion to introduce new programs. Beginning as early as mid-July and continuing through November (after especially heavy season-opening salvos), they intensify the promotion of their programs and their overall image. In addition, networks use newspaper and television guide announcements to list offerings for a particular evening. *TV Guide* magazine is so important to network television that programmers delay schedule changes so that the changes can make *TV Guide*'s deadline for station listings. The promotional value of *TV Guide* is essential both locally and nationally.

On-air promotional announcements play a significant role in the ratings success of a program. Not until a program is safely past the rocks and shoals of its first several airings (or until it becomes clear that nothing will get it past these early trials), does promotion lessen or stop. On-air promotions are apportioned to every program scheduled to appear in a season lineup. Those needing extra stimulus are generally allotted some extra exposure. On-air program promotion continues all year around with extra efforts made during sweeps periods. New slogans and symbols are created for every broadcast year to extol the virtues of overall network offerings and to accompany all promotional announcements.

RETURNING PROGRAM EVALUATION

Evaluation of on-air shows goes on all year long. The final decision on whether or not a program is to return the following fall is usually made by April or May because the networks present their affiliates with the fall lineups at their annual meetings in May.[4] However, last-minute program changes occur right up to the opening guns in the fall. The critical times for most new programs are the four or five weeks at the beginning of the fall season (September/October) and the November sweeps. Traditionally, programs surviving the waves of cancelation at these times and lasting into January or February were safe until June—although a network might decide, as a result of the February sweeps, not to renew some programs for the next season.

Program Lifespan

In the 1970s the lifespan of popular prime-time series grew briefer and briefer. In the 1950s and 1960s, shows like *The Ed Sullivan Show, Gunsmoke, What's My Line* and *The Wonderful World of Disney* endured for more than 20 years. These records for longevity will probably never be matched again. By 1979 a program lifespan of ten years was regarded as a phenomenon. By 1983 stations were purchasing futures on such a ratings wonder as *Three's Company* up to three years ahead of actual production, but even so, betting on longer life, even for top-rated programs, seemed chancy.

Several factors account for this shortened lifespan: the increased sophistication of the viewing audience, the emergence of action/suspense series (a seemingly less durable format than the sit-com), the huge number of people who see each episode of a network series (wearing each episode and series idea out quickly) and the scarcity of outstanding program forms and fresh, top-rated talent. Actor boredom with stereotyped roles also may shorten a program's run. Many stars tire of repetitive characterizations and fail to renew their contracts even when ratings are still high. Jim Arness's leaving killed off the long-running *Gunsmoke,* and the retirement of *M*A*S*H*'s cast in 1983 ended its run, leaving only *After M*A*S*H.*

The shortened lifespan of prime-time series also reflects the complexity of program license contracts, which generally run from five to seven years. When a series first makes it to the air, the network controls the contractual situation and usually requires several concessions from the producer. At this time, the producer has traditionally had to sign over such rights as creative control, spinoff rights, limitations on syndication and scheduling control. The producer also agrees to a specific licensing fee for the run of the contract, regardless of the program's success. Typically, this licensing fee is substantially below actual production cost and makes no concession for sharing the profits should the program become a hit.

However, at the end of the first contractual period, normally five years, the tables are turned. Now the producer enjoys the advantages. The series has a track record with enough episodes in the can for stripping in syndication. In short, since the producers no longer need the network as much as it needs them, producers may demand the return of many of the concessions granted in the original contract. Under renewal conditions, the network often profits by dropping a popular show in favor of an untried newcomer. Both the *Mary Tyler Moore Show* and *Barney Miller* went off the air when agreement on renewal contracts could not be reached.

The Pivotal Numbers

Of the three phases of planning a fall schedule—evaluation, selection and scheduling—deciding which of the programs already on the air will continue and which will be pulled is perhaps the easiest. The decisions are based squarely on the ratings, which in turn reflect the network's profit margin—in essence, a product of cost-per-episode subtracted from advertising revenue. Until the 1980s, a weekday rating below 20 (or an audience share of less than 30) almost always resulted in cancelation on any network. It accounted for the end of *Paper Chase*, an outstanding program aired in the 1979 season.[5] By the mid-1980s, however, the target numbers dropped to a minimum weekday prime-time rating of 17 and a share of 27. They will drop even further if cable's erosion of network viewers continues.

Entertainment programs in the bottom 5–10 percent of the Nielsens are almost always canceled as fast as possible. The most difficult decisions for network programmers involve the borderline cases, programs that show signs of fatigue but are still holding their own or only just beginning to slide in the ratings. Occasionally, the personal preferences of a William Paley or advertiser politics may influence a decision, but the prevailing view is that cancelation had far better come too soon than too late.

Until the 1980s, the three networks differed little in their attitudes toward canceling long-running programs on the decline and were weakly committed if at all to *slow builders* (programs that acquire a loyal audience only after months of patient nurturing). By the mid-1980s, however, all three networks had begun to show slightly more patience with slow builders. NBC led the way in this new approach. Nonetheless, only series with borderline ratings benefit substantially from a longer introduction and promotional period. *Sixty Minutes* proved an exception to this rule; it was on the bottom of the ratings charts for several *years* before catching fire. Programs such as *Dallas, All in the Family* and *Simon & Simon* had much worse than "borderline" ratings for several months before the mass audience discovered them. Ratings strategy is basically the same at ABC, CBS and NBC; cancelation comes quickly more often than not.

Profit Margins

Profit left after subtracting licensing costs from advertising revenues may also influence program cancelation. Two prime-time programs of the same length, on the same network, and with identical ratings will, ideally, produce identical revenues for that network. But if one of them has a slightly higher per-episode licensing cost, say $325,000 vs. $300,000, over a season that difference may mean a half-million dollars in higher costs—to be subtracted from the same advertising revenue. The number of ad minutes remains the same for each program, and advertising rates are based on cost-per-thousand, no matter how much it costs a network to get that thousand. Further complicate the situation by mixing in borderline ratings, and it's clear that the program with the higher licensing cost will be canceled before the lower-cost series. Programs with the same ratings, but lower licensing costs, are often retained.

Program Ratings

There are few aspects of programming that precipitate as much controversy as cancelation. Since television is first of all a business with tens of thousands of stockholders and hundreds of millions of dollars committed for advertising, the networks' overriding aim is to attract the largest possible audience in the ideal demographic range at all times. Prime time is the daypart in which ratings most influence programming strategy, creating in their wake program decisions that are unpopular with some but that always aim the network at the number one position.

The networks have to make many controversial decisions each year: (1) canceling programs that are favorites of millions of viewers, (2) countering strong shows by scheduling competing strong shows, (3)preempting a popular series to insert a special program and (4) using reruns of a series' earlier episodes late in the year.

The three networks do have their own scheduling "styles," however. For example, ABC tends to keep its schedule intact for as long as possible when it has ratings leadership. CBS has a commendable record for budgeting heavy promotional blitzes to give new programs every chance of being sampled. But when CBS recognizes program weaknesses, instead of shifting programs into different time periods, it tends to pull the slow starters off the air and replace them with specials during salvage operations. During the 1970s, however, CBS made exceptions for *Simon & Simon* and *Dallas*, which became late successes, and for *Square Pegs* and *Paper Chase*, which nonetheless failed.

In the mid-1970s and early 1980s, NBC had dozens of program failures. Unable to afford the luxury of patience then, it yanked unproductive entries before they could endanger the overall ratings on a given night. But the amount of program manipulation may, in fact, have increased rather than decreased NBC's rating difficulties during this time. In the mid-1980s, NBC reversed this strategy and began holding onto their almost-successful series. A program such as *Hill Street Blues* illustrates what can happen when a show is left alone for as long as possible to afford the maximum opportunity for audience sampling. After a disappointing start during the 1980–81 season, *Hill Street Blues* was kept in the schedule because of NBC's apparent confidence that ratings would improve as the audience "discovered" the show. That confidence was rewarded. In the 1981–82 broadcast season, *Hill Street Blues* climbed slowly from an average rating of 13.3 to a respectable 18.4 (and an average audience share of 31).

As this series also indicates, critical acclaim can have some effect (in the absence of other rating successes). The kudos for *Hill Street Blues* bolstered

NBC's image at a time when it was in sore need of prestige and may have convinced programmers to stick with the show even in the face of low ratings. That Grant Tinker was head of NBC programming and producer of *Hill Street Blues* may also have been contributing factors. Under Tinker's direction in 1982–83, series such as *Mama's Family, Cheers* and *St. Elsewhere* that might well have been canceled during Fred Silverman's NBC tenure also remained in the prime-time schedule.

Despite these current exceptions, the industry almost totally depends on the ratings to determine a show's fate, a dependence the networks share with the major advertising agencies that use these figures as the primary basis for buying network time. As of mid-1980s, a single rating point translated into an estimated 830,000 homes (out of a viewing audience of over 19 million per network). Over the course of a year, this one point translated into about $50 million in pretax profits. Small wonder then that ratings rule the networks, public irritation with the process notwithstanding.

Sweeps and Overnights

Four times each year a highly controversial rating event occurs—the sweeps, a subject covered in detail in Chapter 2. The results of sweeps rating periods directly affect the rates network-affiliated and network-owned-and-operated stations charge for their advertising time. The stations, therefore, demand that the networks display their highest-quality merchandise during the sweeps period to attract the largest possible audiences and maximize ad revenues. The practice of **stunting** (the deliberate shuffling or preempting of the regular schedule) makes the four sweeps periods highly competitive and, at the same time, not always the most valid indicators of a network's or station's real strength.

As described in chapters 2 and 3, national ratings take several different forms. Aside from sweeps, the **overnights** (available only in New York, Los Angeles, Chicago, Boston, Philadelphia, Detroit, San Francisco, Dallas–Ft. Worth, Houston, Washington, D.C. and Miami, as of 1984) are the most avidly monitored of the other ratings formulas. Overnights provide only total numbers of viewers, without demographic breakouts such as age and sex. Although they give no demographic information, they can be used to monitor overall urban audience reaction to "program doctoring" such as changes in casts, character emphasis and plot line. The overnights also indicate immediately whether a program has "taken off" and captured a sizable audience in the urban markets. Continued low ratings in the overnights during the first few weeks of a newly introduced program's run spell cancelation unless the ratings show a hint of growth—or unless the program is expected to have stronger rural than urban appeal. *Little House on the Prairie* was an example of a rural-appeal program that initially "died in the cities."

Pocketpiece and MNA Report

The ratings report of greatest interest to the creative community is published in a small booklet known as *The Nielsen Pocketpiece*. It includes not only audience size but also audience composition, average ratings by program type,

EVE. SUN. JAN. 8, 1984

ABC TV

Metric	RIPLEY'S BELIEVE IT-NOT	HARDCASTLE & McCORMICK (SD)	ABC SUNDAY NIGHT MOVIE — SLAP SHOT(R) (9:00-11:25PM)(SD)
TOTAL AUDIENCE (Households (000) & %)	15,250 / 18.2	17,770 / 21.2	20,950 / 25.0
AVERAGE AUDIENCE (Households (000) & %)	10,140 / 12.1	14,160 / 16.9	12,570 / 15.0
SHARE OF AUDIENCE %	19	24	24
AVG. AUD. BY ¼ HR. %	8.4	16.9	15.8
Quarter-hour data (Avg% / Share% / ¼hr%)	9.8* / 15* / 11.2 ; 14.3* / 22* / 14.8 ; 13.9	16.9* / 25* / 16.8 ; 16.9* / 24* / 16.9 ; 16.0	16.1* / 23* / 16.4 ; 15.6* / 23* / 15.5 ; 15.0 ; 15.6* / 23* / 15.5 ; 14.9* / 23* / 14.4 ; 14.3* / 23* / 14.2 ; 15.7 ; 14.9* / 23* / 14.8

(W)

CBS TV

Metric	60 MINUTES	ALICE	ONE DAY AT A TIME (SD)	JEFFERSONS	GOODNIGHT, BEANTOWN	TRAPPER JOHN, M.D.
TOTAL AUDIENCE (Households (000) & %)	27,070 / 32.3	20,610 / 24.6				20,280 / 24.2
AVERAGE AUDIENCE (Households (000) & %)	19,780 / 23.6	15,000 / 17.9	16,590 / 19.8	18,690 / 22.3	16,420 / 19.6	17,430 / 20.8
SHARE OF AUDIENCE %	36	26	26	32	29	33
AVG. AUD. BY ¼ HR. %	21.0	17.5	20.1	21.5	19.4	20.3
Quarter-hour data (Avg% / Share% / ¼hr%)	22.0* / 34* / 23.1 ; 25.1* / 38* / 24.9 ; 25.2	17.9* / 26* / 18.2 ; 18.4	18.5* / 26* / 18.2 ; 18.9	23.0		20.8* / 33* / 20.3 ; 20.7* / 32* / 21.2 ; 20.9* / 34* / 20.5

(E) (E) (K)

NBC TV

Metric	FIRST CAMERA (7:34-8:00PM)(OP)	KNIGHT RIDER (SD)	NBC SUNDAY NIGHT MOVIE — BRONCO BILLY(R) (9:00-11:26PM)(SD)
TOTAL AUDIENCE (Households (000) & %)	13,160 / 15.7	17,930 / 21.4	21,960 / 26.2
AVERAGE AUDIENCE (Households (000) & %)	12,070 / 14.4 (2) ; 6,200 / 7.4 (3) ; 7,120 / 8.5 (OP)(–OP)	14,580 / 17.4	13,070 / 15.6
SHARE OF AUDIENCE %	23 ; 11 ; 15.7	25	25
AVG. AUD. BY ¼ HR. %	15.1 ; 7.2 ; 7.4 ; 23.4	15.9	15.2
Quarter-hour data (Avg% / Share% / ¼hr%)		16.7* / 24* / 17.5 ; 18.2* / 26* / 18.2 ; 18.2	15.0* / 21* / 14.8 ; 16.0* / 24* / 16.0 ; 15.8 ; 15.8* / 25* / 15.8 ; 16.0* / 26* / 15.9

(2)

TV HOUSEHOLDS USING TV (See Def. 1)

	1	2	3	4	5	6	7	8	9	10	11	12	13	14	15	16
WK. 1	60.5	60.9	61.3	62.4	63.5	65.1	65.6	66.4	66.6	66.9	65.8	65.5	64.7	63.9	62.5	61.4
WK. 2	64.1	64.6	64.8	66.0	67.9	69.4	70.5	71.0	69.9	70.7	68.1	66.7	64.1	63.3	61.6	60.3

U.S. TV Households: 83,800,000
(1) NFL PLAYOFF GAME–SUN.PITTSBURGH VS LA.RAIDERS.NBC.(4:00-7:14PM)(S)
A-17 (2) AFC CHP GM,SEATTLEVSLA.RAIDERS,NBC,(4-7:18P)(S) (3) AFC CHAMPIONSHIP POST.NBC,(7:18-7:34PM)(S)

For explanation of symbols, See page A.

FIGURE 5-2.

number of sets in use by days and by dayparts, comparison of television usage between the current season and the one preceding, plus other details. Figure 5-2 shows a sample *Pocketpiece* page. The *Pocketpiece* also contains two items of great interest to programmers: program ratings and shares for both the overall audience and specific demographic groups within that audience.

Programmers also find Nielsen's *Multi-Network Area Report* (MNA) very useful. The statistics in the *MNA* cover the 70 most populous areas in the country—all cities with at least three commercial television stations. Since the 70 markets represent about two-thirds of the total number of television homes, only two-thirds of the national Nielsen sample is involved. The networks use *MNA* reports to compare the performance of their three networks without the distortion caused by one- and two-affiliate markets reflected in the national Nielsen reports.

NEW PROGRAM SELECTION

Phase two in planning a new fall season—the selection and development of new program ideas—is more difficult than ongoing program evaluation. As many as 5,000 or 6,000 program ideas are considered over a year by all three networks. These submissions come in forms ranging from a single-page outline to a completed script. Decision makers favor those ideas resembling previous successes and quietly agree that almost all so-called original successes are in fact patterned after long-forgotten programs.

1. *Submissions.*   The three networks invite submissions from established independent producers, such as MCA-Universal, Tandem, Lear, MTM and Lorimar, that enjoy substantial track records. Studios, other independent production companies and individuals are also sought out if some of their prior output ranks high in the ratings. In addition to previous success, these companies or individuals must have financial stability and the know-how required for dealing with network pressures and red tape. It is a given that established organizations have the most accepted writers under contract or can hire exceptional talents, making their submissions more persuasive than those from less well known or experienced sources.

The job of reading and reviewing all of the ideas finding their way into a network's program pool is tedious and time consuming. Many ideas are dismissed out-of-hand; others are read and reread, only to be shelved temporarily. A few get a favorable nod with dispatch. Many times the choices are extremely difficult because decision makers are looking for a program with *staying power*— that elusive combination of elements that will make a series fascinating to viewers over years of new episodes using the same characters and situations.

Once preliminary selections occur, **step deals** are made—that is, producers are given money to develop the ideas. Of the many thousands of submissions that land on the networks' desks, roughly 500 are chosen for further development at network expense. At this point, contracts are signed giving the network creative control over the proposed program and giving it *first refusal rights*—in other words, the producer cannot take the idea to anyone else until the network has actually turned down the show; as a result, a network may hold onto an idea for years.

As a rule, step deals are no more than authorization for scripts and in some cases expanded treatments. The approved concepts often take first form as special programs, made-for-TV movies or miniseries. If a script was submitted initially, a rewrite may be ordered accompanied by specific recommendations for changes in concept, plot or cast (and even writers). ABC has traditionally supported many more program ideas at this stage than CBS or NBC. However, ratings shifts have led CBS and NBC to allot more money to develop new program ideas. Most new program ideas are for half-hour comedies; concepts for one-hour dramas are far fewer, even though a greater number of prime-time programs are one hour in length. Half-hour sit-coms target the much desired demographic group of women 18 to 49, and if successful, may hit the syndication jackpot; they are also the cheapest to produce, and so the networks readily order pilots.

2. *Scripts.* Before authorizing a pilot, the program executive will first order one or more scripts. Although in the early days of television, certain program ideas received immediate pilot funding and even guaranteed places on schedules, such decisions usually depended on the use of a very popular performer as the star or big name participation in a comedy-variety format. This practice has been abandoned as too risky. As of 1984, average expenditures at all three networks ranged from $20,000 for a half-hour comedy script to $40,000 for a one-hour drama script. Exceptional (read *successful*) writers demand even higher prices. Before a pilot is produced, a second or even third script for a proposed series may be called for to test the versatility of the series' idea.

3. *Pilots.* A *pilot* is a sample or prototype production of a series under consideration. Pilots afford programmers an opportunity to preview audience reaction to a property. Each network orders between 45 and 50 pilots to fill about a dozen anticipated gaps in its new season lineup. Once initial decisions are made to film or tape a pilot, a budget is drawn up and start-up money advanced to the producer. The budget and advance may be regarded as the third major step of the program development process. As of 1983, depending on whether videotape or film is used, half-hour pilots cost from $650,000 to $750,000 and one-hour dramas more than twice that amount. These amounts also include license fees.

If the pilot passes final muster and gets into the network's prime-time lineup, subsequent episodes of a half-hour series will cost between $300,000 and $350,000 ($600,000 to $650,000 for one-hour episodes). These costs are average since each property differs as to the number of sets, size of cast and salaries paid. Made-for-TV movies usually cost from $1.3 million to $1.6 million; a miniseries such as *Roots* or *Winds of War* will cost tens of millions of dollars but, unlike most made-for-TV movies, will provide a potential motion picture for theatrical distribution.

The very practice of piloting creates an artificial situation. More money, more time, more writing effort go into a pilot than into subsequent series episodes. All the people involved put their best feet forward, trying to make the pilot irresistable to the network decision makers. It is in a producer's best interests to pull out all the stops and spend even more money than the network has agreed to pay.

Because of its incredible expense and abysmal success rate, some producers have denounced the pilot system, recommending five- to ten-minute presentation films in the place of full-blown pilots.[6] As of 1983, about 150 pilots were produced annually to fill the three- to four-dozen newly opened slots on the three networks each year. Those series failing to make the final selection list for the fall season are often held in reserve in anticipation of the inevitable cancelations. The networks may also "short order" back-up series from some of the pilots. They authorize production of two to six episodes and order additional scripts instead of financing the usual eleven episodes. With the probable investment of over a million dollars in any pilot, inevitably every pilot, as well as all other episodes, will be broadcast sometime during the year—high ratings or not! As a result of increases in pilot expenses, the networks are turning increasingly to the made-for-television movies to try out ideas.

Most contracts require delivery in early spring. When received, pilots are tested on special audiences as described in Chapter 2. Although pilot testing research is admittedly inconclusive, it exerts considerable influence. The pilots are also repeatedly screened by committees of programming experts. The decision to select a pilot for a series may include (1) current viewer preferences as indicated by ratings, (2) costs, (3) resemblance between the proposed program and ideas that worked well in the past, (4) projected series' ability to deliver the targeted demographics for that network and its advertisers and (5) the types of programs competing networks air on nights when the new series might be scheduled. Of secondary weight but also relevant to a judgment are (6) the reputation of the producer and writers, (7) the appeal of the series' performers, (8) the availability of an appropriate time period and (9) the compatibility of the program with returning shows. These considerations and others are juggled by the chief programmer. Fred Silverman, for example, was said to make performer appeal his number one consideration; Paley traditionally supported updated forms of older ideas; other programmers weigh counterprogramming considerations more heavily.

PRIME-TIME SCHEDULING

At the end of the opening week of the 1979 fall television season, Les Brown, former *New York Times'* television columnist said, "For the opening week of the new season, Mr. Silverman [Fred Silverman, president of NBC] mounted a potent schedule of programs that trounced both rival networks and broke a long losing streak for NBC-TV."[7] He went on to say, "Mr. Silverman scored his coup essentially by putting NBC's best movies forward—*Coming Home* and *Semi-Tough*—which had been originally scheduled for the crucial November sweep ratings." This lineup, not representative of NBC's regular programming schedule, was a successful move to lift NBC from its last place position even if only for a brief time. Mr. Brown quotes a rival network's spokesperson: "Silverman bought himself some time and a winning week by 'stacking' the schedule. Now let's see what he does for an encore." Stacking is one kind of scheduling strategy network schedulers employ. Four strategies dominate prime-time scheduling: lead-in placement, tent-poling, hammocking and stunting.

1. *Lead-in Placement.* A strategy all schedulers use is to begin an evening with an especially strong program. Known as the **lead-in**, the first prime-time network show sets the tone for the entire evening. This maneuver can win or lose a night and thus appreciably affect the ratings performance of a full week. The 1979 fall season showed each network using this strategem. ABC placed established hit shows in the 8 P.M. slot Tuesday through Saturday (Monday was exceptional because of *Monday Night Football*). The 8 P.M. lead-in spots were *Happy Days* on Tuesday, *Eight Is Enough* on Wednesday, *Laverne & Shirley* on Thursday, *Fantasy Island* on Friday and *The Ropers* on Saturday. On Sunday, ABC programmed *Mork & Mindy* at 8:00 P.M.

CBS and NBC, lacking ABC's array of ratings hits, placed their new entries in the lead-off time periods three nights out of the week: CBS used *California Fever, The Last Resort* and *Working Stiffs*; NBC used *The Misadventures of Sheriff Lobo, Buck Rogers in the 25th Century* and *Shirley*—all slotted at 8 P.M. Ironically, in spite of its apparent program strength, in the 1979 fall season's first week, only ABC's *Benson* rated within the top 20 shows.[8] Of the new arrivals in the 1979–80 season, a CBS show rated twenty-fifth place, two NBC shows were in thirty-first and thirty-third and two ABC premieres in forty-first and forty-seventh places—early reminders of the high mortality rate for new programs.

By 1982, none of the networks was willing to shift a successful series around just to create a strong lead-in. This new unwillingness to move proven hits followed on the disastrous results of ABC's 1979 hammocking strategy, described below. However, networks still used the lead-in strategy in the mid-1980s, though less consistently. At the beginning of the 1982 season, for example, each network chose to start three nights with strong, established shows. ABC used *That's Incredible* as the lead-in on Mondays, *Happy Days* on Tuesdays and *Benson* on Fridays. They also used the relatively new *T.J. Hooker* as the Saturday lead-in; this show, while not well established, was tried at the end of the 1981–82 season and proved quite strong in this position.

CBS used strong lead-ins in 1982 with *60 Minutes* on Sundays, *Magnum P.I.* on Thursdays and *Dukes of Hazzard* on Fridays. NBC's strongest programs went on Saturdays with *Different Strokes*, Mondays with *Little House: A New Beginning*, and Wednesdays with *Real People*. NBC also chose to use weaker established series as lead-ins on Tuesdays, *Father Murphy*, and Thursdays, *Fame*. Note, however, that most of these series had held the same time slots during the preceding years, and for the most part the networks avoided scheduling their strongest established series against each other.

2. *Hammocking.* Although scheduling strategies can bolster weak programs, it is obviously easier to build a strong schedule from a strong foundation than from a weak one. Scheduling is a matter of taking advantage of the mistakes rival networks commit as well as of making the right moves with one's own programming. It is comparatively simple to add new programs to an already successful evening of highly rated situation comedies.

Moving an established sit-com to the next half-hour and inserting a promising new program in its slot can take advantage of audience flow from a lead-in program to the rescheduled familiar sit-com, automatically providing viewers for the intervening program. This strategy is known as creating a **hammock** for the new program—a possible audience sag in the middle will be offset by the solid support fore and aft. The network may also use the hammock within block programming—placing a new program within a block of similar dramas or sit-coms filling an entire evening, a venerable and respected practice. In using this strategy, the programmer accepts the risk that the new comedy may lack the staying power of its "protectors" and so damage the program that follows. In effect, however, surrounding a newcomer with strong, established programs ensures the best possible opportunity for it to rate as high as the established hits.

ABC's 1979–80 schedule relied heavily on this strategy. On Tuesdays, *Angie*, a new program on ABC, rested comfortably between *Happy Days* and *Three's Company*. *Benson*, a new half-hour, safely nestled between *Laverne & Shirley* and *Barney Miller*. *Detective School* had a comfortable hammock between *The Ropers* and *Love Boat*, and the highly touted *The Associates* was placed between the hit *Mork & Mindy* and the traditionally strong *ABC Sunday Night Movie*. But to create these hammocks, ABC broke up certain adjacencies that had suc-ceeded in the 1978–79 season, and moving proven hits always runs the risk of damaging their ratings.

While ABC's strategies were astute, in practice, the results were a disaster. In only one instance did the hammock strategy work—with *Benson*. *Angie* failed; *Detective School* failed; *The Associates* failed; even the so-called safe bets, *The Ropers* and eventually *Mork & Mindy*, were also canceled. Partly as a result of hammocking, ABC fell from its first place position: Failing new shows dragged down established programs such as the *ABC Sunday Night Movie*, *Laverne & Shirley* and *Happy Days*.

3. *Tent-poling.*   Instead of splitting up successful half-hour adjacencies to insert an unproven half-hour show, in the 1978–79 season ABC and NBC turned to **tent-poling**—an alternative to the hammock. Each network focused on a cen-tral, strong 8:30 or 9 P.M. show on weak evenings, hoping to use that show to anchor the ones before and after it. This strategy is particularly useful when a network has a shortage of successful programs and so cannot employ hammocking.

4. *Stunting.*   The art of scheduling also includes maneuvers called **stunt-ing**—a term taken from the defensive plays used in professional football. Stunt-ing includes scheduling **specials**, shifting a half-hour series to **long-form** or **stack-ing** the program schedule at the last minute. In the late 1970s the networks began deliberately making last-minute changes in their schedules to catch rival networks off guard. These moves were calculated, planned well ahead of time but kept secret until the last possible moment. NBC's surprise movement of its blockbuster movies from the November sweeps into the opening week of the 1979 fall season illustrates stunting. These moves were intended to blunt the effects of competitors' programs. Generally these maneuvers are one-time-only because their high cost cannot be sustained over a long period.

Scheduling blockbuster films, using big-name stars and altering a series' format for a single evening are also attention-getting stunts. They have high promotional value and can attract much larger than usual audiences. Of course, the following week, the schedule goes back to normal, and so these efforts rarely create long-term improvements in series ratings. Creating unusual program **crossovers** of stars from one series to another is a related stunt that affects ratings only so long as the crossover continues.

The Effects of Schedule Churn

Stunting during the 1970s resulted in a continual shifting of prime-time schedules. This *churn* constituted the major difference between 1960s and 1970s programming. (Here the term *churn* refers to the continual shifting of programs within the network schedule, and should not be confused with *churn* as it is used in cable and pay television. In the latter case, it refers to subscriber turnover and not to the programming itself.) The 1960s represented a period of extreme stability in television schedules. New series were introduced during late September; the second season, consisting of only a handful of time shifts and new series, always took place in late December and early January, and virtually no series were canceled in less than 16 weeks (one season). Preempting regular series was held to a minimum and concentrated in particular time periods such as Christmas or Easter when the holidays provided a natural reason for specials. The 1960s were also marked by stability within the audience and within the networks' comparative overall rankings. During the entire decade, CBS came in first, NBC second and ABC third.

During the 1970s, this stability vanished—the combined result of a closer ratings race, pressure from advertisers for "proper" demographics, pressure from public interest groups and declining network audience shares (toward the end of the decade). The number of *time shifts,* the moving of series from one slot to another, for example, went from less than a half dozen in 1969–70 to over 40 by 1981–82. The number of *shows canceled in less than five weeks* went from one in 1969 to a peak of 24 in 1978; cancelations have held at about 20 per year since then. The number of series *frequently preempted* (more than one-third of the time) went from 0 to over 20. The 1970s also saw the collapse of the seasonal system for introducing time shifts and new programs.

Table 5-2 shows the number of series introduced or moved into new time slots during each month from 1971 to 1982. The September/January figures represent the traditional two-season starting points. Therefore, series introduced in other months represent changes in the schedule that took place while the season was in progress. The chart shows the *scheduling churn* caused by moving established series into new time slots (program shifting) and the introduction of new programs (requiring the cancelation of old programs). Included are figures for the two seasons only (32 weeks) as they represent the network's main programming efforts. As can be seen, the mid-1970s saw a massive increase in schedule churn, which has continued. The September 1980 and 1981 figures reflect the effects of the actors' and writers' strikes that delayed the start of those seasons.

A program that a network wants to get rid of can be manipulated (time shifted or churned) until its ratings fall. Examination of the results of program churn shows that an individual program's ratings almost invariably fall when it is moved two out of three seasons (especially when moved in second season too). Programs that are prime candidates for excessive schedule manipulation by the networks include those with higher than average production costs or less than ideal demographics. Also, those that cause managerial decision-making problems as a result of their unusual content or format and those that represent personal judgment failures (even if successful) are likely to be manipulated frequently. Once low ratings, or even a downward trend, is achieved, network programmers can point to the ratings to justify cancelation.

TABLE 5-2.
Prime-Time Churn: Numbers of Time Shifts and New Program Introductions from
1971 to 1982

Year	Sept.	Oct.	Nov.	Dec.	Jan.	Feb.	Mar.	Apr.	Total	Outside of Sept./Jan.
1971	24	-	3	3	14	-	-	-	44	14%
1972	19	-	-	3	13	1	-	-	36	11%
1973	20	-	1	-	20	2	2	-	45	11%
1974	25	2	-	3	13	3	6	1	53	28%
1975	29	4	7	6	17	1	4	-	68	32%
1976	20	-	15	4	21	6	10	-	76	46%
1977	22	7	2	12	13	8	7	12	83	58%
1978	25	5	11	1	20	14	19	4	99	55%
1979	24	8	2	16	11	2	25	8	96	64%
1980	7	4	8	10	13	6	13	8	69	71%
1981	6	13	15	4	13	5	18	20	94	80%
1982	15	10	2	-	12	10	20	9	78	65%
Totals	236	53	66	62	180	58	124	63		

SOURCE: *Variety* ratings, prepared by William J. Adams.

CHANGING FORMAT EMPHASIS

The late 1970s saw several major changes in the kinds of formats dominating prime time. One was the increased use of **specials**—a term encompassing one-time entertainment programs, sporting events, interview shows, docudramas and documentaries. Other changes included increased use of **miniseries, adaptations** of books, movies or foreign TV series and **spinoffs** from existing series.

Specials

Although situation comedies and dramatic series remain the mainstays of nighttime schedules, other formats have found their way into audience affections. In 1953 Mary Martin and Ethel Merman, luminaries of the Broadway stage, made television history when they joined in a song festival that enchanted their audience on *Ford's 50th Anniversary Show*. The setting consisted of a plain backdrop, and the props were two bookkeeper stools; there were no dancers, no gingerbread. It was straight and delightful entertainment for 90 minutes, and it remains one of the medium's highlights—a breakthrough of significant proportions. This program was the *first* special.

In the 1978–79 season, the three networks aired 809 prime-time specials. Of these, **574** were entertainment specials for adults (live, film or tape) or children, such as the Charlie Brown Christmas specials; 14 were unusual interview shows such as those with Barbara Walters and her guests; 49 were sports events, including World Series games; and the remaining 172 were divided among docudramas (79) and 30-minute and long-form documentaries (93). In 1981–82, the pattern was roughly the same: Of 723 specials, **530** were entertainment specials; 14 were interviews; 64 were sports; and 79 were documentaries and docudramas (with 36 "other"). Some specials were motion pictures made expressly for television or had had successful runs in theaters.

Entertainment specials often attract "superstars," whose regular motion picture work or performing schedule prevents them from participating in series programs. Such star-studded specials can invigorate a schedule, encourage major advertiser participation, provide unusual promotion opportunities and generate high ratings.

Because of their popularity, the number of specials steadily increased each season, peaking at the end of the 1970s with the beginning of the economic recession. In the 1980s, specials changed formats: Increasingly they became long-form episodes of regularly scheduled series, presented in their usual time slot. For example, the record-breaking final episode of *M*A*S*H* (77 share) was just a longer episode of an existing series. In 1978–79, this trend was minor; but by 1981–82, one-fifth of the 530 entertainment specials were in fact long-form episodes of regularly scheduled series. Network programmers had awakened to the possibility that too many specials that were very different from the regular programming might interrupt carefully nurtured viewing habits beyond repair. At that point specials would become self-defeating, so they turned to long-form episodes of regularly scheduled series. Such shows also have the advantage of being relatively inexpensive to produce.

Docudramas and Documentaries

The unexpected ratings success of the magazine-format series *60 Minutes* in the late 1970s led ABC and NBC to imitate it with *20/20* and *Prime Time Saturday,* starting in 1979. The success of all three of these programs encouraged the development of other nonfiction forms of prime time, such as *Real People* in 1979, *That's Incredible* in 1980, *Amazing Animals* in 1980, *Believe It or Not* in 1982 and *Monitor* in 1983.

The docudrama, a dramatized version of historical fact, became popular in the 1970s. *Washington: Behind Closed Doors* (based on Watergate events), *Missiles of October* and *Roots* are perhaps the best known of the 1970s docudramas.

Less noticed by the critics but steadily rising in popularity in the same decade were long-form documentaries. Out of 809 specials broadcast in the 1978–79 season, 93 were documentaries, most of which did remarkably well in prime time. On ABC on March 4, 1979, *The Ordeal of Patty Hearst* gained a 34 share. NBC received a 30 share for *The Sea Gypsies* on January 7, 1979 and in 1982, ABC's *Ronald Reagan: At Home on the Ranch,* a "personality documentary" also got a 30 share. In 1983, the highest-rated documentary appeared on PBS rather than commercial television, *Vietnam: A Television History.* The success of these programs in prime time signaled the demise of the myth that public affairs programs are necessarily ratings losers.

Miniseries

The success of specials and limited series on PBS's *Masterpiece Theatre* led the commercial networks into the production of multipart series presented in two to six episodes on successive nights or in successive weeks. Called *miniseries,* they ran for as long as ten or more hours. The best known of recent miniseries are *Holocaust, Shogun, The Blue and the Gray, Centennial* and *Thorn Birds.* In 1983, ABC presented *Winds of War,* a miniseries seen on six successive nights during the February sweeps for a total of 18 hours. Unquestionably, *Winds of War* was the most expensive miniseries on record; its $38 million production cost plus an estimated $25 million for promotion (including ABC's own airtime), however, earned the initial episode half of the total viewing audience, and an average audience share of 53 for its entire run. ABC sold all of its commercial spots at $350,000 a minute, earning revenues in excess of $30 million for the one showing. (Despite ABC's expenditures, this series failed to exceed the all-time high audience share for a miniseries captured by the docudrama *Roots* in 1979. *Roots* attracted an average share of 66 percent over eight consecutive nights.)

ABC's competitors tried to reduce *Winds of War*'s initial audience share. NBC and CBS realized that the first evening contains the **hook** in a miniseries, an element that grabs audience attention. Audiences for subsequent episodes are generally composed of return viewers, sticking with the series, though audiences for subsequent nights may increase as a result of word-of-mouth publicity and heavy network promotion. Both competitors counterprogrammed *Winds of War* with comedy, NBC with a Steve Martin special and later a Gary Coleman movie, CBS with a light Clint Eastwood movie, in an effort to keep viewers away from the initial episode.

Miniseries are typically scheduled so that they begin and end on Sunday nights, the night of maximum television viewing. Shorter miniseries tend to be scheduled on sequential nights while longer series, such as *Winds of War,* are stretched over two weeks and skip evenings on which the network has scheduled its most popular programs. Because of their exceedingly high cost, miniseries are usually only created for sweeps periods.

Both *Roots* and *Thorn Birds* were produced at enormous cost and both gained unusually large audiences and high revenue. *Thorn Birds,* for example, averaged a 41 rating and a 59 share, making it the second-highest rated miniseries, just behind *Roots,* up to that time. Aside from high ratings and beating the competition, the networks derived considerable prestige and critical acclaim from these programs, which help to justify the heavy investment. Some miniseries, such as *Rich Man, Poor Man* and *How the West Was Won,* have been turned into regular series, further reducing the financial risk involved.

Adaptations

The networks have often adapted successful theatrical motion pictures into series formats. Perhaps the foremost example is *M*A*S*H,* derived from a feature picture by Twentieth Century-Fox. Many adaptations use only the feature title on the assumption that it alone will attract audiences. Frequently the adaptation waters down the original film's story line to make it more "suitable" for television. From feature film hits came series like *Mr. Deeds Goes to Town, Blondie, Peyton Place, Hondo, Tarzan, Daktari, Twelve O'Clock High, Shane, Mr. Roberts, Dr. Kildare* and *Seven Brides for Seven Brothers.* Few of these mutations ever enjoyed real success. Adapting British shows for American commercial television goes back about ten years and has been fairly successful. Such adaptations include the hits, *All in the Family* and *Three's Company,* and two failed 1983 series, *Foot in the Door* and *Amanda's Place.*

Spinoffs

Certain supporting characters in a series often become quite popular and are spun off into new series. This practice makes stars of supporting players who demonstrate a potential to carry their own shows. TvQs, ratings measuring a performer's likability and recognizability, give programmers a clue as to which ones are promising candidates to star in spinoffs. Strong performers in lesser roles led to such spinoff series as *Maude, Rhoda, The Jeffersons, Mork & Mindy, After M*A*S*H* and *Benson*.

As much as 10 percent of prime-time entertainment in 1979 consisted of programs based on characters from other situation comedies or adventure/dramas. This technique for creating new programs characterized Fred Silverman's strategy at ABC. Spinoffs bring an experienced production staff from the parent program to support the new series; these staff members are familiar with the stars' personalities and with the characters they play. Because the original writers and directors generally move to a *spinoff* series, they can continue their successful teamwork. *Fresh* program ideas, however, typically involve *new* combinations of producers, directors, writers, technical staff and actors, requiring a lengthy adjustment period. But the overriding advantages of spinoffs are the ready-made audience and built-in promotional possibilities they bring from the parent program. Well-known characters such as Shirley and Laverne brought personal followings to their spinoff series from *Happy Days*, just as Lou Grant brought a following from the *Mary Tyler Moore Show* (though from any perspective his two series had very little in common). A spinoff is most successful when it begins its run while the parent program is still in the schedule. Delay in getting a spinoff on the air can ruin its chances for success.

Made-for-TV-Movies

Many viewers and critics bewail the disappearance of the dramatic anthology format, the single-episode, play-for-TV presented as a series. But in reality, the anthology format went through a style change in the late 1960s and returned as the "made-for-TV" movie. During the 1955–56 season, the very peak of the anthology era, dramatic anthologies made up about **526** hours of prime time. In the 1981–82 season, about **536** hours of made-for-TV movies were offered (excluding miniseries). The best of the made-for-TV movies compare favorably with the best of the dramatic anthologies of the earlier era. For example, *Marty, The Miracle Worker* and *Requiem for a Heavyweight* were classic anthologies, while *The Autobiography of Miss Jane Pittman* and *Bitter Harvest* were made-for-TV movies, themselves immediate classics of the same caliber filling the equivalent gap in programming fare.

In the late 1970s, the made-for-TV movie replaced the pilot as the major method for testing out new series ideas. Programs such as *How the West Was Won, T.J. Hooker, Code Red* and *Seven Brides for Seven Brothers* were all successful TV movies before becoming series. Such movies pay their way whether or not the concept ever becomes a series. And even when a series is created and fails, the networks usually make a healthy profit based on the initial run of the made-for-TV movie and on the normal advertising revenues from the run of the subsequent weekly series.

As a result, the made-for-TV movie-pilot is very popular with networks. Luckily, the format is also popular with audiences. The ratings for some such films equal and even surpass those for feature films shown on television. Of the top ten movies shown on television during 1981–82, five were made-for-TV movies. Some of these films, such as *Battlestar Galactica*, have been strong in theatrical release *after* television airings. Also, made-for-TV movies often command high ratings in later syndication. This popularity, their revenue advantage over regular video tape pilots, the potential for rerun revenues and the fact that the average made-for-TV movie costs about half what an average Hollywood theatrical movie costs, have established this format firmly in the economics of network television. By 1982, made-for-TV movies shown on network television outnumbered feature films made for theatrical release by 268 to 216.

THE CENSORS

The broadcast standards and practices department, a behind-the-scenes group, exercises total authority over all network programming. Cynically and often angrily called the "censors," this department at each network has absolute approval rights over every program—whether a single episode of a half-hour series or a two-hour special. The department acts as cop on the beat and judge for all questions concerning acceptability of material for broadcast. It often finds itself walking a thin line between offending viewers or advertisers and destroying imaginative programming that may pull in high ratings. Only it decides whether an idea is imaginative or objectionable. Members of the department attend every program rehearsal, filming or taping, read scripts beforehand and often preview the final products before they are aired. The broadcast standards and practices department reviews language, dress and concept. Questions of taste are analyzed carefully by this department at the script stage and occasionally in the finished product. If, in the department's judgment, a program fails to conform to network standards, it can insist on changes and be overturned only on appeal to the chairman or president of the company.

Over the years, the department's criteria for acceptability have changed. In the early 1920s, one of the hottest issues was whether such a personal and perhaps obscene product as toothpaste should be allowed to advertise over the air. By 1983, the hottest question was whether or not NBC's censors would permit a new series, *Bay City Blues*, to air a locker room scene that included nude men photographed, as the producer put it, "tastefully from the back."

The department decides acceptability on a show-by-show basis, with no apparent connection between rulings. For instance, in 1978, ABC recalled the premiere episode of *Battlestar Galactica*, demanding that a scene be reshot because one of the characters had his shirt off at what they felt might be considered a sexually suggestive moment. At the same time, the department routinely approved of partially clothed actors in bedroom scenes for programs like *The Love Boat*.

Although decisions may seem arbitrary, the censors normally follow certain guidelines. For example, a program's perceived audience is an important factor. A show appealing to children (or scheduled before 9 P.M.) will be regulated much more heavily than one aimed at adults and scheduled later. The program's daypart is also a major consideration. Traditionally, the censors have been much easier on series run during the morning or early afternoon (most notably, the soap operas) than on programs run during prime time. Also, censors tend to be more liberal with specials, miniseries and made-for-TV movies than with weekly series. The network's implied position regarding controversial material, however, is the most important factor. During the early 1980s, CBS tended to be the most conservative of the three networks, particularly regarding sexual content, while NBC was the most liberal. For instance, during the early 1980s, CBS censors, reviewing scenes from *Capital* concluded a man in jockey shorts was not acceptable but the same man in boxer shorts was. At about the same time, NBC's department cleared *Honeyboy*, a made-for-TV movie having scenes in which the star appeared clad only in bikini briefs, and permitted a prime-time series called *The Shape of Things* to feature male strippers.

Traditionally, the broadcast standards and practices department tries to avoid fighting openly with producers. Its policy is to seek agreement, to compromise if possible, but, in the final analysis, their word is law.

A PERSPECTIVE

For many reasons, in the 1970s television program types narrowed down to situation-comedies, crime dramas and movies. The passing of radio, stage and motion picture stars; the voracious appetite of the medium; the growing sophistication of audiences; the efficiency of film and tape; and a high profit margin for the networks based on relatively low licensing costs for sit-coms and crime series and the profitability of made-for-TV movies all contributed to this change. The westerns, the comedy-variety series, the dramatic anthologies, the high powered quiz shows, the unique panel programs are gone. However, television—like show business in general—is historically cyclical. Once-popular formats are likely to return. The decline in program variety began in the mid-1960s when the networks switched from 30-minute programs that had dominated the prime-time schedule during the 1950s, to the 60-minute format, with the exception of the sit-com. Two-hour movies were also introduced as regular features in prime time in the 1960s. These format changes resulted in an actual decrease in the number of available program slots.

Starting in 1971, the three networks began to concentrate on just three formats: situation-comedies, crime drama and movies (both feature films and made-for-TV). Since that year, these three program types have filled an average of 59 percent of all prime time. Fourth- and fifth-ranked formats fluctuated during the 1970s, but by the 1980s, they were magazine format series, medical shows and soap operas. By 1982, these five formats filled three-quarters of all prime time. All other formats declined until, by 1982, most were represented in only one or two programs in each network's lineup. Although the top three formats are not noticeably more successful than other formats, they appeal strongly to women 18–49, the "ideal demographic" category of especial interest to advertisers. And in the face of competition from the cable television industry, the networks are not likely to change their programming in the 1980s.

All three networks prowl for the breakthrough idea—the program that will be different but not so different as to turn away audiences. *Mork & Mindy* was one such show during the 1978–79 season as was *All in the Family* during the

1971–72 season. Network programmers can only guess what the next hit will be and why it succeeds. A program failure is easier to analyze: It can be the result of the wrong time period, the wrong concept, the wrong writing, the wrong casting, poor execution of a good idea, poor execution of a bad idea, too much strong competition, the wrong night of the week, or any of a dozen other factors. Shows canceled out-of-hand because of low shares might have turned into major hits had they been allowed to build slowly. When scheduled on Tuesdays, *Simon & Simon*, for example, fell to the bottom of the ratings charts in 1981–82, but when moved to Thursdays in 1982–83, it caught on and became a hit. The program graveyard is crowded with shows that were buried alive, but the price tag for even temporary failure is so high that cancelation usually seems safer than delay. The fact remains that anything radically different has very little chance of reaching prime time. Some years ago the unexpected success of *Animal House*, a feature movie staring John Belushi and a supporting cast of unknowns, led all three networks to introduce comedy programs based on the same sort of slapstick antics on a college campus. Not one survived, and *Co-ed Fever*, CBS's 1979 entry, had the questionable distinction of lasting for only one night.

Playing it safe with formats known to satisfy audiences is a normal reaction on the part of network programmers. Considering the high stakes, program executives naturally resist any program that can be described as a trialblazer. Those programmers who dare to depart from the formulas, however, may occasionally enjoy the fruits of such standout hits as *All in the Family* or *M*A*S*H*. Indeed, the current rate of program failure suggests that the unusual might be less risky than sticking to copies of old series. Given the rapid turnover among network presidents and vice-presidents of programming during the 1980s, iron nerves are required to allow a really new idea to remain on the schedule long enough to attract a significant following.

SUMMARY

Television programming remains a high-risk undertaking with large amounts of money, prestige and public interest at stake. For all of their dollars, their care, their studies, their testing, their research, their meetings, their professionalism and their strategies, the networks' high hopes for new programs are repeatedly dashed in a matter of weeks each new season. Cancelation often irritates audiences, but networks point to inadequate ratings and swing the ax anyway. On the other hand, the networks also ensure low ratings for some programs by scheduling them against runaway hits or established series or by excessive churn (time shifts). The nine factors listed earlier that affect program selection from among hundreds of pilots consider resemblance to past successes more important than originality. Scheduling strategies such as leading-in with a strong program, hammocking, tent-poling and stunting are meant to bolster newcomers and create audience flow within a network's prime-time schedule. Although program introductions have shifted from all-in-the-fall to a two-season and then a continuous-season approach, program formulas remain much the same. The only major programming innovation of recent years has been the miniseries. The dramatic anthology was revived as the made-for-TV movie. But the variety that once characterized prime time has disappeared; three formats, sit-coms, crime series and movies, dominate the schedule. Network prime-time programming uses conservative strategies because to do otherwise involves enormous risks to individuals and revenues.

Notes

[1]Jerry Krupnick (syndicated columnist for Newhouse News Service), *Los Angeles Times*, Spring 1979.

[2]William J. Adams, Susan Tyler Eastman, Larry J. Horney and Mark N. Popovich, "The Cancelation and Manipulation of Network Television Prime-Time Programs," *Journal of Communication* 33, Winter 1983, pp. 10–27.

[3]"A New Summer Song," *Broadcasting*, 7 February 1983, p. 35.

[4]Program decisions at ABC, CBS, and NBC are not made by the vice-presidents of entertainment. Vice-presidents recommend, they contribute, they assert themselves. But at NBC Grant Tinker makes the final decisions; at ABC Fred Pierce, Anthony Thomopoloulos, Lew Erlich and Elton Rule decide; at CBS, programming decisions are made by Gene Jankowski, Bud Grant and Jim Rosenfield (William S. Paley also contributed to this process until his retirement in 1982). The bromide that network programs are chosen by three men is false. Many others contribute to the decision-making process from the company presidents to the entertainment division presidents to kibitzers in programming meetings.

[5]*Paper Chase* was the first canceled commercial broadcast network program to be rerun on PBS. In 1983 Showtime picked it up and put some new episodes into production. See also Mitchell E. Shapiro and Lemuel Schofield, "Off-Network Television Program Series in Syndication: A Pilot Study," paper presented to the Speech Communication Association convention, Washington, D.C., November 1983.

[6]"There's Got to Be a Better Way than Pilot System Say Producers," *Broadcasting*, 24 May 1982, p. 54. See also *Broadcasting*, 21 December 1981, p. 35ff; 14 February 1983, p. 69; 24 May 1982, pp. 54–56.

[7]Les Brown, " 'Stacking' the Schedule Put NBC-TV in Top Spot," *New York Times*, 27 September 1979, p. C19.

[8]All three of CBS's 1979 entries and one of NBC's were canceled within two months of the season opening.

Selected Sources

Bedell, Sally. *Up the Tube: Prime-Time TV and the Silverman Years*. New York: Viking Press, 1981.

Brooks, Tim, and Marsh, Earle. *The Complete Directory to Prime Time Network TV Shows: 1946–Present*. New York: Ballantine Books, 1981.

Cantor, Muriel G. *Prime-Time Television: Content and Control*. Beverly Hills, California: Sage Publications, 1980.

Gitlin, Todd. *Inside Prime Time*. New York: Pantheon Books, 1983.

Levinson, Richard, and Link, William. *Stay Tuned: An Inside Look at the Making of Prime-Time Television*. New York: St. Martin's Press, 1981.

Newcomb, Horace, and Alley, Robert S. *The Producer's Medium: Conversations with Creators of American T.V.* New York: Oxford University Press, 1983.

Reel, A. Frank. *The Networks: How They Stole the Show*. New York: Charles Scribner's Sons, 1979.

Variety, weekly trade newspaper of the television and film industry.

CHAPTER SIX

Nonprime-Time Network Programming

Squire D. Rushnell

SQUIRE D. RUSHNELL, *now vice-president of long-range planning and children's television for ABC Entertainment, has been responsible for all of ABC's children's programming since 1974 and was in charge of* Good Morning America *during its climb to the number one position in its time period—1978 to 1981. Mr. Rushnell is widely recognized for his achievements with the multiaward-winning* ABC Afterschool Specials *series and* Schoolhouse Rock. *He has led ABC's long-range planning division since 1982. He started his career by serving in various management and program producer positions with Group W Broadcasting after attending Syracuse University; then in 1969, he joined WLS-TV, the ABC-owned station in Chicago, as an executive producer and assistant program manager, later becoming program manager. Subsequently, he became vice-president of programming for the ABC-owned television stations. In this chapter the author explains the development of ratings winners in each daypart and delineates the constraints operating on children's programming at the network level.*

NONPRIME-TIME NETWORK DAYPARTS

For the broadcast television networks, **nonprime time** generally describes entertainment programming in every daypart other than prime time excepting news and sports, which are handled by separate departments at all three networks. Specifically, the three commercial networks program the following entertainment dayparts (see corresponding list from the affiliates' perspective in Chapter 7, which differs slightly):

early morning (6 A.M. to 9 A.M.)

daytime (from about 10 A.M. to 4:30 P.M.)

children's (Saturday and Sunday mornings)

late night (11:30 P.M. to 1 A.M.)

Although the audience level in any of these dayparts is considerably lower than in prime time, each contributes competitively, economically and in prestige to healthy network performance. Moreover, the network program executives in charge of these dayparts are just as dedicated to competing for available viewers as their prime-time counterparts. Everything is relative: A 4 rating can spell victory for an early-morning program, but in daytime or on Saturday morning, an 8 rating represents success. Compare that to prime time: A program executive feels secure only with 17 or more ratings points.

Another difference between prime-time and nonprime-time programming is the considerable variance in **clearances**. Local stations have the option of clearing (using or airing) or not clearing any network program. If a show is not aired in three or four of the top twenty markets, its average in the national Nielsen ratings will be considerably lower than if it were. Unfortunately for network programmers, affiliates refuse to clear nonprime-time programs much more often than they preempt prime time, making clearances a major variable in nonprime-time ratings.

The three networks have slightly different numbers of affiliates, adding up to different audience sizes, which also affects competition. Major market affiliates, and major market clearances, are naturally most important because they represent the largest audiences. The shifting ratings war between *Today* and *Good Morning America* exemplifies the twin influences of clearances and total affiliates: In 1975, ABC had only 183 primary affiliates, compared with 218 for NBC and 212 for CBS. But by 1983, 210 affiliates were clearing ABC's *Good Morning America* while 209 cleared NBC's *Today* (and about the same number cleared the *CBS Morning News*). An increase to virtually the same number of affiliates was probably one factor in ABC's early morning success in the 1980s, and a loss of affiliates a factor in NBC's ratings weakness in the early 1980s.

Notwithstanding the effects of clearances and numbers of affiliates, programming strategies for different segments of the day do not vary greatly from network to network. For each daypart, the networks give primary consideration to the demographics of available audiences, competitive counterprogramming and economic viability. A network determines which segment of the available audience it will target, mindful of its competitors' programming and influenced in some degree by advertiser support for its programming.

Although advertiser support cannot be dismissed as an unimportant aspect of television programming, it should not be construed as the primary concern of television programmers. There is little direct association between what happens in any given network program and the advertiser. Rarely if ever does a *direct* line of influence exist between an advertiser and the people or policies of network programming. Networks are similar to newspapers in this regard. Editorial departments and advertising departments tend to operate independently of each other.

One network program executive, when asked about advertising influence, said, "My job as a programmer is to spend as much money as I can get away with to attract the largest possible audiences and do programs which make us proud. Whether my company makes a million more or a million less is the responsibility of another department entirely." Of course, if the executive failed to attract the largest possible audience, the sales department would find the programs less attractive to advertisers, and his employment would, in consequence, be jeopardized.

EARLY-MORNING PROGRAMMING

Early-morning programming on the three commercial television networks has followed consistent patterns over the years. Generally, network service has been provided between 7 and 9 A.M., expanded to include the 6 to 7 A.M. hour in 1982. Then an hour or two is returned to the local stations until network daytime programming commences in midmorning.

NBC's early-morning *Today Show* went on the air in 1952 with an information magazine format, eventually becoming one of television's longest running programs. Not far behind in longevity was CBS's *Captain Kangaroo*, a program tailored for preschool children, which began in 1955, ending only in 1982.

The great age of these two programs, relative to the rest of television, has given them classic status. Twenty years passed before ABC's *AM America* (now *Good Morning America*) came on the early-morning scene in 1975. CBS has vacillated among news and magazine formats and children's shows in early morning, but achieved significant popularity only in the early 1980s with *CBS Morning News.*

Today

Today's structure was eventually named the magazine format because of its resemblance to print publications containing a series of articles bound together with a common cover. A television magazine format contains a series of segments bound within a common program framework. In television, one or more central personalities in a single setting provide the sense of continuity in a magazine show. *Today* succeeded so well in part because during the first twenty years of its reign, it had only three full-time hosts. Dave Garroway, bespectacled, bright, articulate, whose memorable sidekick was a mischievous monkey named J. Fred Muggs, was the first. Muggs made faces at passers-by who peered into the ground-floor studio window (the New York *Today* studio had been an RCA product display showroom). Newsman John Chancellor was *Today's* second host (1961 to 1962), followed by Hugh Downs, who remained NBC's pleasant and intelligent early-morning greeter until 1971.

Little turnover in backup personalities occurred: Barbara Walters launched her on-camera career as one of America's best-known reporters through nine years on *Today*, and newsman Frank Blair was on the show longer than anyone else—twenty-two years. Consistency of personalities on a program that offered more national exposure each week than performers could expect in other programs entrenched *Today* as a solid habit.

Today's format has changed even less than its cast. News and weather are still reported on the hour and half-hour, with opportunities for stations to cut away to local news and weather. *Today's* focus has remained on interviews with entertainers, authors and newsmakers.

CBS Morning News

CBS went head-to-head with *Today* using a magazine format hosted by Will Rogers, Jr., in 1956. Failing, they returned to a news block from 7 to 8, the *CBS Morning News*, followed by *Captain Kangaroo*. In 1973 CBS made another attempt at a live morning magazine with Hughes Rudd and Washington reporter Sally Quinn. Six months later, they returned to *CBS Morning News* and *Captain Kangaroo*, and eventually, in 1982, dropped the children's program altogether in favor of an expanded news program.

Good Morning America

Before 1975, ABC did not offer network service until 11 A.M. In 1975 ABC began to compete more rigorously in other dayparts, including prime time, but its station lineup amounted to only 183 primary affiliates, compared with 218 for NBC and 212 for CBS. For ABC to woo away primary affiliates from its competitors, it needed to provide a full network service including early-morning programming.

As might be expected, in many small and medium markets with only one or two television stations, primary affiliations usually went to the older and stronger networks. Station managers who might be impressed by ABC's gains in prime time and daytime would still think twice about switching affiliation because they would have to fill the 7 to 9 A.M. slot with local programming at added cost: NBC and CBS were both filling the time period and compensating their affiliates.

Table 6-1 reveals early morning viewing patterns and ratings prior to ABC's entry into early-morning competition.

NBC's *Today* was clearly ABC's main target as it launched a competitive news and information program. But with a 23-year head start, *Today* had become an institution for early-morning viewers—it was as comfortable as an old friend. Research has shown that the older the viewers, the more entrenched their viewing habits.

However, as it was doing in other dayparts, ABC aimed for a younger early-morning audience, particularly women 18–49. Not only are women in this group less habituated viewers than the over-50 group and thus more easily introduced to a new morning television alternative, they also are the audience segment advertisers most desire to reach.

ABC attempted, when launching *AM America* in January 1975, to present a clear alternative to NBC's *Today*, targeting for younger women. Bill Beutel was chosen as host, and the program was uniquely informal in style, using a living room set with conversation and brief feature vignettes. However, nine months after *AM America* began, *Today* remained the unqualified leader, leading ABC executives to reevaluate their strategies. (See Table 6-2.)

TABLE 6-1.
Fourth Quarter Ratings, 1974

	Rating	Share	Women 18–49 (000)	Men 18–49 (000)	Women 50+ (000)	Men 50+ (000)
7:00–8:00 A.M.						
NBC *Today*	5.5	37	1390	500	1690	930
CBS *Morning News*	1.7	16	480	260	410	260
ABC local programs						
8:00–9:00 A.M.						
NBC *Today*	5.5	36	1330	640	1940	830
CBS *Captain Kangaroo*	3.7	23	640	110	280	90
ABC local programs						

SOURCE: NTI, December 1974. Used with permission.

TABLE 6-2.
Third Quarter Ratings, 1975

	Rating	Share	Women 18–49 (000)	Men 18–49 (000)	Women 50+ (000)	Men 50+ (000)
7:00–8:00 A.M.						
NBC *Today*	4.2	39	920	530	1420	640
CBS *Morning News*	1.5	21	290	200	520	260
ABC *AM America*	0.9	8	200	160	190	110
8:00–9:00 A.M.						
NBC *Today*	4.1	34	970	450	1390	690
CBS *Captain Kangaroo*	2.8	22	460	120	280	110
ABC *AM America*	1.2	10	420	120	240	240

SOURCE: NTI, September 1975. Used with permission.

ABC recast *AM America* as *Good Morning America*, debuting in November of 1975. Actor David Hartman was selected as host because of his warm, caring style and his ability to ask the questions that the viewer at home might ask. A family of well-known contributors was added: Erma Bombeck with humorous reports; John Coleman, the friendly weatherman; Jack Anderson with "Inside Washington"; Howard Cosell on sports; attorney F. Lee Bailey on law; and Rona Barrett with reports from Hollywood.

Good Morning America adopted a framework similar to *Today*'s: news on the hour and half-hour, time and weather services, and interviews with interesting people. By early 1980, some four-and-one-half years after ABC's quest began, *Good Morning America* slipped past *Today* in overall ratings, with impressive gains among its primary target audience of young women, as well as with other demographic groups. (See Table 6-3.) *Good Morning America* had carved out a place for itself at the breakfast table.

TABLE 6-3.
February Ratings, 1980

	Rating	Share	Women 18–49 (000)	Men 18–49 (000)	Women 50+ (000)	Men 50+ (000)
7:00–9:00 A.M.						
NBC *Today*[a]	5.2	27	1360	630	1770	1120
CBS *Morning News*[b]	3.0	18	630	530	790	590
ABC *GM America*[a]	5.5	28	1720	750	1610	1020

[a] 7:30–8 and 8:30–9 A.M. average
[b] 7:15–8 A.M. only

SOURCE: NTI, February 1980. Used with permission.

The Recent Race

In January 1982, two other significant changes took place in early-morning television. *Today's* amiable, inveterate host, Tom Brokaw, was promoted to *NBC Nightly News*, and replaced by a bright young sportscaster, Bryant Gumble. This continued the trend away from journalism toward personality in early morning. Second, CBS made a bold move back into early-morning programming. *Captain Kangaroo*, on since 1955, was pushed back to a 6:30 A.M. time slot, and later, shown on weekends only. Although CBS would deny any connection, some quarters felt that the deregulatory attitude of the new Reagan administration gave CBS the courage to tamper with such an American institution as *Captain Kangaroo*.

CBS was decisive. It replaced Charles Kuralt, the host of *CBS Morning News*, with Chicago news anchor Bill Kurtis, and expanded the program to a morning news and information service fully competitive with NBC's *Today* and ABC's *Good Morning America*.

These events, along with CBS's hiring away of *Good Morning America's* executive producer, George Merlis, put *CBS Morning News* onto the competitive fast track. Table 6-4 shows, by February 1983, CBS was gaining, NBC was fading, and ABC was tentatively number one.

TABLE 6-4.
February Ratings, 1983

	Rating	Share	Women 18–49 (000)	Men 18–49 (000)	Women 50+ (000)	Men 50+ (000)
7:00–9:00 A.M.						
NBC *Today*	4.5	21	980	650	1630	1020
CBS *Morning News*	3.4	16	520	450	1160	760
ABC *GM America*	6.0	28	1710	710	1880	1000

SOURCE: NTI, February 1983. Used with permission.

DAYTIME PROGRAMMING

The magazine formats of *Today, Good Morning America* and *CBS Morning News* have rarely been successful in network **daytime** programming—the period between 10 A.M. and 4:30 P.M. One syndicated program, *The Phil Donahue Show*, with an audience participation/talk format, has provided stations with successful daytime counterprogramming to conventional network offerings. However, daytime talk/variety shows launched by the three commercial networks have repeatedly died.

In October 1962 NBC tried *The Merv Griffin Show* during the early-afternoon hours, and canceled it in March 1963. (However, when Westinghouse reintroduced this program in syndication, it reached impressive audience levels.) In April 1968 ABC scheduled the *Dick Cavett Show* during late morning. It was canceled in January 1969 and rescheduled in late night. In July 1978 NBC made another attempt with *America Alive* during the noon hour. It was canceled six months later. With this record, it is little wonder that network programmers have stuck to the more successful formulas for daytime programming: soap operas, game shows and reruns of popular prime-time series.

Soap Operas

Successful soap operas often build loyal constituencies that last for years. Few television series have lasted as long as *Search for Tomorrow*, which went on CBS in 1951; *The Guiding Light*, in 1952; and *As the World Turns*, in 1956. ABC started *General Hospital* in 1963, *One Life to Live* in 1968, and *All My Children* in 1970. NBC's *Another World* began in 1964 and *Days of Our Lives* in 1965. The subjects of these programs are very mature, but they operate within strict guidelines imposed by network program practices departments.

Women compose 55 to 60 percent of the daytime audience, and soap operas supply much-beloved vicarious experiences for adults at home. As society's values have altered, the themes of soaps have become more and more mature, with familiar characters on the television screen becoming entangled in conflicts beyond the remotest expectations of the average homemaker. The characters in the soaps become so assimilated that it is not unusual to hear viewers discussing them by first name as if they were real people.[1]

Establishing a new soap opera is a long-range commitment for the networks. It takes considerable time to achieve audience involvement with new characters. The development begins with an independent producer providing the network programmer with a basic **concept** for a new series. If it is promising, the network will commission a full length **treatment**, sometimes called a "bible," outlining each of the characters and their interrelationships and describing the setting in which the drama will unfold. For a treatment, the writers receive development dollars or "seed money." The final step is to commission one or more **scripts**, advancing more funds to pay the writers. The entire development process can take one to two years and means an investment of $10,000 to $50,000. Usually, several development projects are abandoned each season; only a few get a chance on the air.

Once a soap opera is picked up by a network, casting begins. Casting the appropriate, charismatic character for each role is seen as crucial to a soap's success. To this end, CBS, ABC and NBC maintain their own casting directors to work with a soap's producers.

Much network television is videotaped on the West Coast, where producers contend they can produce programs for less money than in New York, partly because of more favorable weather conditions for exterior shooting. Soap operas, however, continue to be shot in New York, because nearly all of the shooting is interior, and the Broadway theater provides a large pool of actors.

When a new soap opera goes on the air, the daytime program executives schedule it to maximize the opportunity for audience sampling, frequently slotting the new program opposite the competition's weaker programs. Promoting a new entry is also vitally important. Once a soap is on the air, the day-to-day task of the daytime program executive is to carefully scrutinize scripts to see that they retain the high levels of dramatic conflict and suspense.

Game Shows

Game shows such as *Family Feud* and *The Price Is Right* are another mainstay of daytime programming. They give at-home viewers the vicarious thrill of seeing people just like themselves win thousands of dollars or exotic trips and home furnishings. Game shows can be produced fairly inexpensively for five exposures per week.

The networks seldom invest in pilot programs for daytime programming, because they cannot recoup their investment by airing the pilots, as they do in prime time. Game shows are developed somewhat differently from soap operas. Usually, a game show producer presents a **concept**, and if the network likes the idea, it commissions a **run-through**. The producer then rehearses the shows actors and participants, and network executives are invited to see the run-through. At this stage, if a network is still interested in the show, it may commission a **semipilot**, allowing the producer to videotape various versions of the game show with a studio audience and appropriate production elements such as music but without going to the expense of an elaborate set.

Reruns

Beyond game shows and soap operas, networks rely on the reruns of their own successful nighttime programs to fill out their daytime schedule. Usually, situation comedies such as *Happy Days* or *All in the Family* have performed admirably in daytime, as have such prime-time hits as *Love Boat*. But to strip the programs 5 times a week for at least 26 weeks before repeating, upwards of 130 episodes must have been accumulated, and the networks perennially lack sit-coms suitable for daytime airing.

Situation comedies have not been developed for original play in daytime for a simple reason: The best comedy writers are already working in prime time where they can demand higher incomes. And a prime-time series needs only 22 new episodes per year. For stripping in daytime, 22 programs scheduled 5 times a week would cover little more than a month of the needed programming. The top producers and writers are therefore unavailable (and too expensive) for daytime.

Comparative Costs and Revenues

Daytime is one of the most lucrative dayparts for television networks. Its profit margin often challenges that of prime time because its program costs are substantially less, generating such programming labels as the "golden soaps." Producing the average game show or soap opera is cheaper than making the average prime-time show. While a half-hour sit-com costs about $350,000 an episode, a soap episode averages about $50,000–60,000, and game shows can cost even less.

Moreover, there is a tradition of allowing more commercials in daytime. The National Association of Broadcaster's (NAB) television code (disallowed by the Justice Department in 1982, but still followed by the networks), allowed 9½ nonprogram minutes in a prime-time hour and 16 minutes during daytime. In practice, the networks generally schedule about 14 minutes of commercials per hour in Monday through Friday daytime. (Prime time now averages 9 to 9½; in addition, 1 to 2 minutes per hour are allotted to local station breaks.) Despite much smaller audiences than for prime time, daytime occupies more hours per day, has more advertising time for sale and has lower program costs, resulting in large profits for each network.

Clearly, a successful daytime schedule is vital to a financially sound network. Program investments in other dayparts, such as ambitious prime-time specials, children's dramas or Olympic coverage, tend to cost as much as or more than the advertising revenue they generate. Traditionally, news programming and network documentaries have been loss leaders, providing the viewers with important services, yet produced at a financial loss.[2] Daytime programming supports these efforts.

CHILDREN'S PROGRAMMING

Network children's programming has become a television battleground in recent years, not only because of network competitiveness but also because of increased public concern about the quality of programming designed for children. Historically, Saturday morning has been the time period reserved for children's programs. Children tend to be the most fickle of all viewers. Their attention span is shorter, they have fewer loyalties, and they tend to sample more new programs. As one programmer put it, holding his hands a foot apart, "It's more convenient for them to change the dial—they only sit this far away from the TV."

Until the early 1970s, children's programs tended to look alike on all three commercial networks. Saturday mornings were composed of wall-to-wall cartoons, each striving to present more visual action than the other, which usually translated into violence.[3] Storylines were thin, with writers depending on action rather than plots. One writer described the early days of children's programming in this way, "In the old days the premise for a Saturday morning cartoon was, 'They're coming over the hill' . . . and it was biff-bam, zoom-zoom from there on."

ACT and Other Pressure Groups

Action for Children's Television (ACT), a pressure group formed in 1968 and led by Peggy Charren, has raised network consciousness about children's programs. Although its members were short on the know-how of television production initially, they were certain that networks and stations could do a better job than they had been doing. As public interest in children's programming grew, ACT was joined by the PTA, National Christian Television, the Moral Majority and other groups on some issues.

Among ACT's first acts were complaints to the CBS affiliate in Boston when the local station wanted to cut *Captain Kangaroo*'s air time. Armed with the knowledge that a loud voice from a small group of indignant mothers would probably find widespread coverage in the local papers and with a new awareness about broadcasters' obligations to serve the "public interest, convenience and necessity," ACT, supported by other public interest organizations, took its campaign to Washington. There the Federal Communications Commission (FCC) lent a sympathetic ear and decided to do some investigating of its own.

At about this time, in 1969, the Public Broadcasting Service (PBS) introduced an ambitious new series, *Sesame Street*. It featured a regular cast of likable characters who taught youngsters how to count up to 10 and then 20, with what appeared to be commercials, a form familiar to all children—the 60-second message.

At an FCC hearing in 1972, ACT posed these questions among others: Why was violence necessary in children's programs? Why was it necessary for there to be more commercials—nearly twice as many—in children's programs than in adult programs in prime time? Such questions were hard for network executives (many of whom were parents) to respond to adequately.

From the combined pressure of ACT, the FCC's echoing of their concerns, and *Sesame Street* (whose success embarrassed the networks), a new level of awareness began to take shape on New York's Sixth Avenue, the home of the three television networks. The networks ordered new standards for children's programming. Then-ABC-president Elton Rule, at the Washington hearing in 1972, pledged that ABC would no longer carry children's programs that contained "action devoid of comedy." During subsequent years, outside of slapstick comedy, violence was all but eliminated on network children's programs.

By the mid-1970s, all three commercial networks had named a vice-president in charge of children's programs. Before that, children's programming had been the last thing on the priority list for daytime vice-presidents, whose attention was largely on the more competitive talk shows, soap operas and game shows.

Commercials

Responding to ACT's complaint and that of parent-teacher associations and other groups that commercials in children's viewing hours were as culpable as the programs, the NAB issued new guidelines in 1976. The stipulations cut commercials from the allowable 16 minutes per hour to 9½ minutes; hosts or program characters were prohibited from presenting commercial messages; and vitamin commercials aimed at young people were eliminated. The NAB also developed advertiser guidelines for the presentation of toys, cereals and other products to children. These guidelines, although no longer part of industry code, are still the core of network guidelines for children's programs.

Although ACT had contended from the very beginning that commercials should be eliminated from children's programming altogether, they softened that position through the first decade of their existence. Perhaps they recognized that the total elimination of commercials might result in the cancelation of such quality efforts as the *ABC Afterschool Specials*, CBS's *30 Minutes* or NBC's *Special Treats* as well as other programs they found desirable.

Content Changes

During the early 1970s a new term crept into the jargon of broadcasters: **prosocial.** Violence in children's programs was now considered largely antisocial;

the new approach to programming for young people aimed at integrating pro-social elements: (1) portraying constructive role models in storylines, (2) communicating respect for the feelings of others and (3) providing youngsters with positive messages.[4]

CBS recruited a panel of experts, mostly educators and psychologists, to assist them in reviewing scripts. One of the first programs the CBS panel worked on was *Fat Albert and the Cosby Kids,* an animated program starring Bill Cosby, which wove prosocial themes into a highly entertaining half-hour.

ABC engaged Bankstreet College, noted for its experimental teaching programs, to review all of its children's scripts. The Bankstreet advisers, in concert with ABC's Program Department and Broadcast Standards and Practices Department, issued guidelines on sex roles, role models and age appropriateness for all scripts. They include concepts and policies similar to those advocated at CBS and NBC. An extract from the 1975 ABC script guidelines on children's programming follows:

> The best way to sum up our approach is a list of qualities that we should strive for in our programs. It is keyed to the word "respect," and it includes: "respect for the individual; respect for differences; respect for religious beliefs and ethnic qualities; respect for all animal life and for the environment; respect for private and public property; respect for moral values; respect for the feelings and sensitivities of others; and, not least, respect for oneself."
>
> In short, a program designed for the 2–12 age group must be one in which members of that age group can directly relate or identify with (not passively) but in a positive or prosocial manner. In this regard, having children and/or animals in featured roles is strongly encouraged.
>
> The portrayal of reprehensible or dangerous acts by children's heroes is particularly risky. Boyhood heroes and teenage idols fall hard, and sometimes carry a number of youngsters with them like toppling dominoes. Accordingly, the portrayal of untoward, imitatable behavior by such recent teenage favorites as rock-and-roll stars (including the far too celebrated predilection of a few of them for hard drugs) carries far greater temptation for imitation by youngsters than would the portrayal of similar behaviors by actors with whom they identify in a less hysterical fashion.

Bankstreet College was also commissioned to review all scripts for the *ABC Afterschool Specials,* a series of high-quality dramas for young viewers that commenced twice-monthly broadcasts in 1972. The *ABC Afterschool Specials* were an outgrowth of an ABC-sponsored children's workshop, held a few months earlier, at which critics complained of an absence of good children's programming in the postschool hours.

During the same season, ABC began telecasts of *Schoolhouse Rock,* a series of 3½-minute programs, scheduled each hour during weekend children's programs. The first ten programs taught youngsters the multiplication tables through animation and music. These spots later were augmented with *Body Rock* on nutrition, *Grammar Rock,* the subheading for ten programs on the parts of speech, and *America Rock,* which described, for example, the story behind the Declaration of Independence and how a bill goes through Congress. Later, *Science Rock* further expanded the *ABC Schoolhouse Rock* series, which, along with a computer literacy series called *Scooter Computer & Mr. Chips*, brightened the intervals between Saturday and Sunday morning children's shows.

Meanwhile, CBS augmented their weekend programming with *In the News* shown every half-hour of both mornings. Each miniprogram in this series is a two-minute explanation of a significant news story, so as to make it comprehensible to young viewers. As of 1984, about seven of these were aired every weekend. During the mid-1970s, CBS also created the *Festival of Lively Arts for Young People*, periodic specials introducing viewers to various aspects of the arts, which ran several seasons.

NBC, although slower to react to the critics, won praise with a live Saturday morning half-hour called *GO* using children in the cast. For eight seasons, NBC produced *Special Treats*, dramas designed for telecasting in the afterschool hours. As of 1984, NBC had financed 30 dramas for *Special Treats* over the preceding eight years. Most recently, NBC has shifted its efforts in quality children's programming to prime time, telecasting to a larger audience with *Project Peacock*, an anthology of children's stories.

Retrospectively, it is clear that the outcries of a group of angry parents through Action for Children's Television spurred positive changes in children's programming. The changes, begun in the early 1970s, continued with CBS adding *30 Minutes* (a miniversion of the network's prime time show, *60 Minutes*) to its Saturday schedule in 1978. Also in the late 1970s, ABC started a weekly series of quality dramas for Saturday morning, *ABC Weekend Specials*, and invested in original programming for Sunday mornings with a variety program (*Kids Are People Too*) and an advice column of the air for preadolescents (*Dear Alex and Annie*). In 1983, ABC announced a joint project with the Library of Congress to encourage reading through the introduction of a self-edu-*cat*-ed character known as Cap'n O. G. Readmore, and fostered a series to help kids to think about careers through the advice of a personality called Zack of All Trades. NBC experimented with the unusual *Hot Hero Sandwich*. Whether these network efforts for better children's programs are a sufficient response to ACT and other critics remains to be seen. However, it is clear that such groups have had a positive effect overall.

Cartoons

In devising a children's program, network programmers employ criteria similar to those used in other dayparts. In the final analysis, people of all ages enjoy watching likable characters. This notion is as true with cartoon characters such as Scooby Doo and Bugs Bunny as it is with Lucille Ball, Jack Benny, Henry Winkler (The Fonz), and Penny Marshall and Cindy Williams as *Laverne & Shirley*. A program emphasizing *story* over *characters* is less likely to be attractive to any viewing audience.

The top-rated children's program in the 1983 Nielsens was NBC's cartoon, *The Smurfs*. NBC also had animated hits in *Alvin and the Chipmunks* and *Mr. T*. ABC was top-rated in children's demographics with cartoons such as *Pac Man*, *Rubik the Amazing Cube* and *The Littles*, while CBS's most popular programs were cartoon versions of videogames with characters such as *Dong Kong* and *Pitfall Harry*.

Cartoons are likely to remain the bulwark of Saturday morning programming, as opposed to **live-action shows** (film and tape programs portraying real people), because of cost. A half-hour of animation cost an average of $220,000 as of 1984, while a half-hour of live action was as low as $15,000 in the case of *Mr. Rogers' Neighborhood* or as high as $400,000 for an *ABC Afterschool Special.* Cartoons withstand rerunning better than live action, and—due to higher residual costs for on-camera actors than for off-camera voices—animation is less expensive. The studios have also reduced the production costs for cartoons by moving from individually drawn cells to computerized animating techniques using fewer drawings per second and less hand artwork.

The development of an animated children's series begins about twelve months before telecast, with pickups of new series exercised in February or March to allow producers six to seven months to complete the order for September telecast. A producer—or in some cases a network itself—generates an **idea.** The first step is an **outline** and **artwork.** The outline describes the characters and the setting; the artwork provides sketches of the characters in several poses and dress. If a project passes these stages, the final step is to order one or more **scripts,** which usually go through many drafts before a final script is accepted.

Pilot programs are almost never commissioned for cartoons because of the long production time and high costs. Therefore, the decision to pick up a cartoon series costing nearly $3 million for 13 episodes is based solely on artwork and scripts. Typically, a cartoon program's 13 episodes are aired as many as 4 times each in a year.

Live Action

Development of children's live-action programs is similar to that of an animation program, but substitutes a **casting tape** for animation artwork. The tape shows possible actors for the major roles. Script development for live-action children's programs follows a "writer's guideline" provided by the network. For example, the ABC guidelines explain that the *ABC Afterschool Specials* always deal with problems that many youngsters can identify with; that the main character should be of the age of the target audience, 10 to 14; and that the story's conflict should be resolved by the main character's actions, not by those of an adult. Moreover, there should be a happy ending that exemplifies to young people that they, too, can resolve their own problems. This guideline is typical of those used at all three networks. The *ABC Afterschool Specials* have won acclaim for dealing with such subjects as parental divorce, death of a sibling, appreciation for the handicapped and the problem of having an alcoholic parent.

As with most other segments in the broadcast day, networks produce few children's programs in-house. Instead, independent producers own the rights to the programs, which are licensed to the networks for a certain number of telecasts. This approach is partly due to Justice Department and Federal Communication Commission decisions in the late 1960s that prevented the networks from entering into the syndication of network-aired programs and from sharing in profits from U.S. syndication. Therefore, the networks license one or more runs, relinquishing the profit from subsequent syndication to the producers.

In-house shows may also cost more money to produce because the networks have signed more restrictive union contracts than many independent producers have. However, in cases where the network intends to air more than one or two runs of a program or series, it may make fiscal sense to produce in-house. Such was the case with ABC when it decided to build a library of quality, half-hour children's dramas that could be repeated, like classics, for several years. The *ABC Weekend Specials* resulted.

Conflicts over children's television programming will continue for many years to come. The networks walk a fine line between providing programs that please youngsters, programs that please the growing number of activist groups demanding better quality and programs with adequate space for the advertisers who want to expose young consumers to their toy and food messages. Although children's programming returned to the national spotlight at the FCC in 1983, the Commission took no action.[5]

Warner Amex developed a children's network, Nickelodeon, for cable television that as of the mid-1980s has become one of the more popular basic cable networks. Cable's ability to provide a whole channel dedicated to children's programming gives it the potential for defusing the public's concern over the amount of children's programming.[6] Nickelodeon, however, as of 1984, programs less than a full day, carries advertising and repeats its schedule frequently— although most of its programming consists of original, live-action shows in competition with the best of network children's programming.

LATE-NIGHT PROGRAMMING

The period following the local stations' eleven o'clock news is the domain of the late-night programming. NBC has been most successful in developing new audience viewing trends in that time period. After launching *The Tonight Show* in 1954, NBC won that time period for the next quarter of a century. NBC program executive Pat Weaver gets the credit for initiating the talk/variety format of *The Tonight Show* as well as for *The Today Show* two years earlier.[7]

The Tonight Show

Steve Allen was the first host of *Tonight*, followed by Jack Paar and then Johnny Carson. Each program employs comedy, occasional singers and light conversation with show business personalities. The basic concept is that at that hour viewers are not interested in serious topics. It was a premise that seemed to be right for NBC, but CBS and ABC were never very successful in executing late-night talk/variety formats of their own.

ABC Talk

ABC tried the hardest to win a late-night audience. In less than a decade, the network came up with four different approaches. After the short-lived *Les Crane Show*, from 1967 to 1969 *The Joey Bishop Show* gave *Tonight* a run for its money in the Midwest but lagged far behind in the national ratings for late-night network programs.

TABLE 6-5.
Late-Night Programs, Ratings and Shares, 1960, 1965 and 1970

Network	(Star)	1960 Rating/Share	(Star)	1965 Rating/Share		(Star)	1970 Rating/Share	
ABC		(local)	(Crane)	1	8	(Cavett)	3	12
CBS		(local)		(local)		(Griffin)[a]	4.6	20
NBC	(Paar)	5.9 35	(Carson)	7	36	(Carson)	7.4	31

[a]Ratings and shares for Merv Griffin averaged with the CBS *Late Movie* that filled the time slot during part of 1970.

In 1970 ABC gave the nod to Dick Cavett, who had enormous popularity among the critics despite his poor showing in the ratings with a daytime show. In late night, Cavett remained a favorite among critics, particularly because of the rare appearance of actress Katharine Hepburn and interviews with Alabama Governor George Wallace. However, the mass audience judged him too erudite, finding his topics too heavy for the time of the day. Cavett was cut back to once a week in January of 1973 and canceled in November. Although Cavett claimed the network failed to promote his program, ABC had given him a three-year chance in the time period.

Admiring ABC's determination to offer *Tonight* some competition, many industry observers thought the network had staged a coup when they announced Jack Paar would return to late-night television, alternating with Cavett and specials one week a month starting in 1973. Many thought Johnny Carson was in trouble. Who could better take on the current Goliath of late night than the king of talk himself?

It had been some ten years since Jack Paar had stormed off NBC's *Tonight Show* set. And when he returned, he looked almost exactly the same: the same style sports jacket, same hair length and the same tone of curious astonishment in his interviews. During the opening week, Paar boosted ABC's ratings. Then they began to slide—back to Cavett's level. American viewers were disappointed; Jack was the same, but the audience was not. In ten years, apparently the viewers had become far more sophisticated, discriminating and critical. The ratings stayed low, and Paar was also canceled in late 1973.

CBS Movies

During most of the seven-year period in which ABC tried to go talk show against talk show, CBS was quietly garnering a respectable share of the audience by counterprogramming movies. With the exception of one crack at late-night talk/variety with *The Merv Griffin Show* for six months in 1972, CBS scheduled movies from 11:30 P.M. to 1 A.M., maintaining a comfortable number-two position in the ratings.

ABC Checkerboard

In late 1973 ABC unveiled an ambitious and very expensive plan to program something different every night of the week. On Mondays and Tuesdays there would be dramas, on Wednesdays specials, on Thursdays personalities and Fridays would reach a yonger audience with rock concerts. Although the rock concerts had some ratings success, the enormity of the task of coming up with enough consistently good drama in the early part of the week was staggering, as were the costs. Moreover, it became apparent that the audience was confused by ABC's scheduling, not being sure what they might see when they tuned in on any given night.

By September 1977, several programming factors had emerged that influenced late-night network strategies. ABC's checkerboarding effort still was not offering any serious competition to NBC's *Tonight Show* or CBS's movies. Meanwhile, on another front, the industry was under renewed pressure to eliminate violence from their prime-time programming, particularly before 9 P.M. This trend created a financial hardship for producers who had long counted on subsequent syndication of off-network programming to recoup initial production losses (otherwise known as deficit financing). The movement to eliminate violent programs from time periods when children might be viewing began to dry up the marketplace among television stations that normally would buy such action-packed series as *Starsky & Hutch* and *SWAT*. Capitalizing on this situation, ABC began to approach late-night television from another direction: rerunning successful prime-time series. Shows like *Baretta, Starsky & Hutch, Police Woman* and *Streets of San Francisco* provided counterprogramming to both NBC's *Tonight* and CBS's movie, while resolving the financial problem for producers. The network licensed each episode for additional runs, providing the producers with an opportunity to recoup their initial deficits prior to series syndication.

In the first quarter of 1979, ABC began reaching respectable ratings levels in the late-night time period. (See Table 6-6.) Johnny Carson and his *Tonight Show* on NBC no longer remained the undisputed leader; CBS's movies had gone out in front, and ABC had carved off a larger slice of the available audience. By 1982, however, ABC still remained in third place. (See Table 6-7.)

TABLE 6-6.
First-Quarter Ratings, 1979

	Rating	Share
CBS	7.9	28
NBC	7.3	27
ABC	6.8	23

Source: NSI, January–March 1979. Used with permission.

TABLE 6-7.
First-Quarter Ratings, Late Night, 1982

	Rating	Share
CBS	6.1	20
NBC	5.6	20
ABC	4.7	17

Source: NSI, January–March 1982. Used with permission.

Late-Night Network News

In November 1979, ABC News seized upon the American viewing audience's interest in knowing more about the Iranian hostage crisis and began a nightly newscast to summarize the daily events. Shortly thereafter, in March 1980, ABC premiered *Nightline,* an innovative, in-depth nightly news program. It adopted a satellite-delivered format in which a limited number of stories were covered in depth with extended visuals, rather than early-evening hard news or early-morning talk/magazine format. Satellite availability encouraged a "live from every corner of the earth" approach. Hosted by Ted Koppel, an incisive yet compassionate interviewer, *Nightline* emerged as a strong late-night competitor.

But as the late-night charts for the first quarter of 1983 suggest, the viability of a news-oriented, late-night program varies with the condition of world events and ongoing crises:

TABLE 6-8.
Rating/Shares for Late-Night Network Programs, 1983

	Rating	*Share*
CBS	6.3	22
NBC	5.8	20
ABC	4.0	13

SOURCE: NSI, January–March 1983. Used with permission.

In spite of less than ideal ratings, in early 1983 *Nightline* was expanded to an hour. The network apparently felt timely new programming was a good alternative to entertainment fare on CBS and NBC. Excepting competition from *CBS News Specials* during periods of international or national crisis, ABC also had a clear shot at fortifying its news image in the public's mind. But by the end of 1983, ABC had canceled the second half-hour of *Nightline* after no ratings improvement.

THE FUTURE OF NONPRIME TIME

Apparently, creating dramatic changes in viewing patterns is very difficult to achieve in nonprime time. No early-morning effort, no daytime soap opera and no late-night strategy has ever met with instant success. Only in rare cases with daytime game shows or children's programs has a network been able to dramatically turn around an audience viewing trend. Instead, a steady commitment to long-range achievement is normally required for success.

With cable systems, pay cable, home videorecorders, videodiscs, superstations, direct-to-home-satellite telecasts and any number of other competitors to network television programming on the horizon, it is difficult to imagine that the number of available viewers during any time period will do anything but shrink, thereby making even more arduous the tasks of network programming. The new competitors not only seek part of the same audience, they compete for some of the same programming and raise its cost—especially that of movies and of sports events. The cable networks' inroads on the broadcast networks' combined audience share are forcing ABC, CBS and NBC to consider longer broadcast days. They have already moved into the earlier weekday morning hours and later weeknight and weekend hours. Cable is also redefining the size of an acceptable audience for different dayparts. The future will be an escalating but exciting challenge to the network programmer.

SUMMARY

The commercial broadcast networks allocate responsibility for programming the major nonprime-time dayparts among a group of vice-presidents. Although early morning programming was once dominated by NBC's *Today Show*, as of the mid-1980s, ABC held the ratings honors with *Good Morning America*, with *CBS Morning News* and the *Today Show* close behind. Daytime programming is the province of the soap operas and game shows. They generate the bulk of network revenue that is in turn used to balance more costly programming efforts in other dayparts. Afterschool and weekend children's programming increased and improved substantially in the 1970s, but efforts in this area have slowed because of less public and FCC pressure. Late-night network programming has been consistently dominated by *The Tonight Show* although CBS' movies and ABC's *Nightline* have narrowed the ratings gap.

Notes

[1]For an overview of the literature on soap operas, see Bradley S. Greenberg, Kimberly Neuendorf, Nancy Buerkey-Rothfuss and Laura Henderson, "The Soaps: What's On and Who Cares?" *Journal of Broadcasting* 26, Spring 1982, pp. 519–35.

[2]Programs such as *60 Minutes, 20/20* and *Prime Time Saturday* that once may have been considered loss leaders now sometimes do better in the ratings than the programs they replaced. In 1979 such magazine-documentary programs were used as a form of stunting, like specials, and drew more than satisfactory ratings. By 1983, *20/20* was regularly appearing in the top ten network programs.

[3]See Surgeon General's Scientific Advisory Committee on Television and Social Behavior, *Television and Growing Up: The Impact of Televised Violence* (Washington, D.C.: Surgeon General, U.S. Public Health Service, 1972). See also Thomas E. Coffin and Sam Tuchman, "Rating Television Programs for Violence: A Comparison of Five Surveys," *Journal of Broadcasting* 17, Winter 1972–73, pp. 3–20; and Edward L. Palmer and Aimee Dorr, *Children and the Faces of Television: Teaching, Violence, Selling* (New York: Academic Press, 1980).

[4]The difficulty in defining *prosocial* is illuminated by Dona A. Durham and Timothy P. Meyer, "TV and Prosocial Behavior: A Critical Review of Key Issues and Literature," a paper presented at the International Communication Association Convention, Dallas, Texas, May 1983. See also "Network Kidvid Programs and Advertisers Much the Same, with Subtle 'Prosocial' Growth," *Television/Radio Age*, 21 May 1979, p. 40ff; and "Networks' Efforts to Increase Educational Values of Kidvid Include Inserts, Specials, School Role," *Television/Radio Age*, 4 June 1979, pp. 44ff.

[5]"Children's TV Back in the FCC Spotlight," *Broadcasting,* 2 May 1983, pp. 32–34; and "Too Little or Just Enough," *Broadcasting,* 9 May 1983, p. 68.

[6]See Mark Trost, "Zapped," *View,* August 1983, pp. 30–35; and "Special Report on Children's Television," *Broadcasting,* 29 October 1979, pp. 39–56.

[7]Sylvester "Pat" Weaver, president of NBC in 1954 and 1955.

Selected Sources

Barcus, F. Earle, with Welkin, Rachel. *Children's Television: An Analysis of Programming and Advertising.* New York: Praeger Special Studies, 1977.

Cantor, Muriel G., and Pingree, Suzanne. *The Soap Opera.* Beverly Hills, California: Sage Publications, 1983.

Cassata, Mary, and Skill, Thomas. *Life on Daytime Television: Tuning-In American Serial Drama.* Norwood, New Jersey: Ablex Publishing Corp., 1983.

Grossman, Gary H. *Saturday Morning TV.* New York: Dell, 1982.

Liebert, Robert M. and others. *The Early Window: Effects of Television on Children and Youth.* 2d ed. Elmsford, New York: Pergamon Press, 1982.

Metz, Robert. *The Today Show.* Chicago: Playboy Press, 1977.

Wakshlag, Jacob J., and Greenberg, Bradley S. "Programming Strategies and the Popularity of Television Programs for Children." *Human Communication Research* 6 (Fall 1979): 58–68.

Affiliated Station Programming

John A. Haldi

A QUICK GUIDE TO CHAPTER SEVEN

JOHN A. HALDI, *vice-president of programming for WBNS-TV, Columbus, Ohio, analyzes each daypart in an affiliate's schedule and suggests strategies for effective programming. He served on the Board of Directors of the National Association of Television Program Executives (NATPE) and was elected president of the organization in 1966. His honors include the 1966 Governors' Award from the Columbus chapter of the National Academy of Television Arts and Sciences and "Man of the Year" award from the National Association of Television Program Executives in 1972. He began working for WBNS-TV at the time the station went on the air in 1949, moving from continuity director to program host to producer/director to production director and then, in 1956, to program director, a title he still holds. WBNS-TV has won numerous awards for broadcasting excellence under Haldi's leadership, demonstrating his status as a master of television programming strategy.*

AFFILIATE–NETWORK RELATIONS

The commercial broadcast networks fill about 60 percent of their affiliates' schedules. The remainder is largely syndicated programming (reruns, movies and first-run access shows) or locally originated (mostly news and some sports). As a response to three factors, increased prices for original programming, climbing ratings for some special series and new competition from cable television in some markets, sources for syndicated programming increased dramatically in the early 1980s. Satellite delivery of syndicated television programming allowed affiliates, for the first time, to look beyond their networks to independent distributors, ad hoc networks and group productions for some of their programming. But the three broadcast television networks, ABC, CBS and NBC, still provide the biggest program audiences as measured by the highest program ratings.

When programming a network-affiliated station, the program director ought to regard its network's schedule merely as one of many sources, much as independent station programmers view the many sources of syndicated entertainment programming. In practice, however, a local station enters an affiliation agreement with a network to carry the network's programs in exchange for money the network pays to it for carrying its (the network's) commercials (**network compensation**). This money and the high-quality programs the station receives strongly affect the affiliate's economics and programming strategy. In general, NBC pays higher compensation to its affiliates than CBS or ABC, presumably to offset its liability as the third-place network.[1] As of the mid-1980s, compensation amounts to about 8 percent of television affiliate revenues, and the time periods the networks fill need not be filled by their affiliates, a marked savings. The relationship between an affiliate and its network may sound simple, but an affiliation is like a marriage—until cancelation. And cancelation is like divorce without child support in the view of former affiliates whose networks deserted them for another station in their markets, driving them into independent-station status.

Network Agreement

Television affiliation agreements differ for each network, but in general contain the following elements:

1. The affiliate has first call on all network programs.

2. Acceptance or rejection of network programs (**clearance**) must be made within two weeks (or a minimum of 72 hours for certain programs) by notifying the network accordingly. Upon receiving a program rejection, however, the network has the right to offer the rejected program to another television station in the same market.

3. The network obligation to deliver the programs is subject to the network's ability to make arrangements satisfactory to it for such delivery.

4. The network agrees to pay the affiliate on the basis of an established affiliated station's network rate. This rate is negotiated based on the station's effectiveness in its local market, largely determined by analyzing the station's market size and audience reach.

5. Payment for each network commercial program broadcast over the affiliated station during "live time" is based on a percentage table similar to Table 7-1. Early-evening and prime-time programs are clearly the most profitable to the affiliate. This payment chart, however, is modified by network deductions for BMI and ASCAP music license fees and other minor variances in their contracts.

6. The network can reduce the affiliated station's network rates if market conditions change (after at least 30 days' notice, in which event the

TABLE 7-1.
Network Compensation Rates

Monday through Friday	Percent of Affiliate Station's Network Rate
7:00 A.M.–11:15 A.M.	7
11:15 A.M.– 5:00 P.M.	12
5:00 P.M. – 6:00 P.M.	15
6:00 P.M. –11:00 P.M.	32
Saturday	
8:00 A.M.– 9:00 A.M.	7
9:00 A.M.– 2:00 P.M.	12
5:00 P.M. – 6:00 P.M.	15
6:00 P.M. –11:00 P.M.	32
Sunday	
4:00 P.M. – 5:00 P.M.	12
5:00 P.M. – 6:00 P.M.	15
6:00 P.M. –11:00 P.M.	32
11:00 P.M. –11:30 P.M.	15

broadcaster may terminate the agreement within a predetermined time period).

7. The network agrees to make payments reasonably promptly within a monthly accounting period.

8. The broadcaster agrees to submit reports related to the broadcasting of network programs.

9. Federal Communications Commission (FCC) rules fix the term of this agreement to two years with prescribed periods during the agreement when either party can notify the other of termination. If everyone concurs, the agreement is automatically renewed for another two-year cycle.

10. If a broadcaster wants to transfer its license to another party, the network can examine the new owner before deciding whether to honor the change.

11. The agreement also lists the technical conditions under which the affiliate will carry the network programs (when a broadcast standard signal arrives to insure picture quality, for example). **Clipping** (cutting off the beginnings or ends of programs or commercials), reselling (including permitting noncommercial stations to reair network programs) or altering any of the contents of network shows is expressly prohibited.

12. The rights of the broadcaster, derived from the Communications Act of 1934, are also itemized:
    a. The broadcaster can refuse or reject any newtwork program that is reasonably unsatisfactory or unsuitable or contrary to the public interest.
    b. The broadcaster has the right to substitute programs in lieu of the network's, if the substitution is considered in the broadcaster's opinion of greater local or national importance. The network, in turn, has the right to substitute or cancel programs as it feels necessary.

13. The network must tell the broadcaster of any money, service or consideration it accepted in the preparation of network programs. This condition is in response to Section 317 of the Communications Act of 1934 requiring this disclosure.

14. The network also agrees to indemnify the broadcaster from and against all claims, damages, liabilities, costs and expenses arising out of the broadcasting of network programs that result in alleged libel, slander, defamation, invasion of privacy or violation or infringement of copyright, literary or dramatic rights involved in programs the network furnished.

This list is a condensation of a television affiliation agreement, but it does reflect the basic considerations involved in the affiliate–network partnership. (See Chapter 14 for a discussion of comparable radio affiliation contracts.) However, the network connection is more than a financial arrangement and a source of high-quality programs. By carrying the network programs, the affiliated station automatically has unsold commercial spot time around and within these network programs. The more popular the network programs, the more the affiliate can charge for the spots. On the other hand, the affiliates must clear (not preempt) nearly all network programs for the network to be profitable. The sword that a network holds is the threat to switch affiliation to another station. Networking and affiliating are big business, and, again like marriage, it takes more than a paper agreement to make the relationship work for both parties.

Station Goals

An affiliate's program director makes up a station's local schedule according to the licensee's commitment to the FCC and then blends it with programs the network provides. The remaining hours are filled from the pool of syndicated first-run and rerun series and movies, accompanied by some local news and sport production. Affiliate programming goals are relatively simple even if difficult to achieve: Come up with a schedule that (1) answers the needs of the community, (2) makes a profit for the local station owners and (3) makes the station number one in its market.

In a three-station market with a PBS affiliate as the fourth entity, a programmer's position is more flexible than that of programmers in areas with more than four stations. More competitors mean fewer options in program selection (more programs have already been shown, and there is less visibility for each station's individual programs). Nonetheless, the principles used to program an affiliate are valid and workable in any competitive situation. Generally, the larger the market, the more competing stations and the more likely that new media will become significant competitors for the available audience. At the same time, larger markets typically mean more advertising revenue that in turn means more money to spend on top-rated programs. In the top 50 markets in the United States, competition is hot and gets fiercer as the market size gets larger. In many small and midsized markets, cable already drains a portion of the audience and will eventually get some of the local advertising revenue too. However, as of the mid-1980s, affiliate sales staffs retain a strong edge in advertising competition.

WEEKDAY PROGRAMMING DAYPARTS

The local station goes on the air around 6 A.M. and off the air at about 2 A.M. the next morning, which means 20 hours of programming each day of the week. The broadcast weekday is made up of eight time segments (EST/PST), nearly half of which (about 40 percent) must be filled by the local affiliate programmer:

6:00 A.M.–9:00 A.M.	early morning
9:00 A.M.–12:00 noon	morning
12:00 noon–4:00 P.M.	afternoon
4:00 P.M.–6:00 P.M.	early fringe (late afternoon)
6:00 P.M.–7:30 P.M.	early evening
7:30 P.M.–8:00 P.M.	access
8:00 P.M.–11:00 P.M.	prime time
11:00 P.M.–11:30 P.M.	late fringe (late evening)
11:30 P.M.–2:00 A.M.	late night
2:00 A.M.–6:00 A.M.	all night (overnight)

These dayparts are the standard for Arbitron and Nielsen in the eastern and western time zones, and shift one or two hours in central and mountain time. Ratings researchers use these dayparts to measure audience viewing, and sales departments use them to sell commercial time throughout each day. Programming strategies differ according to the time segment involved.

In four of these dayparts (morning, afternoon, prime time and late fringe), the network provides nearly all the programs. In early morning, early evening and late night, the networks contribute part of the programming. Early fringe, access and overnight are wholly local responsibilities. This chapter looks at the local affiliate programmer's options in surrounding or replacing network programming for each of these successive dayparts. The programmer's strategies include targeting, audience flow, lead-in effects, local appeal and reuse of expensive syndicated programs.

EARLY MORNING

The programming strategies for 6 to 9 A.M. are very simple. The program director for the station commanding first place in local ratings will probably ignore the daypart and stay with what the network provides. The competing program directors whose stations are running second or third (or worse in markets with more stations) have five options:

1. When network news is leading the time period, local or children's programming will attract a segment of the audience not being reached. A *local live 30- or 60-minute* program will find favor with the FCC and encourage sales during the fall and spring quarters of the sales year when certain advertisers most want to introduce fall merchandise and advertise sales.

2. A ploy used in several markets has been to invest in a *women-oriented* program starting as a one-hour entry and expanding to two hours (from 8 to 10 A.M.) when ripe for expansion. Such programming is most successful when directed specifically toward the female audience remaining alone after families have left for school and work. The 8 A.M. start is advantageous because it bridges the 9 A.M. slot that *Phil Donahue* has managed to "own" throughout the United States. A women's show is also highly salable every week in the year. Women's programs can also have frequent community-oriented segments that apply to FCC commitments for public service programming. A good example of this option is WEWS-TV's *Morning Exchange*, 8 to 10 A.M., Monday through Friday. This Cleveland station's program follows the popular magazine format but is wholly locally produced.

3. The most expensive and risky gamble is to challenge the networks' talk and news with a full-blown *local news/talk* program, recommended only if the market is rich with talent, visitors and money to justify the expense. So far, no local station has been successful in the 6 to 8 A.M. time period.

4. *Paid religious* programming will bring in money and figure into the FCC's "other" category; however, its ratings will probably be low in the 6 to 9 A.M. time period. One danger in religious programs is that many raise

controversial issues coming under the Fairness Doctrine without adequate provision for conflicting views. The broadcaster must then find time for presenting opposing points of view.

5. If the program director is desperate, *nonentertainment material* such as public affairs, instructional, educational and agricultural programs can serve immediate needs and free the program director to figure out how to grab a bigger audience after 9 A.M.

MORNING

Between 9 and noon is a frightful time period that has housed *Merv Griffin, Hour Magazine, Edge of Night,* syndicated hours, sit-coms, network repeats and delays, syndicated half-hours and children's programming. The audience during this time consists mainly of preschoolers and homemakers, and the homemaker is the main advertising target. Stations that schedule *Phil Donahue* during this time period have no problems. The networks are no help until the late morning game shows and soaps start at about 10 A.M. (EST/PST). Only one network dominates in any part of the morning—ABC, with reruns of its kiddult nighttime programs (light sit-coms appealing to both children and adults) during the 11 to 11:30 A.M. period. The following are options for the local programmer:

1. Write off the station's investment in *syndicated properties* (after use elsewhere in the schedule) by placing them from 9 to 10 or 10:30; then join the network until noon. Properties such as the reruns of *Happy Days, Laverne & Shirley* and *The Love Boat* have hit the mark.

2. Develop a strong *local live show* that can open up like an accordion to fill more of the morning as the audience grows. A women's service program with provocative overtones and strong talent and popular program segments could capture that part of the women's audience that leans toward magazines for information and emotional stimuli. This option is expensive but worth a try because such a program can be very salable once it gets off the ground.

3. Many markets have tried a *movie* from 9 to 10:30, using the ABC afternoon movie-editing formula (films shortened to 90 minutes) that has been mildly successful in the 4:30 to 6 P.M. period. This option has been mildly successful depending on the competition, but it appears the female audience of the late 1970s did not uniformly support the 90-minute, short-form film, making this an unpredictable approach.

In the 1970s and early 1980s, the 9 A.M. to noon time period was characterized by **passive viewing,** a condition in which viewers often leave the room to perform household tasks. The syndicators and local stations were unable to find the ideal structure to capture enough of the available audience to separate themselves from their competitors. More research is needed, but it is likely that a locally produced program, reflecting the local community, would take the marbles once it established a structure that the female audience could not afford to miss viewing.

With the technical innovation of the **minicam,** morning programs using live cameras became feasible; portable cameras can take the viewers to parts of their community they have never been able to see. Soft features mixed with government and human-interest segments (to direct the rest of their day's activities) could also provide the daytime audience with insight into what goes on in their communities. The major market stations (such as those in Boston, Los Angeles, and Cleveland) have attempted this kind of programming, but because they favor specific local regions, universality does not appear in the subject matter, and their programs have not been syndicatable.

AFTERNOON

Network soap operas dominate the early afternoon daypart (noon to 4 P.M.). Affiliates should not consider preempting soap operas because once the cement of the drama hardens, dedicated viewers are glued—some for as long as ten or twenty years. Preempting a favorite soap for a presidential speech or a news special brings an eruption of ire from addicts. But several alternative programming possibilities should at least be considered for part of this time period. Most programmers divide the afternoon daypart into two chunks: the noon hour and the 1–3 P.M. period.

1. *Noon news* is popular with the stay-at-home audience. The noontime pause in at-home and office activities creates an ideal slot for information. Noon coverage of world and local activities is a ritual, as much for stations as for the audience. Stations aspiring to leadership in news coverage cannot omit the noon news. Furthermore, it makes good money in spot sales and reusing much of the material at 6 and 11 P.M. justifies large news expenditures. Some of the noon news can be gleaned from the preceding night's newscast, which also helps keep costs down.

2. An afternoon *movie* was highly popular with audiences in the 1950s and 1960s, but today most affiliates have abandoned this programming option. The 1 to 3 P.M. period would be nearly ideal for movies were it not for the continued popularity of soap operas in that time period. But movies could be an option for a station from noon to 2 P.M. if its news commitment does not take priority.

3. Although most network affiliates would be committing hara-kiri if they preempted the soaps during this period, a few do manage to get away with substituting either a local or regional *talk show* or a package of *syndicated properties*. Generally, they get no better ratings than the poorest soaps.

EARLY FRINGE

The half hour from 4 to 4:30 P.M. holds no problem for affiliates, but by 4:30 the networks have concluded their afternoon schedules, and the ball sits in the affiliates' court. That leaves a 90-minute span before the early evening newcasts starting at 6 P.M.

90-Minute Options

1. *Merv Griffin, Breakaway, Afternoon* and other *talk shows* designed for this period do rather well, but the viewers will probably be in the 50 + age bracket. Older viewers consider these shows similar to *The Tonight Show*—without requiring them to stay up past 11:30 P.M.

2. The ABC-owned stations designed a movie format that was very successful until abandoned by the stations in the early 1980s. It remains a viable device for affiliates. The ABC O&Os purchased movies and shaved them down to fit a 90-minute time slot. A 100-minute or longer feature film can be edited down to 78 minutes so that 12 minutes of commercials can nestle within the film (filling a 90-minute slot).

There is an apocryphal story about Fred Silverman, later president of NBC in the early 1980s, who (when he was a novice film editor at WGN-TV in Chicago) solved the length problem for an Elvis Presley movie, *Jailhouse Rock*. He merely eliminated the musical numbers! Silverman, too, was almost eliminated. Experienced editors must do the surgery, and it can be and is done every day to the satisfaction of viewers in the 18 to 34 age bracket.

A newer adaptation of shaved-movie editing is the speeded-up movie. New projection processes can mechanically condense a film, cutting its length by a sixth or so, just by speeding up the entire film. It is now possible to run, say, six minutes of film in five minutes without leaving out anything in the original and without the movie appearing "speeded up" to audiences.

3. Another approach to the 90-minute slot in early fringe is to buy *made-for television movies* with a running time of about 75 minutes. They need no editing; they can simply be slotted and filled with commercials and promotional spots. However, the quality of these productions rarely matches theatrical standards, the name value of the stars is less and promotional support is usually weaker. Station ratings of course reflect all these limitations.

Another answer to the 4:30 to 6 P.M. problem is to split the time period into two parts—a 30-minute show followed by a 60-minute unit, or the converse.

4. *Half-hour* programs for the 4:30 period are easily found: *Brady Bunch, Gilligan's Island, Bob Newhart, Sanford and Son* or, if economy is necessary, *Little Rascals, Superman, Spiderman, Gomer Pyle* or *Hogan's Heroes*. The big problem is to find the *following hour show* that will be a good lead-in to the 6 P.M. news. Programming in this time period must appeal to both adult male and female viewers. Historically, the best 60-minute property was *Perry Mason*, but this series has dated considerably and is not in color, a definite drawback. *Bonanza, Mission Impossible, The FBI* and *Emergency*, have also been tried in this time slot, but their ratings did not live up to expectations. The only recent hour-program that has done reasonably well is *Little House on the Prairie*.

120-Minute Options

Some affiliates have solved the early fringe problem by preempting the network's 4 P.M. show. As many as 40 percent of affiliates do not clear the 4 to 4:30 period, which expands the 90-minute period into a two-hour time slot. This combination has been used successfully by independent stations for many years. As a 120-minute segment, the 4 to 6 P.M. slot can be used as follows:

5. *Movies* can be divided into 96 minutes of feature and 24 minutes of commercials, giving a film breathing room and allowing the viewer to see a reasonable amount of the motion picture. The station can also use the two-hour edited version in other time periods. This form is more economical for films than 90-minute edits since the film's licensing cost is based on the entire film. Using all the footage makes sense financially.

6. Instead of leaning solely on Hollywood for feature films, television has started to depend on network reruns. *Comedy series* have been the most successful of these reruns, but also the most expensive (pointing up the problem of the lack of programming in the market). Research shows that sit-coms can capture the early fringe audience and hold them from 4 to 6. The best strategy for a station is to start with kiddult properties around 4 P.M., phase into family-appeal programs, then finally into adult fare as a lead-in to the adult six o'clock news.

An Ideal Example of Early-Fringe Options

4:00 P.M.: *Batman, Gilligan's Island, Beaver* or *Brady Bunch*

4:30 P.M.: *Bob Newhart, Sanford and Son, Good Times* or *Kotter*

5:00 P.M.: *Mary Tyler Moore, Alice, One Day at a Time* or *Rhoda*

5:30 P.M.: *M*A*S*H, Happy Days, Laverne & Shirley* or *Three's Company*

Stripping Off-Network Reruns

Future acquisitions for a comedy block are likely to be expensive. For example, the cost of popular off-network reruns increased from $600 to $8,000 an episode in a three-year period in the Columbus, Ohio, market. Independent stations pay high prices to program off-network reruns against affiliate news between 6 P.M. and 8 P.M. In four-or-more-station markets, the independent attacks the soft underbelly of the affiliate during local and network news by siphoning off the younger audience with such rerun winners as *M*A*S*H, Three's Company* and *Taxi*.

Competition has forced the affiliated stations to vie mightily for the high-priced network reruns, driving the prices up still further. The top 50 market affiliate is, of course, compelled to schedule them only between 4 and 7 P.M. because of the prime-time access rule. As of the mid-1980s, the trend is toward barter rather than cash for off-network and first-run series, alleviating the high capital investment required of stations and providing advertisers with popular vehicles for their spots.[2] The sit-com continues to be a staple, appealing to younger television viewers as well as adults in the early fringe (late afternoon) time period, and all stations compete hard for the best that is available to them.

Long-running network series have been scarce in recent years; in consequence, syndicated properties with the 130 episodes needed to program on a Monday through Friday (stripped) basis are rare. There are actually 260 time slots per year to fill (52 weeks × 5 days). If a program has 130 episodes, each show can be repeated twice a year with a six-month rest between exposures. This cycle is ideal for a good show. If a syndicated series has fewer than 130 episodes, individual episodes must be rerun more often unless the station regularly schedules sports or election-year programming in that slot. If it has more than 130, fewer reruns are needed, or the cycle can be stretched to cover more weeks. Syndicated series with 160 or more episodes command very high prices in the major markets.

The catch is that, as of the 1980s, the networks began licensing only 22, or fewer, new episodes of any series each year. (In the 1960s, as many as 39 episodes were produced for a prime-time slot; see discussion in Chapter 5.) A series now has to run for six years to amass 130 episodes—and very few programs have had that kind of longevity. When a show does stay on the network that long, most stations want to buy it, and the distributor jacks up the price to match the demand. Some shows that have made the golden circle in recent years have been *Mary Tyler Moore, The Waltons, M*A*S*H, Maude, Little House on the Prairie, All in the Family, Hawaii Five-O, Barnaby Jones, The Jeffersons, Laverne & Shirley* and *Happy Days*. Most of these shows came from the great days of CBS.

Futures

In the late 1970s, ABC seemed to have acquired a magic formula for comedy, but by 1979 most ABC series had only about 72 episodes in the can. Consequently, ABC's distributors sold **futures.** Series still on the air came to the marketplace for sale, sometimes three years in advance, at exorbitant prices to be used at future dates. But the futures buyer does not know if the series will last, if the main characters will still be popular, if the network plans to schedule a strip run before the local station acquires the rights. Those questions are tricky, requiring programmers to make tough decisions and take calculated risks. (See also the discussion of futures in Chapter 8 by Aiken.) As of the early 1980s, the collection of precious programs for which stations were willing to purchase futures included *Laverne & Shirley, Kotter, Three's Company, Charlie's Angels, Fantasy Island, Love Boat* and *Mork & Mindy*. These programs reflect ABC's success. NBC's syndicators are hoping that *Hill Street Blues* will sell in futures, but it is less likely to appeal to early-fringe audiences than, say, *Little House on the Prairie*.

EARLY EVENING

The 6 to 7:30 P.M. time period is usually devoted to news. Each network provides 30 minutes of national coverage. Affiliates in markets below the top five adhere to one of two patterns: (a) precede or follow the network news with 30 minutes or 1 hour of local material or (b) sandwich the national news between two local news programs, a 30-minute one preceding and a 30-minute one following.

1. Some stations in the top five markets have instituted *two-hour local news* programs that start around 5 P.M. and stretch to 7, at which time they add the network news, for a total of two and a half hours of news. This much news, of course, must dominate the ratings or fall victim to counterprogramming that usually wins in total audience preference. (Winning the key 18–49-year-old audience is more important to gaining some advertisers than winning the ratings in the local adults 18+ category because the total news audience typically skews old.)

2. For the average affiliate, 90 minutes of news between 6 and 7:30 P.M. is all its market can handle. The most successful structure has been the **sandwich,** which splits the local news into two sections: The six o'clock unit carries the fast-breaking items and the seven o'clock segment handles the follow-ups and feature material. Of course, sports and weather can be sprinkled through both portions.

The affiliate with the strongest news team usually dominates its market. Evening local news is television's front page. Beginning in the 1970s, competition became so fierce that consulting firms sprouted everywhere to advise stations on presenters, content, format structure, set design, program pace and even the clothing to be worn by the on-the-air personnel.

3. How does a station counterprogram against news? If one cannot win with better news, then one can try to split the viewing audience by scheduling *entertainment programs against the news:*

> *Station A*
> 5:30 Local program
> 6:00 Local news
> 6:30 Network news
> 7:00 Local news
>
> *Station B*
> 5:30 Local program
> 6:00 Local news
> 6:30 Local news
> 7:00 Network news
>
> *Station C*
> 5:30 Local news
> 6:00 Network news
> 6:30 Rerun comedy
> 7:00 First-run quiz or game show

The counterprogramming unit, Station C, will score very well since about one-third of the audience does not want to watch the news to begin with; a station can depend on getting about a 20+ share against news at any time. (The top news stations may have a share of 30 or 40, of course.) Programs in rerun that have done well against news are *M*A*S*H, Three's Company, Taxi, Barney Miller, The Jeffersons* and game shows.

ACCESS

Access time is that half-hour moat dug by Donald McGannon of Westinghouse[3] to prevent the networks from further invading affiliates' schedules (and as a self-serving device to strengthen Group W's syndication arm, which was producing first-run programs suitable for this time period). The hope that access time would stimulate quality programs has long since faded, and what remains is largely a nightmare of game shows and recycled quiz formats.

1. Once a bright flower bloomed in the access desert in the form of *The Muppets*; its popularity (ratings) had faded, however, by the early 1980s. As new properties faltered and old programs died from fatigue, the idea of stripping *first-run game shows* accelerated in popularity. If one episode of a show works once a week, why not five times a week? Consequently, television logs are loaded Monday through Friday with such gems as *Joker's Wild, Family Feud, Tic Tac Dough* and *Wheel of Fortune*. The anemia in suitable first-run programs is evident in Table 7-2, a list of the top ten prime access shows from 1982.

2. Some stations, unwilling to wait for the syndicators to develop a long-lasting new program to fit the 6 to 7:30 or 8 P.M. time period, are doing it themselves. In the early 1970s the Group W station in San Francisco, KPIX-TV, applied its budget for prime access to an innovative *local magazine show* entitled *Evening*. This program reflected San Francisco's lifestyle, its people, its oddities and its beauty. The show proved such a success that the remaining Group W stations in Pittsburgh, Boston, Philadelphia and Baltimore adopted the pattern. Eventually, the group-owned

TABLE 7-2.
Top Ten Prime Access Shows; DMA Ratings

Rank and Program	Type*	Dura-tion	No. Stations	DMA Ratings
1 *M*A*S*H*	SC	30	111	13
2 *Family Feud*	QG	30	116	11
3 *Tic Tac Dough*	QG	30	64	11
4 *PM Magazine*	TI	30	86	11
5 *Hee Haw*	CV	60	119	10
6 *Joker's Wild*	QG	30	27	10
7 *Carter Country*	SC	30	7	10
8 *Happy Days*	SC	30	34	9
9 *Lawrence Welk*	MV	60	89	9
10 *Barney Miller*	SC	30	51	9
11 *Entertainment Tonight*	TI	30	79	9
12 *All in the Family*	SC	30	21	8
13 *The Jeffersons*	SC	30	34	8

SOURCE: A.C. Nielsen Company, May 1982. Used with permission.

*QG = quiz/game; CV = children's variety; TI = talk/information; MV = musical variety; SC = situation comedy.

stations started to exchange program segments, and it became apparent that other stations might be able to use this material if a show like *Evening* were begun in markets across the country. *Evening* went into syndication as *PM Magazine* in 1978 and has become the backbone of the access time period for nearly 100 stations.

However, this magazine concept often lacks a proper balance between syndicated material and local stories.[4] If the local material is downplayed, the entire show loses its local flavor, depending entirely on the universality of the syndicated pieces for its appeal, a risky expectation. The Group W *Evening/PM* concept should lead other broadcasters to develop formats producible, at least in part, in their own markets rather than to continue depending on established programs from national syndicators.

3. The most successful first-run access program in recent years is *Entertainment Tonight*. It commands the largest share of audience in access time in most urban markets, though its performance in nonmetropolitan areas has been more uneven. Slick, polished and timely, *Entertainment Tonight* combines some of the most successful elements of *PM Magazine* with fan magazine trivia. The station with this show is generally home free.

PRIME TIME

Prime time is the most highly viewed period of the daily schedule for affiliates. From 8 to 11 P.M., the networks pour on expensive and highly competitive programs, supported by arresting promotional campaigns on the air and in newspaper and magazine ads. Independent stations have been unable to bite into this time period with any consistency, and it remains the payload of the three national networks. The networks must get clearances by affiliates for this time if they are to maintain network **parity.**[5]

Preemption

1. From time to time, an affiliate may identify a section of the network schedule that needs repair but which the network cannot fix until later in the season. Under these conditions, an affiliate might "pick off" a weak night for a local movie *special,* a musical-hour special or a program having some significance to the local community.[6] Networks tolerate these preemptions if they do not happen too often, and the station need only convince its viewers that a preemption is justified. When the public is not convinced, phone calls, letters and the press scold the affiliate for its defection.

2. It is best to preempt on different days rather than pick off the same time slot week after week because regular preemptions irritate viewers who are robbed of certain shows. Preemption of network shows for local *basketball* schedules, for example, can be painful for all concerned, espe-

cially if some network specials are eliminated for the sake of a losing local team.

3. Judgment must be exercised when bumping a new network show that appears to be doomed in the New York or Los Angeles overnight ratings. Many a programmer has been burned by preempting a *big-city loser* only to find that it became a hit in local markets, and that with time it also became a hit in the big city. This situation occurred with *The Waltons, Little House on the Prairie* and *60 Minutes.*

LATE FRINGE, LATE NIGHT AND ALL NIGHT

This time period begins with the half-hour directly following prime time and continues into the late- and late-late-night periods, eventually arriving at morning (6 A.M.) on some stations.

Late Fringe

Affiliates traditionally reserve late fringe, the 11 to 11:30 P.M. time slot, for late local *newscasts.*

1. A carry-over from radio, the eleven o'clock news is part of the ingrained tradition of affiliate programming. Independent stations have tried to break this hold for years, and only one show—*Mary Hartman*—dented the public's late news loyalty; this defection happened in most markets for only a quick 26 weeks, then the news returned to its former dominance.

2. A local affiliate can double its ad avail inventory (available advertising spots) over what a newscast provides if enough programs can be purchased to fill the 260 slots needed for a year's stripping. *Motion pictures* provide a good local advertising vehicle if an affiliate can buy enough recent films to mix judiciously with golden oldies from the rerun files.

Late Night

The last weeknight segment most affiliate programmers must fill is the 11:30 P.M. to 2 A.M. period, late night. NBC's *The Tonight Show* was untouchable in the ratings until Johnny Carson's 1979 contract allowed him to pretape two days a week (nonlive) in addition to having 17 weeks' vacation during the year (co-hosts required). Both ABC and CBS made gains against these irregularities on NBC.

In the early 1980s, ABC's *Nightline* got high ratings, but usually an in-depth news show demands a diet of political crises to survive. Although similar efforts on CBS have not gotten satisfactory ratings, late night is no longer solely the bastion of talk.

The networks scheduled large numbers of reruns, mostly cop and detective shows to fill this period in the late 1970s. By the 1980s, CBS was trying adult action-adventure and doctor reruns such as *Hart to Hart, Quincy* and *Trapper*

John, M.D. NBC attempted its own late-late talk show (following *Tonight*), *Late Night with David Letterman* with spectacular initial success.

1. Of course, an affiliate can try *Merv Griffin* at 11:30 P.M. and fight talk with *talk*. Griffin was on CBS during the heyday of Paar and early Carson and was unable to make inroads, but he might work in some markets today. Recent syndicated entries are *Thicke of the Night* and *Saturday Night Live* reruns.

2. Many affiliates have tried 30-minute shows at 11:30 P.M. and then begun their movies at midnight. Some examples include *M*A*S*H*, *Three's Company*, *Barney Miller*, *All in the Family* and *Maude*. This gambit usually got good ratings for the first half-hour, but the nonmovie people defected at midnight, wiping out the early gains when the two periods are averaged. It appears that the long-form with an 11:30 P.M. start is the wisest structure, especially since *feature films* can be used in earlier time slots to use up all the contractual runs so as to maximize product revenue, an increasingly important tactic in the face of the shorter film contracts starting in the mid-1980s.

Scheduling feature films in alternative time periods became increasingly important in the mid-1980s as film syndicators sought to reduce the length of rental agreements. A **play** or **run** is one exposure of any part of a program or film on the air, and every airing constitutes a valuable property for both the station and the syndicator. Syndicators want to maximize the number of plays on pay television after a film has appeared in syndication, and short contracts allow a movie to return rapidly to the syndication market for resale.[7] This practice forces an affiliate to use up all the runs the station purchased within a short length of time, as short as three years for many contracts beginning in 1983 (for three runs). Affiliates had traditionally commanded contracts of six or more runs over a period of six years for movie packages, but began changing their movie scheduling strategies in the mid-1980s.

Overnight

For some affiliate programmers, usually in urban markets, one time remains to be filled, the overnight slot. In some markets, this time period ends about 4 A.M. or whenever the movie is over. In other markets, stations program all 24 hours, concluding the overnight period at 6 A.M. in time for early-morning programming.

1. Most stations program this time period only on Friday and Saturday nights, but a slowly increasing number of affiliates have copied successful independents in their markets and counterprogrammed a second and even third round of *movies* during the overnight time periods.

2. A second option is the recently developed television version of radio's all night hit, the *Larry King Show*. This program is intended for sleepless major market audiences and should outdraw weak movies on competing stations. Participatory television is the coming trend if the directions taken by radio and cable are any hint. *Call-in programs*, at any rate, are options for affiliates, especially in the overnight time period.

WEEKEND REALITIES

Saturday and Sunday create a different set of programming problems. Football, basketball, bowling, baseball, tennis, golf, auto racing, horse racing and boxing all take turns at capturing the adult male viewer. Cartoons draw children, and dancing captures the female teens.

Saturdays

On Saturdays, if a station schedules a *two-hour movie*, perhaps from 10:30 A.M. to 12:30 P.M., family viewing can be encouraged in a time period historically reserved for children. Scheduling a movie can also yield 52-week advertising sales contracts without depending on kid-oriented commercials, which are usually viable only during the third and fourth quarters (because advertisers buy time to announce back-to-school and Christmas sales). Careful selection of stars and titles can lure parents into watching the films along with the children. Elvis Presley, Jerry Lewis, John Wayne, Francis the Talking Mule, Ma and Pa Kettle and science fiction titles are all sure-fire, split-level audience getters of this type.

Country-western and Nashville *music* can also be used for counterprogramming. Saturdays from 2 to 4 P.M. or 4 to 6 P.M. are ideal time blocks for such programming. These shows usually cost little and can be easily promoted if the community likes the music.

The toughest hour on Saturday for the affiliate to fill is the 7 to 8 P.M. time slot, especially if the competition already owns *Lawrence Welk* and *Hee Haw*. The best attack is to program a *Bugs Bunny* or *Tom & Jerry*-type house show against these giants. The *cartoon half-hour* will garner young demographics (18 to 34 years) and set up whatever is planned at 7:30 to complete the hour. Use the rabbit, mouse or cat to lead the way, and almost anything will work at 7:30 P.M.

The other successful option is the *dance program*. Syndicated weekly shows like *Dance Fever* and *Solid Gold* draw predominantly female audiences with good numbers on early Saturday evenings. The number of new syndicated dance and music programs, following up on the success of MTV, the cable channel programming short videos (performance clips), dramatically increased in the mid-1980s, creating new, albeit untried, options for the adventurous affiliate with plenty of teens in the local market.

Late Saturday night has been traditionally programmed with *feature films*. NBC's *Saturday Night Live* arrived in the late 1970s, developing a large new audience, the college-age group. Their taste for sophisticated comedy relegated theatrical films to second place in most markets. A programmer must choose contemporary box office hits to stay within competitive reach of the syndicated first cast version *Saturday Night Live* (the later cast has been much less successful). If recent movies fail to work, one can try *classic films* (*Citizen Kane, Rebecca, Casablanca*). A *comedy block* could also be tried from 11:30 P.M. to 1:30 A.M., made up of half-hours back-to-back in the genre of *M*A*S*H, All in the Family, Maude, Three's Company* and *Mary Hartman, Mary Hartman*.

Sundays

The affiliate has very little room to maneuver on Sundays. The afternoons contain season-to-season sports, news from 6 to 7 P.M., and network entertainment from 7 to 11 P.M. The only period left for local development is the morning. This ghetto has usually contained public affairs and religious and cultural programs, panel shows and some kids' shows—all of which spell low ratings and low income.

When scheduling Sundays, the affiliate programmer should consider "service people" who work evenings all week and never have a chance to see primetime programming on workdays. The night people are out there; they just need something with mass appeal. And how about all those people who go to church early and all those people who do not go to church?

The most successful property one can schedule on Sunday mornings is a prime-time type *feature film*. Name the 10 A.M. to noon period something other than "Atheist Theater" and watch the numbers roll in. With limited competition, the HUT level will explode, and advertising revenue will follow shortly. If success comes quickly, the station should consider backing up the start to eight o'clock for the fifth and sixth runs of sit-coms that are always tough to play off. A wasteland can be turned into a highly watched and lucrative programming period. Cable television imports such as CBN, PTL and independent stations have relieved most broadcasters of the obligation to provide televised religion on Sunday mornings, although that obligation was always more myth than reality.

Late Sunday night following the 11 P.M. news also remains a difficult time to program—it is the Siberia of the weekly schedule. If the community is large enough, a 60-minute *adventure series* or a short *movie* is the best a programmer can do because of the low number of homes watching television. Using HUT levels as a guide always raises the chicken-and-egg question, however. Perhaps HUT levels are down because little worth watching is ever scheduled in the late-late time period. Certainly, some independents in major markets draw a salable-size audience. It might be worth a gamble to try some better quality films and promote them on Sunday nights.

SUMMARY

Programming is war. You are a general. The object is to win—win in all time periods. Winning means high ratings. High ratings bring top dollars from the advertiser, and top dollars let you control the market for another season. If you can do this and still keep a balanced schedule reflecting community needs, cultural roots and the entertainment demands of your audience, then, indeed, you are a programmer. A program schedule must be analyzed hour-by-hour to take into account available options, the competition and the economic benefits of reusing already-purchased programs. Network affiliates are bound by contract and by economic advantage to their networks, and those in the top 50 markets remain more restricted by FCC regulation than independents. If an affiliate's options are fewer, however, its visibility is generally greater than an independent's (or a public station's), and one of the network affiliates holds top place in nearly every market in nearly every time period. The strategies that get them there include targeting a major demographic group that is unserved to build a new audience (women's programs in mornings) or providing a desirable lead-in to succeeding programs (cartoons on Saturday evenings are one example). Audience flow is the prime consideration in early fringe in order to draw a male-adult audience for local news, whereas local appeal is the key to most effective access programming. Throughout the schedule, unused runs of popular syndicated series (off-network reruns) provide the fodder to build strong ratings.

Notes

[1]"A Side-by-Side Comparison of Network Compensation," *Broadcasting,* 8 August 1983, pp. 54–59.

[2]Robert Sobel, "Music Fills the Air, but Barter Is Calling the Tune," *Television/Radio Age,* 14 March 1983, pp. 139–145.

[3]In 1954, Donald H. McGannon became president and then in 1955 chairman of the board of directors of Westinghouse, the parent corporation of Group W. Group W is the fourth largest broadcasting company in the United States after the three commercial networks. It owns and operates 17 broadcasting stations, a television production and distribution company (Group W Productions, Inc.), national radio and television time sales companies, and is expanding its cable interests.

[4]"'PM Magazine' to be Remade," *Broadcasting,* 18 July 1983, p. 51.

[5]Parity exists when all three networks reach approximately the same number of households in a given daypart. When too many affiliates of one network refuse to clear a particular time period (because a low-rated program is scheduled, for example), that network no longer has any chance of appreciably improving that program's ratings since ratings are a percentage of the *total* U.S. households. And of course, the network's overall ratings are affected—which in turn affects its advertising rates and therefore its profitability.

[6]Preemptions also allow the local station to charge national rates rather than local rates for its prime time, creating a strong incentive to preempt if other program options are available.

[7]Dan Abramson, "Shorter Rental Agreements Seen Forcing Affiliates Out of Features as Pay Impact Hovers over Market," *Television/Radio Age,* 14 March 1983, pp. 146–148ff.

Selected Sources

Austin, Bruce A. "People's Time in a Medium-Sized Market: A Content Analysis." *Journalism Quarterly* 57 (Spring 1980): 67–70.

"News for Sale." *View* (September 1983): 43–45.

"Special Reports on Journalism." *Broadcasting* (16 November 1981): 39–48; (26 July 1982): 39–91; (27 September 1982): 43–71; (25 July 1983): 37–84.

"Television Programming & Production for Profit." *Broadcast Management/Engineering,* monthly series, March 1977 to date.

Television/Radio Age, New York, biweekly magazine, regularly reporting on television station programming and the syndication market.

Wakslag, Jacob J.; Agostino, Donald E.; Terry, Herbert A.; Driscoll, Paul; and Ramsey, Bruce. "Television News Viewing and Network Affiliation Changes." *Journal of Broadcasting* 27 (Winter 1983): 53–68.

CHAPTER EIGHT

Independent Station Programming

Edward G. Aiken

EDWARD G. AIKEN *gained experience as producer/director and promotion manager at WBAY-TV in Green Bay, Wisconsin, before going to WNEM-TV in Saginaw, Michigan, as program director in 1970. He joined KPHO-TV in Phoenix, Arizona, in the same capacity in 1973. In the 1970s, KPHO became a leading independent television station, winning against affiliate competition in several time periods and creating a programming model for other independents. In 1980, Mr. Aiken became vice-president/director of programming for Petry Television Inc., one of the largest station representative firms in New York. He specialized in syndicated television programming, especially movies, for independent client stations, advising stations on syndicated purchases and scheduling, and representing the rep point of view as an industry spokesperson. In 1984, he became vice president and general manager of KMPH-TV in Fresno, California. This chapter shows his wide experience with television station strategies.*

THE REALITIES OF INDEPENDENCE

An independent television station provides a stimulating challenge to its program director since it has no built-in foundation for its schedule in a network feed. However, an independent television station need not assume the posture of an economic stepchild. Although an independent may never rank number one in overall ratings against competing network affiliates, it can lead in key dayparts. Scheduling strong off-network series during prime access time and purchasing ratings-attracting programs from ad hoc networks have dramatically improved independent stations' ratings. A professionally programmed and managed independent with an equally aggressive sales force can attain ratings and economic parity within a given market against affiliates. However, independent programmers must face two unhappy realities—high costs and negative buyer attitude—while learning to use the primary advantage that independents possess: scheduling flexibility.

For the most part, it costs more to program an independent than a network-affiliated station. All the programs on an independent must be *purchased*, and these costs continually escalate. Stations now pay as much for an individual program series such as *Love Boat, Dukes of Hazzard* or *M*A*S*H* as they did for an entire week's schedule not too many years ago. As of 1984, for example, *M*A*S*H* reruns cost a midmarket independent (ranking between the 25th and 50th markets) about $15,000 an episode.

Some national and local spot-time buyers still look down their noses at many independents, making it difficult for some stations to earn their share of advertisers' dollars. However, most ad agencies and advertisers changed their buying habits in the early 1980s as independents became more competitive as a result of top-notch program purchases and scheduling that improved ratings.[1] The programming environment for commercials on an independent is similar to, if not better than, that of an affiliate scheduling the same client's advertising spot.[2] Independents air programs comparable to those of their affiliate competition but have less nonprogram clutter. During prime time, for instance, affiliates can usually only schedule local or national spot advertising at the hour or half-hour breaks; independents can scatter their advertising throughout each hour, typically creating a less-cluttered advertising environment.

These considerations aside, the independent's most important programming reality is its greater scheduling flexibility: It is not tied to the program flow from a network. As a result, it can effectively (1) counterprogram the other stations in a market, (2) target specific audiences the networks are not serving at all or not reaching because their programming is inconveniently scheduled for the potential audience and (3) create the perception among audience members that programming airing at nontraditional times is a viable alternative.

POSITIONING THE INDEPENDENT

Convincing an audience that a station is really different from its competitors is called **positioning** the station. Each station seeks a unique, positive image separating it from its competitors and giving the audience reasons to seek it out. Experience teaches that independents establish their positions by creating "islands of success" using counterprogramming, audience flow and promotion. To develop counterprogramming, flow and promotional strategies, independent programmers must ask themselves what audiences the network affiliates or other independents in the market are reaching, what programs are popular and what images are viable for an independent.

Counterprogramming

Research continually points to a substantial audience that does not watch news. They may not care about what goes on, may want their news in capsule form or may prefer entertainment over news. The independent programmer, using the right kind of programming, can counter the evening news block on the network affiliates and establish an "island of success" of at least an hour's duration. It can extend up to two hours depending on how the competition schedules their programs. Independents in the top 50 markets capture top ratings because they are free to schedule off-network reruns during access time, while the affiliate competition is limited to first-run programming.

Although the news block and prime access time have proved an enormous boon to independents, many other dayparts present similar entree for the independent programmer. Countering the late news and the plethora of weekend sports and public affairs on the networks with comedy/action/adventure programs or movies is also an effective strategy. Countering adult programming with cartoons also works well.

Flow Strategies

Additionally, the independent programmer must maximize the station's potential for audience flow (just as networks and affiliates must—as described in preceding chapters). The goals of flow strategy are to maintain current audience while building on it to take advantage of the rising persons-using-television (PUT) levels of key demographic groups (such as men and women 18–49, for example). An example of audience flow that builds from one audience to another follows:

3:00 *Bugs Bunny*

3:30 *Pink Panther*

4:00 *Scooby Doo*

4:30 *Gilligan's Island*

5:00 *Brady Bunch*

5:30 *Happy Days Again*

6:00 *Laverne & Shirley*

6:30 *M*A*S*H*

In this illustration, the audience is slowly "aged" by targeting programs at children as school ends, at teens as the afternoon progresses, at women still later, and adding men while retaining the children, teens and women in the evening hours. Recall that targeting means selecting programs having especially strong appeal, as demonstrated by research, for a particular age group or gender group. More precise targeting is possible using psychographic program research and other qualitative evaluations of program appeals as discussed in Chapter 2.

Promotional Image

An independent can also counterprogram by developing a program-identified image—as a "sports station" featuring local, regional, professional or amateur sports; as a "movie station" with feature films in every daypart, or as a "local news station" by scheduling news in nontraditional time periods, concentrating on local news and presenting local angles on national stories. In many large markets with more than one independent, a sports image may be the only open avenue, albeit a risky one. Sporting events attract a fickle audience, not a loyal one. Their inconsistency and the probability that superstations and the sports-oriented cable networks have acquired local team franchises (that used to "belong" to local independents), suggests caution in any shift to a sports image. Developing viewer loyalty and habit formation with more traditional series programming may be more effective for midmarket independents (and those in fifth and sixth position in large markets) than developing a particular station image.

Positioning an independent is a complex task. People watch *programs*, not *stations*, so choice programming at the appropriate times is the most important factor to promote. Presenting programs in a quality environment is also important; a shoddy on-air environment creates a negative ruboff that will be lasting and devastating. High-quality film prints and tapes, aired in a tight, professional on-air manner, will do much to create a lasting positive image for viewers and effectively position the independent.

THE PROGRAM SUPPLY

Regardless of the particular strategy for building "islands of success," programming requires money. In large markets with strong competition, it means a lot of money—because an independent does not have a magic button labeled NETWORK supplying up to 15 hours a day of programming and revenue in the form of network compensation. Typically network programming allows network-affiliated stations to operate with fewer personnel than are needed at independents (excepting news personnel). Since average network compensation is about 8–10 percent of an affiliate's revenue, and networks fill about 60 percent of the affiliate's schedule and promote those programs to audiences, many affiliates can focus wholly on sales and spend little staff time on programming and promotion. (The notable exceptions are those affiliates that dive into the news game to see who can outspend the other in people and equipment to gain a valuable rating point advantage.) The independent, however, has to pay cold, hard cash for almost everything it programs, fill an 18–24-hour schedule and promote and advertise every program itself.

Usually, the independent licenses programs from syndicators (off-network reruns, first-run syndication, movies) or produces them itself (e.g., sports, news, talk, children's). Increasingly, stations are trading some of their spot airtime (bartering) to obtain program materials. And ad hoc networks supply another way to compete with the three major broadcast networks in entertainment programming. As pointed out in Chapter 4 on group owners, Metromedia greatly increased its role as a supplier of high-quality entertainment programming to independent stations during the 1980s. However obtained, there are three basic forms of program materials dominating independent programming: syndicated series, movies and local programs.

SYNDICATED PROGRAMS

Varying in length—15, 30, 60, 90 minutes—syndicated programs range in cost efficiency from the "bread and butter" to the "caviar" of an independent station. The bread-and-butter programs cost little, relative to their potential revenue on a per-run basis. All off-network syndicated series are bought on a multiple-run basis. As of 1980, an independent typically licensed a network rerun for six to eight runs in six years. Today, films are a different matter. Syndicators have now reduced the length of performance contracts for feature films to three or four years, with a reduced number of runs, to remarket these films more quickly to pay cable networks. (See Chapter 7 on movie contracts for affiliates because similar contract restrictions apply.)

The most cost-efficient series are those that can be stripped (run Monday to Friday or Sunday to Saturday in the same time period). The most successful syndicated program on independent stations is the sit-com having kiddult appeal. It appeals to both children and adults, especially women 18–34 or 18–49, and draws audiences not interested in affiliate news or sports.

Deciding which off-network shows will work in any given market is often highly frustrating for programmers. They must consider (1) the rating and share of a program while it was on the network—both nationally and in the market in which it will play when purchased, (2) the time period(s) in which the program will prove itself most cost-efficient, (3) whether the program will have staying power as a strip and (4) whether the program will do better as a strip, a single or a two-time-per-week entry (checkerboarded). The independent cannot usually afford to buy the historical data needed to document each program in each market from Arbitron or Nielsen. National sales representatives, however, do buy this data and supply it to client stations. (See Chapter 3 on the role of reps in programming.) But even in the best of circumstances, and given the maximum amount of research and historical data, programmers sometimes must rely on intuition in making program decisions.

Kid Appeal

Syndicated programs whose main appeal is to kids—*Gilligan's Island* and *Little Rascals* and cartoons such as *Bugs Bunny, Tom & Jerry* and recently *Scooby Doo* and *Superfriends*—have worked well for independents in midafternoon (2:30 to 4 or 5 P.M.). Kids take control of television sets immediately after they come home from school. An independent station must entice as many children as possible into watching as early as possible, in order to hold them through the early fringe viewing time.

Kiddult Appeal

Children and women dominate the early fringe (4 to 7 P.M. or 5 to 8 P.M. audience, depending on the time zone) in which potential spot-time buyers look not only at household rating points but also at specific demographics, most often women 18–34 or 18–49. The kids in the audience provide the bulk of household rating points while the women in the audience give programs salability to advertisers. Programs such as *Brady Bunch, Happy Days, Little House on the Prairie* and *Eight Is Enough* and oldies but goodies such as *I Love Lucy, Dick Van Dyke* and *Andy Griffith* have strong appeal in early fringe.

Adult Appeal

Five types of programs have been used to attract adult audiences. Game shows had less audience appeal in the late 1970s and early 1980s but as of the mid-1980s are again popular. *Family Feud* is especially attractive to advertisers since it delivers a predominantly young adult audience (women/men 18–34 and 18–49); other game shows skew toward older demographic groups (adults 25 to 54 or adults 50+). Action/adventure series such as *Charlie's Angels, CHiPs, Battlestar Galactica, Starsky and Hutch* and *Kung Fu* work well in early fringe, in prime time, in early afternoon (as strips) and on weekends as counterprogramming to network sports. On weekends, such shows attract women, which counters the male-oriented sports programming the network affiliates usually offer.

At one time, the talk/variety program such as *Merv Griffin, Mike Douglas, Dinah Shore* and *Phil Donahue* were bread-and-butter series for independents. All these programs except *Phil Donahue* had success stories in virtually every daypart. *Donahue* remains strong in the morning between 9 A.M. and noon in many markets (especially the Midwest). However, syndicated daytime talk/variety is nearly dead. *Merv Griffin*, the only holdout, appeared on the rocks by the early 1980s. Audience interest shifted to magazine-type programs such as *Hour*

Magazine, the reality-based *People's Court* and soft news feature programs such as *PM Magazine* or *Entertainment Tonight.* Music-based programs, the newest trend in the mid-1980s, ranged from first-run dance shows such as *Dance Fever, Solid Gold* and *FM-TV* to dance-oriented game shows. Such programs usually come in once-a-week form for weekend scheduling.

Program Futures

In the early 1970s Paramount Television Sales auctioned the off-network syndication rights to both *Happy Days* and *Laverne & Shirley* as futures. Stations in the same market bid competitively for these programs while they were still on the network. Since then, *Love Boat, Dukes of Hazzard* and *Taxi* have been sold as futures. These sales made Paramount a lot of money and defined an elite class of programs, but the buying of futures is a strategy filled with danger for both the syndicator and the station.[3] Futures buying works as follows: The syndicator has or purchases the right to sell a certain series for individual stations to air either after the series network run or by a certain date, even though the series may continue in network first-run after going into syndication. Such a program has usually had a successful run on the network for four or five years—in some instances, only three or four years. The syndicator assumes the series will continue for a minimum of five years on the network.

Until *Happy Days* was offered for syndication, series pricing was determined for the most part by a formula for each market, as applied to the entire country (times the number of dollars the syndicator paid out for the rights to distribute, and sales costs plus profit). Paramount changed all that with *Happy Days.* Seeing the potential for the program to generate not only large household rating points, but also to reach key demographics (children, teens, women 18–34 and 18–49, men 18–49), they elected to market it on a supply-and-demand basis. Since *Happy Days* was the only series in the late 1970s with unique potential for attracting the kind of audiences stations could sell at premium prices, and since several individual stations in many markets competed for the opportunity to program it, Paramount let the marketplace determine the price after setting a minimum starting point.

The strategy worked: *Happy Days* became the most successful program in terms of syndication revenue in broadcasting history—sold at premium prices to be played two or three years from the time the commitment was made. Many independent stations bid for an elite program to establish a franchise for themselves in prime access time. Affiliated stations in the top 50 markets were prevented from playing off-network programs in access because of the prime-time access rule. The independent stations could charge more for spot advertising within *Happy Days* or require an advertiser to take a less desirable program availability concurrent with a spot in *Happy Days.* Later, Paramount used the same marketing technique for *Laverne & Shirley.* The prices paid for *Laverne & Shirley* far exceeded those for *Happy Days* (as much as $100,000 per episode in the top markets), yet *Laverne & Shirley* has not equalled *Happy Days*'s ratings success, and *Happy Days* itself did not maintain as strong a ratings pull as many experts had predicted. As of 1982, both programs were substantially outperformed by *M*A*S*H, Three's Company* and *The Jeffersons.*[4]

Although some series continue to command record prices as futures (*Love Boat, Dukes of Hazzard, Taxi, Benson*), by 1982 a plateau was reached. Excepting unusual competitive forces in a market, overall prices stabilized near or slightly above the *Happy Days* and *Laverne & Shirley* range. Many stations, however, were burned badly and are still stinging from earlier high-cost/low-yield decisions. Many bought a program as a ratings panacea, an island, without regard to audience flow, and were disappointed when its ratings were lower than optimistic projections. *M*A*S*H*, however, was originally sold at relative low future prices, but has since taken over the record for renewal prices, in major markets often going as high as 10 to 15 times its original license cost.

Program Barter

Traditionally, the independent station's alternatives to purchased or locally produced programs were the relatively rare network programs it begged, borrowed or stole (1) from network-affiliated stations when, occasionally, they preempted network programs; (2) from ad hoc networks such as the one Mobil Oil set up for high-quality programs and miniseries such as *Edward the King;* or (3) from special networks set up for sporting events.

A fourth exception is bartered programs, which are supposedly "free" but in reality are not free. Although no money passes from the station to the program supplier for bartered programs, something of equal and sometimes greater value is given to the supplier—advertising inventory.

Television stations have two customers—viewers and advertisers. Without the first, it is difficult if not impossible to attract the second. Assuming the station attracts a reasonable number of viewers, it can sell time in or adjacent to its programs to advertisers. Time in this context is **inventory.** A television station's inventory (its salable time) acquires an arbitrary dollar value based on the rating each of its programs achieves (or is expected to achieve if it is new programming or in a new time slot). The station's ability to get this dollar value is based on supply and demand for the program itself, the station's overall inventory position and the condition of the market as a whole. If a station pays cash for a program, it can charge advertisers whatever it feels it can get for the inventory within or adjacent to that program, and the station keeps all the money those sales efforts generate. But if the station barters for the program, it must give up part of that precious commodity—inventory—to the program supplier.

If the station, for example, pays a program supplier $1,000 per telecast for a program having an inventory of twelve, 30-second commercial spots, and if the value of each spot (based on ratings and supply and demand) is $500, the total potential return to the station is $6,000 (or a program-cost-to-potential-return ratio of 16.6 percent). In a barter case, the program supplier may say to the station, "I'll give you the program for no cash outlay. All I want is 2½ minutes for my clients, which, incidentally, you must protect against their competitors." Those 2½ minutes cost the station not only $2,500 in inventory it cannot sell (or a program-cost-to-potential-return ratio of 41.6 percent), but also "protecting" the program distributor's clients against possible competitors restricts the station's sales effort, placing another roadblock in the path of the sales department. Using a *nonbarter* program keeps the potential $6,000 in revenues and requires no protection from competitors. Over a 52-week period, using a barter vs. a nonbarter program represents a potential return of $182,000 vs. $312,000—and a restricted vs. an unrestricted field for ad sales.

The programmer must answer some rather critical questions concerning barter programming: Is the cost-to-return ratio too high? Do the program's potential ratings and lead-in possibilities outweigh the cost ratio? Is barter the only way to obtain the program? How many barter programs can the station afford at any given time?

A number of programs that enjoyed successful runs on the networks became available to independent stations via the barter route in the 1970s, some of the most notable being *Hee Haw* and *Wild Kingdom*, in addition to a long list of game shows. In the 1980s, many syndicators began asking for cash as well as barter minutes, particularly in the case of inexpensive, first-run syndication, beginning with *Mike Douglas* (now defunct) and continuing with *Donahue, People's Court* and *Family Feud.* By 1983, barter fever had spread to programs for major time periods and off-network series like *Family, Switch* and the *Nancy Drew/Hardy Boys Mysteries.*[5] Some feature films were also added to the barter group. *Laugh-In* was sold for cash plus barter; *How the West Was Won* became a barter program; and most first-run music programs were going the barter route.

This trend will probably continue for two reasons. First, stations that have purchased substantial amounts of off-network programming at high prices must acquire barter programs to operate within their budgets; their cashflow has been restricted by these previously made, expensive program purchases, and program prices will continue to escalate at nearly 15 percent per year. Second, syndicators have found they can make more money by selling all or part of the advertising themselves for programs stations want, and so the practice is bound to increase among syndicators.[6]

MOVIES

Considered the most cost-efficient form of programming available, movies allow the independent programmer considerable flexibility at relatively low cost. Movies fill many hours in independent schedules and allow the programmer to target key audiences, generally on the basis of sex and age.

Theme Weeks

Movie watchers tend to be women 18–34 or 18–49, especially for familiar titles or superstars. One successful movie strategy is to create theme weeks, heavily promoting "monsters-we-all-know-and-love" or "beautiful ladies week," for example, using horizontal scheduling (stripped across the week).

Stacking

Movies can also be stacked. Stacking allows a programmer to air many hours of the same kind of program in one day while varying the type every few hours. For instance, KPHO-TV (Phoenix, Arizona) has aired a seven-hour block of movies on Saturdays for many years with great success by targeting for four specific audiences.

9:00 A.M.	Saturday Morning	The movies selected for this particular show-case appeal to *children* (to lure them away from the traditional cartoon fare on competing network-affiliated stations). They also *attract young adults.* Examples are *Tarzan* movies, *East Side Kids, Lassie.*
10:30 A.M.	World Beyond	Science fiction and monster films will attract *kids, teens, men and women 18–34* (kiddults).
12:00 noon	Action Theatre	Western, war and sword-and-sandal films have been very successful in attracting *men and women 18–49.* Particular attention is given to picking titles with big-name stars such as John Wayne or James Stewart.
2:00 P.M.	Adventure Theatre	This is similar to Action Theatre with the added dimension of thrillers and long-form sci-fi. It has greatest appeal to *adults 18–49* and draws an especially large proportion of *men.*

Stacking is most successful when used as a thematic showcase device. When purchasing movies, programmers can then select titles for specific showcases and further increase the cost efficiency of the station's movie programming.

LOCAL PROGRAMS

Local programs may be as inexpensive or expensive as the station chooses and can take as many forms as syndicated programs or movies. They include (1) sports of a local or regional nature, (2) news, (3) public affairs, (4) children's programs, (5) talk and women's interest, (6) musical variety and, if the station is so inclined and well-heeled enough, (7) drama.

Sports

Some of the most successful independent stations in the country have a sports image: WGN, Chicago; WTBS, Atlanta; WOR and WPIX in New York; and KTTV and KTLA in Los Angeles, to list a few. Independents have the scheduling flexibility to accommodate sporting events during every daypart, and sports events attract a desirable demographic target (men 18–34 and 18–49). Any number of advertisers are willing to pay premium prices to be identified with a televised sport because it sells their products. This fact makes sports programming a hot strategy for a number of independent stations.

There are three cost approaches to sports programming. In the first, a station purchases telecast rights from the team, produces each game (cost of talent, play-by-play, color) and delivers the signal back to the station (by AT&T Long Lines, satellite or a combination of both). Although very expensive, this route has the greatest potential for revenue because the station can sell all the available advertising inventory. This approach has its risks. All the spots may not be sold, reducing the potential revenue; and the team standing in the won-lost column determines ratings, which in turn determine advertiser support. In another option, the team itself assumes all production and delivery costs and pays the station for the time. The team assumes all financial risk, but it also will reap most of the potential profits. The station is paid for the airtime (but less than if they sold it themselves), and in the minds of viewers gets the credit for bringing them the games. In the third possibility, an outside producer–syndicator pays the team for telecast rights, sells part of the available time within the games and barters with the station for the airtime.

Prime time (7 to 10 P.M. or 8 to 11 P.M.) is ideal for sports programming on independents since that is when they traditionally face the toughest network competition and revenue potential is highest. An independent carrying a lot of sports programming takes risks because the audience composition for sports skews to men both during the game and following, and men are generally not a loyal audience. Also, since women are the primary target for most advertisers, the station may lose out on potential sales. Sporting events also tend to break up audience flow.

News

News programming can be approached with a simple **rip-and-read** formula (announcer rips copy from wire service and reads it on the air) or with a sophisticated, expensive, competitive information showcase. A common independent practice is to program news in nontraditional hours. If the late news airs on competing network affiliates at 10 (C/MST) or 11 (EPST) P.M., successful independents program their news at 9 or 9:30 P.M. in the central/mountain time zones or 10 or 10:30 P.M. in the eastern and western time zones. This strategy allows viewers to see the news on the independent and allows the independent to position itself in two different time periods, initially counterprogramming affiliated stations with news against entertainment and then entertainment against newscasts.

News programs can be cheap or expensive to produce—the station decides. If the rip-and-read approach is used, cost is minimal. A 60-second update every hour or two with a news reader giving details under a slide or series of slides creates few problems and costs little. The ratings, however, reflect the effort and budget expended.

When an independent takes the expensive, sophisticated and thus competitive approach, it must hire a full-time staff of at least a news director, an assignment editor/coordinator, a producer plus weather/news/sports anchors and reporters, photographers, editors and writers. Staff size will vary with the area to be covered and the depth of news treatment desired.

Equipment looms as the next cost consideration. If the station opts to go the ENG (electronic newsgathering) route, thousands of dollars will have to be spent, especially if the station wants "live" capability via microwave. Receiving the satellite-distributed national/international news services requires an earth station, which also adds to capital outlay. The cost for a dish varies according to the level of sophistication the station needs and wants. It can range from $25,000 (plus site) to $500,000. The station can select among many options, such as mechanical reorientation from one satellite to another, an uplink to provide transmit capability, multiple transponder receivers (channels) on each satellite and redundancy in both uplinks and downlinks (backups for safety). Additionally, if the station is located in an area with heavy microwave signals, the satellite receivers must be shielded at yet further cost.

Although some VHF independent television stations have been relatively successful with news, especially when programmed at nontraditional times, few ever equal the total household rating points of network-affiliated stations. Audience perception is that independents cannot or do not do news as well as the affiliates, and it persists although analysis of an independent newscast is likely to show no difference from a network-affiliated newscast in reporting style, content or overall quality.

This audience myth has proven a stumbling block for many independents programming news head-to-head with affiliated stations. For example, the superstation WGN-TV in Chicago tried head-to-head news competition for several years. In May 1979, Arbitron ratings for 10 P.M. in Chicago were:

Station			ADI Rating
WLS	(ABC)	News	20
WBBM	(CBS)	News	18
WMAQ	(NBC)	News	12
WGN	(IND)	News	5
WFLD	(IND)	*Sanford & Son*	5

In response WGN moved its news to 9 P.M. (for one hour) and soon averaged a 6 rating. In February 1980, Arbitron ratings for the 10 P.M. slot were:

Station		ADI Rating
WLS	News	16
WBBM	News	17
WMAQ	News	13
WGN	Soap	7
WFLD	*M*A*S*H*	7

As each ratings point is worth several thousands of dollars in revenue over a 52-week period, most independents have abandoned the head-to-head news strategy in favor of the nontraditional time period. Overall, the amount of locally originated hard and soft news grows steadily on independents.

Public Affairs

Public affairs programs give independent stations an opportunity to excel. As someone once said, "Public affairs need not be dull affairs." If management permits, an inspired and well-budgeted public affairs department at an independent television station can be television at its best. But cost remains a problem. It is difficult to sell public affairs programs to advertisers, and most stations refuse to invest time, personnel and money in programs that don't make money. The documentary and magazine formats best demonstrate a station's public affairs commitment. But few independents go this route. Very few UHF independents do more than a bare minimum of public affairs, and much of that is done in election years. Local weather and other natural disasters, however, offer independent television stations the same opportunity as local radio stations for responding to community events in ways that attract substantial audiences. (See Chapter 16 on news radio for more on local news responsiveness.)

Children's Programs

From both a revenue and ratings standpoint, independents have been successful with locally produced children's programming. During certain dayparts (early morning and afternoon), children usually control the television set. Although live programming eats away at the profit margin, some formats for local, live children's programs are workable. Identifying which segment of the children's audience the station wants to attract is crucial: preschool, grades one through four, grades five through eight or high school. High schoolers are the most difficult to reach since they are the most fickle in their viewing habits. Preschoolers require sophisticated, well-researched material, obtainable only at considerable cost. The age groups easiest to program for are grades one through four and five through eight.

Costs vary depending on production complexity, but the major costs are talent and studio time. Care must be given to continuity acceptance standards (policies covering vocabulary level, pacing, intensity and type of sales pitches and so on) so as not to take advantage of the audience. Some long-running children's shows on independents are *Bozo* on WGN, *Wallace & Ladmo* on KPHO and *Blinky's Club* on KWGN.

Talk and Women's Interest

Women make up most of the daytime audience in most markets, and a number of them want more from television than entertainment. They want to be informed, enlightened and challenged, and a stimulating, local, live (or taped) program can do all three if properly produced (whether on an affiliate or an independent; see discussion in Chapter 7 on this same topic).

Local programs appealing to women are fairly easy to produce and in most instances not too costly. Their most important ingredient is the producer/host or hostess, who must be in tune with what is happening in the community that will be of interest to and challenging for area women. The least expensive way to produce such shows is in the studio with invited guests. More expensive is the **remote,** using ENG equipment to relay (or tape) some or all of the material from wherever activities occur. So far, few independents have seriously tackled local women's programs, but some cable networks have had considerable success with women-oriented programming that might provide models. The talk format can accommodate off-length time periods (following full-length movies and sporting events), has community appeal and low cost, all of which point to their greater use in independents' local production strategy. The talk format always raises the Fairness Doctrine (see Chapter 17), and of course, the program host/hostess is a crucial factor in success.

Musical Variety

These programs are successful depending on the market, although overall musical variety has declined in popularity. For every type of music an audience exists, although some music attracts very small audiences. In certain parts of the Midwest, polka music attracts a loyal and rather large audience on television; country music draws enthusiastic audiences in the Midwest, South and Southwest. Musical variety programs are fairly expensive to produce in spite of using local talent in the station's studio. The largest expense comes from the musicians' fees as determined by the local musicians' union. Other costs (sets, props) can be spread out and amortized over the run of the show, of course. Except for major market efforts, local musical variety programming suffers in comparison to syndicated and network fare. However, it can be scheduled in many time slots as its audience tends to seek it out rather than the station having to seek out the audience.

The latest version of the musical program emphasizes dance numbers rather than the variety format. For no cost, stations can copy MTV's video formula by using videos supplied by recording studios. This kind of program draws a large and loyal teen and young adult audience when it emphasizes rock music and an older audience when it focuses on country music.

Drama

On a local basis, drama is a very ambitious undertaking, and productions should be examined in detail before proceeding. The most expensive items involved are time and people. Rehearsals take up a large amount of time; some station personnel must be present to block the play for television and rehearse the technical people. Although tackling drama can be professionally satisfying, it is very expensive, has a poor cost-to-return ratio, and is rarely attempted by independents (or by affiliates or by the networks).

PROGRAMMING AND SALES

It is imperative for the programmer at an independent station to become familiar with, and involved in, sales. Finding out about, aggressively seeking out, purchasing and effectively scheduling a program that the sales department (for whatever reason) cannot sell is an exercise in futility—a waste of time, effort and money. The programmer must know what budgets spot advertisers have, what target demographics each advertiser seeks, and what effects local and national economics are likely to have on advertising budgets. Programmers must know which programs appeal to national advertisers and which to local advertisers. Ideal programs do both, of course.

An ongoing, working dialogue between the programmer and the sales manager must cover subjects such as rating potentials or projections, pricing for spots within programs, budgets for both national and local advertisers, advertiser resistance to certain programs or time periods, recommendations on spot versus sponsored programs and methods of selling programs other than the traditional cost-per-thousand, cost-per-point and cost-per-person. Programming's escalating costs make it crucial for programmers to know a program's revenue potential before it is purchased. An open relationship with sales management and a program director who understands sales are essential.

Unsalable Programs

Obvious questions arise when certain programs cannot be sold by an effective sales team. For example, a program may be scheduled in a time period not meshing with an advertiser's planned marketing campaign. If an advertiser's marketing plan is to break during the middle part of the second quarter of a given year, but the television station schedules a program that would be an obvious "buy" for the advertiser in the first part of the second quarter, the advertiser is automatically eliminated. The marketing campaign does not correspond with the planned airing of the program. Buying or creating a program that demands a premium price from advertisers but which appeals to advertisers whose sales plans exclude premium prices can also create sales problems. Much time and effort, to say nothing of money, can be fruitlessly spent in seeking out, negotiating for and eventually buying the license rights to programming that later proves to be unsalable.

Risky Programs

Independent programmers must keep up-to-date on changing program possibilities if they expect to compete effectively within their marketplaces. Being aware of available product is only the first step, however; programmers must aggressively pursue and be willing to take a chance on programs their judgment says will work in their markets. Establishing ongoing, candid relationships with program suppliers and producers is quite important for without those pipelines, independent programmers will find themselves out in the cold. Keeping in touch with the business also means reading about program trends and tastes and learning what is going on in the production centers of Los Angeles and New York—though what is a hit in those two unique markets only hints at what might work in other markets and may be very misleading for a station in another part of the country.

The short-term effect of program scarcity is that programs cost more, thus eroding profit margin. But an even worse tactic is scheduling programs that do not attract a large enough audience, reduce advertising revenue and erode the profit margin. The long-term effect of not having access to new programs is that the programmer cannot plan on a long-range basis.

Programmers cannot operate in a vacuum. Program manager, sales manager and general manager working *in concert* create dividends in both audience shares and revenue. Often the perspective of one manager is 180 degrees from that of another. Then the effective programmer must communicate to the general manager and/or sales manager the rationale for programming decisions. Raw research data and extracted data become the tools for determining whether a program should be actively sought, what price should be paid, and how the program should be scheduled. Money must be set aside for research and program development so that fresh, innovative programming becomes an option.

PROGRAMMING AND RESEARCH

If effective communication with program suppliers is the lifeblood for the independent programmer, research is the nerve center. Chapters 2 and 3 review the research all stations should consider as they make programming decisions. Independent programmers, especially, must review every scrap of research material, especially that indicating how an off-network program performed in a given market, especially the market in which that programmer operates.

Tracking Syndicated Series

Tracking an off-network program in similar markets is essential to see how that program might perform in a given market. The programmer can check the Arbitron and Nielsen ratings books for the essential information on how the program performed in rating, share, total women, women 18–34 and 18–49, total men, men 18–34 and 18–49, teens, kids 2–11 and kids 6–11. Although a program may perform very well on the national level, it will not necessarily have appeal in a particular market and vice versa. *Little House on the Prairie* was canceled on the network but outperforms local news when counterprogrammed in the Midwest.

The independent programmer must track that kind of information. Rep firms, discussed in Chapter 3, can supply ratings information to their clients, and syndicated program ratings are, of course, available through both Nielsen and Arbitron as well as from syndicators—although the distributor's information should be taken with a spoon of salt.

OUTSIDE CONSTRAINTS

Most programmers are vividly aware of the many constraints various individuals, groups and circumstance impose. Specifically, budget and equipment limitations may mean the programmer cannot buy and schedule a particular program because the station cannot afford it.

An independent's operating signal may be a major constraint on its ratings potential. UHF stations have traditionally been more disadvantaged than VHF stations in the same market. Cable penetration, however, has made a significant difference, leveling out the technical characteristics of signals and introducing all channels on a more or less equal basis. When cable systems convert UHF channels to unoccupied VHF channels between 2 and 13, these stations have a better opportunity to win viewers. The remote control tuner also improves UHF viewing levels. Tuning all signals in a similar manner (all on consecutive numbers on the same dial or on a keypad) gives underdog independents (and even public stations) frequent chances for viewer sampling.

Community pressures are also of concern to the independent programmer. Organizations such as ACT, NOW, NAACP, Urban League and Chicanos Por La Causa have sought their day in court with the media. They represent viewers that independent programmers must be willing and able to address in their programming. Independent stations are no less responsible for addressing the needs of minority or pressure groups than are affiliated stations. In some respects, independents are even preferred vehicles because they have content flexibility and can make time available in nontraditional time periods.

The FCC's proposed modification of network financial interest and syndication rules also affects independents' programming decisions. The changes have lifted many restrictions on the networks' participation in production and syndication of programs they air. The long-range effects of this increased network program control will not be evident for several years, but many in the industry predict that independents will find the licensing of off-network programs more difficult.

THE FUTURE OF THE INDEPENDENT

One of the greatest problems independent programmers face is the dearth of off-network syndicated programming available for stripping. As of the mid-1980s, syndicated first-run programming is not increasing fast enough to meet the demand. High production costs coupled with network cancelations of programs that do not perform at a given national rating and share level have diminished the supply of strippable programs. Although some relief is available to independent stations from first-run miniseries on ad hoc networks such as Operation Prime Time (*A Woman Called Golda, Blood Feud, Sadat* and other such first-run products), it cannot meet the independent stations' insatiable program appetite. Not enough *proven* product becomes available, which might lead to a situation parallelling that of radio in the early 1950s and 1960s: Radio stations recognized that they could not be all things to all people all the time and consequently specialized in single formats. Many independent stations might have to become specialty stations such as "the movie station" or "the sports station" to survive in the future. Local production, especially of news, will probably fill a greater portion of the program gap.

SUMMARY

The independent television station must purchase, produce or barter programming to fill 18 to 24 hours every day. Syndicated series, movies and sports make up the bulk of independent programming. Licensing practices for key off-network series now commonly require the purchase of program futures; and contract lengths for feature films are shortening to fewer years and fewer runs. Although expensive, series programming can build loyal audiences for independents and kiddult sit-coms generally attract the most desirable audiences. One of the primary jobs of independent station programmers is tracking the ratings of syndicated series. Movies fill large amounts of time and are more successful when thematically stacked; while sporting events also fill large amounts of time with highly visible programming, their male audiences are not loyal and dependable. First-run programs, on the other hand, are often cheaper, but harder to get viewers to sample without a large amount of promotion; they also lack track records on which to base purchasing and scheduling decisions. Increasingly, off-network reruns and first-run series are being bartered, often to the station's financial disadvantage. Independents typically avoid head-to-head news competition with affiliates and are reasonably successful with nontraditional program scheduling. Counterprogramming, flow control and promotion are an independent's primary strategies, and scheduling salable programs is an overriding goal. The advent of cable has been a boon to most UHF stations since being repositioned on the receiver in the home allows the independent (or public) station to compete based on programming, not signal quality or reception difficulty. Programming an independent remains risky and challenging.

Notes

[1] "Advertising: Agencies and Reps Find Growing Favor with Indies," *Broadcasting*, 27 June 1983, p. 71.

[2] This move was first apparent in a major 1977 Arbitron study comparing affiliate and independent audiences in 23 markets; it was later substantiated in the 1980 Burke study comparing advertising environments, based on a survey of 200,000 viewers; and bolstered by several proprietary studies by rep firms. Burke Marketing Research, Inc., *The Effects of Station Environment on Television Advertising Communications: Independent Stations vs. Affiliated Stations, 1981* (New York: Association of Independent Television Stations, Inc., 1981).

[3] As explained in Chapter 7, with the current network schedule of about 22 original programs each year, the syndicator has a minimum of 110 episodes to sell for stripping after five years (130 after six years). Since there are 260 exposures (Monday–Friday strip slots) per year on a station, 110 episodes will fill one year by running each episode 2.36 times. The more episodes produced beyond 110, the much more valuable the series becomes to both the syndicator and the purchasing stations. The series brings a greater dollar return to the syndicator, and it requires fewer repeats in a year's time, which the station can amortize for a better return on dollars spent.

[4] "Sitcoms Pace November Nielsen Syndie Sweeps; Informational, Variety Programs Also Do Well," *Television/Radio Age*, 14 March 1983, p. 152 and p. 328.

[5] Robert Sobel, "Music Fills the Air, But Barter Is Calling the Tune," *Television/Radio Age*, 14 March 1983, pp. 139–145ff.

[6] "Petry Looks at the Future," *Broadcasting*, 21 February 1983, pp. 59–62; and "Independents Taking the Ad Hoc Road to Success," *Broadcasting*, 28 March 1983, pp. 70–72.

Selected Sources

"BM/E's Program Marketplace." *Broadcast Management/Engineering,* monthly series profiling program syndicators, January 1977 to date.

Morgenstern, Steve, ed. *Inside the TV Business.* New York: Sterling Publishers, 1979.

"Special Reports on Independents." *Broadcasting* (30 January 1978): 41–64; (25 January 1982): 47–56; (1 February 1982): 36–48; (17 January 1983): 55–70; (24 January 1983): 66–73.

Television/Radio Age. Biweekly reports on programming, including syndicated program rankings.

Zuckerman, Laurence, and Brown, Les. "Autumn of the Networks' Reign." *Channels* (September–October 1983): 45–48.

PART THREE

Cable Programming Strategies

Part III turns to another aspect of television—programs and services delivered by cable instead of broadcasting. Cable's strategies differ from those of broadcasting because it is a multichannel, wired technology, and its programmers must consider both broadcast stations and cable-only networks in the same competitive arena. In the cable industry, programmers must program many channels, some prescribing for dozens or even hundreds of systems, just as rep programmers consider many broadcast stations. Part III begins with a chapter describing the programming constraints operating on cable systems. The following chapters cover other considerations when programming either a single-satellite-distributed cable network, such as a basic or premium service, or dealing with local origination programs intended just for subscribers in one particular system. A chapter on superstations concludes this part because superstations have played such an influential role in the growth of cable programming. Each of these chapters follows the consistent structural pattern of this book by examining program evaluation, selection and scheduling within a particular programming context.

*Chapter 9 analyzes strategies for operating within **cable system** programming. Law, technology, economics and marketing affect cable programming in ways that differ markedly from their effects on broadcast programming. The author shows how they constrain the system programmer and details options for selecting among premium cable services, other cable-only networks, and distant independent signals including superstations, while leaving channel space for broadcast signals the system must carry.*

*Nonpay or **basic cable networks** use quite different strategies that should, logically, occupy the next chapter in Part III, Chapter 10. Like the premium services, nonpay cable services are types of networks that provide a schedule of programs to cable "affiliates," the local systems. But because the basic cable networks are so diverse and fluctuating in their programming strategies as of the mid-1980s, the chapter can only provide a brief overview of their various services. By the 1990s it should be possible* to generalize about program evaluation, selection and scheduling patterns of the basic cable networks, but the information for such an industry-wide analysis is presently unavailable. Therefore, Chapter 10 analyzes what is available within each of ten sets of content-related basic cable networks and deals with the rising industry problem of program guides.

Chapter 11 examines the well-developed strategies of the **premium** or **pay cable networks.** For an extra monthly fee, a cable system delivers to subscribers nationally distributed channels of programming, called the premium networks. They consist primarily of theatrical movies, so the author focuses on the evaluation, selection and scheduling of feature films. The revenues shared between the premium program suppliers and local cable systems largely account for the resurgence of cable in the 1970s, and they remain central to cable marketing strategy. A dozen premium networks distributed their programming nationally as of 1984, and they are described in detail in Chapter 11.

Chapter 12 looks at cable systems' **local origination programming and services,** separated into subsections on locally produced access programming and ancillary services. These three programming areas have diverse functions, but for the most part, they share the common feature of originating at the local cable system as responsibilities of the local cable programmer. This chapter examines syndicated programs packaged by the local programmer, interstitial programming, cable radio and subsidiary services indicating the direction of local cable programming for the next decade.

Chapter 13 looks at the **superstation** programmer, an individual working for an independent television station whose programs are distributed by satellite-relay throughout the United States. One unusual characteristic of such stations is that, by law, they must program for the audience in their immediate broadcast coverage area when, in fact, they may serve many scattered audiences—one of many special constraints operating on superstation programmers. Like the first of the premium cable networks, superstations played a large role in generating audiences for local cable systems in the 1970s. As of the mid-1980s, only three stations are considered full-scale superstations by the broadcast/cable industry, but the strategies they use to program for their diverse markets in different time zones apply in more restricted measure to dozens of other independent stations whose signals are imported over shorter distances. Chapter 13 therefore examines programming from the point of view of an independent television station distributed nationally.

Part III, then, focuses on the special programming circumstances of cable and the unique constraints operating on different types of cable programmers. This part concludes the portion of this book devoted to **commercial television** programming.

Cable System Programming

Susan Tyler Eastman

A QUICK GUIDE TO CHAPTER NINE

SUSAN TYLER EASTMAN *came to Indiana University in 1981 as an associate professor of Telecommunications, after having taught at Temple University since 1977 in the Department of Radio-Television-Film. She edited and authored* Strategies in Broadcast and Cable Promotion *(Wadsworth, 1982) with Robert Klein, and the first edition of this book,* Broadcast Programming *(Wadsworth, 1981). Both books received Broadcast Preceptor Awards from San Francisco State University for their contributions to knowledge about the industry. She has a B.A. from the University of California at Berkeley; an M.A. from San Francisco State University; and a Ph.D. from Bowling Green State University. In 1980 she was awarded a charter faculty internship by the National Association of Television Program Executives, interning at WCAU-TV in Philadelphia. She coordinated the 1980 Broadcast Education Association's Faculty/Industry Seminar on programming, produces and directs, publishes in scholarly journals, guest-lectures on new technologies at other universities, and regularly consults and teaches courses in programming and promotion.*

THE JOB OF THE CABLE SYSTEM PROGRAMMER

This chapter examines the special characteristics of the cable system programmer's job and details the legal, technical, economic and marketing considerations affecting the selection of programming for cable systems. It analyzes the evaluation and scheduling strategies system programmers use and looks at how pay-per-view will change many current practices.

Choosing among more than 50 satellite-distributed program networks and a growing number of local and regional services is a major dilemma facing a cable programming executive. Figure 9-1 illustrates the range and variety of cable networks jockeying for position on local cable systems. These sources of basic and pay cable programming are described in detail in chapters 10 and 11.

The responsibilities of the local system programmer increase as the number of available program services expands. At one time, the cable programmer was concerned only about finding enough programming to fill all a system's channels.

FIGURE 9-1. Logos of Varied Cable Networks

When only a limited number of national networks were available, cablecasters focused on wiring homes, and program directors were scarce. The few that were employed spent their time producing access programs in local studios. But the dramatic rise in the number of satellite-distributed program networks since 1980 redefined the cable programmer's responsibilities. The programmer now has to decide which national services to add or delete, which services should share time, which local events to televise, which syndicated programs to acquire or barter for, where to place networks and services on the dial, how to organize programs on locally programmed channels and how to keep track of the system's channels and programs.[1]

Responsibility for programming decisions varies greatly from system to system. More often than not, no matter what the system size, no full-time program director is employed. According to a nationwide survey conducted by *Cable Marketing*, more than half of independently owned cable systems and about 40 percent of MSO-owned systems have no programming department.[2] Nationwide, there may be as few as 400 cable system programmers for about 5,000 systems—though accurate numbers are hard to obtain for the small systems. Programmers typically have annual salaries ranging from $15,000 to $25,000. Over 60 percent are college graduates, and about 30 percent have a year or more of graduate or professional school. These salaries are low given the educational level and the many management responsibilities cable programmers have. Additionally, about 60 percent of the programmers responding to *Cable Marketing*'s survey reported prior experience in fields related to cable, most frequently in production or program syndication. In the same survey, however, 90 percent of the respondents rated rapid advancement opportunities as "good" to "excellent," relecting the tremendous growth anticipated in cable management.

At small cable systems, *general managers* make programming decisions. Their challenge is to assemble a basic package and as many additional revenue-producing entertainment tiers as channel capacity allows. Generally, small systems lack interactive channels for shopping, banking or security systems and the like, so the small system programmer's job focuses on scheduling national entertainment and information program services. In many cases, the *program director's* job is largely technical and administrative, not creative; that person mainly coordinates local access programming (discussed in Chapter 12).

At the group headquarters level, programming is usually handled by a director or *vice-president of marketing* who shares decision making with a management team. Programming is usually a broadly defined activity involving elements of marketing and sales, advertising and promotion, technical and engineering matters and general management. In group-owned systems, the multiple system operator (MSO) may program all its systems as Tele-Communications, Inc. and Storer do; or it may, at another extreme, encourage local programming decisions as American Cablesystems does. (See Chapter 4 for a discussion of group managerial styles as they relate to programming.) Tele-Communications, Inc. (TCI), one of the three largest MSOs, has developed a national program package for its 450 systems; its Denver-based group headquarters supplies by satellite an identical package of advertiser-supported cable networks to most of its systems. In contrast, ATC, the second-largest cable MSO in numbers of subscribers, individualizes channel array on its more than 100 local systems.

Cable marketing and programming are intimately connected, and managerial structures in the large MSOs reflect this situation. Programmers must have the skills of a market researcher and a business negotiator to license programming at a financial advantage that will have long-term appeal for sufficient numbers of subscribers. Another aspect of the programmer's job is evaluating possible uses of new technologies and nonentertainment programming capabilities—such as data bases and computer services. Keeping one eye on the competition and another on new revenue sources is part of the current programming game.

PROGRAMMING A MULTICHANNEL SYSTEM

The tasks of evaluating, selecting and scheduling programs for cable and other multichannel nonbroadcast services reflect different legal, technical, economic and marketing conditions than those operating in traditional broadcasting. Although cable and broadcast television signals both require a wide band of frequencies, coaxial cable can handle many simultaneous video signals, each containing different programming, whereas broadcast television is limited to one channel. Cable's ability to carry many television signals is often called its **broadband** capacity. Cable's multichannel nature, the rapid growth in program-supply networks and the franchising of previously unwired, large markets, created cable programming problems in the 1980s.

The Problem of Evaluation

Audience evaluation is one of the cable industry's central problems. Inadequate viewing data especially hamper local cable systems and national advertiser-supported networks. Presumably, the national pay networks face cancelation if their services fail to meet audience expectations. Nonpay services, however, are generally packaged as part of a basic cable service along with retransmitted broadcast signals or **tiered** (marketed at a secondary pay level). Subscribers cannot decline any one of these services. The total number of a system's subscribers is always known, more or less accurately, but how many of them view nonpay cable channels cannot now be accurately measured on most systems.

National audience shares for basic cable networks (excluding the superstations and premium movie networks) rarely exceed 1 or 2 percent of television households at one time. Within most single markets, this percentage is a very small number of people—although in some mature cable markets, the combined audience for cable-only channels exceeds that of the broadcast channels, and when all viewers of repeat showings of a program are summed, that audience may exceed a broadcast station's audience. Cable viewing percentages really represent two audience measurements: One is of the audience watching television at a given time; the other is of the cumulative audience that watches a given program in all its showings. As of 1984, only 40 percent of the United States was wired for cable television. Comparing cable audience shares directly with broadcast television audience shares even in heavily cabled communities remains difficult because cable franchise areas differ in size and shape from markets defined by broadcast station coverage patterns (ADIs or DMAs).

As should now be apparent, most ratings data for cable and the other new technologies are shaky. Typically, early information had a small sampling base. For instance, because of high data-collection costs, early national Nielsen reports on cable used only 250 metered homes to measure 20 million households. Today, the percentage of cabled homes in Nielsen's 1,700 homes (the NTI sample) matches cable penetration nationally. And diarists report both cable and broadcast station viewing in the NSI and Arbitron local market surveys.

But the overriding problem in evaluating cable program audiences has been that cable audience data cannot be compared directly with broadcast audience data. This prevents advertising time buyers from estimating cable's effectiveness in comparison to broadcasting and other media. This lack of comparative data limits the amount of money advertisers are willing to risk on cable commercials; lack of reliable information on audience program preferences limits the capital that financial backers are willing to risk on cable programming; and a lack of information on audience viewing habits reduces much of the programming process to guesswork. Cable has been forced to develop criteria other than ratings for selecting and scheduling national and local services and for wooing advertisers.

The Problem of Churn

A second major problem for system programmers is audience turnover. Subscribers that disconnect, even if replaced by new subscribers, cost the system in hook-up time, record changes, equipment loss and duplicated marketing effort. Initial marketing campaigns usually achieve penetration levels of 55 percent or higher, except in metropolitan areas where penetration runs as low as 25 percent in the first wave. But as many as 30 percent of the initial subscribers may cancel service within the first six months. Turnover on pay channels averages 5 percent of pay subscribers *per month*. The industry refers to such changes in the number of subscribers as **churn**. The churn rate can be calculated for a year, or any length of time, by dividing the number of disconnections by the number of new connections. For example, a system having 200 disconnects while adding 300 new subscribers has a 67 percent churn rate. Usually, rates above 20 or 30 percent presage economic disaster. Not all cancelations can be prevented, of course; many occur because people move, children grow up and leave home, or because of economic recession, unemployment and the like. Whatever the cause, minimizing churn is one of the primary responsibilities a system's programming and marketing executives share.

Cable vs. Broadcasting

The programming problems of cablecasters differ from those of broadcasters. A broadcaster fills one channel all year around; a cablecaster must fill many channels—typically 24 or 36, but increasingly from 50 to 100 or more. A broadcaster purchases and schedules individual programs; only rarely do cablecasters buy or produce specific programs. Instead, they obtain licenses to retransmit whole networks of prearranged and prescheduled programming. A broadcaster with a network affiliation fills about 60 percent of the station's schedule with one network's programs. Except in the cases of multiple affiliates in very small markets, a broadcast station's promotion and advertising can be closely linked to its network's image. The cablecaster, on the other hand, is connected with several networks—perhaps 20 or more—while also retransmitting the signals of local and distant over-the-air broadcasters; its image comes from its total package of channels as well as its local origination programming, public relations, paid local advertising and promotion. Lastly, broadcast stations receive most of their income from spots sold within programs; cable systems are supported primarily by monthly fees paid by subscribers (with growing advertising support).

Other Multichannel Delivery Systems

Delivery systems such as SMATV, MDS and DBS share many programming strategies with cable because they all are multichannel services.

Satellite master antenna television systems (SMATVs) function exactly like small cable systems. Whereas cable systems normally serve wide geographic areas and rely on city franchises, SMATV systems usually serve private properties, typically single buildings or apartment complexes. SMATVs threaten competing cablecasters because they draw their revenues from only the most lucrative locations. This process is known as **cream skimming**.[3] Cable franchises generally require the wiring of low-income neighborhoods or areas with widely dispersed homes, as well as upscale and densely placed housing, which reduces a cable company's overall profitability. Like cable, SMATV has extended channel capacity and usually provides all the local over-the-air broadcast signals, one or more pay networks (such as HBO) and the most popular nonpay networks (often ESPN and CNN).

In 1983, licensees of multipoint distribution services (MDS), using short-range microwave to deliver television channels, received Federal Communications Commission approval to carry up to four programming channels. The National Association of Broadcasters has noted the technical feasibility of expanding the MDS transmission band to as many as 30 television channels, creating multichannel systems comparable to large cable systems.[4]

But the biggest challenge to cable is direct broadcasting from satellites (DBS). Two services began limited operation in the mid-1980s (with about five channels per system).[5] DBS may prove more practical and economical for large cities than cable. Consequently, the wiring of inner city franchises has been slowed to await DBS developments. Eventually, a hybrid of the two may emerge in the cities.

As they develop, the programming characteristics of all these multichannel services will be very much like those of cable systems. Indeed, many of their channels will be retransmissions or combinations of cable networks. Their problems will also be how many and which program networks to carry, how to schedule them, how to market channels, how to minimize churn and how to derive maximum income. These are the evaluation, selection and scheduling questions this chapter addresses. Though the rest of the chapter deals specifically with cable, it applies equally to other multichannel technologies.

Although advertising practices are changing and economic conditions will differ by 1990, for the 1980s the programming strategies of cable systems will continue to be determined by four elements: a system's *legal* responsibilities, its *technology*, the *economic* factors affecting program selection and local *mar-*

keting considerations. All constrain cable programming choices. All limit the system programmer's options because cable industry management makes decisions based on this entire complex of factors. For example, must-carries, addressability, tiering and advertiser appeal all affect the selection and structuring of program networks on a cable system. These are explained in the following sections.

LEGAL CARRIAGE REQUIREMENTS

Identifying the signals that must be placed on a system is the first step in cable programming. The first set of signals are the broadcast station signals the federal government requires the system to provide to all subscribers. A second set is made up of the channels or services stipulated in the local franchise contract. A third set of carriage restrictions may be imposed by the policies of the cable system's owner—generally a corporate MSO.

Must-Carries

Under FCC regulations, every cable system has a legally defined number of local over-the-air signals that must be placed on the system. These signals are the **must-carries**, defined as the "significantly viewed" broadcast stations.[6] They include all local network affiliates, any local independent stations and any local public stations requesting carriage. The number of must-carry affiliates alone ranges from one to a dozen or more because signals from several ADIs/DMAs may overlap a franchise. In some very large markets more than a dozen must-carries are mandated; in very isolated markets, as few as one or two are required. Indeed, Turner Broadcasting System has repeatedly proposed the elimination of all must-carry rules. In the view of cablecasters, the programming of their systems ought to be entirely under their own control.

The total of must-carries in the Los Angeles basin is currently 18, and on some 36-channel systems, must-carries fill half of all channels. The threat of new VHF drop-in broadcast stations leaves most Southern California cablecasters howling since they would be, under current regulations, additional must-carries.

In markets such as Los Angeles, disagreement between operators and lawmakers centers around forced, *redundant* carriage—multiple affiliates of the same commercial network and multiple public stations. Redundant carriage limits the cablecaster's options when a cable system with small channel capacity is located between two large broadcast markets and consequently has must-carries from both. Cable systems operating in the markets between Los Angeles and San Diego, for example, have three commercial affiliates, two independents and a public station from three cities to carry. In the view of one cablecaster, that means that twelve channels are taken up with four channels of programming (because the three sets of affiliates and three public stations repeat the same network programs).

This issue has merit on all sides. Certainly, carrying the local market affiliate is important to *supply local news and local advertising*; but carrying a major market affiliate of the same network will also provide a popular source of news and information that will *draw viewers.* Major market stations have higher budgets, greater technical expertise and larger professional staffs than smaller stations and as a result generally attract most viewers. In areas where a large market affiliate or public station has high visibility, the viewing of small-same-network stations will be minimal when both are available on the same cable system. It is just that small audience service, however, that many lawmakers see as the great social advantage cable has over broadcasting.

At the same time, local broadcasters want all cable systems operating in the same market to carry their stations so they can remain competitive. Without the requirement forcing cable systems to carry all local broadcast stations, cable operators could arbitrarily exclude their competition from easy access to cable viewers—since cable's very installation normally requires disconnecting over-the-air antennas, making broadcast-only reception more than a little inconvenient. The courts have not yet said whether a right to carriage exists, but the FCC established the regulations and has moved very slowly in reconsidering them. Congress may clarify the legal relationship between cable and over-the-air delivery in amendments to the Communications Act of 1934.

Franchise Requirements

Local franchise requirements often specify still more nonbroadcast signals that must be carried as well as access channels that must be provided. Local authorities may even specify that channels be set aside for leasing to local businesses or radio or public television broadcasters. These subjects are covered in Chapter 12. *Federal* regulations no longer require any local access or leased channels nor, of course, do they require a cable system to carry pay channels or superstations. If a franchise agreement specifies them, however, the cable programmer must place them on the system before calculating the number of premium and basic cable channels available.

MSO Policies

Parent corporations frequently impose restrictions on what their local systems can carry. The influence of group-ownership on programming was Klein's subject in Chapter 4. Some MSOs, for example, have policies prohibiting "adult" programming; others require one or more access channels—even when they are not legally stipulated in a franchise contract. One of the largest MSOs, Tele-Communications, Inc. (TCI), adopted standardized carriage on most optional channels throughout its systems in the mid-1980s. This practice obviously improves TCI's position when negotiating contracts with basic and premium networks. Basic networks that fail to be selected by one of the five largest MSOs (TCI, ATC, Group W, Cox and Warner Amex) are less likely to survive.

Many cable companies are owned by nonmedia corporations that emphasize bottom-line profits. When choices must be made between (a) access and specialized services for very small audiences or (b) channels likely to be widely popular, clearly the least profitable services will be cut. From the financial point of view, small audiences should be sacrificed for larger ones because popular programming generates more advertising revenues. Such MSO policies, then, limit the system programmer's options.

TECHNICAL CHARACTERISTICS
AFFECTING PROGRAMMING

A system's technical characteristics also limit the programmer's options. The number of channels a system can carry and the types of cables and converters—whether addressable, and if so, whether one-way or two-way—determine which services are appropriate and which cannot be used.

Channel Capacity

As of the mid-1980s, the average number of channels on cable systems nationwide fell between 24 and 36. Over one-third of the systems still had 12 or fewer channels. These systems are generally located in small towns having already high levels of cable penetration, reducing the economic potential from increasing the number of channels. Upgrading from 24 or more channels progressed slowly even in potentially lucrative markets, in part because of the high cost of capital in the recessionary period of the early 1980s. High interest rates and a shortage of conversion equipment, especially the newest addressable converters and the sophisticated computer software and hardware necessary to implement addressability, held down the rebuilding rate of established systems during the late 1970s and early 1980s.

Two other factors also affect the rate at which cable systems are rebuilt: local contract negotiations with power and telephone carriers and the availability of manpower for installation. The use of telephone poles and underground rights of way is generally shared with other utilities that seek to defend their market positions. Local telephone companies, beginning to view cable as a potential competitor for consumer and business services, are not always quick to respond in negotiations for pole and underground conduit arrangements. The other problem is that most cable installers are either free-lance or employed by a parent corporation (an MSO) and travel among many systems. A shortage of experienced installers exists, and new construction demands generally prevail over rebuilding needs.

The politically unstable relationship between antitrust law and exclusive franchising creates another restraint on system expansion. Cable operators have been reluctant to build high-capacity systems of 100 channels or more without legal assurance that cities will retain the exclusive franchise model or perpetuate **natural monopolies.** The alternative, **multiple franchising** (having more than one cable operator wire the same geographic area), raises the specter of unbalanced competition: Later entrants might build more economical systems offering cheaper services. Early entrants with many nonrevenue-producing features demanded by franchising agencies might be forced out of business.[7]

Additionally, cable equipment manufacturers want to avoid overbuilding their industry, which providing quick response to cablecasters' equipment orders would do. As more and more of the United States is progressively wired, it is not hard to foresee a decreased demand for multichannel conversion equipment. Pacing factory output is practical economics for cable equipment manufacturers. All these factors, then, affect the numbers of channels cablecasters can program on established systems.

All systems built after about 1975, however, have the technical capacity for 24 or more channels. In most midsized cities, systems have between 36 and 56 channels, and in major urban markets 60 to 80 channels are typical. Midband and superband converters permit even the smallest system to add four or more channels without totally rewiring the franchise.[8] On average, programming fills only about two-thirds of the channels on systems with 30 or more channels, the remainder being held in reserve.

In the late 1970s and early 1980s, tough competition for franchise contracts led cablecasters to make big promises, promises that technology and economic conditions cannot readily support. Local franchise boards, seeking the best possible service for their communities, demanded large channel-capacity systems and local origination and access channels (discussed in Chapter 12) without a clear view of what the public actually wanted or would be willing to pay for. Cablecasters promised the moon in some cases to impress local franchising officials and win contracts. In the late 1970s and early 1980s competing MSOs proposed increasing quantities of access, leased and basic channels, interactive services and local origination facilities. But by the mid-1980s, it was evident that the costs of installing cable in metropolitan areas would be much higher than bidders had anticipated, and that the public was sluggish in responding to "advantages" such as access opportunities, interactive channels and large numbers of viewing options.

An economic vise traps the winners of the urban franchises in markets such as New York, Philadelphia and Chicago. They are caught between their franchise promises and the unanticipated high costs of underground wiring in metropolitan areas. Several franchise contracts, however, permit a reduced commitment under adverse economic conditions such as existed in the early 1980s, leaving a question as to whether franchise winners will actually fulfill some of their pie-in-the-sky promises. The amendments to Mile High's franchise commitments in Denver in 1982 are a case in point.[9]

General economic conditions also affect new construction of large market and wealthy suburban cable systems. The total number of systems with more channels than available program networks has remained small. As of 1983, the National Cable Television Association (NCTA) reported channel distribution as follows:

	Number of Systems	Percentage of All Systems	Percentage of Subs
12 or fewer channels:	2,109	37.3	19.7
13 to 35 channels:	2,334	41.4	57.1
36 to 53 channels:	413	7.3	12.4
54 or more channels:	128	2.3	2.1
n/a:	665	11.8	8.7
	5,649	100.1*	100.0

*Discrepancy due to rounding.

Cable networks compete for positions on local cable systems (called **shelf space**). Because channel capacity is limited, only some of the more than 50 cable networks can occupy a channel on systems with fewer than 50 channels. Those networks with similar services vie directly for placement. Most systems would not want to carry all satellite-distributed programs services in any event since many charge the system a fee, and a single representative of the genre would probably satisfy viewers. For example, home-oriented channels such as MSN and SPN compete with each other for shelf space; religious networks such as CBN, PTL and TBN compete; and of course, premium movie networks compete to be the one (or two or five) selected for a system. Nearly all the advertiser-supported and premium cable networks aggressively market their networks to cable-system decision makers.

Addressability: The Systems

Technology defeats the practical limit of 12 broadband channels per coaxial cable in two ways: by installing individual converters in subscriber homes or by adding extra coaxial or fiber optical cables. Current models of converters add midband or superband frequencies to existing frequencies on small cable systems, and these sets of channels can be programmed as one or more pay tiers. When subscribers purchase *basic* cable service, consisting of the local over-the-air stations (must-carries) and a few other advertiser-supported cable networks, they can then choose to purchase one or more additional **tiers** (sets of channels priced as a unit, generally carrying advertising) and one or more **premium channels** (pay networks each priced individually). Choosing, and pricing, these three sets of channels becomes the cable programmer's challenge.

However, the more advanced addressable converters now radically alter cable programming strategies. *Addressability* refers to addressing homes individually with a subscriber-chosen package of programming (one-way); and in more advanced forms, also addressing the cable **headend** (technical headquarters for cable equipment) from individual homes with requests such as to view a pay-per-view program or vote on an interactive channel (two-way). Without addressability, all services, including premium channels, pass every home and are mechanically trapped from entering nonsubscribing homes. With addressability, headend computers direct different sets of channels to individual homes.

At present, *one-way* addressable technology provides strong advantages in accurate and low-cost hook-up (or cancelation) and billing service. One-way addressability keeps churn cost to a minimum by cutting out service calls for adding or changing service (there are no traps to install or remove).

Two-way addressability, also called **interactive cable**, refers to systems in which the subscriber can address the main system computer. The best known of the interactive systems was Warner Amex's Qube. Its technology permitted subscribers to respond to questions posed by live hosts, to shop at home by entering personal account numbers and to purchase pay-per-view programs by pushing buttons on a keypad. The Qube system was installed in Columbus (Ohio), Cincinnati, Pittsburgh, Dallas and other cities, but only experimentally copied by other cable operators. Because the cost of operation outweighed the financial return, in 1984 Warner Amex announced the end of interactive entertainment on the service, retaining only a series of pay-per-view channels.

Eventually, however, per-channel addressability will let subscribers everywhere choose all channels individually instead of purchasing pay channels by the tier. Some subscribers only want to pay for family-oriented channels; others prefer adult entertainment; some want Spanish-language content; others cultural or sports programming; but most subscribers want a customized mix of channels and services, and this facet of addressability will ultimately make the tiering concept obsolete. Being able to sell each subscriber a pattern of channels best suited to that household's desires gives enormous marketing leverage. During the 1980s, however, an educational process must occur: Subscribers must learn about their potential program choices. Only after the public is sufficiently informed to select among a wealth of programming and service options will individual addressability become widespread.

In addition to marketing considerations, addressability conversion is slow in existing systems because of unresolved questions of cost, equipment reliability and signal security.[10] An addressable system costs roughly twice as much as a nonaddressable one. For small and midsized systems with too few subscribers to support multiple pay tiers, adopting addressability means much red ink in the short-term picture. And in such systems, the cost of additional personnel to operate a central computer with complex software (requiring constant back-up and security) may exceed even addressability's long-term financial advantages.

Addressability: The Issues

Some systems with much churn among pay tiers find addressability practical now, however, because it keeps the cost of switching subscribers on and off very low. And addressability's hardware, software and personnel costs may be much reduced if the centralized distribution system TCI pioneered in 1983 proves practical. This plan concentrates the main computer, the experimental software and most of the personnel at the originating site, instead of scattering and duplicating them in each local system. Although TCI's efforts may solve addressability's technical and economic problems, some policy questions surface in exchange. For example, moving the source of programs to another state undermines local governmental control of affiliated cable systems. It also raises questions about the confidentiality of local subscriber records and the security of interactive uses of a system in the absence of federal regulation.

The primary reason for investing in addressable converters to date, however, is **pay-per-view** (PPV) programming. Although the cable industry has little experience with pay-per-view events, its economics appear so favorable to cable systems over the long haul that its potential has become the major selling point for manufacturers of two-way addressable equipment.[11] Consider a hypothetical $5 per-household-per-week for pay-per-view events. Such pricing could effectively *triple* monthly system revenues, not counting revenues from multiple tiers or premium channels. For example, if every household bought only *four* pay-per-view events a month, $20 PER SUBSCRIBER PER MONTH would be added to the approximately $10 that comes in as basic service revenue. In spite of programming and technology costs, pay-per-view looks like a gold mine.

Nonetheless, the installation rate of multistrand addressable cabling and the adoption of midband and superband converters to provide households with a minimum of addressability in small-capacity systems has been very slow, even on the part of the large systems and MSOs—partly because in the beginning equipment tended to break down and supply inaccurate billing records.

Another addressability issue is its lack of security. Devices inside homes are easily tampered with, defeated and stolen, reducing addressability's potential profit. Cox Cable shocked the industry at the 1983 Great Lakes Cable Conference by announcing the results of an audit of a newly installed addressable system: Nearly 90 percent of their converters showed signs of tampering; over half had been defeated. Nearly half of their subscribers were receiving free pay programming.

Estimates of homes illegally receiving basic cable or pay signals range as high as 20 percent in many franchises. This figure suggests one reason many marketing campaigns achieve less than anticipated levels of penetration is that many subscribers targeted for the marketing of additional services are already enjoying them.

The problem involves more than purposeful cheating, however. Subscribers often inadvertently take the converter box with them when they move. Moreover, viewers with more than one television set find the cost of two converters out of line with their expectations, leading to home rewiring, requiring in turn outside or pole-top converters (intended for telephone poles, but which may be located in apartment building basements). Another solution to casual theft or loss being tested in some markets is a converter deposit.[12] Some highly sophisticated systems can even detect illegal converters by remote control. Unreliable billing and service records further compound the problem of theft in many systems, and many MSOs have chosen upgradable one-way systems to minimize financial risk.

ECONOMIC FACTORS AFFECTING PROGRAMMING

The most powerful factor affecting carriage of most cable networks is their cost to the local system. Besides viewer popularity, cost is directly affected by whether the cable network is advertiser- or subscriber-supported and by the financial enticements competing networks offer.

Because of high start-up costs and the slow response of the advertising industry, most advertiser-supported networks find themselves forced to charge local systems a small per-subscriber fee to make up at least some of their advertising shortfall. In addition, the importation of distant independent signals has become an economic factor since the Copyright Royalty Tribunal raised fees for these signals. Sidney Pike in Chapter 13 provides details on copyright royalties for superstations. Spot time on advertiser-supported channels for the local system to sell (local avails) alters these economics, however. Additionally, a provision for print advertising and promotional support from the program supplier can offset per-subscriber fees. In other words, some fees paid to national cable program suppliers are, in effect, returned in the form of co-op advertising funds or prepaid ads in *TV Guide* and other publications benefitting the local system. A further factor that must be weighed in the economic balance is which satellite delivers a network's signal since not all systems have the equipment to obtain signals from all satellites. These factors are discussed in detail in the following paragraphs.

Rate Structures

From a local cable programmer's perspective, cable networks come in four varieties: those that are *free;* those the *subscriber pays for* individually (premium channels); those the system must *license* for a small monthly or annual per-subscriber fee (**minipays**); and those *paying the system* for being carried. (See Chapter 10 for details on basic cable network programming.)

Networks such as Satellite Program Network are advertiser supported; the local system receives them free of charge, although a contract must be signed generally specifying placement on the basic tier. Other networks, the premium channels, require subscribers to pay a monthly fee (typically ranging from $6 to $10 per month for movie services). A portion of that fee, negotiated by the cable system and typically around two-thirds, stays with the local system. For example, $6 of the approximately $10 that subscribers pay for HBO stays with the local system; only $4 goes to HBO per subscriber per month. The fact that a premium channel imposes no cost on the system while actually producing substantial revenue has placed premium services at the heart of cable economics.

In the third and most common option, the cable network charges the local system a fee per subscriber per month while usually also carrying advertising. Those systems carrying advertising typically make some spot time available for local sale as well. Cable News Network (CNN), Music Television (MTV), ESPN and USA Network fall in this category. Networks such as The Weather Channel come free when placed on the basic tier or when a system has a large number of subscribers, but otherwise charge the system a small monthly fee per subscriber. Other specialized channels such as the Reuters Financial Reports and C-SPAN (live coverage of Congress) also charge the cable system a license fee but do not have advertising. Since the per-subscriber charge is in cents-per-month, generally too small to bill individually, networks charging the cable operator for carriage are called minipays. Minipay channels are typically included in basic service or in a "bundled" upper tier for a lump monthly subscriber charge, although a few franchise contracts prohibit bundling of channels. Under most franchise contracts, the local system charges subscribers a monthly fee for basic service that reflects programming and administrative costs. Networks placed on an upper tier are grouped on the subscriber's monthly bill if the subscriber agrees to the additional service.

Religious channels typically come without charge and may come without explicit advertising, being supported by viewers' donations or the parent organization. Religious groups buying time from religious networks, in effect, use "program-length" advertising since the whole program advertises the church. The largest of the religious networks, CBN, also carries traditional spot advertising, however. Another type of no-cost programming is a barter network, operating like the barter programs discussed in Chapter 8 on independent stations. Syndicators offer marginal entertainment programming—that is less than top quality or newly introduced or frequently rerun—on a barter basis to cable systems. In this arrangement, most advertising spots are presold by the distributor, although a limited number of local availabilities are usually included as an enticement to carry the channel. The best known of these barter services is Modern Satellite Network (MSN), which carries only shopping or other information its advertisers supply.

In a few cases, financially powerful program distributors pay the local cable operator to carry their program channels at a rate determined by the number of subscribers. To compete with the well-established Cable News Network, for instance, ABC/Group W paid cable operators the equivalent of $1.50 per subscriber (one time only) to carry the newly introduced Satellite News Channel, and planned also to pay systems 10 cents per subscriber per year for ongoing carriage (see Chapter 10 for an analysis of the demise of Satellite News Channel). To get its Spanish language channel distributed SIN pays cable operators a small amount per month per Spanish-surname subscriber (rates vary with the quarter of the year).

Program content has no bearing on channel-pricing method—with the exception of the premium movie channels. (Their revenues must cover the fees for licensing first-run movies as discussed in Chapter 11.) Smaller than projected advertising revenues have forced nearly all basic cable networks into a similar economic pattern: They charge a fee, sell advertising, make local spots available and, if possible, provide promotional support. Those cable networks charging sizable per-subscriber fees face strong pressure to reduce or eliminate those fees when competition without fees surfaces. Cablecasters argue that all advertiser-supported networks will eventually have to eliminate fees to stay competitive. (The cable networks respond they will be happy to drop fees as soon as the ad revenues they need materialize.)

Spot Availabilities

The quantity of local availabilities (**avails**) is growing on advertiser-supported networks. That they offer local spots is a major bargaining point for the cable networks when renegotiating contracts with local systems. These spots are, for the most part, deducted from program time rather than network advertising time, so they cost the network little. There is, of course, a practical limit on how much a program can be shortened to allow for advertising. Moreover, infrequent interruption is one of the appeals of cable only programming to subscribers. Most advertiser-supported networks, in consequence, offer about two avails per hour and cluster all advertising spots in just a few program breaks.

Availabilities that cannot be sold, however, offer little advantage to a local system, although they can be used for system promotion. Unsold spots generally reflect a weak local sales staff and weak local economic conditions. In major markets, local spot-advertising sales appear to be a promising revenue source. **Interconnects** among several cable systems have been formed in major markets to increase audience size for cable only, regional advertising spots. Gill Cable in San Jose, California, spearheaded the first sizable interconnect. As of 1982, 32 cable systems throughout the San Francisco Bay Area had joined by microwave to carry local advertising on channels such as CNN, ESPN and MTV.[13] This interconnect means that the entire Bay Area cable audience becomes the base for ad rates for those systems. The total potential audience is then large enough to convince advertisers that a substantial number of viewers will watch their ads. Interconnects are becoming the standard pattern for metropolitan areas served by several cable systems.

Promotional Support

When cable programmers are deciding which networks to carry, they should consider how much promotional support a network provides. On-air promos and shared IDs as well as print advertising and merchandising are especially valuable to local systems. Promotion wins new subscribers, reduces churn and creates positive images in the minds of current and potential subscribers, local advertisers and government officials. Local systems can use on-air promotion, paid advertising and publicity (1) to convince the public their channel array is the best available and thereby reduce disconnects, (2) to inform viewers about the programs on the whole package of channels and (3) to identify themselves as the source of highly valued services—such as HBO. Cable networks can provide professional quality consumer marketing and sales materials, including on-air spots and IDs, door-hangers, subscriber information kits, direct mailers, bill stuffers, program guides and other merchandising, to assist low-budget local efforts. National networks can also encourage MSOs to customize promotion for each system by covering part of the cost.

Those national networks purchasing large amounts of national print and broadcast television advertising to promote themselves to consumers have an obvious advantage over their competitors. Many networks pay local systems either at sign-up time or annually for local joint promotion of the network and system. As of the mid-1980s, about half of nonpay cable networks provided start-up assistance, varying from 10 to 50 cents per subscriber; in some cases, the parties negotiate a lump sum. Both pay and basic networks are moving into cooperative advertising (**co-ops**) in which the network and system share the cost of print and radio promotion.

Larger pay cable networks also supply camera-ready materials to the local systems to use in local print promotion, a significant aid because most local systems lack art departments and must hire outside art or advertising firms for all their print advertising. Among the premium networks, Home Box Office (HBO) dominates in market position in part because it supplies far more on-air and print promotional aid than its main competitors, Showtime and The Movie Channel. When competition for an especially lucrative market heats up, the largest cable networks come up with financial incentives such as million-dollar promotional budgets to ensure carriage.

Satellite Placement

For cable, by far the most important of the domestic television satellites is Satcom 3R, which handles the signals of the strongest cable networks. Its immediate predecessor, Satcom I, became established as "the cable satellite" before other satellites began carrying cable television. Consequently, most receive-only dishes are aimed at Satcom 3R. As of 1984, four other satellites also carry cable programs: Satcom 4, Westar, Comstar 4 and Galaxy 1. Satcom 3R is the sole satellite whose signals are received by nearly all cable systems.[14]

Receiving signals from the other satellites usually requires another receiving dish because most dishes pick up only a tiny portion of the satellite orbital arc. Therefore, a cable system must purchase a second dish or a newly developed wide-reception dish or convert to a repositionable dish to pick signals off other satellites.

Program services using transponders on Satcom 3R are more widely carried than their less fortunate competitors, and they retain an advantage in contract negotiations with systems whose receiving dishes draw only from Satcom 3R. Poor satellite positioning (on Satcom 4, Westar 5, Comstar 4 or the recently launched Galaxy 1) initially slowed the nationwide distribution of many cable networks. Some anxious cable networks even subsidized local purchase of an additional dish. CBN, the religious network, supplied a large number of dishes without charge to cable systems with the proviso that CBN be carried. Another religious network, Trinity Broadcasting Network (TBN), the superstation WOR, and GalaVision, the Spanish-language premium network, have also made similar gifts.

The recent development of wide-angle receiving dishes, some capable of receiving transmissions from all 28° of the television satellite orbit, may eventually eliminate the need to purchase more than one earth station, backup units aside. However, as of the mid-1980s, wide-angle dishes capable of multiple-beam reception were not yet cost effective; it was still cheaper to install several standard angle-of-reception antennas. In any case, prices for all types of receiving dishes will probably fall dramatically in the next five years.

Present technical limitations prevent programmers from choosing just any network that might appeal to their audience. They have to weigh the cost of shifting satellites or adding a supplementary dish antenna. In effect, then, the large numbers of networks satellites carry are not equally available to cable programmers. The ones the "dominant" satellites transmit are the most likely to be carried, perpetuating the strong market position of those cable networks that started early and had solid financial backing.

Signal Importation Fees

The Copyright Act of 1976 originally specified such small royalty fees for the importation of distant independent signals that the payments had a negligible effect on programming decisions. The Act, however, contained the proviso that the Copyright Royalty Tribunal might alter the fee schedule if the FCC changed the carriage rules.[15] In 1982, the FCC altered the cable carriage rules, and the CRT raised the copyright fees substantially. Much wailing from the cable industry and much cheering from program producers and distributors (rights-holders) ensued. This subject is discussed in detail in Chapter 13 on superstations since the new fees most affected their carriage. For cable system programmers, the increase in copyright fees adds yet another cost consideration to the selection of some of the most popular program signals.

MARKETING CONSIDERATIONS

Cable programming seeks to attract and hold both the local audience and the local (or regional) advertiser. To achieve this goal, cable programmers must maximize new subscriptions and minimize disconnections. The nature of the local audience determines what programming has appeal. If sheer audience size justifies ad spot rates, then the exact audience demographics will determine whether and which advertisers will want to buy time—just as in broadcast television and radio.

Audience Composition

Research has established that, nationally, the cable audience has two persistent characteristics: It is younger and made up of larger families than the noncable audience. In particular markets, however, system subscribers may differ from the national norm. Data collected when subscribers are signed on and subsequent survey questionnaires included with monthly bills can provide insights into local subscriber psychographics, programming preferences and viewing habits.

In addition, field surveys can supply information on nonsubscribers that helps programmers design advertising to gain new subscribers. Sometimes local franchise authorities commission audience ascertainment research of value to system programmers. And research data may also indicate how to reduce audience churn—another reason to undertake it. The larger MSOs generally have research budgets; typically, they collect systemwide data to aid in marketing decisions and employ their own or outside research staffs to develop and interpret it.

Unfortunately, many small cable systems lack the trained staff to create and administer surveys and to interpret survey data. Some managers in fact prefer to make programming decisions on the basis of their personal experience and informal feedback, failing to see any great value in structured audience research. Thus, the opportunity for spotting unique local market characteristics is often lost or limited to "seat of the pants" audience judgments.

The demographic and psychographic composition of a cable coverage area plays a major role in selecting a channel mix. A young, upscale, urban community, for example, wants sophisticated movies of recent vintage, whereas communities consisting of large families prefer "G" and "PG" movies, children's channels and information on such topics as cooking, gardening and health. Rock music and cultural programming may seem appropriate for college towns; midwestern cities, having strong sports traditions, like all-sports channels. These stereotypical expectations are not always fulfilled, however, when actual subscribers are examined. Families, for instance, often want channel mixes to meet several needs.

The gap between what people say they will or will not pay for and what they actually buy creates considerable programming risk. Even the mere act of discovering what people *say they want* on cable has hazards. The difficulty occurs in composing questions of a hypothetical nature that seek to find out what someone "might do" under a variety of conditions. It is very human to say "no" to proposed services, the value of which is only dimly perceived when monthly fees are involved. Since cable franchise areas do not usually correspond to broadcast ADIs (or DMAs), broadcast ratings data fail to describe potential cable subscribers whose homes are passed. When funds for cable system audience analysis are absent, cablecasters fall back on informal feedback and personal experiences. These data can be misleading and basing program decisions on them risky. Interactive systems, however, can measure audience viewing patterns precisely—provided management budgets for the costs of analysis and interpretation.

Numbers of Channels

Another question both cable programmers and marketing executives must ask is how many channels is the right number. Some evidence suggests the mass audience is unprepared to deal with dozens of cable channels, at least as of the mid-1980s, and that one dozen might be sufficient to attract and hold subscribers—especially if one or two were changed periodically. Cable consultant Paul Bortz has suggested that four or five channels represents a better value for the price in consumers' minds.[16] Unlike broadcast network affiliates, cable affiliates can alter their affiliations among cable networks to always have a "new" service to market.

Gaining Lift

For newly built systems (**new-builds**), scheduling multiple pay channels is a widely adopted strategy. Marketing premium channels along with basic service typically encourages more people to subscribe than might if only basic service were offered, a phenomenon called **lift**. It also operates in established systems when pay channels are added on. HBO, as the best-known pay service, provides the most lift. Initially, lift may increase subscribership from 5 to 30 percent (estimates vary), and other marketing factors influence lift—timing, properly targeted appeals, promotion and other pay channels available. At some point, lift diminishes as systems add more and more pay services, leading to discounts for multiple pay subscriptions in one household, a recent marketing strategy.

Network Concept: Vertical vs. Broad Appeal

Debate persists in the cable industry over which of two network concepts is more likely to succeed: vertical programming (**narrowcasting**) or broad-based appeal. The clarity of a particular national cable network's concept has strategic value. Both subscribers and advertisers seem to feel more comfortable with sharply defined services; certainly, such services are easier to promote in on-air and print advertising and to market to potential advertisers. Defining *sharpness*, however, is more difficult than recognizing it, suggesting that a network lacking sharpness might also create a niche for itself by effective national promotion over a long time period. Nonetheless, some cable networks—Music Television (MTV), The Spanish International Network (SIN) and The Weather Channel, for example, have such clarity of concept; these embody vertical programming at its simplest.

The concept of vertical service has two elements—the *composition of the programming* and the demographically defined *target audience*. Vertical programming may be chosen from a restricted content pool or may represent a range of programming types and formats within one content area; it may appeal to the mass audience or only to a limited group of viewers (demographically or psychographically defined). For example, MTV combines both a restricted content range and narrowly defined appeal to teens and young adults. (**Slivercasting** is the term applied to single services targeted toward still more restricted groups of people—such as pork futures to commodity brokers or games to personal computer owners.) By way of contrast, SIN's content ranges from soaps to movies to newscasts, but it appeals only to Spanish-speaking people. The Weather Channel has a highly restricted content (format) but may be useful to all television viewers for a few minutes daily. The Cable Health Network exemplified a fourth variety of vertical programming. It drew from several formats and content areas, linking its programming to some aspect of human health—broadly conceived to include nutrition, safety, drugs, exercise, maternity, disease, emotional well-being and so on. It was thought this type of vertical service might appeal to everybody at one time or another. (Because of a lack of advertising support, however, Cable Health Network merged with Daytime in 1983 forming Lifetime, a less clear concept; see Chapter 10 for more details.)

It is equally clear that USA Network and WTBS-TV possess broad-based appeal similar to that of the three broadcast networks and that they target the mass audience. USA's longevity and extensive promotional campaigns have given it a sports image in the minds of consumers enabling it to compete with ESPN and WTBS. At the same time, it competes with the national broadcast networks as well as basic cable and premium networks for the daytime soap opera and health audiences, and at night for the movie audience. In other words, USA Network *dayparts* like most broadcast television networks and stations. Superstations such as WTBS create broad demographic appeal by scheduling live sports, off-network reruns and older movies. These cable networks seek the mass audience.

Network concept becomes, then, one more element in the programming mix. The local programmer must gamble that the cable network selected for a system will (1) survive to provide programming for a reasonable length of time and (2) project a clear image to subscribers and advertisers.

Advertiser Appeal

Some channels interest specific types of advertisers. ESPN, the sports channel, an obvious case in point, strongly appeals to the male, beer-drinking, sports-loving audience. That appeal pinpoints a group of products that can be effectively advertised. Similarly, Cable Health Network appealed to manufacturers of patent medicines and exercise equipment. Obviously, mass-appeal cable networks are appropriate places for advertising many consumer products—although their relatively small audiences, in comparison to broadcast networks, reduce their value. Local cable programmers must choose a service that draws the right demographics for *local* advertisers to foster the sale of local avails. This consideration is especially important in small markets with few potential cable advertisers.

Overmarketing

As with the credit card industry, one influence on marketing strategy is the degree to which subscribers have overextended themselves, committing to larger monthly fees than they can afford. On the more sophisticated systems, many subscribers make total monthly commitments of $50, $75 or even $100 at the sign-up stage. When an appealing array of services is initially available or exciting new services are added to an established system, many subscribers overcommit themselves, resulting in nonpayment, late payments or disconnects. To mitigate overmarketing, cable systems set up alternate payment plans to aid indebted subscribers, who must then cut back on total services. Educating subscribers to budget more money for cable service is the long-term solution. In the short run, holding back some channels until subscribers gradually adjust to increased cable bills prevents overmarketing.

SELECTION STRATEGIES FOR SYSTEMS

Designing a system typically involves five steps, in this order: (1) assigning channels for the must-carries, (2) assigning space to local origination channels the franchise requires or the MSO desires, (3) selecting premium networks, (4) selecting distant independent station signals and (5) selecting a composite of nonpay networks to fill out the system. Systems with two-way addressability (interactive capability) can place highly specialized channels in the schedule including pay-per-view, and very large systems with excess capacity may reserve some channels for lease and pace the introduction of upper tiers of service.

The options open to a cablecaster after placing the must-carries depends on the system size. Systems with only 24 channels typically find 8 or more channels immediately filled with must-carries. Franchise agreements or MSO policy may also specify one or more access or local production channels. For marketing and economic reasons (to create lift and gain revenue), operators typically schedule from two to five premium channels. Generally, a superstation fills at least one channel because of the attractiveness of its movies and sports. If the system carries a program guide channel, about half of the 24 channels remain open. Ideally, the demographic and psychographic composition of the local audience determines what goes on them, but in practice the choice is often guided by whatever provides immediate economic advantage.

Programming Source Options

About 50 national networks supply most of the programming designed explicitly for cable (cable only programming). They package entire channels for delivery by satellite relay. A dozen of these are premium networks, and the remaining 40 or so are basic cable networks. Some are hybrid broadcast and cable services such as SIN and the superstations. As of 1984, broadcast network affiliates held on to nearly 80 percent of all viewing while the premium movie channels, superstations, local independents and public stations shared the remaining 20 percent with a few of the basic cable networks. Local origination, leased and access channels taken together represent only a fraction of 1 percent of cable viewing—by the most generous estimates.

For most of a system's channels, the cablecaster functions like a common carrier. The system supplies the technical means for delivering a signal originated by a broadcast station, a national cable network or, less frequently, by local producers. Programming, then, for a cablecaster, means selecting among the available sources to meet system goals. Franchise contracts and federal regulations predetermine much of what must be carried; the number of available channels in a system cannot easily be altered; and economic and marketing realities limit creativity in programming the rest. The cable programmer's decisions are therefore made within a tight matrix.

Channel Balance

The need to balance the content of channels further limits the cable programmer's choices. Although cable networks such as The Playboy Channel and The Pleasure Channel currently limit themselves to soft-core sexual entertainments rather than explicit sexual depictions, they generate protest in some communities. Movies on the popular pay services such as HBO and Showtime rated R because of excessive violence or profane language attract millions of viewers. The presence of such networks or films on local cable systems often generates vocal public disapproval despite large subscriber lists. In 1983, for example, Warner Amex was sued for carrying R-rated material on The Playboy Channel and settled out of court. A number of court decisions in the early 1980s, however, have supported the cable operator's legal right to show sexual (but not obscene) material. The political contest of franchise renewal is another matter. Public pressure from church groups and conservative organizations contrasts with numerous surveys finding adult programming to be one of the most desired of cable services, even in the most conservative of small towns.[17]

Except in the very largest metropolitan markets, then, achieving a balance between family-oriented and controversial material is an important consideration for local operators. One way to *balance* a system is to avoid or bury controversial program content and create an overall image of responsible community service. Consumer promotional materials, for example, can stress the family-content channels, even though the system in fact contains adult programming on other channels. Rock music channels such as MTV generate criticism in some communities; sexually oriented channels such as The Playboy Channel arouse even greater uproar. To protect themselves and still carry highly desired programs most cable systems **piggyback** cultural or religious programming with adult fare in marketing campaigns. For example, the cultural network, Bravo, is often marketed with Playboy to forestall community criticism. Another protective strategy is to place all R-rated and adult content on pay channels, keeping basic cable essentially family oriented. This strategy makes good economic as well as political sense because so many people are willing to pay extra for adult fare.

Piggybacking, Cherrypicking and Flow

Part-time cable networks also complicate the job of local system programmers. Several services program only in the evenings or portions of the day and may share a satellite transponder *(satellite piggybacking)* because transponders are both expensive and relatively scarce. Other part-time services may be delivered by microwave or originate locally. All part-time cable networks must be matched with time-complementing services *(channel piggybacking)* to keep cable channels continuously programmed.

Cautious financial backers generally advise people planning new cable services to start with part-time rather than 18- or 24-hour schedules. But following this advice may be self-defeating. It violates the principle of continuousness, canceling out the benefits of ready audience accessibility—important in encouraging viewer sampling of any new service. It also makes the network difficult to promote and lends itself to delivery problems.

One way around this dilemma is for the programmer to match part-time services for *content flow* so that subscribers perceive the pairing of two or more services as a natural unit. Many part-time cable networks, however, are stacked without regard for marketing effectiveness. Piggybacking a cultural channel (ARTS, for example) in the evenings on top of a children's network (Nickelodeon) or a soap-opera-type daytime service interrupts audience flow and, more important for cable, makes the two services difficult for subscribers to remember. The channel they occupy will lack *position* in the minds of many subscribers.

Piggybacking may also create engineering problems. Daily technical adjustments (for which cable systems generally lack staff) are needed when programmers pair networks appearing on different transponders. Signals coming from different satellites require an even more delicate engineering approach. Engineering inconvenience frequently causes local systems to steer away from part-time networks.

One way of creating a coherent audience identity for a channel is to cherrypick programs. Selecting individual programs from an array of cable networks and syndicators and assembling them on a single channel is called **cherrypicking**, an increasingly common practice. It is used in constructing local origination channels, as discussed in Chapter 12. Some religious and sports networks encourage cherrypicking as a way of increasing the audiences for their most popular programs. Other cable networks and broadcast stations see it as a way to gain larger audiences for advertisers and to acquire visibility as program suppliers. Those programs commonly picked up by many cable systems become vehicles for promoting the originating cable or broadcast service. And, of course, higher rates can be charged for spots in programs with larger audiences. Like piggybacking signals from different sources, cherrypicking requires engineering support.

Four Selection Principles

In sum, four principles operate in the programming selection process for local cable systems: (1) *meet the contract*, (2) *match the system*, (3) *maximize the return* and (4) *maximize audience and advertiser appeal*. These four rules encapsulate the legal, technical, economic and marketing considerations that cable programmers must weigh. When they are in conflict, legal and technical factors override. The weight of various economic factors depends in large measure on the degree of profit orientation of the system owner. Some MSOs greatly exceed others in their public commitment to local service, for example.

To define these four principles, then: *meeting the contract* refers to both federally imposed signal carriage requirements and franchise-imposed requirements such as providing access channels. *Matching the system* refers to engineering considerations such as channel capacity, addressability, satellite placement and hours programmed by part-time services. *Maximizing the return* means getting the greatest possible profit from the system while operating in accordance with the other three principles. The most difficult principle to define and implement is *maximizing the audience and advertiser appeal*. Programmers must estimate appeals before signing service contracts, and pilot tryouts are usually not an option.

Marketing considerations, therefore, become the programmer's primary concern—the area for creative imagination and insight. In the absence of hard data on audience program preferences and on its willingness to pay for cable services, local audience and advertiser characteristics are crucial factors in selecting which cable networks to place on a system and how to arrange them. Subjective analyses of network appeals and clarity of network conception become the tools of the perceptive system programmer. The following chapter assesses the predominant appeals of the basic cable networks.

SCHEDULING STRATEGIES FOR SYSTEMS

Scheduling local cable systems means more than placing programs in an orderly flow. (Chapter 12 covers the scheduling of locally originating programs.) Scheduling also means the strategies for placing whole *channels* on systems. It refers to the line-up of networks on the channels of dials (or keypads). How to switch from one network to another without irritating subscribers is a related topic. Both these activities must be considered in strategies to reduce subscriber churn, a primary goal of cable programmers.

Dial Placement

Cable operators normally place local VHF over-the-air signals on the same channels they broadcast on (e.g., Channel 4 on cable channel 4). A distant broadcast signal is not always so lucky since its number may be occupied by a local station. This switch frequently happens to superstation WGN licensed as Channel 9 in Chicago. Signals originating as UHF stations, whether local or distant, tend to be relocated on one-digit channels if space is available and if the system has relatively few channels (fewer than fourteen or so). Cable-only networks, both basic and premium, appear in a variety of positions on cable systems across the nation.

The primary constraint on dial placement is simply the number of channels a system has. Until the number exceeds a dozen, dial position is largely irrelevant—except as a benefit or irritant to over-the-air broadcasters who then must promote one or several channel numbers. With more than a dozen channels, however, subscribers become increasingly vague about the location of all except their favorite channels—generally the ones "most often viewed in the past." When systems have 20 or 60 or more channels, national research shows subscribers viewing, on average, about 10 channels. Even so, with effective dial placement strategies, systems can markedly increase the number of channels viewed in long stretches and the number regularly sampled.

The most successful systems encourage viewer sampling and user satisfaction by grouping their networks and signals on the subscriber's dial (or channel list) in meaningful sets through *content clustering* and *promotional packaging*. Content clustering is placing similar networks adjacent to each other on the dial whether on basic or an upper tier, making a set that is easy to promote and easy for subscribers to remember. (Chapter 10 groups basic cable networks into ten classes or categories linked by common subject matter.) Except in the very largest metropolitan systems, few cable operators carry networks falling in more than seven or eight of these classes. Over-the-air local signals, superstations and other distant independents, premium networks and local origination channels comprise added categories. Most cable systems will have fewer than a half-dozen networks or signals *within* each of these classes—except in the case of broadcast must-carries in a few between-market locations.

As an example of content clustering, a 36-channel system might place all local over-the-air signals on channels 2 to 9, if possible. Channels 10 to 19 could then be used to group a second set of services—often the movie channels on 10 to 15—with the balance as an extended basic group. This extended group can be made up of ESPN and the superstations, de facto lumping sports together and placing them next to movies. In this example, the "twenties," channels 20 to 29, can be marketed as a separate upper tier of family entertainment, and the channels from 30 to 36 packaged as an additional group, perhaps as a business or news group.

What defeats this easy subscriber-oriented logic is short-term marketing strategy. Subscribers buy additional tiers only if something on a tier strongly appeals to one or more members of a household. Therefore, systems mix networks to create a tier with varied appeals, and then place second tier networks adjacent to each other on channel lists (or dials) and third tier networks adjacent and so on. The marketing problem lies in conceiving of tiers as sequenced rather than concurrent buys, a result of historical evolution of systems rather than long-term planning. A related scheduling problem lies in using adjacent rather than scattered elements to create a tier. This practice has a technological rather than a marketing base. When established systems add midband converters, for example, they add a set of two or four channels, which tend to be filled with a mix of channels bearing no relationship to the structure of the rest of the dial placement.

Arranging channels to satisfy the home subscriber who buys all offerings ought to be the goal. A sophisticated strategy takes advantage of both the marketer's and subscriber's needs and creates tiers of networks out of sets of networks that are scattered across a signal range. That way, once a subscriber has signed up for multitier service, all of the holes in the sequence of channel numbers are filled in, and filled in to create easy to remember content groupings. For example, if channels 20 to 29 contain women's programming and channels 30 to 36 contain news services, they naturally fall into two tiers of alternate channels with broad appeal. At the same time, *where* the channels are becomes relatively easy to remember, generating greater subscriber *use*.

The second element in dial placement is promotional packaging. Placing networks in content sets lends to effective audience and advertiser promotion.

Sets of channels then can be grouped in customized cable program guides—which become increasingly unwieldy as the number of system channels increases. (See Chapter 10 for more detail on guides.) Content clusters indicate similar target audiences; creating sequences of content-related networks in turn fosters easy sales promotion to advertisers—with the goal of selling a package of spots spread across those demographically related channels.

The Art of Switchouts

Cable programmers sometimes find it necessary to change from one cable network to another. An important marketing problem, with possible policy implications, occurs when **switchouts** are from one premium service to another. The largest switchout to date occurred in the early 1980s when Times Mirror, Cox and Storer removed HBO and Showtime networks in favor of their jointly owned Spotlight movie service. Hundreds of thousands of their subscribers were affected.[18] Such a switchout has antitrust implications that have not been addressed in federal cable regulation and raises questions about unfair competition. Switchouts have also occurred among basic cable networks, the largest of which occurred when Group W and ABC introduced the Satellite News Channel (SNC), knocking Cable News Network (CNN) off hundreds of systems. (Later, both Spotlight and SNC were themselves switched out.) Numerous unplanned switchouts also were forced when CBS Cable and The Entertainment Channel failed in the early 1980s.

Converting subscribers from an old service to a new one requires careful timing and promotion. A successful switchout strategy will not eliminate subscriber complaints, but it can reduce disconnects. The first strategic consideration is timing. Switchouts create maximum subscriber resistance when some big event is scheduled on the disappearing network. A switchout during the middle-of-the-month during nonratings periods best serves the cable system dropping well-known networks. Choosing a time when no blockbuster movies or important sporting events are scheduled and allowing viewers to sample replacement channels make an effective strategy. A second element in timing is the length of notice given subscribers. Very short notice, as little as one or two weeks, minimizes viewer complaints. What is simultaneously required is extensive advertising and subscriber promotion during those and subsequent weeks. Direct subscriber mailings and on-air and print promotion will inform and soothe subscribers at switchout. The obvious strategy is to advertise the benefits of the incoming service.

Switchouts can be turned from negative to positive events if they coincide with lagging subscriber interest in a cable network. When called **switch-ins** and conceived as a marketing inspiration to stimulate interest among current subscribers, they can reduce churn and attract new subscribers. Such a strategy, however, requires careful tracking of audience tuning behavior on a monthly basis to isolate weaker networks and time their demise. Most cable systems lack the technical equipment to monitor daily tuning, and some having the data fail to budget for interpreting it. Eventually, switch-ins will become a standard programming strategy for cable systems—just as they presently characterize consumer product marketing in everything from toothpaste to cars.

PAY-PER-VIEW PROGRAMMING

Pay-per-view (**PPV**) would seem to have enormous revenue potential for cable systems (recall the earlier discussion on addressability). If 50 million homes (more than half of U.S. homes) were wired for cable, and all of those were addressable, and if 10 percent of them were willing to pay $10 to see a major movie on the same evening, revenues for that one program on one evening would be $50 million. By contrast, very few theatrical feature films gross that much in a month.[19] Such numbers enthrall much of the cable and the Hollywood production industries. Which of the two would acquire most of that hypothetical revenue is an open question, however, since it necessarily awaits the wiring of millions of homes. As of 1984, about 3 million homes could receive PPV. The earliest PPV events were delivered to most of these homes by STV stations and a very few cable systems, so estimates of what cable could do are just guesses. For some offerings, penetration of PPV homes ran up to 30 percent (as high as 50 percent for the Cooney–Holmes heavyweight boxing match), and cable is increasing its share of the PPV sales. Producers and distributors continue to experiment to find the programming content that will have maximum appeal to PPV audiences.

Two conflicting concepts of the ideal content for pay-per-view programming exist. The blockbuster boxing events that have demonstrated PPV's enormous earnings potential to date reflect the most common view: Program *out-of-the-ordinary events* that generate immense audience excitement. The Cooney–Holmes prize fight was clearly such an event—although it took an unexpected post-ponement (due to an injury) to generate the kind of national superexcitement the fight's promoters and cable operators had hoped for. Along with outstanding sporting events, superstar concerts are considered appropriate material for PPV. Concerts by The Rolling Stones and The Who were moderately successful as PPV events in 1983. Unfortunately for PPV operators, there are probably only four or five events a year of national blockbuster stature.[20] Two other efforts in 1983, a Broadway play, *Sophisticated Ladies,* and a musical movie, *The Pirates of Penzance,* drew small audiences well below programmers' expectations. Cable operators also complain that program suppliers seek too large a proportion of revenues during the developmental stages—as much as half the subscriber gross for some events.

The opposing PPV programming concept is that PPV events should be self-promoting; otherwise, the cable rights cost too much. In this view, the key to long-term PPV success is determining a reasonable cost per subscriber for program promotion, which can be achieved only by moving to *regularly scheduled PPV events.* Proponents of this vision of PPV see addressability as the means for reaching small, targeted audiences on a regular basis with highly specialized programming (e.g., first-run films with narrow appeal, possibly opera or, perhaps, pornography). When such programming is offered as a series, once or twice a week in the evenings at a predetermined hour, the promotional and advertising costs can be absorbed and steady profits realized over a long time period. Both Gill Cable and Warner Amex cable systems are testing this concept on several PPV channels, using first-run theatrical movies and sporting events.

One key to PPV subscriber penetration appears to be customized weekly or bimonthly cable program guides that heavily promote PPV events. Another key appears to be very precise calculation of the time period in which subscribers will perceive a movie as "worth paying extra for." Group W Cable research suggests that movies should appear on PPV two or three months after theatrical release, allowing time for the growth of public awareness from advertising and word-of-mouth promotion; at the same time, industry practice is that movies appear on PPV at least nine months prior to appearing on a premium network (premium window). Finding answers to the programming questions raised by PPV will be a major industry concern in the late 1980s.

THE FUTURE OF MULTICHANNEL PROGRAMMING

The operant strategy for cable programmers in the 1980s is survival. For most of the basic networks for years to come, the costs of producing and distributing programs will far outweigh expected advertising revenue. The amount of capital behind those basic networks having inadequate numbers of cable affiliates will determine the survivors. Those basic networks reaching more than 10 million homes as of the mid-1980s may eventually become financially successful. For competing premium movie networks, money spent on national and local promotional/advertising support and the availability of marketable program product are likely to determine the winners. Economic benefit to cable systems, perceived value to viewers and, in the case of advertiser-supported networks, appeal to national and local advertisers are also considerations in determining the future of multichannel programming.

Most basic networks that carry advertising will discontinue minipay charges to local cable systems as they become profitable because the large cable MSOs will refuse to subsidize profit-making program suppliers. It is likely that the industry as a whole will continue to provide financial support for new basic services during their start-up periods and for unusual public services such as C-SPAN.

The industry must soon deal with other programming problems. Too many similar services are available (or proposed), and many are only part-time. Many advertiser-supported services are threatened with extinction as a result of slow system acceptance and a slowly recovering national economy. The economic power of the largest multiple system owners will probably become the overriding factor in winnowing the basic cable networks and influencing the character of cable programming. The largest systems can demand quantity discounts from producers because they can place the same programming on hundreds of systems.

At the same time, these systems owners will be seeking program content that draws the largest possible audiences irrespective of local audience ethnic composition and the system's geographic location. This programming approach places pressure on producers and writers to come up with bland, mass audience programming—suitable for all markets—resembling the content of national broadcast television. The trend toward specialization in cable programming is heavily countered by a pressure for mass appeal programming from the very largest multiple system owners.

From the perspective of the local system, the fierce competition among the program services means an active marketplace in which building a positive system image is difficult, lift is minimal, and churn is high. Turnover among pay channels will persist, and local systems must, in consequence, move toward addressability and improved system promotion. Customized promotion of basic service through program guides, consumer merchandising, on-air contests and image promotion and external advertising are survival tools in the multipay (and multibasic) environment.

The cable programmer operates in a matrix of constraints, the strength of many unknown. Estimating the rate of return on services is highly uncertain. Yet the programmer must choose among "cheap" alternatives that might pay off in "big" dividends and among competitive services that might return greater profits than projected. If Showtime's exclusive specials and first-run series should achieve extraordinary popularity, then the programmer selecting Showtime over other options has a winner. But the odds on picking services that will develop unusually widespread followings are poor. Selecting the next MTV is a significant challenge for cable system programmers.

As the cable subscriber base levels off in the coming decade, following completion of the wiring of the major metropolitan markets, cable operators will begin altering their array of pay channels on an irregular basis as a marketing strategy, hoping to lure new viewers with new offerings. Although operator-instigated churn will damage national advertising and promotional campaigns, it will become a fact of life to be faced in a stable cable universe. The program suppliers should respond to this development by offering even stronger schedules of original programming and much more pay-per-view programming. One strategy that some pay services will inevitably adopt with strong financial backing is loan support to cable systems to speed the introduction of reliable addressable technology, bringing nearer the day when pay-per-view programming can reach most cable households.

And on the horizon lies a profusion of interactive shopping, banking, security, computer data base and yet-to-be-named services that may provide economic underpinnings for cable systems in the 1990s and beyond. For the 1980s, information and entertainment networks will dominate cable programming. Basic cable will reflect a pluralistic, mass audience while premium channels will target those upper-income families willing to pay for specialized programming. Although much cable programming copies that of broadcasting, unique programming forms will increase in the 1980s. Popular new ideas will then be recycled to feed the endless programming appetite of the established broadcasting and cable networks.

SUMMARY

The multichannel natures of cable, SMATV, MDS and DBS services are central to their programming strategies, but the cable industry faces severe audience measurement and churn problems. After placing the federally mandated must-carries and franchise- or MSO-required stations and services on a system, the job of the programmer is to select among the more than 50 premium and basic cable networks to fill all or most of the system's channels. Two technical factors constrain the programmer's choices: channel capacity and the presence or absence of addressability. A very large number of economic considerations also affect the selection process, chiefly the four different program cost patterns that exist: premium pay, minipay by the system, free or barter and pay-to-the-system. When the system's cost for basic networks is high, selling spot availabilities can produce additional local revenue and offset costs. Promotional support from the cable network also reduces costs and churn, but satellite placement and signal importation fees must be paid. Then there are marketing considerations such as the composition of the local audience, means of gaining lift among new subscribers, vertical vs. broad audience, advertiser appeal and overmarketing. The key to cable programming, from the system operator's perspective, is selecting among the available cable networks and over-the-air signals to design a package that meets federal and franchise regulations as well as special local marketing needs, and that is balanced in its appeal to subscribers and advertisers and is economically practical for the operator. Scheduling the selected channels on a cable system to maximize sampling and minimize churn involves strategies for dial placement and reducing negative audience reactions to switchouts. Whether the blockbuster or regularly scheduled concept of pay-per-view programming will dominate in the coming decade is an interesting unknown. For the 1980s, cable systems will be programming for multiple audiences in a multipay and multibasic environment in which sets of networks war for shelf space on local cable systems.

Notes

[1] Alan Radding, "Who Is the Cable System Program Director and What Does He *Really Do?" Cable Marketing,* March 1982, p. 31.

[2] The former may be an underestimate since the survey underrepresents small independent systems. "Cable Marketing Survey: Not Many Full Time Program Directors But Their Value to the Management Team Increases," *Cable Marketing,* March 1982, pp. 14–17.

[3] Four basic modes of receiving television coexist: (1) conventional broadcast systems consist of stations transmitting signals through the air received directly by home television sets; (2) cable systems use special antennas to receive satellite signals and over-the-air signals and then retransmit them to homes via coaxial cable mounted on telephone poles or buried under streets; (3) SMATV systems receive satellite signals by means of ground or rooftop satellite dishes and deliver signals by wire to points within a building; and (4) DBS is a version requiring no stations or intermediate companies; the household receives signals through its own satellite dish and decoder. MDS is a modification of SMATV in which the received signals are retransmitted by microwave relay, picked up by a local receiving dish and then delivered to receivers by wire.

[4] Peter Frank and John Schackelford, *Business Opportunities For Broadcasters In MDS Pay Television,* Com/Tech Report, Vol. 1, No. 2 (Washington, D.C.: National Association of Broadcasters, August 1982), p. 7.

[5] Marsha DeSonne, *New Technologies Affecting Radio & Television Broadcasting* (Washington, D.C.: National Association of Broadcasters, November 1981), pp. 17–19; see also *Countdown: Direct-to-Home Satellite Broadcasting in the Eighties* (Washington, D.C.: *Television Digest,* 1982).

[6] Mel Friedman, "How Many Must-Carries Must a Cable System Carry?" *View,* August 1982, pp. 38–41. The FCC defines "significantly viewed" as an affiliate receiv-

ing at least a 3 percent audience share and a net weekly circulation of at least 25 percent; independents need only a share of 2 percent and circulation of 5 percent to become "significantly viewed" and therefore a "must-carry." See *Cable Television Report and Order,* 36 FCC 2d 143, 24 RR 2d 1501 (1972). Also see FCC, Sec. 76.51, 76.54, 76.57, 76.59, 76.61 and 76.63.

[7]"Cable: Coming to Terms with Adulthood," *Broadcasting,* 3 January 1983, p. 74. Fewer than a half dozen franchises have actually been wired by more than one cable company.

[8]Converters electronically shift special cable channels located on the frequencies between VHF channels 6 and 7 (midband) and above channel 13 (superband) to unused VHF channels on the home television set. Block converters allow a different set of channels (than those normally appearing in those positions) to appear on channels 7 through 13; tunable converters shift tuning from the set dial to a new dial or keypad capable of tuning large numbers of channels. See Thomas F. Baldwin and D. Stevens McVoy, "Home Drop," in *Cable Communication* (Englewood Cliffs, New Jersey: Prentice-Hall, Inc., 1983) for more technical details.

[9]"Denver OKs Franchise Amendments," *Multichannel News,* 7 February 1983, p. 1.

[10]"Addressable Converters: Competition Heats Up for Lucrative Market," *Cable Marketing,* August 1982, pp. 31–35ff. As of 1983 addressable converters range in price from $90 to $125 per unit.

[11]A skeptical point of view suggests that program producers may demand so much for their product that the cable operator will be left in an economically untenable position after the large investment that addressability demands.

[12]Alan Radding, "The Great Converter Debate," *Cable Marketing,* October 1981, p. 6. See also Ellis Simon, "Addressability: Cable's Newest Frontier, The Computer Connection," *Cable Marketing,* 1 August 1982, p. 19ff.

[13]Interconnects vary between "hard" ones that are physically joined and "soft" ones in which an advertising representative is shared but with no electrical connection. "Cable Interconnects: Making Big Ones Out of Little Ones," *Broadcasting,* 1 March 1982, pp. 59–61.

[14]*The Home Video & Cable Yearbook, 1982–83* (White Plains: Knowledge Industries Publications, Inc., 1983), pp. 89–98.

[15]The basic formula was set by Congress and cannot be altered by the Tribunal. "Copyright Royalty Tribunal—Reimposes Distant Signal Rules," *CATA Cable Newsletter,* November 1982, p. 1.

[16]Jack T. Pottle and Paul I. Bortz, with the firm of Browne, Bortz and Coddington. *Cable and Its Competitors: An Analysis of Services, Economics and Subscribership; The Impact of Competitive Distribution Technologies on Cable Television* (Washington, D.C.: National Cable Television Association, March 1982).

[17]Michael O. Wirth, Thomas F. Baldwin and Jayne Zenaty, *Consumer Demand for Sex-Oriented Pay Cable Programming,* 25 April 1983; see also Albert R. Tims, *Community Attitudes and Preferences Concerning Cable Television Program Services: A Survey of Cable Television Subscribers in Bloomington,* Bloomington Telecommunications Council and Horizon TeleCommunications, Inc., February 1982.

[18]J. A. Trachtenberg, "Switchouts Without Switchoffs," *View,* November 1982, pp. 89–91.

[19]Susan Paul, "Marketing Pay-Per-View: A Key to Addressability's Success," *Cable Marketing,* August 1982, pp. 26–28ff. See also Savannah Warning Walker, "Pay-Per-View: Opening Nights at Home," *Channels,* November/December 1982, p. 38.

[20]Seth Goldstein, "Pay Per View in Retrospect: An Apparent Underachiever," *View*, April 1983, pp. 29–34.

Selected Sources

Baldwin, Thomas F. and McVoy, D. Stevens. "Home Drop," "Satellite-Delivered Programming and Cable Radio," "Audiences and Programming" and "Marketing and Advertising." In *Cable Communication*. Englewood Cliffs, New Jersey: Prentice-Hall, Inc., 1983.

Cable Age, biweekly trade magazine of the cable advertising industry.

Cable Marketing, monthly cable industry trade magazine focusing on marketing cable television.

CableVision, monthly cable industry programming magazine; includes monthly status report on the number of cable subscribers, the scheduling of feature films, top MSOs and top cable systems.

Kaatz, Ronald B. *Cable: An Advertiser's Guide to the New Electronic Media*. Chicago: Crain Books, 1982.

Rice, Jean, ed. *Cable TV Renewals & Refranchising*. Washington, D.C.: Communications Press, 1983.

CHAPTER TEN

Basic Cable Networks

Susan Tyler Eastman

A QUICK GUIDE TO CHAPTER TEN

Biographical material on Susan Eastman appears in Chapter 9. She assembled this chapter on basic cable networks from articles in trade periodicals, personal interviews and promotional materials, updated by National Cable Television Association's most recent statistics and the summaries in the Home Video & Cable Yearbook 1982–83. *This chapter provides an overview of basic cable as of 1984.*

TYPES OF BASIC CABLE CONTENT

All satellite-distributed cable networks other than the premium (i.e., pay) networks are called *basic cable* networks, and they can be placed on a cable system's basic tier. This chapter describes all the operational, basic, cable-only networks as of 1984. All of these services come free to the basic cable subscriber (unless grouped on a pay tier, but even then at least a dozen channels would come free as basic service). The reader can use the information in this chapter to track the growth of cable networks in the coming years and to examine changes in programming concepts and scheduling strategies. It provides reference material that college libraries frequently lack and supplies a 1984 baseline for comparison. The premium networks, local origination channels and superstations are covered in subsequent chapters.

This chapter considers basic networks based on their content because competition for shelf space on cable systems occurs largely among similar services. The following ten content groups classify the programming of the more than forty basic cable networks:

> sports
>
> news/information/public affairs
>
> music
>
> arts/culture
>
> games/children's
>
> full service/women's
>
> adult
>
> religious
>
> foreign language/ethnic
>
> educational/instructional

Just as the premium channels compete for shelf space as movie channels, so basic services vie for inclusion on basic cable service. Placement on an upper tier reduces a network's total potential audience since not all basic subscribers pay for higher tiers. An upper tier position especially hurts advertiser-supported networks as they depend partly on measures of total potential audience size to sell spots.

Basic cable networks are typically advertiser supported, and about half of them use program forms similar to those of broadcast television. The other half represent innovations in long-form content (all-weather, all-health) or adaptations from other media (games from computerized software, teletext-type news and financial information adapted from print media). Many forecasters predict

COMPARATIVE POTENTIAL AUDIENCES

as of January, 1984
(Rounded to nearest million)

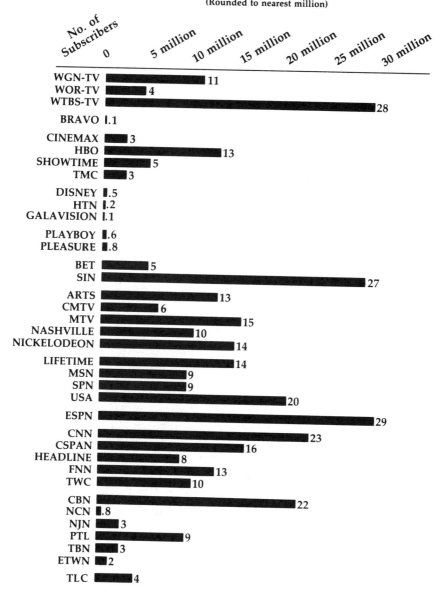

FIGURE 10-1. Cable Network Audiences

that less than two dozen of these basic services will survive as national services. At present, four basic networks lead the field: ESPN in sports, CBN in religion, CNN in news and USA Network in full-service programming. The number of competing services, however, continues to grow, and the shakedown period will continue into the 1990s. Figure 10-1 shows the comparative sizes of basic, premium and superstation audiences for most of the cable networks at the beginning of 1984.[1] In reading the bar graph keep in mind that premium audiences are paying subscribers while the rest are *potential* audiences subscribing to basic cable service.

SPORTS CHANNELS

Six cable services supply most sports and sports-related programming: ESPN, WTBS, WGN, WOR, USA Network and HBO. They compete with each other and regional sports channels for the adult male audience.

ESPN

ESPN, the leader, schedules a wide variety of sporting events including many national contests (college football and basketball, regional football contests and so on), a limited amount of sports-talk and interview programming, a morning newscast and a daily business program. ESPN is a well-established cable network with a clear vertical program format appealing to men of all ages (but especially men 18–49) interested in sports, although women make up about 20 percent of its audience, according to ESPN research.

The fact that major sporting events have ready advertiser appeal has turned ESPN into one of the first financially viable basic cable networks. Unlike many cable and broadcast networks, however, ESPN lacks efficiency of scale. That is, the larger its audience grows, the more team owners charge for the rights to sporting events. In addition, its production costs are high. Because of slow advertising sales, in 1983 ESPN altered its sports-only format to offer a two-hour business–news program on weekdays during the breakfast hours. This experiment marked the first major alteration in one of the vertical cable formats.

When ESPN began service in the fall of 1979, it charged cable systems 4 cents per subscriber per month. Intense competition led the company to drop cable system fees in 1982 and provide its service without charge while it strived to establish itself as a basic cable service, not a second tier service. As of 1984, however, because of disappointing advertising revenues, ESPN returned to monthly per-subscriber charges of 13 cents (still a minipay). ESPN reaches nearly 30 million subscribers on over 7,000 cable systems. Originally owned by Getty Oil and ABC, ABC bought out what was the Getty share in 1984.

Sports Competitors

The three superstations also program large amounts of sports in direct competition with each other and ESPN. Even HBO programs some events, such as reruns of the 1980 Olympic trials that target the same male audience, and it regularly includes sporting events in its weekend line-up. USA Network also contests for rights to sporting events with national appeal (when not outbid by one of the three broadcast networks). Madison Square Garden (MSG) sports form a major component of USA Network programming. Several MSOs have begun regional sports channels such as Cablevision and the *Washington Post* in New

York and the northeast, Group W in the Washington D.C. and Seattle areas and Warner Amex in Ohio. Anheuser-Busch, Multimedia, Inc. and Tele-Communications, Inc. began a pay regional sports network in the Midwest in 1984 (called Sports Time). In addition, ABC/Sports offers a major sports presentation each month on pay-per-view. Of the sports services available in 1984, ESPN still has the highest national visibility and the strongest vertical appeal in the minds of viewers and advertisers, but it may be effectively challenged in the late 1980s as regional networks expand.

NEWS, INFORMATION AND PUBLIC AFFAIRS

Twenty-four-hour all-news was one of the most competitive of cable programming areas in 1982 and 1983. The battle between Ted Turner, owner of Cable News Network (and also of superstation WTBS-TV), and ABC and Westinghouse, owners of Satellite News Channel, illustrates most of the elements that make for survival or defeat in basic cable network competition.

Cable News Network and Satellite News Channel

From its beginning in 1980, CNN led the cable news services in audience popularity and wide distribution. CNN is now the only long-form news network in the United States. It operates 24 hours a day with in-depth news coverage and feature stories. Although broadcast news tends to appeal to older demographic groups, cable all-news brings in more of the younger and more upscale demographic groups that especially interest advertisers. CNN reaches about 23 million homes on over 4,000 systems, carries both national and regional advertising and schedules two local avails per hour.

Satellite News Channel (a joint venture of Group W and ABC Video) entered the news service field in 1982, and for a year its entry clouded the outcome of the long-term race for news shelf space on cable systems. SNC provided a 15-minute, headline-only news service. Its combination of programming support from ABC network television news and sports plus use of the Group W facilities created an immediate challenge to Turner Broadcasting. CNN (in the person of Ted Turner) responded to the new competition by adding Headline News (CNN2), a 24-hour service consisting of a 5-minute, repeating cycle of news headlines. This service, marketed to broadcast stations as well as cable systems, is free when systems also carry CNN 1, 5 cents per subscriber per month without CNN, increasing to 10 cents when placed on a tier.

It was on this economic side, moreover, that SNC's challenge to Turner Broadcasting lay. CNN *charges* cable systems 15 or 20 cents per subscriber per month (the amount depends on whether WTBS-TV is also carried) while SNC *paid* a system up to $1.50 per subscriber for inclusion in the basic cable line-up. (One-third of the total amount per subscriber actually came in promotional launch support.) After the initial payment, Satellite News Channel came to systems without a payment in either direction. Thus, a financial advantage came with carrying SNC, a strong appeal for many struggling cable systems. To counter

SNC's strategem, for a brief period, Turner paid new cable affiliates $1.00 per subscriber per year if they contracted to carry all three services—WTBS-TV, CNN and Headline.

A third factor also had a part in the outcome of this all-news contest: satellite carriage. The industry's main cable satellite, Satcom 3R, transmits CNN. Westar 5 carried the SNC network—requiring cable systems to use a second receiving dish (or a sophisticated one capable of drawing from both satellites). In addition, over $2,000 in special switching equipment was needed to use SNC's regional feed format that addressed varied news items, sports scores and the like to different geographical regions.[2]

Of the three variables, journalistic quality, fee structure and satellite position, per-subscriber fees would seem to have had the most influence on subsequent negotiations between MSOs and CNN as contracts came up for renewal. CNN, however, retained its momentum: In 1984 Turner purchased SNC and merged it with CNN.[3] CNN bought out the competition and survived. The quality of CNN's newscasts continues to satisfy viewers and advertisers and, therefore, system affiliates.

Financial News Network

The specialized business news networks are the second major set of cable news sources. Although all-news has vertically defined content, the individual networks have different target audiences. CNN seeks mass appeal while several business-oriented news networks slivercast. The most widely distributed of these is Financial News Network (FNN), which reaches homes as a part of broadcast newscasts as well as on cable. FNN, using live anchors, programs a cycle of business news events, news interviews and stock and commodity listings. In addition to regular hourly newscasts, it schedules programs interpreting domestic and international news events in light of their impact on U.S. business interests. FNN reaches about 13 million cable homes on 730 systems via Satcom 4 (piggybacked with Bravo) and has actively sought shelf space in major markets where business viewers are concentrated.

Text News Services

Besides *live* news formats using anchors and video, cable systems can use *text* news services. These services provide alphanumeric news in short repeating cycles of news headlines, sports, features and stockmarket reports within a text and graphics format. UPI, the international wire service, offers UPI Cablenews in a 15-minute recycling format that can include local advertising; Reuters News View offers two channels of alphanumeric news reports—a 24-hour all-news channel and an encoded weekday financial news channel including stock and commodity listings. Each of these services reaches about 4 million homes (on 400–500 systems) and costs systems between $150 and $300 per month, depending on the number of subscribers and whether both Reuters channels are carried. Dow Jones Cable News is a similar service consisting of 24 hours of business, financial and economic news in 15-minute cycles by the Dow Jones newswire, *Barron's* and the *Wall Street Journal*. All these services use transponders on Satcom 3R.

The Weather Channel

Another unique 24-hour cable offering competing with news channels in a limited way is The Weather Channel. Landmark Communications began the service in 1982 to provide a continuous round of national, regional and local weather delivered in short segments. The Weather Channel carries advertising and is free to cable systems (if placed on basic service) from Satcom 3R. Its highly specialized content and easily identifiable name generate immediate consumer recognition. Unlike most other cable audiences, viewers of The Weather Channel are expected to tune in only for brief checks—but to tune in reliably from day to day in large cumulative numbers. According to one study Landmark conducted, viewers used the channel an average of 18 minutes a day. As of 1984, its advertising revenues were down, creating a shaky financial position—despite the 10 million homes it reaches (on 1,000 systems) and its carriage by the NASA space center (who said they needed the weather reports!).

C-SPAN

The Cable-Satellite Public Affairs Network (C-SPAN) is the only public affairs channel on cable. C-SPAN provides live coverage of the U.S. House of Representatives and tapes of House and Senate hearings, political interviews and conferences and daily live phone-in programs; it carries no advertising. Its unique public-service image makes C-SPAN especially attractive to cable systems with sufficient shelf space to accommodate it. A nonprofit, cable system cooperative owns C-SPAN, and despite its minipay charge of 3 cents per subscriber per month, it is likely to receive continued support from large numbers of cable operators. Its 24-hour service reaches over 16 million homes on more than 1,000 cable systems and conveniently comes from Satcom 3R.

MUSIC NETWORKS

Borrowing from radio, cable programmers have created several all-music channels with rock and country formats. Of these, the 24-hour Music Television (MTV) from Warner Amex is the most widely distributed and the first to become financially successful, becoming a model for other cable music networks.

Music Television

MTV programs a mix of video clips provided by record companies promoting their rock groups and very short, live interviews with rock celebrities. MTV maintains an active roster of about 750 video clips (called **videos**), repeating the top 4 or 5 daily and adding to the playlist from new clips provided weekly by the record industry. MTV zoomed to extraordinary popularity in early 1984.

An unusual feature of MTV is that home viewers are urged to subscribe to cable FM service as well to receive the Dolby stereo FM sound simulcast with MTV. Without this addition, MTV's sound comes through the usual monaural television speakers. With it, a multiplexed pair of sound signals is decoded at the home FM tuner providing two channels of high-quality stereo sound. Cable systems charge subscribers a monthly fee for the FM service, typically $1–2 per month, and the service may include several other FM signals.

MTV carries advertising and comes to the cable system as a minipay cable network. For systems targeting the 18–34 age group, MTV has clear vertical appeal, and two minutes per hour are open for local commercial sale. One of MTV's initial problems was demonstrating its value to advertisers because most viewers *listened* to MTV rather than *watched*. In 1983, MTV shifted to radio-style spots emphasizing audio copy and drew more advertisers; its rates, however, more nearly equal radio than television spot rates. As of 1983, MTV reached about 15 million homes on about 2,000 systems via Satcom 3R, and had high national visibility among teens and young adults. As might be expected, its unique programming was rapidly copied in a half dozen new music services.

The Nashville Network

Beginning in 1983, Opryland Productions in conjunction with Group W offered The Nashville Network, combining country music-oriented variety, interview, comedy and game shows mixed with hit country music songs. Unlike MTV, The Nashville Network programs a wide range of formats, often of uneven quality. As of 1984, The Nashville Network reached 10 million homes on about 1,200 systems as a minipay service. It carries advertising and comes on Westar 5; two minutes per hour are offered for local sale.

Country Music Television

The Country Music Television network (CMTV) follows the MTV pattern more closely. Owned by Telestar and others, it programs only country music with an urban emphasis, using short videos produced by record companies and showcasing country music performers. At the beginning of 1984, after six months of operation, CMTV reached over 5 million cable homes as a minipay service via Comstar 4 and appeared likely to grow quickly in the Midwest and Southeast.

Other Music Services

A popular music service in Atlanta, Georgia, Video Music Channel, is also seeking national cable distribution. It programs rock videos and concerts and competes directly with MTV. Unlike MTV that does not vary its content by the time of day, Video Music Channel programs top 10 in the evening, soul music in the afternoons and so on. It is currently available on many cable systems in the southeastern United States. WTBS and NBC also program rock music videos on weekend nights, capitalizing on their popularity with young audiences and their extraordinarily low programming cost.

In addition to simulcasts of MTV's stereo sound, many cable systems offer **cable radio** service. Using related technology, a cable system can deliver radio as well as television programming. This subject is covered in Chapter 12.

ARTS/CULTURAL PROGRAMMING

In addition to Bravo, the premium cultural network, the ABC and CBS television networks have both tried arts/cultural programming. As discussed in Chapter 11, Bravo stresses the performing arts, carrying ballet, dance, theater and music. This content area has had the greatest failure rate in cable programming. Two large-scale, well-funded efforts lasted less than a year each. CBS formed CBS Cable in 1981, an arts/cultural network, showing drama, opera, music, variety programs, Broadway plays, cabaret performances and documentaries. Its productions were of high technical and performance quality. They were aired in three-hour blocks, repeated three times, making a twelve-hour daily schedule. CBS Cable reached 4 million homes but failed to sell its service effectively to advertisers, lost $30 million for CBS and went out of business in 1982 after one year of operation.

The Entertainment Channel, launched in mid-1982 as a cultural pay channel, had failed by mid-1983. Announced as a cultural network, the operation obtained the American rights to BBC productions previously unexposed on U.S. public television and moved rapidly into broader-appeal programming, hedging its bets with movies and British action-adventure series. Lacking a clear definition in the market, the service folded. The surviving cable cultural networks, ARTS and Bravo, as well as PBS, are now bidding for rights to the BBC productions.

ARTS

ARTS, an advertiser-supported, joint venture of ABC Video and the Hearst Corporation, reaches 12.5 million homes on over 2,000 systems with three prime-time hours devoted to the performing and visual arts. It plans to expand to five hours of prime-time programming in 1984. Its program schedule includes formats using drama, music, ballet and other dance forms, opera, literary works, sculpture, painting, photography and design. ARTS competes directly with public television and Bravo to get programming from a quite limited number of sources, especially for original American programming. ARTS is offered free to systems carrying Nickelodeon through a special arrangement with Warner Amex since the two channels are piggybacked on the same transponder on Satcom 3R. ARTS carries advertising, and three minutes of spot time are available per night; it does not supply co-op funds or launch assistance. ARTS has gotten very little national promotion and lacks visibility among consumers.

GAMES/CHILDREN'S PROGRAMMING

Videogames are an area where cable's unique capabilities contrast quite favorably with over-the-air broadcasting. Cable systems with enough channels can offer interactive and semi-interactive computerized games to subscribers who must first purchase the home-end equipment permitting participation in the game. However, these services have been slow to capture subscribers.

PlayCable, The Games Channel and Atari

PlayCable was the first popular system utilizing cable to carry game formats, but it ended operations in early 1984. The specific games were varied every hour or so and had to be coupled with a $200 Intellivision console. This system varied from the usual pay cable arrangement in that the subscriber dealt directly with the PlayCable company or a retail store to obtain the home decoder equipment. PlayCable did not require a fully dedicated channel because the games were sent via an FM signal that could be multiplexed on any channel. The Intellivision console **downloaded** or decoded the scrambled signal. After two years of operation, PlayCable reached only a few thousand homes, and Mattel stopped Intellivision production.

Group W in California is now testing The Games Channel. Like PlayCable, it requires an extensive investment in headend equipment, and consumers must pay a one-time installation fee of $50 and a monthly fee of about $15 for 20 repeatable games.[4] This rate structure is slightly higher than PlayCable's monthly fee of about $13. Unlike PlayCable, The Games Channel requires its own fully dedicated video channel.

A potential competitor to these cable game services is Atari, the giant of the videogame manufacturers. But to date, Atari provides only personal game computers and has not announced a cable service. Observers feel that Atari will inevitably move into cable because it is owned by Warner Amex, the third-largest owner of cable systems. An era of multiplay has been predicted when some homes will subscribe to several games channels just as they do to multipay premium movie channels today. But the early demise of PlayCable pushes the expectations of multiplay into the 1990s.

Nickelodeon

The only basic cable network consisting exclusively of children's fare, Warner Amex's Nickelodeon, provides a 14-hour daytime service targeted toward young people (preschool through teen). (The Disney Channel, a pay service, targets women 18–49 as well as children and promotes itself as a family-oriented network.) Nickelodeon schedules teen-oriented films, concerts and several child-oriented series and became an ad-supported service in 1984. It has won several national awards for excellence in children's programming. Nickelodeon dayparts, targeting preschoolers in the morning hours and older children in the late afternoon. Warner Amex charges cable systems 15 cents per subscriber per month for the service (and it piggybacks with ARTS). As of 1984, Nickelodeon reached 14 million homes on about 3,000 cable systems, and its name was widely recognized.

Other Children's Services

In addition to Nickelodeon and The Disney Channel, several hours of child-oriented programming appear on USA Network under the title *KidVid*. KidVid was nationally distributed to systems beginning in 1984 as KidVid Network, a part-time service telecasting on weekday afternoons and weekend mornings. It contains animated films but no live or hosted children's programs, and targets children ages 2 to 11.

Other cartoon services are expected to start operation in the next few years. Cable MSOs consider games and children's channels especially useful bargaining points when negotiating franchises because of their well-defined target audiences and the shortage of broadcast programming for children. Child-oriented networks purport to serve a wide range of age groups (ten years is a very long time when considering developmental stages in children) and may have few programs for subgroups of children such as preschoolers or ages six to eight. Excepting Nickelodeon, there is still a shortage of original live-action programs for children, the form encouraged by ACT and other concerned groups.

FULL-SERVICE, WOMEN'S AND ADULT CHANNELS

USA Network is the sole full-service cable-only network. It reaches over 20 million homes, making it one of the largest of the cable only networks. Although the superstations and SIN, the Spanish-language network, also program full services, they have broadcast as well as cable audiences. MSN, SPN and Lifetime compete for shelf space.

USA Network

USA Network is scheduled like a broadcast network with once-a-week and stripped daily programs of varied formats to mesh with at-home activities (**dayparting**). USA carries news, sports, talk and movies in its schedule grouped in four programming blocks: *Sportstime, Daytime, Kidstime* and *Nighttime.* It includes The English Channel, a cultural service of British origin. USA Network combines advertising support with a system charge of 11 cents per subscriber per month if the cable system includes it on basic service (raised to 20 cents if the system places USA on a pay tier). Local avails can be sold by its 3,500 local affiliates. USA Network is carried on Satcom 3R.

Modern Satellite Network

Modern Satellite Network (MSN) operates only in the mornings on weekdays and provides a consumer information service for about 9 million shoppers on over 500 systems. MSN is essentially a shopping service, carrying a key program called *The Home Shopping Show,* accompanied by public service and informational programming. Advertisers, business and government produce the individual programs and pay MSN for including them in its schedule. It is free to cable systems, and two spots per day are available for local advertising, but MSN provides no co-op or launch support. It is carried on Satcom 3R piggybacked with varied other services. According to its management, it has been a financial success from the start due to its immediate advertiser appeal and absence of program costs.

Satellite Program Network

The Satellite Program Network (SPN) offers a broad array of programming in a 24-hour lifestyle service that includes talk shows, business, how-to and classic movies along with self-improvement segments. SPN approaches a full-service concept in subject matter but uses a magazine format with a regular host rather than a distinct program-by-program line-up. Until 1983, SPN carried TeleFrance-USA's foreign language movies and programs in the afternoons, but that service failed as a result of inadequate advertising revenues. SPN remains advertiser supported and is free to cable systems. It reaches about 9 million homes on 460 systems via Satcom 4.

Lifetime

Although all of the networks described above carry some consumer health information, only the Cable Health Network (CHN) restricted itself to information and features on the general topics of health, nutrition, fitness and better living. CHN featured Dr. Art Ullene in its on-air and external promotion and targeted adults 25+. Begun in 1982, CHN was advertiser supported and free to systems; two minutes per hour were available for local advertising along with 15 cents per subscriber per year in launch and co-op funds. CHN also had an advantageous position on Satcom 3R. An all-health network would seem to possess a precisely identifiable vertical programming concept, with appeal to a broad range of demographic groups and advertisers. Unfortunately, health-related programming can be found on at least a dozen or more broadcast and other cable networks in small segments. Even local broadcast stations often include special medical reporters (often doctors) in their newscasts. Whether this trend demonstrates a virtually insatiable appetite for health-related information or indicates a dissipation of CHN's potential audience is an interesting question. In any case, because of weak ad revenues CHN and Daytime merged, forming the new network, Lifetime, which began operation in early 1984.

Daytime was an afternoon only network aimed at women at home, reaching 9.5 million homes after a year and a half of operation. A joint venture of Hearst and ABC Video, Daytime's advertiser-supported programming focused on beauty and health care, fashion, cooking and similar self-improvement subjects in a magazine format.

Lifetime, launched early in 1984 on Satcom 3R, incorporates programming from both Daytime and Cable Health Network (and retains CHN's apple logo). To encourage systems to promote the new service, Lifetime offered 15 cents per subscriber in support at launch and plans on an additional 15 cents to support first-year consumer campaigns for those systems that participate. The 24-hour, advertiser-supported service offered 2 minutes per hour for local sale and had 16 million subscribers on about 1,600 affiliates at launch.

Adult Channels

As of the mid-1980s, programming containing nudity and/or explicit sexual behavior did not appear on basic cable networks, which tend to program family-oriented movies, series and specials. However, racy material, R-rated movies and soft-core pornography do appear on several premium networks. Two of the networks advertising as sexually oriented services, The Playboy Channel and The Pleasure Channel, are carried primarily by cable systems operating in large, urban markets. This practice takes into account community political pressure while targeting high density urban markets. Nationally, however, sizable numbers of people have demonstrated their willingness to pay an additional premium for adult content, but local and state elected officials are reluctant to approve carriage, causing several MSOs to announce that they prohibit adult networks on their cable systems.

RELIGIOUS NETWORKS

The evangelical Christian movement generated some of the first cable networks and long-form programs. Since the late 1970s, however, CBN and other religious networks have turned increasingly to family-oriented entertainment programming, reducing the proportion of overtly religious content.

Christian Broadcasting Network

CBN, the Christian Broadcasting Network, is one of the very largest of the basic cable services, reaching more than half of all cabled homes (over 22 million on nearly 4,000 systems). The tone and direction of this network come from the Reverend Pat Robertson. CBN programs 24 hours a day of religious and family entertainment including an innovation in the soap opera format—a Christian daytime series emphasizing prosocial and family-life values. College sports and classic movies also make up part of CBN's schedule. CBN is free to systems and is supported both by viewer contributions and advertising. It makes one minute an hour available for local spot sale and provides 10 cents per subscriber per year in co-op funds (up to a limit of $7,000). CBN encourages cable system affiliation by giving satellite receiving dishes to systems that contract to carry the network and lack the capacity to draw from Satcom 3R.

Other Religious Networks

Five other religious networks also supply Christian messages in mixes of entertainment, news, movies and sermons. Three of these networks take an interdenominational approach to their programs by using a variety of evangelists: PTL (Praise The Lord), TBN (Trinity Broadcasting Network) and NCN (National Christian Network). The largest of these services, PTL, reaches 8.5 million homes while TBN is available in about 3.4 million homes and NCN in less than 1 million homes. All three services program 24 hours a day.

Also competing for carriage on cable systems are Eternal Word Television Network (EWTN) reaching 1.6 million homes and the Episcopalian Television Network (ETN). EWTN offers predominantly Catholic programming in a daily prime-time schedule (8 P.M. to midnight); ETN emphasizes the Episcopalian perspective in a two-hour Sunday morning service. These two services are relatively restricted, programming for less than a full day, and ETN reaches only a few hundred thousand people. These smaller networks do not conduct on-air solicitation of funds, but the three leaders, CBN, PTL and TBN, actively pressure viewers to donate or become members to support the network. All religious networks come free to cable systems. Ironically, at one time EWTN piggybacked with Eros (a premium adult service) on Westar 4. PTL and EWTN have the advantage of being carried on Satcom 3R; the others are on other satellites.

FOREIGN LANGUAGE/ETHNIC SERVICES

This section discusses services targeted toward specific demographic groups on the basis of their language or ethnic heritage. Although these services strive for broad programming appeal, the size of their potential audiences is necessarily limited to the number of people with cable in the target group.

Spanish International Network

The 24-hour, Spanish-language SIN Television Network (SIN stands for Spanish International Network) is one of the five most widely distributed cable services. One-quarter of all U.S. television homes can view it through a mix of over-the-air and cable carriage. (Combining its nine-station broadcast network, low-power stations and other part-time affiliates and 251 cable system audiences makes a total potential audience of over 27 million homes.) The network pays cable operators 10 cents a month for each Spanish surname household among their subscribers. SIN carries Spanish-language news, novelas (Mexican-produced series), soap operas, variety and children's shows, movies and specials, all advertiser supported. SIN is transmitted on Galaxy 1, the newest cable satellite.

Black Entertainment Television

BET (Black Entertainment Television) is the only cable service oriented toward black viewers. BET strives for broad appeal by mixing movies, specials, sports, public affairs, and a children's program. About 5 million homes can view BET over 240 systems. It charges systems 1 cent per subscriber per month and makes two spots an hour available for local advertising during its daily six hours of operation (8 P.M. to 2 A.M.). BET also provides 6 cents per subscriber per year in co-op funds.

Although AET (Apollo Entertainment Television) is planned for late 1984, it will concentrate on urban music and music-related video programming using taped concert and nightclub footage of black performers. After one year of service, AET ended operations in 1982, but plans to return two years later with fresh programming and advertiser support.

National Jewish Television

National Jewish Television provides a limited afternoon schedule of talk-magazine programming targeting the national Jewish community with discussions of social and political issues. It programs only three hours on Sunday afternoons, is free to systems and reaches about 3 million homes nationwide on 175 systems.

Other ethnically oriented networks are projected but only as regional services. Buena-Vista Channel, for example, plans to offer bilingual programming in Spanish and English in southern California.

EDUCATIONAL/INSTRUCTIONAL NETWORKS

Although self-instruction and educational programming make up a part of several services, to date there is only one network concentrating on instructional materials, in addition to the services provided by over-the-air public broadcasters.

The Learning Channel

The Appalachian Community Service Network, now called The Learning Channel, concentrates on college credit courses and life-long adult education. TLC is a daytime only service funded by cable system fees, charging systems 5 cents per subscriber per month, and by fees viewers enrolled for courses pay. As of 1984 TLC reached about 4.5 million homes on about 500 cable systems largely in the Appalachian Mountain regions of Ohio, Kentucky and Pennsylvania. Altogether, it had enrolled over 5,000 participants in its for-credit programs during four years of operation.

PROGRAM GUIDES

In order to let subscribers know what is scheduled on these basic cable channels, cable systems with more than 30 channels typically provide a program guide. The major pay services also supply printed guides for their own channels.

Guides to a cable system's programming can be printed and mailed to subscribers or they can be electronically generated and placed on a dedicated channel. Printed guides permit fuller descriptions of program content and allow subscribers to plan their viewing as much as a month in advance. Electronic guides give easy-to-read summaries of what is currently on an array of channels or what is scheduled for the remainder of the day on a single channel. Both carry advertising and can be wholly or partially subscriber supported, though the trend is toward advertiser support. System programmers often consult on guide format and design, and in some systems, the local system programmer supplies monthly information on specific programs to the guide's editor.

As of the mid-1980s, printed guides were more common than electronic guides, but in the largest MSO-owned systems electronic guides are slowly replacing print.[5] The costs of printed guides are rising rapidly, while electronic guides offer greater consumer convenience.

Printed Program Guides

There are three types of printed guides: single channel guides to pay channels, generic multichannel guides and customized guides. They vary in size from about five-by-six inches to tabloid-size, though small ones are more common. The paper varies from rough newsprint to glossy pages with high-quality color illustrations. Typography and layouts vary from cluttered and crowded to customized, artful designs.

HBO sells its guide, the most widely circulated single channel guide, to systems to mail to their subscribers with their monthly statements. It contains an illustrated, hour-by-hour listing of all shows on HBO, in a handy, colorful, easy-to-use format, without advertising. The Disney Channel distributes a similar guide for its programs. Both guides cost the cable system about 4 cents per subscriber, and versions for the four U.S. time zones are printed.

Generic program guides cover several cable networks, usually the most widely distributed premium channels such as HBO, Showtime and The Movie Channel, and the most popular basic cable networks such as ESPN and WTBS. Generic guides carry advertising, and the same guide is sold to many systems. *TV Guide* now covers the most popular cable channels in its broadcast listings so that it functions as a generic guide to cable channels as well as to broadcast television stations. Generic guides do not cover all cable-only networks and emphasize prime time and late night while skimping on daytime listings; they of course omit all local origination programming. Some guides provide detailed descriptions of show content and include feature articles, while others are bare bones. *Cableview* and *Premium Channels,* two of the most widely available generic guides, have about 30 to 60 pages and cost the cable operator between 20 and 50 cents a copy (plus mailing costs).

As systems expand and carry more uniquely scheduled channels, an individualized guide to show just what that system carries becomes increasingly important. Market-wide guides such as *TV Guide* carry only a few cable only channels, and not all of them are available to every cable subscriber; at the same time, *TV Guide* listings exclude whatever local cable progamming subscribers do have. Without a localized guide, viewers have no way of knowing what many cable channels carry and cannot plan their viewing to take advantage of unusual programs. From the operator's perspective, much of the promotional value of having local origination channels disappears if viewers do not know what can be seen on them. And their revenue potential is nil without viewers.

The inherent problem with customized printed guides to a whole system, however, is that more channels means more program listings. To provide a complete information service, all programs on all channels must be listed half-hour by half-hour (or hour by hour). Guides to large systems are fat and awkward to use. To keep printing costs down, pages are crowded, and cheap paper and poor typography are the rule. The cable operator usually eliminates space for feature articles to run advertising to cover the costs of printing and mailing, further reducing the guide's appeal.

The operator is actually in a no-win situation. Systems that do not encourage sampling of their off-beat channels find subscribers reporting dissatisfaction with service. Customized guides do stimulate viewer sampling, provided they are clear and easy to use. At the same time, they are so expensive that operators generally charge subscribers for them, while subscribers who may be unconvinced of the value of the cable service in the first place are not likely to want to pay for a guide—creating ill will if the payment is required.

In one effort in 1983, Tele-Communications, Inc. (TCI) created *Cabletime,* a generic guide for all its cable systems—which were located in different time zones but carried the same cable networks, more or less. Instead of separate guides for each time zone, TCI distributed the same guide with an elaborate grid for deciphering when a program was scheduled in each time zone. Subscribers quite naturally refused to learn the coding system and rejected the guide. This failure was expensive, and the company retreated to single-channel premium guides while "reformatting" *Cabletime.*

A tough question for creators of customized guides in large markets is whether to include the broadcast channels that are must-carries on the system. If they are not included, viewers must use *TV Guide,* newspaper supplements or other program guides to find out about the most-watched channels. On the other hand, including them greatly increases the number of listings, making the guides even more unwieldy, and they then duplicate much information available elsewhere.

Electronic Program Guides

Although electronic guides may be the solution to many of these problems, as of the mid-1980s, they tend to be supplementary rather than complete guides to cable services. On most systems, program information appears in alphanumeric form (as text only) and has no graphics. Because the resolution of television screens is much lower than that of printed pages, individual words must be large and clearly separated to be readable; therefore, video screens display only 20–22 lines of copy at one time.

Some cable systems adopt a limited electronic format, placing the names of important films in a heading on text news channels. Only a very few titles can be promoted at one time, and such listings contain only premiere premium films and specials, rarely local origination. In another option, electronic program listings are used as filler on access channels when there is no other programming to run. The disadvantages of this practice are that viewers cannot predict when they will find program listings, and the information is usually sketchy because this service is only offered part of the time and receives little attention from the cable programmer.

Other systems dedicate a full channel to alphanumeric listings of program titles that continuously scroll past the viewer. Twenty-four hours of programs, half-hour by half-hour, however, occupies a very large number of frames. Because of the immense number of program titles appearing on a system with 24 or more channels, listings typically include only the titles of featured films and specials on pay channels and exclude the descriptive addenda so popular with viewers. Figure 10-2 shows a page from one such electronic guide.

Several MSOs have experimented with more complete electronic listings. Creating the pages demands a big investment in graphics development, and current systems are still in the experimental stage. One problem is that making the listings useful requires the widespread availability of interactive cable or teletext decoders; to work effectively, the viewer must be able to select portions of the listings to examine on the screen. (Scrolling through pages and pages of titles that do not interest the subscriber would make a complete guide channel unappealing.) Warner Amex, owner of the interactive Qube systems, dedicates a guide

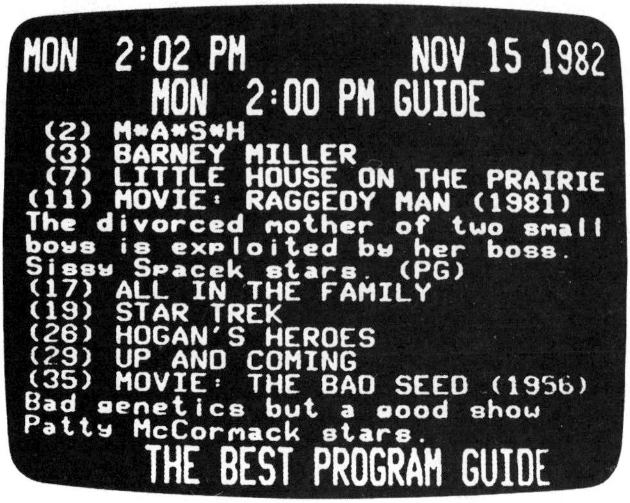

```
MON 2:02 PM          NOV 15 1982
     MON 2:00 PM GUIDE
(2)  M*A*S*H
(3)  BARNEY MILLER
(7)  LITTLE HOUSE ON THE PRAIRIE
(11) MOVIE: RAGGEDY MAN (1981)
The divorced mother of two small
boys is exploited by her boss.
Sissy Spacek stars. (PG)
(17) ALL IN THE FAMILY
(19) STAR TREK
(26) HOGAN'S HEROES
(29) UP AND COMING
(35) MOVIE: THE BAD SEED (1956)
Bad genetics but a good show
Patty McCormack stars.
     THE BEST PROGRAM GUIDE
```

SOURCE: Courtesy of TV Watch, Inc.

FIGURE 10-2. Frame of an Electronic Program Guide

channel on the basic Qube service to listing of the programs on other channels and to promoting the system's special services, although it also supplies a printed guide. Its electronic guide does not take advantage of cable's graphics and interactive capabilities. By the late 1980s, electronic guides will be highly developed, and the adoption of consumer teletext decoders will permit interactive program listings on cable systems. Teletext decoders will allow subscribers to display one page from a menu thereby getting desired detail, but such services will probably require a monthly fee.

SUMMARY

Many observers of cable advertising economics predict fallout among cable services will eventually reduce the total number of advertiser-supported networks to about a dozen, perhaps as soon as 1990. If this prediction proves accurate, clearly CNN, CBN, USA Network, SIN, ESPN and MTV will be six of the survivors. Based on the analysis in this chapter, the following are also likely to survive: Nickelodeon, Lifetime, Modern Satellite Network, Financial News Network and CMTV. Two other services, those economically supported by cable operators, will almost certainly survive because they do not need advertising revenue and possess unique appeal for some cable systems: C-SPAN and ACSN. Other services need more memorable names, clearer concepts, greater promotional support and, of course, long-term advertising revenue potential to survive. What this chapter does not reveal are the yet-to-be invented cable program forms that will emerge as competitors for shelf space in the second half of the 1980s.

Notes

[1]As of April 1982, 48 pay and basic cable networks were operating using 41 satellite transponders. An additional 20 networks (pay and basic) have been announced, and 15 of them have reserved transponders. Source: *Current and Projected State of the Cable Business,* Michael Wirth, April 1982. See also Evelyn DiSante, "Who Will Survive?" *Multichannel News,* 19 July 1982, pp. 6ff. The National Cable Television Association, *Broadcasting,* 3 May 1982, p. 52; *The Home Video & Cable Yearbook, 1982–83;* and *View Magazine* provided the data on total number of main subscribers and systems for each network and were the sources for programming content information for the less widely distributed networks. Since 1982, at least three networks have failed: CBS Cable, The Entertainment Network and Satellite News Network (absorbed by CNN); several have been withdrawn or postponed; and two merged: Cable Health Network and Daytime.

[2]Allen M. Charlene, "96 Hours of Cable News," *View,* January 1982, pp. 26–31.

[3]"Turner the Victor in Cable News Battle," *Broadcasting,* 17 October 1983, pp. 27–29.

[4]Mark Trost, "Waiting for Atari?" *View,* December 1982, pp. 29–31.

[5]Fred Dawson, "What's On?" *Multichannel Programming,* insert in *Multichannel News,* 19 July 1982, pp. 18–25; Joseph Lisant, "Electronic Guides," *View,* February 1983, pp. 37–41.

Selected Sources

Broadcasting, the trade magazine of broadcasting and cable.

Cable Age, the cable counterpart to *Television/Radio Age.*

CableVision, one of the major cable trade magazines.

The Home Video & Cable Yearbook, 1982–83. White Plains: Knowledge Industries Publications, Inc., 1983.

View: The Magazine of Cable TV Programming, monthly trade magazine on cable programming.

CHAPTER ELEVEN

Premium Programming Services

Jeffrey C. Reiss

A QUICK GUIDE TO CHAPTER ELEVEN

JEFFREY C. REISS, *vice chairman and chief executive officer of Cable Health Network, Inc. was one of the founders of both Showtime and Cable Health Network. Before forming his own company in 1981, Reiss Video Development Corporation, he was president of the parent corporation, Viacom Entertainment Group. As president of Showtime Entertainment, he helped create multipay marketing and was responsible for several original pay television productions, including the first made-for-pay series,* What's Up America. *Under his direction, Showtime developed from a stand-alone, in-house operation to a national premium cable network distributed to local cable systems by satellite. Prior to founding Showtime, Mr. Reiss was director of feature films for ABC Entertainment. Before joining ABC in 1973, he was in charge of program acquisitions and development for Cartridge Television, Inc., the producer of the first home videocassette recorder. As a partner in Kleiman-Reiss Productions, he presented several theatrical productions, and earlier worked as a story editor for Norman Lear's Tandem Productions and in the literary department of General Artists Corporation. In 1982, Mr. Reiss became the first president of Cable Health Network, moving into development of additional satellite program services for the cable industry after the CHN/Daytime merger. He has also taught at Brooklyn College and New York University. In this chapter, Mr. Reiss details the programming formats and strategies monthly pay cable services use and the program sources available to premium movie programmers. He describes the national premium networks available as of 1984.*

THE PAY TELEVISION SYSTEMS

The term *pay television* is an umbrella for *premium* programming. It may be distributed by cable systems, by subscription television using over-the-air scrambled signals (STV), microwaved signals (MDS) or by satellite-distributed, direct-to-home services (DBS) (see Figure 11-1). The premium programming services described in this chapter are available in any of these technologies but are most commonly delivered by cable operators to individual homes. All require a monthly subscriber fee. The content of a cable system's pay channels comes from about a dozen national programming services, each distributing a program schedule to local cable systems by satellite. The home subscriber pays a fee (or premium) for a pay channel in addition to the charge for the basic cable service, hence, **pay cable.**

Shelf Space

One way to understand the cable programming business is to consider the wholesaler–retailer analogy: National cable programming services are like national wholesalers in that they sell their product—programming—to regional and local outlets, the operators. Cable operators are like retailers because they sell that same product to consumers—their subscribers—one by one. The wholesalers' functions are: (1) acquiring programming from the Hollywood studios; commis-

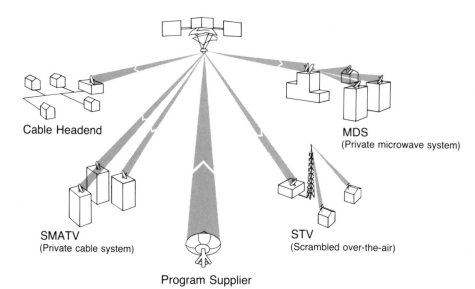

Cable Headend

MDS
(Private microwave system)

SMATV
(Private cable system)

STV
(Scrambled over-the-air)

Program Supplier

FIGURE 11-1. Satellite Delivery of Pay Program Signals

sioning independent producers; doing international coproductions; (2) packaging that programming in a form acceptable to consumers (wraparounds, titles, on-air hosts, graphics); (3) delivering that programming to the cable operator (usually by means of a satellite transmission); and (4) supporting their products with national advertising and promotion while supplying their retailers with local advertising materials and co-op dollars.

As indicated in the preceding chapter, the operator (or retailer) must decide how best to market the channels in the local system's inventory. Just as a supermarket manager has to allot shelf space to products, deciding to display some more prominently than others, a cable system operator must decide which premium and basic cable services to offer and promote to subscribers. Channel capacity, the number of must-carry stations in the franchise, the demographics of the subscribership, the distributor's (wholesaler's) pricing and so on influence these marketing decisions. The cable industry uses the term *shelf space* to mean available channel capacity on local cable systems. The premium services compete with each other for a share of the shelf space on local cable systems. Unlike basic or ad-supported networks, local systems promote their pay services extensively to increase subscription revenue. (See the discussion of **lift** in Chapter 9.)

Virtually every cable system in the United States carries at least one premium service, and over three-quarters carry two or more premium services.[1] If a system has only one premium channel, the odds are very high it is Home Box Office (HBO) since HBO is carried on 5,000 systems out of a total of just under 6,000. A very few systems carry only Showtime or have no pay channel. Increasingly, systems carry several premium channels, and competition then focuses on shelf space as the second, third or fourth premium service. The contenders are *Bravo, Cinemax, The Disney Channel, Home Box Office, Home Theatre Network, GalaVision, The Movie Channel, The Playboy Channel, The Pleasure*

Channel, Showtime and *The Sports Network*. Both *Eros* and *Spotlight* dropped out of the competition in 1983–84. But three regional pay channels have strong followings: Prism in Philadelphia, The Sports Channel in Washington, D.C., and Z Channel in Los Angeles; and others are growing.

Multipay Environments

Until the 1980s, most cable experts thought subscribers would only be willing to pay for one, at the most two, premium channels. A ceiling for total cable bills was assumed; many thought that subscribers would resist paying more for cable than they did for their telephone bills (around $30 per month on average for upper-income families). However, in the early 1980s, multipay arrived. When offered two or more pay channels, a large percentage of pay subscribers signed up for two or more services—especially in newly constructed cable systems **(new-builds)** where enthusiasm for cable was high and promotion strong. In one case, research for Showtime (the second largest premium movie network) showed that when HBO and Showtime were marketed in a newly installed system (undergoing first-time sales), 98 percent of basic subscribers took at least one premium service. But the big news was that 70 percent of that 98 percent took *both* HBO and Showtime. Similar research findings heralded the era of multipay cable—in which subscribers could be offered several pay services and be expected to subscribe to at least two and possibly more. This phenomenon encouraged HBO to launch Cinemax, a second premium movie channel, marketed jointly with HBO.

The earliest pay networks offered a mix of movie programming with a small amount of sports and entertainment specials, using a pricing system having broad appeal to a heterogeneous audience. Multipay subscriptions, however, stimulated the creation of several *specialized premium services* that target a narrowly defined (homogeneous) interest group with programming—for example, adult males or children or culture buffs. The specialized premium services typically schedule movies like the *general services* but add a larger proportion of specials, documentaries and other nonmovie programs.

By the mid-1980s, the phenomena of service substitution and subscriber churn modified the multipay picture. When a new premium service was marketed in an established cable system already having one or more premium services, subscribers tended to cancel one service when they took on a new one **(substitution)**. This substitution happened in several communities when Playboy, an adult programming channel, or The Disney Channel, a Disney Studios service, was introduced. Moreover, after some years, many subscribers appear to perceive the major movie services as too much alike and cancel one service **(churn)**. Nationally, as of the mid-1980s, about half of the basic cable subscribers take one or more premium channels. About 40 percent of those premium subscribers take a second premium channel when one is offered; a much smaller percentage take three or more premium channels. In 1983 more than 20 percent of basic subscribers canceled at least one pay service for reasons other than a change in address.

The strategies pay cable programmers have adopted to combat these phenomena are to develop a unique identity or image through advertising and promotion (**differentiation**) and to develop more original programming and acquire exclusive rights to some movies (**exclusivity**). Those services competing with HBO tend to target their movies to more carefully defined audiences while consciously counterprogramming HBO's lineup. Exclusive rights to hit movies have become the key to pay movie success. Premium services narrowcasting to specific audiences have fewer problems with differentiation, but to remain economically viable, they must provide programs of high value to subscribers.

Multipay's short history suggests many subscribers will become increasingly willing to pay for several premium channels (how many no one knows), but each channel will need to provide a sharply distinct service with significant value, appealing to a well-defined target audience.

Revenue Split

Economic considerations come strongly into play when a local system is deciding which premium network to carry. As discussed in Chapter 9, cable systems charge their subscribers about $8–$10 above the basic monthly cable bill to receive a premium channel. The local system operator sets the exact monthly charge, usually within a range negotiated with the program supplier. The revenue for a premium channel is distributed between the programming service, which licenses the programming and is responsible for delivering it to cable headends (engineering headquarters), and the cable system operator, who invests in a satellite dish to receive the signal and delivers it by coaxial cable to subscriber homes and bills them. About 40 percent of the monthly revenue goes to the program service, and 60 percent (sometimes more) goes to the cable operator. For example, Showtime typically costs subscribers about $10 per month; the operator keeps about $6, and Showtime receives $4. To gain carriage and achieve broad local acceptance, the premium programmers also offer cable operators discounts and revenue incentives. Because of this favorable revenue split, premium services have become an important component of operators' revenues. In fact, revenues from pay services stimulated a cable industry resurgence in the late 1970s and made the difference between profit and loss for many operators.

Between 1975 and 1983, pay programming became the top moneymaker in the cable television business, with total revenues of more than $240 million per month as of 1983. Premium services significantly increased the cable industry's subscriber base, as well as operators' average revenue from each subscriber. Consumer desire for pay programming also spurred dramatic expansion of the cable industry into major urban and suburban markets where cable is not usually needed for adequate reception of broadcast television signals.

MOVIES

The staple of pay cable remains the Hollywood *feature film* aired soon after theatrical release and well in advance of its commercial television premiere. None of the premium cable services carry commercials. Pictures are shown unedited and uninterrupted, including those rated PG and R (containing strong language and behavior normally censored on commercial television).

Rotation Scheduling

Rotation scheduling is a major area of difference between pay cable and broadcast television. The premium services offer a range of 20 to 50 programs per month, some first-run and totally new to the service, and some repeated from the previous month. In the course of a month, they are scheduled from four to six times on different days and at various hours during the daily schedule. Different movie services offer varying numbers of monthly attractions, but all services schedule most of their programs more than once, typically from four to six times. (Programs containing nudity or profanity, however, rotate only within prime time and late night on most networks.) The viewer therefore has several opportunities to watch each film, special or series episode. These repeat showings maximize the potential audience for each program. The programmer's scheduling goal is to find the various complementary time slots delivering the greatest possible audience for each attraction during the course of a month, not necessarily in one showing.

In contrast, broadcast television's scheduling practices result in the weekly series, the daily soap opera, the nightly newscast. In most cases the program or episode is shown only once, and the largest possible audience is sought. As premium networks adopt more of the short-length formats of broadcast television, such as 60-minute episodes of *The Paper Chase* and stripped 30-minute soap operas, the difference between pay cable and broadcast scheduling will remain the frequent repetition of current episodes within a week in different dayparts (and across one or two months) on pay cable networks.

Several of the specialized premium networks are part-time services. The Playboy Channel programs from 8 P.M. to 6 A.M., and Eros, formerly an adult pay service, now bankrupt, programmed only the overnight daypart—from midnight to 5 A.M., on only three nights (Thursdays, Fridays and Saturdays). GalaVision concentrates on early fringe through late night, and Bravo is a prime-time-only service. These specialized networks use rotation patterns within the daypart they program similar to those of the general movie networks. Individual episodes, specials and films are repeated on different days and in different dayparts—permitting all subscribers multiple opportunities to view each program.

Monthly Audience Appeal

Another major contrast between broadcast television and the premium programming services lies in their revenue strategies. To maximize ad revenues, the commercial networks and broadcast stations program to attract the largest possible audiences every minute of the programming day. Premium networks, as explained in Chapter 2, try to attract the largest possible cumulative audiences over the period of a month. The lifeblood (read daily operating revenues) of a pay service is its direct subscriptions; pay services must satisfy their subscribers over the long term, forestalling disconnections. A premium service's success is not determined by the ratings of its individual programs but by the general appeal of its overall schedule. Insofar as ratings reflect that appeal, they are useful measures. But cable has a more valuable measure of success in the count of subscriber *turnover*. Since both schedules and subscriber billings are arranged by the month, viewers tend to evaluate one-month blocks of programming. Viewers who use their pay television program service two or three times a week and see benefit in (1) its varied viewing times, (2) uninterrupted program content, (3) lack of commercials and (4) unique entertainment programs and theatrical feature films continue the service for another month.

Discontinuing a pay service seldom reflects subscriber dissatisfaction with one or two individual shows. When viewers disconnect, they feel the service as a whole is lacking. Customers repelled by violence, for example, may disconnect a movie service if a large number of a particular month's films contain a great deal of violence. A family may determine that its desire for wholesome, G-rated fare is not being filled by the programming mix of one movie service and cancel after a trial month or two. This process also works in reverse. Favorable word of mouth is the most potent way of attracting new customers, particularly in non-urban communities.

A handful of individual programs each month makes the difference between success or failure when a premium service is new in a community and the local operator lacks a large and stable subscriber base. Having one or two blockbuster films on the order of *Star Wars* or *Raiders of the Lost Ark* undoubtedly attracts new subscribers to the service and holds current subscribers even if their reaction to the balance of that month's schedule is negative.

ENTERTAINMENT SPECIALS

In addition to feature films, several of the pay movie services offer series and specials created expressly for their subscribers, typically entertainment specials featuring Broadway shows and popular Las Vegas nightclub acts. Such performances are not available in their original, uncensored form on broadcast television. Other programming formats have been developed, including made-for-pay television movies, original documentaries, magazine-format series and blends of entertainment and documentary styles. A few made-for-cable series using soap opera or situation comedy formats have been created, and a rare few off-network series have been licensed to premium networks. More recently, pay services have emerged that do not base their programming solely on feature films; they target narrowly defined audiences and program a mix of live action and film for which they feel those consumers will pay. The Playboy Channel, The Pleasure Channel, Bravo, The Disney Channel, GalaVision and The Sports Network constitute such services. Home Theatre Network is narrowly targeted also but uses only movies.

Selecting performers to star in original pay cable specials and choosing properties to adapt to the television medium require an intense examination of cable subscribers' expectations. The broadcast networks frequently offer variety specials, and most leading entertainers can be seen either there or on the many daily talk/variety shows. To offer something fresh and different, premium programmers have three options: Use performers who, though well known, appear infrequently as network television guests; use performers often seen on broadcast television but who rarely headline their own programs; develop programs having a format or content not available on broadcast television.

The premium networks have made a major asset of taping shows on location, offering subscribers a front-row seat at theaters, nightclubs and arenas around the world. A Las Vegas nightclub special provides the cable subscriber with the same performance that costs $40 per couple to see in person. Although there is no substitute for being there, the broadcast of a concert from Central Park or a country music festival in West Virginia makes the viewer in Cleveland, Ohio, or Agoura, California, a part of that one-time event. At their best, these shows are vivid reproductions of live performances, unlike conventionally packaged broadcast network specials. Every effort is made to preserve the integrity of a complete performance without guest stars, dance numbers and other window-dressing used to widen the audience base of individual broadcast network variety programs. Pay cable's time flexibility also permits nightclub acts and concerts to run their natural lengths, whether 1 hour and 11 minutes or 1 hour and 53 minutes, without the artificial compression of performances into 1-hour or 90-minute broadcast formats.

As with theatrical feature films, premium network nightclub and concert specials feature material commercial television does not provide and, in some cases, could not provide without expurgation. An "HBOnly" *Richard Pryor Special* in 1983 is a case in point. The Showtime schedule for July 1979 contained six specials, one of which rated as adult entertainment not suitable for families. By the mid-1980s, Showtime and HBO schedules included as many as a dozen specials every month.

By the close of the 1980s original programming (including made-for-pay movies, series and specials) may make up as much as 50 percent of the premium network's monthly schedules. Showtime spent between $6 and $7 million on original programming in 1979, entering into production and development deals with a variety of studios and independent producers. By the mid-1980s, this budget had increased to over $20 million and was expected to keep climbing. HBO, as of the mid-1980s, was spending approximately $30–$40 million annually on original productions.

SPORTS

The third major component in pay programming is sports. The Sports Network began service in 1984 to cater to this devouring national interest. HBO, which is primarily movies, also schedules national sporting events on weekdays in prime time. Sports programming creates a divergence of opinion, however, in the pay movie community. Showtime and The Movie Channel have opted not to offer any sports programming. They argued that sports blurs a movie service's image. Austin Furst, former vice-president of programming at HBO, argued that two-thirds of HBO's subscribers watch sports and that those subscribers were *more pleased* with HBO than subscribers having no interest in sports.[2] Because of the broadcast networks' financial strength and audience reach, ABC, CBS and NBC acquire the rights to most major sporting events. Premium movie networks have to settle for events of lesser national interest. Nevertheless, an audience can be found for some sports broadcast television does not adequately cover such as nonheavyweight boxing, regional college sports, track and field, swimming and diving, soccer and equestrian competitions.

The premium networks' advantage in sports programming is that they can present sports as entertainment rather than cover events in journalistic fashion. New formats are emerging that focus on sports personalities and dramatize memorable past sports events. Such approaches can broaden sports' appeal and offer intriguing programming possibilities not characteristic of broadcast television. Certain of the basic cable networks and superstations—ESPN, WOR, WTBS, WGN, USA Network—have large appetites for major and minor sporting events, and pay-per-view is moving into the sports arena. Several regional networks, such as Sports Channel and Prism, offer sports as pay options. The premium movie channels probably will not increase their sports programming; original entertainment such as films and series and specials creates more differentiation for them than does sports.

THE GENERAL PREMIUM MOVIE SERVICES

Home Box Office (HBO), the first of the premium movie services, became a satellite-transmitted signal in 1975. Up to that time HBO used microwave relay or shipped its program on videocassettes. Its pioneering use of a satellite to distribute its programming simultaneously across the United States demonstrated the feasibility of a national cable program network. In 1976 Viacom, an MSO and program supplier, founded Showtime, and two years later that service, too, went up on the satellite. In 1979 Warner Cable, merging with American Express, made its in-house pay television service, Star Channel, available to the industry at large as a satellite-delivered movie-only service, renaming it The Movie Channel (TMC). The following year, 1980, Time Inc. formed Cinemax as a complementary, movie-only service. Several cable MSOs owned Spotlight, another movie-only service launched in 1981 and offered only to their subscribers. However, Spotlight was discontinued in 1984. The other premium services were launched between 1982 and 1984, and many more may be added as shelf space on local cable systems expands. The top four movie services, capturing 90 percent of the pay cable market, are HBO, Showtime, Cinemax and The Movie Channel. (See the logos for some premium services in Figure 11-2.)

Cinemax

Cinemax, a division of Home Box Office, owned by Time Inc., was set up in 1980 to compete with Showtime as a multipay alternative by complementing the mother service based on an alternative selection of feature films. The two networks are marketed jointly, and Cinemax had 1,800 affiliates and 2.5 million subscribers at the beginning of 1984. Cinemax dovetails its daily 24-hour schedule with HBO's so that when a movie ends on one service, another begins on the other. In 1983 Cinemax modified its programming to include entertainment specials. Although Cinemax had carried only films since its inception, it added a mix of specials to help foster a personality distinct from HBO's. It also carries the comedy series *SCTV Network*. Although one of Cinemax's initial tenets was

FIGURE 11-2. General Premium Networks

that it would not duplicate HBO films (within a given month), the smaller service now premieres major movies like *Rocky III* at the same time as HBO. This change permits Cinemax to take advantage of HBO's major promotional campaigns.

Home Box Office

As of 1984 Time Inc.'s Home Box Office had 5,000 affiliates and 12.5 million subscribers. It constantly fine-tunes its programming strategy, but its basic thrust is to license feature films from the motion picture studios as soon as possible after their theatrical release, many of them on exclusive contracts. The service also programs originally produced specials with big-name entertainers (including Dolly Parton, Willie Nelson, Hall and Oates); "docutainment" series (*Time Was*, with Dick Cavett); *Consumer Reports* (working with the Consumers' Union); comedy programs (*Not Necessarily the News*); and boxing matches. Consistently popular, high-quality programming gives HBO 50 percent of the pay market.[3] Since its parent corporation, Time Inc., has extensive financial resources, HBO can finance some films during their early production stages in return for exclusive pay cable rights (called **prebuying**).[4] In this way HBO withholds some movies from its competitors and promotes them as "HBOnlys."

In 1982 and 1983, seeking to further differentiate itself from competitors, HBO greatly accelerated its pursuit of *exclusive* titles. It produced a number of made-for-pay movies, designed to have their first showing on HBO. The first of them was *The Terry Fox Story*. HBO also signed exclusivity agreements with two motion picture studios, Orion and Columbia Pictures, obtaining first crack at films those studios release (for a substantial price). In addition, the company raised $125 million in the investment community through a venture known as Silver Screen Partners for the production of a dozen or more motion pictures exclusive to HBO. Several coproduction ventures were begun with foreign partners, and in a 1983 coup, HBO signed an agreement with CBS and Columbia Pictures to create another major motion picture studio in Hollywood, Tri-Star. Each of these moves gives Home Box Office exclusive access to a considerable number of film titles that it plans to promote to cable operators and consumers as uniquely available on HBO.

HBO has also joined with Metromedia to license to independent television stations programs HBO originally produced. This alliance represents a breakthrough for pay television and broadcasting; for the first time, broadcasters agreed to telecast programs that had already appeared on a pay cable network.

The battle for differentiation began with the advent of multipay marketing. Exclusive rights to major motion pictures are one of the most powerful weapons for winning a distinct, positive image for a pay network. HBO now monopolizes exclusive licensing of theatrical feature films through its aggressive program of prebuys and production financing arrangements.

The Movie Channel

The Movie Channel, like HBO, Showtime and the other theatrical movie networks, runs feature films as soon as possible after their theatrical release.[5] But unlike its competitors, TMC does not program any specials or other kinds of programming (travel, sports). Living up to its name, TMC promotes itself as the channel that offers an unadulterated diet of films. It generally shows the same first-run motion pictures as the other services, but because it has no specials, it has more time to fill. As a result, TMC programs a greater number of titles per month, drawing upon older features to fill the gaps. Owned by Warner Communications and Viacom International, Inc. (with a minority interest by American Express), in 1983 TMC and Showtime managements were merged, pooling their assets including three transponders, in an attempt to increase their competitive stance relative to HBO. The two companies now share the financing, production and distribution of feature films through the joint venture. In 1984, they concluded an exclusive licensing agreement with Paramount, further improving their competitive position. TMC appears on 2,700 systems (including those owned by its parent, Warner Amex, and by Viacom), with about 2.6 million subscribers as of 1984.

Showtime

Showtime relys on feature films for a major portion of its audience appeal but it has moved increasingly into dramatic and comedy series programming. It now regularly schedules a children's program series starring big-name performers and an ongoing series featuring the comedian Gallagher. In addition, Showtime airs two adult soap operas (*Loving Friends and Perfect Couples* and *A New Day in Eden*) and the first-run cable continuation of *Paper Chase*, the canceled CBS series. Through series programming, Showtime is trying to create the same kind of program loyalty that the broadcast networks generate with their soaps and their prime-time situation comedies. Showtime generally appears as the second or third premium channel on a system, not as a stand alone. Formerly owned by Viacom and Group W Communications (a subsidiary of Westinghouse), it has 2,900 affiliates and over 4.7 million subscribers as of 1984, and participates in the joint production and licensing venture with TMC already described. Like TMC, Showtime is now owned by Viacom, Warner Communications and American Express.

The Demise of Spotlight

Spotlight, with 230 affiliates and 750,000 subscribers as of 1984, was disbanded. It was the only pay cable movie service cable operators owned, and it was offered solely to their subscribers. The rationale behind Spotlight was that cable operators (Cablevision, Cox, Storer, Tele-Communications, Times-Mirror) could buy films directly from the Hollywood studios, thus cutting out the middlemen suppliers (HBO, Showtime, The Movie Channel) and keeping a larger slice of the revenue for themselves. However, subscription numbers at Spotlight never reached the critical mass necessary to accomplish this goal. Cablevision Systems pulled out of the partnership in 1983, and the service ended in 1984. Their assets were sold to both HBO/Cinemax and Showtime/TMC.

Spotlight's programming resembles that of its rivals. Over a month, Spotlight aired five to seven G-rated and PG movies, some R-rated films but no "hard-R" films. Spotlight also presented movie festivals featuring a performer or a theme. For instance, it ran a "Woody Allen Festival" and a "Vintage Peter Sellers Festival." In addition, the service involved viewers in the programming by giving them a chance to participate in picking certain films via a 900 number and by holding film trivia contests. It programmed only movies. Its demise illustrates the effects of movie economics: Current film **production rates** can support only a few pay movie services.

MOVIE-BALANCING STRATEGIES
FOR GENERAL SERVICES

Premium services relying primarily on feature films generally use the same overall strategy, balancing several elements in their programming. These elements include premieres of major box-office hits, family and children's films (G-rated), adult-appeal films and specials, a select number of foreign films and repeat presentations of previous months' pay releases (euphemistically called *encores*). To these programs, a few dramatic or sit-com series, specials and, in some cases, sports are added.

Decisions on which films and specials to purchase and which performers or events to feature in original specials are based on several criteria. The overriding consideration is that each program be *value-justified* to subscribers. To warrant purchase or licensing and a prominent schedule position on a premium service, a film must either have proven popularity at the box office or have especially strong appeal for a particular segment of the audience. Premium services usually air only distinctive specials and series; they either present the top talent in the entertainment industry or explore unique television formats. Specific monthly schedule choices hinge on the availability of theatrical feature films and on showcasing entertainers and program forms that best complement these films so as to appeal to a variety of psychographic and demographic targets each month.

Selecting programs appealing to different target audiences through the course of a month becomes the programmer's challenge. For example, if a particular month's feature films have strong appeal to teenagers and men 18–49, the obvious choice for an entertainment special would be a show appealing to women 18–

49. Pay television programmers break down their audiences according to urban–rural classifications, age groups of 18–24, 25–49 and 50+, and by sex.[6] By scheduling programs each month that will appeal to all these groups, the programmer creates a balanced schedule.

Premieres

Films subdivide into five groups with overlapping appeals. The major audience attractions for any month are the film premieres—the recent box-office hits or special appeal films being offered for the first time on that premium service. These films may be rated G, PG or R. In August 1983, for example, Showtime headlined three films in on-air promotion and in its program guide as premiere audience attractions:

> *The Best Little Whorehouse in Texas,* co-starring Burt Reynolds and Dolly Parton in a comic hit about the attempts to launch a moral crusade against The Chicken Ranch, a favorite Texas hotspot. Rated R; shown six times during the month.

> *Firefox,* starring Clint Eastwood as a U.S. pilot who sneaks into the Soviet Union to steal the Firefox, Russia's newest and most deadly weapon. Rated PG; seven August playdates.

> *Nightshift,* comedy directed by *Happy Days'*s Ron Howard, in which Henry Winkler and Michael Keaton bring life to the city morgue by opening up a call girl operation. Rated R; shown six times in August.

Family and Children's Appeal

The second group of films placed in the schedule are G- and PG-rated, family-oriented movies. Four films appeared on Showtime during August 1983, establishing a strong pattern of family and children's appeal in the schedule:

> *Secret of N.I.M.H.* uses Disney-style animation in the story of a mama field mouse's efforts to save her home and family from a farmer's plow. Rated G; played six times in the month.

> *Black Beauty,* the classic family film based on the friendship between a boy and his colt. Rated G; shown six times.

Adult Appeal

The third group of films have varied adult audience appeals. Films without notable box-office success usually fall in this category. They are repeated less frequently than premieres and G-rated hits. In August 1983 Showtime had scheduled these films, among others, targeting young adults at the end of summer:

> *Homework,* showing that afterschool homework is not of the reading, writing and arithmetic kind for sixteen-year-old Tommy when *Dynasty'*s sexy Joan Collins gives him his first lesson in love. Rated R; four August playdates.

Humongous, story of a group of teenagers looking for a fun Labor Day weekend who become trapped in a nightmare of death and destruction when their boat is stranded on a deserted island. Rated R; three August playdates.

In other months, this group of films has included films such as *Somebody Killed Her Husband,* starring Farrah Fawcett, which was not a big box-office success. But as part of the monthly line-up in which 40–50 films cost the subscriber about what it costs for two people to go out to see one movie, a film like the above can be readily enjoyed by the pay cable viewer. Many passable films will attract viewers when they can see them at little cost.

Foreign Films

Other films that were not major theatrical hits may still rate as important acquisitions for pay television services. Viewers may value seeing a film on television that they might not be willing to pay three or four dollars to see in a movie theater. Foreign films fall in this group. One August, Showtime scheduled:

Gregory's Girl, starring Gordon John Sinclair and Dee Hepburn in a critically acclaimed sleeper about a high school boy who becomes enamoured with a female classmate. Rated PG; shown three times in August.

Encores

Encore films are repeat showings of films that premiered nine to twelve months earlier and features that premiered in the latter part of the previous month's schedule. Late premieres are always aired once or twice the following month to ensure an adequate number of plays and to use up all the contracted runs. One August, Showtime's line-up included five encore presentations, individually repeated from five to eight times. *Arthur* is one example:

Arthur, starring Dudley Moore in the hit about an eccentric young millionaire. Rated PG; six playdates in August.

MOVIE SCHEDULING CONSIDERATIONS

Balancing the number of major films and lesser-known but promotable titles every month, then adding a handful of encore presentations, is one of the key challenges a premium movie programmer faces. A crucial factor in preparing the line-up is title availability. Most films with good track records at the box office are obtained from the major film distributors, but an increasing number can be purchased directly from independent producers and distributors.

Film Availability

Theatrical films distributed by major studios are typically available to pay television services nine to eighteen months after their initial theatrical release.[7] This time period varies depending on the box-office success of the film. Twentieth Century-Fox kept *Star Wars,* a huge box-office success, in theatrical release for almost two years and then held off its theatrical rerelease for at least another year, substantially delaying its availability on pay television. In a similar situation, Universal rereleased its enormously successful film *Jaws* after the introduction of a sequel, *Jaws II*, postponing the pay television exhibition of *Jaws* for more than four years. Conversely, Irwin Allen's disaster epic *The Swarm* fell short of box-office expectations, had a limited theatrical run, and was not rereleased. It therefore became available for pay television almost immediately after its initial theatrical release.

Time constraints on the use of films also affect steady product flow, including how long and when a film is available to pay cable. Commercial broadcast television buyers, for example, have the financial clout to place time limitations on distributors' sales of films to premium and STV services. The broadcasters seek early telecast of key films to bolster their ratings during the Nielsen and Arbitron sweeps. This tactic shortens the period of time during which the films are available to premium networks. Since most top-grade films are released in time for theatrical showings in the summertime, and broadcasters often want those same films for the November and February sweeps, premium networks must use them at an accelerated rate in the early fall and in December/January. Because those same films might be useful to the largest premium cable networks that also seek ratings points in the sweeps, this practice operates to the especial benefit of broadcasters. On the other hand, some desirable films are unsuitable for broadcast sale altogether, which increases their pay television availability. Films such as *Carnal Knowledge* and *Lenny* would require such massive editing for broadcast television that they would be destroyed in the process. Therefore, distributors allow premium networks to schedule them as many times as they like for as long as they like.

Most of Hollywood's film classics are licensed to broadcast television stations on an exclusive basis, but a limited (and growing) number are available to pay television. Exceptions to the standard pattern include independent productions and major studio films removed from syndication or network release from time to time. Unfortunately, the rule prevails and not the exception; such classic favorites as *Casablanca*, *Citizen Kane* and *Adam's Rib*, which would be enhanced by being shown without editing, commercial interruption or inconvenient scheduling, are not available to pay television.

Occasionally, the major pay movie services disagree about whether or not to schedule a movie *after* it has already had a commercial broadcast network run. Some recent theatrical films, *Animal House* and *The Godfather* for example, played on pay services after they aired on the broadcast networks. Indeed, HBO and Showtime have found a pay cable following for such movies when they are shown unedited and without commercials. Some survey research even demonstrates viewer support for the reshowing of films that have been badly cut for commercial television presentation or that have exceptionally strong appeal for repeat viewing. Almost all pay services show a few selected off-network movies, which often draw sizable audiences.

Film Licenses

Feature films are licensed to pay television networks in one of two ways: per-subscriber payments or by flat fee. Per-subscriber means the film's producer or distributor negotiates a fee per customer for a specific number of runs within a fixed period. Such a fee is based on the actual number of subscribers who had access to the film (though not necessarily the number who actually saw it). In a flat fee arrangement, the parties negotiate a fixed payment regardless of the number of subscribers who have access to the film.

In the 1970s per-subscriber fees were small compared to theatrical distribution revenues and broadcast license fees and suited the rapid growth of the premium-network subscriber base. The film distributors were satisfied to get a share of every subscriber household receiving the premium network's programming. But once the premium networks grew large enough to have to pay substantial amounts for the pay television rights to a movie under that method, they often abandoned the per-subscriber formulas and negotiated flat fee arrangements with the program suppliers. The flat fee method is also used for acquiring originally produced programming.

Pay Windows

Distributors create a distribution **window** for a film's release when offering it to pay cable. In this arrangement, premium programmers have only a limited time, generally 12 months, in which to schedule first-run and second-run plays. For example, a given film may be made available to pay cable from April to March. It might premiere in April, encore in August and then be rescheduled as a G-rated or adult appeal film in February, possibly encoring in the following month to complete the run. Programmers must project ahead to see that the scheduled play periods for similar films from different distributors do not expire at exactly the same time. Otherwise, viewers could be treated to five blockbusters or four westerns or three Paul Newman films in the same month, an inefficient use of scarce resources. Ironically, inadvertent clustering of films can be packaged successfully and marketed as a "festival" or "A Night of _____," thus turning a potential problem into a promotable benefit.

Selective Viewing

Premium schedules are designed for selective rather than continuous viewing as in commercial television. Promotion stresses the values of convenience and choice in pay programming. If pay cable viewers cannot see *Best Little Whorehouse* on Monday, August 1 at 8 P.M. on Showtime, they will have several other opportunities to catch it during the month, on various nights of the week and in different time slots.

Despite this selective viewing, the audience flow concept that operates in broadcast television is inevitably at work on the premium networks as well. A strong attraction early in the evening will create a larger audience for subsequent programs. Strong 7 or 8 P.M. lead-ins maximize viewing of all features during an evening, but strategies enhancing viewing over the period of a month are even more important to pay cable. Encores of popular films, for example, can be assets to monthly premium schedules. Rescheduling them effectively is as important as placing them appropriately the first time they appear in the line-up. By scheduling the same film in a variety of time slots, the premium programmer avoids alienating viewers.

Film Placement

General rules of thumb for film scheduling include beginning weeknight programming at 8 P.M. and starting final showings (of major offerings) as late as 11:30 P.M. to 12:30 A.M. Those networks concentrating on the overnight daypart employ still later final-showing schedules. For most of the premium movie services, an evening consists of three to five programs, depending on individual running lengths. Entertaining short subjects, elaborate animated titles and promotional spots for other attractions fill the time between shows. All-movie networks especially favor movie-oriented shorts such as interviews with directors or location tours. Most movie services operate for 24 hours, but for the short-schedule services, Saturday, Sunday and holiday schedules generally begin at 2, 2:30 or 3 P.M. and may include as many as six programs up to the final major show at 11:30 P.M. or 12:30 A.M. The pay services use filler materials, usually old movies, to fill out their overnight and daytime schedules.

The premium services no longer **front-load** their films (that is, schedule most of them at the start of the calendar month). Using 20 new films each month (not counting final encores of the previous month's premieres) usually means scheduling four premieres each week, gradually integrating first-, second-, third-, and up to sixth-run presentations week by week so the viewer has a constantly changing line-up from which to choose, and new movies appear every week.

Counterprogramming broadcast network schedules is another strategic consideration. For example, on Monday nights, when *Monday Night Football* is a strong attraction on ABC, premium networks schedule films with female appeal. Preceding or following a popular broadcast network show with a program of the same genre creates a unified programming block (requiring channel switching, an easy move in cable homes with remote control keypads). Beginning programs on the hour as often as possible—especially during prime time from 8 to 11 P.M., makes it convenient for viewers to switch to and from pay cable.

Films and specials containing mature themes are usually scheduled at later hours even though pay television is not bound by broadcasting's traditions. PG features are offered throughout premium schedules. Monthly program guides encourage parents to prescreen all films rated PG or R early in the week to decide which are appropriate for their children to watch on subsequent airdates. Premium movie scheduling practice encourages parental control—which explains why there is little outcry from pay cable viewers about the content of R-rated films. Protests, when they occur, come from conservative groups that, as a whole, do not even subscribe to the mass-appeal or adult-oriented premium networks.

THE SPECIALIZED PREMIUM SERVICES

Several premium services narrowcast to specific interest or demographic groups. Movies make up most of their schedules (with the exception of The Sports Network, The Sports Channel and Prism, which emphasize sporting events). Movies on these networks are chosen for their strong appeal to a target group rather than any appeal they may have for a heterogeneous audience. Target audiences for the specialized premium services are variously defined by sex and age, as in the case of The Pleasure Channel and The Disney Channel or by ethnic groups such as the Spanish-language GalaVision or by common interests as in the case of Bravo. As of 1983, seven national premium networks and several regional and in-house pay services targeted their programming toward specialized audiences. (See their logos in Figure 11-3.)

Bravo

Bravo, a division of Rainbow Programming Services, schedules a mix of performing arts and feature films for ten hours a day (focusing on prime time and late night). Twenty-five percent of its programs are produced by Bravo itself. Bravo has featured internationally known performing companies such as the Bolshoi Ballet (in a performance of *Romeo and Juliet*), the New York Y Chamber Orchestra (performing Bach's Brandenburg Concertos) and the Jerry Mulligan Jazz Quartet in concert. When the service first began at the end of 1980, movies were much less prominent, but to boost subscribership, film now fills half of Bravo's schedule. The feature films presented on Bravo, however, differ sharply from those seen on the other premium movie services as some typical titles indicate: *Madame Rosa* (1977), *La Strada* (1954) and *Atomic Cafe* (1982), major foreign films—classic and current. Bravo had 97 affiliates and 140,000 subscribers at the start of 1984, and its programming is designed for affluent, sophisticated performing arts fans and classical-movie buffs.

The Disney Channel

The Disney Channel, launched in April 1983, trades on the name of the Walt Disney Studios. While its boosters say that no premium service has been launched with so much product recognition, it is equally true that no service has as much to live up to. Programming for The Disney Channel does not include the famous Disney movies like *Snow White* and *Bambi* that the public normally associates

FIGURE 11-3. Specialized Premium Networks

with the Disney name. They have been held back because the Disney executives prefer to keep their great classics fresh for theatrical rerelease every seven years and to prevent the massive home recording of these classics that would surely occur. Instead, The Disney Channel emphasizes original pay programs appealing to viewers of all ages. For the very youngest it has *Dreamfinders*, a weekly one-hour program tracing the adventures of six children in the "realm of imagination," and *Mousercise*, an exercise show. For adults, The Disney Channel carried in its first year *Epcot Magazine*, containing daily, evening and weekend editions focusing on the futuristic technology being developed and merchandised at Disney's Epcot Center. Already existing Disney product, nonclassic films such as *The Love Bug* and television series programming such as *True Life Adventures*, is also scheduled with these series in a mix of about half original productions and half Disney library materials. The Disney Channel's biggest challenge is to appeal not only to children but also to their parents who make the decision to purchase a pay service. As of January 1984, The Disney Channel had 1,100 affiliates and 530,000 subscribers.

Eros, a Canceled Service

Subscribers to this cable premium service were interested in program material with soft sexual content, similar to that appearing in *Eros* magazine, owned by the same company. The programming attracted a predominantly male audience using a mix of theatrical and made-for-videocassette movies, largely of European origin, dubbed in English. All programming had an R or X rating, but the schedule avoided hard-core pornography. Eros tried to minimize controversy over its material by programming only the overnight hours from midnight to 6 A.M. Eros appeared largely in urban markets, but failed due to a lack of financial backing. The Playboy Channel offers an equivalent level of adult programming (hard R or very soft X), and *Penthouse* magazine announced its intention to create a similar service in the late 1980s.

GalaVision

GalaVision programs in the Spanish language for the growing Hispanic population in the United States. It has 130,000 pay subscribers on 200 cable affiliates. Its 4 P.M. to 3 A.M. daily schedule consists of movies, Latin American daytime soap operas (called *novelas*), sporting events (weekly Tuesday night boxing) and specials. On weekends, it programs an 18-hour schedule. GalaVision uses Spanish and Latin American productions and some U.S. films dubbed into Spanish. Begun in 1979, it targets an adult audience of all ages and is jointly marketed with the co-owned Spanish International Network (SIN), a broadcast and basic cable network. Both appear on Galaxy 1.

Home Theatre Network

Home Theatre Network, which began limited satellite operation in 1978 (one movie per night), was restructured as a 12-hour service in 1982. It relies on feature films but limits its offering to G- and PG-rated movies, even excluding some films that other cable programmers consider suitable for family viewing. HTN advertises itself as a service for the entire family, appealing to those viewers offended by the "strong language, nudity and adult situations" that have become identified with some pay cable programming. HTN's policy includes showing blockbuster titles such as *Superman II* and *Star Wars*, which it shares with the other premium movie services. HTN further differentiates itself, however, by offering occasional family concert specials and several hours a week of travel programming, consisting of picturesque documentaries of the world's cities and more exotic locales. HTN is owned by Group W and programs from 4 P.M. to 4 A.M. It has 400 affiliates and 230,000 subscribers, largely in the Midwest.

The Playboy Channel

The Playboy Channel, a premium service owned by *Playboy* magazine in conjunction with Rainbow Programming, which includes Cox Cable, has over 300 affiliates and 560,000 subscribers. Like the Disney Channel, the Playboy Channel elicits instant brand recognition from consumers. Most people have a notion of what it is like before they see it.[8]

In 1982 Playboy Enterprises bought into Escapade, Rainbow's adult movie service, and reformed it introducing original programming bearing the Playboy stamp—such as *The News According to Playboy* and *Playmate Playoffs*. Playboy provides what it calls "a video magazine" of adult material targeted mainly at male adults 18 +. Early Playboy research, however, demonstrated that subscribing couples tend to watch the programming together and that nearly 50 percent of its audience was women. This research stimulated the inclusion of programming targeted specifically toward women in its 8 P.M. to 6 A.M. schedule. The result is a service composed half of adult movies (e.g., *Fanny Hill*) and half of original specials, catering to an adult male audience. Like The Pleasure Channel, it is a highly differentiated premium service.

The Pleasure Channel

After two years as a regional adult pay service, The Pleasure Channel was launched in 1984 on Westar 5 as a national premium service. Like its predecessor Eros, it programs only a short overnight schedule (the six hours from 11 P.M. to 5 A.M., EST). The Pleasure Channel carries harder adult content (more X) than The Playboy Channel (closer to R ratings), but all adult satellite services avoid hard-core pornography (drawing the line at explicit penetration). At the time of launch, The Pleasure Channel had about 40 affiliates with 75,000 subscribers, mostly in rural areas, but including many hotel subscribers. Although adult services have fewer political difficulties in sophisticated metropolitan areas, they also face greater competition for the leisure dollar. In consequence, their subscribers tend to live in rural areas.

The Sports Network

Launched in 1984 by Group W, The Sports Network uses the resources of Sportsvision (Chicago), Pro-Am Sports Systems (Detroit), Wisconsin All-Sports

Network (Milwaukee) and several other smaller regional sports networks. Using four satellite transponders and drawing various games from its regional affiliates, The Sports Network tailors sports packages for the four geographical regions of the country. The Sports Network is piggybacked with Showtime in some areas and developing slowly on a part-time basis. It includes magazine-style sports talk and interview programming, some repeats of historically important sporting events, dominated by live games.

Regional Services

Regional premium services provide programming to many cable systems within a limited geographical area. Prism, a mixed sports and movie service, supplies its programming largely to restaurants, bars and other public places and some clustered residences in the greater Philadelphia metropolitan area. Buena Vista Channel supplies a mix of Spanish- and English-language programming in the Los Angeles area. Z Channel, a movie service in the Los Angeles market, appeals to the Hollywood film community by programming thematically to satisfy film buffs and aficionados. Its programmers select older, often overlooked movies to appeal to the special tastes of the educated Hollywood audience. A few other pay services provide in-house programming for their parent cable systems. Also, several regional sports channels appear on cable systems as premium channels.

FUTURE DIRECTIONS FOR PREMIUM PROGRAMMING

Some national studies have shown that the high cost of pay services and the repetition of feature films on competing pay networks contribute to service cancelation in multipay households.[9] Churn will be even more pronounced as cable systems wire low-cost housing in metropolitan markets. Increasingly sophisticated packaging of core services with value-added premiums such as remote control, stereo sound, extra set connections and discounted fee structures will ultimately affect churn rates and increase the number of multipay households. Showtime's Pactime marketing strategy in 1983 (drawing on the Pac Man videogame fad) set the standard for packaging a range of multipay offerings. HBO/Cinemax has pioneered the differentiated, low duplication strategy.

The problem of repetitive or overlapping programming on different services is already being addressed by aggressive acquisition campaigns that seek exclusive rights to feature films, and by joint ventures to produce theatrical made-for-pay movies and specials. HBO's domination of the pay television marketplace resulted in the 1983 merger of Showtime and The Movie Channel to guarantee them the financial clout to obtain a supply of quality, first-run theatrical movies and to expand their production capabilities. The strategies of differentiation and exclusivity will guide the actions of most premium programmers in the late 1980s.

The amount of pay-per-view "event" programming will expand dramatically in the late 1980s, including movies, sports and live entertainment. By the end of the decade, single pay events will be a major part of all general premium services and of the programming of a new competitor, direct broadcasting (DBS). Subscription television services will try to merge with premium networks or become regional competitors for shelf space on local cable systems. Another competing form of mass-audience pay television will emerge by 1990: electronic delivery of videogames and computer software, combined with data base information retrieval and transactional services. Cable companies will alternately compete and create joint ventures with telephone companies for a major share of this market, and entertainment services will compete with nonentertainment services for the public's attention, time and dollars. The specialized premium services will find small but loyal audiences and will probably turn to advertising to supplement their subscriber revenues. Although the addition of advertising will be controversial, subscribers will eventually accept it as an alternative to higher monthly fees.

Exclusive programming and pay-per-view will be the dominant concerns of the premium networks and cable operators through the balance of the 1980s. Increasingly, however, their attention will turn to marketing information services via satellite and cable to the burgeoning universe of home computers. Premium services will vie for a role in the growing information and transaction business that will emerge in the latter half of the 1980s.

SUMMARY

Premium cable networks, for which subscribers pay over and above the cost of basic cable service, primarily provide theatrical feature films and an increasing number of entertainment specials and sporting events. The services divide into general pay services, scheduling movies aimed at a broad-based audience, and specialized pay services, targeting narrowly defined demographic or interest groups with cultural programming, sports, adult films, family films or Spanish-language programming. In the multipay environment, the premium services compete for shelf space on cable systems by offering revenue splits so as to acquire attractive positions on systems. The movie networks rotate their feature films and seek complementary programming with different audience appeals to balance their schedules. Pay cable programmers must consider film availabilities, licensing practices and pay windows in selecting and scheduling theatrical motion pictures. The major strategies for the late 1980s focus on the need for differentiation among services and exclusivity in programming. Pay-per-view, when it arrives, holds the promise of enough revenue to support original programming for pay cable.

Notes

[1] *Television & Cable Factbook*, 1982–83, pp. 317–1498.

[2] "Austin Furst on HBO's Programming," *Cablevision*, 26 February 1979, pp. 63–65.

[3] "Special Report: The HBO Story," *Broadcasting*, 15 November 1982, pp. 48–52.

[4]Jefferson Graham, "Guess Who's Amassed a Fortune in Feature Films?" *View,* June 1983, pp. 2–36. See also Hoyt Hilsman, "The Price of Pictures," *View,* February 1983, pp. 56–59.

[5]Herbert Swartz, "Movies, Movies, Movies: What Makes the Movie Channel Work?" *Cable Marketing,* January 1982, pp. 51–53.

[6]Pay cable typically uses the age categories 18–24 and 25–49 because they best separate people with similar entertainment tastes, whereas broadcasters focus on consumer buying habits. The 18–24 group is important because it watches more films since the bulk of films are directed toward that age group, in part because their lifestyles permit easy attendance at movie theaters.

[7]Sophisticated distributors have been extremely successful with several rounds of alternating theatrical rereleases and pay television exhibitions. A pay **run** is a playing period of about 30 days in which an attraction is telecast three to eight times. This pattern applies to premium network, subscription television and other pay services.

[8]In 1983, a grand jury indicted Warner Amex Cable on charges of carrying on the Playboy Channel two adult films that "pandered obscenity." Warner Amex settled out of court, agreeing not to present programs that would receive an X rating (if they were rated) or other sexually explicit materials in Hamilton County (Cincinnati), Ohio. See "Cincinnati System's Carriage of Playboy Brings Obscenity Charge," *Broadcasting,* 20 June 1983, pp. 74–75.

[9]"B&B Study Sees Pay Cable as Goldmine," *Broadcasting,* 30 May 1983, p. 50, referring to *The New TV Technologies: The View from The Viewer—I* (New York: Benton & Bowles, Inc., May 1983).

Selected Sources

Baldwin, Thomas F., and McVoy, D. Stevens. "Pay Television." *Cable Communication.* Englewood Cliffs, New Jersey: Prentice-Hall, 1983.

CableVision, monthly trade magazine covering the cable industry.

Electronic Media, weekly trade newspaper emphasizing new television technologies.

Multichannel News, monthly trade articles on national cable programming.

"Special Reports on Cable," *Broadcasting* (6 December 1982): 35–36; (15 November 1982): 48–69.

View: The Magazine of Cable TV Programming.

CHAPTER TWELVE

Local Origination Cable Programming

Donald E. Agostino and Susan Tyler Eastman

A QUICK GUIDE TO CHAPTER TWELVE

DONALD E. AGOSTINO, *associate professor and chairman of Telecommunications at Indiana University, was also chair of the Bloomington Telecommunications Council in 1983 and a consultant to the cable industry. After taking degrees at Gonzaga University (B.A.), the University of California at Berkeley (M.A.) and Ohio University (Ph.D.), he joined Indiana University in 1973 as an assistant professor. In 1978 he worked for the National Science Foundation, developing funding for projects in science education via the mass media. In addition to producing and directing credits, he has published in the* Journal of Broadcasting *and* Journal of Communication *and authored reports on videotex, videodiscs, radio programming and cable access programming.*

SUSAN EASTMAN'S *credentials appear at the start of Chapter 9. Together, these authors appraise local origination and special services on cable in the mid-1980s.*

PROGRAMMING AT THE SYSTEM HEADEND

Cable systems deliver satellite-distributed basic and premium networks, including the superstations. They also program special services and originate channels intended only for their subscribers. This kind of cable programming is called **local origination** or **LO.** Most frequently, it refers to live cablecasting of community meetings and playbacks of videotaped programs community organizations produce about their activities; LO subdivides into *local production* and *access.* This chapter examines the selection, scheduling and evaluation of LO programming, and also covers *ancillary services* such as leased and subsidiary business services and cable radio.

Increasingly, cable systems produce their own local newscasts and cover high school sporting events, local parades, festivals, state fairs and the like. Programming that community groups or individuals produce—church groups, college students, video artists, local politicians and so on is called *access programming* to separate it from programs the cable staff produces. By the mid-1980s, many local cable programmers were supplementing local production and access material with syndicated programs to round out the schedules of their local origination channels. Like broadcast programmers, then, local cable programmers must choose programs, place them in a meaningful arrangement and judge their success or failure.

Many systems also provide pay services to generate additional system revenue. These extra services range from cable radio and teletext to leased channels and computerized data services.

The programmer handling local origination for the system functions much like a television or radio station programmer. But instead of scheduling just one channel, that person schedules many, purchases syndicated programs and services and also acts as producer/director for some of the programs. In addition, the LO programmer generally supervises access channels and administers ancillary program services.

LOCAL PRODUCTION BY THE SYSTEM

Most major market cable franchises require locally produced programming. When the franchise does not require it, the cable operator may provide local programs anyway, as a service or a moneymaker. Nationally, local cable production ranges from the extremely simple—a fixed camera panning the faces of a clock, thermometer and barometer—to the relatively complex—live productions from cable headend studios. In a few systems, local production includes fully produced high school sports, little theatre or nightclub performances. On the other hand, it may only be a frame of text presenting information such as program listings for other cable channels or the dates of community meetings. Increasingly, systems cablecast local newscasts specializing in community events and purchase syndicated movie packages and old off-network series to stimulate viewing of local only channels. The purpose of such expensive programming is to provide a hospitable advertising environment.

National distributors syndicate taped sporting events and reruns of entertainment specials to cablecasters at low rates since their audiences are likely to be very small. In addition, syndicators supply program shorts, brief programs of varying lengths intended to fill out an hour after an odd-length sporting event or movie. Many cable systems combine this kind of syndicated programming with live and taped replays of local productions.

Community Service and Franchise Renewal

In keeping with the principle of localism in the regulation of broadcasting, in 1972 the FCC began to require cable operators to provide programming to the community of franchise. All but the smallest systems were required to provide local programming "to a significant extent." Many cable operators reluctantly provided facilities and originated programming—though most preferred to limit cable service to delivery of must-carry broadcast signals, superstations and national cable networks. Much LO programming, therefore, consisted of whatever could be acquired for the lowest cost per-screen-minute. Initially, local cable operators saw no advantage to supporting production and sales efforts.

By the late 1970s, when the courts overturned this FCC requirement, LO was seen as a way large cable systems might narrowcast, that is, reach narrow, specific-interest groups within the community and generate more ad revenue. Program quality improved, and LO producers and programmers learned what programs and approaches were successful. LO demonstrated cable could originate programming that met viewer needs other media could not fill. Live cablecasting of community meetings typifies such programming. Furthermore, some MSOs, such as ATC, Group W and Warner Amex, have committed their systems to providing LO as a way of serving their franchise communities and as a defense against cable's technological competitors. STV, MDS and DBS services cannot match the subscriber orientation evident in effective LO programming.

Impending franchise renewal created another reason for continued LO. Now MSOs promise to upgrade their LO facilities and expand programming to get support for franchise renewal. Nationally then, the pressure to renew franchises and the lure of advertising revenue stimulated LO programming.

Advertising Revenue Potential

By 1980 the average annual advertising revenue generated by those cable systems offering advertising was $1.70 per subscriber. By 1982, the average had climbed to $3, and by the end of the 1980s, it is expected to reach $40 per subscriber.

A small system of 20,000 subscribers, even in a market unlikely to attract national spot advertising or ad agency placements, may generate as much as $800,000 in annual ad revenue by 1990. Local advertising revenue may exceed that from premium channels on some systems. (Premium cable pay-back economics were explained in Chapter 9.) Especially in systems where basic cable fees were set artificially low in franchising agreements, advertising will be increasingly important as a revenue source. And in most systems, local origination will be the most flexible advertising vehicle for local spot advertising.

Types of Local Production

As of the early 1980s, about 10 percent of the cable systems having more than 10,000 subscribers offered LO programming. A survey of cable systems offering LO in 1982 showed that the number of LO hours varied from 1 to 264 per week, and that most programs were frequently repeated.[1] About 40 hours per week, one-third of which was first run, was a typical LO operation.

About 24 percent of LO programming in 1982 fell into the category of public affairs, 22 percent was entertainment, 17 percent was religious, 13 percent instructional, 9 percent sports, 9 percent government and 3 percent news. The remaining 3 percent consisted of an extraordinary variety of shows and is perhaps most indicative of what LO programming can become.

U.S. Cable of Lake County in Waukegan, Illinois, for example, cablecasts over 80 hours of LO per week. The most-viewed programs are a 30-minute sports talk show, an auto racing program, health programs and local sports events. Cable 6 of San Francisco cablecasts "the only regularly scheduled prime-time television program dealing with arts and entertainment in San Francisco" and *Lovestyles,* a half-hour late-night show dealing with the concerns of the gay community. In Oklahoma City, Cox Cable televises the local rodeo as well as the Stars' ice hockey games. The ad availabilities in both programs are sold out. In several systems, a video dating service is the most popular local-only program.

Such programs indicate cable technology is easily and cheaply adapted to serve the community in ways that other media cannot because their costs are significantly higher. Low-power broadcast television (LPTV), a new class of station with signal coverage of less than 10 miles, is cable LO's only likely competitor. Cable programmers have learned to make localism an asset to both advertisers and cable systems. Production quality, however, affects audience appeal, and as with all television programming, well-produced LO is expensive. To recover costs, therefore, LO productions must have broad appeal, a characteristic often at odds with localism.

Syndication and LO Networking

As with other mass media, popular LO programming is eventually networked to a larger audience. This fundamental media distribution principle holds that expensive, high-quality material distributed to a mass audience achieves the lowest per-viewer cost, and some LO programs have been popular enough to follow this pattern. A coproduction by the Cox Cable System and the Grumbacher Paint Co., for example, was distributed in 1982 over 62 Cox systems. The program was a six-part series on art instruction, and it included promotion of a paint kit available by direct mail from the sales of which Cox received a percentage. Thus, this cable programming reached a very specialized audience in many locations by networking and so multiplied its producers' profits. This pioneering effort illustrates the coming pattern: Small-scale, independent producers and manufacturers wanting to make sales will syndicate or barter programs and series to LO programmers having access to program networks.[2]

LO is on its way to becoming a more specialized version of a commercial, independent broadcast station. It relies on the most popular entertainment forms such as sports and music; purchases and barters syndicated material of established appeal; produces some local programming of high visibility within the community; and builds an advertising clientele among local businesses. Syndication of LO programs has become another potential revenue source for some MSOs.[3]

Program Shorts

A rising cable-related business syndicates packages of very short programs, some as brief as 30 seconds, called interstitial programming. Used singly and in groups, these shorts serve as filler between odd-length programs to complete an hour. Although travel-related companies (airlines and the like), tourist offices and the U.S. government (especially the departments of Defense and Labor) supply some of this programming for free, increasingly, commercial firms are producing shorts especially for the cable television market. LO channel programmers purchase a lot of interstitial programming when budgets permit. The appetite for off-beat, original shorts is growing, fueled in part by the generally higher quality of professionally produced programming over in-house productions.

HBO used shorts extensively between telecasts of uncut films in the late 1970s. These shorts provided a breather for audiences as well as a national outlet for independent filmmakers. The content and style of shorts varied from silent walks in an autumn forest to zany cartoons using pinched-clay figures. HBO's need for shorts as filler decreased as more feature films were produced to fit cable's program lengths and as the premium networks began using the breaks between programs for promotional announcements and music videos.

Shorts remain popular with audiences, however, so suppliers market them in cable systems. Sometimes shorts are sequenced together to form half-hour features on local cable systems—much as music videos are put together to form full-length programming.

ACCESS CHANNELS AND ACCESS PROGRAMS

Cable's multichannel capacity provides an opportunity for "people's television," a way for relatively small groups to gain access to the nation's most popular entertainment and information-processing medium. Access, in cable television, is both a means of giving a small group a sense of identity and providing them with a channel of communication to the larger community. Television helps special interest groups reinforce their common interest and relate their purpose to others—in effect, to become a recognized entity in the information culture. The common bond of these access user-groups might be age, ethnic background, political cause, intellectual interest or hobby. Minority groups, antiwar activists, readers of Tolstoy, model railroad club members, off-road racers and a myriad of special interest groups all want to be on television.

A system can dedicate a whole channel to access or reserve time on LO channels for access programs. Historically, access programming divided into four types: *public, educational, governmental* and *leased.* In practice, scant programming material and the overturning of the FCC's regulation mandating cable systems to set aside a channel for each type reduced the four to a combined or community access channel.

Community Access

In 1972 the FCC promulgated rules for new cable systems of 3,500 or more subscribers requiring four access channels to be used by (1) individuals within the general public, (2) educational institutions, (3) local government and (4) those wishing to lease a channel. In addition, cable systems had to provide the production facilities and organizational structure needed to produce access programs for these groups.

Those rules dramatically enlarged the role local franchise authorities envisioned for cable service in their communities, elicited a flood of dull, amateurish television productions, and set up an adversary relationship between cable operators and access program groups that lasted well into the 1980s.

Even so, public access channels did make some cablecast time and production support available free on a first-come, first-served basis. Production support and technical facilities were available at an at-cost rate for additional time, and most access operations also offered instruction in the rudiments of studio and field electronic video production. Thus, in the 1970s, candidates for local public office used access channels because no requirements for equal time applied. Independent filmmakers and video artists used the channels for their production work though much of it was essentially personal rather than public communication. Some individuals undertook regularly scheduled series. The most notorious was perhaps *The Ugly George Show* on New York City's Manhattan Cable.

Host Ugly George approached women on the street and asked them to take off their clothes for his camera. Enough did so to give public access a vulgar image among both viewers and policymakers.

Only about 5 percent of the public access programming of the 1970s was actually planned, produced and scheduled. Most was material that might be best classified as home movies by local producers or lengthy rap sessions. Public access programming, in fact, was viewed mostly by its principal participants. For example, in one study, a videotaped replay of a senior citizens dance was found to be viewed almost exclusively by persons who attended the dance.[4] This systematic study of the audience for a well-run and promoted public access channel in a small city with no local television broadcasting showed an average weekly audience share of less than two-tenths of 1 percent.

In short, the concept of unstructured public access really never took off. It failed to attract groups willing to submit to the organizational discipline necessary for success in any mass medium—clear purpose, cost and equipment control and a coherent plan of audience appeal. Without these elements, and with growing disenchantment among policymakers and cable operators, it was clear access had to take a different line of development.

In 1979 the Supreme Court forced the issue in the *Midwest II* decision, holding that the 1972 FCC access requirements violated a section of the 1934 Communications Act holding that broadcasters and, by extension, cablecasters, are not common carriers.[5] Federal regulation could not require cable operators to carry programming over which they had no say (except the broadcast must-carry stations).

Though the FCC rules mandating access channels were thrown out, most new franchise agreements still require provisions for access channels, now more broadly referred to as *community access channels*. Some group in the community, such as the library system, an appointed council of access users, the school or hospital board, leases a channel from the cable company and manages the access operation. Under this structure the users must abide by the operator's policies concerning access to production facilities and cable time. The access channel management has discretionary authority over content and scheduling. Most community access channels have policies prohibiting cablecasting of commercial or sectarian material.

As with LO, exceptionally successful examples of access programs and access operations suggest viable directions for the future. Some cable operators are now more inclined to see access not as a "them vs. us" obligation but as an opportunity to win both subscribers and franchise renewal. But across the United States to date, fewer than two dozen community access channels have successfully combined the functions previously divided among public, educational and governmental access.

Community access programming's singular characteristic is localism, often to the level of "neighborhoodism." A number of reports describe the organization, policies and programming of thriving community access operations, but as one might expect, they take on the particular interests and emphases of their communities.[6] Four general characteristics have emerged, however, that provide a model for community access programming:

1. *Broad Community Support.*   Viable access operations usually enjoy the backing of city officials, cable system officers, community institutions, volunteer groups and, most importantly, subscribers. This coalition quite often convinces the city to turn over a sizable portion of the cable franchise fee to the access channel, and enlists the support of persons knowledgeable in the arts, business, sports and public service. This money and expertise, in turn, help the access channel operators cover local events and issues with reasonable technical and conceptual quality. Such programming does attract a small, interested audience and is recognized as a worthwhile public service. At its best, access television provides the clearest example of localism in the electronic media, and it benefits subscribers, user groups and the cable operator.

2. *Consortium Approach.*   Community access operators typically see themselves as facilitators of community interaction, not as imitators of low-budget independent television. The access operator prefers to provide live coverage of a public discussion on a local zoning issue, for example, rather than produce a documentary on zoning problems. Access channels tend to be communications resources for the community, not production centers. Thus, creating viable access programming involves (a) helping community groups form consortia and (b) helping them integrate television communication into their own quite specific activities and interests.

3. *Live, Involved Programming.*   Successful access operators accentuate their community service function by live, full-length telecasting of significant meetings of local legislative bodies, advisory councils, school boards, community groups and other such deliberations on community business. Recognizing the importance of such coverage in a democracy, some city councils allow persons watching at home to participate by phone in the televised public discussion or to make an appearance using split-screen presentation from a neighborhood access studio.

Such live, interactive community programming is not likely to be duplicated by any other media services and, during debate of important community topics, commands a measurable share of the cable television audience. Such programming gives access a clearly defined and positive image in subscribers' minds and becomes a selling point for basic cable service.

Conversely, programming generic how-to shows, frequent repeats and lengthy blocks of viewer-requested replays dilutes the subscribers' notion of access programming's value. Many community access channels are overly dependent on just such programming.

4. *Regular Programming Service.*   Although the philosophy of access television includes the notion that individuals should, on their own terms, be able to address the television audience, sequences of unrelated, stand-alone presentations cannot build audience loyalty and often alienate drop-in viewers. Access programming builds support with coherent, thematic, predictably scheduled programs and video services. This approach may smack of commercialism to access purists, but the experience of *successful* access operations indicates that what works in commercial and public television broadcasting and cable networking also works for access.

Capital and Operating Budgets

A successful access operation, therefore, has the same technical make-up—though in lesser measure—that a local origination or instructional video facility has, and, additionally, needs a staff that can work effectively with a wide range of community institutions. Such a program costs money; a sizable amount of capital is needed just to begin operation. An adequately equipped, industrial-quality access facility needs about $300,000 in electronic equipment and about 6,000 square feet of secure space convenient to the public and served by backfeed lines to the cable headend.[7] A well-equipped operation that can easily support multiple projects needs three times that amount of money and space.

Salaries, rent, maintenance, repair and expendables for a minimum access operation—one that is heavily dependent on volunteers—cost about $60,000 a year. More typical access facilities have about eight full-time employees and an annual operating budget of $200,000 a year. Many failed access centers tried to start small and then grow, not realizing that an initial critical mass of capital and committed personnel was needed. Others started successfully but could not develop funding sources to replace grant monies used for initial equipment and operating funds. Video production, even by volunteers (and sometimes especially by volunteers) is expensive, and the most common way of holding costs down is to cablecast exchange or syndicated programming and performances by school-age amateur groups. Such programming, more and more tangential to the original idea of access, illustrates how access programming is growing indistinguishable from local origination (LO) programming.

Educational and Governmental Access

The terms *educational access* and *governmental access* are holdovers from the 1972 *Cable Television Third Report and Order* in which the FCC mandated access channels. As required in the 1970s, cable systems offered a reserved access channel (dedicated) for both the local school board and for local government. In most cases these institutions did not utilize the channels. Public or community access groups rather than government itself cablecast government meetings; and school districts interested in using television in their classrooms had already developed distribution systems—by broadcasting, microwave or videocassette. The *Midwest II* decision legally confirmed the real situation in the schools and government offices—the availability of a dedicated cable channel did not usually mean implementation of access television.

Notable exceptions are worth mentioning, however, because they illustrate the possibilities for educational and governmental narrowcasting. An impressively planned and engineered cable loop in Spokane, Washington, links classrooms, homes and headend, carrying a set of cable channels dedicated to instructional use.[8] Students at home are linked to the classroom, standardized in-class materials are cablecast throughout the unified school district's classes, and students can do assigned home viewing or view repeats of classroom materials during evening hours. Such a system provides a model reflecting a well-organized school administration, an enthusiastic faculty and a service-oriented cable operator.

Medical schools have developed similar cable loops with hospitals and clinics to instruct both medical practitioners and patients. In general, however, schools and colleges are not operating educational channels. They use cable as they use broadcasting, for distribution of specific continuing education courses or series programming such as *Civilization* that might be of value to classroom viewers.

Leased Access

A leased channel is one turned over to another entity to program, either as a subscriber service or as an advertising vehicle. Leased channels account for less than 1 percent of all cable channels and occur, in all cases, in the larger markets.[9] A Markle Foundation study concluded that most systems provide *no* leased access, but that one-quarter of systems having more than 30 channels provide at least one channel for lease.[10] Systems with a small number of channels lack space for leased channels, and franchise agreements rarely require leased access. In any case, leased channels are used for only a very small percentage of total available time. Experiments with shopping and security services, however, have shown positive audience reaction, making them viable leased channel concepts. Classified advertising is also proving a big success on some leased channels. *Optional* leased channels are discussed below as a part of the ancillary, revenue-producing services cable systems offer.

Leased *access* channels raise the issue of whether cable is a common carrier or a publisher with full First Amendment protections. The requirement of leased access suggests a common carrier model, and in consequence, the cable industry opposes it. Optional leasing allows the cable operator to form joint publishing ventures on one or more channels, thereby establishing itself as a publishing entity, presumably with the same rights as newspapers. Although a forced leasing contract can supply exactly the same content as an optional leasing arrangement, it is the optional arrangement that clearly establishes the cable operator's intention to be a publisher.

The Future of Access Programming

As with cable itself, access began in the small and medium-sized markets where it often provided the only source of local news and community information. These operations were hampered by low budgets and high personnel turnover. In 1976 the National Federation of Local Cable Programmers (NFLCP) began to coordinate the efforts of access managers and users in the nation, circulating programs and information, and providing leadership and training. One of the results of the franchise wars of the early 1980s in the major cities was the arrival of professionally equipped and staffed access centers in cities such as Cincinnati, Pittsburgh and Boston. These cities have a strong sense of community that access can both utilize and serve. User groups in midsize and large cities are more extensive, more professional and more inclined to use video than their counterparts in smaller markets. It seems likely, therefore, that access users will continue to coordinate program production in these cities.

Access program content will include continuing professional education, popular discussion of local political topics and candidates, and presentations by local musical, theatre, environmental, preservation and other groups. Such productions may be successful both as local access programming and as networked access programming.

Except for live coverage of public meetings and the like, access programming, by and large, will meld with local origination programming. Programming from the two sources is already difficult to distinguish.

Access operations will have to develop new revenue sources, similar to those LO channels have. User fees, advertising and full-fledged rate cards for equipment use will become commonplace as revenue-starved local governments divert franchise fees and federal regulations limit the access support a franchise authority can demand from a cable operator.

SCHEDULING LO PROGRAMMING

The programming goals of a local cable channel are similar to those of a broadcast station: to acquire and produce programs appealing to a target audience marketable to advertisers. Scheduling goals are also similar: to develop as broad, loyal and large an audience as possible. The challenge for cable programmers is to achieve these goals under franchise, economic and competitive constraints. Franchise contracts often require cablecasting programs of very limited appeal. Budgets, facilities and numbers of personnel scarcely compare to those, say, of the smallest independent television stations. And the rest of the channel array introduces programs of the highest quality and popularity with which LO must compete for audience attention.

Block Programming

LO cable's strengths, however, can overcome some of these problems. Because of its time flexibility, LO can carry live, local events such as public meetings and sports events of unpredictable length. The timing of *live* programming of course depends on the producers or authorities actually in charge of the event—the cable programmer cannot usually influence it. But the audience such coverage draws can be maintained by scheduling related, pretaped programming *after* the live event, using a block programming strategy. Cablecasting of a school board meeting might be followed by a documentary on local school planning or a syndicated program dealing with education. In the same manner, a football coaching film might follow a live high school football contest. These related, taped shows can easily be repeated with the repeat cablecast of the originally live event and promoted jointly.

Repeat Scheduling

Repeat scheduling is an essential narrowcasting strategy for LO as well as the national cable networks—and even public television as explained in chapters 18 and 19. On LO, Friday night's game, for example, should be recablecast at a fixed, predictable time and promoted on the air and in a program guide so interested viewers who could neither attend nor view the live coverage can watch the later telecast. LO scheduling practice seeks cumulative rather than one-time-only audiences.

Cherrypicked Channels

When live coverage is a large part of the schedule, some cable programmers use another programming strategy. They schedule a potpourri of unrelated but individually interesting programs, similar to the format strategy of some public radio stations. (See Chapter 20 on eclectic radio.) Selecting among cable networks, syndicators and local programs is called cherrypicking, as described in Chapter 9. Such a channel offers a kind of curious surprise for the viewer, a jumbled toy-box of programs. Group W, on its Manhattan system in New York, mixes sports, movies, inspirational and access programming into a single channel, and promotes the composite as "WWW," giving it a stationlike identity.

Instead, then, of programming an LO channel with a narrow range of programs giving it a distinct, uniform identity, cable programmers may schedule on the basis of individual program appeal, availability and community interest. Such an approach seeks surprise rather than audience flow. On-air graphics and promotional copy during breaks give such an LO channel its visual identity. As Smith points out in Chapter 20, this program concept is quite difficult to master. It depends on greater knowledge of the audience and greater sensitivity to nuances in program content than other programming strategies.

Program suppliers also have reservations about cherrypicking. They worry that their carefully targeted programs will be scheduled among incompatible shows, discouraging audience flow, or that viewers will not be able to find their offerings within the scheduling hodgepodge. Most LO cable channel schedules are neither published nor listed on a menu channel. Moreover, networks offer co-op advertising, sales guarantees and other incentives usually only to those cable systems carrying the network's entire schedule without time shifts or preemption. In consequence, extended cherrypicking is rare on LO cable.

EVALUATING LO PROGRAMMING

As with broadcast programming, peer recognition and viewer response indicate cable programming success. Public acknowledgements—through awards, for example—signal critical and peer approval and provide promotion for specific programs and channels. They are also useful ammunition for the cable system at franchise renewal time.

Ace Awards

The cable industry recognizes excellence in programming with its annual Ace Awards, presented at the Cable Software Symposium & Exposition, sponsored by the National Cable Television Association. Like an Oscar (film), Emmy (broadcast television) or Clio (advertising), an **Ace** is awarded for superior effort to programs, actors or producers (or other behind-the-scenes talent) in numerous categories, including "community programming" and "distinguished achievement in programming" as well as "national programming," "cabletelevision advertising" and so on.

Subscriber Feedback

Cable systems want information on the number and characteristics of their viewers for two reasons: to program better for them and to aid in selling advertising spots. As pointed out in Chapter 2, Arbitron and Nielsen television rating services do not report audiences with an average overall rating of less than 1 percent of all the available television homes in the market. Typically, less than half the homes in an NSI (Nielsen) or TSA (Arbitron) are cabled. LO programming practically never shows up in the rating reports advertising agencies use, and commissioning independent audience studies to measure LO audiences on non-addressable systems is prohibitively expensive. However, other measures of response can indicate the approximate size and interest level of an LO audience. The viewer response to discount coupons or other incentives announced only on an LO channel is a fair gauge of the size and characteristics of that LO audience. The number and street addresses of respondents to per-inquiry advertising can be compared with responses to ads broadcast over radio or television. Local retailers can report the size of their store traffic before and after using LO advertising. Finally, old-fashioned "cards and letters" from supporters and critics offer unsystematic guidance about current programming. They can reveal what an LO audience wants to see and how they want it scheduled.

LO audience measurement, then, is much like very small-market radio. Anecdotal and testimonial data must be sought out to convince advertisers to buy time. And programmers must instigate direct feedback from the audience to get a sense of the community's program and schedule preferences.

ANCILLARY SERVICES

Cable operators are developing a wide range of ancillary services as supplementary revenue sources, adding to the monthly fees from cable television subscribers. Leasing their production facilities is one option. In addition, systems are introducing ancillary program services—dividing into those intended for the general public (all cable subscribers) on a free or pay basis, and those intended only for closed user groups. Cable radio and teletext, for example, are for all who want them and are willing to pay for them; subsidiary services for businesses are private. Leased channels may carry either type. For many of these extra services, the cable programmer serves as supervisor or administrator.

Although the economics of ancillary services are just developing as of the mid-1980s, there are at present three payment models. In one pattern, the cable operator carries a service to increase basic subscriber rolls and returns a percentage of the monthly subscriber fee to the service supplier. Teletext follows this pattern. In another model, the cable operator leases a channel for a monthly fee, and the lessor programs the channel and promotes it among subscribers. Shopping services, newspaper headlines and classified advertising and security services usually follow this model. In a third pattern, an entity leases the channel for a monthly fee but does not market to the general public; it uses the channel to communicate private information (such as findings in the day's court hearings). If the system is not addressable, then this kind of information must be scrambled so that it can be used only by those people with decoders; if addressable, security is assured by sending the private channel only to those "drops" the leasing entity intends to reach. Ancillary services must be divided, then, according to their intended audience and according to their payment method. The cable programmer typically plays a central role in pay services intended for the general subscribership and a minor role in leased services.

Cable Radio

Cable radio, also called cable audio and cable FM, resembles cable television. Program suppliers use relay satellites to distribute FM music networks to local cable systems.[11] The cable operator installs cable drops to home stereo receivers, and subscribers pay a small monthly fee for basic audio service on top of their fee for basic television service. When systems offer cable radio as part of the franchise agreement, they usually carry local radio stations and draw from several cable-only radio networks to create a marketable service. A cable radio array may include over-the-air AM and FM stations, radio superstations and cable-only audio networks and single signals. The four primary influences on cable television programming, legal, technical, economic and marketing, apply in theory to cable radio as well. Cable radio, however, is much less well developed as of the mid-1980s than cable television, but many observers expect a parallel development in the late 1980s.

On the legal side, must-carry rules similar to those for broadcast television signals do not exist; the choice of channels remains entirely with the cable programmer. But if an operator has offered cable radio in franchise negotiations to win the overall cable contract (or as a renewal concession), then the agreement may specify local radio station carriage. If so, the local stations are usually cablecast as a single technical entity and imported signals added on unoccupied frequencies. The franchise may specify only local FM signals or both AM and FM since the cable operator can convert AM to frequency-modulated signals for reception on unoccupied FM channels. If Congress confirms must-carry laws for broadcast television, eventually over-the-air radio broadcasters will seek the same protection.

The technical side of cable radio is changing rapidly. Although many cable operators deliver over-the-air broadcast radio signals and taped, syndicated audio services, the national audio networks are shifting to the new digital technology. Satellites relay digital audio at low cost to cable systems who in turn deliver the very high-fidelity signal in digital form to home receivers. Home Music Store, for example, uses digital technology to distribute seven channels of stereo music, each in a different format.

The economics of cable radio operate somewhat differently from the economics of cable television as of the mid-1980s, although similar patterns can be expected by the 1990s. At present, most audio suppliers (nonbroadcast sound signal distributors) offer cable systems whole sets of audio channels, each with an identifiable musical format, so that the whole package can be marketed as a unit. Because the cost of producing audio is so much less than video, suppliers typically offer many channels, and cable operators purchase the whole package. Subscribers then pay the cable system for a basic cable radio service having a variety of channels. Some networks provide time for local advertising sales and offer some promotional support. Satellite placement and signal importation fees also affect the economics of cable radio networks.

Cable radio can be a basic or premium service, and superstations already exist:

1. *Basic Cable Radio.*   Two of the largest suppliers of cable FM music as of the early 1980s were WFMT-FM in Chicago and Lifestyle. WFMT-FM, a hybrid broadcast and cable service, programs fine arts radio, largely classical music and arts talk, 24 hours a day. WFMT-FM is called a radio superstation because it is satellite relayed to cable systems across the United States by a common carrier (United Video). Lifestyle, an instrumental, easy-listening, music-only service owned by United Video, is a digital audio signal programmed only for cable systems and is satellite distributed. As of the mid-1980s, WFMT reached only about 850,000 homes, and Lifestyle reached 2 million.

Like television superstations, cable FM superstations increase revenue by selling their advertising time at higher rates because they reach huge audiences. And because subscribers usually pay extra to receive cable radio service, they can be expected to listen to it. When cable radio becomes an important revenue-producing service, cable radio networks will acquire the same audience evaluation problems characterizing cable television. These problems are discussed in Chapters 2 and 9.

A single channel jazz service, The Jazz Network, supported by a combination of advertising and operator fees, began operation in 1983. In addition, at least four services provide satellite delivered religious audio programming to cable systems. The audio to Cable News Network (CNN) is marketed (for a fee) as CNN Audio and can be placed on cable radio as a 24-hour news channel. Other competitors are expected to rapidly swell the number of cable radio networks—including broadcast radio stations seeking 24-hour stereo outlets.

2. *Premium Cable Radio.*   Beginning in 1983, the Home Music Store offered its seven music channels as a tiered pay service (all seven channels for one monthly fee). Its varied formats are transmitted digitally and converted to analog by home decoders. This unusual service lets subscribers record very high-quality musical selections at home.

Other premium audio networks do not exist as yet, although NPR, HBO and other companies are investigating that possibility.[12] Many people might subscribe to a cable radio service to receive public radio, for example, if cable were the only way to receive it.

On the marketing side, cable operators must consider the lift potential of cable radio service—in other words, whether cable radio services will increase cable television subscriber rolls. Currently, cable operators do not market radio service independently; subscribers must pay for basic cable television to take cable radio. The cable operator structures radio as an ancillary service to television. This structure will not last into the 1990s, and cable systems may eventually employ separate radio programmers whose responsibilities will be entirely separate from those of the television programmer. As with cable television, advertiser appeals and overmarketing will become important considerations. Unlike cable television, the over-the-air radio industry has settled the question of whether most stations will have vertical or broad appeal. Broadcast radio is strictly a vertical appeal operation.

Leased Channels

Optional leased channels, those not required by a franchise agreement but offered at the cable operator's discretion, raise the legal questions discussed earlier under "Leased Access," but for large cable systems with channels to spare they are potential revenue producers. Only systems with 30 or more channels lease more than a single channel, and most smaller systems lease none.

Pay leased channels operate much like premium movie channels and nonpay leased channels like basic services. The difference is that the leasing company, not the cable operator, administers the channel. These administrative duties include billing, collecting, advertising, promoting and customer relations, in addition to programming.

The shopping service is one common variety of leased channel. A local department store or retail chain operator rents a channel from the cable system and programs whatever content it desires, generally a continuous run of demonstrations of products for sale. Two other open leased operations are text news channels and classified advertising channels. Both of these are clearly intended for all who will watch. Many of these channels are jointly operated by a local newspaper and the cable operator. Newspapers serving cabled areas usually want to lease a channel for classified advertising on cable. Increasingly, cable operators want to participate in such a leasing arrangement because of the legal advantages publishing provides and because of revenue potential.

The cable system must use descramblers or traps distributed to subscriber homes or must have addressable technology for a leased channel to go only to paying subscribers. (Channels supported by advertising or a sponsor like a newspaper, are open to all cabled homes, of course.)

One unusual instance of pay leasing occurs in the state of Washington where the Supersonics lease time on one channel on cable systems throughout the Puget Sound area for showing their basketball games. Only addressable systems or ones providing special box combination security can participate. The Supersonics sell the right to view the cable channel like a season pass, so they have no churn.

Although from the point of view of government and the public, two types of optional leased channels exist, those for everybody and those for restricted groups, from the cable operator's point of view, profit participation vs. a flat lease fee is the issue. Those leasing agencies offering the cable system increased revenue as subscriber rolls increase are likely to command much more of the optional channel space than those requiring long-term, fixed leasing agreements.

Teletext

Teletext commonly refers to signals sent on the vertical blanking interval of broadcast television stations to subscribers who pay for decoders (and in most cases, pay a monthly fee for the service). Since the FCC has refused to establish must-carry status for broadcast teletext, and has been upheld by the courts in limited tests, cable systems are free to create their own teletext service or license syndicated services. Teletext has advertising potential. The subscriber can switch from broadcast channels to teletext to get additional information on advertising appearing in the broadcast frame—or to find a classified advertisement. For example, car advertisers can purchase teletext ads amplifying their brief, 30-second on-air spots that would be of interest primarily to people wanting to buy a new car. Extravision was a local classified advertising service, reached by switching from the local CBS affiliate to Extravision, and programmed by the affiliate (except for a minimum number of ads supplied by CBS). CBS's role in Extravision was largely to develop the technology, clarify the economics and market the service to its affiliates. Extravision was withdrawn in 1984 after a weak affiliate and advertiser response.

Cable systems can also license teletext services from syndicators such as Southern Satellite Systems (SSS). This common carrier distributes a teletext service by satellite relay on the vertical blanking interval of WTBS, the superstation described in Chapter 13. It can be given a dedicated channel on a cable system, requiring no decoders, or decoders can be sold to subscribers so they can switch between WTBS and the teletext service. The future of teletext appears problematic to date as neither advertisers nor affiliates have rushed to participate.

Videotex

Videotex differs from teletext in that it is a fully interactive service, requiring a full 6 Mhz channel on a cable system, and access to a personal or main frame computer. Subscribers commonly interact with videotex via telephone lines; when received on an unoccupied cable channel, the term *cabletext* applies. On cable it is a pay service subscribers purchase directly from software suppliers such as CompuServe, Dow Jones and The Source. They program news and information data bases intended for the paying general public. If a cable system supplies a dedicated channel for a videotex service, it receives a small monthly user fee. Cable has the advantage of bringing information more quickly and more accurately to computer users than telephone lines. Only systems with 40 or more channels can spare a channel for such a limited use, however. The number of homes with personal computers is expected to double every couple of years for the rest of the 1980s, and consequently, videotex service will expand.

Subsidiary Services

Other ancillary cable services are also for limited groups of subscribers. The difference between most videotex and other subsidiary services is that the latter are typically for private businesses or organizations, and their information has to be secure from unauthorized use. Chain retailers, for example, can lease cable channels to distribute information to their local outlets; Sears and J.C. Penney are considering this option. Large businesses can distribute information from their headquarters to local offices, related businesses and their subscribers, such as stock and commodity listings from Dow Jones to local brokers, farm wholesalers and farmers.[13] Corporations relying on common data bases for sales or quick rate changes can also benefit from satellite relay from national headquarters to local offices and plants. Insurance agents, for example, need access to main computers to determine rates and rapidly register new clients; using telephone lines for this purpose is expensive and the service of low quality. Cable systems with enough capacity can afford to lease bandwidth for such private use.

FUTURE DIRECTIONS IN LOCAL ORIGINATION AND SERVICES

Though the technologies, users and policies affecting cable's local origination and services are rapidly changing, current practices point the way to future developments. Local productions will improve in quality and increase in number; the development of advertiser support and the pinpointing of narrow target audiences will determine the kind of programming produced. Programs originating from access groups or centers will increasingly be intermixed with programs the cable operator produces locally. LO programmers will need to use sophisticated programming strategies to attract and hold a salable audience share against competition from local independent broadcasters, LPTV and other television distribution technologies. Independent producers and advertising agencies will develop a variety of informational, interstitial and series programming for LO cablecasting, and successful LO programs will be networked within MSOs, regions and user groups. MSOs will form subsidiary production companies to create and syndicate LO programming. LO and ancillary services will be critically managed and evaluated in terms of net profit to the cable system.

MSOs will shuffle the configuration of cable-based services based on profitability. Cable deregulation and the inability of regulatory agencies to keep up with advances in cable technology will allow LO programmers to experiment with new forms of commercial messages, direct catalog sales, shop-at-home marketing, coproductions and barter arrangements. This high level of activity holds the promise of large numbers of jobs for recent college graduates with a willingness to participate in the development of new cable programming.

SUMMARY

This chapter traced the transformation of federally mandated access programming into community access channels producing much the same programming as that produced by many system staffs (local origination or local production). The authors predict a gradual merging of the two forms into commercially viable formats targeted at specialized audiences as a vehicle for community service and advertising. The two forces driving this process are MSOs' need to demonstrate effective public service at franchise renewal time and their need for advertising revenues. Although at one time access channels consisted of four separate varieties: public, leased, educational and governmental—in practice, these have become the single entity of community access. LO scheduling follows some of the principles of program placement on broadcast stations. Ancillary services are a growing part of local cable, and in the 1990s, services such as cable radio will probably follow the pattern set by cable television. Optional leased channels are increasingly a source of revenue-participation for cable systems, but closed-user group services will find space only on the very largest cable systems.

Notes

[1]Donald E. Agostino, "LO Programming Types: A Survey of 134 LO Cable Programmers." Unpublished report, Bloomington, Indiana, March 1983.

[2]Laurie Winer, "Bartering Without Reservations," *View*, January 1982, pp. 34–36.

[3]Kathleen Lane, "How to Syndicate LO," *View*, June 1983, pp. 99–104.

[4]Kenneth Ksobiech and others, *The Columbus Video Access Center: A Research Analysis of Public Reaction* (Bloomington, Indiana: Institute for Communication Research, 1975) pp. 45–51.

[5]*FCC v. Midwest Video Corp.*, 440 U.S. 689 (1979).

[6]*Access Operating Rules & Procedures* (Washington, D.C.: National Federation Local Cable Programmers, 1983). See also C.J. Hirschfield, "An Innocuous Concept Becomes a Hot Issue: Leased Access," *View*, May 1982, pp. 131–32.

[7]A backfeed line uses a separate coaxial cable between the point of origination and the headend on one-way cable systems. Signals are carried to the headend on a frequency other than that on which they are cablecast to avoid interference.

[8]Cox Cable TV in Spokane, Washington, is a 35-channel system with 6 channels set aside for educational access use.

[9]Herb Swartz, "Leased Channels: The Issue of the '80s," *Cable Marketing*, August 1982, pp. 14–17.

[10]Only one in a hundred cable operators make more than one leased channel available, according to *An Economic Analysis of Mandatory Leased Channel Access for Cable Television*, a report prepared by Stanley M. Besen and Leland L. Johnson for the Markle Foundation. Santa Monica, California: Rand Corporation, December, 1982.

[11]Ed Shane, "Radio and the Cable Challenge," *Broadcast Communications*, July 1982, pp. 35–36; Dennis Gros, "Cable FM: The New Sound in Town," *Broadcast Communications*, July 1982, pp. 38–39.

[12]Joshua Noah Koenig and Ann Stookey, "Cable Audio Sounds Promising: A Summary of National Public Radio's Reports on Cable Audio Services," *Broadcast Communications*, July 1982, pp. 42–43.

[13]Susan Tyler Eastman, "Policy Issues Raised by the FCC's 1983 and 1984 Subcarrier Decisions," *Journal of Broadcasting*, in press 1984.

Selected Sources

Baldwin, Thomas F. and McVoy, D. Stevens. "Over-the-Air, Access, Community and Automated Channels." *Cable Communication*. Englewood Cliffs, New Jersey: Prentice-Hall, Inc., 1983.

Forbes, Dorothy, and Layng, Sanderson. *The New Communicators: A Guide to Community Programming*. Washington, D.C.: Communications Press, 1980.

Hollowell, Mary Louise, ed. *The Cable/Broadband Communications Book, Vol. 3, 1982–83*. Washington, D.C.: Communications Press, 1983.

Jesuale, Nancy, ed., with Smith, Ralph Lee. *The Community Medium*, Vol. 1. Arlington, Virginia: The Cable Television Information Center, 1982.

Shaffer, William Drew, and Wheelwright, Richard. *Creating Original Programming for Cable TV*. Washington, D.C.: National Federation of Local Cable Programmers, 1983.

Sigel, Efrem, *The Future of Videotex*. White Plains, New York: Knowledge Industry Publications, 1983.

CHAPTER THIRTEEN

Superstation Programming

Sidney Pike

A QUICK GUIDE TO CHAPTER THIRTEEN

SIDNEY PIKE, *after more than 30 years in television, became president of the Turner Program Services, a program distribution development division of Turner Broadcasting Systems, Inc. He started in television as a producer/director for WBZ in Boston, later becoming director of program development for WHDH in Boston and station manager of WQXI in Atlanta. He then joined Ted Turner's WTCG in Atlanta as station manager in 1971, moving up to vice-president and director of television operations of WTBS. He lectures at nearby colleges and often represents the pro–superstation viewpoint on industry panels. In this chapter he describes the economics of the superstation concept, the roles of common carriers and cable operators, and the programming strategy that has made WTBS the most widely distributed station in the country.*

THE NEW INDEPENDENTS

The **superstation** is an extension of the familiar broadcast station–cable relationship. A superstation is an independent television station having its signal delivered nationally by satellite and distributed by many cable systems. Ted Turner, chairman of the board of Turner Broadcasting System, Inc., and owner of WTBS, originated the idea. Currently, three independents are nationally distributed by satellite relay to local cable systems and called superstations: WTBS, WGN and WOR. The idea of distributing a UHF independent's program schedule over a huge area of the United States led to a restructuring of part of the television industry in the late 1970s. WTBS-TV of Atlanta was the first independent to become satellite–cable distributed and is linked inextricably with the term *superstation.*

A superstation capitalizes on two technological advances: cable television and satellite television relay transmission. A superstation comes into being when a common carrier company picks up an independent television station's broadcast signal, retransmits that signal by microwave via an **uplink** to a satellite transponder (channel) leased for the purpose; in turn, the satellite redistributes the signal to receive-only earth stations (**downlink** dish receivers) that local cable system operators maintain. Local cable operators dedicate a channel to the superstation signal, adding it to the other off-air and cable-originated material they provide. Figure 13-1 depicts the process.

The operators pay a percentage of their gross revenue to the Copyright Royalty Tribunal as a royalty for the use of copyrighted material the superstation carries. Cable systems also pay the common carrier company a fee to receive the satellite signal, an amount based on the total number of cable subscribers. As of 1983, cable operators paid about 10 cents per subscriber per month to common carrier companies for satellite reception of a superstation signal. The fee to the common carrier covers its equipment and transmission costs of about $1 million a year and profits of between $90,000 and $130,000 per month (as of 1983).The superstation gains revenue by increasing its advertising rates according to its gain in audience size.

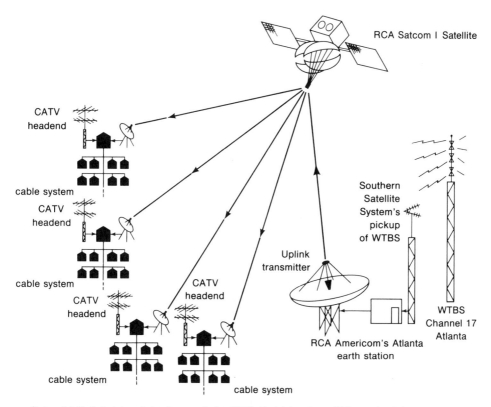

Southern Satellite System's transmission of programming from WTBS, Atlanta independent, to CATV system headends uses uplink in RCA Americom's Atlanta earth station, and transponder in Satcom I satellite SSS pickup of WTBS signal off the air is at site adjacent to the RCA's Atlanta earth station nine miles from indie's transmitter. Transponder retransmits signal direct to CATV systems' earth stations.

FIGURE 13-1. Diagram of the Distribution of WTBS-TV

CABLE GROWTH IN THE 1970s

Historically, restrictive Federal Communications Commission regulations inhibited cable growth. In particular, the 1972 regulations—limiting both the distance over which cable companies could import independent station's signals (**leapfrogging rule**) as well as the number of imported signals—diminished the appeal of distant independent programming. These regulations, combined with the high cost of building and maintaining microwave relay systems to distribute television signals to cable headends, slowed cable industry expansion into new markets in the late 1960s and early 1970s. Growth occurred only near major cities, such as the Chicago suburbs where a common carrier economically exported two of the city's independent stations on a single microwave line to cable systems several hundred miles away.

Cable growth in the early 1970s came largely through attracting new cable subscribers within existing cable communities. They paid a basic subscription fee, typically from $7 to $12 per month, that generally provided off-the-air broadcast television stations, signals from nearby independent stations and locally originated services such as automated weather information readouts and alphanumeric news channels. The addition of other programming services, not available over the air, lured many viewers into subscribing to cable service. Premium cable services, originated typically by companies owning several cable systems and offering recent, unedited, uninterrupted motion pictures, came into being in the late 1970s, as described in Chapter 11. Premium channels cost subscribers an additional $9 to $12 above the basic cable service rate.

During 1975–76, a series of events broke cable loose from its relatively dormant state. In 1975, the FCC authorized cable systems to install receive-only earth stations, permitting reception of pay programming transmitted by domestic satellite. As pointed out in Chapter 11, Home Box Office (HBO) was the first satellite-delivered service offered to cable systems. Under FCC regulations then in effect, the receiving antennas (or dishes) could not be less than nine meters in diameter (to permit a "broadcast quality" reception of the satellite signal) and were originally priced at $85,000 to $125,000. Despite the high cost, a large number of cable systems purchased antennas, foreseeing an income potential from premium subscriptions.

In January 1976, the FCC dropped its distant-signal requirements and permitted cable systems anywhere to receive any distant independent station from whatever sources.[1] In response, the common carrier called Southern Satellite Systems (SSS) formed the first satellite-to-cable relay system, distributing the signal of WTBS-TV, Channel 17 in Atlanta. The common carrier acts as a broker or middleman between the program supplier, the satellite provider and the cable system.

At the end of 1976, the FCC reduced the minimum size of receive-only antennas to 4.5 meters, markedly reducing their cost, which eventually fell to between $8,000 and $60,000, depending on size and complexity. This move encouraged even more cable systems to buy receive-only dishes. By the end of 1983, all of the more than 5,000 cable systems in the country had installed earth stations, some costing as little as $2,500.[2] Inexpensive access to satellite-delivered program services spurred a cable revolution in which HBO and superstation WTBS-TV were the most popular services.

SUPERSTATION ECONOMICS

As was pointed out earlier, superstations receive no direct revenue as a result of their superstation status. Any additional compensation they earn is generated by increased rates for advertising to match increased audience size. However, this rate increase challenges tradition. In the early days of cable, ad agencies felt television advertisers should not pay for increases in audience size due to cable penetration beyond the local market. Station sales staffs and national representative firms gave the added audience from cable penetration to their advertisers gratis, referring to cable-only homes as the "bonus audience."

Breaking advertisers of the bonus habit did not occur until the cable audience became significantly larger than the direct broadcast audience. Superstation ad rate increases are justified not only by the increase in audience, but also because penetration of distant markets costs the station higher licensing fees for motion pictures, off-network series and certain sports events.[3] Program syndicators demand this increase because they assume they will not be able to sell those programs for as much money to local television stations competing with the superstation signal.

Program suppliers continue to sell to superstations—even though competing local broadcast stations try to negotiate reduced fees for these duplicated programs—because (1) suppliers can charge superstations higher program licensing fees and (2) rights holders collect Copyright Royalty Tribunal (CRT) payments from cable systems. In more detail:

1. Most syndicators, even successful ones, lack sales forces large enough to penetrate all 210 television markets. Eighty percent of program sales income derives from the top 50 markets (though many stations in smaller markets are co-owned by corporations purchasing for all their stations). The remaining 160 television markets are too small to support the expense of a visiting sales staff. Program suppliers collect rentals, their programming sales income, through sales to superstations that penetrate these "ignored areas."

2. Based on a detailed payment schedule, the Copyright Tribunal (CRT) awards program rights holders money collected from cable systems' basic fees for program use in homes outside the superstation's market of license. As explained below, cable systems must pay a larger amount for a distant independent signal than for a local or nearby independent. This money returns to the same sources that licensed their programs (or events) for use.

Copyright Royalties

Cable systems can bring in an unlimited number of distant independent stations. However, they must pay additional money for each signal to the CRT. The size of the copyright royalty fee increased dramatically in 1983 from 1.21 percent to 3.75 percent of the cable systems' gross income from basic service, causing much industry controversy. Cable systems claim the rate is too high while program rights holders and broadcasters claim it is too low. In addition nearly all participants find the formula for delivery of copyright royalties unsatisfactory. Under the system in effect in 1983, the CRT determines the amount to be received according to the form of programming. In 1983, the CRT awarded most of the $42 million in 1982 *television* reuse royalties to the following copyright holders:

Motion Picture Association of America (syndicated programs and feature film producers):	61.0%
Joint Sports Claimants (baseball, hockey, basketball, soccer) and NCAA:	13.5%
PBS:	4.7%

NAB/U.S. Television:	4.6%
Music Performing Rights Societies (ASCAP, BMI, SESAC):	3.8%
Multimedia:	1.0%
CBC (Canadian commercial television):	.8%
SIN:	.4%
National Public Radio (new in 1979):	.2%

The royalty pool the CRT divided in 1983 was $63.2 million; it is expected to hit $145.5 million by 1990. The tribunal used three primary criteria for payment:

1. The harm caused to copyright owners by secondary transmissions of the copyrighted works by cable systems.
2. The benefit to cable systems from the secondary transmission of certain copyrighted works.
3. The marketplace value of the works transmitted.

Criteria of secondary importance were:

4. Quality of copyrighted program material.
5. Time-related considerations.

The 1982 fee of 3.75 percent of gross basic subscriber revenue is figured for EACH additional distant signal equivalent (DSE) carried in excess of those the FCC allowed prior to 1982. (An independent station counts as one DSE while public stations and network affiliates count as one-quarter of a DSE; the issue, therefore, focuses on the independents.) In one example of a small system importing two superstations, the copyright fee (including signal delivery cost and fee to the common carrier) comes to almost 50 cents per subscriber per month. This amount far exceeds the charges for CNN and ESPN together. Large market systems permitted to import several signals before the new carriage rules were not affected so severely. Although many in the industry predicted a dramatic loss of cable affiliates for superstations as a result of the increased copyright royalty fees, in fact, the number of cable affiliates for each of the three superstations has climbed since 1982.

THE NATIONAL SUPERSTATIONS

Satellite-carried independents did not exist prior to 1977, and their potential proliferation remains a prickly legal and economic issue in the minds of many broadcasters. To date, only three independents qualify as superstations, and this group is unlikely to grow in the near future. Until local cable systems add many more channels, these three (in addition to about forty basic cable networks, local independents and nearby imports) would seem to fill the demand for independent station programming.

WTBS

WTBS was the first of the superstations and encourages identification with the word *superstation* by incorporating it in its letterhead, using it over the air, promoting it to advertisers and proselytizing it to the industry and the public. By 1983, WTBS reached 28 million viewers on about 5,800 cable affiliates. Its UHF signal penetrated 205 out of the 210 markets (DMAs/ADIs), over one-third of U.S. homes. Ninety percent of WTBS's audience, in consequence, lives outside its home Atlanta market.

It pays affiliates an initial 25 cents per subscriber (up to $10,000) and an additional annual 16 cents per subscriber for promoting WTBS. When affiliates carry WTBS along with Cable News Network (CNN I) and CNN Headline News, they receive another $1 per subscriber per year for three years. In addition to these promotional payments, WTBS is the only one of the three national super-stations to have a national rate card (in addition to a local advertising rate card). The station generates most of its income from the sale of national advertising.

Like most independents, WTBS programs largely movies, off-network series and sports. It carries baseball's Atlanta Braves and basketball's Atlanta Hawks, as well as some NCAA football and basketball games. The station also produces a significant number of entertainment series and specials intended for national syndication after airing on WTBS. It has won numerous awards for its local programming, including ACE and IRIS awards in 1982 and 1983.

WGN

Although WGN's VHF signal is satellite relayed to participating cable systems, it did not seek out superstation status. Its management remains more impressed by the potential disadvantages of superstation identification than by its advantages. As the station sees it, one of WGN's main attractions is live sports, and wide distribution of these events occasionally interferes with rights sales by the owners of the Chicago teams to stations outside of the Chicago market because of the loss in local exclusivity. Similarly, WGN wants to avoid paying national rates for movies and syndicated programs. Since it is an old, established, highly successful station in its market area, WGN lacks incentive to seek out controversial changes in its way of operating. However, like WTBS, WGN purchased a major league baseball team (Chicago Cubs) to strengthen its future sports programming plans. It also carries some Chicago Bulls games and college sports such as Big Ten conference games.

As of 1983, WGN reached approximately 11 million cable homes (largely in the Midwest) through nearly 4,800 cable affiliates. Its signal appears in nearly 200 markets (DMAs), and 48 percent of its audience lives outside the Chicago market. Sports gives WGN a distinct identity, and counterprogramming the broadcast networks contributes to its success, according to Sheldon Cooper, former President of WGN-TV. Theatrical and made-for-TV films have been important programming for WGN. Management feels they provide, dollar for dollar, the most entertainment value because they have big stars and strong viewer appeal. WGN was a pioneer in movie "theme" weeks, such as *Clint Eastwood Week*. At one time, they hired Basil Rathbone to do introductions and segue pieces for old Sherlock Holmes movies.

WOR

WOR, also a long-established major market VHF independent with local economic strength, reaches about 4.3 million cable homes in nearly 100 markets, on over 850 cable affiliates. In addition, more than 8 million New Yorkers can receive the station's broadcast signal. It originates in New York City and carries New York news and sports having broad appeal for viewers throughout the northwest. Over 30 percent of its audience lives outside the New York market.

WOR carries more sports than any other U.S. independent. It broadcasts the games of seven professional teams such as the New York Mets (baseball); the New York Rangers, New York Islanders and New Jersey Devils (all hockey); the New York Cosmos (soccer) and the New York Knicks and New Jersey Nets (basketball). In addition, WOR carries relatively new off-network series as well as older movies and syndicated programs.

Both WGN and WOR used their increased coverage to increase their advertising rates. They have not altered their programming strategies to please audiences outside their local markets, however, because these independents already program entertainment for very large, heterogeneous local audiences.

A Regional Superstation: KTVU

KTVU, Oakland, has in fact been a regional superstation distributed by land-based relays since the early 1960s. Although it concentrates on programming for the Oakland–San Francisco area, its UHF signal has been imported up and down the coasts of California, Oregon and Washington, as well as inland into California, for two decades. In many places along the mountainous coast, reception requires cable, and KTVU is one of the few metropolitan, West Coast independents for cable systems to carry. (In the West, stations are more widely separated because of the scattered population and mountainous terrain in many places. Only major cities, generally hundreds of miles apart, have independent stations.)

KTVU's signal was picked up by a common carrier and distributed to more distant locations (still in the West) via satellite for two years (1978 to 1980), but the distributor failed to convince sufficient numbers of cable systems to affiliate and dropped the effort. KTVU is now distributed largely by microwave. It carries movies and off-network reruns of varying vintages.

Like WGN and WOR, KTVU is concerned that becoming known as a superstation may hurt its program acquisitions. Its management claims that possible rises in the cost for films will override any benefit derived from superstation status. Consequently, KTVU declines to cooperate with common carriers desiring joint promotion of its signal; it does not advertise its cable distribution in trade publications, nor does it assist cable companies in promoting its schedule.

PROGRAMMING FOR THE SIGNAL COVERAGE AREA

When a station's signal reaches audiences in different regions and time zones, its programming strategy should be changed. Most commercial broadcast independents are located in densely populated areas—the large markets. Superstations supply smaller markets with independent programming they could not otherwise support. Because advertising revenue in these smaller markets can only support the one, two or three affiliates, the markets rarely have their own independents.

Rural Audiences

Superstations have their greatest viewer density in the regions nearest their points of origination: WGN in the northern portion of the Midwest, WTBS in the Southeast and WOR in the Northeast. Cable markets, however, are scattered rather than grouped closely together. Many rural areas have cable television service bringing distant signals. Superstation signals often leapfrog populated areas, reaching more rural homes than urban. And understandably, in rural cable areas promotion of superstation programming will lure new audiences.

WTBS is more nationally oriented than WOR or WGN, although both have increased the number of newly released off-network series they carry, partly as a result of their superstation status (and partly to remain competitive in their local markets). In the coming decade, a superstation willing to invest in program development could generate a much larger share of the total television audience; it could function much like one of the national television networks—providing a schedule of first-run programs for its cable affiliates. However, a superstation, under present FCC rules, must serve the particular market reached by its over-the-air broadcast signal as defined in its license. It must cater to that market's needs and present programs serving the local community. Inevitably, some of the broadcast schedule, as well as some program development efforts, must address this responsibility. However, WTBS's cable audience exceeds its broadcast audience more than 50 times over. The station's management also acknowledges a responsibility to that audience.

Time Zone Conflicts

The map in Figure 13-2 showing the location of the cable systems distributing WTBS's signal clarifies the wide availability of its programming. The WTBS signal is even carried on cable systems in Alaska, Hawaii, Puerto Rico and Guam. This wide distribution could lend itself to new programming strategies if the FCC permitted. At present WTBS programs mostly for its own broadcast time zone, the eastern zone. It cannot satisfy the needs of all the various time zones it is carried in without disrupting local service.

For some viewers in different time zones, this situation is not a problem—for example, Western viewers may enjoy a favorite sport in the late afternoon even though it originates at 7:30 P.M. in the East. But time zone difference can create absurdities: *Romper Room,* a preschool children's program, is aired at 8 A.M. in the East, but is of little interest to viewers on the West Coast at 5 A.M. when children of that age ought to be asleep.

Like most cable services, superstations repeat many of their programs to ensure reception in all homes at appropriate hours and to maximize viewing opportunities. Repeat showings to accommodate different time zones is one of a superstation's major scheduling strategies.

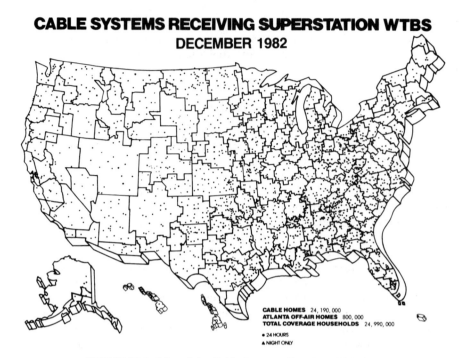

FIGURE 13-2. Map of the Cable Systems Carrying WTBS-TV

Competition, Not Blackout

The FCC no longer requires local cablecasters to black out imported programs duplicating locally available programs.[4] But debate on the blackout rules goes on within the FCC and the industry. Some members of the FCC express the view that local-station profits are now large enough to weather the economic vagaries of increased competition. Others insist elimination of blackout rules will eventually harm local stations. However, a two-year economic inquiry by the FCC found cable systems had little or no impact on broadcast stations from the vantage points of exclusivity or distant signal importation. As of 1983, these conclusions are supported by the Mass Media Bureau of the FCC.[5]

Irrespective of FCC rules, a superstation wanting to make its programs attractive to cable systems is wise to originate as much new or unduplicated programming as possible. Hometown sports are a good example of such unduplicated programming. Specials such as rock concerts, public affairs, documentaries and news are also invulnerable to repeat coverage by the local television stations in the markets the superstation reaches.

TWENTY-FOUR-HOUR SERVICE

Most television stations stay on the air about 18 hours a day. To operate 24 hours a day, seven days a week, is too costly for most stations: Early morning programs generate insufficient advertising revenue to defray feature film amortization, station labor and operating costs. But for the superstation, 24-hour service becomes profitable once a wide audience is reached, even though initially it may be a loss leader. Some cable systems that do not have a 24-hour broadcast station available to fill out the day, sign up with a superstation's common carrier (or CNN) just to get late-night or all-night programming.

Providing 24-hour service can be vital to a cable system's success, the "extra" that attracts enough additional cable subscribers to make the system profitable. Moreover, a 24-hour superstation offers programming attractive to shift workers who cannot watch television during regular programming hours. Many workers who are either on their jobs or sleeping during the normal television day will watch daytime-type programming in the 1 A.M. to 6 A.M. period. As advertisers realize that this new audience is available to them, even the early morning hours become profitable for both cable systems and 24-hour superstations.

PROGRAM ELEMENTS IN SUPERSTATION STRATEGY

The success of the local independent station is based on its ability to counterprogram the network affiliates in its market at specific peak-audience time periods of each day. However, the success of the superstation lies in providing alternative programming *throughout* the broadcast day. Not surprisingly, the superstation's programming mix is heavy on sports, movies and specials.

Sports

One of the biggest attractions of superstation programming is a heavy schedule of live sports events. For example, each year WTBS originates 150 Atlanta Braves baseball games and 40 Hawks basketball games.[6] WGN has a similarly large schedule of Chicago Cubs games and other local teams. And WOR remains the station with more sports than any other independent in the country, using sporting events as the cornerstone of its programming strategy.

In addition, each of the superstations covers one-time sports specials such as the annual Masters Water Ski Championship, golf tournaments, occasional major college football and basketball playoffs and championships, and some track and field events.

Typically, a superstation first broadcasts these events live, and then repeats many of them on tape one or more times, but it is not desirable to delay a sporting event receiving wide press coverage since the winner will be known before the event airs. Some professional sports events are repeated on superstations for a new, early morning audience about 1 A.M. (EST). Viewers on the West Coast can see the same games about 10 P.M.

ABC, CBS, NBC and the independent national sports promoters obtain exclusive national rights to many important games. Nonetheless, individual stations and groups can originate a huge number of games attractive to large cable audiences. Technical production quality must match that of major network sports producers if viewer and advertiser interest is to be maintained. For this reason, WTBS owns two complete remote trucks with 16 top-of-the-line cameras (and four smaller trucks). It can televise a complete golf tournament, one of the most technically demanding of sporting events. Owning remote equipment gives superstations flexibility when they cover sports and guarantees technical quality as well.

In the future, superstations may form special networks of independents and affiliates to compete for the rights to special sporting events with the broadcast networks. WTBS alone outbid CBS for the 1982 University of Virginia vs. Georgetown basketball game, paying approximately $600,000.

Movies

As measured by air time, movies make up the largest element in superstation programming. Particularly for the 24-hour station, an abundant supply of theatrical films is essential. WTBS uses up to 40 feature films per week—about 1,800 movies a year. To support this appetite, WTBS maintains a library of about 3,000 feature films, providing more rest for individual films than the once-a-year scheduling most broadcast stations use. (The film library at KTVU, Oakland, one of the best stocked in the country, contains over 2,000 high quality titles.)

Independent station film libraries are generally a mixed bag of made-for-television movies and theatrical films of varying age. A few of these old warhorses get better ratings than newer films, but these films generally do not compete with the top pay cable offerings.

Syndicated Programs

Most independent television stations generally counterprogram network affiliates' news and adult programming with recently released, strip-scheduled, mass-appeal syndicated shows. (See the strategies for independents in Chapter 8 by Aiken.) For example, they often schedule programs that appeal especially to children in the early fringe time period. But superstations actually find these syndicated programs their weakest counterprogramming strategy. Recent, widely syndicated programs are the most duplicated form of programming, especially in the top 50 markets where most advertising revenue is generated. The newest, most popular off-network series such as *Laverne & Shirley* and *M*A*S*H*, because they are licensed to lots of stations, are most likely to be duplicates when introduced into a distant coverage area. Therefore, superstations stick to older syndicated series, such as *Father Knows Best* or *Leave It to Beaver* that are no longer as heavily distributed nationally and so appear on fewer competing stations.

Specials and Syndication

The remote equipment superstations use for sports telecasts is also useful for occasional specials such as rock concerts, holiday events, local children's or adults' theatrical performances and important public affairs events. Many programs that serve the local community also serve as unduplicated entertainment for a much greater region when cable extends coverage. One of the main benefits of the superstation is its ability to distribute unique specials of wide appeal to most parts of the United States.

Superstations and some of the cable-only networks, however, are beginning to produce extensive programming and to syndicate it to other independents and small-market affiliates. Their audience reach justifies the expense, and they can afford to produce programs having more than strictly local appeal. Superstation specials (as well as movies and series) provide new opportunities for small, independent producers to reach the public and share in future syndication rewards (if successful).

In an effort to generate fresh, competitive programming for WTBS airing and the syndication market, WTBS produces *The Catlins*, a southern family soap opera competing with the daytime broadcast network fare, and *Starcade*, a video-arcade game show aired (for the local market) in late afternoons to attract older children and teens. WTBS also originates *Night Tracks*, a widely popular overnight music program, using videos, scheduled on Friday and Saturday nights (midnight to 6 A.M.). WTBS combined with other stations to form Turner Network Television (TNT) in 1984 to air *Miss World 1984* and certain Bowl games.

News

Superstations find both special opportunities and special hazards in dealing with news and public affairs programming. A superstation's locally oriented news is inappropriate for viewers in other markets. Nor can the superstation compete effectively with local coverage in the many areas where it is carried. The solution is a national newscast from another source.

Cable News Network (CNN), also owned by Ted Turner, provides WTBS with access to news facilities and staff. WTBS's one-hour 10 P.M. news, produced primarily by CNN, is tailored for a national audience. News from such major markets as Chicago, Los Angeles and New York also has wide regional appeal— though typically not national appeal.

The best news strategy for superstations is to confine spot news to bulletins on fast-breaking regional and national events, saving most of their news departments' energies for documentaries and in-depth coverage of current public affairs issues. Here superstations can take advantage of the fact that the national television networks often treat subjects briefly then drop them even when they still have current interest. Superstations can capitalize on the original network coverage as a kind of promotion for their own subsequent in-depth treatments of such topics.

One example of this type of news follow-up was WTBS's in-depth treatment of new religious groups (cults) in a series called *In the Name of God*. Following the Guyana incident in 1978 (a shocking mass suicide–murder among members of a religious cult), WTBS devoted ten hours in prime time to this subject. Hare Krishnas, Moonies and Children of God were represented on the series along with a well-known deprogrammer and leaders of the conventional religious faiths and former cult members.

SUPERSTATIONS' FUTURE ROLE

Cable television homes and audiences are increasing monthly, nationwide, and so is the amount of advertising money available. Superstations increase the opportunities for national television exposure for talented producers, directors, writers, comedians and musicians. They also nurture that talent as they increase the amount of their own television programming. A growing population with increased average education wants better-quality, more specialized programming. In addition, expanding advertising budgets seek new outlets. There is a limit on how much the commercial broadcast stations can charge for spot commercials, so advertising will need more outlets—resulting in more program sales opportunities and in a demand for talented people. Superstations and the other cable-only services with their growing audiences can provide producers and distributors as well as advertisers the air time for new programming. In the end it is the viewers who benefit from national distribution of independent television station signals because of their increased opportunity to choose programs that interest them.

SUMMARY

Superstations are UHF or VHF independents imported from distant locations by satellite. Common carriers arrange for the uplink, and local cable systems provide the downlink and distribution to homes. Superstation revenue rises because with a larger audience, they can charge more for advertising. But program costs and copyright fees go up. The managements of the three stations historically known as superstations differ in the benefits they see in satellite distribution and in how much they tailor their programming for audiences beyond their immediate coverage area. Some structure their program service solely for their local over-the-air audience; others schedule programs to counterprogram in other time zones and serve rural audiences. Most superstations program for 24 hours a day with major blocks of sports and movies and smaller segments of syndicated series, specials and news. The future holds greater competition for superstations from the increasing numbers of basic cable networks, but as yet audiences and cable systems find superstations especially appealing additions to cable channel arrays.

Notes

[1]In 1980, the FCC eliminated the ceiling on the number of distant signals cable systems could import.

[2]An orbiting satellite covers the entire Northern Hemisphere; thus a superstation signal falls on Alaska, Hawaii and Puerto Rico, as well as on the continental United States. Illegally, any of these signals can be picked up in Central America, Canada and Cuba. (Castro has been known to watch CNN; it prompted him to invite Ted Turner to Cuba.)

[3]WTBS sales penetration was made by opening sales offices in major agency cities such as New York, Chicago, Los Angeles and Detroit.

[4]In 1980, the FCC eliminated the syndicated program exclusivity (blackout) rules.

[5]*Inquiry into Economic Relationship Between Television Broadcasting and Cable Broadcasting*, Docket 21284, 71 FCC 2d 632, 7 May 1979.

[6]Ted Turner owns the Atlanta Braves and Atlanta Hawks.

Selected Sources

Broadcasting, periodic reports on independent television stations.

Strong, William S. *The Copyright Book: A Practical Guide.* Cambridge, Massachusetts: The MIT Press, 1981.

"Superstations: An Independent Phenomenon." *Broadcasting* (27 June 1983): 68–70.

PART FOUR

Commercial Broadcast Radio Strategies

Part IV of this book is about radio. Although the approximately 9,000 commercial radio stations far outnumber television stations, their combined revenues fall far below those of television stations. As of 1983, listening levels, however, reached 3½ hours per person each day, just short of the average amount of individual television viewing. Radio is a local medium with lower production costs and correspondingly lower revenues. But the sheer number of stations gives radio programming a major industry role and creates thousands of jobs for programmers.

Part IV covers programming strategies both from network *and* station *perspectives, but emphasizes the local orientation of most radio programming. It has chapters on commercial networks and syndicators, local music programming, station news programming and talk programming. Each author deals with the evaluation, selection and scheduling of radio programming.*

Chapter 14 on **networks and syndicators** *provides an overview of the radio broadcasting industry. Networks play a major role as suppliers of information programming to music, news and talk stations. About half of all commercial stations affiliate with a network to obtain national and international news items, and some networks act as feature resources to stations that otherwise originate most of their own content. Music format syndicators supply geographically scattered, automated-music stations with a complete programming schedule. Chapter 14, then, takes a national perspective on radio programming. Some of the issues raised about national news and talk programs also apply to national television newscasts and public affairs programming; some of the issues raised about national program syndication also apply to cable.*

Chapter 15 on **music programming** *follows. Music format stations outnumber all other formats combined by a ratio of better than 90 to 1. Chapter 15 concentrates on rock music programming, but its strategies can also be applied to other music formats. To illustrate music radio programming strategies, the author of this chapter creates a hypothetical radio market into which he introduces a new station, step by step. Choosing a commercially viable format for any given market indicates how radio programmers are restricted and the methods they adopt for operating* *within those constraints. Chapter 15 continues the examination of the triple aspects of programming—evaluation, selection and scheduling.*

*Chapter 16 examines the locally programmed **all-news station**. Although this format occurs in its pure form only in very large markets, where a high degree of specialization can be supported economically, it occupies an important media role in times of local emergencies and national history-making events. All-news is advancing as an AM specialty in response to the shift of music formats to FM. However, many of the concerns of the all-news programmer apply equally to five-minute hourly interruptions inside music formats as well as to more lengthy newscasts. Chapter 16 takes a local perspective on news programming on radio. Many of the issues raised in this chapter also apply to local television newscasts.*

*The last chapter in Part IV, Chapter 17, focuses on **talk radio**, another major market specialty format varying from all-talk to news/talk mixes called information radio. From a programming perspective, talk radio differs from news radio because talk draws on audience members and guests to create large portions of the programming, whereas professional journalists occupy center stage in news radio. The typical talk format carries live celebrity interviews, but its most distinctive feature is the telephone call-in show. One talk station stands out from another primarily on the basis of the proportions of interviews, call-ins, conversations and news it uses. Chapter 17 discusses ways of structuring the talk radio format. The author also delves into the touchy issues of fairness and community pressure that operate in any size market and in any radio, cable or television format deviating from "canned" material.*

Radio programming may not seem complex when compared to broadcast television or cable, but these chapters demonstrate that radio programming strategy is highly developed within music, news and talk formats and that radio networks and syndicators play increasingly important roles in an essentially local medium. Part IV completes this book's overview of commercial programming.

CHAPTER FOURTEEN

Broadcast Radio Networks and Syndicators

Rolland C. Johnson and Edward F. McLaughlin

A QUICK GUIDE TO CHAPTER FOURTEEN

ROLLAND C. JOHNSON, *professor and former chairman of Telecommunications at Indiana University, is also president and a major stockholder of Indiana Communications, Inc., owner of an FM station with applications pending for a television station and an MMDS facility, and director of broadcasting for Duchossois Enterprises, owner of three radio stations. Johnson began in radio in 1959 and has since associated with it in every capacity of local operation—announcing, programming, sales, management, ownership. He also consults on station acquisition, programming and management. His B.J. and M.B.A. degrees come from the University of Missouri and his Ph.D. from Ohio University. In addition to articles on network compensation rates in the* Journal of Broadcasting, *he was co-author of the 1975 NAEB Book of the Year,* The Federal Role in Funding Children's Television Programming *(with K. Mielke and B. Cole). He has also worked for the federal government at the National Science Foundation and was visiting Howard R. Marsh Professor of Communication at the University of Michigan in 1980.*

EDWARD F. MCLAUGHLIN, *president of the ABC Radio Networks since 1972, has a long history with ABC. Before becoming president, he was vice-president and general manager of KGO Radio, the ABC owned-and-operated station in San Francisco. He joined KGO in 1964 and became general manager in 1967. Earlier, he had been general sales manager of KGBS in Los Angeles, office manager of Peters, Griffin & Woodward, and an account executive with KEWB, both in San Francisco. Currently, he is chairman of the Radio Network Association, a member of the board of governors of the North American Rock Radio Awards and a member of the board of the International Radio and Television Foundation. He graduated from San Francisco State University and, in 1972, was named alumnus of the year. Jointly, these authors analyze network and syndicated radio programming.*

HISTORICAL PERSPECTIVE ON NATIONAL RADIO

This chapter describes the economic relationship between radio affiliates and their networks and the program services the major radio networks supply as of the mid-1980s. It then examines the role of national radio syndicators in radio programming. Just as the evolution of both networks and syndicators was profoundly affected by the development of satellites and precise content targeting, future programming directions in each area are similarly entwined.

Radio programming has undergone remarkable changes in the last 50 years. In the 1930s and 1940s, radio was the major live, electronic mass medium. It supplied the primary national sales vehicle for consumer products. The radio networks provided both entertainment and news programs that captured the devoted attention of Americans before and during World War II. The programs resembled what can be seen on television in the mid-1980s—dramas, variety shows, comedies and so on—and were called **long-form** programming. By 1950, network radio advertising represented over $215 million in total revenue—and that amount probably represents over $1 billion in 1983 dollars.

The Impact of Television

But by 1953, network radio revenues had shrunk to less than $40 million because of television's inroads. Network radio was nearly replaced by a second electronic medium, and the changeover in the 1950s was swift, almost complete and nearly fatal. Television not only captured most of the national advertising dollars, it also attracted the best talent and the biggest stars. Television not only affected radio revenues, but perhaps more significantly, the programs and the nature of the services radio networks provided. The percentage of stations affiliating with one of the four largest networks dropped from 97 percent in 1946 to 30 percent in 1955.[1] American families began to huddle in front of television sets instead of radio sets. National radio programs failed to draw significant, measurable audiences to sell to advertisers, and radio networks crumbled. CBS, NBC and ABC survived in part because of revenues from their co-owned television operations. They cut expensive entertainment programming from their radio networks and concentrated on the delivery of short newscasts—usually five minutes or less—or **short-form** programming. A fourth major network, Mutual, did not own a television operation, but it also changed from long-form to short-form programming.

This change was a profound one for the networks and brought about change at the local level as well. No longer could stations look to their networks for most of their programming. On the other hand, few stations, even in major markets, could afford to produce elaborate live shows. By 1960, recorded music had become the mainstay of radio programming because it was inexpensive, universally available and appealed to the younger listeners who increasingly made up the radio audience.

The value of the radio networks dropped as their role diminished. To maintain visibility, they became short-form news and sports programmers, providing stations with services that would support their local identities. But rock and roll, the car radio, transistors, Elvis Presley's music and that of other superstars, plus the maturation of the postwar baby boom, gave local radio new life. As networks provided less and less material for local stations, program syndicators tried to fill the void, producing features or short musical programs and making them available on tapes or discs to stations throughout the United States. In the late 1960s, syndicators also developed long-form, formatted products for use on automated stations—provided on tape and disc and also syndicated to other locally programmed stations. But not until the 1980s did national radio networks again provide long-form entertainment programming. A major element in this recovery was the advent of satellite-relayed radio programming.

The Impact of Satellite Distribution

Until 1983, radio networks hooked up with their affiliates by wire or telephone land lines. The modern distribution method—the satellite—allows radio program suppliers to make their programming available simultaneously to every station in the United States relatively inexpensively. Additionally, satellite technology permits the distribution of more than one signal at the same time and provides a high-quality audio signal. A supplier can provide program A to one station and program B to another using the same satellite channel (transponder). High fidelity and stereo are possible over long distances without significant quality loss. The considerable cost savings achieved through satellite distribution effectively eliminated the major barrier to entry—the expense of land lines. As a result, a broad array of full-service or ad hoc radio networks appeared.

Using satellites allows radio networks and format syndicators to overcome two distribution weaknesses that had plagued them for many years: program scarcity and poor signal quality. Since the introduction of satellite distribution, networks and syndicators have been able to provide several offerings simultaneously with signals of the same quality as the originating signal. Stations can now mix locally produced, network-originated and syndicated features or programs without uneven audio characteristics (such as unmatched presence, signal-to-noise ratio, stereo and Dolby.)

The Influence of ABC's Program Targeting

The desire to package programs that would appeal to radio audiences with certain demographic characteristics was just as important as the arrival of relatively inexpensive satellite distribution in the proliferation of radio in the early 1980s. Both program targeting and satellite distribution led to the formation of new competing networks and long-form syndicators. The change in programming came first. Historically, radio stations targeted a specific demographic group whereas networks usually designed their programming for broad appeal to integrate with many station formats. But in the late 1960s, ABC decided to target its network programming to *specific* audience demographics. It began to program news written and delivered for specific demographic types ("cells" in ratings books) and specific affiliate formats. Its Contemporary and FM services identified and then tried to fill the youth-oriented music stations' need for news and other entertainment- or information-oriented features. (ABC's TALKRADIO followed a decade later, packaging hosted, telephone call-in programs.)

ABC targeted specific audiences by introducing a multiple network of four separate news services. At that time, a network leased land lines from the telephone company to connect it with its affiliates. It was cheaper for the network to lease the lines full-time, 24-hour-a-day, than to lease hourly for five-minute segments. This practice also allowed them to cover breaking spot news as it occurred. But newscasts were normally only for five minutes each hour, so for fifty or more minutes the line was not in use. As might be expected, renting telephone lines throughout the country was extremely expensive. To take advantage of the unused time on the lines and to try to recoup some of its money, in 1967 ABC created four different types of newscasts and staggered the transmissions on the same line. Thus, a station could affiliate with ABC Entertainment, for example, and get news during the second quarter of each hour (news *targeted* to that station's demographics). A second station in the same market could affiliate with ABC Information and get news of interest to its audience perhaps in the first quarter of each hour; other stations could affiliate with ABC Contemporary or FM and get their newscasts at other times. This pattern allowed ABC to use its news personnel more efficiently while the cost of the land lines remained the same. And the network became attractive to a broader array of stations—

potentially four times as many as when ABC had only a single news service. As a result, the number of ABC affiliates jumped dramatically in the late 1960s.[2] Surprisingly, the other networks did not copy this innovation until the late 1970s.

Networking vs. Syndication

Until the mid-1980s, several important distinctions separated networks and syndicators. A commercial *network* was usually defined as a group of affiliated stations, generally interconnected by wire, microwave or satellite, depending on a common source for the origination, simultaneous distribution and sale of programs. Traditionally, *syndication* differed from networking in that it lacked interconnection and simultaneous distribution. (Early syndicated short-form or long-form programs were distributed to stations on disc or tape and used whenever the station chose.)

During the 1980s, however, these traditional distinctions between networks and syndicators blurred. Networks started behaving as syndicators—providing short features and long-form entertainment programming—while many syndicators hooked up via satellites with affiliates and could therefore be classified as networks. The arrival of satellite distribution brought about this change.

The distinction that persists is that network programming is free to the affiliate although the affiliate must carry the programs' commercials. Syndicated programming is either sold or bartered to stations. In addition, networks focus on providing news; syndicators do not supply newscasts. While network programming is typically short-form, a syndicator's may be long or short. A station can both subscribe to a format syndicator and affiliate with a network.

CRITERIA FOR NATIONAL DISTRIBUTION

Five interrelated criteria guide networks or syndicators in selecting programs for national distribution. The overriding factor is talent availability for writing, performing and producing the show. The original notion behind networking and syndication is that talent is scarce and its cost can be most easily covered by pooling resources. A first criterion, therefore, is that a program must meet the network's or syndicator's standard of professionalism in writing, production and performance. A second criterion for national distribution is that the program must offer some element—be it location, star or budget—that the individual station cannot match. Once these two criteria are met, a program's third most important asset is its potential appeal. Whatever its precise demographic target, a program must capture the interest of most people in that target group.

A fourth standard in how unique a program's style, talent or presentation is. While star power draws radio audiences, the combination of top talent *and* a unique program format can give a network a franchise for a time in the competitive battle for affiliate clearance.

Fashion trends become a fifth consideration. Determining what is or will be "hot" requires intimate involvement with, and understanding of, the medium and its audiences. Trends in other media often provide clues, and widely appealing subjects or forms jump to other media. The programmer must also know when something that is popular will lose its appeal. Periodic program revitalization and replacement are critical if a network or syndicator is to remain acceptable to both audiences and affiliates, and therefore salable to advertisers.

The hallmark of the best network and syndicator programmers is how well they use these five criteria to evaluate programs and whole formats, irrespective of specific content. This chapter now turns to the kinds of programming networks are likely to provide in the late 1980s and, after detailing the syndication process, the kind of programs syndicators are likely to distribute.

NETWORK NEWS PROGRAMMING

Prior to revision of the radio guidelines in 1982, the FCC suggested certain minimum percentages of radio air time be filled with news and public affairs as a part of a station's community service obligation (otherwise, stations risked FCC examination at license renewal time). Once live entertainment ceased to be profitable for radio networks in the 1950s, the FCC's "suggestions" directed network attention to news. Thus, news became the mainstay of network programming until the late 1970s, and it is likely to remain an important ingredient in what networks provide and in what distinguishes them from syndicators. Even after the FCC relaxed its news and public affairs requirements, stations continued to affiliate with all-news networks, indicating the value stations place on network news programming.

Identifying the Need

To cover global news events, local stations rely on the national wire services and networks. Most stations expend nearly all their news budgets in covering local news and cannot mount effective national and international coverage. Wire services provide copy, but usually it must be rewritten and delivered in a credible manner (with a variety of voices) to compete with top-line news productions. Stations can blend wire reports with local news (using their own staff) or affiliate with a national network that will deliver the broader news perspective for them.

Nationally, just under two-thirds of stations affiliate with a network for national and international news coverage.[3] Fewer than two dozen stations nationwide program all-news, many owned and operated by CBS (see Chapter 16). Other affiliates receive their news in short bursts, typically less than five minutes in each hour. The evolution of demographically formatted news services made this strategy all the more attractive to major market stations that once generated their own national newscasts.

Identifying the Right Network

Once a station decides to affiliate with a network for network news services, it must decide which network to approach. After eliminating networks already having affiliates in a given market, the station next considers networks that target the demographics it tries to reach. A rock music station aimed at the 18–

34 category, for example, might affiliate with ABC's Rock Radio, CBS's RadioRadio, NBC's The Source or RKO's I. A country music station might choose Associated Press's Music Country, which includes newscasts. A black-oriented station could choose Unity's National Black, American Black or Sheridan's black-oriented programming. Each of these networks programs only for its target group, and one cannot be readily substituted for another. For example, the black-oriented networks each create a news sound that fits best in one radio format.

NETWORK SPORTS PROGRAMMING

Although a station rarely chooses an affiliation based solely on the sports coverage a network provides, sports does affect the extent of affiliation (hours of clearance) and the popularity of the entire service. ABC, CBS and NBC use the same nationally known sportscasters to cover the games appearing on television and radio. Most radio network sports programming, however, is regional—set up to broadcast sporting events in particular geographic areas—such as the Notre Dame Football Network or the Nebraska Football Network.

Sports has been a good money-maker for radio networks because it delivers a clearly identifiable audience, largely male adults 18–49, having strong appeal to many advertisers. From the national network programmer's perspective, however, there are not enough attractive sports events to cover. Only games with national appeal are suitable for national distribution. To remain competitive, the four radio networks will have to offer both news and sports programs that distinguish them from fare syndicators supply. Because of the limited number of nationally appealing sports events, the cost for the rights to these games can be expected to climb, reducing the networks' potential profit from sports coverage.

NETWORK TALK AND ENTERTAINMENT PROGRAMMING

In the 1980s, the established networks returned to long-form entertainment programming—most notably talk shows. Mutual's *Larry King Show*, ABC's TALKRADIO and NBC's TALKNET combine overnight long-form talk and interview programs, covered in detail in Chapter 17. Most talk affiliates are AM stations, many with long commitments to information/personality/sports, and strong information images in their communities. In this area, the distinction between the programming *networks* provide and *syndicators* offer blurs.

NETWORK MUSIC PROGRAMMING

Network music programming was also reborn in the late 1970s. The success of syndicated services after the introduction of satellite distribution and the birth of music-only services stimulated the established news and sports networks to expand their music offerings. Music programming divides into individual programs and series, or *short-form*, and continuous formatted music, or *long-form*.

The major broadcast networks typically provide only the short-form programs, but during the early 1980s, some new networks began supplying long-form, formatted musical programming via satellite.

Concerts and Specials

For the networks operating in 1975, special music programs generated little or no money, but in 1983 sales for such programming hit $30 million. These shows consist largely of live concerts or specials featuring star interviews intercut with songs. Access to these concerts and major performers has been, and still remains, beyond the financial reach of most local stations so they turn to syndicators that record the shows and sell them at prices ranging from $25–$50 per hour in small markets to several hundred dollars per hour in large markets. Networks also provide music specials within the context of full-service programming—news, sports and music—and as part of appropriate 24-hour format services.

Advertisers will pay a premium rate (above the normal network commercial rate) for music concerts and specials because the commercials in these shows are fixed, assuring clearance in advance within a specific program environment. Commercials can therefore target the exact demographics of the affiliates clearing a music special, and the advertiser can also enjoy the benefit of being associated with a major musical event.

Concerts and specials are often a factor in a network's financial negotiations with an affiliate. When a network supplies programming many affiliates want, it gains leverage in the annual battles to set compensation rates. Even a slight diminution of compensation payments, en toto, balances increased production costs for special programs.

As with any other type of network program, the key to revenue for a music special is the size of its cleared audience. Fitting a particular concert or series of concerts to a demographic category and selling it to complementary affiliates is more difficult than clearing a targeted newscast. Most programs target either the youth demographic of roughly 18–49 years (it may include teens) or the adult demographic of 25–54 years. Each presents separate problems. In general, the youth demographic requires a more careful fit between programs and formats in the affiliate line-up than the adult demographic. The biggest distinction networks must make however, is whether programming is for the pure or the mixed format.

Pure and Mixed Formats

The album-oriented-rock format (AOR) represents a pure format. It has an easily definable audience, predominantly male 18–24, interested in varied, offbeat rock music accompanied by a laid-back DJ style. Country music, despite the rise of "urban country" over "country/western," is also a relatively pure format appealing to a more adult audience (25–54). For both AOR and country formats, the list of acceptable artists, groups and even songs is generally agreed on by stations nationwide. Or at the least, stations agree on broad exclusions from each of these musical formats.

Both formats enjoy strong audience followings with salable demographics, making them ideal for network program series. What a network must supply is superior production quality, top artists, merchandising support and protection in the local market. (Protection means that the network will supply the program only to a single station, irrespective of the number of affiliates it has whose signals overlap, a form of **exclusivity**.)

The adult contemporary (AC), Top 40 and contemporary hit radio (CHR) formats are mixed. Stations using them perceive a wide variation in acceptability. One station claiming to be AC may clear an artist totally refused by another station claiming the same format. Thus, network programmers have difficulty identifying programs that will build audiences of salable size.

For a network seeking musical concerts and specials, three strategies exist. The first is to produce many shows of varied appeal to capture fragments of the youth or adult audiences. The second is to concentrate on the relatively small number of stars that appeal across the broadest format spectrum. Neither of these strategies has the economic efficiency of producing programs directed toward the pure format groups, however. The third option is to buy or produce programs that have unique, broad appeals such as *Dick Clark's National Music Survey* or special hosted-shows. They succeed best as regularly scheduled features, and audiences seek them out. A broad range of affiliates will clear unique music programs, thus accumulating sizable audiences and potentially making them the most profitable of network music programs, competitive with top-rated radio sports.

Format Music Networks

Until the late 1970s, format syndicators were the sole source of long-form, all-music programming unless stations programmed their own music. The major networks concentrated on news, sports and music specials. With the arrival of satellites, however, a new generation of format music networks appeared. Like format syndicators, these networks supply 24-hour music services targeted to a single demographic or ethnic group.

As of the mid-1980s, music format networks and syndicators were supplying a product targeted at a defined audience, accompanied by minor leavening of news and, in some cases, a small amount of public affairs. The sole practical distinction between some networks and some syndicators is that hourly news-casts are included in a *music network* service while separate network news affiliation may be needed to accompany some *syndicated* formats.

The New Networks

From the beginning of radio until the very late 1970s, ABC, CBS, Mutual and NBC were the principal radio networks, due initially to the limited number of stations with sufficient broadcasting power and, subsequently, to the expense of interconnecting stations via telephone lines. But by the mid-1980s, more than 30 networks blanketed the nation with long-form and short-form audio programming. Table 14-1 lists the most established of these networks and indicates the types of programming they make available to the local station.

TABLE 14-1.
Radio Networks

ABC:	RKO:
Contemporary	RKO I
Direction	RKO II
Entertainment	
FM	Satellite Music Network:
Information	Country*
Rock Radio*	AC*
TALKRADIO*	Black*
	Beautiful*
Associated Press:	
AP Network News	Sheridan
Music Country Radio Network*	
	Starfleet Blair*
Bonneville*	
	Transtar*
CBS:	
CBS Radio	Turner:
RadioRadio	CNN Radio*
Mutual	Unity:
	American Black
NBC:	National Black
NBC Radio	
The Source	UPI
TALKNET*	
	Wall Street Journal

*Indicates long-form or format networks

RADIO NETWORKING ECONOMICS

Commercial radio networks make money by selling advertising time (inventory) to advertisers, generally through the mediation of advertising agencies. As in television, acquiring local affiliates provides the potential audience. The combined audiences of all a network's affiliated stations thus becomes the audience for the network spots advertisers buy. Networks sell advertisers time within their newscasts and programs on the condition that a substantial number of stations will carry the ads and a substantial number of listeners will be reached.

Contracts

The FCC allows a station to contract with a network for no longer than two years (at which time renewal is necessary). Radio station program managers agree to carry network programming for many reasons—but principally to add to the attractiveness of the station's offerings at minimal cost. Network programmers produce national and international newscasts, credibly delivered by nationally known reporters and announcers. Thus small market as well as large market stations receive high-quality, reliable, on-the-spot news coverage of national and international events. The network supplies the programming to the station in exchange for an outlet for the network's commercials. The usual contract allows the station to preempt the news but requires the station to broadcast the commercials. For most stations, therefore, the network is viewed as a "free" service.

Compensation

In large metropolitan markets, Arbitron's top 50 ADIs, radio stations typically have large enough audiences to demand more than programming for carrying a network's commercials. They usually ask for network compensation, similar to the arrangement between a television network and its affiliate (see Chapter 7 on television affiliate contracts). This payment is negotiated on the basis of the size and type of the station's audience and the number of network commercials it agrees to carry, influenced by the competitive market conditions at the time the compensation is arranged. Radio affiliation differs from television in that a radio station's audience typically counts only in the demographic group it targets; compensation is based only on the number of persons reached among its target demographic group (rather than the total number of persons reached).

Networks pay compensation either in the form of a flat monthly rate or a per-unit rate for commercials actually aired. Thus a network pays less compensation to its affiliates when it sells a smaller percentage of its—the network's—inventory, although the station rate remains fixed. Under either contractual arrangement, the network assesses penalties for commercials the network carries but the station does not air. Stations, therefore, almost always carry the network commercials even though they may preempt the programs.

In the past, compensation negotiations also involved payment for the telephone lines that delivered the network signal. Although a network might absorb the cost of telephone lines for stations not in the top 50 markets, telephone line costs substantially reduced the metropolitan station's profit from compensation. This issue has become moot, however, since the introduction of satellite program distribution. The network pays satellite distribution costs, and the affiliated station provides its own receiving dish. Some of the networks even covered affiliates' costs for receiving dishes to speed the transition to satellite technology.

Network compensation, whether in television or radio, is not a big part of a typical station's revenue total. On average, compensation for television affiliates amounts to about 8 percent of their revenue. As of 1983, compensation usually accounts for less than 1 percent of radio affiliate revenue. This difference occurs because there are so many more radio stations (nearly 9,000 commercial stations). Fewer are affiliated with any network (about 60 percent as of 1983 compared with 80 percent of television stations), and the majority are located in small markets where affiliates receive no compensation.

RADIO SYNDICATION

Syndicators fall into two distinct classes. One group produces format packages, typically a species of rock, easy listening, country, nostalgia or classical music. They supply stations with tapes or satellite interconnection for a monthly fee based on market size. The second syndicator group produces special features such as weekly top 40 countdowns, concerts or religion (sermons, talk or gospel music), supplying stations with tapes, discs or interconnects for cash or barter. The two classes of syndicators correspond to the two types of music networks, format (long form) and fixture (short form).

Syndicator Compensation

In contrast to the networks, few syndicators pay any station compensation. Instead, the syndicated program is provided in one of three ways: (1) free to the station on a bartered basis (see Chapter 8 for an explanation of barter), (2) for a fee and containing no advertising or (3) for a fee and containing some advertising. To determine how to pay for the programming, a programmer usually consults with the sales manager and often the station manager in selecting syndicated material; local spot revenues must exceed program costs as a rule. As syndicators prepare more long-form programming for simultaneous satellite distribution, however, the current fee arrangements may alter substantially. As the costs of distribution decline, and competition among producers increases, syndicators may begin compensating more stations for carrying their product.

Format Syndicators

Ten of the major companies providing formatted music programming in long-form for radio stations throughout the United States are listed below.

Toby Arnold and Associates, Dallas, Texas
Nostalgia, Contemporary, Soft Hits

BPI, Bellevue, Washington
Easy Listening, Country, AC and others

Century 21, Dallas, Texas
Nineteen formats varying from Country to Religion

Drake-Chenault, Canoga Park, California
Country, Top 40, Nostalgia, AC, Soul

Al Ham Productions, Dallas, Texas
Nostalgia

Musicworks, Inc., Nashville, Tennessee
Country, AC, Easy Listening

Parkway Productions, Washington, D.C.
Classical

Peters Productions, San Diego, California
MOR, AC, Top 40, Country

Schulke Productions, South Plainfield, New Jersey
Beautiful Music

TM Programming, Dallas, Texas
Beautiful Music, Country, Urban Contemporary, Top 40,
Nostalgia, Adult Contemporary

Besides these major suppliers, hundreds of regional syndicators market single packages to limited numbers of stations.

In the 1960s, the FCC's nonduplication policy (limiting the amount of duplicated programming on co-owned AM and FM stations) spurred FM stations to find inexpensive programming. At this point, syndicators proliferated. They took advantage of the increasing desire among programmers for tightly formatted stations, and microprocessor technology to provide long-form, adopted packages. Consequently, the number of automated stations using format packages grew from a handful to over 2,000 in the 1970s. The syndicators selected the music and suggested the order in which tapes should be played. Typically, this type of syndicator consulted with individual client stations about promotion, advertising spot placement, the length of the broadcast day, the role of announcers, the amount of news and so on. Using syndicated format packages, a small market station could achieve a consistent "big market" sound with recognized advertiser appeal.

Feature Syndicators

The number of syndicators providing shorter programs or features also increased dramatically during the 1970s. Syndicated feature programs range from daypart packages, such as sports shorts or Sunday morning religious programs, to very brief inserts such as 90-second interviews with star performers—for example, *Earth News Radio*. Stations producing their own programming use short features to add spice and variety to a stretch of recorded songs and use the longer programming to fill unsalable time periods. Radio broadcasters also use features as a strategy for attracting a specific target audience, frequently subgroups of the station's overall demographic group management wants to strengthen.

Syndicated feature programming is as varied as its producers. Many of the companies syndicating long-form format packages also supply short features that fit within the long formats. The shorts are also made available to other stations in the same market (on a format-exclusive basis). Drake-Chenault, for example, produces *The Weekly Top 30, The Great American Country Show*, and *The Golden Years*, and it produces format packages such as country, top 40, MOR, AC and Soul.

One of the most successful short-form programs, a weekly two-hour program created by Tom Rounds and his Watermark Company in 1969, is *American Top 40* featuring Casey Kasem. It targets young people 12–25, and as of 1983, is heard on over 1,000 radio stations. Another syndicator, DIR, came out with *King Biscuit Flower Hour* in 1973, targeting a slightly older group, generally 18–25, and its popularity continues a decade later.

Listed below are ten syndicators supplying primarily short-form or feature programming (including samples of their most widely distributed features).

The Broadcast Group, Los Angeles
American Voices, In Depth Magazine

DIR Communications, New York
King Biscuit, Robert Klein Show, Supergroups in Concert, DIRect News, The Rock Radio Awards

Multimedia Broadcast Associates, New York
Celebrity Corner, The Stan Martin Show

Narwood Productions, New York
Country Closeup, Minding Your Own Business, Outlook

O'Connor Creative Services, Universal City, California
Kids Say the Darndest Things, Howard Ruff Commentary, Ronald Reagan Commentary, More for Your Money

Radio Arts, Burbank, California
Your Hit Parade, Country Countdown

Radio Works, Hollywood, California
The Unexplainable, Line on Tomorrow, Stay Healthy

Watermark, Inc., Los Angeles
American Top 40, TV Tonight, American Country Countdown

Weedeck, Inc., Hollywood, California
Country Report Countdown, The Great American Spirit

Westwood One, Culver City, California
Live from Gilleys, Dr. Demento, Playboy Advisor, Off the Record with Mary Turner

TRENDS IN NATIONWIDE RADIO

As we pointed out earlier, satellite distribution of radio programming obliterated many of the distinctions traditionally separating radio syndicators from radio networks. By the mid-1980s, established news and sports networks were also providing long-form, formatted music programming and special feature broadcasts, and some had purchased syndicators as subsidiary companies. ABC, for example, purchased Watermark, Inc., in 1982.

On the other hand, by the mid-1980s, many long-time syndicators were distributing most of their long- (format) and short-form (feature) programming by satellite, reaching stations simultaneously across the nation. As the economics of satellite relay became favorable, Bonneville and Starfleet Blair, for example,

TABLE 14-2.
Types of Programming from Syndicators and Networks

	Syndicators	Networks
Format	(Drake-Chenault; TM)	Satellite Music Network
Feature		
Long-form	(*Dick Clark's American Top 40*)	Starfleet Blair
Short-form	(Earth News Radio)	Paul Harvey
News		
Long-form	(none provided)	Cable News Network
Short-form	(none provided)	ABC, CBS, Mutual, NBC

shifted to satellite distribution and became networks, after previously being thought of as syndicators. The former produces a beautiful music package, and the latter distributes AOR and AC concerts. Table 14-2 summarizes the types of programming that networks and syndicators offered at the beginning of 1983.

Other services introduced since 1982 include Satellite Music Network and Country Music Network. These 24-hour services reserve a minute or two per hour for commercial sale and charge stations a monthly fee, typically around $1,000. Although two such services failed in their first year, Enterprise Radio carrying sports and Continental Radio carrying religious programming, the number of national radio services will grow and the expansion of existing services continue. According to the National Association of Broadcasters:

> Radio's flexibility uniquely positions it to track the growth, mobility and interests of the U.S. population in the changing environment of the 1980s and 1990s. Program specialization or narrowcasting can be predicted to emerge as a typical marketing strategy designed to meet the needs of an increasingly diversified and sophisticated radio audience.[4]

Four trends in radio programming will continue. The distinctions between networks and syndicators will further blur, and following the pattern cable television set, the term *services* will probably acquire general usage. The amount of long-form format programming produced at a single source will expand. The number of narrowly targeted music and information services will increase. And the number of automated stations using nationally distributed format packages will rise.

From the local station programmer's perspective, programming source is immaterial as is delivery method just so long as the programming appears quickly, reliably and has high quality. The station programmer focuses on the nature and quality of the programming itself, requiring innovative, trendy, timely and polished programming that will deliver an audience to advertisers. The expanded array of nationally available programming permits the station programmer to cherrypick—to select the best of what is available to accomplish station goals. More and more radio programming will come from national networks and syndicators in a mix of long-form, formatted packages and short-form, feature elements, blended at the local level to fit a program manager's ideal mix.

SUMMARY

The business of nationwide radio programming has altered drastically since the 1950s. Defeated by television, the national radio networks abandoned most entertainment programming and turned to news and sports until the advent of inexpensive satellite relay and formatted radio in the 1970s. By the early 1980s, more than a dozen new satellite-distributed music or news networks had joined the traditional "big four": ABC, CBS, Mutual and NBC. CBS and NBC remain suppliers of news, sporting events and occasional short-form concerts and specials. ABC has a half dozen target news services and an all-talk network, as does NBC. Mutual has been joined by several full-service entertainment networks.

Stations affiliate with a network news service when they cannot afford their own national news staffs or need the prestige of the network sound to compete. They affiliate based on target demographics and cost. Music networks either provide features for a locally originating format or a package for an automated station. Both the total number of networks and syndicators greatly increased during the 1970s. In the late 1960s, syndicators began supplying a significant portion of FM programming, and by the mid-1980s, they rivaled the old-line networks as major suppliers of feature materials, while also providing most packaged music formats. Both networks and syndicators face a period of intense growth in the 1980s as they respond to changing interests and fads. As the distinctions between the two continue to blur, they will come to be called program services rather than networks or syndicators.

Notes

[1]Christopher H. Sterling and Timothy R. Haight, *The Mass Media: Aspen Institute Guide to Communication Industry Trends* (New York: Praeger, 1978), p. 47.

[2]Ibid. By 1970, half of all commercial radio stations were affiliated, the largest number with ABC; by 1980, the percentage had climbed to just over 60 percent.

[3]In one of a series of six nationwide surveys conducted in 1983 by Torbet Radio, half of the station managers surveyed said *news* was the main reason they affiliated, followed by compensation, prestige, national sound, news actualities and features. The most preferred features were celebrity interviews geared to the station's demographics. The managers reported airing somewhat over half of the network news feed, cutting it to shorter length, using only the actualities or reducing the quantity of aired network newscasts as the day progressed. Mariann DeLuca, *Survey of Radio Stations* (New York: Torbet Radio, 1983). (See 1 February, 7 April, 15 June, 25 August and 21 September Torbet press releases.)

[4]Marsha L. DeSonne, *Radio, New Technology and You* (Washington, D.C.: National Association of Broadcasters, April 1982), p. 5.

Selected Sources

Bortz, Paul, and Mendelsohn, Harold. *Radio Today—and Tomorrow.* Washington, D.C.: National Association of Broadcasters, October 1982.

Shooshan, III, Harry M., and Jackson, Charles L. *Radio Subcarrier Services,* Com/Tech Report. Vol. 2, No. 1. Washington, D.C.: National Association of Broadcasters, May 1983.

"Special Report on Radio." *Broadcasting* (15 August 1983): 47–52; (29 August 1983): 47–94 (and annually in August issues).

"Special Report: Satellites." *Broadcast Management/Engineering* (July 1983): 41–78.

Television/Radio Age, weekly reports on the radio industry.

Trubia, Charles, "Pros and Cons of Radio Syndication." *Marketing and Media Decisions* (June 1979): 88–90.

CHAPTER FIFTEEN

Music Programming

Edd Routt

A QUICK GUIDE TO CHAPTER FIFTEEN

Music Format Popularity

Choosing a Format
    Comparing Technical Facilities
    Defining the Competitive Market
    Identifying Target Audiences
    Knowing the Available Budget
    Estimating Potential Revenue

Step-by-Step Selection Process

Implementation

The Music
    The Music Wheel or "Hot Clock"
    Music Research

News
    Journalistic Content
    Nonentertainment Programming

Air Personalities and Dayparting
    Morning
    Midday

    Afternoon
    Evening
    All-night

Advertising and Promotion
    Contesting
    Commercial Load
    Call Letters
    Jingles

FCC and Other Constraints
    Contests and Games
    Plugola and Payola
    Sounds That Mislead
    Program Logs

Radio's Future

Summary

Notes

Selected Sources

EDD ROUTT, *as a general manager of several radio stations and writer on radio, brings a wealth of expertise in news, sales and station management to this chapter on music programming. He creates a hypothetical market in which the reader goes step by step through the process of selecting a competitive format. After deciding on rock music for this proposed station, he details a system for song classification and delineates the role of research. This chapter draws on the author's experiences as broadcast consultant and general manager of KSLM/KSKD, Salem, Oregon; vice president and general manager of WKRG/WKRG-FM; general manager of KLIF; general manager of WRR-AM/FM; and sales manager of WFAA/KZEW. In addition he has taught station administration for six years at Southern Methodist University and written three books on broadcasting:* The Business of Radio Broadcasting *(TAB Books, 1972);* Dimensions of Broadcast Editorializing *(TAB Books, 1974); and* The Radio Format Conundrum *(with McGrath and Weiss, Hastings House, 1978). This chapter covers the strategies that work with popular music formats and the problems in presenting news within music format schedules.*

MUSIC FORMAT POPULARITY

Some stations may play country, classical, beautiful music, ethnic or nostalgia, but rock is the prevailing genre in radio. Rock music encompasses soft rock, hard rock and even country rock, but it is most commonly classed as top 40, adult contemporary, album-oriented rock (AOR), hot hits, urban contemporary and contemporary hit radio. More people listen to rock, in one form or another, than to any other music style. Unquestionably, rock's passionate, relentless beat is as firmly established in America as country, jazz and classical. Fueled by a resurgent interest in the top 40 format, 1983 saw more radio format shifts than any year since the mid-1960s.[1] In all sections of the United States except the South, adult contemporary, including top 40, is the most popular format, with AOR and country music close behind (see Figure 15-1).

CHOOSING A FORMAT

The first step in analyzing an unfamiliar market is to evaluate its stations and their current programming. This information can then be used to modify or replace existing program formats or to decide which property to buy and what to do with it after purchase. Such an evaluation takes into account: (1) the technical facilities, as compared to those of the competition; (2) the character of the local market; (3) the delineation of a target audience; (4) the available budget; and (5) the potential revenue. Once completed, this evaluation will determine which music format is commercially viable and can win in the ratings in a given market.

Comparing Technical Facilities

The best facility has the best chance to succeed. Thus, AM's power and frequency and FM's power and antenna height are important considerations.

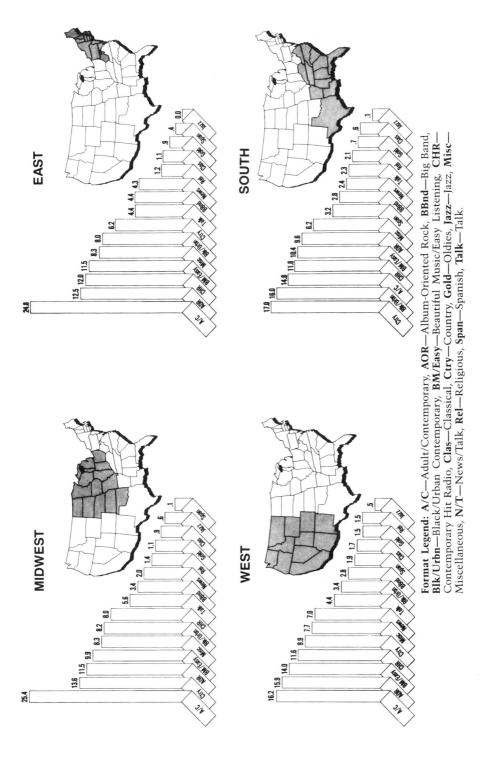

FIGURE 15-1. Format Preferences by Region Based on 1983 Radio & Records Ratings Report, Vol. 1.

Format Legend: A/C—Adult/Contemporary, **AOR**—Album-Oriented Rock, **BBnd**—Big Band, **Blk/Urbn**—Black/Urban Contemporary, **BM/Easy**—Beautiful Music/Easy Listening, **CHR**—Contemporary Hit Radio, **Clas**—Classical, **Ctry**—Country, **Gold**—Oldies, **Jazz**—Jazz, **Misc**—Miscellaneous, **N/T**—News/Talk, **Rel**—Religious, **Span**—Spanish, **Talk**—Talk.

Generically, these elements determine signal quality. A clear, undistorted signal is less tiring to the listener than one that is distorted, faint or accompanied by natural or artificial interference. All other qualities of similar formats being equal, the station with the best signal will be the listener's choice. Emotional fatigue unconsciously sets in after a period of straining to hear a program with a noisy, uncomfortable signal.

An FM station with 100,000 watts of **effective radiated power (ERP)** with its antenna assembly mounted on a 1,000-foot tower is a much better facility than a station with the same power but with the antenna mounted on a 500-foot tower. The AM station with a power of 50,000 watts on a clear channel (820 kHz) is a much better technical facility than a station with 5,000 watts of power at 570 kHz. Usually the low-power station is at the mercy of the higher power station. A 5,000-watt facility with a country or beautiful music format may be very vulnerable to a same-format station broadcasting at 10,000 or 50,000 watts.

This rule of thumb does not hold in all cases. For example, a 10,000-watt facility at 1600 kHz might easily fall victim to a 1,000-watt station at 710 kHz. In AM, both power and dial position are important. The lower the frequency, the greater the range of the AM signal. A 1,000-watt station at 710 kHz might easily reach a bigger population than a 10,000-watt station at 1600 kHz.

In FM, tower height and power are the principal considerations. A low-power (Class A) FM station with a 1,000-foot antenna might cover more territory than a full-power (Class C) station with its antenna mounted 200 feet above average terrain. Dial position is much less important in FM, although the center of the dial gets more sampling. An FM station at the fringe of the band needs an advertising and promotion blitz when altering its format. But always, having the best or one of the best facilities in the market is crucial to beating the competition.

In the AM vs. FM competition, the victories since the early 1970s have been going to FM, when music competes against music. A beautiful music format on FM will win in ratings against a similar format on AM, simply because FM reproduces music with greater fidelity. This situation is true also of FM rock vs. AM rock and FM country vs. AM country. In fact, in recent years, FM has scored greater audience gains than AM in every music format.

The station's technical facility plays an important part in the initial decision to enter music programming competition. It would be aesthetically foolish and economically disastrous to pit, say, a daytime AM against a full-power FM in the contemporary rock field. Conversely, if the leading contemporary music station in a market is AM, and the new facility is a high-quality FM, the AM station will be extremely vulnerable to a programming assault.

Defining the Competitive Market

In deciding on a radio format, the programmer's essential first step is to review the competition thoroughly. Television, cable and newspaper competition can be ignored: Television and newspapers stay relatively stable media no matter what radio does; and cable companies compete principally for audience time, not for advertising dollars (though in a few markets with advertising interconnects, cable is indeed an adversary and will become more so in the late 1980s).

One of the prospective buyers' first steps toward a purchase decision might be to profile each station's demographics in a bar graph, to show what percentage of each of the six standard demographic groups each station has. The bars in such graphs display the age "leaning" of a station's audiences, suggesting the industry name of **skew graphs**. Arbitron is the principal source of the data; the 6 A.M.–midnight, Monday–Sunday page of a ratings book breaks out all individual demographic groups. However, any audience analysis service providing demographic separation has the necessary information. Table 15-1 shows skew graphs for two stations in the hypothetical market considered in this chapter.

With skew graphs of all stations laid out, program strategists can quickly analyze which age groups are best served by which stations and therefore which stations represent major competition. The examples in Table 15-1 show only age, but sex breakout would also be useful. For example, an AOR (album-oriented

TABLE 15-1.
Skew Graphs for a Hypothetical Metro Survey

WMMM-AM

Age Group	Size of Group	Percentage of Total Audience
		5 10 15 20 25 30 35 40 45 50
Teens	35,400	▓▓▓▓▓▓▓▓▓▓▓▓ (≈30)
18–24	29,500	▓▓▓▓▓▓▓▓▓▓ (≈26)
25–34	23,500	▓▓▓▓▓ (≈13)
35–44	11,400	▓▓ (≈7)
45–54	7,400	▓ (≈3)
55–64	8,700	▓ (≈4)
Total	115,900	

WNNN-AM

Age Group	Size of Group	Percentage of Total Audience
		5 10 15 20 25 30 35 40 45 50
Teens	6,000	▓ (≈4)
18–24	7,000	▓ (≈5)
25–34	11,900	▓▓▓ (≈10)
35–44	6,300	▓ (≈4)
45–54	13,600	▓▓▓ (≈10)
55–64	20,100	▓▓▓▓▓▓ (≈30)
Total	64,900	

SOURCE: April/May 1978 Arbitron. Used with permission.

rock) operation might show 30 percent adults 18 to 34 years, but the males in the audience usually account for 60 to 70 percent of the total.

Identifying Target Audiences

It is not enough to study population graphs and other research data about a market's radio listeners. It is essential to go into the community to find out specifically what people are doing, thinking and listening to. It is helpful to observe lifestyles by visiting restaurants, shopping centers, gas stations, discotheques, bars, taverns and other places where people let their hair down.

The 40-year-old lawyer who dresses in dark suits during the week and has lunch at a stuffy club may be found in the evenings wearing jeans and a T-shirt in a favorite disco. He is hip, married, has two children and loves to go dancing with his wife. A potential listener to a new rock station? Absolutely! Are there more like him? They number in the thousands in most markets of the nation.

Formal research can supplement personal investigation. Most cities have research firms that can be hired to make special studies, and national firms such as Frank N. Magid Associates and McHugh-Hoffman specialize in broadcast station research. Other well-known radio consulting firms include Reymer & Gersen Associates; Jhan Hiber & Associates; and McGavern Guild Radio. A study assessing current formats using lengthy, in-depth telephone interviews might get interesting responses: too many commercials, bad commercial production, too much kinky music, too many contests, can't win contests, or jocks are idiots. As you can imagine, a station getting answers like these is ready for a major overhaul.

Many broadcasters employ university instructors and students to do summer studies that can be very beneficial. Later on, staff involvement in the community often provides feedback on how the community is reacting to the station's new programming strategies. DJ-manned student discos can provide an additional input channel.

As an example of the kind of findings that prove useful, a station in Dallas identified its typical listener as male, about 30 years old, earning $25,000 a year (in the 1970s), driving a Corvette, drinking a foreign beer, going out at least twice a week with a date to a good restaurant and playing tennis. The station sold this audience description to advertisers and to listeners. Promotional material stressed joining the "in" crowd who listened to this particular station.

Knowing the Available Budget

The usual hit music operation requires six to eight disc jockies, along with a production director and, perhaps, a music director. In a market of 500,000, the program director may earn as much as $35,000 a year, the morning DJ probably gets $25,000, and the production director's salary falls in the middle. The afternoon-drive DJ may get $20,000. The other five or six jocks will average $12,000 to $15,000 per year. In the top ten markets, one may have to double or triple these salaries.

In a medium-sized market (500,000), television and billboard advertising might run $15,000 a month for good exposure. It may cost five times that in a

Dallas- or a Chicago-sized market. Not only are unit prices higher in large markets, but usually more territory must be covered. A set of billboards reaching the whole population in one market may require 35 billboards, for example, while a similar showing in Dallas would require 125 billboards.

Consultants are available to advise on every conceivable aspect of operations. Programming consultants find market voids, spot competitor weaknesses and frequently even assemble a staff to work up a specific format. One may employ legal, technical, management, personnel and sales as well as programming consultants—all of them may be useful at one time or another. Consultation is expensive, however. An engineer may charge $300 a day plus expenses; a programmer may charge $2,000 a month on a three-to-six-month contract; for a complete station overhaul, consultants range from $200 to $1,000 a day. In addition, a syndicated program service like Schulke or Bonneville, depending on market size, could run as high as $10,000 a month. Nevertheless, a neophyte licensee may be literally unable to start up without using one or more consultants. A great deal of highly specialized knowledge and experience must be brought to bear immediately once the Federal Communications Commission has given the licensee authority to start operations.

Estimating Potential Revenue

In any area, advertisers most desire the 18- to 49-year-old audience. In radio, this group is subdivided into ten-to-fifteen-year segments that specific formats target. Following Arbitron's pattern, radio audience segments end in a 4. The target audiences of most advertisers are age 17 to 24, or increasingly, as the baby boom generation ages, 25 to 34 or 44 to 54 years. Rarely does an advertiser seek the audience aged 55 to 64. Advertisers assume older people are set in their buying habits; they are regarded as saving money rather than spending it, having bought about everything they are ever going to buy. But they see the youth market as having money, responding to advertising and as receptive to buying, even if it means going into debt. Increasingly, stations are tracking the largest population group in the market and adjusting their music formats to continue to appeal to this group as it ages. By the late 1990s, the baby boom generation may be too old to interest most advertisers—unless new products emerge.

STEP-BY-STEP SELECTION PROCESS

Format strategy can be examined by working through a hypothetical market—say a metropolitan area of 500,000 inhabitants in which 17 stations are heard, licensed either to the metro area or to its suburbs. Further assume that a small group of radio enthusiasts is about to buy one of these stations and to design a program format from scratch. Table 15-2 lists the stations in the market.

All stations are licensed in the metro area except for two suburban stations. WEEE, the suburban AM daytimer, programs strictly for its local audience. WIII, the low-power FM station, block programs its schedule, running three hours of country music followed by three hours of rock, followed by an hour of gospel

TABLE 15-2.
List of Stations, Types, Formats, Facilities

Station	Type	Format	Percent Share	Facility[a]
WAAA	AM day	Religious	1.0	1 K @ 1500 kHz
WBBB	AM day	Country	4.2	1 K @ 1600 kHz
WCCC	AM day	Talk	2.6	5 K @ 840 kHz
WDDD	AM day	Ethnic	4.8	1 K @ 900 kHz
WEEE	AM day	Local	0.9	1 K @ 710 kHz
WFFF	FM	Classical	1.1	100,000 @ 700'
WGGG	FM	Schulke	7.6	100,000 @ 600'
WHHH	FM	Bonneville	8.7	100,000 @ 540'
WIII	FM	AC(MOR)	0.8	3,000 @ 250'
WJJJ	FM	Ethnic	6.1	100,000 @ 540'
WKKK	AM	Country	9.9	5 KD/1 KN @ 970 kHz
WLLL	FM	Country	12.1	100,000 @ 700'
WMMM	AM	Rock	16.5	5 KD/5 KN @ 1480 kHz
WNNN	AM	News/Info	5.0	10 K @ 1010 kHz
WOOO	AM	Rock	0.6	1 KD/½ KN @ 1310 kHz
WPPP	FM	AOR	12.1	100,000 @ 540'
WQQQ	FM	MOR/Contemporary	4.9	100,000 @ 1,000'
Other	(Distant signals)		1.1	

[a]K = 1,000 watts; 5 KD/1 KN means that a station uses 5,000 watts in the daytime and reduces to 1,000 watts at night.

and so on. The station about to be sold is WQQQ in the metro competition with a 4.9 audience share of the market—not bad, but well behind the leaders.

In going over the list of stations in the hypothetical market, the planners identify those with which they do not expect to compete seriously. The prospective facility is FM (a decided plus); it is full power (most desirable); and its antenna is on the highest tower in the market (bingo!). It is otherwise a dog. But, the facility is superior to anything in the area.

First, the planners can scratch all AM daytimers as potential competition. That narrows the competition from 16 to 11. Next, they can knock out any good classical operations (one in the market, WFFF-FM) as most markets can accommodate only a single classical station. That leaves ten. It would be foolhardy to tackle two beautiful music operations with syndicated programming by Schulke and Bonneville (program consultants and group station owners providing taped music and program counseling)—which is the situation with WGGG-FM and WHHH-FM. These two stations are among the most successful beautiful music stations in the country, and two beautiful music stations should be quite sufficient for this market. Scratching these cuts the field to eight. The FM suburban station (WIII-FM) can be eliminated since it will never be in competition with a high-powered metro FM; the latter certainly is not interested in duplicating WIII's limited and suburban-oriented format.

Two ethnic stations (WDDD-AM and WJJJ-FM) have a combined share of 10.9. The market shows a black population of only 25,000, or about 5 percent, and no other substantial ethnic population. It would appear that black-oriented radio is well represented by the two stations, showing a combined audience of twice the black population. Scratch one more (the FM ethnic WJJJ as well as WDDD, already counted out as a daytime AM). The field is down to six, plus the proposed buy.

The three country stations together have 26.2 percent of the market, and need to be considered. If country were adopted, WQQQ (the proposed buy) could easily defeat the AM daytimer with the country format (WBBB, already written off) and maybe even the AM full-timer (WKKK). But the FM country station (WLLL) would be a serious problem even with WQQQ's signal superiority and top-grade programmers. Although the country format targets an age and occupation group of great interest to many advertisers and is usually profitable, the planners estimate the market is already well served with country formats. Eliminating these two stations leaves four:

A full-time AM rocker with a 16.5 percent share (WMMM)

A 10,000-watt news/info AM facility with a 5 percent share (WNNN)

A full-time AM rocker with a 0.6 percent share (WOOO)

A full-power FM with an AOR format and a 12.1 percent share (WPPP)

Even if deciding how to program WQQQ is still not easy, at least the field of competition is much clearer, and the prospective new owners have weeded out the strong, effective stations from the also-rans. These circumstances surround the final four stations. The full-time AM rocker with the 16.5 percent share is an old-line, top 40 that has held top ratings for ten years, although in the last three years its shares have slipped from a high of 20 to the present level. As an AM, WMMM is vulnerable to attack by a well-done FM rocker, using basically the same formula: hit music, personalities, limited news, a few singing logos, games, contests and a lot of community involvement. But this rocker will be a fierce competitor! No new programmer can go into a market and knock off the number one rocker without a long and costly fight, even if the competitor is an AM.

The 10,000-watt AM station is another old-line operation. WNNN affiliates with several news networks, has a heavy sports schedule, and generally attracts a 25-to-64-year-old audience, with the largest segment being 35 to 64 years. This station is not competing for the young audience, just the 25 to 54 age group.

WOOO, the full-time AM rocker with the 0.6 share, may be written off. It is poorly financed, and the staff is less than mediocre. It will not be a problem to WQQQ unless it is sold to someone with plenty of money and know-how. Even then, WOOO would be unlikely to reenter the rock field against high-powered FM (WQQQ), the other established rocker (WMMM), and the AOR (WPPP).

WPPP'S full-power FM with the AOR format may be a problem but not as long as it holds onto its present formula. The AOR plan is a pure format, meaning that the DJs are very laid back, and the music follows the traditional album line. The format is laced with Van Halen, AC/DC and Rush, and the audience has a much larger proportion of males than other music formats draw. New artists are introduced weekly, and new product from known artists is almost automatically sent to the station. WPPP might change formats if the new WQQQ (1) captures a substantial portion of the big AM rocker's audience and (2) cuts into the AOR station's predominantly male audience. Any programmer takes these chances:

Sleeping giants are sometimes awakened when new people come to town beating drums to build audiences.

In the hypothetical market, counting both ethnic stations with disco formats, total contemporary listenership is about 45 percent. The AM rocker and the AOR-FM pull an inordinate portion of the audience, 28.6 percent. Three country stations combined have a 26.2 share of the market. There is only one news/information station, but a market of 500,000 will barely take care of one such station, much less two. Also people who listen to these adult-oriented, all-news or news-talk stations are much older and spend their nonnews listening time either with the beautiful music stations or the country stations.

The 18–49 age group represents 56.1 percent of the hypothetical market, and teens make up another 15.1 percent. Altogether, 71.2 percent of this market may be available to tune in WQQQ-FM, leaving a mere 28.8 percent potential for the adult-oriented stations. Advertisers should readily buy time on a new rock station, which clinches the decision to buy WQQQ and rock.

IMPLEMENTATION

The program director's first step is to get out the word through personal contacts and the trade press that WQQQ is hunting top 40 jocks, a production manager and two people to handle the news. Since this station is going to rock, news will play a minor role. The program director will act as temporary music director to structure the music, and later one of the jocks can take over those duties and audience research. The music director works for the program director, doing research and preparing proposed additions and deletions to the playlist. The program director usually makes the final decision; the music director does the background work.

Getting records is fairly easy. The program director contacts friends in the record business (promotors, pushers) to get on their call schedules and mailing lists so the station will receive all the current material immediately. Belonging to both ASCAP and BMI gives a station the right to play all the popular music, a necessary expense for any music station. (Classical stations also need to join SESAC to obtain foreign and other specialized music performance rights.)

Someone will have to dig for the recent hits (**recurrents**) and the **gold**—especially the latter. Because of their age, these records are scarce; distributors are often out of stock, and pressings are no longer being made. It may take months to build the gold library, and these recordings should be kept under lock and key to forestall avid collectors among staff members.

The program director may decide to "cart" all music, that is, dub it onto cartridges, so the station can play its music inventory without damaging the actual disks. Carting is also a control factor. The announcer who wants to "swing out" a bit simply will not have the opportunity, if all turntables are removed from the control room, if all music is carted, and if the only available carts are those the program director wants played. But carting is costly, time consuming and risky, and some programmers believe dubbing inevitably lowers quality. (The new digitally recorded compact disks, using laser-based technology, are improving the quality of aired recordings, but as of the mid-1980s, too few recordings are available on these disks, and playing a whole disk on the air makes a perfect master for recording pirates.)

THE MUSIC

Jim Mahanay, a highly successful program director for WKRG-FM (Mobile, Alabama) and former director for three years of WQUA (Moline, Illinois), developed a music system that is this chapter's model. This system represents one way to program a rock format station. It evolved from Mahanay's association with Jim Davis, former RKO programmer, and much research went into its formulation. It is designed to achieve maximum attractiveness to the 17–34 (primary) and the 18–49 (secondary) demographic targets. The system has seven major music categories: power, yellow, blue, super-recurrent, recurrent, super-gold and gold.

1. *Power.* Eleven songs are in the power category. Four are played each hour for a turnover rate of 2 hours and 45 minutes—the time elapsing before the eleven-song cycle begins again. These songs are the most important in the system and, consequently, receive more air play than any other music. They attain power status through a combination of high national *chart ranking,* high local *sales ranking,* high *research status* and the unanimous *verdict as winners* by the music selection board, usually composed of the program director and music director. *Billboard, Radio & Records,* and *Rudman* are the three major sources for charts (or lists) of national ranking. They show the position of current hits this week compared to last week. These publications chart the paths of hundreds of pieces of music each week and are consequently referred to as the "charts." Information on local sales comes from telephoning a dozen or more retail stores. In large cities, 40 or more stores may be canvassed.

2. *Yellow.* The yellow category contains nine or ten songs comprising the *lower status records on the current chart.* They are all *up-tempo or fast songs* and are positioned within the music clock to achieve a tempo balance. These records may be either rising in popularity to power status or songs recently withdrawn from the power rotation because research indicates their popularity is declining. The yellow category songs are played at the rate of two per hour and are recycled every 3 hours and 15 minutes.

3. *Blue.* The blue category is exactly the same as the yellow category except they are *down-tempo or slow songs.* In fact, the most important thing about these two categories is that they are tempo categories. They comprise the *bottom 18 to 20 songs on the current playlist,* and two are played in an hour.

Note that the content of the power, blue and yellow categories changes weekly to conform to changes in the current playlists. These three categories comprise what might be called the radio station's "core contemporary music marketing strategy."

4. *Super-recurrent.* The super-recurrent category contains 15 songs recently on the playlist. To qualify as super-recurrent, a song must have had *a number*

one ranking in one or more of the trade magazines and be absolutely accepted by the prime target demographic audience as measured by the station's own research. One super-recurrent song is played every hour for a rotation of 15 hours.

5. *Recurrent.* The recurrent category contains 30 songs *recently in the super-recurrent* rotation. These songs are also played at the rate of one per hour. This category is designed to increase the amount of very recent popular music aired on the station. It creates the impression that the station plays more varied music than it actually does because one current song (power, yellow, or blue) is cut to make room for a recurrent. Listeners get the impression the station airs a broad range of music although only one song is added per hour. The recurrent songs are proven winners and do not harm format attractiveness. The whole list is heard only once in 30 hours.

6. *Super-gold.* The super-gold category contains 53 songs that have climbed the ladder to the *top and moved downward* through the recurrent list. These songs are the "never-dies" the target audience will always recognize and immediately identify as *classics.* These 53 *songs change periodically* to make way for newer songs. The age of records in this category may vary from three months to two years, but they are the all-time winners and greatly enhance a music format.

7. *Gold.* The gold category completes the formula. Gold songs are played at the rate of four to five per hour depending on the daypart and the availability of audience with the desired demographics within each daypart. For a song to make the gold list, it must be a *proven winner.* A gold stays a gold *forever.* One source for many gold libraries is the *Miles Chart Display*, which lists every song by its national chart status over several weeks.[2] Other sources are available from which to compile the gold library such as *Billboard, Radio & Records, Gavin, Record World, Rudman* and *Broadcasting*, but the credibility of the national rankings in the *Miles Chart* cannot be overlooked. All gold records receive a daypart code as follows:

0—May be played any time in the 24 hours, and any day in the week.

1—May be played only in A.M. drivetime.

2—May be played from 9 A.M. to noon.

3—May be played from noon to 3 P.M.

4—May be played from 3 P.M. to 6 P.M.

5—May be played from 6 P.M. to midnight.

6—May be played from midnight to 2 A.M.

7—May be played on weekends.

Each song may have several codes, making it available at different times during the day. The recordings in the gold library are coded "A" or "B," meaning "recent" or "older." This designation ensures that each receives the right demographic exposure whenever played.

Depending on daypart, a station uses three A golds to two B golds. This formula is obtained by making a simple demographic curve of the target audience. For example, there are many more 25–44-year-olds available during the 7

P.M. to midnight daypart than any other demographic group. Consequently, a station will expose more A gold than B in that period, achieving higher identification with the available audience.

The Music Wheel or "Hot Clock"

When not busy interviewing potential DJs, talking to prospects on the telephone or obtaining music, the program director constructs a **hot clock** or **wheel.** A hot clock is a design, looking like a clock face, in which the formula for producing the station's "sound" is visualized. It divides an hour into portions for music (by category), weather, news, promos and commercials.

Hot clocks are examples of dayparting, that is, estimating who is listening and what their activities are, and then programming directly to them. Each daypart has its own clock. The morning clock includes news, for example, but the 7 P.M. to midnight clock does not. News is principally for the morning audience on a rock station. Figure 15-2 shows a morning clock; the hour makes room for 10 commercial minutes. There are only eight commercial minutes in the evening clock in Figure 15-3. The gold, power and recurrent songs are slotted in; liners are DJ comments; and PSAs are public service announcements.

Music stations generally use four clocks for weekdays and as many as two additional ones for weekends. Morning clocks apply to the morning drive period; midday clocks to the 10 A.M. to 3 P.M. period; afternoon clocks from 3 P.M. to 7 P.M.; and the nighttime clocks from 7 P.M. to midnight. Other clocks may be developed for certain weekend dayparts and days on which special events occur.

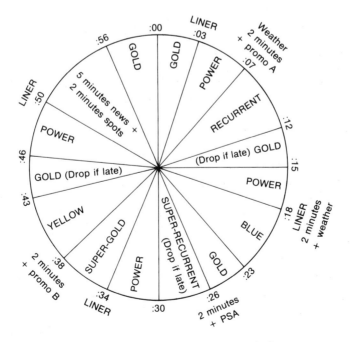

FIGURE 15-2. Morning Drive Hot Clock

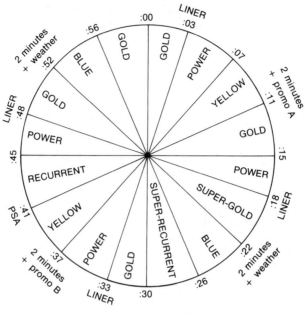

Used 7 P.M. to midnight

FIGURE 15-3. Nighttime Hot Clock

Music Research

Most music stations employ one or more people to handle call-out research and assemble statistics. A rock station's music researcher compiles the list of the 15 local, top-selling LPs and singles based on local record store sales. The researcher also keeps tabs on records the station does not play but that are selling due to air play on other stations and nightspot exposure. The researcher may be employed full- or part-time and usually works for the music director.

Trade publications such as *Billboard* and *Radio & Records* are studied when adding new music to a playlist. Each week the researcher compiles a chart of the top 30 songs from each magazine and averages them to get composite ratings. Analysis of chart movements of newer songs and news regarding air play in other areas are also helpful in choosing the "adds." In markets with a sizable black population, the researcher tracks the soul charts as well as pop in *Billboard* and *Radio & Records.* In markets where country wins in the ratings, the country music charts can suggest cross-over songs. The *more* objective information the researcher gathers, the easier it is for the programmer to evaluate the record companies' advertising and sales. Record promoters will naturally emphasize their products' victories, neglecting to mention that a record died in Los Angeles or Kansas City. The station must depend on its own research findings to rate a piece of music reliably.

As explained in Chapter 2, call-out research gets reactions directly from radio listeners.[3] Two versions of the technique are used—"active" and "passive." In active call-out research, the names of active listeners are obtained from contest entrant lists. The passive version selects names at random from the telephone directory. In either case, respondents are asked to listen to extracts from the songs being researched or to lists of titles and to rate them on a scale running from 1 to 7 as follows:

1 = "Never heard of it."

2 = "Dislike it strongly."

3 = "Dislike it moderately."

4 = "Don't care."

5 = "Tired of it."

6 = "Like it."

7 = "My favorite record."

When a sample is completed (50 to 100 calls is typical), the votes for each number on the scale are tabulated. The various totals are then manipulated to obtain interpretations in terms of ratios or percentages (see Table 15-3).

For example, assume 50 contest winners are called within a week, and 25 records are discussed. Ten listeners say they like song number four, and fourteen say it is their favorite record. Twenty-four of 50 rate number four as a 6 or a 7. For the "positive acceptance" measurement, divide 24 by 50; the result indicates 48 percent of the audience want to hear number four played.

Compare the top 30 to 40 pieces on the current playlist to rankings in *Radio & Records*, *Billboard*, *Gavin*, *Rudman* and *Record World*. If song number four is number one in *Radio & Records*, it gets 30 points. If it rates number two in *Rudman*, it gets 29 points; a rating of number three in *Record World* gives it 28 points, and so on. After charting each song against the five trade publications, the researcher divides the total by five to get the average ranking. Trade publication rankings are based on data supplied by hundreds of reporting stations. If the researcher finds from the call-out test that number four is burned out locally but was nevertheless still running in the top three or four nationally, the song would be retained but assigned a lower rotation position.

TABLE 15-3.
How to Calculate Votes

Total Votes for	Divided by Total of	Equals a Ratio That Measures
6 + 7	sample	Positive acceptance
2 + 3	sample	Negative rejection
5 + 6 + 7	sample	Positive recognition
2 + 3 + 5	sample	Developed dislike
4	sample	Neutral
5	sample	Burnout
6 + 7	2 + 3	Acceptance
6 + 7	2 + 3 + 5	Tolerance
1	sample	Unfamiliarity
2 + 3 + 4 + 5 + 6 + 7	sample	Familiarity

NEWS

News has always been a problem on rock 'n' roll stations. Many broadcasters do not want it, cannot afford it, feel their listeners are bored with it, but think they must provide news to satisfy unwritten FCC requirements. They dutifully promise in their license applications to program a certain percentage of news and are stuck with their commitments.

Do listeners want news on music stations? Frank N. Magid Associates, in a study of Los Angeles radio, found that a large percentage of rock listeners were "turned off" by news.[4] These same listeners also hated commercials, PSAs and anything else not related to music and fun. On the other hand, an Associated Press study published in 1978 found that everybody wanted lots of news on their music stations.[5] The Associated Press, which is in the business of selling news services to radio stations, is not likely to publish a study indicating young listeners do not want to hear news. Consultants, however, are in the business of finding out what is wrong with radio stations and have a vested interest in finding things wrong that can be fixed. A 1982 study by R. H. Bruskin Associates for CBS found that news and information make up eight of the top ten elements listeners say they listen for, on both AM and FM stations.[6] No studies have definitively resolved this issue.

In any case, listeners expect to hear news on the hour and the half-hour, and the radio networks still schedule news at those times. Knowing this, some programmers schedule news at odd hours (20 minutes after and 20 before the hour, for example), hoping to pick up new listeners when competing stations schedule their news more conventionally on the hour and half-hour.

Some recent thinking on news scheduling hinges on the habits of some listeners and Arbitron's diary method of surveying listeners. The idea is to hold a listener for at least five minutes in any quarter-hour by playing some music (even on a talk/news station) so the station will get credit in a listener diary. On popular music stations, news is therefore buried in the middle of one or two 15-minute periods each hour. This strategy assumes listeners are turned away by news. Increasingly, stations targeting younger listeners are experimenting with eliminating newscasts except in morning drivetime.

Journalistic Content

Having decided where to put news, the programmer must then decide how to handle it, whether to go the low road or the high road. On the low road, jocks rip and read news wire copy as it comes out of the machine. Some low-roaders satisfy the need for local news by simply stealing from the local newspaper (the news itself cannot be copyrighted, although specific versions of it can). Programmers who set higher goals for themselves do well to hire at least two persons to staff the news operation. One staffer does the air work in the morning while the other develops local stories, mostly over the telephone. The two news staffers reverse their roles in the afternoon. The morning person leaves **voicers** (stories recorded by someone other than the anchorperson) for use during the afternoon and evening newscasts, and the afternoon person leaves them for use early the next morning. This news operation would be relatively luxurious for a music station, however. The typical full-time news staff in radio stations throughout the country is only one person.

Nonentertainment Programming

The deregulation of radio has substantially eased FCC-imposed requirements for nonentertainment programming on radio stations. Minimum amounts of nonentertainment programming for AM and FM stations have been abolished as have the Commission's formal ascertainment requirements, although a licensee is still required to "informally" ascertain the problems, needs and interests of the community. On the anniversary date of license renewal, a narrative statement of the problems, needs and interests of the community and the programming the licensee has broadcast to meet those needs must be placed in the station's public file.

Section IV of the new FCC Form 301 requires, for radio stations, only a brief narrative description of the planned programming service explaining how the projected programming relates to issues of public concern in the proposed service area. Programming in general, for new applicants and for renewal applicants, has become progressively less and less an area in which the Commission intrudes.

However, programming representations to the Commission, once made, should be kept. A discrepancy between the amount of programming promised and that actually broadcast (a promise versus performance issue) may mean the Commission denies a renewal application (or, at least, instigates legal hearings). Moreover, if a competing application is filed against the renewal applicant, the licensee has an advantage over the competitor only if the FCC can find a "solid and substantial" service record. This record must include news and information programming, PSAs (public service announcements) and community-oriented programming.

News, public affairs and "other" nonentertainment programming create a flow or continuity problem for the formula format. The complaint is that "we have to shut down the radio station to air that junk." Junk, of course, is any programming not directly related to the music format. In stations with an information-oriented format featuring network news, local news, talk and sports, little flow problem exists, of course. Nonentertainment material may be effectively woven into this format. Public service announcements are both nonentertainment and community-oriented programming, and a station can make significant contributions to the community welfare with an aggressive PSA policy.

Radio will probably always be a service medium, and broadcasters will always differ on what constitutes community service. In a competitive major market served by a number of communications media such as newspaper, cable, television, radio, MDS, ITFS, LPTV and DBS, the FM radio station that plays wall-to-wall rock music is doubtlessly providing a service, even though it is merely a music service. In information-poor markets, owners may elect to mix talk shows with music, air editorial comments on community affairs and in general, provide useful information to the community. The services provided should be based on competitive market factors, the owners' and managers' personal choices and a realistic understanding of the role a radio station can play in some market situations.

AIR PERSONALITIES AND DAYPARTING

In contemporary radio, there are SCREAMERS!!! And there are very laid-back jocks who just talk conversationally when they open the microphone switch. Then, there are those "friendly" jocks who fall somewhere in between the screamers and the laid-backs. Once there was also the big-voice-boss who told the listener this was a Big DJ, a know-it-all, but this style faded in the early 1970s.

Dayparting is one of the major strategies of the music station programmer. The programmer's challenge is to make each daypart distinct and appropriate to the audience's characteristic activities and at the same time keep the station's sound consistent. The most important ingredient in making daypart distinctions is the personality of the jock assigned to each time period.

Morning

By and large, modern jocks are friendly or very, very laid-back. They "relate" to the target audience. Morning jocks, for example, probably will talk more than jocks on other dayparts, because their shows are service oriented. They have lots of time and temperature checks. They may chat with the newscasters before the news, may bring the traffic reporter on and off the air, and, in fact, manage the morning team. Listeners preparing for work or school are keen on the time and weather conditions. And the larger the market, the more important traffic reports become. Reports of a pile-up on one expressway give listeners a chance to switch their commuter routes—and the stations a chance to earn a Brownie point.

On most stations the morning jock is the only performer permitted to violate format to any appreciable extent. The trend in the early 1980s was toward paired morning jocks, teams generally having a joker and a straight man or an upbeat and a sexy voice, frequently one male and one female. Normally, morning drivetime personalities are also the most highly paid. They have a greater responsibility than other jocks because the audience is bigger in the 6 to 10 A.M. period than at any other time of day. As the saying goes, "If you don't make it in the morning drive, you don't make it at all."

Midday

The midday jock is friendly, but the incidental services (requiring talk) during this daypart are curtailed in favor of more music. Although there is considerable out-of-home listening in the 10 A.M. to 3 P.M. period, Arbitron data show the majority of the listeners are at home. Many midday jocks capitalize on a large female audience by being sexy, using **liners** (brief continuity between records) having special appeal to women and by talking about what the listener might be doing at home. Some jocks even get off-color at times. In sum, the midday jock is more laid-back than the morning jock and tries especially hard to be warm and friendly.

Afternoon

The afternoon jock (3 P.M. to 7 P.M.) is more up-tempo, as is the music in this period if the station is dayparting. Teens are out of school, and adults are driving home from work, necessitating a delicate balance between teen-oriented music and music suiting the moods and attitudes of the going-home audience. Again, traffic and weather are important in this period but not as much as in the morning. The afternoon jock alludes frequently to evening activities—about how good it must be to finish work and to look forward to playing for a few hours, to taking your honey out, to being with your guy tonight or to doing whatever else people are planning. This jock relates!

Evening

Many contemporary stations program their 7 P.M. to midnight slot much differently from the other dayparts. The music may become heavily disco, heavily black, or laced with teen-oriented pieces. Teens are more available to listen at night than the 18 to 49 listeners. Evening jocks may be screamers with a special appeal to teens. They may talk with teens on the phone and air some of the conversations. They may open the request lines and play specific records for specific people. In major markets, and even in many middle-sized ones, this practice creates problems for the phone company. In Mobile, Alabama, WKRG-FM asked the phone company to make a record of calls that did not get through to its four request lines. In one week, there were 65,000 such unsuccessful calls. Imagine what the number might be in Los Angeles or New York! In many major markets in the last decade the telephone company has appealed to station management to stop listener call-ins.

At some 40 operations, the nighttime slot is regarded as a time for AOR music, but this stratagem has not been notably successful in highly competitive markets—mostly because such a drastic departure from format destroys consistency. A station should maintain basically the same sound in the 7 P.M. to midnight slot as it has in the other dayparts.

All-night

In the all-night period, from midnight to 6 A.M., the jock's attitude is usually one of camaraderie. "We're all up late tonight, aren't we? We have to work nights and sleep days." This jock must commune with the audience: the taxi drivers, revelers, police officers, all-night restaurant and grocery store workers, insomniacs, parents up giving babies two o'clock feedings, shift workers at factories, bakers and the many others active between the hours of midnight and 6 A.M. The commercial load is almost nil during this period, so the jock can provide listeners with a lot of uninterrupted music. Many stations use the period to beef up their PSA quotient, although this burying of PSAs in low-listener hours could be a problem if the owner is challenged at license-renewal time.

Under a strong program director, a kind of "sameness" can develop among all the jocks in a specified format—without the drabness or dullness normally associated with sameness. Sameness here means predictability. Listeners tuning in the station at odd hours hear the same "sound" they heard while driving to work in the morning or home in the afternoon.

ADVERTISING AND PROMOTION

The modern radio station pays almost as much attention to advertising and promotion as to programming. They are essential to keep a station from simply disappearing in the crowd. Nowadays stations are even using television in addition to their traditional use of newspapers, billboards, bumper stickers, cards and other graphic media. Promotional stunts are the special province of radio and involve the cooperation of programming personnel. A national group owner who went into the Dallas market in 1977 was rumored to have allotted a $600,000 budget solely for promotion. By the mid-1980s that figure would have doubled. Many hit music operations, seeking a general (mass) audience with emphasis on the 18–49-year-old group, might give away as much as $200,000 a year in cash!

Contesting

The traditional promotional stunt is the *contest*, but the industry favors the word *game.* Many people think they cannot win contests, but they like to play games. For many stations, a contest approach emphasizes a superprize of $25,000 or more. Such amounts can be offered only once or twice a year (during the Arbitron survey sweeps). And because a station cannot afford to risk losing the big prize on the first day of the game, winning has to be made difficult.

People are more likely to think they can win a small prize than a $25,000 treasure hunt or open a safe containing $50,000. With a superprize, one person is made happy, but thousands are disappointed. Consequently, it is better to break up the $25,000 prize into $25 prizes and scatter them through the year.

Currently popular games include "cash-call," in which the jock makes one call-out per hour. The jackpot goes to the person naming its exact amount. This game involves a small prize, added to with each call until the correct amount is guessed.

Jock:	Is this Mary Jones at 1212 Elm Street?
Listener:	Yes, I'm Mary Jones.
Jock:	Well, this is Jocko at station WPPP, and if you can tell me the exact amount in our WPPP jackpot, you'll win!
Listener:	Mmmmmm. Last I heard it was $485.
Jock:	You win! You're right. Mary Jones, you've just won yourself 485 American greenbacks!!! You've ripped us off, you lucky lady you!!!
Listener:	Oh, wow! I can't believe it.

The more exaggerated the winner's response to his or her victory, the better the programmer likes it. Later the station will air promos in which each winner's response is repeated and repeated. Hyperbole is the element sought.

Cash-call is but one of many games. The "people's choice" gambit provides a variety of prizes and allows the contestants to identify ahead of time the prizes they want if they win. Magid's Los Angeles study determined that color television sets were very desirable prizes. A thousand dollars in cash was also popular, along with free trips to Hawaii. Prizes and contest rules should be carefully targeted to appeal to the exact age, sex and economic groups the station wants to listen.[7]

Exercise caution in recording and airing telephone conversations. The law requires that the person being called be informed immediately, "This telephone conversation is being recorded, and I'm Jocko from WPPP." Then the dialogue can begin. It is a troublesome law that ruins many such calls because once informed the listener does not respond spontaneously. Management should seek legal counsel on this question and should write specific instructions to programming personnel on how such calls are to be handled.

Community involvement projects are as important as contests in programming a successful radio station. The station must be highly visible at local events to gain a strong, positive, local image. The following are community promotions benefitting both the station and the community:

The station's van (complete with disc jockey, albums, bumper stickers and T-shirts) shows up at the entrance to the hall that features a hot rock group tonight.

Two or three jocks take the van and disco equipment to the beach (or any public park) on the Fourth of July to provide music and "freebies" to listeners and friends.

Jocks provide free music for high school and junior high school dances, local fairs and nonprofit benefits.

Commercial Load

More arguments arise over commercial load than any other aspect of programming a rock format. Before the 1970s, FM stations had few commercials because they had few listeners. Researchers began hearing listeners say, "I like so and so because they don't play commercials" or "because they play so much more music than other stations." Lights flashed and bells rang throughout the industry. Listeners hate commercials! Schulke and Bonneville, two of the major radio programming syndicators, began to employ the strategy of music sweeps and stop sets. A **music sweep** is an uninterrupted period of music; a **stop set** is an interruption of the music to air commercials or other nonmusic material such as news headlines.

Herein lies conflict. Sales personnel must have commercial availabilities (unsold spot time) if the station is to make money. Programmers rightfully argue that if the station is to score big in the numbers, it must limit its commercial load. The answer is compromise. Salespeople agree to raise rates, and programmers agree to provide 10 to 12 commercial minutes per hour instead of the 8 to 10 of other formats or the full 18 the sales department wanted. (In 1982, the FCC stopped expecting radio stations to adhere to the now-defunct NAB radio code that specified a maximum of 18 minutes of commercials per hour except during political campaigns and other local, seasonal events when increases were permissible.)

Not only do many successful rock operations run a reduced commercial load, but they also often program (and promote) commercial-free periods. Further, the quality of commercial production is critical. Commercial design must complement the format rather than clash with it. A typical commercial for a rock show coming to town indicates how to achieve relatedness: The commercial opens with a piece of the rock group's music, followed by a popular jock touting the show, and ends with more of the group's music. Many rock stations refuse to advertise funeral homes, intimate patent medicines such as hemorrhoidal creams and other products and services they believe will offend their listeners.

One key to understanding radio programming strategy is to compare stations in the number of commercial spots per break ("load") and the number of interruptions per hour. Too many spots in a roll creates clutter, reduces advertising impact and encourages listeners to twirl their dials (or push buttons). Too many interruptions, on the other hand, destroys programming flow and encourages listeners to migrate on their dials. Since advertising is necessary, management must establish a policy reflected in music wheels ("hot clocks") and stick to it.

In the past, stations have kicked off new formats with no commercial load whatever. They typically offer huge prizes to listeners to guess the exact time and date the first commercial will be aired. Another popular audience-holder is the two-, three-, four-, five-in-a-row concept, with the announcer saying, essentially, "We've got five in a row coming up *without* interruption." The longer the listener stays with the station, the more the station quarter-hour shares are improved. This programming technique is becoming commonplace in music-oriented formats. A tension will continue to exist between the number of commercials and the number of interruptions that can be tolerated.

Call Letters

Gordon McLendon, early innovator of the top 40 format, was one of the first broadcasters to recognize the value of *sayable call letters*. His first big station was KLIF, Dallas, originally named for Oak Cliff, a western section of the city. The station call was pronounced "cliff" on the air. Then there is KABL ("cable") in San Francisco, KOST ("coast") in Los Angeles, WWSH ("wish") in Philadelphia and KEGL ("eagle radio") in Fort Worth. These call letters are memorable and distinctive noms de guerre and get daily usage. When the Belo Corporation in Dallas developed a new format for WFAA-FM, the historic letters were changed to KZEW, and the station is now known as "the zoo." (Gagsters used to try to pronounce WFAA, and it came out "woof-uh.")

In recent years, FM stations often combine call letters and dial position in on-air promotion—especially if they are rock stations. WKRG-FM in Mobile is G100; the RKO station in New York, WXLO, calls itself 99X; in Indianapolis, an AOR station, WFBQ, calls itself Q95; a Bloomington station calls itself 97WB. However, one potential by-product of the introduction of cable radio is shift in dial position; another is the importation of competing distant radio signals. These factors may herald a return to call letter identification (instead of frequency).

Jingles

The day of the minute or half-minute singing jingle ID is, sadly, gone. Nowadays, having a chorus of singers praise the station for a minute or half-minute is out of the question. That would take time away from popular music, which people tuned in for in the first place. Now most stations either do not bother with jingles at all, or they keep them very short and to the point. Automated stations sometimes effectively use jingles since they lack a live DJ to fill gaps in programming and repeat the station's name.

FCC AND OTHER CONSTRAINTS

Even with radio deregulation, a myriad of rules, regulations and guidelines exist of which radio broadcasters should be aware. To keep up with them, radio programmers read trade journals and join the National Association of Broadcasters (NAB) and the National Radio Broadcasters Association (NRBA). Programmers, too, have to be aware of legal constraints that may limit their ingenuity. Illegal or unethical practices such as fraud, lotteries, plugola and the like can cost a job or even a license.

Contests and Games

The principal point to remember about on-air contests and games is to keep them open and honest, fully disclosing to listeners the rules of the game. Conniving to make a contest run longer or to produce a certain type of winner means trouble. Perry's newsletter, *Broadcasting and the Law,* is useful for flagging potential difficulties.

The perennial problem with many brilliant contest ideas is that they are lotteries by the FCC's definition, and lotteries are explicitly and vehemently prohibited. If a contest includes "prizes, consideration and chance," it is probably a lottery. Consult the station's lawyers or the NAB legal staff if there is the slightest question.

Plugola and Payola

Announcers who "plug" their favorite bar, restaurant or theatre are asking for trouble for themselves and the licensees (**plugola**). Similarly, a jock who accepts a color television set from a record distributor in exchange for air play of a record is guilty of **payola**. But the big payola payoffs usually come in drugs, conveniently salable or consumable so they rarely leave evidence for the law. Nonetheless, such practices eventually surface, because talk gets around, leaving the people concerned subject to prosecution. Drugs make station management very nervous because the legal penalties can include loss of the station's license, a $10,000 fine and jail. Certainly any tainted jock's job is likely to disappear instantly. Most responsible licensees require air personnel to sign statements usually once every six months confirming that they have not been engaged in any form of payola or plugola.

Sounds That Mislead

Commercials opening with sirens or other attention-getting gimmicks (such as "Bulletin!") unjustifiably cause listeners to believe they are about to receive vital information. Listener attention can be gained in other more responsible ways that do not offend FCC rules or deceive listeners. Monitoring locally produced commercials for misleading production techniques is especially important.

Program Logs

Any announcement associated with a commercial venture should be logged commercial matter (CM), even though the FCC has done away with requirements for program logs per se. Program logs have many practical applications, aside from the former legal requirement, including billing for advertising, record-keeping, format maintenance and format organization. Common sense dictates a continuation of the old method. Advertisers demand proof of performance, and an official station log is the best evidence of whether and when spots were aired. If a station is challenged on the number of PSAs or nonentertainment programming it has aired, an official station log provides the best evidence of performance.

RADIO'S FUTURE

Music is the main course in radio, and FM does it better. FM will win over an AM facility whenever a showdown occurs. The exceptions occur among information and country music formats and then only for powerhouse AM facilities. A case in point is the sad story of the AM station in Dallas, KLIF, once the unquestioned national leader in rock radio. For 20 years KLIF held number one position in the market and was respected nationally as the station to imitate. Since the mid-1970s, however, Dallas has been an FM market. KVIL-FM is the leading station and shows no signs of weakening. KLIF no longer places among the top ten stations. Eight of the top ten in any market with more than twelve stations will probably be FM. KRLD (AM) and WBAP (AM) number in the top three in Dallas, but these are 50,000-watt stations on clear channels, programming news/sports and country music/baseball, respectively. The Dallas picture is being repeated in market after market across the country.

FM has become the home of adult contemporary and a whole package of rock formats. What lies ahead for AM radio? Not pop music, that seems certain. Country music? Maybe. MOR music? Perhaps. But in no case can an AM stand up to a well-programmed FM station. One strong and recurrent view is that AM must program information to older audiences, even though doing so is expensive and complicated. So news and talk become viable alternatives for AM radio. Continued strength in the radio industry nationwide, however, suggests there is room enough for both AM and FM. Spot advertising revenues for radio continue to rise, and increasing numbers of new advertisers are learning radio is an effective medium for them. The programming problem is to locate a sizable audience not being served by a stronger facility in the same market.

For daytimers, religion has become a mainstay, along with limited-audience ethnic formats. However, the difficulties are illustrated by KKDA (Dallas), once a country music station. New owners launched a black-oriented format and quickly gained position in the market. When they then acquired an FM facility and duplicated their format, all of the AM listeners switched over to the FM station. The AM daytimer that once fared well was reduced to an also-ran. Frequently an FM will show 7 and 8 shares in markets with more than 12 stations, while an AM daytimer plods along with 1s and 2s. AM stereo appears to be little more than a gimmick for the foreseeable future. Stereo may be useful in promoting an AM station, but until the industry settles on a single standard *and* a large turnover in receivers occurs, there will be few AM stereo listeners.

"New wave" was the latest and hottest thing in the music business in the early 1980s. It was a refinement of punk rock, but having more lyrical content and appealing to an audience with downscale demographics. By the mid-1980s, it was being called "new music" and showing Australian and British influence along with danceable, Americanized lyrics. The massive return to top 40 occurring under labels such as contemporary hit radio, hot hits and adult top 40, uses faster rotation times and top-rated songs, incorporating the new music in a flexible, trendy format, influenced by MTV, the cable music channel.

But many programmers overreact to fads in music. When disco first appeared, WKTU-FM in New York embraced it and zoomed to first place in one book. Several years ago, someone conceived of a solid gold format. One station in Detroit tried it, made good gains in the first book, then fell back into obscurity. Another station tried commercial-free radio for three months, soared in the ratings, then fell back into ninth place. Such formats are like the hula-hoop: a craze today, forgotten tomorrow. What works is consistency—in service, in music, in technical quality, in station identity. The fast-buck artist does not stand a chance in the marathon race for big audience and big dollars.

This chapter has touched on only the more obvious strategies involved in the fascinating art of programming a modern music station. To the uninitiated, all radio music formats may seem much the same. In actuality, each is replete with subtle and not-so-subtle variations. To program a formula successfully in today's competitive market requires never-ending ingenuity, insight and professional growth. The name of the game is change, but it must be accomplished by consistency in the on-air sound. Radio programming is constantly evolving, and for those who enjoy innovation, it offers a rewarding challenge.

SUMMARY

Five factors determine which music format will win the largest audience market. Of these, the most influential is the quality of the technical facility. FM produces inherently higher-quality sound than AM, and that gives it an undisputed advantage in music competition. Among FMs, tower height and power give decided advantages, but among AMs, power and dial position matter. The remaining factors of market, target audience, budget and potential revenue indicate what programming is most competitive. Once a format has been selected, a staff must be hired and a record library created. The next big job is to program the music wheels for all the major dayparts and weekends. In broadcasting, dayparting means altering the programming at different times of the day to fit the audience's activities. Different styles of disc jockey patter match different dayparts on a popular music station. This chapter described a rock music rotation system composed of power, yellow, blue, super-recurrent, recurrent, super-gold and gold song classifications. How to classify songs and rate them are the functions of the station's music research department and depend heavily on the radio trade press. The role of news and nonentertainment programming on a popular music station remains controversial, but once promises are given to the FCC, adherence must follow. Drug payoffs persist as a payola problem. The amount and kinds of on-air promotion and the number of commercials and breaks in programming also delineate stylistic differences among competing popular music stations. In the mid-1980s, stations are returning to top-40-type formats.

Notes

[1]Robert Sobel, "Top 40 Revival, New Artists Rock Music Radio," *Television/Radio Age*, 29 August 1983, pp. 25–27ff.

[2]Daniel J. Miles, Betty T. Miles and Martin J. Miles, *The Miles Chart Display of Popular Music: Volume II, 1971–1975* (New York: Arno Press,   /7).

[3]James E. Fletcher, and Roger D. Wimmer, *Call-Out Research in Managing Radio Stations* (Washington, D.C.: National Association of Broadcasters, n.d.).

[4]KHJ-AM audience study by Frank N. Magid Associates, 1976, reported by Chuck Martin, program director, 1979.

[5]"Radio News Listening Attitudes," survey conducted by Frank N. Magid Associates for Associated Press in 1977, abstract, 11b.

[6]R. H. Bruskin Associates study, August 1982, commissioned by CBS Radio and presented to CBS Radio Network Affiliates, Phoenix, September 1982. See "AM and FM Listeners Have a Lot in Common," *Broadcasting*, 27 September 1982, pp. 81–82.

[7]For a more detailed discussion of contesting and prize structures, see "Commercial Radio Promotion" by Harvey Mednick in *Strategies in Broadcast and Cable Promotion* by S. Eastman and R. Klein (Belmont, California: Wadsworth, 1982).

Selected Sources

Billboard, weekly trade magazine for the record industry, 1894 to date.

Bortz, Paul, and Mendelsohn, Harold. *Radio Today—And Tomorrow*. Washington, D.C.: National Association of Broadcasters, 1982.

"Special Report on Radio." *Broadcasting* (27 September 1976; 25 July 1977; 24 July 1978; 10 September 1979; 25 August 1980; 17 August 1981; 8 February 1982; 8 March 1982; 6 September 1982; 20 September 1982; 11 October 1982; 29 August 1983; 5 September 1983).

Routt, Edd; McGrath, James B.; and Weiss, Fredric A. *The Radio Format Conundrum*. New York: Hastings House, 1978.

"Radio Programming & Production for Profit." *Broadcast Management/Engineering*, monthly series, January 1977 to date.

Radio & Records, *R&R Ratings Reports*. Los Angeles: Radio & Records, Inc., semiannual.

CHAPTER SIXTEEN

News Radio

Don J. Brewer and Susan Tyler Eastman

DON J. BREWER and SUSAN TYLER EASTMAN *write of the day-to-day strategies of all-news radio. After more than 15 years with KYW News Radio, the nationally known innovator in the AM radio field owned by Group W Broadcasting, Mr. Brewer brings an extensive background in radio broadcasting to this chapter. He has been regional affairs director for KYW as well as food and wine editor for all seven Group W radio stations for more than a decade. He was a station manager for a Department of Defense radio station in Germany after World War II, civilian director of the American Forces Network, Europe, and program director of Radio Free Europe before coming to KYW as an executive producer in 1970. He brings an insider's perspective to radio journalism. Susan Eastman, one of the editor–authors of this book, provides a national perspective on news radio strategies and scheduling. Her background appears at the start of Chapter 9. Together, these authors review news programming options.*

FORMAT PREREQUISITES

News radio holds a unique position in listeners' media behavior. In cars and offices and stores, nearly everyone turns to radio for news at times of disasters and historic events. Radio has a long tradition of bringing fast-breaking headlines to listeners more quickly than other media. This chapter looks at local *all-news* radio programming, a continuous source of news headlines and features. It examines the advantages of affiliation and independence and their different format wheels. It covers the program elements making up a newscast and their placement, repetition and priorities. It then analyzes the characteristics of the news audience and the management practices and policies that make the all-news format difficult to adopt but important to its listeners and its practitioners.

Cost and Commitment

The all-news format strains the infrastructure of current broadcasting establishments—whether group-owned or independent—because the cost commitment is high. News cannot be automated, as so many other radio formats have been. Consequently, all-news is limited to major markets where sales revenue can match program outlay and where the potential news audience is large. And even under these conditions, the format is not likely to be very profitable. The same investment in another format would bring a much greater return both initially and once established. For the foreseeable future, all-news is a prestige format, practiced best by major network affiliates and group owners willing to absorb initial high costs and low ratings.

In the 1980s, several all-news stations moved into the news/talk format. This format is more flexible than all-news. For example, when a series of significant national events occur, such as hot events in the Near East, the stations shift to all-news; as the amount of hard news diminishes, they incorporate more talk and soft news features. The early morning television newscasts and overnight television news services now compete with radio all-news stations, forcing many to add original feature programming to their formats to remain competitive. However, flexible formats and popular features may threaten the news station's credibility. The farther the programming moves from journalism, the more it becomes an entertainment medium. And a gain in the entertainment column seems to mean a loss in the information column in the audience's long-term view. The basic caveat for any all-news programmer rests in one word: *credibility*. It must be maintained in every program element from headline to commercial; it goes a long way to ensuring an enterprise's success. It is the unique thing an all-news station has to offer audiences.

The product manager of an all-news station lives with a very forthright credo: "Communicate credibility by commitment." The unspoken C in this dictum is *cost*. The resources needed to operate an all-news station are considerable. Attracting an audience of sufficient size and loyalty is a formidable task. Maintaining basic journalistic standards *and* program innovation is constantly challenging. Management must be aware of these factors if the format is to survive. No format demands more management involvement. The heartening thing is that, once firmly entrenched, all-news programming commands a fanatically loyal audience. If creatively programmed, the all-news station can capture a broad range of listeners attractive to advertisers.

Founding Stations

In the mid-1960s, two major broadcast establishments laid the foundation for operating all-news radio stations as we know them today. The first was Group W, Westinghouse Broadcasting Company. It converted three AM stations—WINS (New York) and KYW (Philadelphia) in 1965 and KFWB (Los Angeles) in 1968—to all-news programming. CBS followed suit with WCBS-AM (New York), KCBS-AM (San Francisco) and KNX-AM (Los Angeles); later, WBBM-AM (Chicago) and WEEI-AM (Boston) were converted, and in 1975, WCAU-AM (Philadelphia).[1] By the mid-1980s, more than two dozen all-news or news and information stations were operating in major cities.

In 1974 NBC began an abortive experiment of providing an all-news network service called News and Information Service. Its demise in 1976 worked hardship on many of its medium- and small-market affiliates, most of whom subsequently dropped the all-news format or modified it to talk/news. The emergence of AP and UPI audio news services in the late 1970s, plus major network news and information divisions such as the ABC Information Network, gave heart to the survivors. But what was a tough, tentative format for many in major markets became an impossible, costly burden for stations on the economic fringe going it alone. As of the mid-1980s, the national news networks played an important role in supporting local news gathering by providing headline services and national and international news stories. But all-news is essentially a locally programmed format. Network affiliation provides coverage most local stations could not supply; group-ownership can provide shared features and investigative reports; but in the end, each station must support a full staff to fill the broadcast day.

INDEPENDENT AND NETWORK COMPETITION

A competitive pattern has emerged in the brief history of all-news stations: A well-operated, all-news station in a major market can count on a 5–10 percent audience share. If there are two all-news stations, they divide the audience share (given relatively equal effort and appeal). The format is not normally subject to radical ratings swings, perhaps because its audience is quite loyal.

All-news competition usually occurs between a network outlet and an independent station. The network-affiliated station programmer has the advantage of network resources but must air obligatory network news at key times. Thus, if the breaking story is local, the affiliate may be running behind the story, being forced to air the network feed that ignores a big local event. Added to that is the gnawing feeling among the staff that they are second-class citizens because the network voice automatically preempts their voices. The other side of the coin is that they must scramble to equal the network staff's professionalism to create a consistent sound. Although the independent does not have the same problems, it does have the entire burden of staffing and reporting national and local news, aided only by the wire services.

Aside from head-to-head combat, all news stations face a subtler form of competition arising from the *drivetime newsblock confrontation*—usually instigated by a well-established music station in the market with a fairly strong news department. To cope with the all-news station's intrusion into its market, a music station will often expand its news programming, particularly in morning drivetime. Since the music station can afford to compress its news staff effort into a two- or three-hour period, the facade of an important news effort can be erected. This tactic, coupled with a well-regarded local disc jockey, can be formidable indeed. Pulling away from such a station over a stretch of time is not too difficult, however, because sustained, tight utilization of news team strength will tell. Heavy use of well-researched and well-programmed series, made up of short vertical or horizontal documentaries in morning drivetime, is one of the most effective countermeasures. (**Vertical documentaries** are stories aired in brief segments throughout one day; **horizontal documentaries** occur in segments over several days, perhaps weeks.)

Programming the Coverage Area

Difference in signal strength among stations is often mentioned as a key advantage or disadvantage. For news stations, too strong a signal may lead to spreading its resources too thinly. For network-owned or affiliated news stations this is not a hazard because the network base is broadly appealing without the constant need for as much local back-up as the independent programmer has to muster. Concentrating on the smaller metro-area audience can be more rewarding for the independent station in terms of audience loyalty than trying to be too many things to too many people at once. Such a situation exists in the Los Angeles area. There, listeners can tune (within the L.A. primary-coverage zone) to a 5,000-watt independent, while a 50,000-watt network outlet serves a much greater audience area. Power limitation, translated to audience limitation, is an obvious programming constraint. The programmer must be aware that many in the metro audience relate to outlying population groups and want to know, to some degree, what is going on "out there." Still, the metro-limited station cannot afford to cover the fringe audience too generously. Adding a metro-assignment reporter to the staff of the metro-only station tends to pay bigger dividends than making a spread gesture by setting up a suburban bureau in an area with few listeners. Suburban bureaus are for stations with wide-area signal coverage and adequate support budgets.

Setting up suburban bureaus, however, manned by outside reporters, ensures regional coverage. This strategy has its limitations—cost factors and areas of necessary concentration—but it works to great station advantage. When economic factors dictate, **stringers** (free-lance reporters paid per story) can often cover an entire geographic area for the station, an especially useful approach for small- and medium-sized stations. The prime advantage of full-time reporters is the visible and audible station presence in the outlying areas. Serving the major market bedroom communities nets the station their involvement and empathy. If, however, population is sparse or mainly rural, stringers are the cheaper alternative. A well-managed pool of stringers can add informed reporting of local issues without requiring local bureaus.

Sources of Programming

The all-news program manager has a multitude of programming resources available. If the station is a network outlet, most of the basic feature input is supplied, often by glamorous newscasters who lend a touch of extra authority. In most cases, these network features are line-fed at fixed times, and local program managers have little room for imaginative scheduling.

In the network wheel in Figure 16-1, the *N*s indicate live network feeds that usually restrict the local programmer's options. The letter *f* refers to features that may originate at the network or locally. If the features can be tape delayed, local news directors have space to develop their own matrices, shuffling the tapes to fit around local news items. In either case, feature handling is usually a mix of advantages and disadvantages for the programmer. The main network support comes in the form of network personalities, often from the television side, reinforcing "name" prestige through features, promos and special series production.

The programmer connected with a group or chain of stations will probably have major cross-feeds from sister stations and possibly a Washington or New York bureau on which to draw. A bureau provides stories, analyses of national political and economic news, and covers special events such as press conferences, U.N. developments and personality interviews. Added to these highly professional programming sources is the freedom to develop local staff and resources. The degree of station independence varies considerably among group-owned stations, but scheduling is normally left to the local manager.

FORMAT DESIGN

The news wheel, or programming infrastructure, forms the skeleton on which hang the sections of hard news, features, sports commentaries, editorials et al.

News is repeated in 20-, 30-, 45-, or 60-minute sequences. Cycle length affects spot and headline placement, time, traffic, weather and sports scheduling, major news story development and feature scheduling. As illustrated in the following sections, advantages and disadvantages accrue to all lengths; *which* a programmer chooses depends on local market conditioning to the format, staff capability, editorial supervision and content elements.

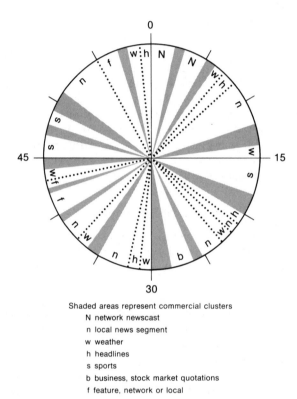

Shaded areas represent commercial clusters
N network newscast
n local news segment
w weather
h headlines
s sports
b business, stock market quotations
f feature, network or local

Source: Prepared by Don J. Brewer, KYW-News Radio

FIGURE 16-1. Network Affiliate All-News Wheel

Spot Placement

The initial task of the all-news programmer, in company with other department heads, is to create the wheel (see Figure 16-1). The wheel is a pie chart of an hour divided into segments denoting points for insertion of commercials and public service announcements, normally clustered to minimize clutter. The general, sales and program managers start by agreeing on just how confining or flexible the wheel is going to be.

Typically, each hour contains 12 to 16 minutes of spot announcements spaced out in 18 interruptions (see Figure 16-2). Frequent breaks in the flow for commercial spots creates less interruption in news than in music formats; voice shifts accompanying content changes are typical of news delivery and, in fact, contribute to its appeal. Commercial spots are usually less out of place in an all-

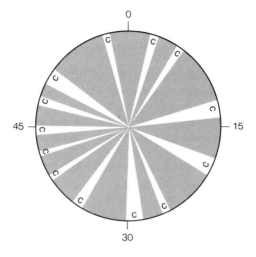

c   commercial clusters

FIGURE 16-2. Commercial Spot Spacing

news format than in an all-music format. Restricting each spot break to one or two minutes of commercials and returning quickly to news content is important.

Headlines

Headlines are the handle to the news wheel. Normally programmed at the top of the hour and at the half-hour (see Figure 16-3), their presentation style

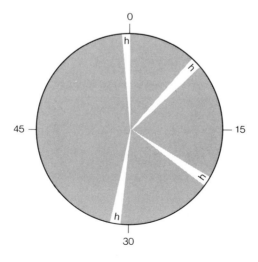

h   headlines

FIGURE 16-3. Headline Placement on the Wheel

and substance must be determined carefully. If they tease or bear only a slight relation to the stories that follow, credibility suffers. The program manager who fails to define headline policy carefully and fails to oversee how the staff applies it has a stuck zipper in the format.

For example, a tease headline might be written, "And, in Salem, Oregon, today, a wife who cried rape got an answer." This tabloid approach is damaging sensationalism. The ethical headline for an all-news format is more closely approximated as, "A Jury in Salem, Oregon, has ruled in favor of a husband, charged by his wife with rape while they were living together." If listeners are teased by the first kind of headline and distracted from hearing the follow-up story in detail, they have been deprived of valid information and will resent the station that "half-informed" them.

Sound beds (music backgrounds), gimmicky writing or flashy delivery weaken credibility and the cycle's rhythm. One common practice that works is to repeat a single, top story headline at the quarter- and three-quarter-hour points, usually as a prelude to weather, sports or some other format basic. As a subtle form of audience-attention reinforcement, it has wide acceptance.

Time and Traffic

Once the wheel's spots and headlines are set, basic format components such as *time, traffic, weather* and *sports* can be keyed in (see Figure 16-4). Time and traffic announcements gain in importance during certain dayparts, especially morning drivetime. Determining their length is a pivotal decision, as is their frequency. And when time lags occur between on-site observation and actual broadcast, inaccurate traffic information seriously undermines the all-news station's believability.

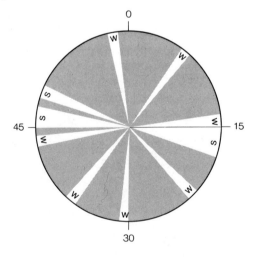

w   weather
s   sports

FIGURE 16-4. Weather and Sports on the Wheel

Weather

The arrangement of basic format components such as weather and sports is most important. These *personal-service elements* should be extremely flexible within the wheel. At times, of course, both become hard, major stories in and of themselves, such as during a major blizzard or when a local team wins a championship or fires its coach.

Weather is a key to an all-news station's prime programming periods. If a professional meteorology service is used, the station gains a special kind of credibility. Even in-house use of National Weather Service wires, area airport reports, Coast Guard data or standard wire service reports can be mixed to fit local audience needs. It is desirable, however, for the announcer to supplement wire reports by looking out the window.

Drivetime weather reports are usually short, covering only immediate-area conditions. An occasional forecast can be added to tell commuters what to expect going home and for the night to come. When a significant number of boaters, private pilots or farmers occur in the audience, special weather reports are useful at intervals. And the long-distance business commuter should get at least a spot-check two or three times a day on weather in major cities the local airport serves.

Special weather reports can run from 30 seconds to 2 minutes and can be tied to a hard news story if conditions warrant. In general, weather is increasingly important as it becomes extreme (affecting commuting), during holidays (affecting travel) and as the weekend nears (affecting leisure plans).

Sports

Sports is generally granted the quarter- and three-quarter-hour slots, with local interest, volume, time of day and pressure from other news features determining its length. Sports reporting is anchored to scores and area team activities, but sportscasts are normally expanded on weekends to cover many more games or contests at distant points—after all, in the farthest reaches of Maine and California, Notre Dame alumni associations persist. Although weekday sports segments are usually held to about two minutes at the quarter- and three-quarter-hour marks, weekend sportscasts are easily expanded to ten or twelve minutes.

In both weather and sports reporting, accuracy and timing are critical. A careful study of the market for various kinds of weather and sports information will dictate if segments should expand or contract. As in all other news areas, being right is more important than being first. The programmer who neglects a sizable special-interest group will find the competition filling the gap.

THE NEWS PROGRAMMING

The station news programmer can creatively mix the elements of news programming within the format limits. The major elements, news, editorials and features, fill about 75–80 percent of an all-news wheel. Commercials, public service announcements and promotional announcements make up the balance.

Hard News

Typically news occupies about 75 percent of airtime. Within this general category fall **hard news copy**; recapitulations of major stories (**recaps**); question-and-answer material from outside reporters via mobile radio or telephone (**actualities**). These elements form the bulk of radio newscasts. To them, stations add in-studio *interviews, news conferences, roundtable discussions,* and special *remotes* to balance coverage and add local flavor and variety.

Editorials

Most stations use an editorial director as writer, and the general manager often "voices the copy" (reads the material on the air). The most common schedule for editorials, running a minute or slightly longer, is a "26 Plan," entailing 26 plays per week for a given editorial occurring in all dayparts.[2] Depending on the number of editorials produced in a given week (usually two to four), they are salted throughout the schedule, Monday through Saturday, and each is repeated no more than once in each daypart.

For editorial content, most stations stick to local issues, avoiding national controversies and unresolvable social problems. Station management credibility is strained if the issues are too large, too unresolvable or require credentials management lacks. Widely reported local problems on which closure will occur in the coming months are especially suitable; they fit easily into the very brief format used for most editorials since listeners already know a great deal about the subjects. Issues that will be resolved by coming elections or events of moderate interest are usually safe for editorial comment. Also those problems about which all listeners agree (public safety, drunk driving, utility rate hikes, the dearth of cable television, violence in the streets) provide targets for numerous editorials.

Some stations take their editorial responsibility seriously, seeking to shape community opinion on controversial issues. Most do this by having a management executive read copy off a teleprompter. But in the early 1980s, a new wave in television editorials surfaced, involving taped footage of events (such as dead bodies, crashed cars and mangled bicycles) and tough-talking copy that urged public action. Only major market stations (less than two dozen as of 1983) had adopted this visual approach to editorials because of the cost and managerial commitment on-location editorials require. Many editorial subjects raise fairness doctrine issues, requiring airtime for opponents to respond, and on-location shooting requires camera crews and extra staff, carrying too high a price tag for many midsized and small-market stations. Even so, some editorials have stimulated legislative action and public awareness because of their hard-hitting visuals.[3]

Editorials are best scheduled in a section of the wheel farthest from the top stories, assuming that the news items are mainly local and that the editorials deal with local issues. Such scheduling means editorials appear toward the end of a 60-minute cycle. Local editorials and syndicated or network commentaries can be easily confused in some listeners' minds because they come from "strange" voices and are both persuasive statements, seeking to alter the listener's point of view. Separating editorials and commentary by at least 15 to 20 minutes is best, but one of each can fit into a 60-minute cycle. In any case, features, including editorials, should never be clustered, causing the listener to lose identification with the station as a hard news voice.

Features

Features are the salt and pepper in the format. In most cases, the reports or miniprograms are between 1½ and 2 minutes long. Independent all-news stations either hire their own commentators and feature editors or purchase syndicated material from production houses or network sources without market presence. Group all-news stations usually do both; network affiliates, of course, share in the popularity of established news personalities. Public affairs, 7–8 percent of the mix, usually falls into one of six categories:

1. *Cultural segments* review local theater and films, food and wine shows, or report on local galleries and major museum exhibitions.

2. *Features* on science and medicine are well received, particularly those on personal health matters. This subject is handled either by a recognized local authority prominent in the medical community or by a national authority, who usually gives a lay summary of new material from leading publications for the professions.

3. *Business commentary* is another category frequently aired, going beyond stock market reports (basic news). A local brokerage house, a regional stock exchange or a syndicator such as Dow Jones, AP or UPI provides them.

4. *Religious features* normally dwell on area judicatory meetings, plus church news of a social nature. But occasionally an all-news station will add a national commentator, usually syndicated, such as Norman Vincent Peale with his series of short homilies.

5. *Educational features* are an important building block in the format, particularly since so much hard news erupts from the school system nowadays. This area is a delicate one. The programmer obviously can get burned by a controversial commentator. Still, the material has to go beyond a recital of PTA meetings and social notes to be meaningful. Some risk-taking is necessary.

6. *Commentary* is authoritative personal opinion, as distinguished from station editorials reflecting management policy and opinion. Commentaries and commentators are delicate balancing acts. Many all-news stations shy away from local commentary because it is easily confused with the station's editorial policies. But, once a given format has matured, there is no real reason to steer away from local commentaries as long as they are not placed too close to the editorials and have a distinctive character of their own.

SCHEDULING CONSIDERATIONS

In a full-hour cycle after playing *commercial clusters, headlines* and *basic format elements* (time, traffic, weather, sports), eight fairly stable sections for news are left. The first and fifth sections contain the *hard news* (see Figure 16-5). The second and sixth segments normally deal with *news stories* of less immediate importance. The remaining sections incorporate some *soft news* and a mix of carefully selected *features* and news of local value. The fourth or eighth section often includes a station *editorial*—meticulously identified as management opinion. This pattern gives the listener headlines, hard news, more news, soft news and features in a repeating hourly cycle although the sources and specific content always vary.

Priorities

Within the basic format design, programming priorities should be explicitly recognized. First, programmers must disabuse themselves of the idea that earthshaking news developments on a global or national scale are uppermost in the audience's notion of what is news. Since the morning drivetime is the peak period of audience interest for most stations, and, therefore, the most viable period commercially, it is then that personal services should be most frequent and varied. Schedule in this way: Time announcements at least every two minutes; weather information (of the moment and forecast) no more than ten minutes apart; traffic information every twenty minutes (as accurate and close to the flow as humanly possible although the ideal will vary from market to mar-

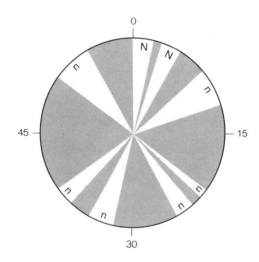

N   network newscast
n   local news segment

FIGURE 16-5. Network and Local News on the Wheel

ket); plus interspersed, allied information such as school closings, major area sports events and so on. In other words, the top priority in any all-news format is local, personal service programming. Item repetition slows during the day and is stepped up during evening drivetime (4 to 7 P.M.).

Flexibility

Although the mechanics of the format formula vary, its strategy is closely constrained. Many outside forces dictate the degree of a manager's flexibility within the format around the wheel. If the station is network affiliated, the program manager must work around prior commitments to network segments; consequently, local discretion diminishes. If the all-news station is an independent, choice is wider (see Figure 16-6). Other sources of program material, however, often dictate placement. For example, sponsored segments may be sold as fixed positions in the wheel.[4]

Live-feed items also interrupt the cycle's rhythm. Adjusting program elements within the fixed dimensions of the product base is a continual process. The programmer must guide the process, but those decisions are strongly influenced by cost considerations, staffing patterns and the like.

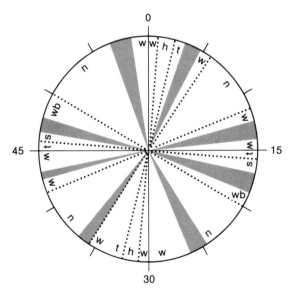

Shaded areas represent commercial clusters.

w weather forecast
h headlines: news, sports, business
t top story of the hour
n news block
s sports
b business, stock market quotations

Source: Prepared by Don J. Brewer, KYW-News Radio

FIGURE 16-6. Independent All-News Station Wheel

News Repetition

Next to credibility, predictability demands primary consideration in news format construction. The programmer may wrestle a long time with this issue because program elements such as time, weather and sports are usually fixed within the cycle for audience access. But too many predictable items reinforce the canard that all-news is little more than endless repetition.

Programmers must remember that they and their staffs are *handling* not manufacturing the product. The placement and rotation of its basic elements become important, in a sense, inversely to momentum. In time periods in which local, national or world news creates a **critical information pile**, the cycle almost moves itself. When an event dominates all news sources, the editor has many opportunities to choose among wire services, external story angles and a variety of reaction sources. In effect, the story runs itself. In the slow news spaces, product management becomes crucial. The news programmer then controls the story, planning a measured release of information on the air, affecting the news event's very real impact on the audience. News management means carefully watched story placement, creative rewriting of leads and precisely calculated lifespan for individual stories.

Feature Repetition

Scheduling features is the fine art of format structuring. Beware of three pitfalls: scheduling repeats too frequently, scheduling material requiring more listener retention than they find convenient or including irrelevant nonlocal material. For example, if a feature segment is aired on a Wednesday at 10:40 A.M., then aired on Thursday and Friday at the same time or within an hour either way, chances are the audience will be largely the same. Scheduling the repeat of a morning-drive feature in evening drivetime merely causes resentment in many drivers that catch both broadcasts.

The important question is how much soft (as opposed to hard, fast-breaking news) material is available? When? How often? What kind? Most soft material based on an audience's natural interest in medical and health information, the entertainment industry or hobby material, finds a catholic reception. Local audiences vary, of course, in what they need and will accept. The lesson from the consumer reporter fad of the 1970s was that when a special feature blurs into the normal flow of news, the program manager should take a hard look at its value as a separate program item.

COST AND QUALITY

In a 24-hour period the average all-news operation takes in about 400,000 words from all sources, including teletype; telephone; line-feeds from network, group, or contract services; stringers; and its own beat reporters. Of this data, less than half will be aired. Control of product vis-à-vis control of cost requires a finely honed strategy. Cost control cuts in many directions, but it counts most when the opportunity arises to "own a story." A lack of budget reserve at those crucial moments leaves a manager unable to capitalize on strength and gives competition an audience edge hard to overcome.

Original Reporting

The shrewd all-news programmer will be keenly aware of news themes that are being "ridden" in the market—a tendency among radio reporters and editors to follow on a story a local newspaper or television station generated, such as series on child abuse or auto repair swindles. If a radio news reporter picks up such a theme and converts it to a series of reports, it is not only duplicative (even when new material is exposed) but also drains budget. Rather, the prudent programmer hoards a portion of the operational budget for other opportunities— a local disaster, major storm or an original investigative project by the station staff—and then goes all out to swamp the story from every possible angle, thus "owning" it compared to the competition. One dividend of this maneuver is that such coverage is very likely to be an award winner in one of the several national or regional competitions that wire services, universities and professional associations sponsor. The station not only owned the story but picked up some prestige along the way. Corporate management likes to see awards on the wall as visible proof of station status and enterprise.

Reporting Assignments

In building audience and meeting competition, one crucial decision is selection and assignment of outside reporters. If there is any one place for a programmer to spend money on the grand side, it is with this group. The determination of station outreach is critical, but merely advertising the station's coverage is quickly pegged as public relations sham if actual beat coverage is slighted or faked. Listeners are acutely (if often subliminally) attuned to their environment, especially the sound of it. Cold handouts, studio copy, voice cuts, sound effects cannot replace the presence of a live reporter. The programmer should study the community's needs to define an appropriate geographical extent to the station's commitment. Political centers such as city halls, statehouses or county seats should get staffing priority. Beats in education, transportation, health, crime, urban affairs (ethnic concentrations), suburban centers and any special regional or local priority deserve close attention. A **correlator** (inside or telephone reporter), creating an actuality, often adds a local dimension to a story. The quick taping of a phone call can make the difference between a vaguely pertinent off-wire rewrite and a story with a local angle that has local audience impact and appeal.

Boilerplate Programming

One trap for the programmer is **boilerplate** programming—the purchase of canned generic features. These are packaged, syndicated features such as *One Moment Please*, a boilerplate in the form of short morality talks. Since they have no local association, they usually dilute the station's commercial momentum and should be avoided by large-market all-news stations having better alternatives. The programmer at a well-financed station should generate local feature segments on health, personal finances, local cultural activities, leisure time activities and entertainment—prepared and announced by station talent.

Commercial Copy

If union contracts permit the prerecording of announcement material, rather than requiring it to be aired live, the programmer has a distinct advantage in achieving voice change and more efficient staff utilization. If contracts do not permit it, the anchorperson suffers from the constant stress of changing gears from hard news copy to often widely disparate, even frivolous, commercial copy. A highly skilled announcer–reader can manage this feat, but many come off badly in the process, and credibility takes a beating. The ideal tactic is to have the anchorperson totally involved in news preparation as well as in delivery and accompanied by supporting announcers at the microphone.

Another problem is that many feature contributors come from the print media and are not accustomed to writing material to be read aloud. A radio listener's attention span is shorter than a print reader's, and there is no rereading on radio. Each all-news segment must be as brief as possible; the giving of involved directions, recipes and the like is an irritant.

Union Contracts

In most major markets union rules govern production personnel—a very real constraint for management. Most unionized radio stations have contracts with the American Federation of Television and Radio Artists (AFTRA) although many stations also have Newspaper Guild writers in-house. Union contracts set work rules, pay provisions and exclusivity that can manacle all-news programming. These elements are all tied to working conditions in the various union contracts. Contracts exist in which the repeat of a story in later shifts or dayparts carries a residual payment to the original reporter, writer or anchorperson. Sometimes this kind of provision is designated a "within-shift" rule allowing the story's use within the individual's scheduled shift, but adding a fee when used outside the particular shift. Added to that may be special tape-reuse fees or added cost for use by another station in the network or group. When reporters cannot edit tape, write their own extraneous wraps or do simple editing because of contract constraints, delay becomes handicap. And handicaps create daily dissension and threaten cost control.

News breaks; it doesn't wait. If management cannot afford a story because complex costs surround its on-air repetition (from marching to union labor shifts, taped amplification and extension or multiple-fee burdens of one kind or another), the story gets short shrift, if any attention at all.

Staff Size

As is immediately obvious, especially in a union shop in which AFTRA or the Newspaper Guild controls most positions, personnel costs take a big jump.

The average all-news station in a major market starts with a news team of 25 to 35. Format evolution and union negotiations in the past several years have tended to tighten the staffing pattern, but all-news remains a labor-intensive format. Round-the-clock operations, living up to the slogan "All News All the Time" (KYW, Philadelphia), leave little room for staff economies without compromising the format's promise.

During the average shift, the "product communicator" is on the air between two to three hours, and does some writing, collating or ancillary production work in the off-air period. Using taped segments on the overnight daypart (1–4 A.M.) is widely practiced, and curtailed staffing on the slower weekend shifts works reasonably well. Other options depend on availability of free-lance talent, overtime budgets, technical maintenance requirements and a basic assessment of market needs. For example, if an appreciable audience exists for the wee hours, then live newscasting becomes appropriate; if the audience is miniscule, then taped repeats become an option to preserve the budget for important news events. This choice faces all news programmers.

NEWS AUDIENCE DEFINITION

Most all-news stations have a relatively easy time with the 50+ age group and generally build strong cumulative audiences (cumes). Attracting and holding the 18–49 group and women present the greatest problems. The AQH (average quarter hour) span is another tough block in audience-building schemes. Listeners tune in and out of all-news stations. In contrast, music stations may hold some listeners over long periods, giving them a leg up on total time spent listening (long TSL). (These measures were described in Chapter 2 under radio ratings.) The countermove is not to cater to random pressures but rather to choose the news mix in as catholic a fashion as possible and "be there" with a steady diet of quality reporting at all times.

Strategic use of audience research by the all-news program manager is important, but only if it is regarded as *one* factor in judging format suitability. It cannot be the governing force. Most stations subscribe to the monthly audience assessments of *Mediatrend*, now a feature of The Birch Report, and to Arbitron's highly detailed, quarterly reports. Other services fall between these two in the details they provide. One of the most important research tools is The Birch Report, based in Coral Springs, Florida. As described in Chapter 2, it relies solely on telephone research rather than diaries and now has subscribers in most major markets. From time to time, new services arise, but they emerge slowly and tend to be marginally useful.

The sales keys are the October/November Arbitron reports on which most annual buys are made and on which most advertising agencies rely for guidance. A newspaper strike, severe storms, major sustained disaster stories and so on, can "wobble" a report book in an all-news station's favor. Such measurement devices as **ESF (expanded sample frame** that culls new and unlisted telephone respondents) may hurt or help from book to book. Format changes in the market, such as a new talk station or FM proliferation, can alter audience measurements remarkably.

THE STRAINS AND PAINS

All-news radio presents an almost Kiplingesque "if" situation: If the general manager is interested mainly in short-term corporate tactics; if the sales manager musters a sales force that sells only numbers rather than the all-news product; if the promotion manager has no appropriate promotional strategy; if the chief engineer sees fit not to apply maximum special support requirements; if, in other words, management regards the format as an ideological loss leader and insists on "yo-yo" format deviations to compete in the ratings scramble—then the all-news programmer is in deep trouble. All-news demands complete support from all parts of the organization.

Problems Inside and Out

Here are a few internal problem areas with which programmers must be prepared to deal:

1. *The incompatible commercial:* Many advertisers think it is just the thing to submit copy that sounds like a fake news bulletin (that contains verbiage that seems interwoven with hard news copy) or that requires an anchorperson to do ethnic dialects. Erosion of credibility is obvious.

2. *The jingle jokers:* Many in promotion and, sadly, even in programming feel that the all-news format is inherently dull and repetitious and, therefore, needs hyping. They frequently insert jingles unrelated to the basic format sound package. They recommend promos that tease, non–news-related contesting and sensational headlines. They become especially frantic with promotional distractions during periods in which ratings firms are known to be gathering their listening data.

3. *The tech wreckers:* The demands of processing a heavy daily load of tape material, extra production requirements and sudden, awkward remote broadcast assignments have forced more than one technician to retreat to the sanctity of the transmitter. The chief engineer then announces sharp increases in "obligatory" meter readings and adjustments. Engineers will make themselves inaccessible if they feel they are being asked to do more than they think fair.

4. *The bottom line is all there is:* "You've blown the budget on the snowstorm, and we'll have to cover the capital hearings off the wire." Programmers often hear such talk from general managers. Programmers have to challenge poor-mouthing, perhaps, their most dangerous confrontation with management. Many have fought with too little, for too much, at the wrong time, and over the wrong issues. The successful programmer finds out where the land mines have been placed before rushing into the fray.

Piling onto internal constraints are the ones coming from the audience. A programmer without a disciplined philosophy about how to deal with external complaints has an uphill struggle from the start.

1. *Repetition:* The initial cry from listeners when the format is introduced is "repetition." What the audience is really saying, however, is, "The way I listen to and use radio is not comfortable any more. You demand full attention, but I hear the same stories over and over." It takes a fair span of time before the audience begins to understand how all-news radio works.

2. *Bad News:* The need to convey "bad news" creates another external pressure. All-news never provides calming background music for the routines of the day, nor will it offer a stimulating, continuous round of exciting rock music or spirited talk and debate.

3. *Bias:* Audience mail will complain that the station promotes horrid fascist ideals and reprehensible communist plots. If the volume of letters on each side is about even, the station must be doing about right.

4. *Pressure Groups:* Another powerful external pressure comes from civic groups and consumer bands bent on attacking the station's license. These attacks can trigger enormous legal expense and create much inconvenience. However, the station that practices ethical journalism and uses sound broadcasting management has little to fear from these onslaughts.

Promotional Effectiveness

An important key to successful competition is well-thought-out promotion. Clever slogans, jingle packages and spot promotional efforts are not enough; good promotion requires the sustained use of a valid theme underlying major programming *and* staff recognition of it. If the newsroom staff does not identify with a station promotion "theme," it will not be communicated to the audience. Amazing as it sounds, management often fails to convey its short- or long-range thinking behind a promotional theme or campaign to the news staff. Although overuse of cute promos dilutes the effectiveness of news material, programmers and promotion managers can work closely to judge the value of in-house promotional themes and external campaigns to the benefit of the entire format.

Another great weakness in most broadcasting is lack of on-air communication. Sometimes programmers forget to tell the audience what comes next in the program. The solution is called "promoting off the desk," meaning that the editor (with back-up from writers, correlators, and anchorpersons) must be foresighted enough to create audience expectations for an upcoming special series, phone interview sequence or other special item. This sort of promotion can be formalized to some extent.

Program Monitoring

Another aspect of maintaining a competitive edge is close monitoring of what goes on the air. A monthly review of script packages will show which writers and anchorpersons are "dogging it," that is, either using excessive paste-up of wire copy (necessary and permissible within reasonable limits on stories outside the station's coverage area) or simply using carbon copies of stories from previous news segments. Repetition of exact copy is an insidious tendency that may eventually bore the audience and drive it away. Many program managers have neglected this syndrome to their later sorrow. Keeping on top of script packages is a prime responsibility, and the competition will be quick to notice if a station fails to do so.

Last, programmers should not find themselves forced to play catch-up. They must listen to the competition regularly for the same reasons the competition listens to them.

FANATICS WERE YESTERDAY

Many practitioners of all-news radio remind one of Winston Churchill's definition of a fanatic: "He not only won't change his mind, he won't change the subject!" All-news programming tends to suffer from two extremes: those programmers who periodically want to revolutionize the format and those who are so locked into a format they will not consider change. All-news, in fact, is an evolutionary service, used by many different types of listeners at one and the same time. The programmer who does not dare to "dump the format" for an event that lends itself to another obvious form of coverage will lose crucial ratings battles. The judicious use of format openings such as massive team reporting efforts from remote locations, proper invocation of telephone programming and even the airing of play-by-play sports can have creative benefits. Little touches the life of any major audience group that is not compatible with the meaning of the word *news*. Conversely, there are very few things an all-news station can attempt into which a satisfactory amount of straight, hard news coverage cannot be inserted.

Despite the increase in news networks and syndicated news programming, it is doubtful that all-news can be profitable in small- or even medium-sized markets until the FCC lifts its limit on the number of stations one group can own. Without sufficient personnel and money (such as group ownership usually provides), all-news operations are almost bound to revert to the old rip-and-read practice of earlier days. They then collapse in the ratings and lose advertising support. To be sure, technology is cutting costs—slowly. ENG (electronic news-gathering) equipment is widening the audience's appetite for information that broadcast television alone cannot satisfy, ironically because of its own slavery to the old network radio formats and, of course, its own cost problems tied to the personality cult. The day of the self-transmitting remote reporter has come and the computer with audio-speech capacity is not far down the road. And satellite-distributed audio signals are reducing the cost of radio networking. But cable news networks are filling some of the public's news appetite, and all-news radio is likely to remain most competitive in major markets.

SUMMARY

The all-news format is costly and demanding, but, if given time to build an audience, it can command a highly loyal audience—although the demographics skew toward older listeners, and it is most successful in major markets. Six key content elements make up the fundamental structure of the news wheel: commercial spots, headlines, time and traffic, weather and sports. Once these elements are placed, the remainder of the open spaces in the wheel are divided among hard news (including remotes and recaps), editorials and features. In scheduling, the highest priority should go to those items (whether hard or soft news) providing local personal service such as time, traffic, weather and local events, especially during morning and afternoon drivetime. Flexibility in restructuring the news wheel for highly unusual events creates an image as a responsive and professional station that, in turn, fosters loyalty and strong cumes. Misplaced or too frequent repetition of hard news and feature elements encourages listeners to dial away. To remain competitive a news station requires a high budget and a high level of commitment from management. With a large budget, a station can provide original reporting, quality features and extensive beat reporting. Union contract limitations affect day-to-day programming, and news programmers must understand how contracts do so. Both the public and higher-up management contribute to the constraints operating on news programmers, but the successes provide immense personal rewards. The future will hold greater competition from cable all-news services and an increasing number of network and nationally syndicated news suppliers. Some cost relief will come from new technological developments.

Notes

[1] WCAU's format was modified to news and information in December 1978.

[2] The number 26 is an arbitrary one, a hangover from traditional 13-26-52 week programming cycles; editorials could be run as readily in 18- or 30-unit schedules, but 26 is most common.

[3] Edwin Kiester, Jr., "Bull's Eye! Those Editorials Are Now Drawing Blood," *TV Guide*, 17 September 1983, pp. 18–21.

[4] Some all-news stations sell five- or six-minute blocks of news time to a single advertiser, allowing identification of that sponsor with a certain feature or news segment.

Selected Sources

Fang, Irving E. *Television News, Radio News.* 3d. ed. Minneapolis: Rada Press, 1980.

Kierstead, Phillip O. *All-News Radio.* Blue Ridge Summit, Pennsylvania: TAB Books, 1980.

Routt, Edd. "The Information Format." In *The Radio Format Conundrum.* New York: Hastings House, 1978.

"Special Report on Journalism." *Broadcasting* (27 September 1982): 60–65; (19 September 1983): 50–56.

"Special Report on Radio." *Broadcasting* (29 August 1983): 48–104. See also "AM and FM Listeners Have a Lot in Common." *Broadcasting* (29 September 1982): 81–82.

CHAPTER SEVENTEEN

Talk Radio Programming

Bruce W. Marr

A QUICK GUIDE TO CHAPTER SEVENTEEN

BRUCE W. MARR   *is president of Bruce Marr and Associates, a broadcast consulting firm specializing in news, talk and information radio programming. He has introduced the talk radio format to many client stations across the country. From 1975 to 1981, he was director of news and programming at KABC, Los Angeles, one of the creators of the all-talk format. Before joining KABC, an ABC-owned station, Mr. Marr worked for KFWB, a Group W-owned AM station in Los Angeles. He has lectured on radio programming at the University of Southern California (USC) and the University of California at Los Angeles (UCLA) and served as a director of the National Leukemia Broadcast Council. His chapter looks at many related formats ranging from all-conversation at one extreme to half-news/half-talk at the other, the format often called "information radio." Since nearly all stations at some time include elements of talk, the discussions of fairness and public pressure in this chapter have relevance for all programmers.*

THE BEGINNINGS OF CONTEMPORARY TALK

This chapter covers the special characteristics of news inside the news/talk format, and then concentrates on structuring talk programming, the unique attribute of the format.

The term *talk station* was generally adopted when KABC in Los Angeles and a few other major market stations discarded their records around 1960 and began airing nothing but the sound of the human voice. KABC started with a key four-hour news and conversation program entitled *News/Talk* from 5 to 9 A.M. KGO in San Francisco later adopted that designation for its overall format. KGO used news blocks in both morning and evening drivetime and conversation programs throughout the balance of the day. KABC focused on live call-in programs, interviews and feature material combined with informal and formal news coverage.

Though KABC originally promoted itself as "The Conversation Station," *news/talk* stuck as the generic industry term for stations that program conversation leavened with news during the drive periods. News/talk radio includes some half-and-half formats as well as all-conversation programming.

During the latter half of the 1970s, radio broadcasting changed drastically. At that time the hares of the industry—the AM broadcasters—paused to look over their shoulders at the tortoises—the FM stations. When they did so, they found themselves being overtaken. When they glanced forward toward the finish line, they saw that some of the FM tortoises were already leading the race. By 1977 an entire generation of listeners had grown up with their radios permanently locked on the FM dial.

In 1978 a number of AM broadcasters assessed the situation and recognized that FM had become the music medium of choice for a large part of the radio audience. To retain their audiences, several notable AM stations counterprogrammed: They shifted their formats away from music to the spoken word. Information programming proliferated.

FLEXIBLE STRUCTURE

The talk format is fluid *and* stable. Its framework is fixed, but flexible enough to respond to issues on a day-to-day basis and quickly reflect changing community moods. Good broadcast personalities can sense audience mood and respond accordingly. Talk hosts, unhampered by a music rotation list and the like, can alter the tone of on-air talk more rapidly than announcers working in other formats.

Major Event Coverage

When an issue or news event is significant enough to color the outlook of an entire community or even the entire nation, the sound of the talk station will reflect the audience temper. Coverage of significant events preempts the regular schedule and previously booked guests. Like most broadcasters, a talk station responds to major news events on the air; but talk and all-news stations respond to events more *rapidly* with on-hand personnel and equipment resources, and when appropriate, can devote all of the station airtime to the event. Television newscasts require visuals (videotape) to accompany stories, and reporters are generally locked into morning/noon/night/late-night newscast patterns—except in times of local disaster. Radio news/talk reporters have hourly deadlines, needing only fresh event coverage, new perspectives and the taped or live voices of participants.

The November morning in 1978 when San Francisco Mayor George Moscone and Supervisor Harvey Milk were shot and killed in city hall provides a vivid example of talk radio's responsiveness. That morning, San Francisco's KGO radio had been planning to air a discussion on holiday loneliness and depression, followed by programs on taxation and alcoholism. When the city hall story broke, the entire Bay Area went numb. All of northern California wanted the details of a single story: the city hall shootings.

KGO's news team responded immediately, deploying its field reporters and assigning inside staffers to telephones. From the moment the story reached the station, the atmosphere within the station altered, and the change was reflected in the on-air product. Scheduled guests were canceled; talk hosts instantly became anchorpersons. KGO mixed field staff reports with reactions from civic officials its inside newspeople gathered by telephone. Audience comments were aired constantly. The station stayed with the city hall shooting story exclusively throughout the day, discarding its planned programming in favor of a strong response to its community's needs and concerns.

Informal News Breaks

Because the news/talk format generally presents information, the audience readily accepts a news break. The interruption may be a network bulletin or a casual sounding "visit" from a member of the station news staff who joins the talk host in the studio to break a story fresh from a wire service or a local reporter. The newsperson's presence in the studio on such occasions provides the opportunity for questions and answers or conversation between the host and the newsperson. Assuring the audience that the station's news staff will follow the story and keep listeners informed as the story develops will keep them from shifting to an all-news station.

Local Responsiveness

News department resources and personnel vary substantially from station to station. Certainly, mobile radios, helicopters and station cars make possible live, exciting, on-the-spot reports as an event is happening, but even a small station with a tiny news staff can cover a breaking story using the primary tools of electronic journalism: the telephone and enterprising production people. With a little ingenuity, a few credible contacts and a reverse telephone directory (arranged by addresses instead of names), studio assistants can put the talk host in touch with officials, eyewitnesses and other involved parties even before a news crew can reach the scene of a story. During periods of disaster, the news/talk station can become a vital clearing-house for information.

When wide-ranging brushfires swept through thousands of acres of southern California in October 1978, KABC dealt with the disaster continuously throughout the day and evening—through news staff reports and through the liaison it established between those in need and those willing to help. One caller pleaded for safe pasture for his threatened livestock, and another listener responded with an offer. Other listeners, unable to reach their homes in the fire areas, heard neighbors call in to report on the fire-fighting efforts. Temporary housing offers were relayed on the air to evacuees. People who had lived through other devastating fires in the brush country around Los Angeles called with tips on how to protect homes and property. Beyond such valuable services, the station also delivered to its entire audience the story of the fire in very human and personal terms. Fortunately, this type of event is rare, but when it happens live coverage adds drama to the news/talk format. When preparing a budget, metropolitan market programmers should anticipate three or four events a year requiring live coverage.

Role of the Program Director

A special kind of partnership, involving a great deal of mutual trust, grows up between on-air personalities and their program directors in talk programming. Program directors establish station policies that ensure not only high journalistic standards but also take into account the bounds of good taste, Federal Communication Commission rules, libel laws and industry codes. Having established and communicated such policies, an individual program director must recognize that day-to-day errors and deviations will occur. The individual on the air has to make instant decisions and respond immediately. A conversation host interacts with phone callers for two, three or four hours a day. Callers can be assertive, aggressive, even belligerent. And no format is easier to second-guess, after the fact. Program directors should therefore avoid impulsively calling air personalities to task; in almost every case, the personality is the first to know when something has gone wrong.

In fact, talk radio is radio waiting for something to go wrong. When things do go wrong, the first approach of the program director should leave an opening for the personality to say, "I know it was bad. The reason was . . ." Although program directors are responsible for determining that the air talent understands what happened, they must then act as intermediaries and arbitrators between management and on-air personnel.

NATIONAL PROGRAM SOURCES

Music programmers can turn to a large number of outside music syndicators to augment their locally produced programs or to program their entire broadcast day. Talk radio programmers, however, were largely on their own until the early 1980s. Syndicators offered short features of five minutes or less, but only the Mutual network offered a major long-form program, *The Larry King Show.* This midnight-to-dawn program was first aired in January 1978 on a 28-station network. The demand for such live call-in programming was so great that by its fifth anniversary, 266 affiliates were clearing the King program.[1]

By the late 1970s, the other major radio networks were exploring their affiliates' (and potential affiliates') need for long-form information programming. In November 1981, NBC launched TALKNET, which delivered continuous nighttime programming from 8 P.M. to 2 A.M. (See its logo in Figure 17-1.) It had 115 stations on the line as of 1983. Meanwhile, ABC also tested the appeal of network talk programming and in May 1982 began delivering 18 hours of it, filling most

FIGURE 17-1. TALKNET Logo

of the hours between 10 A.M. and 9 A.M. ABC's TALKRADIO reached 60 affiliates by 1983, and both networks continue to assess the need for additional information programming—especially for AM stations. As of 1984, neither CBS nor RKO were planning long-form talk programming.

TALKNET

The executive producer of TALKNET, Maurice Tunick, pointed out in an interview that NBC's decision to introduce the service grew solely from needs potential affiliates had expressed. "Our network is responsive," Tunick says. "Our original ideas are worthless if they don't meet the needs of stations. A reasonable number of stations must express interest in clearing programs we are considering *before* we can go into production."

NBC's original TALKNET programming included advice on personal finance on the *Bruce Williams Program*, aired weeknights from 8 to 11 P.M. (EST); and personal advice from *Sally Jesse Rafael*, from 11 P.M. to 2 A.M. (EST). In 1982, the network also began offering two Sunday night programs, *Bernard Meltzer*, with personal and financial advice from 8 P.M. to midnight, and psychiatrist *Dr. Harvey Ruben* from midnight to 3 A.M. (EST). On these programs audience members call in to the network studio to ask questions, deliver opinions, respond to comments and so on. TALKNET is a barter program, coming to stations with most of the advertising spots presold; another 3½ minutes per hour can be sold locally. Stations can carry all or part of the TALKNET programming, but by contract, all the nationally originating commercials must be aired during the hours stations agree to carry.

TALKRADIO

While NBC originates programming specifically for the TALKNET network, ABC takes a different approach to talk radio. Because it owns two well-established talk stations, KABC in Los Angeles and KGO in San Francisco, ABC uses the programs and personalities of those stations as TALKRADIO's core. KGO's *Owen Spann* airs nationally from 10 A.M. to noon (EST) and *Michael Jackson* of KABC is heard from 2 to 4 P.M. (EST). Both host general interest talk programs. Psychologist *Dr. Toni Grant*, originating from KABC, appears on the network from 4 to 7 P.M. (EST). Similarly, KABC's *Ira Fistell* is heard nationally from midnight to 3 A.M. (EST), and *Ray Breim*, a late-night program, is aired from 3 to 9 A.M. (EST). A program featuring psychologist *Dr. Susan Forward* originates from Los Angeles to provide programming for stations in the eastern and central time zones from noon to 2 P.M. (EST). Altogether, then, these programs fill 18 hours daily. TALKRADIO is packaged as a barter program coming with most of the advertising spots presold; four minutes each hour are available for local sale.

Mutual

The *Larry King Show* continues to dominate radio talk in popularity and numbers of affiliated stations. The five-hour show divides into a three-hour guest interview and a two-hour national call-in segment. King supplies a smorgasbord of comment, questions and sports trivia. Mutual also distributes 2½-minute mini-interviews by King for daytime airing.

Affiliates and Networks

As of 1983, a station clearing programs from two or more national radio networks could fill 15 or more hours of each broadcast day. However, some broadcasters feel that such network dependency deprives the local audience of programs dealing with local issues. Others point out that national programming has big budgets, extensive resources, major talent and access to nationally known guest experts that no single local station could expect to acquire. The president of ABC Radio, Ben Hoberman (who as general manager had created KABC's talk format in 1960), said in an interview, "The very nature of radio is changing, but not for the first time. Much of the radio was networked until the 1950s when it had to adapt to the advent of television. Radio virtually became an exclusively musical medium, and the best way to deliver music was with local disc jockeys playing records. But now, as we enter the information age, there is a clear need for the kind of programming the networks can do best."

The national networks recognize that news/talk stations must program key dayparts locally. The networks structure their programming so that morning and afternoon drivetime can be all or mostly local, and stations can present individual local programs. One major structural difference between music and news/talk programming is that music forms a continuous, never-ending single program, while talk and news break into discrete units that can be added, deleted or reassembled into customized program structures.

LOCAL TALK PROGRAMS

To complement nationally distributed talk programs, programmers schedule local talk programming that provides an opportunity for local listeners to call in. As of the early 1980s, trendy local shows targeted specific demographic groups with participation formats focusing on services, not issues. Radio flea markets and swap shops in which callers describe something they have for sale on the air have broad audience appeal; dating services target younger audience demographics. By capitalizing on fads and hobbies, these specialized programs try to attract new groups of listeners to talk radio. The key element is that the listener contribute to the program within a highly controlled structure. ("Tell the audience what you have for sale, what's special about it, what your price is, and how they can get in touch with you . . .") In some markets, these programs have succeeded in attracting new groups of listeners.

TALK HOSTS

Conversation program hosts are often generalists, as are most broadcast journalists. They have developed the ability to grasp a subject's essence. The host of a general interest talk program will discuss world and local affairs, politics, medicine, economics, science, history, literature, music, art, sports and entertainment trivia—often on a single program. Talk hosts typically are inveterate readers: Some even find speed-reading courses helpful.

In the view of David Graves, General Manager of Chicago's WIND, a good talk host, like a great author or filmwriter, creates a vehicle that operates on more than one intellectual level. "The great talk show host," said Graves, in an interview, "uses humor, pacing and interesting phrasing to create a program that works as a pure audio entertainment form which will appeal to a large segment of the audience. On the other hand, the well-educated, sophisticated listener should not be offended by the level of the conversation."

Bias

The best of talk radio is either broadcast journalism or closely akin to it. Much of it, however, stresses entertainment over completeness of information and opinions over facts. As the talk format matured, it embraced more of the journalistic tradition, introducing a content conflict. Professional newspeople filter out their own biases as they write and prepare stories. In live talk radio, the on-air person cannot always keep personal points of view in check. Many talk hosts do not see themselves as journalists but as entertainers. When a station adopts a live talk format, management has to admit that the members of the on-the-air team have individual biases and must be allowed to express their viewpoints on issues discussed on the air. Management can, however, expect program hosts to treat guests with respect when the guests represent opposing sides of issues. This philosophy has grown from the experience of finding it fruitless to ask on-air personalities to be unbiased. Program hosts are often investigators, sometimes advocates, and biases are doubtless part of their stock-in-trade. Some talk hosts represent the listeners' own opinion or cases of "the man you love to hate."

A new trend, however, stresses presentation of factual information in expert interviews rather than the volatile, listener call-in format. Experience has shown that angry, screaming hosts with call-in programs rarely get more than a 5 audience share, while informative, witty, content-oriented programs using expert-guest interviews draw substantially higher audience shares in most markets.

Turnover

When a newcomer takes over an on-air slot on a talk station, a certain amount of audience turnover occurs. Many listeners and callers go elsewhere; new ones find and accept the new personality. Initial reaction is usually negative when a host is removed and replaced, a natural response to a change that disrupts the listening habits of regular listeners. Even when ratings and other indicators confirm the need for a change, the followers of the departed personality will react vigorously enough to make programmers question their own judgments. The new host's first programs will find callers responding timidly, as they would with a new acquaintance. This newness will color the tone of the program for a time since the audience is an integral part of any conversation program.

Structuring Issue Debates

The discussion of controversial issues is a central part of talk programming. In structuring programs on controversial subjects, a key question arises: Is it wiser to invite representatives of each point of view to a single program and structure a debate or to invite individuals to express their points of view separately on consecutive hours of a single program or on successive programs?

Answers differ by station, but the common denominator is how to maintain control. Program producers cannot manipulate what individuals will say, but they can design program segments so that listeners perceive that the content is "under control." At a minimum, two persons participate in a telephone talk program: the host and the caller. A program guest adds a third presence. If two guests appear on the program, there are now four voices. Because it is radio, listeners have no visual reference and can easily lose track of who is speaking. If a debate gets out of control, listeners hear a cacophony of voices, one speaking over the other. As a rule of thumb, have few voices on a single show and keep them easily identifiable. The host can do the latter by referring to guests by name when prefacing their statements or asking them questions. Hosts must also soft-pedal their own views during interviews to time-broker shows.

AUDIENCE

The talk format appeals to an older audience than most music formats attract. The most frequent talk target is the 25–54 group. Even when directed at this demographic group, the format will usually attract a substantial proportion of those 55 and over.

During the 1960s and 1970s, these demographics were a disadvantage: Most advertisers were trying to reach that large segment of the population that fell into the 18–34 category. During those years, programmers tried to lower the average age of their audiences, but with little success. KABC, for example, experimented on more than one occasion with youthful program hosts to appeal to the younger segment of the market. Each time the effort failed. Moreover, not only did the attempts fail in drawing young listeners, they also alienated the older, hard-core listenership.

By the early 1980s, that inordinately large population segment that once fell into the younger demographic groups had moved into the 25-years-and-over bracket that talk radio effectively reaches. The format therefore became more attractive to advertisers (who in turn had raised their demographic target and begun cultivating the older audience). Even so, programmers should keep the audience from skewing toward the top age demographics.

Targeting the Content

Programmers can manipulate a demographically top-heavy talk audience downward by rigidly controlling subject matter. The program manager and the on-air staff must construct each programming hour to appeal to the target demographic group. Freeform (sometimes called "open-line") programs in which callers set the agenda must be severely limited or entirely prohibited.

KTRH (Houston), for example, aired a significant amount of freeform programming when it began its talk format in 1961 and found that it reached a predominantly older audience. Moreover, the older listeners added to the problem since they dominated the call-in air time. They felt free to dial the station at any time and discuss issues that were of interest to them but not to younger listeners. In 1975 the station imposed controls on the on-air subject matter and markedly reduced the average age of its audience.

One stratagem for forcing down the median age of an audience is the sports conversation show. Aired in late afternoon or evening, such a program will attract a significant audience younger than the normal 25 + target group without relinquishing males 25–49 that are the backbone of the station's potential evening drive audience.

Call-in psychology programs also have broad demographic appeal, reaching both men and women of all ages. The key to such programs is the nature of the subject matter itself. When properly produced and controlled, the on-air therapist is dealing with the most absorbing subject possible—the audience members themselves. In general, casual surveys of listener habits and opinions during the call-in portions of such programs are effective ways of targeting specific audience demographics.

Impact

If a talk station is sufficiently involved in the community it serves, it attracts influential civic and business leaders, political figures and intellectual leaders from all walks of life. It is not unusual, even in a radio market the size of Los Angeles, for public figures to call an ongoing program in response to the mention of their names on the air.

The talk audience is as active as the station itself. Conversation stations are foreground stations, designed to involve listeners. Seldom do listeners use conversation radio as a background the way they may a beautiful music station. This attribute represents an important sales advantage. Commercials are particularly effective within the conversation environment because they reach an audience that tuned in *to listen.* A commercial read live by an authoritative talk host has added impact.[2] The talk audience is also above average in education, spendable income and many other attributes that attract a broad range of advertisers.

GUESTS

Effective guests for talk radio come from all walks of life. They range from well-trained actors and politicians to unknowns on the air for the first time. A good guest must have something to communicate that interests the audience— unsuspected facts, offbeat experiences, unusual opinions or a unique mode of self-expression—and that usually generates argument. The most popular shows investigate issues and explore the facts, using guests who can supply a strong informational component.

Interviews

Every talk program director receives hundreds of audition tapes as part of the job applications of aspiring talk hosts—on which they interview nationally known celebrities. It follows that the applicants must think these interviews are their best. Too often, however, celebrities have nothing new to say. (Aspiring interviewers must feel that some of the "celebratedness" rubs off onto them.) The best audition tapes are those that give the program director an opportunity to hear how the host probes substantive issues, to learn how well the individual prepares and how agile his or her mind is. Celebrity interviews rarely offer such opportunities. Most of them include a few brief, pat questions from the host and lengthy answers from the interviewee. The person who stands to gain the most recognition from the interview is the celebrity.

Too often talk stations and hosts pursue well-known names as guests, people who will bring "star value" to their programs. But often the best guest will be a local person whose name is unknown to the listeners. The local station in the small community can program relevant topics without looking beyond its own coverage area for guests. Stations quite distant from the "talk show circuit" need not avoid locally produced talk programming for lack of interesting guests. An hour spent with a major movie star might better be spent with a mayor, school superintendent, game warden, newspaper publisher, football coach or auto mechanic. Many movie actors have plenty of eye appeal, but are of little interest as voices. Good radio conversation requires ideas and opinions, not good looks. Public relations firms representing nationally known figures deluge major market stations with offers for celebrity appearances. Those responsible for scheduling guests on such stations should consider carefully the relevance of every guest's contribution to its listeners' needs or desires, not merely the impact of the person's name.

Stations can interview by telephone guests that otherwise would never be available, and a conference call permits local callers to participate in the conversation. Programmers still prefer to have guests in the studio when possible to maximize the host's effectiveness and minimize the guest's defenses.

Commercial Interests

Of all radio formats, the talk format is the most vulnerable to unscheduled commercial matter. The terms *payola* and *plugola* have been associated with the music industry, but the talk format offers the greatest opportunities for such abuses. An hour of friendly conversation presents endless opportunities for the on-air host to mention a favorite resort or restaurant or to comment on a newly acquired automobile. Moreover, the program host is often in the position of booking favored business acquaintances as guests. The on-air personality therefore receives many offers, ranging from free dinners to discounts on major purchases. Policies aimed at preventing violations must emphasize that management will severely penalize violators. Most stations require their on-air talent and producers to sign affidavits showing that they understand the law on these points, and some stations hire independent agencies to monitor programs for abuses. More than one station has reinforced this message by billing on-air performers for time if their casual conversations become commercials.

However, guests representing commercial enterprises may certainly appear on the station. It is appropriate, for instance, for a local travel agent to discuss travel in mainland China or for the proprietor of a health food store to present opinions on nutrition. And, obviously, many personalities on the talk show circuit have something to sell—a book, a movie, a sporting event, a philosophy and so on. Some mention of the individual's reason for appearing is appropriate because it establishes the guest's credentials. An apt reference might be, "Our subject today is solar energy, and our guest is John Smith, author of a new book entitled, *The Many Uses of the Sun.*"

To summarize, two criteria should govern the booking of all guests:

1. The guest must contribute to building or maintaining audience.

2. Neither the station nor any individual in the station's employ may benefit from the appearance of the guest unless the remuneration is properly accounted for, and commercial references are logged and announced.

ON-AIR TECHNIQUES

Call-in programs are the backbone of talk radio. The **call screener** (or producer) is a vital part of the talk radio staff because this person serves as the center who delivers the ball, in the form of the telephone call, to the on-the-air quarterback.

Telephone Screeners

Screeners add substantially to station budgets, but only through careful screening can a station control its programming. Airing "cold" or unscreened calls can be compared to a disc jockey reaching blindly into the music library and airing the first record that comes to hand. Few programmers would relinquish control in that manner. The telephone call represents the playlist of talk radio.

The screener constantly manipulates the line-up of incoming calls, giving priority to a more appropriate caller and delaying or eliminating callers of presumably lesser interest. The situation changes constantly as new calls come in, and the good screener orchestrates them to provide the most appealing program for the listener. If, for instance, the subject under discussion is the city fire department, and ten callers are standing by when the fire chief calls, the chief's call obviously should move to the front of the pack and air at the first opportunity.

The screener filters out the "regulars" that call the station too frequently as well as drunks and others unable to make a coherent contribution. Callers thus dismissed and those asked to hold for long periods often complain of unjust treatment, but the screener must prevail, insisting on the right to structure the best possible sequence of talk. Effective screeners perform their jobs with tact and graciousness.

When screeners must dump a caller, they say something like "I'm sorry, your call doesn't fit into the programming we're doing at the moment, but thank you for calling."

Most stations prohibit the use of the caller's full name to forestall imposters, callers identifying themselves as prominent people in a community and then airing false statements to embarrass the individuals they claim to be.

When a program depends on callers, what happens in those nightmare moments when there are none? For just this emergency, most talk show hosts maintain a clipping file containing newspaper and magazine articles they have saved from their general reading to provide the background for monologues when no calls come in. Another strategy is the "expert phone list." A list of ten or twenty professionals with expertise in subjects of broad appeal should yield at least one or two able to speak by phone when the host needs to fill time to sustain a program.

Screening Systems

Various systems are used for the screener to signal to the on-air host which incoming call has been screened and is to be aired next (see Figure 17-2 for call screener's equipment). Most talk stations now utilize computers, and some stations have even developed their own software for this function, although appropriate programs are now sold commercially. Using computers places greater control of the program in the hands of the on-air host. The computer display indicates the nature of the calls prepared for airing so the host can alter the complexion of the program by orchestrating the order of calls. Usually the information displayed for the host includes the first name, approximate age and sex of the caller and may specify the point the caller wishes to discuss. Frequently the display includes material of practical conversational value such as the current weather forecast. (See Figure 17-3 for a host's computer display.) Hosts often use a timer to monitor the length of calls. Many hosts cut a caller off, as politely as possible after 1½ to 2 minutes (3 minutes tops).

Delay

All talk stations use a device (usually an electronic digital delay unit) to delay programming a few seconds between the studio and the transmitter to "dump" profanity, personal attacks and other unairable matter. The on-air host generally controls a "cut button" that diverts offensive program material, although the engineer should have a back-up switch.

Because the program is delayed (generally four to seven seconds before it reaches the air), the screener instructs all callers to turn off their radios before talking on the air. Failing this, callers hear their voices coming back at them after some seconds delay and cannot carry on a conversation. Listening only on the telephone, they hear the real-time program material and can talk normally with the host.

FIGURE 17-2. Call Screener's Equipment. Photo courtesy of David Graves, WIND Talk Radio 56, Chicago.

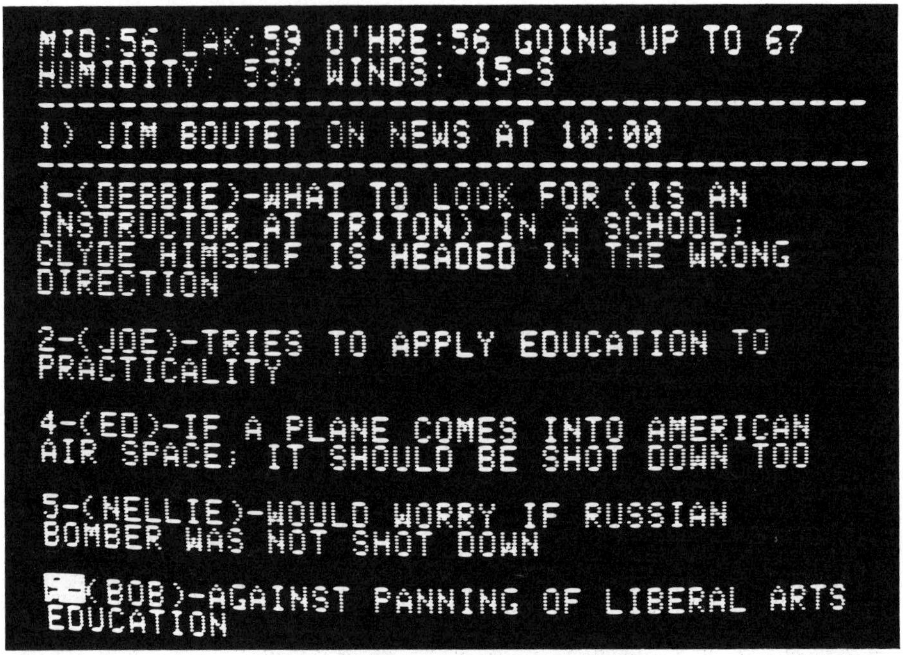

FIGURE 17-3. Screen of a Host's Computer Display. Photo courtesy of David Graves, WIND Talk Radio 56, Chicago.

Electronic Logs

Most talk stations consider a round-the-clock, tape-recorded log a necessity. Such a log allows the station to retrieve and reconstruct precisely what was said on the air in the event of threatened legal action. These tapes are made on special slow-speed monitoring recorders running at $^{15}/_{32}$-inches per second; a tape then lasts for 12 hours. The program can be recorded on one track while a telephone company time check is recorded on the second track, thus providing the exact time of all on-air events. Such tapes were recognized as official FCC master logs and, although the FCC no longer requires them, should be kept for at least three years.

Access to these log tapes by outside parties should be limited to those with a bona fide need. Many stations require a written request that is examined by the station's legal counsel before the station complies. Such tapes have been requested as evidence in litigation not involving the radio station but concerning guests that have appeared on the station. In such cases, many stations require the tapes be subpoenaed. Law enforcement agencies may also request access to log tapes. The Los Angeles Police Department once requested KABC's aid in establishing the exact time a play occurred in a baseball game it aired, which helped them pinpoint the precise time of a crime. The station, of course, granted access to the tapes for that purpose.

CONTROVERSY, FAIRNESS AND PRESSURE

Although talk radio programmers get many opportunities for creative ...sion, they also must devote considerable time to administration. Because the station deals almost constantly with public affairs issues, its programmers spot-monitor the station's programs for compliance with FCC rules such as the fairness doctrine and equal time for political candidates, and to avoid legal pitfalls such as libel. A programmer, however, having many other duties as well, rarely knows as much about the minute-by-minute program as heavy listeners. Therefore, back-up systems must be established.

Fairness Doctrine

Compliance with the FCC fairness doctrine occurs naturally and without the program director's daily evaluation as long as the on-air personality's calls actively represent a broad cross-section of divergent points of view. Caller input presents a whole range of opinions that add to those of the guest and host. Over the period of a month or two, so many points of view are presented on a single talk station that it is impossible to identify any facet of an issue that has not been covered.

Nonetheless, management must maintain a reporting system to ensure compliance with the doctrine. The program director, acting for management and the licensee, must be able to document full and fair coverage of controversial issues. The following steps ensure compliance:

1. Indoctrinating on-air talent when they join the station staff including reading a primer prepared by the station's legal counsel on this and all legal restrictions.

2. Annual meetings with the on-air staff to reinforce the FCC requirements. (Some station staffs meet every other month or more often.)

3. Monitoring the station's output to detect uncovered points of view or personal attacks.

4. Summarizing in writing the subjects covered on each program and which sides of issues were discussed.

Almost without exception, when an outside party charges the *well-pro-grammed* talk station with failure to adhere to the fairness doctrine, the station, using program reports or tape logs, can prove that all sides of controversial issues have been aired.

All stations conducting live on-air programs have detailed policies governing call-ins and on-air interviews. The self-regulatory ethical codes of professional organizations such as the Radio-Television News Directors Association (RTNDA) apply to their members although the NAB Radio Code no longer exists.

Public and Private Pressure

Talk stations frequently find themselves the targets of pressure groups, activist organizations and political parties trying to gain as much free access to the station's airtime as they can. Although most partisans deserve some time on the station, management must turn away those seeking inordinate amounts of time.

Political parties are well aware of the impact of talk stations and have been known to organize volunteers to monitor programs and flood the incoming phone lines with a single point of view. Politicians seeking airtime have sometimes misused the fairness doctrine. These partisans confuse it with the equal-time provision for political candidates—sometimes through ignorance, at other times to confuse the program executive.

For example, in the late 1970s, a national group opposing the use of nuclear power objected to a statement Ronald Reagan made on his nationally syndicated radio commentary. They claimed personal attack on the integrity of one of their members, Daniel Ellsberg, and demanded equal time on his behalf from all stations that carried the original commentary. They submitted to the stations a tape-recorded comment of about seven minutes duration, presenting their organization's antinuclear position.

The group demanded "equal time" although in fact the issue involved a personal attack on a single individual who was not a political candidate. One station (KABC) disregarded the demand for time and instead scheduled an interview with Ellsberg. Because he is a well-known and controversial figure, the discussion was lively and informative, covering a wide range of topics. Notably, he declined to reopen the subject about which the personal attack had been claimed. Instead, he waived in writing any claim to further time to dispute the issue.

Because an effective talk station frequently deals with controversial issues, its management can expect threats of all kinds from irate audience members. A provoked listener will demand anything from a retraction to equal time and, on occasion, will support such demands with threats of legal action. Such threatened lawsuits usually vanish, however, when management explains the relevant broadcast law to the complainant. When the station is even slightly in the wrong, it is usually quick to provide rebuttal time to an overlooked point of view.

Often the issue that draws the audience's wrath is not a serious, controversial subject but a frivolous one. One recent statement that drew many shouts of righteous indignation was a Los Angeles sportscaster's opinion that Notre Dame's basketball team was superior to UCLA's. That remark drew phone calls and letters demanding the statement be retracted and the sportscaster discharged. Such teapot-sized tempests, although not serious, make demands on the time of talk programmers.

THE COST AND THE REWARD

By the mid-1980s, many stations had shifted from limited-appeal talk to broader audience appeal by switching from a caller-orientation to a listener-orientation. Talk radio programmers realized that listeners would tune out a poor phone call just as they would a weak record on a music station. Station programmers therefore began controlling the on-air subject matter and the flow of program material in preference to letting callers dictate the programming. By 1983, the talk stations with the highest ratings had adopted the strategy of focusing on the needs of the listeners, not the wants of the callers. The talk host that in the past had generated telephone calls because of an argumentative personality or an "over-the-back-fence" nature was replaced or redirected toward informational radio programming. Interviews with knowledgeable people replaced random phone calls, and programmers targeted specific demographic groups when choosing subject matter and determining the amount of time to devote to each topic. The strategy, then, became listener-orientation through informational programming. At its best, talk radio now focuses on content quality and depth of coverage, not on stimulating outrageous comments.

A primary ingredient in the recipe for success in any talk format is commitment at the top—at the station management level. A timely and innovative music format can catapult a station from obscurity to the number one ranking during a single rating period. Talk stations and all-news stations, however, generally take years to reach their potential. But once success is achieved, the talk station enjoys a listener loyalty that endures while the more fickle music audience shifts from station to station in search of the hits. High figures for time-spent-listening and long-term stability in cumulative ratings demonstrate audience loyalty. (See Chapter 2 on radio ratings to review these measurements.)

The talk station producing a significant amount of local programming generally is more costly to operate than a music operation. Good talk personalities are often higher paid than disc jockeys, and they must be supported by producers, call screeners and, frequently, extra administrative personnel. Salaries of talk hosts vary a great deal, of course, from city to city. Some, in smaller markets, earn $20,000–$30,000 while major market personalities are paid as much as $200,000. Screener and producer positions are often entry-level jobs paying the minimum wage or just above, but they offer an opportunity to enter the industry and acquire experience.

The talk radio station of the 1980s combines news and conversation formats in a blend of programming characterized by live interviews, telephone actualities and on-air audience feedback. It has great journalistic flexibility and local responsiveness but will continue to be known best for its colorful host personalities.

SUMMARY

Talk radio varies from station to station in the proportions of live call-in programs, on-air interviews and news. In addition to the now classic *Larry King Show* Mutual distributes, local stations have recently acquired national programming from such sources as NBC's TALKNET, ABC's TALKRADIO and other networks and syndicators. One key to effective, live talk programming is the on-air personality who may introduce journalistic bias into programs but stimulates loyal listening. Most talk radio targets an audience of prime interest to advertisers, although the station must rigidly control content to avoid attracting too large a proportion of older listeners. In-person and telephone guests and callers supply the content for talk radio, and the screener plays a pivotal role in structuring the flow of call-in programs. Talk radio has become listener- rather than caller-oriented, striving for a broad appeal through general informational programming, but any controversial coverage will always generate public and private pressures on the station. In such cases, detailed, written station policies and electronic logs provide the best offense and defense for the talk programmer.

Notes

[1]Beginning in 1983, a 90-minute version of *The Larry King Show* was produced for television and syndicated to television stations to fill their overnight hours. Using three 30-minutes interviews, it includes a short call-in segment at the end. The television version is produced by Post-Newsweek and distributed by MCA. Within months of its announcement, the program was sold to 79 stations representing 72 percent coverage of television markets. "Mutual's Larry King: Five Years of Questions and He's Still Curious," *Broadcasting*, 7 February 1983, p. 103.

[2]Station policies differ on the degree to which hosts can be involved in commercials. Many individuals fear losing their journalistic credibility, and personalities known for their balance want to avoid a persuasive role. Ironically, it is the outspoken advocate host who often makes the most appealing salesperson.

Selected Sources

Broughton, Irv. *The Art of Interviewing for Television, Radio and Film.* Blue Ridge Summit, Pennsylvania: TAB Books, 1981.

FCC Sensitivity Training Guide for TV Program Directors. Washington, D.C.: National Association of Broadcasters, 1979.

King, Larry. *Larry King.* New York: Simon and Schuster, 1982.

"The Many Faces of Format." *Religious Broadcasting* (September 1982): 24–26.

Sterman, Art. "A Look at KABC/ABC TALKRADIO." *Broadcast Engineering* (July 1982): 51–59.

Tramer, Harriet, and Jeffries, Leo W. "Talk Radio—Forum and Companion." *Journal of Broadcasting* 27 (Summer 1983): 297–300.

PART FIVE

Public Broadcasting Strategies

Part V steps away from the commercial perspective on programming to examine the strategies operating in national and local public broadcasting. This part includes two chapters on **noncommercial television** and one on **noncommercial radio** programming. Noncommercial or public stations differ from their commercial counterparts in their lack of uniformity in means of support. This varied support affects both national programming for PBS and NPR member-stations and individual station strategies. As with commercial broadcasters and cablecasters, how the public station pays its way limits the programmer's options even as technological advances expand them. The chapters in this section follow the pattern of considering evaluation, selection and scheduling of programs as the major elements of the programmer's job.

Chapter 18 introduces the **national network** perspective on noncommercial television. The author examines the philosophical contradictions operating within the Public Broadcasting Service and the means for resolving them in a national core schedule of promotable prime-time programs. The chapter shows how the national schedule of satellite-delivered programs is achieved and how national commercial ratings are adapted to meet the purposes of public broadcasting. Public television's audience characteristics are discussed in light of its philosophical goals and financial needs. This chapter raises many of the controversial issues affecting noncommercial programming and shows how economic pressure is forcing public broadcasting to make use of many commercial strategies.

Chapter 19 turns to the local public **television station** to analyze the programming effects of different types of public licensees. It shows how the philosophies of the nearly 300 public stations arise from their means of economic support and how these philosophies in turn affect their programming. It analyzes how public station programmers learn about their audiences. The authors then describe the various program sources for public television and list the main scheduling priorities for most public television stations. It concludes by examining competing perspectives on counterprogramming strategy for public television.

Chapter 20 deals with **noncommercial radio station** programming strategy. Out of nearly 10,000 radio stations, approximately half AM and half FM, about 1,300 are noncommercial—nearly all FM broadcasters.

Public radio occurs in seven basic formats, and stations may be affiliated with one or more networks or independent. Satellite transmission has changed public radio's structure by making new networks possible and stimulating program syndication. The author shows how the technological changes that have profoundly affected commercial radio syndication are affecting public radio. The author then uses the example of KUSC's rise as a case study illustrating station programming strategy for public radio. The chapter considers the sources of public radio programs, the effects of various methods of placing programs in the schedule and the procedures for evaluating public radio programming.

Part V, then, examines the noncommercial side of broadcasting. It draws analogies with the commercial world and points out distinctions and similarities in programming strategies. The book concludes with an afterword by Sydney W. Head on how proliferation, synthesis and convergence among technologies are affecting broadcasting, cable and new media and will change programming in the 1980s and 1990s.

CHAPTER EIGHTEEN

National Public Television

John W. Fuller

A QUICK GUIDE TO CHAPTER EIGHTEEN

JOHN W. FULLER,   *associate director of research at PBS, came to the national noncommercial network in 1980 from the position of research project manager at Arbitron in Laurel, Maryland. He started in television as studio director of WJKS-TV in Jacksonville, Florida, in 1966, moving to promotion manager in 1968. From 1972 to 1976 he was research director and program manager for WTLV-TV in Jacksonville. He went to Arbitron in 1976. He holds a B.A. in radio-television from Florida State University and an M.A. from the University of Florida in communications research. S. Anders Yokom, Jr., author of the first edition's chapter on national public television, asked John Fuller to make a fresh start on the subject because the national situation changed markedly in the last four years, and this chapter shows Mr. Fuller's intimate knowledge of the current issues in noncommercial broadcasting.*

THE PROGRAMMING ENVIRONMENT

This chapter deals with **national** perspectives on public television. (Local station programming options and regional network offerings are explored in the following chapter.) This chapter covers the similarities and differences between commercial and public television and the special character of the responsibilities and pressures in public broadcasting. The chapter then addresses scheduling issues raised by the special circumstances of member control of the public network and, lastly, analyzes the problems in applying the national commercial ratings to national public television. Programming the national public broadcasting service is a little like trying to prepare a universally acclaimed gourmet meal. The trouble is that a committee of 160 plans the menu, and the people that pay the grocery bills want to be sure the meal is served with due regard for their images. Some people coming to the dinner table want the meal to be enjoyable and fun; others want the experience to be uplifting and enlightening; still others insist that the eating be instructive; and the seafood and chicken cooks want to be sure the audience comes away with a better understanding of the problems of life under water and in the coop.

The analogies are not far-fetched. A board of 35 appointed and elected representatives of its member stations governs the Public Broadcasting Service. The board is expected to serve some 160 public television licensees operating 300 public (PTV) stations all over the country and in such remote areas as Guam, American Samoa and Bethel, Alaska. Since PBS produces no programming, it uses a host of program suppliers and tries to promote and schedule their programs effectively. In addition, constituencies ranging from independent producers to minority groups constantly pressure public television to meet their special needs. And, of course, the program funders have their own agendas too.

THE NETWORK MODEL

A national, commercial, American television network, as generally understood, acts as a centralized programming, sales and distributing agent for its affiliates, program suppliers and clients (advertisers). A commercial network supplies about 60 percent of an affiliate's entire program service, and the affiliate gets paid for the time it makes available. Commercial affiliates have little voice in choosing the network programs they air or the way they are scheduled. The commercial network's great strength lies in its ability to program some 200 television stations simultaneously with a lineup of popular programs that the network itself either produces or, more commonly, commissions for production, usually under its close supervision. As important as the network programmers' choice of individual programs is their expertise in melding them into a sequence that holds the attention of national audiences.

How closely does the Public Broadcasting Service conform to this model? In commercial television, programming and money flow from network headquarters to affiliates. Production is centrally controlled and distributed on a one-way line to affiliates, paid to push the network button and transmit what the network feeds. Most of the economic incentives favor affiliate cooperation with the network, placing tremendous programming power in network hands.

In public television, money flows the opposite way. Instead of being paid as loyal affiliates, member stations pay PBS dues. PBS in turn supplies them with programs sufficient to fill only 4 to 11 P.M. weekdays and 8 to 11 P.M. on Sundays. No regular PBS service airs on Saturday. Morning and late-night PBS programs are available on a user-pays basis to stations desiring them. A station's remaining broadcast hours are typically filled with leased syndicated fare (movies, off-network reruns, made-for-syndication series), local productions and selections regional public television networks offer.

Four regional networks are headquartered in and serve the eastern, southern, central and western sections of the United States. One, the Eastern Educational Network, formed the Interregional Program Service in 1980 to distribute its programs nationally. It now serves a large group of stations in all regions, functioning as a second major PTV distributor. The parallel between the regional networks and PBS is strong: Member stations pay a regional network dues, and it then delivers programs to them. PBS, however, delivers its programs in a prearranged schedule whereas the regional networks distribute their programs during off-hours via satellite for local taping and scheduling.

Clout with PBS, then, rests with the stations. They spend their revenues as they see fit, expecting to be treated fairly and with the deference due any consumer. PBS, as a consequence, has a limited ability to get stations to agree on program scheduling. Quite naturally, local station managers display considerable scheduling independence. After the multi-transponder satellite system was phased in during 1978 and as low-cost recording equipment became available to the stations, they carried the PBS schedule less and less frequently as originally programmed. Until a networking agreement (the **common carriage** agreement) was worked out with the stations in 1979, no two station program schedules were alike. National promotion, publicity and advertising placement were, if not impossible, extremely difficult to achieve.

Implementing the common carriage agreement in October 1979 partially ordered this networking chaos. The nonbinding agreement, in effect to this day, established a **core** schedule on Sunday, Monday, Tuesday and Wednesday nights. During the hours of 8–10 P.M., PBS feeds its best programs (providing delayed feeds for the Central, Mountain and Pacific time zones) (see Figure 18-1). In turn, stations committed themselves to airing the PBS core offerings (1) on the night they were fed, (2) in the order fed and (3) within the prime-time hours of 8 to 11 P.M. Some flexibility remained in station hands; if desired, stations could tape and air the two-hour core feed from 7 to 9 P.M. instead of 8 to 10 P.M.

Common carriage has worked well. In its first four years, audiences grew at a faster rate than ever before, advertising efforts flourished, and **underwriter** (program-funder) interest increased, all because station line-ups stabilized on core nights. As of 1983 over 80 percent of the member stations telecast the PBS core programs at the time they were actually fed.

Programs fed on noncore nights, however, tend to receive pre-1979 treatment. Noncore programs get live carriage (telecast when PBS feeds the program) less than 40 percent of the time. However, those noncore programs with proven popularity such as *Sneak Previews, Mystery!, Washington Week in Review* and *Wall Street Week* routinely air as fed on 50–80 percent of the system's 293 satellite-interconnected stations. Station program managers commonly tape delay programs with limited appeal and air them in early fringe or weekend daytime slots, using the vacated prime-time slots for station-acquired programming.

PBS RESPONSIBILITIES

Since its founding, PBS has had two undisputed responsibilities: to carry or reject programs offered for national distribution and to schedule available programming. The program acceptance/rejection responsibility is grounded in the technical and legal standards the membership voted during the 1970s. The technical standards protect stations from Federal Communications Commission violations and maintain high levels of video and audio quality. By their very nature, they can be applied with reasonable consistency. The legal standards protect stations from libel and rights infringements and alert them to equal time and fairness doctrine obligations that may result from PBS-distributed programs. As the steward for underwriting guidelines, PBS's legal department also established the form for on-air crediting of PBS program funders.

Program Scheduling Task

Scheduling responsibility rests with the PBS Program Department, which develops strategies, and Program Operations, which manages the daily details of the national schedule much as a traffic department would at a commercial station. Program Operations must plug all the pieces of the jigsaw puzzle into place across the three satellite transponders, seeing to it that when an 11-episode series ends, another is ready to occupy its slot; when a drama has profanity, an edited feed of it is available; when the Saturday morning schedule of how-to programs runs short, a forgotten cooking series is resurrected to fill out the summer; and so on.

A senior vice-president heads the PBS Program Department, whose concerns include the long-range development of major program series and supervision of

PBS FALL '83 PROJECTED SCHEDULE
Week-at-a-Glance

	Sunday	Monday	Tuesday	Wednesday	Thursday	Friday	Saturday
4:00	AMERICAN INTERESTS	SESAME STREET (rpt)					UNDERSTAND HUMAN BEHAVIOR (rpt)
	THE COMPUTER PROGRAMME (rpt)						UNDERSTAND HUMAN BEHAVIOR (rpt)
5:00	THE ART OF BEING HUMAN (R)	MISTER ROGERS' NEIGHBORHOOD (rpt)					BUSINESS OF MANAGEMENT (rpt)
	THE ART OF BEING HUMAN (R)	THE ELECTRIC COMPANY (rpt)					BUSINESS OF MANAGEMENT (rpt)
6:00	BRADSHAW ON THE EIGHT STAGES OF MAN	THE MACNEIL LEHRER NEWSHOUR					MATINEE AT THE BIJOU / FOC. ON SOC. (rpt)
	NEWTON'S APPLE (rpt)						FOC. ON SOC. (rpt)
7:00	INSIDE BUSINESS TODAY						NEWTON'S APPLE
	ISRAELI DIARY						MOVING RIGHT ALONG
8:00	NATURE	THE OIL KINGDOMS / THE MAKING OF A CONTINENT / TBA	NOVA	SPECIALS	SNEAK PREVIEWS	WASHINGTON WEEK IN REVIEW	PBS DARK
					WILD AMERICA	WALL $TREET WEEK	
9:00	MASTERPIECE THEATRE	GREAT PERFORMANCES	VIETNAM: A TELEVISION HISTORY		INSIDE STORY	DINNER AT JULIA'S	
					THE NEW TECH TIMES	INTERNATIONAL EDITION	
10:00	RAPHAEL / SILKSCREEN SOUNDINGS / TBA		SPECIALS	SPECIALS	THE LAWMAKERS	FIRING LINE	
					TONY BROWN'S JOURNAL		
11:00	THE DICK CAVETT SHOW (R)						
	LATENIGHT AMERICA						
12:00							

Shaded area is the Sun.–Wed. core. SOURCE: Public Broadcasting Service, used with permission.

FIGURE 18-1. Core Lineup for One Week

the PBS National Program Service (4–11 P.M. Monday–Friday and 8–11 P.M. Sunday). Other executives concerned with program administration, development and acquisition assist this vice-president. Subdivisions within the department concentrate on the acquiring and scheduling of specialized program forms such as news and public affairs, children's shows, cultural productions and minority-interest programming. One subdivision, Station Program Services, offers feeds of daytime and late-fringe programs on a user-pays basis. An entirely separate department, Educational Services, provides a schedule of instructional programs for in-school use and a selection of adult education courses for home study.

PBS Fund-Raising Assistance

Through it all, one enormously successful PBS activity is its Station Independence Program (SIP), a division in PBS's Development Department, that helps stations conduct on-air fund-raising appeals. The stations pay PBS dues for this fund-raising assistance. A key SIP service is consulting with the PBS Program Department on the acquisition, funding and commissioning of special programs for use during local station pledge drives. Mass-appeal programming with emotional payoff—such as heavy dramatic impact, warmly received performances, emotionally charged documentary subjects—seems to work best.

PROGRAM SOURCES FOR PBS

PBS has developed its own pattern of dramatic miniseries and anthologies, science and nature documentaries, concert performances, public affairs documentaries and a few other types—none of which the commercial networks offer on a regular basis. British programs such as *Masterpiece Theater* and *The Shakespeare Plays* appear on American public television because they are available, high-quality programs at one-tenth the cost of producing comparable fare in the United States. Very few government or commercial institutions in the United States have the financial resources and willingness to see major program ideas through from conception to broadcast. That power does exist in a handful of places, all of which compete with one another for people and production resources and, within PBS, for national attention. But PBS lacks the unified national authority necessary for coordinated planning.

PBS programmers must balance program types. Unlike the program chiefs at ABC, CBS and NBC, PBS cannot simply order pilots, choose those with promise, then send production companies scurrying to produce what has been chosen. In theory, it should be possible to develop a national program schedule by aggregating licensee needs. The programming needs common to the greatest number of stations would determine what programs were proposed, funded and produced. They would be delivered at times when the maximum number of stations could take them off-line (i.e., off the satellite) to best serve their local audiences. Many programs could have educational components built in and ancillary print material produced for distribution when the programs are released. The national schedule could be balanced to ensure that no major programming areas (such as news and current affairs) were neglected and to assure no surfeit of specific content forms (such as televised performances by symphony orchestras). What in fact happens is not controlled by PBS programmers. They must choose among those programs producing stations and independent producers offer them.

Most programs PBS distributes are someone else's idea and someone else's creation. PBS cannot schedule what the producers do not produce. The producers are not bound by any set of national programming priorities. They produce whatever their analyses, instincts and funding dictate. In practice, they produce what the various funders are willing to fund.

The major producers have portfolios of program ideas that they constantly shop around to potential funders. The few ideas that do get funded become the programs presented to PBS for the national schedule. The programs are *not* produced to play a part in a national plan addressing a particular philosophy and set of objectives. By haphazard means and some aggressiveness on the part of the producers, they get produced.

STATION PROGRAM COOPERATIVE

But productions that come in "over the transom" (fully underwritten) are not the only source for the PBS schedule. The Station Program Cooperative (SPC) is another source. PBS funds and manages the SPC, in which most public stations participate. The participants meet every October at the PBS Program Fair to screen some 50-odd programs, many of which are program pilots, and to hear producers of long-running series plead the case for refunding their shows. Afterward, several rounds of voting are held to winnow out the affordable programs, the final round occurring in late winter (usually February). The "winning" producers are notified, and the rush begins to complete episodes in time for the fall PBS premieres.

Out of this process a slate evolves of some 25–30 programs for which the stations pay.[1] Its beauty as an avenue to additional program sources is that the SPC funds programs unattractive to or too controversial for underwriters—investigative news documentaries, children's series, minority programs—and so restores some balance to the national program schedule. However, SPC's electorate uses the democratic voting process and in consequence, chooses conservatively, tending to refinance long-running series again and again and to bypass untried program ideas.

CONSTRAINTS ON THE NATIONAL SCHEDULE

The PBS Program Department thus receives programs from two major sources: the stations and independent producers. The results of the SPC determine most of PBS's options. And with program selection comes pressure from producers for the best scheduling positions.

Corporate Pressure

Most programs PBS distributes enter the system via a station that develops, produces and finally delivers its program to the Washington PBS headquarters (hence, a variety of station credits appear fore and aft PBS programs). Local station producers often have corporate underwriters that actively participate in program production or purchase programs outright. Corporate executives in charge of underwriting invest not only prodigious sums from corporate treasuries but also personal effort and reputation, and they feel entitled to choice slots in the prime-time schedule—invariably, during the core period. Of course, PBS cannot fit in all such programs and maintain a balanced schedule.[2] A fully funded series must be played off, however, within and only within the underwriting corporation's fiscal year irrespective of audience response and schedule needs if the corporation is to receive a tax break. Because money flows into PBS rather than out, PBS program executives wield almost no power, and usually must acquiesce to corporate demands.

The major producing stations, too, attempt to influence program decisions at PBS; for some, financial stability depends on preserving the income from their underwriters. Underwriter funding pays for salaries, equipment loans and other production expenses for turning out programs seeking systemwide distribution. Were a major underwriter to withdraw support, the financial effect on the station might be devastating.

Member Pressure

Other programming pressures occur. Many stations, for example, may refuse to telecast a program at the time fed because they feel it (1) does not deserve a prime-time slot, (2) contains too much profanity or violence to air in early evening, (3) will fail to attract contributors at fund-raising time, (4) occupies a slot the stations want for their own programs or syndication purchases or (5) has no appeal for local viewers. PBS program executives assembling a schedule must anticipate these problems to minimize defections from the live feed.

Program Rights and Delivery

PBS programmers must also wrestle with two problems common to both commercial and noncommercial programming: program rights and late delivery. In public television as in commercial television, standard program air-lease rights are set by contract with the producer, who owns the rights. PBS has traditionally negotiated with producers for as many plays as possible so that by airing the same program several times the typically small (per-airing) PBS audience snowballs. Extra plays also fill out the program schedule. At the same time, the program syndicator seeks as few airings as possible over the shortest time period to retain maximum control and revenue potential for a program. A compromise between various producers and PBS permitting four program plays within three years is now the standard rights agreement in public television. To fully amortize an underwriter's investment, PBS must therefore shoehorn programs into fewer seasons (three) than airplays (four).

Late delivery has obvious trouble-making possibilities. So many productions were behind schedule in 1981 that the fall schedule premiered without a single new series. As a consequence, in that extraordinary year, the "second season" premieres in January 1982 were so choked with overdue new programs that the popular *Mystery!* series had to be popped out and shelved until the following fall!

NATIONAL SCHEDULING STRATEGY

How, with so many conflicting interests and confounding considerations, can a national scheduling strategy emerge? In truth, none can, at least not in the fashion of commercial broadcasting, which allows network programmers to assemble their schedules, program by program, for maximum audience impact. In spite of the PBS program department's herculean efforts to hammer out a schedule for fall, for winter or for summer each year, what finally emerges is a monument to compromise and appeasement. Agreeing on program schedules requires a round of marathon meetings with the research and program operations departments, accompanied by meetings with producers, meetings with station executives, countless phone calls and assorted conversations over lunch and dinner. After all interested parties have been heard from, one or two programs may actually remain where the programmers had initially scheduled them.

Nowadays, PBS programmers want to maximize audiences. Gone are the educational television days when paying attention to audience size was looked upon as "whoring after numbers." The prevailing attitude at PBS recognizes that a program must be seen to be of value, and that improper scheduling prevents full realization of a program's potential. Member stations now recognize that bigger audiences also mean a bigger dollar take during on-air pledge drives.

Still, opportunities occur throughout the year when the programmers and research people can put their heads together to solve scheduling problems one at a time, removed from the charged atmosphere attending fall scheduling meetings. The PBS program department does act alone sometimes, adding or subtracting from the schedule, reversing program order and so on; and at those times, scheduling strategies come into play.

Counterprogramming the Commercial Networks

Competition, of course, is a key consideration. The three ways of responding to it are offensively (attempting to overpower the competitor), defensively (counterprogramming for a different segment of the audience than the competitor's program is likely to attract), or by ignoring the competition altogether and hoping for the best. PBS has never been able to go on the offensive; its programs lack the requisite breadth of appeal. Prime-time PBS shows in midwinter, for example, average a 3 rating. ABC, CBS and NBC regularly collect ratings of 15–25 and sometimes higher. (ABC's *The Thorn Birds* in March 1983, for example, averaged 42 rating points.)

PBS, then, must duck and dodge. By studying national Nielsen data, programmers learn the demographic make-up of competing network program audiences so they can place their own programs more advantageously. For example, a symphony performance that tends to attract well-educated women over 50 living in metropolitan areas would perform well opposite *The Dukes of Hazzard* or *CHiPs*, having downscale (lower socioeconomic) audiences. Similarly, in searching for a slot for the investigative documentary series *Frontline*, PBS did not consider for a moment the 8–9 P.M. slot on Sundays because football overruns frequently push *60 Minutes* into this slot.

PBS tries to avoid placing a valued program against a hit series in the commercial schedules. Pressure to avoid these situations frequently comes from individual program producers. PBS also has traditionally avoided placing important programs during the three key all-market audience-measurement periods (sweeps) in November, February and May—times when commercial television throws its blockbusters at the audience. Recently, however, PBS has revised this strategy, acknowledging the value of ratings. Since the public television stations are also measured during the sweeps for all time periods and for the all important cumulative audiences reached over a week (cumes), the major public stations demand priority programming. As one PBS programmer put it, "When they announce the start of the contest, that is hardly the time to head for the sidelines." Ratings periods now display PBS's best—not weakest—programs, and this fresh approach has paid off. Recent audience figures show a rise in public television viewing.

Bridging

Another competitive strategy PBS uses is **bridging**. Most viewers stay with a program from start to finish. A lengthy program prevents an audience from switching to the competition's programs at the time where one network's programs end and others begin (crossover points). This strategy can be applied offensively or defensively. PBS generally defends. For example, all three commercial networks air one-hour programs in the 8–9 P.M. period every night thus bridging any PBS show scheduled at 8:30 by eliminating the 8:30 crossover point. Were PBS to schedule a pair of half-hour shows in the 8–9 P.M. period, the 8:30 program would draw away very little of the network audience. Viewers of the hypothetical 8:30 PBS program would have to flow out of the lead-in program or come from homes where the television set had just been turned on at 8:30. At times, however, PBS *avoids* being bridged. For example, in the fall of 1983, all three commercial networks began shows at 9:00 P.M. every night of the week. PBS's *Life of Verdi* starts at this time too but bridges CBS at 9:30 and 10 P.M. (see Figure 18-2).

Otherwise, PBS counters the commercial networks simply by scheduling according to their general scheduling patterns. If two of the commercial networks have long-form nights (nights with two-hour movies or specials running 9 to 11 P.M., (EST), PBS may schedule its own long-form programming opposite. The theory holds that when two of the networks tie up audiences from 9 to 11, no viewers are released to come to public television for a program starting at 9:30 or 10. Since all of the commercial networks break every night at 9, the PBS schedule does too, in the hope that if any dial twisting occurs at 9, some of the viewers might come to public television.

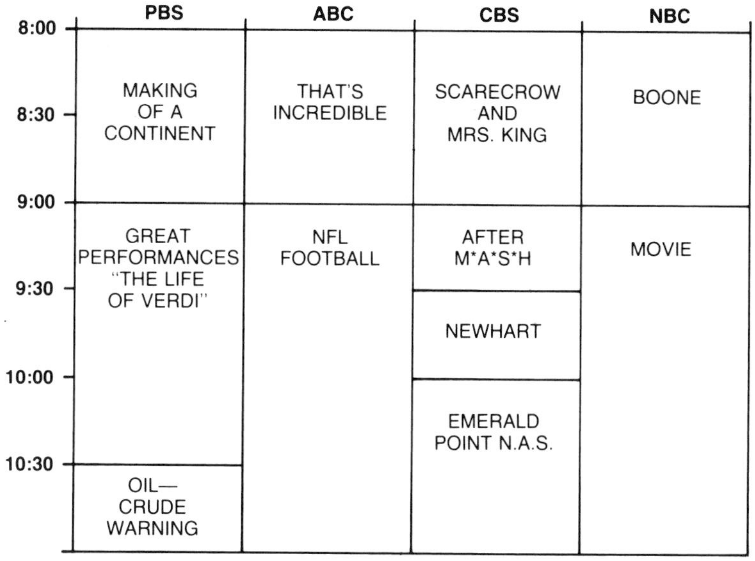

	PBS	ABC	CBS	NBC
8:00				
8:30	MAKING OF A CONTINENT	THAT'S INCREDIBLE	SCARECROW AND MRS. KING	BOONE
9:00				
9:30	GREAT PERFORMANCES "THE LIFE OF VERDI"	NFL FOOTBALL	AFTER M*A*S*H	MOVIE
			NEWHART	
10:00				
			EMERALD POINT N.A.S.	
10:30	OIL— CRUDE WARNING			

FIGURE 18-2. Illustration of Bridging at 9:30 and 10:00

Audience Flow in the Core Schedule

Certain PBS series are especially dependent on audience flow from a strong lead-in. The anthology drama series *American Playhouse,* presenting an entirely different cast and story from the week before, cannot build a loyal following the way a predictable series such as *Sneak Previews* can. Thus, a healthy series should precede it. *NOVA* has supplied an effective lead-in for *American Playhouse. NOVA,* with its reputation for well-crafted science investigations, draws large audiences almost any place it is scheduled, and thus has no particular need for a strong lead-in. Nor would a heavily advertised *National Geographic Special.*

PBS gains an advantage on nights or in periods when commercial television is not at its competitive best. One such night occurs every two years in November during national elections. While ABC, CBS and NBC are busy seeking every last ratings point from their simultaneous election coverage, public television and independent stations have a rare opportunity to score with counter-programming.

National Promotion

A fledgling program needs help for viewers to discover it. Two forms of help, advertising and promotion, can alert potential viewers to a new program and persuade them to try it. Unfortunately, public television budgets rarely permit advertising, although major underwriters now include some promotional allotment in most program budgets. *National Geographic Special* is one such case.

Still another PBS strategy is to schedule on-air promotion for its programming on nights having the greatest number of viewers. Since HUTs (households using television) are highest on Sunday nights, and *Masterpiece Theater* (which has traditionally done well in audience size by public television standards) has played on Sunday nights since its premiere, PBS takes this opportunity to promote core programs scheduled later in the week.

NATIONAL AUDIENCE RATINGS

Careful scheduling is necessary because public television must always demonstrate its utility. Many have contributed to its continuance—Congress, underwriters, viewers. If few watch, why should contributors keep public television alive? Programmers have come to realize that critical praise alone is insufficient; they need tangible evidence that audiences feel the same way. The most meaningful evidence comes from acceptable ratings.

Nielsen Data

The Nielsen Television Index (NTI) provides audience data based on the only national, electronically metered sample of television households in the United States. Nielsen's local market diary service, the Nielsen Station Index (NSI), provides the individual market data for PBS. Arbitron does not supply ratings data to PBS because they lack a national sample and because Arbitron's corporate policy does not allow public station program titles to be collected and published in their rating books. (Arbitron books show ratings data, but without program identification.)

PBS's research funds can only cover the cost of ten 1-week national surveys (NTI) annually. (Forty-two weeks must go unreported.) The commercial networks, as described in previous chapters, purchase continuous, year-round national data. Beginning with the fall premiere week in October, NTI collects national viewing data at roughly five-week intervals for PBS. Another research firm (Statistical Research, Inc.) obtains station line-ups (play dates/times) via telephone the week following each survey. Nielsen then marries the two computer files of meter viewing data and station line-ups to produce the equivalent of a national PBS rating book.

Public television stations use the same Nielsen local station mail-diary surveys during the four sweeps as do the commercial stations. Nielsen surveys a few large markets with additional diaries in October, January and March, and public stations in those markets can also purchase these reports.

Commercial network programmers, much to the irritation of advertising agency time-buyers, try to inflate affiliates' ratings by stunting with unusually popular specials and miniseries during the sweep weeks (see chapters 1 and 5). These higher ratings provide the local affiliates with an opportunity to raise advertising rates. PBS programmers lack enough topnotch programming to stunt for an entire four-week period. PBS does, however, try to schedule a representative mix of PBS offerings during each of the national survey weeks. No more than one opera is permitted, for example, nor are too many esoteric public affairs programs scheduled during that week. Furthermore, PBS programmers are not above allowing an occasional *National Geographic Special* to drift into a national survey week.

PBS indulges in unabashed stunting during its 16-day fund-raising Festival every March. Just as networks stunt for economic reasons, so too does public television. The difference is structural: Rather than raise revenue by selling advertising time on the basis of ratings, PBS stations raise revenue by direct, on-air solicitation of viewer contributions. In general, large audiences mean large contributions. Hence, programs scheduled during a fund raiser must deliver large audiences.

Cumulative Audience Strategy

At all other times, PBS strives for maximum variety in its program schedule to serve as many people as possible at one time or another each week. Unlike commercial network programs, not all public television programs are expected to have large audiences. Small audiences are acceptable so long as the weekly accumulation of unduplicated households is large. PBS's programming success is therefore assessed largely in terms of its weekly *cumulative audience data* or **cumes.**

As explained in Chapter 2, Nielsen defines a cumulative household audience as the percent of all television households (in the United States for network ratings or in a local market for stations ratings) that tuned in for at least six minutes to a specific program or time period. The public television national cumes for prime time (8–11 P.M., Mon.–Sun.) averaged from 28 to 33 percent of U.S. households in 1983. This measurement is based on the number of U.S. television households that watched public television programs in prime time for at least six minutes during the survey week. Cume ratings for prime-time programs have ranged from under 1 to over 19 percent; the higher figure earned by a *National Geographic Special* on sharks. When all times of day are included, the weekly cume rises to more than 50 percent of the country's households, a respectable figure for the impecunious fourth network.

Based on prior experience, PBS programmers apply informal guidelines for what rating levels constitute adequate viewing. Nature and science programs are expected to attract a cumulative audience of 5 to 10 percent of U.S. house-holds, dramas 4 to 5 percent, concert performances should attract 3 to 4 percent, public affairs documentaries 2 to 4 percent. Because of the way PBS programs are funded, failure to meet these levels does not mean cancelation. But failure to earn the minimum expected cumes could lead to nonrenewal by the Station Program Cooperative.

Loyalty Assessment

PBS researchers also study audience loyalty to evaluate program performance. Nielsen's overnight reports (based on data from the on-line metered sample homes in the top six markets) permit detailed audience analysis station-by-station and quarter-hour-by-quarter-hour in these markets. If the audience tires quickly of a program, the overnight ratings will decline during the telecast (a fate to which lengthy programs are especially susceptible). If the audience weakened to the appeal of network competition, such as a special starting a half-hour or more later than the PBS show, the overnight ratings suddenly drop at the point where the competing special began. This information tells the programmers (roughly, to be sure) the extent to which the program engaged viewers. Noncompelling programs are vulnerable to competition. Shows failing this test have to be scheduled more carefully when repeated, preferably opposite soft network competition.

Demographic Composition

Still another concern researchers address is who is watching. Households tuning to public television each week are, as a group, not unlike television viewers generally. Many, in fact, use television heavily and, in search of variety, frequently turn to public television. Research has revealed, however, that audiences for individual programs can vary widely in demographic compositition. Intellectually demanding programs such as *Cosmos* or *Brideshead Revisited* or *Tinker, Tailor, Soldier, Spy* attract older, college-educated, professional/managerial viewers. Because these "demanding" shows are scattered throughout the prime-time schedule, the cumulative prime-time audience exhibits an upscale tendency. Many programs, though, have broader-based followings, among them *Life on Earth, NOVA* and *Sneak Previews.*

Public television's audience grew dramatically in the late 1970s and early 1980s. Audience figures reached nearly 90 million viewers per week. Viewing per week reached 3½ hours, and public television's demographics mirror the nation's in education, income, occupation and race composition.[3] (See Figure 18-3.) The growth of cable television has been a major contributor to this trend. Local cable systems make UHF public stations as easy to tune in as VHF stations with similar picture quality—resulting in much greater use of PTV channels.

THE AUDIENCE ISSUE

Public television representatives frequently are called upon to explain a seeming paradox: How can public television's audience duplicate the demographic make-up of the country when so many of its programs attract the upscale viewer?[4] The question is second in importance only to that of how many people are watching; it is often tied to charges of elitism in program acquisition, implying PBS is not serving all the public with "public" television. PBS replies that it consciously attempts to provide alternatives to the commercial network offerings; to do so, the content of most PBS programs must make demands of viewers. Demanding programs tend, however, to be less appealing to viewers of lower socioeconomic status. The result is underrepresentation of such viewers in certain audiences. But this underrepresentation is, on balance, only slight, being offset in the week's cumulative audience totals for other programs having broader appeal. Critics often overlook that underrepresentation does not mean no representation. *NOVA,* for example, is watched each week in some 1.4 million

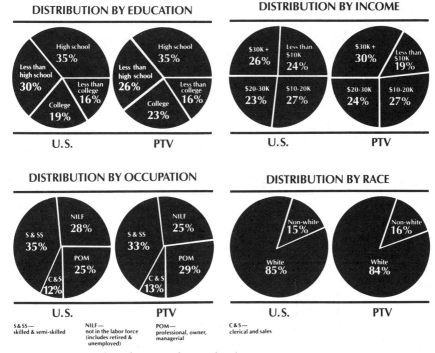

SOURCE: PBS Research/Nielsen TV index. Used with permission.

FIGURE 18-3. U.S. Population and PTV Audience Composition

households headed by a person who never finished high school. Even operas average over one million such downscale households in their audiences.

The kinds of audience statistics just cited serve a unique function: justification of public television. Commercial broadcasters justify their existence when they turn a profit for their owners and investors; public broadcasters prove their worth only when survey data indicate the public valued (i.e., viewed) the service provided.

SUMMARY

PBS operates in a more constrained environment than the commercial networks. Its member stations pay dues, and PBS serves them with programming. Corporate underwriters, independent program producers and member stations exert pressure on PBS in the selection and scheduling processes, constraining PBS's programming strategies. The SPC process also favors programs popular with stations in the largest markets as votes reflect market size. Counterprogramming, bridging and audience flow operate as major scheduling strategies in the prime-time core schedule. Promotion builds ratings, but funds for it are often lacking. SIP provides stations with special fund-raising programs and assistance and is among the most successful of PBS's services. While PBS uses the Nielsen ratings, it focuses on cumulative audiences and measurements of loyalty. A long-standing controversy in public broadcasting is whether its programming is elitist; analysis of audience demographics shows that the composite schedule has broad appeal. Although specific programs may draw largely upscale viewers, all programs capture some viewers from all demographic groups. Cable television has significantly increased the pool of available viewers for public broadcasting.

Notes

[1]Some programs arrive at the Fair with partial corporate funding, accompanied by requests to SPC to make up the difference. Failing SPC support, the producers must either persuade their corporate funders to fully underwrite the programs or turn elsewhere (usually to additional corporations) for the balance.

[2]"Not Much Schedule Juggling at PBS," *Current*, 12 July 1983, p. 4.

[3]PBS Research/Nielsen Television Index, 1983.

[4]Dale Rhodes, "Upscale, Downscale: PTV's Demographics," *Current*, 16 April 1982, p. 6.

Selected Sources

Agostino, Don. "Cable Television's Impact on the Audience of Public Television." *Journal of Broadcasting* 24 (Summer 1980): 347–65.

Attracting Minority Audiences to Public Television. Washington, D.C.: Corporation for Public Broadcasting, 1981.

Current, weekly Washington newspaper focused on public broadcasting, 1981 to date.

Fowler, Mark S., and Bresser, Daniel L. "A Marketplace Approach to Broadcast Regulation." *Texas Law Review* 60 (1982): 207; 250–55.

Frank, Ronald E., and Greenberg, Marshall G. *The Public's Use of Television: Who Watches and Why.* Beverly Hills, California: Sage Publications, 1980.

Mahony, Shiela; Demartino, Nick; and Stengel, Robert. *Keeping PACE with the New Television: Public Television and Changing Technology.* New York: Carnegie Corporation, 1980.

Public Television Station Programming

James Robertson and Bruce L. Christensen

A QUICK GUIDE TO CHAPTER NINETEEN

JAMES ROBERTSON *recently retired as the president of Robertson Associates, Inc., an independent consulting firm focusing on public broadcasting. He was its principle consultant to more than thirty clients in the last nine years. Prior to this time he had been successively employed from 1954 to 1973 as director of programming for WTTW, Chicago; vice-president for network affairs for National Educational Television (NET), the predecessor of PBS; vice-president and general manager of KCET, Los Angeles; director of broadcasting for the University of Wisconsin's WHA; and executive director of National Educational Radio for the National Association of Educational Broadcasters (NAEB). His role as president of Robertson Associates involved the evaluation of the effectiveness of existing stations, planning for new ones, and research and community surveying preparatory to the development of statewide public broadcasting plans for public radio in Ohio, Nebraska and Virginia and for public television in Indiana and Illinois.*

BRUCE L. CHRISTENSEN, *president of PBS and formerly president of the National Association of Public Television Stations in Washington, D.C., represents public television's legislative, regulatory and planning interests in the nation's capital. Prior to joining NAPTS in 1982, he was director of media services and general manager of KUED-TV and KUER-FM at the University of Utah in Salt Lake City and taught classes in public broadcasting as an adjunct associate professor in the department of communications. Before moving to the University of Utah, Mr. Christensen served as director of broadcast services for Brigham Young University and general manager of its radio and television facilities. He holds a master's degree in journalism from Northwestern University. He was elected to the board of directors of the Public Broadcasting System in 1979 and has also served on the boards of the Pacific Mountain Network and Rocky Mountain Corporation for Broadcasting. Together, these authors bring wide-ranging experience to this discussion of programming public television stations.*

STATION PROGRAM PHILOSOPHY

Public television, its mission and its public service objectives occupy a unique position in American broadcasting. Contrary to broadcast development in nearly every other country in the world, public service broadcasting in the United States developed long after the commercial system was in place. This fact has had an immense effect on the general public's attitude toward American public television programming and on public broadcastors' self-definition.

The public debates whether or not public television programs are even necessary and whether they should occupy the time and attention of the nation's communications policymakers in the Congress, the Executive Branch and the Federal Communications Commission. Some argue that the advent of the new technologies of cable, direct satellite broadcasting, multipoint distribution systems, videotapes and discs and so on, in the marketplace obviate the need for public television. Others counter that the marketplace fails to provide the special audience programming that public television offers and that any belief that emerging technologies will be different from existing media is unfounded. They point to CBS's and RCA's failures when they offered arts and cultural programming on cable and to the very limited success of Bravo and ARTS, who supply cultural programming on pay and basic cable. Marketplace critics also state that only public television programming has special audience services for children, the elderly and ethnic minorities.

The debate over programming content has persisted within the industry since public television began. For stations, the debate centers on the meaning of "noncommercial educational broadcasting," which is what the Communications Act of 1934 and the Federal Communications Commission call public television's program service. Noncommercial service came into existence in 1952 when educational interests lobbied the FCC into creating a special class of reserved channels within the television allocations—exclusively dedicated to "educational television."

One extreme argument defines *educational* in the narrow sense of *instructional*. From that viewpoint, public television (PTV) should teach—direct its programs to school and college classrooms and to out-of classroom students; the last thing PTV should do is to compete for commercial television's mass audience. At the other extreme are those people that define *educational* in the broadest possible sense. They want to reach out to viewers of all kinds and generate mass support for the public television service. This group perceives "instructional" television as a duty that sometimes must be performed, but their devotion goes to the wide range of programming the public has come to think of as public television.

The Carnegie Commission on Educational Television introduced the term *public television* in 1976. The commission convinced many in government and broadcasting that the struggling new service had to generate wider support than it had in its fledgling years. One of the impediments to such support, the Commission felt, was the word *educational*, which gave the service an unpopular image. They suggested *public television* as a more neutral term. Thus, a distinction has grown up between ITV (instructional television) and PTV (public television)—a distinction not altogether desirable or valid.

Lacking a truly national definition for public television's program service, a public television station's programmer must deal with the unresolved, internal questions of what it means to be a "noncommercial educational broadcasting" service. The PTV programmer must come to grips with a particular station's particular program philosophy. Philosophies vary widely from one station to the next, but one common theme persists: being noncommercial. This term implies that public television must directly serve "the people"; it must be, at the very least, different from—if not better than—commercial television. One of the implications of such a fundamental difference is that public television programming need not pursue the largest possible audience at whatever cost to programming. Public broadcasting has a special mission to serve audiences that would be otherwise neglected because they are too small to interest commercial broadcasting. This difference in outlook has great programming significance. It means that the public station programmer is relieved of one of the most relentless constraints limiting a commercial programmer's freedom of choice.

At the same time, public television cannot cater only to the smallest groups with the most esoteric tastes in the community. Broadcasting is still a mass medium, whether commercial or noncommercial, and can justify occupying a broadcast channel and the considerable expense of broadcast facilities only if it reaches relatively large numbers of people. As explained in Chapter 18, public broadcasting achieves this goal cumulatively by reaching many small groups. As long as they add up to a respectably large cumulative total in the course of a week, the PTV programmer has a "large" audience.

TYPES OF STATION LICENSEES

One of the difficulties in describing PTV programming strategies is that the stations are so diverse. The 158 licensees (as of 1983), operating nearly 300 stations, represent many management viewpoints.[1] Much of this diversity is explained by the varying auspices under which they operate. Licensees fall into four categories: community, university, public school and state agency, and each constrains programming in different ways.

Community Licensees

In larger cities—particularly those with many educational and cultural institutions but without a dominant institution or school system—the usual licensee is the nonprofit community corporation created for the purpose of constructing and operating a public television station. Because the governing board of such a station exists solely to administer the station (as compared with university trustees who have many other concerns), many feel community stations are the most responsive type of licensee. As of the mid-1980s, 69 such stations operated in the United States.

Compared with other licensees, community stations derive a higher proportion of their operating support from fund-raising activities—about 50 percent, compared with 32 percent for licensees overall. As a result, much of their programming reflects the urgent need to generate funds from the viewers they serve. Programmers at these stations, therefore, are more likely to be sensitive to a proposed program's general appeal. They will lean toward high-quality production values to attract and hold a general audience. These stations cannot grow or improve without a rapidly ascending curve of community support.

Recent cuts in federal funding for public television have forced a greater reliance on public donations. Most stations now rely more heavily on revenue from nonfederal sources in general and on public donations in particular. Ten public television stations, including all types of licensees, with Congressional approval, experimented with limited advertising from April 1982 through June 1983. Preliminary results that the National Association of Public Television Stations released in early 1983 showed the public accepted the commercials on those stations, at least in the first year, and that direct costs of sales commissions and salaries ran about 20 to 30 percent of gross sales, creating a substantial station profit. Undoubtedly, the results of this experiment will influence future legislation dealing with federal funding for public television.

Within the community category, eight stations stand somewhat apart because of their metropolitan origins, their large size and their national impact on the entire noncommercial service as producers of network-distributed programs. These flagship stations of the public broadcasting service are located in New York, Boston, Pittsburgh, Washington, Chicago, Los Angeles, San Francisco and Philadelphia. The first four are particularly notable as production centers for the nation, originating such major programs as *MacNeil/Lehrer, Nova* and the *National Geographic Specials*. Although other public stations and commercial entities often participate in their productions and financing, these stations produce most of the PBS schedule.

University Stations

In many cases colleges and universities activated public television stations as a natural outgrowth of their traditional role of providing extension services within their states. As they see it, "The boundaries of the campus are the boundaries of the state,"[2] and both radio and television can do some of the tasks extension agents formerly did in person. Fifty-two licensees make up the university group.

Here, too, programmers schedule a fairly broad range of programs, often emphasizing adult continuing education and culture. Some, typically using student staff, produce a nightly local newscast, and many produce a weekly public affairs or cultural program. None, in recent history, has produced a major PBS series for the prime-time core schedule. University-licensed stations such as WHA (Madison, Wisconsin) and KUHT (Houston, Texas) contribute occasional specials and single programs to the PBS schedule. Moreover, WHA began *The New Tech Times* in 1983, a weekly prime-time (noncore) series on the home computer revolution, and other university licensed stations have supported short-run series aired in the daytime PBS schedule.

As operating costs mount and academic appropriations shrink, university stations also ask their communities to supplement their budgets from their licensee institutions. Expanded fund-raising efforts are generally accompanied by broadening program appeal.

Public School Stations

Local school systems initially became licensees to provide new learning experiences for students in elementary school classrooms. From the outset, some augmented instructional broadcasts with other programming consistent with the school system's view of its educational mission. By the early 1980s only 14 of these school licensees remained. Most of them have organized a broadly based community support group whose activities generate wider interest and voluntary contributions from the community at large. As a result, the average local licensee now draws from 15 to 20 percent of its income from subscriber contributions. Naturally, programmers at these stations are heavily involved with in-school programming (instructional television on ITV), but because they desire community support, they are also concerned with programming for children out of school and for adults of all ages. Other than ITV series, most rarely produce original entertainment programs for PBS, and they obtain most of their schedules from national, state and regional suppliers of instructional programming. Of course, they usually carry *Sesame Street* too.

State Television Agencies

More than a hundred of the nation's public television stations are part of state networks operated by legislatively created public broadcasting agencies. Networks of this type exist in 23 states. Most of them were authorized initially to provide new classroom experiences for the state's schoolchildren. Most have succeeded admirably in this task and have augmented their ITV service with a variety of public affairs and cultural programs furnished to citizens throughout their states.

State networks such as those in South Carolina, Maryland, Kentucky, Nebraska and Iowa, are very active in the production and national distribution of programs. Their efforts range from traditional school programs for primary and secondary grades to graduate degree courses offered in regions where colleges and universities are few. These production efforts are the counterpart to the national production centers of the community-based licensees. Although state networks rarely produce core PBS series, they frequently join consortia generating specific programs for series such as *Great Performances* and *American Playhouse*. Others, such as the Maryland Center for Public Broadcasting and the South Carolina ETV Commission, have produced many long-lived PBS series such as *Wall Street Week, AM Weather* and *American Short Story*.

Although in recent years these state network stations have increased foundation, underwriter and even viewer support, state legislatures still appropriate more than three-fifths of their budgets. This fact, plus the perception of their "community of service" as an entire state rather than a single city, gives programmers at these stations a different perspective.

It should be evident from these brief descriptions that each category of public television station poses special problems and special opportunities for programming strategies. Each station type is ruled by a different type of board of directors—community leader boards, university trustees, local school boards, state-appointed central boards. Each board affects program personnel differently. University boards, preoccupied with higher education programs, tend to leave station professionals free to carry out their job within broad guidelines. School boards likewise are preoccupied with their major mission and in some cases pay too little attention to their responsibilities as licensees. State boards must protect their stations from undue political influences. Community representatives try to balance local power groups. All licensees struggle to function with what they regard as inadequate budgets, but there are wide funding discrepancies between the extremes of a large metropolitan community station and a small local public school station.

Significantly, all types of stations have broadened their financial bases in recent years to keep up with rising costs and to improve program quality and quantity. Licensees having the greatest success in securing new funding have, in general, made the strongest impact on national public television programming, partly because the firms or agencies that underwrite programs want to get maximum favorable impact from their investments. In turn, successful public television producer–entrepreneurs are motivated to create attractive new public television programs with broad audience appeal in the hope of securing still more underwriting. These kinds of programs increase viewership and draw more support in the form of memberships and subscriptions. Although this trend has its salutary aspects, it has also diverted noncommercial television from some of its original goals. For example, controversial public affairs programs and programs of interest only to specialized smaller audiences now tend to be eliminated.

THE PROGRAMMER'S AUDIENCE INFORMATION SOURCES

Before attempting to build a public television station's program schedule, a programmer must know the people who live in the area the station serves—not as objects for commercial exploitation but as constituencies entitled to special program services. An in-depth study undertaken in 1977 under the auspices of the television station managers themselves shows much about how programming decisions are actually made. It revealed the kinds of information on audience needs programmers have available and the programming sources that fill those needs.

Robertson Associates, Inc., studied how local stations developed their program service and the role that PBS and other nonlocal program sources played in the total local offering. On-site visits were made to 20 PBS member stations, carefully selected to make the sample group proportional to the total PBS membership in several respects: UHF vs. VHF facilities, geographic location, licensee type and size of market. The results of those interviews were measured against questionnaire responses from program managers at 20 other stations, equally representative of total PBS membership. Thus, the study's findings (many of which are reported in this chapter) were based on a sample that included more than 25 percent of all public television station programmers in the country. The study revealed that public television programmers secure information on the public's needs and interests in at least seven ways. The information sources are ranked by importance, and the general pattern has remained constant in the 1980s.

1. *Rating services.* Between 50 percent and 75 percent of U.S. public television stations use commercial ratings services, most of which now include profiles of commercial and public channel viewing within a given market. Public television programmers use this information to plan their schedules. For example, the Pacific Mountain Network (a regional public television organization) has worked with David LeRoy Associates to develop specific public television program ratings strategies based upon commercial rating service data.

2. *Station-commissioned local studies.* Since many public television stations are licensed to educational institutions with research capabilities, they can enlist faculty members and students to measure program impact and to ascertain community needs. Several stations in metropolitan areas retain professional polling

organizations to conduct periodic studies for them. Of stations visited, 70 percent used specially commissioned research, as did 50 percent of those polled.

3. *Formal ascertainment.* Since 1977 the FCC has required noncommercial as well as commercial television stations to determine—through interviews of key community leaders and random sampling of the general public—the needs, interests and problems of the station's local community. When needs or interests not being served are identified, most public stations take this as a cue to develop programming in response. Of stations polled in the 1977 study, 70 percent said the results of their local ascertainment efforts had made a difference in their programming decisions.

4. *Mail and phone calls from viewers.* Public television stations generally keep fairly detailed records of viewer mail and phone calls. Of stations visited, 20 percent keep very specific records and furnish reports to program decision makers on numbers of letters and calls, topics mentioned and attitudes expressed—both positive and negative.

5. *Viewers' evaluations through questionnaires and screening.* Nearly half of U.S. public television stations use questionnaires (often published in their program guides) to solicit viewer responses to programs already aired and suggestions as to types of programs desired in the future. Some stations hold screening sessions for program advisory groups to tap a more representative sampling of opinion than can be acquired from the staff alone.

6. *Exchange of information with other programmers.* Program executives of public television stations can exchange information on programming strategies when they meet at frequent executives conferences and during the annual PBS Station Program Cooperative (SPC).

7. *PBS-supplied information.* Partly in response to requests from television managers, the PBS administration decided in 1977 to acquire more audience information from both stations and national ratings services and to share it with stations. As of the mid-1980s, PBS supplied monthly audience size and composition reports.

PROGRAM SOURCES FOR STATIONS

After discovering the needs of their service areas, program managers face a second task: evaluating the full range of program sources at their disposal. Public broadcasting sets out to be different from commercial broadcasting, and the development of unique program sources has been one of its most difficult problems. PTV stations have to have a national program service but do not want a network organization that would dominate station programming (as happens on the three commercial broadcast networks). PTV needs commercially syndicated material but cannot always compete with commercial broadcasters for it. It needs the revenue from syndicating its instructional programming but lacks the backlog typical of syndicated entertainment programs. And finally, PTV needs to produce local programs since commercial programming neglects them, and PTV has a special obligation to serve local needs and interests. These five sources supply most PTV programming.

As shown in Figure 19-1, the Public Broadcasting Service distributes the largest amount of programming public television stations air (67.1 percent). Stations in major cities produce many of the series PBS offers, but local programming (produced locally for local audiences) fills just over 6 percent of airtime. Since instructional programming is generally no longer produced locally, less than 1 percent of that 6.2 percent of local programming is instructional. The total hours devoted to instructional programming *not* produced locally (from AIT, GPNITL and other instructional suppliers) amount to 8.2 percent of airtime. Regional and state networks, commercial syndicators and miscellaneous others supply the remainder of the programs (18.5 percent).

The National Program Service

Clearly, the satellite-delivered PBS programming is the most significant program source for most public television stations. As explained in the preceding chapter, PBS is not a network organization in the customary commercial sense. It does not have "affiliates"; it undertakes no program production itself; it does not own or operate any stations. It is a membership organization to which nearly every public television licensee belongs and for whom it administers and distributes the national program service according to policies and patterns the stations themselves set.

Most of the PBS schedule is determined each season through an unusual mix of member station preference and PBS Program Advisory Committee action. The mechanism is far from simple but assures the needs and interests of the

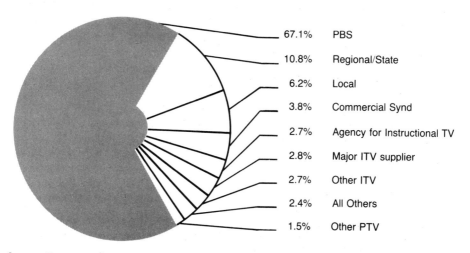

67.1%	PBS
10.8%	Regional/State
6.2%	Local
3.8%	Commercial Synd
2.7%	Agency for Instructional TV
2.8%	Major ITV supplier
2.7%	Other ITV
2.4%	All Others
1.5%	Other PTV

SOURCE: Corporation for Public Broadcasting, Policy Development and Planning. Used with permission.

FIGURE 19-1. Sources of Public Television Programming, 1982

local licensee will not be overlooked as the national schedule takes shape. (See the discussion of the SPC in Chapter 18.) PBS develops a programming book containing production proposals for the stations to consider about a year and a half in advance of when the programs are to air. After individual station programmers respond to it, the book proposals are refined and reduced in number. Every October, local station programmers gather to meet with program producers to discuss program offerings and suggest how to make the programs offered even more attractive to the local audiences. PBS calls this its Annual Program Fair.

PBS's program department takes the information gathered at the Program Fair, works with the producers to incorporate the station recommendations and then meets with a group of station programmers the entire system has elected. Their purpose is to create a national program schedule to recommend to the stations for purchase. Since the money for program purchases flows from the stations to the national organization, everyone concerned wants to buy the best programs possible at the lowest cost to meet the greatest number of licensee needs. The amazing thing is that it seems to work. The ultimate program decisions rest with the local stations. Their programming staff must decide whether or not to purchase the offered program package. They may refuse by withholding their money, or they may buy only a few of the offered programs, giving them the opportunity to program their station as they believe makes the most sense for the audience they serve.

Subnational Networks

Programmers are not limited to PBS for network programs. Four regional telecommunications associations exist: the Eastern Educational Television Network (EEN) with members from Maine to Virginia; the Southern Educational Telecommunications Association (SECA) including stations from Maryland to Texas; the Central Educational Network (CEN) in the upper Midwest from Ohio to the Dakotas; and the Pacific Mountain Network (PMN) serving stations from the Rockies to the West Coast. These associations serve not only as forums for discussions of stations' policies and operating practices but also as agents for program production and acquisition. Set up to make group buys of instructional series, the regionals' role in providing nonlocal programming for general audiences as well as for ITV use was firmly established by the early 1980s. This trend was accelerated by the availability of the public television satellite distribution system, enabling any of these organizations or any combination of them to deliver a program to any public television station in the country.

The state networks in more than 20 states, as mentioned earlier, provide both instructional and general audience programming, including legislative coverage and special events of statewide interest. In some states (such as Kentucky, Georgia and Nebraska), a central office makes programming decisions for the entire state. In other states (such as New York, Ohio and Florida), station program managers within the state jointly plan the schedule on the state interconnect. Although state networks are another program source for local stations, materials they produce do not usually serve stations beyond the state's boundaries.

Noncommercial Syndication

Because of its role in formal education, public television has had to develop its own unique body of syndicated material. The only precedent for such program stockpiling is the audiovisual film distribution center, an educational adjunct that came into being long before television. Public television gradually created a new appetite for instructional material, introduced technological resources for its production and stimulated the founding of new centers for program distribution that perform the same function as commercial syndication firms except on a noncommercial or cooperative basis.

The Agency for Instructional Television (AIT) in Bloomington, Indiana, for example, produced ten new series for syndication during 1982–83. Altogether, its catalog lists 71 series for primary grades, 40 for high school use and 8 for postsecondary students. Among the best known are *Ripples, Inside Out, Trade Offs, Thinkabout* and *Give & Take.* By the mid-1980s, AIT had developed innovative instructional programming in the classrooms in conjunction with microcomputers, creating interactive lessons on videodiscs.

The Great Plains National Instructional Television Library (GPNITL) in Lincoln, Nebraska, offers dozens of series for elementary school use along with a great many materials for college and adult learning. Titles in the 124-page catalog for 1980 ranged from *The Art Consumer* and *I Can Read* for first graders to *Anyone for Tennyson* and *The Media Machine* for high schoolers and adults.

The International ITV Co-op, Inc., Falls Church, Virginia (known to most programmers for *Cover to Cover, Write On!* and other widely used instructional series) has won international awards for its earth–space science series, *L-4.* And Western Instructional Television, Los Angeles, offers more than 500 series in science, language arts, social studies, English, art and history. The abundance of cooperatively planned and produced ITV materials means that most instructional programming is no longer produced locally, except where certain subject matter is unique to a local area or community.

Local school authorities usually select instructional materials for in-school use, although the public television station's staff often serves as liaison between sources of this material and users. Stations that serve schools usually employ an "instructional television coordinator" or "learning resources coordinator" to work full-time with present and potential users, assist teachers in proper use of the materials, identify classroom needs and select or develop materials to meet the specific goals of local educators.

More quality programming for adult learners is now available to public stations than in the earlier decades of public broadcasting. By the late 1970s, consortia efforts in higher education were turning out television courses to be integrated into the curriculums of most postsecondary institutions, yet produced in a way that made them attractive to the casual viewer as well. Budgets for such series range from $100,000 to $1 million for a single course. These efforts center particularly in community colleges, led by Miami-Dade (Florida), Dallas (Texas) and Coastline Community College (Huntington Beach, California).

Meanwhile, faculty members at other leading postsecondary institutions began developing curriculum materials to accompany several outstanding public television program series distributed nationally through PBS for general viewing.

Of these, the first was *The Ascent of Man* with the late Dr. Jacob Bronowski, a renowned scholar as well as a skillful and effective communicator on camera. More than 200 colleges and universities offered college credit for that course. Quickly others followed (*The Adams Chronicles, Cosmos, Life on Earth, The Shakespeare Plays,* etc.) as programmers discovered such series furnished the casual viewer with attractive public television entertainment and simultaneously served more serious viewers desiring to register for college course credits.

This experience led many public television programmers to realize that too much had been made of the supposed demarcation between ITV and PTV. Too often during earlier years, many program producers would not even consider producing so-called instructional television. The first Carnegie Commission in 1965 strengthened this presumed gap by not concerning itself with television's educational assistance to schools and colleges and by adopting the term *public* television to mean programming for general viewing.

In 1980 PBS began its adult learning service. After three years of development, 230 stations offered this service. By spring 1983, over 6,000 colleges and universities were using the service, and enrollment in the courses had reached 75,000 per semester. This service offers public television programmers one of the most challenging additions to the program schedule. Because such programs require close cooperation with institutions offering the credit, they require a reliable repeat schedule that permits students to make up missed broadcasts, while the quality of the programming must also interest the general viewer who may not sign up for credit.

Recent experience has demonstrated that ITV and PTV programs can appeal to viewers other than those for which they were especially intended. The Bronowski series, *The Ascent of Man,* is only one example. Another is *Sesame Street,* initially intended for youngsters in disadvantaged households, prior to their school years. Yet one of the significant occurences in kindergarten and lower elementary classrooms throughout America in the 1970s was the **in-school** use of *Sesame Street.*

Commercial Syndication

More extensively tapped sources, however, are such commercial syndicators as Time-Life, David Susskind's Talent Associates, Wolper Productions, Granada TV in Great Britain and several major motion picture companies such as Universal Pictures. Public television stations sometimes negotiate individually for program packages with such syndicators; at other times they join with public stations through regional associations to make group buys. Commercially syndicated programs obtained in this way by PTV include historical and contemporary documentaries, British-produced drama series and packages of highly popular or artistic motion pictures originally released to theaters.

The proportion of commercially syndicated programming in specific public television station schedules may range from none at all to as much as 25 percent. The variation has two derivatives. First, those commercially-syndicated programs public television stations find appropriate are relatively expensive. Unless outside underwriting is secured to cover license fees, many stations simply cannot afford them. The second factor is philosophical. Although much commercially syndicated material has strong audience appeal, its educational or cultural value is arguable.

Local Production

The percentage of airtime filled with locally produced programming has gradually decreased over the years, as both network and syndicated programming have increased in quantity and quality. The percentage of total on-air hours produced locally by public television stations declined from 16 percent in 1972 to just over 6 percent in 1982. Moreover, production quality expectations have risen. More time and dollars and better facilities must be used to produce effective local programs than before. A medium-sized station intending to produce 200 to 320 hours of local programs per year (or up to 1 hour a day, six days a week) should have at a minimum the following equipment:[3]

One studio of 3,000 square feet

Three broadcast-standard color cameras

Six broadcast-standard videotape machines

Two programmable videotape editing units

Two film islands

One graphic font character generator

For film production: two 16-mm cameras and one 35-mm slide camera

For remote production: one electronic newsgathering (ENG) unit

The total cost for this equipment can range from $1.5 million to $4 million. With such equipment and a reasonably proficient engineering and production staff, a station should be able to turn out an hour a day of creditable local programming.

Increasingly, programmers now spend their limited local budgets on regular, nightly broadcasts devoted to activities, events and issues of local interest and significance. These newscasts are somewhat different from those of the network-affiliate. Commercial broadcast television stations concentrate on spot news and devote only a minute or less to each story; public television stations see their role as giving more comprehensive treatment to local affairs. (As of the mid-1980s, a few local cable systems were adopting a similar style of local news coverage.) Further, the use of ENG units has made live and recorded news coverage outside the public television station easier to handle.

THE SEQUENCE OF SCHEDULE BUILDING

No PTV programmer ever builds an entire schedule from scratch. A public television program schedule is a series of compromises meant to serve the total audience in the best manner possible, but doomed to serve no single viewer's needs entirely. The program schedule is built on what the programmer thinks the audience will watch at a particular time.

A public television programmer must consider and balance these elements: *licensee type* (each carries its unique program priorities), *audience demographics, competition* from commercial and other public television signals, *daypart targeting* (such as afternoons for children's programming, daytime for instructional services), *program availability* and *equipment capacity*. No single element overrides the others, but each affects the final schedule.

Public television programmers seek programs that meet local audience needs and schedule those programs at times most likely to attract the target audience. Since all audience segments cannot be served at once, the mystery and magic of the job is getting the right programs in the right time slots. High ratings are not the objective; serving the appropriate audience with a show they will watch that adds to the quality of their life is. (See Figure 19-2 for a breakdown of PTV program types.)

Instructional Programs

Most public television stations carry some in-school instructional programs. Broadcasting is still the least expensive way to reach millions of students in elementary schools scattered across the nation. In 1983 over 3 million students watched instructional programs each week on public television stations.

Hours of Programs, by Type, 1982

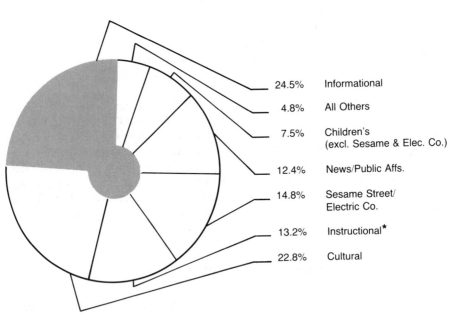

24.5%	Informational
4.8%	All Others
7.5%	Children's (excl. Sesame & Elec. Co.)
12.4%	News/Public Affs.
14.8%	Sesame Street/ Electric Co.
13.2%	Instructional*
22.8%	Cultural

*Excluding the ITV portion of the *Electric Company.*
SOURCE: Corporation for Public Broadcasting, Policy Development and Planning. Used with permission.

FIGURE 19-2. Types of Programming Broadcast by Public TV Stations

State agency licensees and school board stations carry the heaviest instructional schedules, but most public television stations have contracts with state school boards or local districts to provide instructional services. For the programmer this means that instructional programming is often the first part of the program schedule to be filled since it can only be broadcast during specific hours of the day and times of the year.

PBS Programs

Another major element most stations schedule early on is network programming from PBS because (1) about two-thirds of PTV stations depend on PBS programs to generate their largest audiences and (2) a number of PBS series have become staples in the local audience program diet, and viewers expect them to remain in the same time period from season to season. For these reasons as well as to capitalize on national promotion, local programmers usually carry major PBS features in the prime-time spot PBS programmers propose so that a given telecast is seen more or less simultaneously on all PBS stations. Generally, then, station schedules are consistent with the core feed from PBS on Sunday through Thursday nights. (Officially through Wednesday, Thursday is de facto part of the core because many stations carry *Sneak Previews* and *Mystery!* as feed then.)

Member stations, however, control PBS and are free, without fear of reprisal, to rearrange PBS programs in any way they wish. As explained in Chapter 18, when the satellite is feeding two programs simultaneously, the station has three scheduling choices: to air Program A without delay, recording Program B; to air Program B without delay, recording Program A; or to record both for later use. Programmers cannot always take advantage of these options, however. Videotape recording machines are expensive to operate and maintain and may be tied up with other functions when needed to record off the network.

More than 155 earth terminals feed 90 percent of the public television stations in the United States and associated territories, and as a result, individual stations now control access to national programs. By 1983 every public television station had its own earth station, shared one or had access through a network to satellite signals.

Commercially Syndicated Programs

Programs acquired from commercial syndicators are usually the next priority in building a schedule. These features possess the same high quality and broad appeal as PBS's best offerings and add variety to a station's schedule (as long as they remain consistent with its philosophy). In many cases they are motion pictures of artistic or historical value as well as strong audience appeal.

Local Programs

Locally produced programs do not necessarily come last in the sequence of schedule building. In fact, some stations block in time for certain local programs (for example, the nightly magazine-format programs devoted to local activities and interests) before considering anything else in their proposed schedule. The appropriate maxim is, however: Secure the best of whatever is needed from elsewhere, then use local production resources to make programs that cannot be obtained elsewhere precisely because they are local.[4]

Just where in a public television station schedule should the programmer insert local programs? Practices of PTV stations across the country vary on this point. For example, some schedule their local nightly news-and-feature magazine adjacent to *The MacNeil-Lehrer Newshour*, an in-depth news interview program PBS supplies. Because viewing habits differ from one time zone to another, some stations cannot do this without running opposite local commercial news programs. Some stations air their local news-and-feature programs twice, once in early evening and again late at night. Here, as in other instances, the public television programmer must make a judgment based on local viewing habits and preferences, programs on other local channels and programs available from the PBS incoming satellite channels.

COUNTERPROGRAMMING BY STATIONS

PTV station programmers do not engage in fierce counterprogramming warfare with their commercial colleagues. For example, most station programmers avoid putting their strongest dramatic program opposite another station's strongest drama, preferring to play theirs at an hour when other stations are not appealing to the drama devotee. Instead, against a commercially broadcast drama they may play their strongest public affairs features or their strongest programming of some other type. In areas with more than one public television channel as well as the usual array of commercial channels, the public television programmers usually confer and develop schedules designed to give viewers the greatest possible choice of viewing times for programs. Most PBS member stations play most PBS programs at least twice, and some also repeat selected local features a second time since there is always a potential audience for repeats.

AUDIENCE FLOW WITHIN THE LOCAL SCHEDULE

Public television programmers wrestle with the question of how to keep an audience tuned to their station just like commercial programmers do. For the PTV programmer, however, the question is more difficult since the programs most often appeal only to a particular or special audience. It is possible, with due regard for related interests and tastes, to schedule a sequence of programs that holds viewers from one time period to another. One musical program followed by another may keep viewers interested in music tuned to a PTV station. The same principle applies to public affairs programs, science and natural history broadcasts, drama and performing arts productions, business and economic reports.

Some station programmers consider it unwise to devote an entire evening to one type of programming because it excludes viewers not interested in that particular program type. Others contend that within the course of a week, it is possible to attract all audience segments. Every programmer faces the dilemma of deciding between greater diversity in program offerings versus the desirability of increasing the time viewers with a particular interest spend watching public television programs.

FUTURE DEVELOPMENTS

Many people in the noncommercial field believe the public television station of today will become the public telecommunications center of tomorrow—a place where telecommunications professionals handle the production, acquisition, reception, duplication and delivery of all types of noncommercial educational-cultural-information materials and stand ready to advise and counsel people in the community. In this scenario, existing public television stations will transmit programs of broad interest and value to relatively large audiences scattered throughout their coverage areas; but they will also feed these and other programs to local cable channels and transfer programs of more specialized interest to videocassettes or videodiscs for use in schools, colleges, libraries, hospitals and industry or for use on home video equipment.

By the late 1980s antennas capable of picking up superb quality video and audio signals directly from satellites without going through any ground-based broadcasting station (direct broadcasting) will be available for about $200. When the problem of scheduling multichannel satellite traffic is solved, public television programming could be distributed directly from satellites to schools, colleges, libraries, industrial locations—and even homes—by the end of this decade.

Companies with billions of dollars in assets are investing heavily to bring these new communications systems into daily use. Every program decision maker at every public television station must be aware of these technological advances. Today's programming challenges—complex, difficult and rewarding—may be simple when compared with those of the future.

SUMMARY

The disparate philosophies guiding public television programmers have in common the elements of noncommercialism and special audience service. The four types of licensees, community, university, public school and state agency, follow different mandates in programming to serve their constituencies, although all tend to appeal more and more to the general, entertainment-oriented audience that supports public television with subscriptions. The public television station programmer draws information from seven sources to evaluate the success of the station's programming strategies. Ratings are only one indicator since so few public stations have large enough one-time audiences to receive ratings. Public stations count their cumulative audience rather than per-program as commercial stations do. PBS is the main source of PTV programming; regional and state networks, local production, commercial and noncommercial syndicators and other sources supply only about 30 percent of station programs. A PTV station usually schedules instructional programming first, then core PBS programs, commercially syndicated programs and local programs, excepting local newscasts. Although both audience flow and counterprogramming strategies affect program placement on public stations, actual PTV practices differ somewhat from those of commercial television. In the future, inexpensive satellite transmission may bypass PBS and permit direct distribution from program production centers to each PTV member household.

Notes

[1]More stations than licensees exist because in 20 states a legislatively created agency for public broadcasting is the licensee for as many as 11 separate stations serving its state. Also, in several communities, one noncommercial educational licensee operates two television channels. In these cases (Boston, Pittsburgh, San Francisco and Milwaukee, among others), one channel usually offers a relatively broad program service while the second channel is used for more specialized programming, often instructional material. With the addition of KCWC-TV in Riverton, Wyoming, in 1983, licensed to Central Wyoming College, Montana becomes the only state without a public television station.

[2]This particular expression was coined by President Charles Van Hise of the University of Wisconsin in the early 1900s, but all land-grant colleges espouse similar traditions.

[3]Based on *Facilities Guidelines for Public Television Stations*, prepared by the PBS Engineering Committee, coordinated by Kenneth S. Dewire, June 1978. Similar guidelines are furnished for smaller and larger stations.

[4]Percentage of total on-air hours public television stations produced locally, as reported by the Corporation for Public Broadcasting, was 16.1 percent in 1972, 11.4 percent in 1974, 10.1 percent in 1976, 7.4 percent in 1978 and 6.8 percent in 1980.

Selected Sources

Alternative Financing Options for Public Broadcasting, Vols. I & II. The Temporary Commission on Alternative Financing for Public Telecommunications, Report to the Congress of the United States, 1982.

Frank, Ronald E., and Greenberg, Marshall G. *Audiences for Public Television*. Beverly Hills, California: Sage Publications, 1982.

Koughan, Martin. "The Fall and Rise of Public Television." *Channels* (May/June 1983): 23–31.

Lewis, Raymond J. *Meeting Learners' Needs Through Telecommunications: A Directory and Guide to Programs*. Washington, D.C.: Center for Learning and Telecommunications, American Association for Higher Education, 1983.

The Project Team in Instructional Television. Washington, D.C.: Corporation for Public Broadcasting, 1983.

Schenkkan, Robert F.; Thurston, Carol M.; and Sheldon, Alan. *Case Studies in Institutional Licensee Management*. National Association of Educational Broadcasters, 1980.

CHAPTER TWENTY

Public Radio Programming

Wallace A. Smith

A QUICK GUIDE TO CHAPTER TWENTY

WALLACE A. SMITH *has been involved in public radio broadcasting, com-munications teaching and university administration and counseling for more than a decade—first at Occidental College and then at the University of Southern California. A graduate of Waynesburg College and Pittsburgh Theological Seminary, both in Pennsylvania, he holds a master's degree and Ph.D. in telecommunications from the University of Southern California. He is active in public radio locally, statewide and nationally. As general manager, he shepherded KUSC-FM through its transition from a low-powered student-run operation to its position as one of the leading public radio stations in the nation. He served as a member of the board of directors of National Public Radio and two terms as president of the board of directors of the California Confederation of the Arts. He is a founding member of the American Public Radio Associates and a member of its board of directors. He has served as chairman of the radio advisory committee of the California Public Broadcasting Commission, on the executive committee of the Association of California Public Radio Stations, and is past president of Alpha Epsilon Rho, the national radio/television honor society. Dr. Smith uses the station he manages, KUSC, as a dramatic case study of public radio's potential.*

PHILOSOPHY AND FORMAT

This chapter focuses on the programming strategies of public radio, relating a station's philosophy to its audience and fund-raising capability, its degree of localism and its integrity. The author describes the seven main public radio formats, concentrating on their program selection and scheduling strategies and the effects of satellite relay of programming on public radio networking. Using the adoption of a classical music format by KUSC-FM as a case study, the chapter illustrates how public radio programmers do their jobs, showing the roles of promotion, fund raising, financial accountability and ongoing evaluation in success.

Audiences and Fund Raising

The purpose of noncommercial, educational (public) broadcast licenses is intentionally different from the purpose of commercial broadcast licenses, but both licensees are challenged to use their channel assignments in the most productive manner to reach the largest possible audience given their program services. Even though a public broadcast station may serve a disparate audience with highly specialized programs, its overall objective is to reach as many listeners as possible. (In Chapter 18 Fuller discussed the use of cumulative audience measures that apply to public radio as well as public television broadcasting.) Commercial broadcasters want to attract large audiences to generate operating revenue and profits for their stockholders. Public broadcasters have the same objective but reinvest their profits (nonprofit revenue) in the program service.

The challenge to the public radio programmer is to design an alternative program service that differs significantly from program formats other commercial and noncommercial stations in the market offer. The selected format must attract sufficiently large audiences to generate direct listener support of the station and encourage philanthropists, government agencies, foundations, business, industry and corporations to invest. Motivating support for a public radio station requires evidence that substantial numbers of people in a community use, want and need the program service.

Localism and Integrity

A unique sound captures the imagination of the potential listening audience. Programming elevates a public station into a position competitive with other radio services. It is not enough to say, "We are public, therefore we are better," or to rely on the lack of commercial announcements to build an audience. Localism is a key factor in developing radio formats. Radio is a flexible medium using lightweight equipment that enables it to respond quickly to spontaneous events. The more live local events and happenings included in a broadcast schedule, the higher the probability for success.

Public broadcasting's most valuable asset is the integrity and quality of its programs. Whatever format is selected, success is predicated on the delivery of a program service that will inform, entertain and enhance the life of each listener and improve the quality of life in the community. Those goals are idealistic, but they create the margin of difference that will attract listeners to public broadcasting regardless of the station format. Commercial broadcasters are less able to pursue such lofty ideals. They must turn a profit, so even their most deliberate attempts to achieve excellence are often compromised.

Seven Format Options

Public radio uses six basic formats: classical music and fine arts, jazz, news and public affairs, community service and public access, eclectic and instructional; a seventh option mixes two in a dual format. Americans are accustomed to selecting radio stations according to format. Nothing annoys radio listeners more than tuning to a news station *for news* only to hear classical music. Educating the public to accept more than one sound from radio is a slow process. Most public as well as commercial broadcasters therefore deliver the expected format. By 1983, however, some evidence had emerged that radio audiences were beginning to listen to radio for individual programs and that public radio stations were challenging the rigid rule that people listen to radio stations, not programs. The extraordinary success of programs such as *All Things Considered, Prairie Home Companion* and radio adaptations of *Star Wars* and *The Empire Strikes Back*, inserted in any of the basic formats discussed below, suggests a change in the audience's expectation of uniformity in radio programming. It is still too early to decide if these programs indicate a new trend or are the exceptions that prove the rule.

CLASSICAL MUSIC AND FINE ARTS

All-music formats depend on prerecorded music for the majority of their broadcast schedules. Public radio stations choosing the classical music and fine arts format have a competitive edge over their commercial counterparts because they can broadcast long, uninterrupted performances of classical works. They can surround these performances with informational modules to enhance the audience's listening experience but avoid the abrasive intrusion of advertisements. Public radio stations' ability to put aside time restraints contributes substantially to the quality of presentation of classical music.

The classical music format has become a staple in public broadcasting. Because it is considered a safe format, many social activists criticize managers that select it. Their criticism is usually a result of misplaced values. The priority for arts and music in our society is low; music and arts are tolerated, but most people have a limited understanding of their value in stimulating many higher aspirations. And a format that feeds those aspirations is as important as any service public radio provides. The size of audiences and financial support for the classical music and fine arts format are sufficient evidence of the need for them.

The classical music and fine arts format can take several forms. WNED-FM (Buffalo, New York) broadcasts all classical music with only the briefest interruptions for information about the performers.[1] KUSC-FM (Los Angeles), licensed to the University of Southern California, has a schedule that is 85 percent classical music. The other 15 percent includes news, fine arts modules on subjects besides music and programs about classical music.

Public radio has contributed greatly to the return of live classical music concerts on radio. Quite unlike the stereotype of a classical music juke box using scholarly announcers to introduce one record after another, public radio now produces major programs featuring live concert music from concert halls throughout the world. KUSC, for example, recorded more than 90 live concerts in 1982, including the seasons of the Los Angeles Philharmonic and other major orchestras and chamber ensembles in Southern California. Minnesota Public Radio, WGBH in Boston, KQED in San Francisco and WNYC in New York also recorded many live concert events and major American music festivals. Moreover, live broadcasts from Bayreuth and Salzburg have arrived via satellite for listeners throughout the United States.

National Public Radio developed the ultimate classical music variety program, *The Sunday Show*, in 1982. This program featured documentaries and concerts of classical music, jazz, musical theater and popular music, combining these segments with highly produced features about the spoken and fine arts. The programs utilized a satellite relay to include live segments from all over America. The idea worked, but the program was too expensive to produce, and it was canceled before the concept had time to jell.

JAZZ

A new public radio format emerged during the late 1970s as certain stations began featuring jazz music programming. Like the classical station, these stations combine recordings with live events. Although they often record concerts in clubs and from concert stages, they also produce jazz events themselves—which are then recorded or transmitted live to local and national audiences.

KLON-FM, Long Beach, California, and WGBO in New Jersey are the two public radio stations currently producing the largest number of jazz concert events. The Long Beach Blues Festival, featuring some of the nation's best-known blues performers, has become a national event as a result of KLON's efforts to record and promote the annual day-long concert.

National Public Radio was once again a pioneer in regenerating interest in live radio broadcasts of jazz performances. *Jazz Alive* presented jazz concerts from all over the United States. The program went under during NPR's financial crisis in 1982, but producing stations such as KLON and WGBO continue to make original jazz programming available to other public radio stations.

Public stations selecting the jazz format usually do not find much audience support for this program service. The audience for jazz music tends to be less affluent than the classical listening audience. As a result, many public stations emphasize jazz programming but include other program elements that attract more financial support. The format is popular with some university-licensed public radio stations such as WRTI-FM, at Temple University in Philadelphia, which does not seek financial support from its audience.

NEWS AND PUBLIC AFFAIRS

The news and public affairs format, although seemingly a natural for public radio, is less used than one might expect. National Public Radio supplies most news programs for public radio. Most stations integrate local news into NPR's 90-minute daily news magazine, *Morning Edition*, using preestablished cut-aways from the national news service. A few stations completely dismantle the national service and build a local news service that includes segments from the national programs.

Only two public radio stations use an all-news format. WEBR-AM in Buffalo, New York, was the first to do so, but it fills out its broadcast day with jazz. Minnesota Public Radio has one station, KSJN-AM, carrying largely news. WEBR-AM and KSJN-AM follow the traditional, commercial all-news format described in Chapter 16, using cycles of national and local headlines, local news coverage, commentary, public policy discussions, business news coverage, agriculture, sports, weather and so on. The major difference between noncommercial and commercial all-news stations is that public stations have no commercial restraints. Thus, topics local advertisers might consider touchy are not given "kid glove" treatment, and individual item length can be as long as necessary to adequately cover the topic.

Statewide, public radio news gathering organizations are just emerging in the 1980s. A subsidiary of the Association of California Public Radio Stations produces a daily, 15-minute news and feature service financed primarily from state funds. California Public Radio (CPR) also produces statewide coverage of major news events, and public radio stations use this service much in the way they use NPR programs. KSJN-AM in Saint Paul, Minnesota, is the anchor station for the owned-and-operated stations of Minnesota Public Radio that has also developed a statewide hourly news service for commercial stations. This new business venture is an imaginative way for a public radio organization to use its resources to earn revenue through a commercial business whose profits then subsidize its noncommercial programming.

The Pacifica stations—WBAI-FM (New York), WEFW-FM (Washington, D.C.), KPFT-FM (Houston, Texas), KPFA-FM (Berkeley, California) and KPFK-FM (Los Angeles)—pioneered the news and public affairs format for noncommercial public radio.[2] The Pacifica Foundation, licensee of the stations in this group, has a specific social and political purpose that influences their approach to news and public affairs. The listener has little difficulty recognizing the bias, and Pacifica is open about its philosophy. These stations were especially successful during the late 1960s and early 1970s when the nation was highly politicized over Vietnam and Watergate. They demonstrated the vital role of broadcasting that is free from commercial restraints in their reporting of the war and surrounding issues.

WEBR, KSJN and the Pacifica stations differ in both format and point of view. WEBR and KSJN concentrate on hard news reporting and investigation, similar to all-news commercial stations. They use their noncommercial status to provide more complete news coverage than is possible in commercial all-news operations. The Pacifica stations present a variety of news and public affairs programs in a somewhat eclectic format. One may hear an in-depth news report on Third World nations, followed by a program on automobile maintenance with a consumer emphasis, followed by a dialogue on Marxism, followed by a gay symphony concert, followed by a lecture on socialism. Listeners cannot predict what they will hear but can usually expect the ideas expressed and programs broadcast to reflect a nonestablishment, nontraditional point of view, whether the content is hard news reporting, commentary, news analysis, documentaries or public affairs programs. Although the majority of program ideas are oriented to the political left, the managers of the Pacifica stations recognize their responsibility to present unrepresented right-oriented political philosophies. They tend to leave the broad middle, the traditional point of view, to other noncommercial and commercial broadcasters.

News and public affairs programming is becoming increasingly viable in public radio because an information society demands high-quality news programs. The extraordinary popularity of NPR's news programs, *All Things Considered* and *Morning Edition*, have created audiences for news programs on public radio. These two programs have won many awards for broadcast journalism, and they provide a prestigious base for local station newscasts and supply sufficient national and international coverage to support expanded news programming in all public radio formats.

NPR's news programs also attract private and corporate financial support. News programming was difficult to underwrite locally or nationally until NPR pioneered a fund-raising strategy, the News & Public Information Fund, that enabled corporations, foundations and individuals to invest jointly. This fund in turn supports individual news programs.

COMMUNITY SERVICE AND PUBLIC ACCESS

Often considered the only legitimate format for public radio, community service and public access programming is essentially directed at the specific needs of unserved or underserved minorities. The programs provide information needed for social and economic survival and the opportunity for the public to use radio to vent emotions or solicit political support. KBBF-FM (Santa Rosa, California) is one of the few minority-owned public radio stations in America.[3] Its programming is directed at Spanish-speaking and bilingual audiences in the Santa Rosa Valley, and it has become a major production center for the network of radio stations serving the Spanish-speaking farm workers in California and other special-interest constituencies within the Latino community.

KYUK-FM (Bethel, Alaska), licensed as a community station to Bethel Broadcasting Co., serves its community with programs that include the broadcast of personal messages to individuals isolated by weather and geography. Moving from ice to deserts, KEDB-FM (Ramah, New Mexico) is licensed to the Ramah Navaho School Board and provides instructional services and specific education in the culture and history of the Navaho Indians.

One of the best examples of a more diversified community service format station is KPBS-FM (San Diego). It leads the nation in the development of bilingual programs for local and national distribution. For example, KPBS produces National Public Radio's *En Folke Nacionale.* Because San Diego, California, and Tijuana, Mexico, are border cities poised to become a truly international city, their social, political and economic lives are inextricably woven together. Recognizing this reality, the manager of KPBS-FM boldly discarded the station's evening classical music service, replacing it with a bilingual news and information service targeting the needs of the vast Hispanic community that hears KPBS on both sides of the border. The station also multiplexes SCA subcarrier services for the print-handicapped.[4] Its daily program services include city council hearings and comprehensive local news coverage. The program format is carefully designed to meet the needs of subsets of the San Diego community. No matter how obvious the justification for selecting this format appears to be for public broadcast stations, few managers successfully merge the components of community service and broadcasting. KPBS-FM is a rare example of success with the public service format.

The community service and public access format is highly individualized. As such, it is often so specialized that it fails to serve the community's broader needs. It frequently becomes the instrument of a vocal minority and fails to reach the people who need it. When people scream at people about a need that the people who are being screamed at already know exists, it accomplishes little beyond catharsis for the speaker. Those who could actually do something about the need being expressed listen to a different radio format, and those in need are likely to be so bored by discussion of issues they are already familiar with that they also listen to something else.

ECLECTIC

The most common public radio format is the eclectic format, which operates on the premise that public radio should have a little something for everyone. Although eclectic stations will occasionally emphasize one theme, listeners expect anything from a symphony concert to a school board meeting, to jazz, to cooking lessons, to folk music, to news, to soul music, to lectures on almost any topic. Increasingly, public radio stations are adopting a version of the eclectic format (or a two-part format). Many listeners enjoy turning on a radio station knowing it might broadcast a concert, a lecture by Herbert Marcuse, a community forum or a discussion of motorcycle riding. Essential requirements for this format are good quality and a logical program sequence. Listeners will depend on a program service that delivers a variety of programs as long as they can reconcile its scheduling logic and theirs.

The key to an eclectic format is achieving continuity—making the diverse parts a whole. The eclectic is the most difficult to design of all radio formats because it requires a logical program sequence that enables the listener to follow from one program to another with a sense of appropriateness. This logic comes from carefully planned program blocks that lead from one set of ideas or listening experiences to another. Listeners must be able to anticipate what they will hear when tuning to the station. The program manager must satisfy that expectation by programming so that listeners identify that station whenever they tune that frequency on the dial.

The critical difference between a successful eclectic format and an unsuccessful one is whether the listener gets a meaningful sequence of diverse programs or a program hodgepodge broadcast at the whim of a programmer attempting to keep the listener off balance. In communities where the commercial stations rely primarily on popular or beautiful music, the eclectic public radio service provides an interesting option for listeners who will be attracted by the station's diversity.

KCRW-FM (Santa Monica, California) is one of the best examples of an eclectic station.[5] It programs jazz, classical music, folk music, esoterica, coverage of local school board and city council meetings, Santa Monica College sports, political opinion, arts, news and music/talk mixes, such as its *Morning Becomes Eclectic*. Although this format may seem to be the hodgepodge for which public broadcasting is notorious, people who listen regularly to KCRW know what to expect when they tune to the station.

INSTRUCTIONAL

The instructional format was at one time the dominant format for noncommercial educational licensees. Some public radio stations licensed to school boards still broadcast classroom instruction, but in-school programming has generally moved to public television to gain the visual element. KBPS-AM in Portland is the prime example of the radio instructional format. It broadcasts other public radio program material but designates a part of its broadcast day for instructional broadcasts.

THE DUAL FORMAT

Dual format stations appeared in public radio in the 1970s. This format is similar to the eclectic but concentrates on two specific program forms—such as news and jazz. The dual format station focuses on building two distinct but comparable audiences for the station. WEBR-AM, Buffalo, for example, is all-news during the day and jazz at night; no attempt is made to mix the two formats. WUWM-FM in Milwaukee is also news and jazz. During the early morning and late afternoon drivetimes, WUWM broadcasts news; late morning, afternoons and evenings are for jazz. But WUWM's manager includes one or two jazz recordings in the news wheel to provide continuity and tries to maintain similar announcing styles for news and jazz. Continuity of style and an occasional reminder of both formats during the news and music segments provide the essential glue for both versions of the dual program format.

NATIONAL PUBLIC RADIO NETWORKS

Although one network, National Public Radio (NPR), has had long visibility as the national noncommercial service, two other radio networks emerged in the 1980s to compete for public radio affiliates. This section describes the economics and programming of these three networks.

National Public Radio

Less than one-fifth of public radio stations are members of National Public Radio (NPR). This system of about 220 noncommercial, nonprofit radio stations broadcasts to communities in 48 states, Puerto Rico and the District of Columbia. Each station, itself a production center, contributes programming to the entire system. Each station mixes locally produced programs with those transmitted from the national production center.

NPR, a private nonprofit corporation, distributes informational and cultural programming by satellite to member stations daily. Funds for the operation of National Public Radio and for the production, acquisition and distribution of radio programs come from corporate underwriting, private foundations, government agencies, the Corporation of Public Broadcasting and member stations.

NPR has traditionally programmed news, public affairs, art, music and drama to fit into whatever format member stations choose. The news and information programs already discussed, *Morning Edition* and *All Things Considered*, are NPR's most distinguished trademark and the core of its program service. It also has provided leadership in music and arts programming for the public radio system, such as *The World of F. Scott Fitzgerald, Jazz Alive, NPR Playhouse* (featuring new radio dramas), live broadcasts of musical events from Europe and from around the United States. NPR has also provided stations with in-depth reporting on education, bilingual Spanish news features and live coverage of Senate and House committee hearings. Satellite distribution of the NPR program service has meant better-quality transmission of existing programs and the distribution of up to a dozen stereo programs simultaneously.

NPR member stations are not required to use any given number of programs. Each station selects the programs that fit its format. However, the quality of national programs frequently entices stations to use NPR programs differing markedly from local station efforts.

In addition to Programming, two other NPR divisions, Representation and Distribution, also provide valuable services to member stations. The Representation Division, like a trade organization, represents NPR and public radio before the FCC, the Corporation for Public Broadcasting, Congress and any government agency involved with matters of importance to public radio. Member stations pay dues to support the Representation Division since it acts as an advocate for member stations in disputes with NPR and so must be funded separately. The Distribution division operates and maintains the satellite relay system. It also works with some autonomy within NPR because it has broad responsibility for the overall management of the information system.

NPR's Financial Crisis.   In the early 1980s, the Reagan administration advocated a phaseout of federal funding for public broadcasting. In response, NPR began a campaign to end its reliance on federal dollars. One part of that effort was the creation of NPR Ventures in 1983, a company joining commercial partners in new business activities to develop profits to replace federal dollars. Because the new ventures business is highly risky, many of NPR's first ventures failed to materialize.

A naive optimism on the part of NPR management was the major cause of a serious financial crisis in 1983. The attempt to realize huge profits from venture activities distracted NPR's officers from the daily operation and administration of the company, allowing a major failure of the budget control and financial accounting system to nearly destroy NPR.

Nonprofit organizations traditionally downplay the importance of financial accountability and frequently move revenue from budget category to budget category without careful controls on dollar flow. NPR's imaginative attempts to stretch income to serve too many budget purposes created a revenue shortfall that resulted in an insurmountable deficit. Another related characteristic of nonprofit companies affecting NPR's deficit was overly optimistic income projections. That NPR had no plan to reduce operational costs in the event of a financial crisis was also typical of nonprofit company problems.

NPR was saved from bankruptcy by a $9 million loan from the Corporation for Public Broadcasting. NPR member stations agreed to pay $1.6 million annually for three years (1984–86) to NPR to assist in repaying the loan. Some member stations also agreed to forego their entire annual community service grant to collateralize the loan. The Corporation for Public Broadcasting forced NPR to sell its satellite equipment to a special public trust to secure the future of the public radio interconnection system in the event of a loan default or other financial crisis.

NPR's president and several NPR officers were forced to resign as a result of the financial crisis, and more than 140 NPR employees lost their jobs. *All Things Considered* and *Morning Edition* were given top budgetary priority, but most of NPR's cultural and arts programs were lost. Partial recovery in 1984 allowed NPR to expand from 13 to 24 hours of classical music, seven days a week, and to add a daily ten-hour jazz service.

The Public Radio Satellite System. In the 1970s, public radio switched from land line interconnection to satellite interconnection. The Corporation for Public Broadcasting, NPR and public stations created a system of earth satellite stations that freed public radio from dependence on low quality, monaural telephone lines. Public radio leased 24 channels of full fidelity stereo transmission on Westar I to transmit and receive radio programs and data information. Sixteen uplinks and 280 downlinks were built.

The main originating terminal was constructed in Washington, D.C., and NPR was to manage the new distribution system. The system's primary purpose is to provide high-quality NPR programming to public radio stations, but the system is interactive, permitting origination of whole or partial elements of programs from all 16 uplinks. Through the Extended Program Service (EPS), producing stations and independent producers can distribute their programs by satellite to interested stations. Interconnection with European and Canadian satellite systems also enables U.S. public radio to use live programs originating outside the country.

The introduction of the satellite distribution system greatly increased the number of high-quality programs available to individual public radio stations. It also provides public radio with its best opportunity for generating commercial revenue to support NPR and member stations. By selling unused satellite time (excess capacity) to commercial users, public radio generates badly needed revenue without decreasing program availability.

American Public Radio and Other New Competition

In 1982, a group of five stations formed a second national radio network. American Public Radio Associates, composed of Minnesota Public Radio, KUSC-FM in Los Angeles, KQED-FM in San Francisco, WNYC AM/FM in New York and WGUC in Cincinnati, joined together to market and distribute programs they produced and to acquire other programming to distribute to affiliates.

American Public Radio differs from NPR in two ways. First, APR is not a membership organization but a network of affiliated stations paying fees to become the primary or secondary outlet for APR programs in their community. Unlike NPR (but like commercial networks), APR offers its programs to only one station in each market (exclusivity). However, when a primary affiliate refuses a program, it is offered to the secondary affiliate, much in the way small-market affiliations operate in commercial television. Second, APR's charter does not permit it to become a national production center. Like PBS, all its programs are acquired from stations or other sources. A program fund, supported by major foundations and corporations and administered by the APR board of directors, provides revenue for producers with ideas that fit the APR program schedule.

The most successful program APR distributed in its first year, 1982, was *A Prairie Home Companion,* produced by Minnesota Public Radio. By 1984, the majority of its schedule consisted of original performances by orchestras, soloists and ensembles, but a broader array is anticipated. Like commercial network affiliates, APR affiliates select programs individually for use in their schedules. APR does not supply a continuous long-form schedule. Over 230 public radio stations (95 percent of NPR's members) joined APR as affiliates in its first year, while continuing their membership in NPR.

In 1983, another national distribution organization, U.S. Audio, was formed by Eastern Public Radio, Audio Independents and the Longhorn Network. Like APR, the new network markets and distributes programs nationally. The appetite for more programming than NPR can supply is strong, but how many and which competing entities have economic and marketing viability remains to be seen.

A variety of station programming consortia also have emerged in public radio, parallelling those in public television, commercial broadcasting and cable. The Public Radio Cooperative (PRC), a joint venture of individual public radio stations largely in the northeastern United States, supplies programs to stations that pay a broadcast fee. Member stations produced many of the programs; the rest come from commercial syndicators.

THE FINE ARTS/CLASSICAL MUSIC FORMAT: A CASE STUDY

The largest class of public radio stations in America is that licensed to colleges and universities. The emergence of public broadcasting generated a substantial dilemma for many of those institutional licensees. Traditionally, campus radio stations were training grounds for journalism and broadcasting students and assorted radio freaks—students interested in careers in broadcasting or looking for an extracurricular activity. When the Corporation for Public Broadcasting, under a mandate from Congress in 1969, began to develop a national public radio system, it found many of the most desirable noncommercial licenses were held by colleges and universities. CPB provided special grants to selected holders of educational and noncommercial licenses to explore their institutions' and communities' support of a public radio service. Forming a public station generally meant relinquishing many educational opportunities for students.

The University of Southern California has held the license for KUSC-FM since 1946. Captain Alan Hancock—an oil wildcatter, marine biologist and amateur musician—decided it would be nice to share the concerts his string ensemble played with the citizens of California, or at least those few with FM receivers in 1946. Over the years the station served as an outlet for Captain Hancock and variously as laboratory for the Broadcast Communications Department of the university and toy for any given generation of students. The station was on the air from 4 to 24 hours per day, and the budget seldom exceeded $4,500 per year. It was typical of most college campus radio stations: It fluctuated between ingenuity and disaster.

In 1972 USC hired the first full-time employee to manage its radio station. The general manager's mandate was (1) to provide management continuity, (2) to work with the students operating the station and (3) to explore the station's potentials for the university and the community. The students had great ambitions for the station and encouraged the manager to expand KUSC's service to the broader public and to build the station into a strong public radio station.

The first requirement was to convince the university to adequately fund the operating budget and invest in capital improvements. Second, it was necessary to plan the transition of the staff from students to professionals. Third, a format had to be chosen that would have the greatest potential for success in a market saturated by more than eighty radio stations, six of them public. After four years of advocacy, the university invested $150,000 in capital improvements and dramatically increased the operating budget from $26,000 to nearly $100,000. CPB granted KUSC $775,000, and in December 1976 new facilities became operational.

Objectives

The strategies employed to achieve success in radio are grounded in the very nature of the medium. People listen to radio stations, not radio programs. They compare stations with stations, not programs with programs. Therefore, the successful radio broadcast builds a sound image that distinguishes one station from all the others. KUSC's management set an ambitious goal: It wanted KUSC to become the premiere fine arts and classical music broadcast station in America—the standard against which all public or commercial classical music stations would be measured.

The format includes a significant number of nonmusic features and programs with an overall emphasis on quality in performance, language and writing. A careful integration of high-quality news, cultural affairs and modular features on the arts, drama, poetry and literature enables KUSC to develop a consistent sound image with a variety of aural experiences. Although 85 percent of its programming is music, the format also uses local, national and international news about the arts. Working on the premise that arts are not an escape from everyday life but rather a vital part of it, KUSC also airs significant news and public affairs programs from NPR.

Competition

The Los Angeles market has 82 commercial and noncommercial radio stations, sharing an audience of nearly 10 million, the second largest in the United States. Establishing a new service and building an audience in such a market were major challenges.

KUSC's primary competition is a commercial classical music service with a long and well-established tradition as "the" classical AM and FM music source in Los Angeles. Changes in ownership over the years left the stations in the hands of individuals who did not take seriously the broadcast audience for traditional classical music. First shorter works, then movements of major works, then themes from movements of major works took over programming. An increasing number of commercials offended dedicated classical music and casual listeners.

In the mid-1970s, KUSC decided to counter with a program service empha-sizing quality in all programming aspects—signal, performance, information about the music and nonmusic broadcast programs. The result was that many classical listeners alienated by the commercial AM and FM services began to listen. KUSC's audiences grew from 30,000 to 230,000 in less than two years, but the commercial FM station also maintained its audience or grew slightly in listenership. This phenomenon suggests that KUSC shares a large part of its audience; that KUSC provides an alternative classical format for listeners to select if they are dissatisfied with a given program on the competition; and that listeners turned away from the classical format to another format such as beau-tiful music before KUSC emerged.

In addition to entering a crowded radio market, KUSC had a dial location problem. The main FM competition was adjacent to KUSC on one side of the broadcast band and KPFK—the Pacifica station that programmed a lot of classical music until KUSC emerged—on the other. Creating a sound image that would make it impossible for listeners to confuse KUSC with either of the other sta-tions was enormous.

While KUSC's primary competition is from commercial stations, the grow-ing number of noncommercial stations in the Los Angeles market has become an additional challenge. By 1983, the noncommercial stations numbered seven, three offering serious competition to KUSC. KPFK, the Pacifica station, is the oldest challenger. KCRW, licensed to Santa Monica College, is the newest and most formidable competitor for the public radio market. A change in its trans-mitter facilities provided KCRW with a coverage area identical to KUSC's, and careful positioning in the market has attracted some of the audience that used to rely solely on KUSC for its NPR programming. The dilemma facing KUSC is whether to concede certain programs to KCRW and build competitive alternative program offerings or to continue to share the audience for many programs with KCRW.

This situation illustrates the conflicting strategies among both public radio and public television programmers. One view holds that a community should have several options for hearing public radio programs (or seeing public television programs). By presenting the same program at different times, a larger number of people are able to hear each program (and the cumulative audience builds). On the other hand, by presenting the same program on several stations, the audience has fewer total program choices than if each station had a unique schedule (eliminating some diversity, although increasing diversity is an acknowledged goal of public broadcasting). In addition, stations airing the same programs divide the audience rather than lure new listeners from commercial radio or other activities. And most crucial for community-supported stations, sharing programming blurs station image and divides financial support.

As of 1984, KUSC had taken a middle ground, offering both duplicate and some alternative programs. This strategy let it maintain its competitive position by keeping all major NPR programs in the schedule, while counting on KCRW's NPR schedule to free it to present some alternative programs. The new programs give KUSC something unique to promote and a chance to build new audience loyalties.

KLON, Long Beach, is the third station making significant progress in the Los Angeles market. It has a weak signal in much of the area KPFK, KCRW and KUSC serve, but is nonetheless significantly increasing its audience within the area. KLON's format combines jazz and local news. It includes NPR's national news programs as more of a courtesy than as competition since all NPR programming is available to KLON's audience on other stations. If KLON turns to more original programming or joins another network service, it could become a major threat to the Los Angeles-based stations.

Staff

The transition from a completely volunteer staff (mostly students) to paid professionals was tedious and long. Fortunately, students suggested that a fully professional staff was needed to provide a high-quality, competitive public broadcast service. Tying salaries for professional staff to university faculty and staff pay scales also complicated staff development. (Public radio in general has disproportionately lower salaries than public television.)

The first staff under the new management combined volunteers, students and full-time paid employees. But as community expectations for a high-quality broadcast service increased, upgrading the professional experience and specialized skills of the staff was necessary. As KUSC drew more sophisticated listeners, the mail regarding employee errors and mistakes increased in volume and intensity. Staff unable to meet audience expectations for informed opinion, commentary and programming were let go. The need for excellence in performance and content forced the station to search for personnel in all areas of operation who were knowledgeable about concert music. All of the persons presently working at KUSC know, understand and love classical music. Even administrative, clerical and engineering personnel are expected to have a working knowledge of classical music and fine arts. Many successful commercial and noncommercial radio stations employ as few as four or five employees. KUSC's 38 people are the margin of difference in its service, and the station makes a substantial financial and personal investment in its employees.

Promotion and Development

The critical role of promotion, advertising and public relations in establishing a public radio service cannot be overemphasized. All the program strategies in the world are useless if people do not know that the program service exists. A major public relations firm was engaged to develop KUSC's promotional and public relations programs. The senior officers of the firm were fans of the station, believed in its potential and agreed to handle KUSC at a rate far below charges made to commercial clients.

Their first assignment was to design and implement a graphic image to complement the sound image. Next they embarked on a campaign to get every inch of print copy and electronic media coverage possible. The judicious use of meager sums of money to purchase the best possible advertising space was helpful in introducing new listeners to the station. The radio editor of a major trade paper once commented that in his career with that trade paper, he had never seen any radio station get as much ink as KUSC.

KUSC eventually internalized its public relations department and staffed it with one officer from the public relations firm. An aggressive public relations campaign is still a major component of the station's management strategy.

Fund Raising

Another major component of the KUSC strategy is fund raising. A fatal flaw in most public broadcasting entities is the failure to provide for a diversified financial base. Developing a competent fund-raising department requires time and professional leadership. Success comes to any public broadcasting station only through the commitment and support of the *local* community. The amount of support that a station generates is relative to the size, wealth, support of nonprofit organizations and the pure pride of its community. But no community can expect federal and state revenues if it does not demonstrate its willingness to invest its own resources in its public broadcast service. Either the licensee fully subsidizes the station or commits itself to fund raising.

However, some institutions prohibit their public broadcasting stations from fund raising. Such a decision deprives the institution and its station of money essential to station growth and community service. Academic institutions are typically the most restrictive of the public broadcasting licensees. They usually fear that fund raising for the public broadcasting station will compete with the institution's other fund-raising activities. This attitude is shortsighted and fails to acknowledge that public broadcasting and education are distinct and separate businesses. Donors are able to make distinctions between gifts to a university and gifts to a broadcast station licensed to the university.

The University of Southern California allowed and encouraged KUSC to raise funds. As a result, KUSC has generated substantial operating funds. Careful coordination between KUSC and the university's development office avoids embarrassing conflicts with potential donors.

Accountability

Finally, a major failure of many public broadcasting entities is financial accountability. NPR's near disaster, described earlier in this chapter, underscores the need for sound fiscal management. Public broadcasters often get so caught up in the design and development of their program service that they neglect to establish sound business practices, especially financial record-keeping. Lionel van Deerlin, chairman of the House Communications Subcommittee, told a gathering of public radio managers attending the Public Radio Conference in San Francisco in 1978 that the state of financial record-keeping in public broadcasting was appalling. Other government agencies, corporations and foundations also show concern about the lack of sound business procedures in the administration and accounting practices of nonprofit organizations, including public broadcasting.

The call for accountability in public programs by consumer activist organizations, the reduction of tax revenues and changes in tax laws greatly reduce the amount of revenue available for nonprofit entities. As a result, government agencies, foundations, corporations and individual donors are increasingly interested in the best use of their investments. Financial accountability serves as one measure of the effective management of limited resources. It also provides additional security against wastefulness, duplication of services and misappropriation of funds.

KUSC maintains its own business office working in tandem with the business offices of the university to keep accurate records of business transactions and administer finances. KUSC's decision to hire a full-time business manager has been repaid a thousandfold.

Evaluation

KUSC has established goals for its service. The station believes it should reach at least 0.5 percent of the available audience of 12 million people in southern California and should eventually have a weekly cumulative audience of 750,000. The initial goal was to reach that number in five years. Every scrap of available data is used to evaluate reaction to the program service. Mail response, telephone response, program guide questionnaires, direct-mail solicitation, community ascertainment, personal contact and Arbitron ratings are basic evaluative tools.

A radical change in listenership between one rating period and the next revealed the importance of audience data in program evaluation. During one year the station had a very high weekly cume followed by a rating period with significantly lower numbers. The staff noted several contributing factors in the ratings decrease, and most of them were tied to programming. First, the commercial station broadcast a program unavailable to KUSC that greatly reduced the Saturday morning audience. Second, KUSC aired a series of programs on experimental composer Arnold Schoenberg during the same ratings period. Because of the low audience appeal of experimental music, that program registered the lowest ratings ever for a series on KUSC. Third, the afternoon classics program had a drop in ratings because the announcer had included more than the normal quantity of new and unfamiliar music.

The strategy for combating such ratings vagaries is, first of all, to identify the few programs the competition has that are not available to KUSC. If it is not possible to secure rights to those programs, KUSC must broadcast stronger programs opposite them. Second, during a ratings period the station will not broadcast a series of programs that is likely to draw a limited audience. This tactic does not imply that only "safe" programs will be broadcast, only that the timing of the broadcast of limited appeal programs will be more carefully selected. One can afford such programs when other programs are stronger and the overall ratings are higher. Third, the daily programming will be corrected to maintain the proper balance of familiar music.

As a whole, public radio station managers are devoting more effort to audience research. Many stations subscribe to the Radio Research Consortium, a company public radio stations created to provide detailed analyses of Arbitron data for individual subscribers. Audience data enables programmers to make informed decisions about audience flow and listening trends when creating program schedules and so build audience size.

Some persons argue that public broadcasting stations should not seek high ratings. Nonsense. Ratings provide a relative measure of success, and success is a desirable objective. The more individuals public radio serves, the better. Although public broadcasters may rely less on the number of people they reach than on the delivery of alternative program services to special audiences, it is imperative that they serve the largest number of individuals within those areas of special interest. To aim for less is to misuse a public trust and underutilize a scarce commodity—the broadcast spectrum.

TRENDS

Public radio grew considerably in the 1970s and has grown more in the 1980s. Both public and commercial radio audiences will continue to expand as long as radio provides local, personal, informational, educational and entertainment services. Public radio audiences, especially, will increase as public stations mature and become more professional.

The introduction of the Public Radio Satellite System opened up opportunities for independent producers, production companies, syndicators and public radio centers. This inexpensive distribution means created competing networks of program suppliers, increased the program market and diversified program offerings. The emergence of American Public Radio and U.S. Audio signals the end of National Public Radio as the dominant supplier of public radio programs. Although NPR will continue as a major programming producer, the new networks will supply alternative programming sources, increasing the competition for funds for program support. The new competition has three positive side effects: (1) more and diversified programs will be available to local communities through their public radio stations, (2) increased competition will stimulate donor interest in public radio and (3) public radio will no longer rely on a single programming source, minimizing the effects of any future NPR financial problems.

The chief threats to public radio continue to be lack of funding and the government bureaucracies that manage the system. Public radio is relatively inexpensive. Because it costs less, it is often difficult to convince the persons and agencies that finance public broadcasting to allocate sufficient funds to accomplish the quality of service listeners demand. Bureaucrats also tend to consider radio and television as one—lumping them together as "the media"— ignoring their subtle but substantial differences. This view is as disastrous as expecting a basketball team to use a football because both basketball and football are sports that use a ball. If public radio is left with its existing structure intact, it has a great future.

SUMMARY

Public radio seeks to combine localism and programming integrity to attract big cumulative audiences that will actively support its fund-raising activities.

Public radio stations use six formats to meet this challenge. The classical format, illustrated here by the case study of KUSC, shows how a clear set of objectives, a high-quality staff and ongoing evaluation help a public station meet its commercial competition in the ratings. Although only two public stations use the all-news format, news itself is playing a greater role in all public radio, partly due to the strong news base NPR provides. Jazz is one of the most recently developed public radio formats among community licensees, and its listeners are not usually financial donors. Community service and public access programming typify public radio in many people's minds, and the format generally serves minority audiences with informational rather than entertainment programming. Eclectic programming is the most common and most difficult format to succeed with, whereas the instructional was once the easiest, usually having a built-in market. But radio now plays a diminished role in schools; television has preempted its function. The dual format combines programming for two separate audiences by shifting from a daytime format to a nighttime format. Promotion, development, fund raising and strict accountability are the major tools that assist the public radio broadcaster to high levels of achievement in programming. NPR's high-quality news and arts programming have occupied center stage in public radio programming, but partly as a result of NPR's financial crisis and partly as a result of cheap satellite distribution technology, joint ventures, consortia and new networks challenge its role in the mid- and late 1980s. The future holds greater competition among public radio stations within many markets and a greater number of program sources to aid them in differentiation.

Notes

[1]WNED-FM is one of three stations licensed to Western New York Educational Foundation. WNED-FM and WEBR-AM were commercial stations the foundation purchased to operate as noncommercial broadcast stations. The price of approximately $1.8 million is believed to be one of the highest outright purchase prices ever paid for a noncommercial station.

[2]The Pacifica stations were founded in 1949 in Berkeley, California. All of the stations qualify for financial support from the Corporation for Public Broadcasting, but only one—KPFT-FM in Houston—is a member of the national public radio system. Primary support for Pacifica stations comes from listener donations, and the stations generally refuse support from business and industry.

[3]KBBF-FM is licensed to the Bilingual Broadcasting Foundation. The station was established by support from the National Campaign for Decency of the Roman Catholic Church and was set free to develop its own support in the community. While the station struggles to survive, it has become a major training center for Spanish-speaking personnel for local public radio stations and National Public Radio.

[4]The FCC authorizes FM stations to transmit two or more signals in the same channel (multiplex), and expanded this opportunity in 1983 to include commercial ventures for public stations.

[5]KCRW-FM is licensed to Santa Monica Community College. The majority of the staff are professionals or community volunteers; however, some students work at the station for college credits.

Selected Sources

Freiberger, Paul. "Western Public Radio: The Independent Producer Gets a Chance." *Public Telecommunications Review* 7 (September/October 1979): 12–14.

Listening to the Future: Cable Audio in the 80s. Washington, D.C.: National Public Radio, 1982.

Lukoff, Manny. "The University and Public Radio: Who's in Charge?" *Public Telecommunications Review* 7 (September/October 1979): 22–26.

Public Radio and State Governments. Vols. 1 & 2. Washington, D.C.: National Public Radio, 1981.

Williams, Jr., Wenmouth, and Krugman, Dean M. "Innovativeness and the Public Radio Audience." *Journal of Broadcasting* 25 (Winter 1981): 61–69.

Afterword

PREPARING FOR THE FUTURE

This section, written by Sydney W. Head, summarizes some of the newer types of programming made possible by innovative technology. It points out that programmers of the future need to be aware of these new opportunities and willing to think of novel ways of filling screens and loudspeakers with new sights and sounds. Much of the programming of the future will not be programming as we know it, but will incorporate material hitherto alien to conventional notion of what constitutes programming. Sydney W. Head's biographical information appears at the start of Chapter 1.

A PROGRAMMING PROGNOSIS

At the beginning of this book, I said that programmers must be futurists, able to foresee social trends that will affect public tastes and interests and to program accordingly. They need to be futurists in another sense as well—able to understand technological trends and to evaluate their probable impact on future programming and its strategies.

No one, of course, can predict with certainty where the new technology and the new regulatory (or better, deregulatory) trends will ultimately take us. But it behooves the programmer to keep up with developments in technology, regulation and the business of telecommunications. More specific advice would be outmoded before this book gets into print. All we can say is, "Be prepared, hang loose, monitor developments, track the experiments and jump on whatever bandwagon you think will take you toward your goal."

In organizing your perceptions, it may be helpful to think in terms of *proliferation, symbiosis* and *convergence.* Proliferation refers to the recent exponential increase in numbers of new technologies. Symbiosis refers to their interdependence and mutual sharing. Convergence refers to the fact that current technological developments tend to bring together into new configurations elements that formerly seemed entirely separate. First came technological expansion, with broadcasting wedded to satellites, computers and other new technologies such as videodisc. Then came programming symbiosis, with all the media sharing versions of the same products and being influenced by the same trends. Cable, for example, shares off-network syndication and movies with DBS, videocassette and pay-per-view. We even have videogames prompting the creation of television programs such as the *Pac Man* cartoon. The success of Music Television (MTV) illustrates convergence of radio, television, the record industry, cinematography and even publishing. Newspapers must prepare for the likelihood that teletext and videotex will cause their hitherto separate medium to converge with broadcasting and cable. Once we had clearly labeled pigeonholes, one named "broadcasting," the other named "common carriers." But with symbiosis and convergence have come a blending of sound, pictures and print into a variety of new services for some of which new pigeonholes have yet to be invented. All these new services clamor for program material and for the skills of the programming specialist. Following is a list of the major types of services, along with some speculations about what convergence might mean for programmers.

Broadcasting

After years of gathering in over 90 percent of the available audience, the television networks began a steady decline in the late 1970s—down to 78 percent in 1984 accompanied by a concommitant increase in audience shares for independent stations, cable and public television. Forecasters expect the network decline to continue throughout the 1980s, reaching a percentage in the low 60s by 1990. Not all of the loss will be due to cable television, though the greatest decline will occur in heavily cabled areas.

Independent television stations gained shares as their counterprogramming strategies began to pay off. Some critics also blame network decline on short-sighted programming policies—especially the tendency to cancel promising new series before they had a chance to build a following.

In the early 1980s the National Association of Broadcasters began bombarding its members with information about investment opportunities in the new technologies—just in case. No one expected broadcasting to disappear, but most observers expected its programming to change. They recalled how radically the coming of television altered radio programming in the 1950s. Radio's solution—leaving to television the role of mass entertainer, concentrating instead on formula programming designed to win the allegiance of narrowly defined slices of the local audience—will not work for television. Video programming costs too much.

Among programming changes suggested as the salvation of broadcast television are: concentration on news and information, leaving big entertainment to cable, more local production (along with cuts in production costs involving improved production technology and changes in union rules and pay scales), more repeat scheduling (pioneered by public television and adopted by cable television). The success of superstations and the example of the more successful basic cable services suggest that the compatibility principle in television programming remains a vital ingredient in the programmer's strategic arsenal.

Subscription Television

The over-the-air version of pay television, known as subscription television or STV, is a hybrid combining functions of normal broadcast television with pay television. As an example of imaginative STV programming, consider the case of UHF station KSTS-TV in San Jose, California: During the daytime it offers business-oriented programming; from 7 to 9 P.M. it switches to STV programming in Japanese; from 9 to 11, STV programming in Chinese; and from 11 onward

X-rated STV programming. FCC deregulation liberalized STV rules, opening the way to new opportunities for innovative programming. Many predict, however, that STV will soon be supplanted by cable, MDS or direct broadcasting because of their multichannel capacity.

LPTV

A new class of stations, beginning to be licensed in the 1980s, called low power television (LPTV), will create new programming challenges. LPTV stations, which could number in the thousands, will be more highly localized in coverage area than regular television stations, offering opportunities for narrowly targeted local programs. Many LPTV outlets will probably be programmed as subscription television stations, at least part of the time, but will initially supply informational and public affairs programming during most of their hours rather than the feature films now characterizing STV. LPTV faces an agonizing battle for survival unless the FCC permits large networks of stations with duplicated programming.

Basic Cable

All services cable subscribers receive for the minimum subscription rate qualify as basic services. As discussed in Chapters 10 and 12, they include locally originated programs, superstation programs and a wide range of services designed especially for cable and delivered to cable headends by satellite. Most are highly specialized, from all-news to all-health, from programs for children to programs for art lovers, from weather to religion, from ethnicity to rock. Basic cable services offer opportunities for imaginative programming, whether in terms of access channel fare amateur producers and performers prepare, local features the cable system itself produces, or highly sophisticated specialized information on a satellite channel.

The history of MTV illustrates cable's potential for creative program ideas. Television had always been regarded as an inhospitable setting for rock music, which remained a province of the radio station. But on cable, MTV (for "Music Television"), consisting essentially of songs by one rock group after another accompanied by promotional clips known as videos, won instant acclaim. The videos accompanying the music, though originally simply promotional pieces prepared by record companies to sell their records, became virtually a new cinematic genre, often highly abstract and evocative. The ripple effect from the success of MTV has had a marked influence on radio and television broadcast programming, on how the record companies market their products and on independent filmmakers.

The basic cable networks face a shakedown and merger period, leading to a reduced number of services programming to substantial numbers of homes nationwide. Although targeting is the key to any marketing plan, over the long run, advertising support will have the same effect on cable that it had on broadcast television—forcing it to program for the largest possible cumulative audiences.

At the same time, local origination cable (LO) represents an opportunity for local television and radio broadcasters. Increasingly, broadcasters are leasing channels from cable systems to forestall newspaper competitors and lay the groundwork for possible new revenue (from teletext and videotex services, for example). LO channels need attractive programs that will encourage advertisers to buy time.

SMATV

Another hybrid service links master antenna systems in apartment complexes with satellites, hence the name satellite master antenna television (SMATV). It avoids costly franchise applications because it has no need to use municipal rights of way to string cables and therefore pays no fees to municipalities where it operates. Since SMATV is merely an alternative way of delivering the same programming that cable systems deliver, it offers the same opportunities as cable for programming innovations.

MDS

Pay television supplies the programming for multipoint distribution services (MDS), a common-carrier, over-the-air version of cable television. MDS uses radio transmission paths in the superhigh frequency band, above VHF and UHF broadcast television. Conventional sets cannot receive it without converters. Once a single channel, now averaging four, MDS may eventually rival cable in its multichannel capabilities. An NAB study showed MDS' technical potential for 30 channels. From the perspective of management, MDS is an economical alternative to a cable system in areas with many high-rise apartment buildings. Again, it offers programming opportunities identical with those of cable.

Pay Cable

Pay cable costs cable subscribers extra monthly fees, over and above the basic cable fee. In the pay arena, about a dozen of the big guns of the entertainment world lay down barrages of movies and special productions. A major preoccupation of pay programmers is how to schedule the maximum number of repeat performances of their relatively few, but very expensive, productions without disillusioning subscribers and causing costly audience churn. Pay cable appears to be strengthening as a result of the mergers the Justice Department permitted, and most services will continue throughout the 1980s without advertiser support. The financially weaker pay cable services, however, will probably have to incorporate some advertising by the late 1980s, much in the manner of the public television experiments of the early 1980s. Pay cable has become the mainstay of cable programming, and the number of pay channels can be expected to increase, creating new programming opportunities.

DBS

Direct broadcast satellites promise to challenge the existing heirarchy of broadcasting and cable in signal delivery. If home satellite receiving antennas become sufficiently cheap and easy to install, they could render huge investments in broadcasting stations and cable installations redundant, except for purely local services. (Local cable could, of course, include many functions other than disseminating entertainment and information, such as home shopping and banking or home security systems.) But DBS can reach widely scattered homes that will always be uneconomical to wire, and DBS may supplant MDS and SMATV in metropolitan apartment complexes and other dense housing units. Using a single receiving antenna for many subscribers appears financially practical in cities. Barely beginning operation in 1983, DBS remains an unknown but promising potentiality for programmers' future.

Two-way Cable and Pay-per-View

Warner Amex (also owner of The Movie Channel, MTV and Nickelodeon) pioneered in the installation of interactive, or two-way, cable. Trade-named "Qube," the Warner Amex system enabled viewers to respond to questions or express preferences by "keying in," using extra buttons on the channel selector keypad. This facility opened up a whole new range of innovative possibilities for programmers and producers alike. Though Qube has been on the air only in a few cities (Columbus and Cincinnati, Ohio, Pittsburgh, Detroit), viewers in the rest of the nation had opportunities to see how it worked on national broadcast television. For example, *Tony Brown's Journal* on PBS routinely used the Qube facilities to secure the Columbus audience reactions, the results of which the national PBS audience saw on the screen. Although local programming has been discontinued on Qube, interactive facilities lend themselves to pay-per-view operations that let subscribers order up specific programs for which they pay a stipulated price per program. Qube's Pittsburgh system devotes five channels to pay-per-view options, for which subscribers pay "admission" fees varying from $2.50 to $4.00 per program. Two-way cable opens up almost unlimited opportunities for innovative program ideas—provided an economic base for them can be found.

Pay Radio

Another new technology on the horizon, covered from the cable radio programming perspective in Chapter 12, is pay radio. Local cable systems carry radio into homes and offices just as they carry television programs. Cable systems can hook an array of audio signals into home high-fi sets, exceeding the number and technical quality of locally available radio signals by drawing upon national satellite offerings. Small audiences wanting specialized channels could subscribe to individual services—as in pay cable television. The question here is the cost to the subscriber. Cable radio, however, represents a potential drain on over-the-air audiences, and thus a threat to radio broadcasters that ignore the opportunity to negotiate to get their signals carried by the cable systems in their coverage areas.

Videotex

Textual and graphic material can be delivered to home television receivers by means of a piggyback signal encoded in regular television channels or on cable as discussed in Chapter 12. When delivered in the vertical blanking interval it is called teletext, a one-way delivery medium. The generic term *videotex* also covers interactive systems using ordinary telephone lines as well as cable interconnections to deliver two-way videotex.

Videotex services developed more rapidly in Europe than in the United States, where lack of a common standard delayed implementation (the FCC wanted to leave the choice of standard to "the market"). U.S. experimental installations have tried out four incompatible systems developed by Canada, France, Great Britain and Japan. Videotex has been described as "essentially a hybrid of mass-communications and computer technologies. Combining television, print and data processing, it blurs the traditional distinctions between publishing a message, broadcasting a message, transmitting a message and reporting a message. As a result, videotex defies easy categorization."[1]

Videotex programming consists of material best displayed as letters, numbers, line-drawings, graphs, charts, designs and maps. Interactive videotex has proved of interest to banks and business publications, one-way teletext to newspapers and cable. Games as well as information form part of teletext's program resources. But the industry's current problem is defining the ideal content for these media, how often content should be updated, how much detail should be supplied, what price should be charged. Teletext has very limited information capacity and limits on how long subscribers will wait between frames (cycle time). Videotex requires personal computers (or specially constructed keyboards and decoders) and will be a subscriber service with charges based on both time and specific content used. It awaits improvements in user operations to make its technology easy for nonexperts to use and is tied to the problems arising from equipment incompatibility. Videotex has potential for educational services and other highly specialized uses; teletext appears to be a general consumer service—if it succeeds at all.

Teletext and videotex require programmers to think in terms of new categories of program material, neither quite like written text nor much like conventional video material. Advertising, too, takes on new forms in videotex services. Indeed, videotex "programs" do not seem like programming in the traditional sense at all; nevertheless, programmers will be needed to invent new ways of filling videotex pages and to adapt content to fit within the severe constraints imposed by the page-by-page format.

Subsidiary Radio Services

Radio stations can now distribute several simultaneous signals over subcarriers, in addition to stereo—either to paying subscribers or to the general public. For the next decade, such services are likely to be business-oriented data services rather than audio, supplying stock and commodity listings or paging services for mobile trucks. Subcarrier services also challenge programmers to think of content types quite different from the information-entertainment types that have been the stock-in-trade of radio programmers in the past.

SUMMARY

To recapitulate, the programmer needs to know how to find program materials, to negotiate effectively, to define suitable target audiences, to select programs for these audiences and to construct effective schedules. The programmer needs research analysis skills and the ability to read shifts in lifestyles, attitudes and social trends. The industry's evaluative benchmarks are moving from gross ratings to subscriber satisfaction as increasing numbers of services require monthly renewal. Though underlying common strategies apply, the particular strategies employed must be suited to the particular medium employed, the type of programming it furnishes and the audience it reaches. Programmers must be alert to the implications of new technologies for their profession. Media proliferation has created symbiosis and convergence in content, technology and economics. Some of these innovative media require types of content never before considered as programming. Developing this new content will require new partnerships, and the product will be distributed by multiple media, some still in their infancy. Unlimited opportunities exist in the programming field for those with sufficient imagination and inventiveness to grasp them.

Note

[1] "Videotex: The Electronic Word," *The 1983 Field Guide to the Electronic Media* (New York: *Channels*, 1983), p. 42.

Abbreviations and Acronyms

Italicized terms are explained further in the Glossary.

AAA	Association of Advertising Agencies
ACT	Action for Children's Television
ADI	*Area of dominant influence*
AFTRA	American Federation of Television and Radio Artists
AID	Arbitron Information on Demand
AIT	Agency for Instructional Television
AOR	Album-oriented rock (radio music format)
AP	Associated Press (news service)
AQH	*Average quarter hour*
ARB	Arbitron Research Bureau
ASCAP	American Society of Composers, Authors and Publishers
BMI	*Broadcast Music, Inc.*
CAB	Cabletelevision Advertising Bureau
CATV	Community antenna television
CBC	Canadian Broadcasting Company
CBN	Christian Broadcasting Network
CEN	Central Educational Network
CHN	Cable Health Network (now Lifetime)
CHR	Contemporary hit radio (radio music format)
CM	Commercial matter
CNN	Cable News Network
CP	Construction permit
CPB	*Corporation for Public Broadcasting*
C-SPAN	Cable-Satellite Public Affairs Network
CTAM	Cable Television Administration and Marketing Society
DBS	Direct broadcast satellite
DJ	*Disc jockey*
DMA	*Designated market area*
EEN	Eastern Educational Television Network
ENG	Electronic newsgathering
ERP	Effective radiated power
ESF	*Expanded sample frame*
ESPN	Entertainment and Sports Programming Network
FCC	Federal Communications Commission
FTC	Federal Trade Commission
G	Movie code: general audiences
GPNITL	Great Plains National Instructional Television Library
HBO	Home Box Office
HHs	*Households having sets*
HUTs	*Households using television*

ID	Station identification
IN	Independent News (was INN)
INN	Independent Network News (now IN)
INTV	Independent Television Station Association
IRTS	International Radio-Television Society
ITNA	Independent Television News Association
ITV	*Instructional television*
LPTV	Low power television
LULAC	League of United Latin American Citizens
MBS	Mutual Broadcasting System
MDS	Multipoint Distribution Service
MNA	Multi-Network Area Report
MOR	Middle-of-the-road (radio music format)
NAACP	National Association for the Advancement of Colored People
NAB	National Association of Broadcasters
NAEB	National Association of Educational Broadcasters
NATPE	National Association of Television Program Executives
NCTA	National Cable Television Association
NET	National Educational Television
NFLCP	National Federation of Local Cable Programmers
NOW	National Organization for Women
NPR	*National Public Radio*
NRBA	National Radio Broadcasters Association
NSI	Nielsen Station Index
NTI	Nielsen Television Index
O&O	*Owned-and-operated station*
OPT	Operation Prime Time
PBS	*Public Broadcasting Service*
PDG	Program Development Group
PG	Movie code: parental guidance suggested
PMN	Pacific Mountain Network
PSA	Public service announcement
PTAR	*Prime-time access rule*
PTL	Praise The Lord (religious program service)
PTV	*Public television*
R	Movie code: restricted
RAB	Radio Advertising Bureau
RPC	Radio Programming Conference
RTNDA	Radio-Television News Directors Association
SCA	Special Communications Authorization (FCC subcarrier permit)
SECA	Southern Educational Telecommunications Association
SESAC	Society of European Songwriters, Artists and Composers
SIN	Spanish International Network
SIP	Station Independence Program (service of PBS)
SMATV	Satellite master antenna television
SMPTE	Society of Motion Picture and Television Engineers
SPC	*Station Program Cooperative* (service of PBS)
SRA	Station Representatives Association
SSS	Southern Satellite Systems
TBN	Trinity Broadcasting Network

TvB	Television Bureau of Advertising
TVPC	Television Programmers' Conference
TvQ	Television Quotient (program and performer ratings)
UPI	United Press International (news service)

Glossary

Italicized words in the definitions also appear as defined terms.

AC Adult contemporary, a soft rock music format targeting the 25–54 age category.

Access Public availability of broadcast time. In cable, one or more channels reserved for public use, possibly requiring fees to cover facility costs. See also *Prime-Time Access Rule.*

ACE Awards sponsored by the National Cable Television Association for original cable programs.

Action News Television news reporting style emphasizing films, rapid pace and visuals; frequently includes informal dialogue among anchors.

Actuality An on-the-spot news report or voice of a newsmaker (frequently taped over the telephone) used to create a sense of reality or to enliven news stories.

Adaptation A film or video treatment of a novel, short story or play.

Addressability Having equipment that permits the cable operator to send a separate set of signals to each household that can be turned on or off at the cable *headend*; provides maximum security; usually associated with the potential for *pay-per-view* channels.

Ad Hoc Networks Temporary national or regional hook-ups among stations for the purpose of program distribution; especially common in radio sports.

Adjacencies A commercial or promotional spot next to a specific program or type of program, especially spots next to prime-time programs. Also programs (usually compatible in type) in consecutive time periods.

Affiliate A commercial radio or television *station* receiving more than ten hours per week of *network* programming. Occasionally applied to individual cable operators contracting for *pay, basic* or services, or to public stations airing noncommercial programming from the *Public Broadcasting Service* or *National Public Radio.*

Aided Recall In survey research, supplying respondents with a list of items to stimulate their memory.

Alphanumeric News Service Television news created on a character generator and distributed as lines of text to be displayed on television receiver screens.

American Society of Composers, Authors and Publishers (ASCAP) An organization licensing musical performance rights. See also *Broadcast Music, Inc.* (BMI).

Amortization The allocation of syndicated program series costs over the period of use to spread out total tax or inventory and to determine how much each program costs the purchaser per airing.

AOR Album-oriented rock, a rock music format appealing to a strongly male audience, ages 18–34, consisting of less well-known songs by avant-garde rock artists and groups as well as their most popular works.

Area of Dominant Influence (ADI) One of 211 geographical market designations defining each television market exclusive of all others; indicates the area in which a single station can effectively deliver an advertiser's message to the majority of homes. ADI is Arbitron's term; Nielsen's comparable term is designated market area (DMA).

Ascertainment A two-part examination of local audience needs the FCC requires to retain broadcast television licenses.

Audience Flow The movement from one program or time period to another, either on the same station or from one station to another; includes turning sets on and off. Applied to positive flow encouraged by similarity between contiguous programs.

Audimeter Nielsen's in-home television rating meter.

Audio-Speech Capacity A computer able to create sounds representing human speech (not natural sounding in present state of technology).

Auditorium Research In radio, mass testing of song *hooks* to measure their popularity.

Automation Use of equipment, usually computerized, that reproduces material in a predesignated sequence; includes both music and commercials and produces a *log* of airings acceptable to advertising agencies. Also used for traffic and billing and in some television production processes.

Avail Short for *availability*.

Availability Spot advertising position offered for sale by a *station* or *network*.

Average Quarter Hour (AQH) Rating showing the average percentage of an audience that tuned a radio or television *station*.

Barter Exchange by a *station* of commercial announcements for the use of a television program (the commercials usually are aired within the program being bartered but sometimes elsewhere in a station's schedule). Purpose is to eliminate the exchange of cash and thus reduce the station's financial commitment and provide a program vehicle for the advertiser. *Hee Haw, Lawrence Welk, Mickey Mouse Club, Mike Douglas* and *Phil Donahue* are bartered or partially bartered programs.

Barter Incentive Extra inducement to encourage negotiation of a barter deal.

Basic Cable Those cable program channels supplied for the minimum subscriber rate, including all local broadcast stations and assorted advertiser-supported cable networks. See also *basic networks* and *must-carries*.

Basic Networks Those cable services for which subscribers do not pay extra on their monthly bills (although the cable system may pay to carry them); contrast with *pay networks*.

Beat The geographic area or topic-related area in which a reporter gathers news (for example, White House, state government, northern suburbs).

Beautiful Music A format emphasizing low-key, mellow, popular music, generally with extensive orchestration and many classic popular songs (not rock or jazz).

Bicycling Transfer of *syndicated* or *group* program tapes or films by means of wheeled delivery services or mail (in contrast to wired or microwave transmission).

Blackout A ban on airing an event, program or *station's* signal. Also FCC rules for blocking imported signals that duplicate other stations' programs, eliminated in 1983.

Black Week A seven-day period during which no network ratings were taken until the early 1970s; generally, the week before the beginning of the fall television season,

Christmas week, and a week in April and in June; programs with low *ratings (documentaries, reruns)* usually were programmed during this time.

Blockbusters Special programs or big-name films that attract a lot of attention and interrupt normal scheduling; used especially during sweeps to draw unusually large audiences; usually exceed 60 minutes in length.

Blocking Placing several similar programs together to create a unit with *audience flow.*

Block Programming Several hours of similar programming placed together in the same *daypart* to create *audience flow.* See also *Stacking.*

Boilerplate Syndicated program packages using low-cost *formats.*

Bonus Audience Generally, any audience coverage for which the advertiser does not pay; specifically, households increasing the total *households using television (HUTs)* for a program as a result of cable distribution.

Bridging Beginning a program a half-hour earlier than competing programs to draw their audiences and hold them past the starting time of the competing programs.

Broadband Having a wide bandwidth capable of carrying several simultaneous television signals; used of coaxial cable.

Broadcast Music, Inc. (BMI) A music-licensing organization created by the broadcast music industry to collect and pay fees for musical performance rights; competes with *American Society of Composers, Authors* and *Publishers* (ASCAP).

Broadcast Window Length of time in which a program, generally a feature film that was made-for-pay cable, is made available to broadcast stations in syndication. See also *Pay Window.*

Bumping Canceling a showing, as in *preempting.*

Buying Renting by station of programs from *syndicators.* See also *Licensing, Prebuying* and *Presold.*

Cable Audio Radio signals converted to FM and delivered to homes along with cable television, usually for a separate monthly fee; same as *cable radio.*

Cablecasting Distributing programming by coaxial cable as opposed to broadcast or microwave distribution; also, all programming a cable system delivers, both pay and basic, except over-the-air signals.

Cable Penetration The percentage of households subscribing to basic cable service.

Cable Radio Radio signals converted to FM and delivered to homes along with cable television, usually for a separate monthly fee; same as *cable audio.*

Cable Subscriber A household hooked to a cable system and paying the monthly fee for *basic* cable service.

Cable System One of nearly 6,000 franchised, nonbroadcast distributors of both broadcast and cablecast programming to groups of 50 or more subscribers not living in dwellings under common ownership. See contrasting *SMATV.*

Cable System Operator The person or company managing and owning cable facilities under a *franchise.*

Cabletext *Videotex* on an otherwise unoccupied cable channel.

Cable TV All programming, both *basic* and *pay,* transmitted to subscribers by a cable system.

Call-Out Research Telephone surveying of audiences initiated by a station or research consultant; used extensively in radio research especially to determine song preferences in rock music. Contrast with call-in research referring to questioning listeners who telephone the station.

Call Screener Person screening incoming calls on telephone call-in shows and performing other minor production functions as assistant to a program host.

CATV The original name for the cable industry, standing for "community antenna television" and referring to retransmitting of broadcast television signals to homes without adequate quantity or quality of reception.

Canned Prepackaged or prerecorded; commonly applied to *syndicated* mini-lectures, automated music, commercials and other program elements that arrive at a station preproduced.

Checkerboarding Scheduling five *stripped* programs alternately, one each day in the same time period, that is, five different shows five days of the week; used of prime-time access television programming on *affiliates*, in any *daypart* on *independents*.

Cherrypicking In cable, selecting individual programs from several cable networks to assemble into a single channel (as opposed to carrying a full schedule from one cable network).

CHR Contemporary hit radio, a format that plays the top songs, but uses a larger playlist than top 40.

Chromakey The special-effect mechanism for inserting one picture on top of another by electronically eliminating background of a specific frequency (usually blue).

Churn Turnover; in cable, the addition and subtraction of subscribers or the substitution of one pay cable service for another; in broadcast network television, shifting of the prime-time schedule; in public broadcasting, changes in membership.

Clearance Acceptance of a *network* program by *affiliates* for airing; the total number of clearances governs a network program's potential audience size.

Clear Channel AM radio station the FCC allows to dominate its frequency with up to 50kw of power; usually protected for up to 750 miles at night.

Clipping Illegally cutting off the beginning or end of programs or commercials, often for the purpose of substituting additional commercials.

Closed Captioning Textual information transmitted in the vertical blanking interval that appears superimposed over television pictures.

Clutter Excessive amounts of nonprogram material during commercial breaks; includes credits, *IDs*, *promos*, audio tags and commercial spots.

Commercial Load The number of commercial minutes aired per hour.

Common Carriers Organizations that lease transmission facilities to all applicants; includes firms that provide network signal distribution by telephone, microwave and satellite.

Compensation A broadcast network payment to an affiliate for carrying network commercials (usually within programs, but sometimes radio affiliates carry only the commercials embedded in a local program).

Composite Week An arbitrarily designated seven days of program logs from different weeks, reviewed by the FCC in checking on licensee program performance vs. promise (until 1982 for radio).

Contemporary FCC radio *format* term covering popular music, generally referring to rock.

Continuous Season Network television scheduling pattern spreading new program starts across the September to May year (rather than concentrating them in September/October and January/February).

Converter An electronic device that shifts channels transmitted by a cable system to other channels on a subscriber's television set.

Co-Productions Agreements to produce programs in which costs are shared between two or more corporations or stations.

Core Schedule Two hours of programs fed to PBS member stations for simultaneous airing four nights per week; begun in 1979.

Corporation for Public Broadcasting (CPB) Government-funded financial and administrative unit of national public broadcasting since 1968.

Correlator An inside or telephone reporter on radio who aids the editor; frequently responsible for *actualities* for news broadcasts.

Cost per Thousand The ratio of the cost of a commercial spot to the size of the audience, reported in thousands; basis of comparison of advertising rates among media. Other bases are cost per point and cost per person.

Counterprogramming Scheduling programs with contrasting appeal to exploit competitors' weaknesses and lure audiences.

Cream Skimming Marketing only to high-return portions of an audience, generally upper income households.

Critical Information Pile A quantity of important news breaking simultaneously that causes massive alterations in planned news coverage.

Crossover Using characters from one program series in episodes of another series.

Crossover Points Times when one network's programs end and another's begin, usually on the hour and half-hour, permitting viewers to change channels easily (although a long program such as a movie may *bridge* some hour and half-hour points).

Cume Cumulative rating; the total number of different households that tune to a *station* at different times, generally over a one-week period; used especially in commercial and public radio, public television and commercial sales.

Cycle Span of news flow between repeat points in all-news radio.

Daypart Period of two or more hours, considered as strategic unit in program schedules (for example, morning *drivetime* in radio—6 to 10 A.M.—and *prime time* in television—8 to 11 P.M.).

Dayparting Altering programming to fit with the audience's changing activities during different times of the day (such as shifting from music to news during *drivetime*).

Daytimer An AM radio station licensed to broadcast only from dawn to dusk.

DBS Programming from *direct broadcast satellites* going from satellite to home receiving dishes, bypassing a ground-based distributor such as a broadcast station or cable system. DBS operations began in 1983.

Dedicated Channel Cable channel restricted to a single type of program or aimed at a single audience (for example, sports or children's channels).

Delays Programs taped for rebroadcast at another time; contrast with *live*.

Demographics Descriptive information on an audience, usually the vital statistics of age and sex, possibly including education and income.

Demo Tape Demonstration tape of a program, used for preview without the expense of producing a *pilot*.

Designated Market Area (DMA) See *Area of Dominant Influence (ADI)*.

Diary Instrument for recording stations and hours of listening or viewing, used by Arbitron, Nielsen and other researchers; filled out by audience members.

Differentiation Perceived separation between networks, stations or services by the audience and advertisers, generally based on programming differences and promotional images.

Direct Broadcast Satellites Special satellites intended for redistribution of *DBS* television programming to individual subscribers' receiving dishes.

Disc Jockey (DJ) A radio announcer who introduces records.

Disconnects Cable subscribers who have canceled service.

Dish Receiving or sending antenna with bowl-like shape intended for transmitting satellite signals.

Distant Signals Broadcast station signals imported from another market and retransmitted to cabled homes; usually *independents*. See also *Superstations*.

Docudrama Fictionalized drama of real events and people.

Documentary Program that records actual events and real people.

Dolby A circuit incorporated in audio equipment to improve the ratio of *signal-to-noise*.

Downlink Satellite-to-ground transmission path, the reverse of *uplink*; refers also to the receiving antenna.

Download Transmission and decoding of signals at receiving end; used of satellite program (and computer) signals.

Drama Prime-time series program format, usually one hour long, contrasting with situation comedy; includes action-adventure, crime, doctor, adult soap and other dramatic forms.

Drivetime In radio, 6 to 10 A.M. and 4 to 7 P.M.

Early Fringe In television, the period preceding the early news, usually 4 to 6 P.M. See *Fringe*.

Earth Station Ground receiver/transmitter of satellite signals; when receiving, the purpose usually is to redirect satellite signals to a broadcast station or to cable *head-end* equipment; also used to receive *DBS* signals without a broadcast or cable intermediary. Most are receive only stations, also called antennas or *dishes*.

Eclectic Mixed; applied to varied programming in radio incorporating several types of programs; a recognized *format* in public radio.

Effective Radiated Power Watts of power measured at receiving antennas on average; used to measure the strength of antennas.

Emmys Awards to top broadcast television programs and performers.

ENG Electronic news gathering, refers to portable television equipment used to shoot and tape news stories on location.

Entering Stations In public broadcasting, those stations participating in an SPC bid or a production venture.

Episode One show out of a series.

Equal Time An FCC rule incorporated in the Communications Act of 1934 requiring equivalent air time for candidates for public office.

Ethnic Programming by or for minority groups (for example, Spanish-speaking, American Indians, blacks).

Exclusivity The sole right to air a program within a given period of time in a given market; imported signals can violate exclusivity agreements.

Expanded Sample Frame (ESF) The base unit for a sampling technique that includes new and unlisted telephone numbers.

Extraneous Wraps Reusable closings for radio news, prerecorded by an announcer or reporter for later on-air use.

Fairness Doctrine An FCC policy upheld by the Supreme Court requiring that *stations* provide airtime for opposing views on controversial issues of public importance.

Family Viewing Time A short-lived NAB code reserving the first two hours of television prime time—7 to 9 P.M. (EST)—for programs suitable for both children and adults; later determined to be illegal (if done at the FCC's behest) by a federal court.

Feature Radio program material other than hard news, sports, weather, stock market reports or music; also called *short-form*. In television and cable, generally short for theatrical films used as features.

Feature Film Theatrical motion picture, usually made for theater distribution; feature films occupy about one-fifth of the total syndication market.

Feature Syndicator Distributor of short, stand-alone programs or series, as contrasted with long-form (continuous) programming; used in radio, television and cable.

First Refusal Rights The legal right to consider a program proposal until reaching a decision on producing or not producing it; can stymie a program idea for years.

First-Run The first airing of a television program (not counting theatrical exhibit of feature films).

Flat Fee Method of payment involving a fixed lump price; contrast with sliding scale (usually based on number of viewers).

Flow See *Audience Flow*.

Focus Group People participating in a joint interview on a predetermined topic as a method of research.

Format Overall programming design of a station, cable service or specific program, especially used of radio and cable program packages.

Formula The elements that define a format.

Franchise Legal permit a local government awards to allow a cable operator to use public rights of way to install wires in a community or portion of a community; delineates geographic area to wire.

Frequency In advertising, the number of times the audience was exposed to a message.

Fringe The television time periods adjacent to *prime time*—from 4 to 7 P.M. and 11 P.M. to midnight or later (EST). *Early fringe* means the time preceding the early local newscast; *late fringe* usually starts after the end of late local news.

Frontload In pay television, to schedule all main attractions at the beginning of the month.

Futures Projected episodes in a series that have not yet been produced; typically, network series programming intended for syndication that may be purchased while the series is still on the network for a negotiated price that takes account of the purchaser's risk.

General Premium Channels Cable movie networks targeted at a broad audience, seeking appeal to all or nearly all demographic groups.

Gold A hit song or record generally with lasting appeal; in sales, a song selling a million copies, an album selling 500,000 copies.

Graphics Titles and other artwork used in a program, promo or commercial spot.

Group Parent corporation, owners of several broadcast stations or cable systems.

Group-Owned Station Radio or television station licensed to a corporation owning two or more stations; cable system owned in common with many other cable systems. See also *MSO*.

Hammock The position between two successful programs; they support a new or less successful program by lending their audience to it.

Hard News Daily factual reporting of national, international or local events. See also *Soft News*.

Headend Technical headquarters for receiving and transmitting equipment for a cable system.

Homes Passed The total number of buildings cable wires pass, irrespective of whether the occupants are or are not cable subscribers.

Hook A plot or character element at the start of a program that grabs audience attention; also, in radio research, a brief song segment characterizing a whole song.

Horizontal Documentaries Multipart treatment of a news subject spread over several successive days or weeks. See also *Vertical Documentaries*.

Host Personality that moderates a program or conducts interviews on radio, television or cable.

Hot Clock See *Wheel*.

Households Having Sets (HHs) Ratings industry term for the total number of homes with receiving sets (AM or FM radio, UHF or VHF television or cable hook-ups), that is, total potential audience.

Households Using Television (HUTs) Ratings industry term for the total number of sets turned on during an *average quarter hour*, that is, actual viewing audience to be divided among all stations and cable services in a market.

House Show Program produced in the station's studios rather than purchased as a syndicated property.

Hyping Excessive promotion of a program or airing of special programs to increase audience size during a *ratings* period.

Independent A commercial television broadcast *station* not *affiliated* with one of the national *networks* (by one FCC definition, carries fewer than ten hours of network programming per week).

Infomercial A long commercial, usually incorporating a demonstration and sales pitch lasting from 3 to 15 minutes, typically presented on cable television or videotex.

Instructional Television (ITV) Programs transmitted to schools for classroom use by public television or radio stations.

In-Tab Diaries that are actually returned in usable form and counted in the sample.

Interactive Cable Two-way cable that permits each household to receive one stream of programming and also to communicate back to the cable headend computer; *Qube* is the best-known interactive system.

Interconnects Transmission links among nearby cable systems permitting shared sales and carriage of advertising spots.

Interstitial Programming Short programs intended to fill the time after an odd-length program is completed. Also called *shorts.*

Inventory The amount of time a station has for sale (or the commercials or programs that fill that time).

Iris Awards for television advertising commercials.

Jock See *Disc Jockey.*

Joint Venture Cooperative effort to produce, distribute or market programs.

Kiddult Television programs appealing to both children and adults.

Kidvid Television programs for children.

Latch-Key Children Children whose parents work who are given their own keys so that they may return home by themselves after school.

Lead-In Program preceding others, usually intended to increase *audience flow* to the later programs.

Leapfrogging Importing distant (noncontiguous) signals without importing all intervening station signals; used of cable systems picking up independent station signals.

License Fee Charge for the use of a syndicated program or feature film.

Lifestyle The way different people live; in research, measures of people's attitudes, interests and opinions.

Lift Added audience gained by combining popular and less popular cable services in marketing.

Liners Brief ad lib comments by *disc jockeys* between records on music radio.

Live Not prerecorded; or in the record industry, recorded as performed, not edited.

Live Feed A program or insert coming from a network or other interconnected source without prerecording and aired simultaneously.

Local Programs or commercials generated 50 percent or more within a station's broadcast coverage area.

Local Origination Cable programs the cable system produces or licenses from syndicators to show locally, including *access* programs, as contrasted with basic cable networks or *pay cable networks.*

Log The official record of a broadcast day, kept by hand or automatic means such as tape, noting opening and closing times of all programs, commercials and other non-program material and facts mandated by the FCC.

Long-Form Longer than the usual length of 30 minutes for most television series and 60 minutes for *dramas* or *specials* (for example, a 60- or 90-minute fall season introduction to a new prime-time *series*) or playing the entire two or three hours of a feature film in one evening; also, in radio, nationally distributed programming using a single musical format, as in automated beautiful music or rock, as opposed to syndicators and networks of *short-form* programming.

Loss Leader A program (or *format*) broadcast because management thinks it is ethically, promotionally, culturally or aesthetically worthwhile rather than directly rewarding financially; used in image building.

Low-Power Station A newly created class of broadcast television stations covering less than ten miles with a signal.

Made-for-Pay Programs, usually feature films, produced for pay cable distribution; may later be syndicated to broadcast stations.

Made-for-Television Movie feature produced especially for television, usually fitting a 90-minute or two-hour format with breaks for commercials.

Magazine Format A television or radio program composed of varied segments within a common framework, structurally resembling a printed magazine.

MDS Multipoint distribution service, a system of distribution of pay television using microwave to rooftop antennas; generally distributes pay cable networks (without using cables outside buildings).

Merger Legal joining of two separate corporations or companies into one legal entity.

Minicam A small, portable television camera.

Mini-Doc A short documentary.

Minimote A small television remote unit.

Minipay A basic cable network that charges cable systems a small amount per subscriber per month for its programming.

Miniseries Series shorter than the traditional 13 episodes.

MSO Multiple system operator, owner of more than one cable system; see also *group owner*.

Multiaffiliates Stations with affiliation contracts with two or more networks, generally specifying a primary and a secondary affiliation.

Multiple Franchising Licensing more than one cable company to wire the same geographic area and compete for subscribers; occurs very infrequently.

Multitransponder Satellites having many *transponders* and thus capable of carrying many simultaneous television signals; all communications satellites have 18–24 transponders nowadays.

Music Sweep Uninterrupted period of music on music radio.

Narrowcast Targeting programming, usually of a restricted type, to a defined demographic or ethnic group; used when either the programming or the audience is of a narrow type.

National Public Radio (NPR) The noncommercial radio *network* service financed primarily by the *Corporation for Public Broadcasting (CPB)*; serves *affiliated* public radio stations.

National Representative See *Station Rep(resentative)*.

Network An interconnected chain of broadcast stations or cable systems that receive programming simultaneously; also refers to the administrative and technical unit that distributes (and may originate) preplanned schedules of programs (for example, ABC, CBS, NBC, Mutual, PBS, NPR, HBO, Showtime).

News Block Extended news programming; in radio, the time immediately before and after the hour when stations program news; in television, the period between 5:30 and 7:30 P.M. (varies with market).

Nonprime Time In network television, the hours outside of prime time, especially morning, day and late night; nonprime-time programming usually excludes news and sports since they are handled by separate network departments.

Oscars Awards for feature films and performers.

Off Line Use of program elements as they are fed from a network or other source.

Off-Network Syndication Selling programming (usually series) that has appeared at least once on the national networks directly to stations or pay television.

Off Syndication Programming, usually feature films, made available to pay cable after a broadcast station syndication run.

Open-Entry Policy FCC policy permitting *common carriers* unrestricted access to commercial satellite channels. See also *Retransmission Consent*.

Operation Prime Time (OPT) An association of stations and producers contributing funds on a prorated basis for the production of high-quality, *first-run* drama intended for prime-time airing.

Overnight Radio airtime in the small hours, usually from 1 to 4 A.M.

Overnights National television *ratings* from metered homes in major cities, available the following day.

Owned-and-Operated Station (O&O) Broadcasting station owned and operated by a network or group. Number of stations licensed to a single entity is limited to seven television stations (five VHF and two UHF) and seven AM and seven FM stations.

Parity Equivalence; in network television, equal numbers of affiliates with equal circulations so that each network has a fair chance to compete for ratings/shares based on programming popularity.

Passive Viewing Watching television without actively consulting all the competing program options.

Pay Cable Cable television programming service for which the subscriber pays an extra fee over and above the normal monthly cable fee. See also *Pay Television*.

Pay Cable Networks National satellite-distributed cable programming for which subscribers pay an extra monthly fee, over and above the monthly fee for basic cable service. See also *Premium*.

Payola Illegal payment for promoting a recording or song on the air.

Pay-per-View Cable or subscription television programming that subscribers pay individually for, billed per-program viewed.

Pay Television An umbrella term for any programming for which viewers pay a fee; includes *pay cable, subscription television, pay-per-view, MDS* and *DBS*.

Pay Window A period of time in which a program, usually a feature film, is made available to pay cable, generally from six to twelve months.

Pick Off Preempt.

Piggybacking Scheduling two part-time cable networks on the same satellite channel, usually one in daytime and one in nighttime; also, scheduling two cable networks on the same channel, irrespective of source; also, in advertising, promoting two cable services as if carrying one (or subscribing to one) were conditional on carrying (or subscribing to) the other.

Pilot A sample first program of a proposed television series, often longer than regular episodes; introduces characters, set, situations and style of the program, generally accompanied by heavy promotion when aired.

Plateauing Leveling off in successive ratings; can characterize a single program or an entire *station's* or *network's* programming.

Play Showing; also, one to two showings of each episode of a program until all are shown as specified in a licensing agreement.

Playlist Strategically planned list of records to be played on music radio.

Play Off Last games in a sports series; also, last showings of episodes of a licensed program series to get full value for the program expenditure.

Plugola Inclusion of material in a program for the purpose of covertly promoting or advertising a product without disclosing that payment of kind was made; penalties for violating *payola* or plugola regulations may be up to a $10,000 fine and/or a year in prison for each offense. See also *Payola.*

Positioning Making the audience believe one *station* is really different from its competitors; especially important for *independent* television stations and music radio stations.

Prebuying Paying for future airing of theatrical properties while they are still in production or being shown in movie theaters. See also *Buying* and *Presold.*

Preemption Cancelation of a program by an *affiliate* after agreement to carry the program, or cancelation of an episode by a *network* to air a news or entertainment *special*; also applied to cancelation of a commercial sold at a special preemptible price to accommodate another commercial sold at full rate.

Premium In cable, pay networks costing subscribers an extra monthly fee over and above *basic cable.*

Presence Quality of audio that seems close to the speaker (rather than faraway).

Presold Series episodes or film idea sold before being produced (generally related to high reputation of the producer). See also *Buying* and *Prebuying.*

Prerun Showing before network television air date (usually on pay television).

Prime Time Television *daypart*; in practice, 8 to 11 P.M. (EST) six days a week and 7 to 11 P.M. Sundays. Technically, any three consecutive hours between 7 P.M. and midnight).

Prime-Time Access Rule (PTAR) FCC rule that, in general, limits evening *network* programming to three hours of entertainment material between the hours of 7 to 11 P.M.

Program Practices Department Network department that clears all programs, *promos* and commercials before airing, responsible for administration of network guidelines on such subjects as sex, race and profanity. Also called "standards and practices" or "continuity acceptance department." Function also performed at every station.

Promo A broadcast advertising spot announcing a new program or episode or encouraging viewing of a *station's* or *network's* entire schedule.

Promotion Informational advertising of programs, *stations* or *networks.*

Prosocial Behavior and ideas that appear to provide constructive role models and uphold the highest traditional social values.

Psychographics Descriptive information of the lifestyles of audience members; includes attitudes on religion, family, social issues, interests, hobbies and political opinions.

Public Broadcasting Service (PBS) The noncommercial, federally supported interconnection service that distributes programming nationally to member public television stations; serves as a representative of the *public television* industry.

Public Radio The noncommercial radio service in the United States, nearly all FM licensees.

Public Station Noncommercial station; prior to 1967 called *educational station*; licensed by the FCC as a noncommercial educational broadcast station.

Public Television (PTV) Overall term replacing educational television to describe noncommercial television.

Qualitative Research Systematically gathered information on broadcast and cable audiences and program viewing other than ratings collected by the industry; also used in sociological research to contrast with other research methods.

Qube Warner Communications' two-way, interactive cable system first installed in Columbus, Ohio; now in Pittsburgh and other cities.

Rating Audience measurement unit representing the percent of the potential total audience tuned to a specific program or station for an *average quarter hour* period.

Reach Cumulative audience or total circulation of a station or service.

Recurrents Songs that have been number one on *playlists* in the recent past; used in scheduling songs on popular music stations.

Remote Live production from locations other than a studio (such as football games, live news events).

Rep See *Station Rep(resentative).*

Rerun Repeat showing of a program first aired earlier in the season or some previous season. Commonly applied to series episodes.

Rest Length of time a feature film or other program is withheld from cable or broadcast syndication to avoid losing audience appeal from overexposure.

Retransmission Consent Control by originating station of right to retransmit that station's signals for use by cable sytems; also a proposal to require agreement from copyright holder before programs can be picked up by resale carriers *(common carriers)*; issue particularly affects *superstations*, cable operators and writers/producers. (The disintegration of the 1978–79 Communications Act *rewrite* effort along with a key 1979 FCC decision permitting an *open-entry policy* for common carriers has tabled this issue, although inadequate 1978 Copyright Act retransmission provision remains.)

Reverse Telephone Directory   A phone book arranged by addresses instead of names; can be purchased from urban telephone companies.

Rewrite   Proposed redrafting of the Communications Act of 1934, introduced in early 1970s but dropped in 1979.

Rip and Read   Simplest form of newscasting; announcer rips copy from wire service and reads it on the air.

Road-Blocking   The simultaneous airing of a program or commercial on all three networks to gain maximum exposure for the content (for example, presidential addresses, political campaign spots and commercial spots).

Rocker   Colloquial term for a radio station with a rock music *format.*

Rolling Averages   In radio research, using different daily audience samples and averaging them together; used in telephone ratings research by Birch.

Rotation Scheduling   Repeating programs (usually movies) four to six times during a month on different days and often in different dayparts to encourage viewing, creating a cumulatively large audience; used by pay cable and public television services.

Royalty   *Compensation* paid to copyright holder for the right to use copyrighted material.

Run   The play of all episodes of a series one time.

Run-Through   Staging of a proposed show for preview by program executives; often replaces script for game shows.

Sandwich   For affiliate news, splitting the local news into two sections placed before and after the network newscast; in promotion, standardized opening and closing segments of a *promo.*

Schedule   The arrangement of programs in a sequence.

Screener   An assistant who preinterviews incoming callers or guests on participatory programs; also called *call screener.*

Screening   In research, locating individuals fitting specific age or gender criteria.

Second Season   Traditionally the 13 weeks of episodes (of new or continuing programs) beginning in January; vitiated by practice of ongoing program changes called *continuous season.*

Self-Transmitting Reporter   One with a "lunchbox" or miniature transmitter; does not need telephone lines to reach the broadcast studios.

Semipilot   Sample videotape version of a proposed game show with audience and production devices (such as music) but no finished set.

Series   Program that has multiple *episodes* sharing a common cast, plot line and situation.

Share   A measurement unit for comparing audiences; represents the percentage of total listening or viewing audience (with sets on) tuned to a given station; total shares in a designated area in a given time period equal 100 percent.

Shelf Space Vacancies on the channel array of a cable system.

Shorts Very brief programs, usually five minutes or less in length; see also *interstitial programming.*

Signal-to-Noise Ratio Relationship between the amount of transmission noise in a signal and the intended sounds or data.

Sit-Com See *Situation Comedy.*

Situation Comedy A program (usually a half-hour in length) in which stereotyped characters react to new plots or altered situations.

Skew Graphs Bar graphs showing the percentage of each of six demographic groups a station reaches; used to compare all stations in a market.

Slivercast Very narrowly targeted programming, used of cable networks that distribute only to small total audience, especially programming in foreign language or appealing to a hobby group.

Slow Builders Programs acquiring a loyal audience only after many months on the air.

Small Sweeps July ratings period. See *Sweeps.*

SMATV Satellite master antenna television; "cable" television distributed within a restricted geographic area (private property) not requiring a franchise to cross city streets or public rights of way; otherwise similar to cable television systems; charges a monthly fee and usually delivers a mix of pay and basic cable channels.

Soap See *Soap Opera.*

Soap Opera A serial drama generally scheduled on broadcast networks during weekday afternoons. Advertisers (such as laundry detergent manufacturers) targeting homemakers dominate soap advertising time.

Soft News Opposite of *hard*, fast-breaking news; consists of *features* and reports that do not depend on timely airing (for example, medical reports, entertainment industry stories, hobby material).

Sound Bed Musical background; an instrumental beginning and ending for commercials, station identifications or other on-air talk, applied especially to radio.

Special One-time entertainment or news program with special interest; usually applied to *network* programs that interrupt regular schedules.

Specialized Premium Networks *Pay cable* services targeting a less broadly defined audience than a *general premium service*, usually carrying a more restricted schedule of programs (all adult, all children, all Spanish-language).

Spectacular Older term for network television one-time-only programs interrupting regular scheduling. See *Special.*

Spinoff A series using a secondary character from another series as the lead in a new series (for example, *Rhoda* was a spinoff from the successful appearances of the character Rhoda in episodes of *Mary Tyler Moore*).

Stacking Sequential airing of several hours of the same kind of programs; similar to *block programming.*

Standards and Practices Department See *Program Practices Department.*

Station Facility operated by licensee to broadcast radio or television signals on an assigned frequency; may be *affiliated* by contract with a *network* (for example, ABC, NPR) or may be *independent* (unaffiliated); may be commercial or noncommercial (public).

Station Program Cooperative (SPC) The vehicle for public station participation in choosing the national program schedule carried by PBS.

Station Rep(resentative) Firm acting as sales agent for client station's advertising time in the national market.

Staying Power A series idea's ability to remain popular year after year.

Step Deal Agreement to supply funds to develop a program idea in stages from expanded concept statement to scripts to *pilot* to four or more episodes.

Stockpiling Preemptive buying of *syndicated* programs for future use that also keeps them off the market and unavailable to competitors.

Stop Set Interruption of music on radio to air commercials or other nonmusic material.

Stringer A free-lance reporter paid per story rather than by hour or month.

Stripping Across-the-board scheduling; putting successive episodes of a program into the same time period every day, five days per week (for example, placing *Star Trek* every evening at 7 P.M.).

Strip Run/Strip Slot See *Stripping*.

Stunting Frequent shifting of programs in schedule; also using *long-form* for a program's introduction or character *crossovers*; goal is to attract audience attention and consequent viewership; frequently used in the week preceding the kickoff of a new fall season combined with heavy *promotion*.

Subscription Television Over-the-air *pay television* (scrambled).

Substitution Changing one pay-cable network subscription for another.

Superstation An *independent* television *station* that has its signal retransmitted by satellite to distant cable companies for redistribution to subscribers (for example, WTBS-TV, formerly WTCG, from Atlanta, Georgia).

Sweeps The periods each year when Arbitron and Nielsen gather audience data for the entire country; the ratings base from a sweep determines the network and station rates for advertising time until the next sweep. For television, the four times are November (fall season ratings most important, becomes ratings base for the rest of the year); February (rates fall season again plus replacements); May (end-of-year ratings); and July, when a small sweep takes place (summer replacements). Radio sweeps occur at different times and vary from 48 weeks to two to six occasions annually depending on market size.

Switch-In Adding a new cable network to a cable system line-up.

Switch-Out Cutting a cable network from a cable system line-up.

Syndication The marketing of programs on a station-by-station basis (rather than through a *network*) to *affiliates, independents,* or *pay television* for a specified number of plays; *syndicators* are companies that hold the rights to distribute programs nationally or internationally. See also *Off-Network Syndication*.

Syndication Barter Practice in which advertiser rather than *station* buys rights to *syndicated* program and barters remaining spots to stations in exchange for free airing of its own spots in the program. See also *Barter*.

Syndication Window Length of time a program, usually a feature film, is made available to broadcast stations, generally ranging from three to six years; may be as short as two months for pay television. See also *Pay Window*.

Talk Radio format characterized by conversation between program hosts and callers, interviews and monologues by personalities.

Targeting Aiming programs (generally by selecting a similar group of appeals) at a demographically, psychographically or ethnically defined audience.

Tease A very brief news item or program spot intended to lure potential audience into watching or listening to the succeeding program or news story; referred to as the "teaser" when used as a program introduction.

Teletext One-way electronic publishing service, using the vertical blanking interval of the broadcast signal. See also *Videotex* and *Cabletext*.

Tent-Poling Placing a highly rated program between two series with lower ratings (often new programs), intended to prop up the ratings of the preceding and following programs.

Tiering Arranging cable networks in sets marketed as a pay unit to potential subscribers.

Titles Text portion of a program with the name of the program or stars or credits or source.

Tonnage Raw audience size (as opposed to demographic subgroups); used in advertising.

Tracking Charting a program's *share* of audience over time and in different markets.

Transponder One of several units on a communications satellite that both receives *uplink* signals and retransmits them as *downlink* signals (amplified on another frequency). Some users lease the right from satellite operators to use entire transponder (40 MHz bandwidth); others lease only a part of a transponder's capacity.

Treatment Outline of a new program (applied especially to *soap operas*); describes characters and setting of program (before a script is prepared).

Trending Graphing ratings/shares over a period of time or on a series of stations to anticipate future ratings/shares, especially of syndicated series; same as *tracking*.

Turnover Changes in the numbers of subscribers, listeners or viewers; in cable, the ratio of disconnecting to newly connecting subscribers. See also *Churn*.

TvQs Program popularity ratings characterized by viewer surveys asking respondents to tell if a program is "one of their favorites" and typically measuring familiarity and liking.

UHF Ultra high frequency television signals having less advantageous positions on the broadcast band than VHF, requiring separate receiving antennas in the home. Most public and many commercial independent television stations are UHF.

Underwriting Grants from foundations or private corporations to cover costs of producing or airing a program or series on public television or radio.

Unduplicated Said of programming that is not available on any other local or imported station signal in a market.

Universe In cable, the total population of cable subscribers within all franchises.

Uplink Ground-to-satellite path; also the sending antenna itself (the reverse of *downlink*).

Upscale People who rank toward the upper end on socioeconomic scales measuring income, education and the like (work/profession, housing).

VCR Videocassette recorder, also used for playback.

Vertical Documentaries In-depth factual treatment of a subject in many segments broadcast on the same day. See also *Horizontal Documentaries.*

VHF Very high frequency, the segment of the electromagnetic spectrum in which television channels 2–13 fall, the most desirable broadcast television stations.

Videocassette Packaged videotape unit for recording or playback.

Videodisc Prerecorded video information for playback only.

Videos Taped musical performance shorts used for promotion and programming (on MTV and others).

Videotex Two-way interactive electronic signals requiring telephone line or cable to connect a central computer with the home user's computer screen. See also *Teletext* and *Cabletext.*

Voicers Stories prerecorded by someone other than the announcer or *disc jockey.*

VTR Videotape recorder, also used for playback.

Warehousing Purchasing and storing series and movies primarily to keep them from competitors.

Wheel Visualization of the contents of an hour as a pie divided into wedges representing different content elements; used in radio to visualize a program *format,* showing designated sequences and lengths of all program elements such as musical numbers, news, sports, weather, *features, promos,* PSAs, commercials, IDs and time checks.

Window Period of time in which a feature film or other program is made available to the broadcast networks, pay television or broadcast stations (generally after the first theatrical distribution if the program was not made-for-pay); windows vary from a few months to many years. See also *Pay Window, Syndication Window, Broadcast Window* and *Off Syndication.*

Bibliography of Books, Reports and Articles on Programming

This is a selective, annotated listing of books, articles, guides, reports, magazines, theses and dissertations on broadcast programs and programming, emphasizing publications since 1980. An item is included if it contributes unique or otherwise useful insights into the factors affecting television, radio or cable program content or programming strategy. The bibliography lists major trade publications, books published since 1970 and scholarly research into scheduling strategy, but specific articles and reports only appear if an item has unusual value to the study of programming. For articles published before 1980, consult the bibliography and chapter sources to the first edition of this book, the National Association of Broadcasters' annual bibliography, scholarly journals, *Topicator* and other sources.

Abel, John D. *Television Programming for Children: A Report of the Children's Television Task Force,* Vol. IV. Washington, D.C.: FCC, October 1979.

> *The fourth volume in a series the FCC contracted comparing the amount and scheduling of children's television programs for two television seasons, 1973–74 and 1977–78.*

Adams, MaryJo. "An American Soap Opera: As the World Turns, 1956–1978." Ph.D. dissertation, University of Michigan, 1980.

> *A longitudinal analysis of one soap opera, showing its historical contribution to the genre.*

Adams, William J.; Eastman, Susan Tyler; Horney, Larry J.; and Popovich, Mark N. "The Cancelation and Manipulation of Network Television Prime-Time Programs." *Journal of Communication* 33(Winter 1983):10–27.

> *Multipart analysis of new and established program cancelations by the three commercial networks in the last decade showing some effects of program schedule manipulation.*

Adler, Richard P. *All in the Family: A Critical Appraisal.* New York: Praeger, 1979.

> *Anthology of scripts and critical and descriptive articles about the 1971–79 program.*

Adler, Richard, and Baer, Walter S., eds. *The Electronic Box Office: Humanities and Arts on the Cable.* Palo Alto, Calif.: Aspen Institute Program on Communications and Society, 1974.

> *Six contributed chapters on the potential of pay cable as an alternate programming mechanism; includes a summary chapter on the Aspen Program Conference on the Humanities and the Arts on Cable.*

Agostino, Don. "Cable Television's Impact on the Audience of Public Television." *Journal of Broadcasting* 24(Summer 1980):347–65.

> *Scholarly analysis of Arbitron ratings data showing improved cumulative audiences for public broadcasting as a result of cable carriage.*

Alternative Financing Options for Public Broadcasting, Vol. I & II. The Temporary Commission on Alternative Financing for Public Telecommunications, Report to the Congress of the United States, 1982.

> *Major report on the options in new technologies, advertising and fund raising for public television and radio for the 1980s.*

Alvarado, Manuel, and Buscombi, Edward. *Hazell: The Making of a TV Series.* London: The British Film Institute, 1978.

> *The story of the compromises that went into the making of a British peak-viewing dramatic series.*

Analysis of the Causes and Effects of Increases in Same-Year Rerun Programming and Related Issues in Prime-Time Network Television. Washington, D.C.: Office of Telecommunications Policy, February 1973.

> *Analysis of the extent, causes and effects of reruns during prime time on the networks, including useful historical statistics.*

Andrews, Bart. *Lucy & Ricky & Fred & Ethel: The Story of I Love Lucy.* New York: E. P. Dutton, 1976.

> *Anecdotal narrative of the* I Love Lucy *program of the 1950s.*

Arbitron Company. *Research Guidelines for Programming Decision Makers.* Beltsville, Md.: Arbitron, 1977.

> *Explains how to use Arbitron radio audience reports.*

Armstrong, Ben. *The Electric Church.* Nashville: Thomas Nelson, 1979.

> *Informal history and discussion of current trends in religious radio and television.*

Armstrong, Ben, and Sheldon, LaVay. *Religious Broadcasting Sourcebook.* Morristown, N.J.: National Religious Broadcaster, 1976.

> *Concepts of religious broadcasting, research, operations of religious stations, religious commercials and editorials and programming; essentially evangelical point of view, presented in a series of articles reprints.*

Attracting Minority Audiences to Public Television. Washington, D.C.: Corporation for Public Broadcasting, 1981.

> *Report prepared by Booz-Allen & Hamilton based on data collected in conjunction with Ronald E. Frank and Marshall G. Greenberg public television studies; segments minority audience on common interests and needs.*

Austin, Bruce A. "People's Time in a Medium-Sized Market: A Content Analysis." *Journalism Quarterly* 57(Spring 1980):67–70.

> *Analysis of commercial network-affiliate programming during the 4:00 to 8:00 P.M. time period.*

Austin, Bruce A. "Prime Time Television in a Medium-Sized Market: A Content Analysis." *Communication Quarterly* 27(Summer 1979):37–40.

An analysis of commercial network-affiliate programming during the 8:00 to 11:00 P.M. time period.

Austin, Bruce A. "Public Interest Programming by Commercial Network Affiliates." *Journalism Quarterly* 56(Spring 1979):87ff.

A quantitative analysis of the prime-time programming on affiliates of the three commercial networks.

Avery, Robert K.; Ellis, Donald G.; and Glover, Thomas W. "Patterns of Communication on Talk Radio." *Journal of Broadcasting* 22(Winter 1978):5–17.

An analysis of the cycles of interaction between hosts and callers on talk radio programs.

Avery, Robert K., and Pepper, Robert. "Politics in Space: The Struggle over PTV Satellite Governance." *Public Telecommunications Review* 7(January/February 1979):19–28.

A historical perspective on the struggle over public television's use of the satellite interconnection. Last part of an extensive series.

Bagdikian, Ben H. "Pensions: The FCC's Dangerous Decision Against NBC." *Columbia Journalism Review* 12(March/April 1974):16–21.

Discussion of fairness doctrine issues raised by the FCC's decision against NBC's public affairs program, Pensions: The Broken Promises.

Balakrishnan, Trichur R. "A Game Theory Approach to Programming Prime Time Network Television." Ph.D. dissertation, University of Illinois, 1974.

Mathematical model of network prime-time decision making using game theory; focuses on decisions intended to increase ratings to increase advertising rates.

Baldwin, Thomas F., and McVoy, D. Stevens. *Cable Communications.* Englewood Cliffs, N.J.: Prentice-Hall, 1983.

Definitive text on the technology and operations of cable systems; detailed, readable and scholarly.

Baldwin, Thomas F.; Wirth, Michael O.; and Zenaty, Jayne W. "The Economics of Per-Program Pay Cable Television." *Journal of Broadcasting* 22(Spring 1978): 143–54.

Discussion of policies promoting the development of competitive pay cable industry while maintaining the present "free" television program delivery system.

Barcus, F. Earle, with Welkin, Rachel. *Children's Television: An Analysis of Programming and Advertising.* New York: Praeger Special Studies, 1977.

Compilation of three content analyses done for Action for Children's Television; ACT since has issued additional studies by Barcus.

Barnes, Rey L. "Program Decision-Making in Small Market AM Radio Stations." Ph.D. dissertation, University of Iowa, 1970.

Analysis of interviews with program decision makers at twenty stations in five midwestern states.

Barnouw, Erik. *The Sponsor: Notes on a Modern Potentate.* New York: Oxford University Press, 1978.

Scholarly essay on the development and current influence of sponsors on programming.

Barnouw, Erik. *Tube of Plenty: The Evolution of American Television.* New York: Oxford University Press, 1975.

Based on his monumental History of Broadcasting in the United States *in three volumes, this book is an anecdotal history of television and the influences on it.*

Barrett, Marvin, ed. *Broadcast Journalism 1979–1981: The Eighth Alfred I. Dupont-Columbia University Survey of Broadcast Journalism.* New York: Everest House, 1982.

Biennial survey of trends in news programming at the network and local level.

Bedell, Sally. *Up the Tube: Prime-Time Television and the Silverman Years.* New York: Viking Press, 1981.

An informal, anecdotal excursion through recent network entertainment programming.

Besen, Stanley M., and Johnson, Leland L. *An Economic Analysis of Mandatory Leased Channel Access for Cable Television.* Santa Monica, California: Rand Corporation, 1982.

Analyzes cable regulation and the access issue from an economic standpoint; prepared for the Markle Foundation.

Billboard. 1894 to date.

Weekly trade magazine of the record industry.

Bortz, Paul, and Mendelsohn, Harold. *Radio Today—and Tomorrow.* Washington, D.C.: National Association of Broadcasters, 1982.

In-depth analysis of the current radio audience and usage patterns, assessing the trends affecting radio in the 1980s.

Bowman, Gary W. "Consumer Choice and Television." *Applied Economics* 7(1975): 175–84.

Research study employing a model of past viewing to predict future viewing.

Breitenfeld, Frederick, Jr. "Public Broadcasting: A Two Party System." *Public Telecommunications Review* 4(March/April 1976):19–23.

Delineation of the centralist and localist political approaches to the Corporation for Public Broadcasting and the Public Broadcasting Service.

Broadcaster: The Magazine for Communicators. 1942 to date.

Canadian trade magazine on the radio, television and cable industries, with especial emphasis on news.

Broadcasting. 1931 to date; cable added in 1972.

> *Major weekly trade magazine of the broadcasting industry; see special reports on journalism, radio, independents, sports, new technologies and television program formats.*

Broadcasting and the Law. Knoxville, Tennessee: Perry Publications, 1972 to date.

> *Twice-monthly newsletter and supplements explaining findings of the Federal Communications Commission, courts and Congress affecting broadcast operations.*

Broadcasting/Cablecasting Yearbook. Washington, D.C.: Broadcasting Publications, 1935 to date, annual.

> *Basic trade directory of radio and television stations and support industries; added cable in 1980.*

Broadcast Management/Engineering. 1965 to date.

> *Trade magazine with management and engineering focus, containing regular columns on television and radio programming and production.*

Brooks, Tim, and Marsh, Earle. *The Complete Directory of Prime Time Network TV Shows: 1946–Present.* Rev. ed. New York: Ballantine, 1981.

> *Annotated directory of most network television programs with details on casts and content of the program; updated from 1979 edition.*

Broughton, Irv. *The Art of Interviewing for Television, Radio and Film.* Blue Ridge Summit, Pennsylvania: TAB Books, 1981.

> *Anecdotal guide to eliciting entertaining live interviews.*

Brown, Les. *Les Brown's Encyclopedia of Television.* New York: Zoetrope, 1982.

> *Expanded version of the* New York Times Encyclopedia of Television; *descriptive and analytic comment on facts of network television programming, economics and personalities in the 1970s.*

Brown, Les. *Television: The Business Behind the Box.* New York: Harcourt Brace Jovanovich/Harvest, 1971.

> *Detailed narrative analysis of the problems and policies of network television in 1970–71.*

Browne, Bortz and Coddington. "The Impact of Competitive Distribution Technologies on Cable Television," In *Cable and Its Competitors: An Analysis of Services, Economics and Subscribership.* Washington, D.C.: National Cable Television Association, March 1982.

> *Report commissioned by NCTA assessing the demand for single-channel STV in competition for cable; also examines the findings of the Arthur D. Little DBS Study.*

Bryant, Jennings, and Anderson, Daniel R., eds. *Children's Understanding of Television: Research on Attention and Comprehension.* New York: Academic Press, 1983.

> *Compendium of funded research reports covering the process aspects (rather than the effects) of children's television viewing and learning.*

Burke Marketing Research, Inc. *The Effects of Station Environment on Television Advertising Communications: Independent Stations vs. Affiliated Stations, 1981.* Washington, D.C.: Association of Independent Television Stations, 1981.

Analysis of telephone survey comparing audience response to and perception of ads on independent television stations and network-affiliated stations.

Burns, George A. *The Burns Media Report on AM Radio.* Studio City, California: Burns Media Consultants, 1982.

Assessment of the future of AM radio, stressing format marketability.

Cable Marketing. New York, 1980 to date.

Monthly trade magazine covering the marketing and promotion of cable systems and programming.

Cable Services Directory. Washington, D.C.: National Cable Television Association, 1978 to date, annual (title varies).

Annual directory of information on individual cable systems including amounts and types of local origination.

"Cable Television Symposium." *Comm/Ent: A Journal of Communications and Entertainment Law* 3(Summer 1981):557–767.

Special issue devoted to legal concern in cable television touching on programming.

CableVision. 1975 to date.

Monthly cable-industry trade magazine devoted to programming, economics and marketing of cable and new technologies.

Cantor, Muriel G. *The Hollywood TV Producer: His Work and His Audience.* New York: Basic Books, 1972.

Unique study of working producers of prime-time television programs based on interviews with 80 producers.

Cantor, Muriel G. *Prime-Time Television: Content and Control.* Beverly Hills: Sage Publications, 1980.

Research-based text on prime-time entertainment using a verbal model of constraint patterns; covers program forms, legal and organization contexts and audiences from a sociological perspective.

Cantor, Muriel G., and Pingree, Suzanne. *The Soap Opera.* Beverly Hills: Sage Publications, 1983.

Scholarly overview of the soap opera format, content and audience, placing them in a social and historical context.

Cassata, Mary, and Skill, Thomas. *Life on Daytime Television: Tuning-In American Serial Drama.* Norwood, New Jersey: Ablex Publishing Corp., 1983.

Scholarly content analyses of daytime network soap opera genre, including lifestyles, social issues and interactions.

Chamberlin, Bill F. "The Impact Affairs Programming Regulation: A Study of the FCC's Effectiveness." *Journal of Broadcasting* 23(Spring 1979):197–212.

Evaluation of the effectiveness of 75 television stations in public affairs programming.

Channels. 1980 to date.

Bimonthly consumer magazine focusing on television programming, edited by Les Brown, former New York Times *television critic.*

Clancy, Thomas H. "Nine and a Half Theses on Religious Broadcasting." *America* (7 April 1979):271–75.

Popular overview of the state of religious broadcasting, covering its limitations and successes.

Clift, Charles, III, and Greer, Archie, eds., *Broadcasting Programming: The Current Perspective.* Washington, D.C.: University Press of America, 1974 to date, revised annually.

Facsimile reprints from trade and scholarly programming literature on ratings, network prime-time programming schedules, network program types, local television programming, public broadcasting, radio programming, program regulation and the role of citizen groups in broadcasting.

Cole, Barry G., ed. *Television Today: A Close-Up View: Readings from "TV Guide."* New York: Oxford University Press, 1981.

Compendium of reprints of TV Guide *articles from the 1970s.*

Cole, Barry G., and Oettinger, Mal. *Reluctant Regulators: The FCC and the Broadcast Audience.* Rev. ed. Reading, Mass.: Addison-Wesley, 1978.

An analysis of FCC policies and the constraints under which they are drawn. Revised edition is available only in paperback and includes index and updating chapter.

Coleman, Howard W. *Case Studies in Broadcast Management: Radio and Television.* Rev. ed. New York: Hastings House, 1978.

Short case studies of problems in managerial decision making, many of them relating to programming.

Comm/Ent: A Journal of Communications and Entertainment Law. San Francisco: Hastings College of the Law, 1978 to date.

Law journal, published quarterly, containing articles summarizing the law on specific issues including broadcasting and new technologies.

Compaine, Benjamin M., ed. *Anatomy of the Communications Industry: Who Owns the Media?* 2d ed. White Plains, New York: Knowledge Industry Publications, 1982.

Original edition subtitled "Concentration of Ownership in the Mass Communication Industry"; contains eight original articles providing tabular and text information on ownership of the major media, including radio, television and cable.

Comstock, George; Chaffee, Steven; Katzman, Natan; McCombs, Maxwell; and Roberts, Donald. *Television and Human Behavior.* New York: Columbia University Press, 1978.

Substantial overview of the social and behavioral effects of television; summary of the research literature.

Cowan, Geoffrey. *See No Evil: The Backstage Battle over Sex and Violence in Television.* New York: Simon and Schuster, 1979.

The story of the legal battle over the family viewing hour written by one of the lawyers who took part.

David, Nina. *TV Season.* Phoenix, Arix.: Oryx, 1976 to date, annual.

Annotated guide to the previous season's commercial and public network and major syndicated television programs.

De Luca, Mariann. *Survey of Radio Stations.* New York: Torbet Radio, 1983.

Series of 1983 surveys of radio managers on their programming practices.

Dengler, Ralph. "The Language of Film Titles." *Journal of Communication* 25(Summer 1975):51–60.

A content analysis by title of nearly 8,000 American movies suggesting a shift in style from the "public and good" to the "personal and perverse."

DeSonne, Marsha L. *Radio, New Technology and You.* Washington, D.C.: National Association of Broadcasters, April 1982.

Overview of new radio technologies as revenue-producing options for radio broadcasters.

Dessart, George. *Television in the Real World: A Case Study Course in Broadcast Management.* New York: Hastings House, 1978.

A simulated case study of a new VHF television station with 65 pages on programming issues.

Dominick, Joseph R., and Pearce, Millard C. "Trends in Network Prime-time Programming, 1953–74." *Journal of Communication* 26(Winter 1976):70–80.

A historical study of the economic factors affecting prime-time television programming.

Dranov, Paula. *Inside the Music Publishing Industry.* White Plains, New York: Knowledge Industries Publications, 1980.

Overview of the structure of the music publishing industry, covering copyright, royalties, contracts, domestic and foreign markets; with charts, tables and a directory of music publishers.

Duncan, James H., Jr., ed. *American Radio.* Kalamazoo, Mich.: Duncan Media Enterprises, semiannual.

Reference source on Arbitron and Birch audience, programming and sales ratings and statistics on both national and local market levels; spring and fall editions annually.

Duncan, James H., Jr., ed. *Radio in the United States: 1976–1982.* Kalamazoo, Mich. Duncan Media Enterprises, 1982.

Historical statistics on radio formats in the late 1970s.

Durham, Dona A., and Meyer, Timothy. "TV and Prosocial Behavior: A Critical Review of Key Issues and Literature." Paper presented at the International Communication Association, Dallas, Texas, May 1983.

Analysis, based on dissertation research, of the issues, concepts and literature of prosocial behavior.

Eastman, Susan Tyler, and Klein, Robert A. *Strategies in Broadcast and Cable Promotion.* Belmont, Calif.: Wadsworth, 1982.

Text on strategic planning for marketing networks, stations and cable systems to audiences and advertisers.

Eberly, Philip K. *Music in the Air: America's Changing Tastes in Popular Music, 1920–1980.* New York: Hastings House, 1982.

Illustrated history of musical radio concentrating on the developmental period before 1955.

Ellens, J. Harold. *Models of Religious Broadcasting.* Grand Rapids, Mich.: Williams B. Eerdmans, 1974.

Discussion of programming approaches with many case studies of religious programming past and present.

Eliot, Marc. *Televisions: One Season in American Television.* New York: St. Martin's Press, 1983.

Anecdotal overview of the people, programs and events of the 1981–82 season as seen by a producer and critic.

Epstein, Edward J. *News from Nowhere: Television and the News.* New York: Random House, 1973.

Classic study of gatekeeping in the television news process at the commercial broadcast networks based on 1969–70 research.

An Evaluation of "Over Easy": A Television Series for and About Older People. Washington, D.C.: Corporation for Public Broadcasting, 1980.

Evaluation of this targeted and purposive program series prepared by the Office of Communication Research using innovative program evaluation methodologies.

Federal Communications Commission. *Annual Programming Report for Commercial Television Stations.* Washington, D.C.: FCC, 1973 to 1979, annual.

Market by market statistical analysis of annual programming reports filed by all commercial stations, providing national and per-market data on nonentertainment content, noting proportion locally produced.

Fisher, Michael G. "A Survey of Selected Television Station Program Managers: Their Backgrounds and Perceptions of Role." Master's thesis, Temple University, 1978.

Survey of 160 members of the National Association of Television Program Executives on personal experiences, background and position in management hierarchies.

Fletcher, James E., ed. *Handbook of Radio and TV Broadcasting: Research Procedures in Audience, Program and Revenues.* New York: Van Nostrand Reinhold, 1981.

Compendium of rating and survey research procedures for television and radio researchers; includes reprints of articles and ratings.

Fletcher, James E., and Wimmer, Roger D. *Call-Out Research in Managing Radio Stations.* Washington, D.C.: National Association of Broadcasters, n.d.

Manual for telephone surveys of listener song preferences to aid in construction of music playlists.

Fletcher, James E., and Wimmer, Roger D. *Focus Group Interviews in Radio Research.* Washington, D.C.: National Association of Broadcasters, August 1981.

Practical guide to conducting focus group interviews on radio listener preferences and lifestyles using a facilitator.

Forbes, Dorothy, and Layng, Sanderson. *The New Communicators: A Guide to Community Programming.* Washington, D.C.: Communications Press, 1978.

Originally published by the Canadian Cable Television Association, written to aid cable programmers in focusing community television efforts.

Foster, Eugene S. *Understanding Broadcasting.* 2d ed. Reading, Mass.: Addison-Wesley, 1982.

Introductory text on the technology, economics, regulation and programming of television and radio.

Fowler, Mark S., and Bresser, Daniel L. "A Marketplace Approach to Broadcast Regulation." *Texas Law Review* 60:207(1982):250–55.

Statement of the legal and policy implications of the competitive market approach to broadcast regulation by the current chairman of the Federal Communications Commission.

Frank, Ronald E., and Greenberg, Marshall G. *Audiences for Public Television.* Beverly Hills: Sage Publications, 1982.

Analysis of national survey data on the viewing habits and leisure patterns of the public television audience, translated into strategies for programming public stations.

Frank, Ronald E., and Greenberg, Marshall G. *The Public's Use of Television: Who Watches and Why.* Beverly Hills: Sage Publications, 1980.

Interest segmentation analysis of the public television audience.

Gans, Herbert J. *Deciding What's News: A Study of CBS Evening News, NBC Nightly News, Newsweek and Time.* New York: Pantheon, 1979.

Sociological analysis of the journalists and their day-to-day decision making in developing a cohesive news policy.

Gantz, Walter, and Eastman, Susan Tyler. "Viewer Uses of Promotional Media to Find Out About Television Programs." *Journal of Broadcasting* 27(Summer 1983): 269–77.

Report of survey of viewers' uses of promotional media such as guides, listings and promos and the value placed on them.

Gates, Gary Paul. *Air Time: The Inside Story of CBS News.* New York: Harper & Row, 1978.

Gossipy "inside" review of the personalities behind 20 years of CBS domination of network journalism.

Gerrold, David. *The World of Star Trek.* New York: Ballantine Books, 1973.

Account of how the series concept was developed. Similar to The Making of Star Trek *by Stephen E. Whitfield and Gene Rodenberry, New York: Ballantine, 1968. See also David Gerrold's* The Trouble with Tribbles, *New York; Ballantine, 1973, about the creation, sale and production of one episode of Star Trek.*

Gianakos, Larry James. *Television Drama Series Programming: A Comprehensive Chronicle, 1975–1980.* Metuchen, New Jersey: Scarecrow Press, 1981.

Cross-referenced list of dramatic series and special programs on the three commercial television networks, including date, day and cast; supplements earlier volumes covering programs since 1947.

Gingras, Richard. "The PTV Satellite System: Turning Point or High Anxiety." *Public Telecommunications Review* 6(May/June 1978):5–13.

A discussion of the possibilities and likelihoods resulting from public broadcasting's acquisition of satellite channels.

Gitlin, Todd. *Inside Prime Time.* New York: Pantheon, 1983.

Mass market book based on 200 interviews with network executives, producers, writers, agents and actors, delving into the process of prime-time program selection and cancelation.

Gohring, Ralph J. "Influences on a Children's Program Decision-Maker on a National Commercial Television Network." Ph.D. dissertation, Ohio State University, 1975.

Analysis of one network's children's program decision making based primarily on participant observation and interviews with a network vice-president.

Goodhardt, G.J.; Ehrenberg, A.S.C.; and Collins, M.A. *The Television Audience.* Lexington, Mass.: Lexington Press (Saxon House), 1975.

Scholarly analysis of research on program scheduling assessing audience flow, lead-in effects, loyalty and viewing patterns, published originally in Great Britain.

Greenberg, Bradley S. *Life on Television: Content Analyses of U.S. TV Drama.* Norwood, New Jersey: Ablex Publishing Corp., 1980.

Studies of the content of dramatic series on prime-time network television.

Greenberg, Bradley S.; Neuendorf, Kimberly; Buerkey-Rothfuss, Nancy; and Henderson, Laura. "The Soaps: What's On and Who Cares?" *Journal of Broadcasting* 26(Spring 1982):519–35.

Analysis of soap opera content and survey of soap viewers to determine viewing motives, involvement and possible effects.

Gross, Lynn Schafer. *The New Television Technologies.* Dubuque, Iowa: Wm. C. Brown Co., 1983.

Overview of the technology and economics of the new electronic media, including videodisc, videotex, cable and direct broadcasting.

Grossman, Gary H. *Saturday Morning TV*. New York: Dell, 1982.

Popular essay on the cartoon fare delivered by the three commercial networks to children on weekends.

Grote, David. *The End of Comedy: The Sit-Com and the Comedic Tradition*. Hamden, Connecticut: Shoe String Press, 1983.

Scholarly tracing of the historical evolution of the comedic form from its origins to the present form of comedy on network television programs.

Gunn, Hartford. "Inside the Program Cooperative." *Public Telecommunications Review* 2(August 1974):16–27.

Interview on the workings of the public television program cooperative.

Gunn, Hartford, N., Jr. "Window on the Future: Planning for Public Television in the Telecommunications Era." *Public Telecommunications Review* 6(July/August 1978):4–54.

Overview and recommendations for long-range planning for public television.

Gutman, Jonathan, and McConaughy, David. "Ambivalence and Indifference in Preference for Television Programs." *Journal of Broadcasting* 22(Summer 1978): 373–84.

Application of ambivalence/indifference analysis to adult tuning behavior.

Hadden, Jeffrey K., and Swann, Charles E. *Prime Time Preachers: The Rising Power of Televangelism*. Reading, Mass.: Addison-Wesley, 1981.

Brief overview of the major religious television personalities and their audiences.

Halberstam, David. *The Powers That Be*. New York: Alfred A. Knopf, 1979.

Inside history of four of the largest media institutions in America including CBS; emphasizes the role of Paley and his influence on CBS's programming.

Hall, Claude, and Hall, Barbara. *The Business of Radio Programming*. New York: Billboard Publications, 1977.

Informal analysis of radio station management with focus on programming; includes verbatim interviews with key industry figures.

Harmonay, Maureen, ed. *Promise and Performance: The Arts. ACT's Guide to TV Programming for Children*. Vol. 2. Cambridge, Mass.: Ballinger, 1979.

Second of two volumes reviewing network television programs from the perspective of Action for Children's Television.

Head, Sydney W., and Sterling, Christopher H. *Broadcasting in America: A Survey of Television and Radio*. 4th ed. Boston: Houghton Mifflin, 1982.

Basic reference text on American broadcasting, covering technology, economics, regulation and programming.

Heeter, Carrie; D'Alessie, Dave; Greenberg, Bradley S.; and McVoy, D. Stephens. "Cableviewing." Paper presented to the International Communication Association, Dallas, Texas, May 1983.

Preliminary report on patterns of cable viewing based on minute-by-minute data collected from interactive cable households with 34 channels, showing viewing of a subset of about 10 channels in string, ministretch and stretch lengths.

Heighton, Elizabeth J., and Cunningham, Don R. *Advertising in the Broadcasting Media.* 2d ed. Belmont, Calif.: Wadsworth, 1984.

Expanded text on the history, campaign strategies and principles of electronic media from the perspective of the advertiser and agency; includes case studies.

Hesbacher, Peter; Clasby, Nancy; Anderson, Bruce; and Berger, David G. "Radio Format Strategies." *Journal of Communication* 26(Winter 1976):110–19.

A case study that tests the theory of relationships between music programming and audience size and composition.

Hofacker, Kristine H. "An Analysis of the 'Donahue' Show from 1967 to 1978." Ph.D. dissertation, University of Michigan, 1979.

Chronicle of a top-rated daytime talk show, examining the aspects that contributed to its success in syndication.

Hollowell, Mary Louise, ed. *The Cable/Broadband Communications Book, Vol. 3, 1982–1983.* Washington, D.C.: Communications Press, 1983.

Most recent in a series tracing policy changes and problems in cable and related technologies.

The Home Video & Cable Yearbook, 1982–83. White Plains, New York: Knowledge Industries Publications, 1982.

Compendium of statistics on cable systems, networks and program services, operators and other aspects with brief summaries.

Howard, Herbert H. *Group and Cross-Media Ownership of Television Stations in 1983.* Washington, D.C.: National Association of Broadcasters, 1983.

Most recent of a series of reports on ownership commissioned by the National Association of Broadcasters; useful tables.

Howard, Herbert H., and Kievman, Michael S. *Radio and TV Programming.* Columbus, Ohio: Grid Publishing, 1983.

Station-oriented text on broadcast programming, covering history, appeals, audience, station management and criticism for commercial and noncommercial stations.

Jeffries, Leo W. "Cable TV and Viewer Selectivity." *Journal of Broadcasting* 22(Spring 1978):167–77.

A before/after study of the effect of cable on the viewing behavior of subscribers.

Jesuale, Nancy, ed., with Smith, Ralph Lee. *The Community Medium: Vol. I.* Arlington, Virginia: The Cable Television Information Center, 1982.

First of two parts (second: A Guide for Local Policy*), this book discusses cable technology and services within a historical perspective, including state-of-the-art options, intended for local government regulators.*

Johnston, Jerome, and Ettema, James S. *Positive Images: Breaking Stereotypes with Children's Television.* Beverly Hills, Calif.: Sage Publications, 1982.

Review of the creation and audience viewing of the PBS series Freestyle.

Johnson, Joseph S., and Jones, Kenneth K. *Modern Radio Station Practices*. 2d ed. Belmont, Calif.: Wadsworth, 1978.

Radio station programming from a practical management perspective.

Johnson, Nicholas. "Broadcasting in America: The Performance of Network Affiliates in the Top 50 Markets." 42 FCC 2d. (*Reports*, 1973):1–72.

A case study of stations in three states—Arkansas, Louisiana and Mississippi—prepared as a statement of dissenting opinion by retiring Commissioner Johnson and his staff.

Johnson, Rolland C.; Groth, Gary; and Lynch, Edith. "Trends in Broadcasting, Broadcast-Related Media, and Film." In *A Study on Creative Personnel in the Media Fields of Radio, Television and Film*, by Robert J. Anderson, Gary Groth, Roland C. Johnson, Edith Lynch, Sonia P. Maltezou, and Robert J. Wuthnow. Washington, D.C.: National Endowment for the Arts, 7 July 1980.

Chapter summarizing trends in industry structure and economics, including programming, emphasizing the impact of new technologies.

Johnson, William O., Jr. *Super Spectator and the Electric Lilliputians*. Boston: Little, Brown, 1971.

Book-length collection of five-part series from Sports Illustrated *(1969–70) exploring the impact of television on sports and vice versa.*

Jones, Kenneth K., and Kimmel, Joel K. "How Cable (and small UHFers) Can Compete in Programming." *Television/Radio Age* (13 March 1978):31ff.

Analysis of the advertising dollars and audience shares potentially available to cable franchises and small UHF independents.

Josephson, Larry. "Why Radio?" *Public Telecommunications Review* 7(March/April 1979):6–18.

Addresses Carnegie Commission's request for justification of public funding of public radio; this issue of PTR *focuses entirely on radio and includes several articles on the future of public radio in the 1980s.*

Kaatz, Ronald B. *Cable: An Advertiser's Guide to the New Electronic Media*. Chicago: Crain Books, 1982.

Handbook on media buys on national and local cable, intended for potential advertisers and agencies.

Kaplan, Stuart J. "The Impact of Cable Television Services on the Use of Competing Media." *Journal of Broadcasting* 22(Spring 1978):155–65.

An investigation of the media-use behavior of subscribers to cable services.

Kasindorf, Martin. "Archie and Maude and Fred and Alan: A TV Dynasty." *New York Times Magazine* (24 June 1973):12–22.

Analysis of the major programs and characters created by Norman Lear.

Katzman, Natan. *Program Decision in Public Television: A Report for the CPB/NCES Programming Project*. Washington, D.C.: National Association of Educational Broadcasters, 1976.

Statement on program strategy in national, local and school public broadcasting.

Katzman, Natan, and Wirt, Kenneth. *Public Television Programming by Category: 1976.* Washington, D.C.: Corporation for Public Broadcasting, 1977.

Latest in biennial series on national and local programming trends in public television, including ITV; tables and charts.

Kierstead, Phillip O. *All-News Radio.* Blue Ridge Summit, PA: TAB Books, 1980.

Handbook for programming the all-news format on commercial stations.

King, Larry. *Larry King.* New York: Simon and Schuster, 1982.

Popular, anecdotal autobiography by the nationally known late-night talk personality.

Klein, Paul. "When Men Who Run TV Aren't That Stupid . . . They Know Us Better Than You Think." *New York* (25 January 1971):20–29.

Statement of Klein's programming strategy at NBC including the concept of the least objectional program.

Korn, Alexander, and Korn, Stanley D. "A Look at the Economics of a New Independent Television Station Entering the Market" and "Adding One More Independent TV Station to the Market: What's the Success Potential?" *Television/ Radio Age* (6 June 1977):29ff., (18 July 1977):32ff.

Parts one and two based on a report to the Federal Communications Commission on the "Economics of New Entry of Independent Stations into Television Markets" (Docket No. 20418).

Koughan, Martin, "The Fall and Rise of Public Television." *Channels* (May/June 1983):23–29 ff.

An informal overview of the political strengths and weaknesses of public television from a popular perspective.

Krasnow, Erwin G.; Longley, Lawrence D.; and Terry, Herbert A. *The Politics of Broadcast Regulation,* 3d ed. New York: St. Martin's Press, 1982.

Introduction to the five determining institutions in regulatory policy; includes five case studies, one of which deals with format changes, another with comparability for UHF television stations.

Kressel, Marilyn, ed. *Adult Learning and Public Broadcasting.* Washington, D.C.: American Association of Community and Junior Colleges, 1980.

Report of a project examining the use of television as an effective mode of offering educational options to adults.

Kushner, James M. "KDAS (FM): Want-Ad Radio in Los Angeles." *Journal of Broadcasting* 16(Summer 1972):267–76.

Analysis of an experiment in radio programming, the all-classified ad format.

Levinson, Richard, and Link, William. *Stay Tuned: An Inside Look at the Making of Prime-Time Television.* New York: St. Martin's Press, 1981.

Insiders' view of the history of selected prime-time series by two commercial television producers.

Lewis, Raymond J. *Meeting Learners' Needs Through Telecommunications: A Directory and Guide to Programs.* Washington, D.C.: Center for Learning and Telecommunications, American Association for Higher Education, 1983.

Guide to programs and projects completed and underway for the commercial and noncommercial instructional markets.

Lichty, Lawrence W., and Topping, Malachi C. *American Broadcasting: A Source Book on the History of Radio and Television.* New York: Hastings House, 1975.

Collection of more than 90 readings and dozens of tables including 150 pages on programming developments.

Liebert, Robert M., et al. *The Early Window: Effects of Television on Children and Youth.* 2d ed. New York: Pergamon Press, 1982.

Analysis of the research literature on children and television, including the 1972 Surgeon General's Report.

Lindsay, Carl A.; Leroy, David J.; and Novak, Theresa A. "Public Television: Whose Alternative?" *Public Telecommunications Review* 6(March/April 1978): 18–23.

A study of the audience of public television by viewing habits and age, based on reinterviewing of 208 households from an Arbitron sweep sample.

Listening to the Future: Cable Audio in the 80s. Washington, D.C.: National Public Radio, 1982.

Report of research conducted principally by NPR's staff on the potential of cable audio, especially for public radio broadcasters.

Lloyd, Mark L. "A Descriptive Analysis of the Syndicated Religious Television Programs of Jerry Fallwell, Rex Humbard and Oral Roberts." Ph.D. dissertation, The University of Michigan, 1980.

Examination of the production of three nationally syndicated evangelical or fundamentalist television programs and their on-air personalities.

Lull, James T.; Johnson, Lawrence M.; and Sweeny, Carol. "Audiences for Contemporary Radio Formats." *Journal of Broadcasting* 22(Fall 1978):439–54.

Demographic profiles of radio audience listener types, showing the comparative uniqueness of audiences for several formats.

MacFarland, David T. *The Development of the Top 40 Radio Format.* New York: Arno Press, 1979.

Reprinted 1972 doctoral dissertation on the philosophies and policies governing the development of the top 40 format.

MacKenzie, Alexander C., Jr. "Descriptive Analysis of the Factors That Influenced the Creation, Introduction and Impact of Selected Television Programs of the Years, 1946–1976." Ph.D. dissertation, Case Western University, 1979.

Interview-based analysis of nine selected trend-setting prime-time programs, showing their derivation from radio programming, and the networks' lack of empirically based program decision making.

Mahony, Sheila; Demartino, Nick; and Stengel, Robert. *Keeping PACE with the New Television: Public Television and Changing Technology.* New York: Carnegie Corporation, 1980.

Review of the developments in new technologies as they affect public television, prepared by three members of the Carnegie Commission's staff, proposing a nonprofit cable network for performing arts, culture and entertainment.

Mankiewicz, Frank, and Swerdlow, Joel. *Remote Control: Television and the Manipulation of American Life.* New York: Times Books, 1978.

Informed critical review of programming controversies.

Manning, Willard G., Jr. *The Supply of Prime-Time Entertainment Television Programs.* Memorandum no. 152. Stanford, Calif.: Center for Research in Economic Growth, 1973.

An economic and policy analysis of program supply and domestic syndication, the competitiveness of supply and prospects for cable.

Mayer, Martin. *About Television.* New York: Harper & Row, 1972.

Examines the decision-making process as one part of a review of the television industry.

McAlpine, Dennis B. *The Television Programming Industry.* New York: Tucker Anthony and R.L. Day, January 1975.

Analysis of costs to the networks of prime-time programming since 1969; predicts a rise in fees the networks pay to program suppliers.

Metz, Robert. *CBS: Reflections in a Bloodshot Eye.* Chicago: Playboy Press, 1975.

History of the CBS radio and television network from its inception to 1975 from an insider's perspective.

Metz, Robert. *The Today Show.* Chicago: Playboy Press, 1977.

Anecdotal narrative of an important television program.

Metzger, Gale D. "Cable Television Audiences: Learning from the Past and the Present." *Journal of Advertising Research* 23(August/September 1983):41–47.

Review of the history of the impact of television on radio and the 1982 CONTAM report, concluding that cable will have little impact on radio and total television viewing and no impact on prime-time viewing.

Meyers, Richard. *TV Detectives.* San Diego, Calif.: A.S. Barnes & Co., 1981.

Anecdotal behind-the-scenes view of television detective dramas, tracing their historical development.

Milam, Lorenzo W. *Sex and Broadcasting: A Handbook on Starting a Radio Station for the Community.* 3d ed. Los Gatos, Calif.: Dildo Press, 1975.

An antiestablishment guide for prospective station licensees providing useful information on management, regulation and programming.

Miles, Daniel J.; Miles, Betty T.; and Miles, Martin J. *The Miles Chart Display of Popular Music: Volume II, 1971–1975.* New York: Arno Press, 1977.

Week-by-week graphs of the chart history of nearly 10,000 records and 2,300 artists; one of the bibles of music radio programming.

Miller, Merle, and Rhodes, Evan. *Only You Dick Daring! How to Write One Television Script and Make $50,000,000.* New York: William Sloane Associates, 1964.

Inside humorous account of television from the writer's perspective using one program proposal as a case study.

Monaghan, Robert R.; Plummer, Joseph T.; Rarick, David L.; and Williams, Dwight A. "Predicting Viewer Preference for New TV Program Concepts." *Journal of Broadcasting* 18(Spring 1974):131–42.

A research study locating two distinct types of viewers, Mr. Happy World and Mr. Realistic Conflict, that describe television preference patterns.

Morgenstern, Steve, ed. *Inside the TV Business.* New York: Sterling, 1979.

Eight chapters by outstanding figures on aspects of network programming.

Mossberg, Irene B. "A Study of the Identification of Prosocial Behaviors in a Commercial Television Program." Ed.D. dissertation, West Virginia University, 1980.

Field experiment testing the effects of teacher intervention on the ability of children to identify prosocial content in television programs.

Mullally, Donald P. "Public Radio: Options in Programming." *Public Telecommunications Review* 6(March/April 1978):8–13.

Discussion of the limitations inherent in block and format programming strategies.

Multichannel News. 1979 to date.

Weekly newspaper of regulatory, programming and technical events affecting the news media.

NAB Legal Guide to FCC Broadcast Rules, Regulations and Policies. Washington, D.C.: National Association of Broadcasting, 1977. Regularly updated.

Loose-leaf, one-volume compilation of selected FCC broadcasting regulations (many on programming) with analysis and commentary designed for station managers.

Newcomb, Horace, and Alley, Robert S. *The Producer's Medium: Conversations with Creators of American T.V.* New York: Oxford University Press, 1983.

Interviews with eight producers of commercial television programs critically analyzing their work and perspectives.

The New Television Technologies: The View from the Viewer-II, An American Consensus Report. New York: Benton & Bowles, May 1983.

Second of two mail surveys on new television technologies focusing on cable and home videorecording.

Nielsen, Richard P., and Thibodeau, Thomas. "Applying Market Research Methods for Formating Decisions for Radio." *Feedback* (Spring 1979):19–24.

Aid to format decision making supplied by a format-market matrix comparing market shares across markets and formats.

Noll, Roger G.; Merton, J. Peck; and McGowan, John J. *Economic Aspects of Television Regulation.* Washington, D.C.: The Brookings Institution, 1973.

Chapters on new technology and institutional impacts on FCC regulation of commercial, public and cable television.

O'Bryan, Kenneth G. *The Project Team in Instructional Television.* Washington, D.C.: Corporation for Public Broadcasting, 1983.

Prescription for the job-functions of production personnel involved in instructional program or series making. Companion book to Writing for Instructional Television, *1981.*

O'Donnell, Thomas, and Gissen, Jay. "A Vaster Wasteland?" *Forbes* (24 May 1982): 109–16.

Popular assessment of the direction of cable programming emphasizing economic limitations.

Orton, Barry, ed. *Cable Television and the Cities: Local Regulation and Municipal Uses.* Madison: University of Wisconsin-Extension, 1982.

Booklet on the process of municipal franchising.

Owen, Bruce; Beebe, Jack H.; and Manning, Willard, Jr. *Television Economics.* Lexington, Mass.: Lexington Books, 1974.

Scholarly study analyzing the economic working of the television industry with heavy emphasis on program supply using economic modeling.

Paley, William S. *As It Happened: A Memoir.* New York: Doubleday, 1979.

Personal reminiscences of an important figure in broadcast history; includes remarks on programming strategy with numerous annecdotal examples.

Palmer, Edward L., and Dorr, Aimee, eds. *Children and the Faces of Television.* New York: Academic Press, 1980.

Collection of contributed articles on children's television emphasizing research and policy making.

Pearce, Alan. *NBC News Division: A Study of the Costs, the Revenues, and the Benefits of Broadcast News and the Economics of Prime Time Access.* New York: Arno Press, 1979.

Reprint of a doctoral dissertation on the economics of news and sports programs telecast on NBC in the 1969–70 period, and an economic analysis of prime time prepared for the FCC.

Pearce, Alan. "The TV Networks: A Primer." *Journal of Communication* 26(Autumn 1976):54–59.

A review of the basic facts of network existence, economic structure, profitability and power.

Pekurny, Robert G., and Bart, Leonard D. "'Sticks and Bones': A Survey of Network Affiliate Decision Making." *Journal of Broadcasting* 19(Fall 1975):427–37.

An attempt to determine how television station executives and program directors make decisions.

Pennybacker, John H. "The Format Change Issue: FCC vs. U.S. Court of Appeals." *Journal of Broadcasting* 22(Fall 1978):411–24.

History of the issue of radio format changes and the disagreement between the FCC and the U.S. Court of Appeals.

Persky, Joel. "Twenty Years of Prime Time." *Television Quarterly* 14(Summer/Fall 1977):50–52.

Results of a quantitative study of prime-time television program logs for the three commercial networks in 1955–56, 1965–66, 1975–76.

Powers, Ron. *The Newscasters.* New York: St. Martin's Press, 1977.

An exposé of the trends behind the scenes in television news; includes attack on the role of program consultants, influence of advertising and encroachment into journalism of entertainment values.

Powers, Ron, and Oppenhein, Jerrold. "The Failed Promise of All-News Radio." *Columbia Journalism Review* 12(September/October 1973):21–28.

Discussion of the content and programming methods all-news radio stations use.

Public Radio and State Governments. 2 vols. Washington, D.C.: National Public Radio, March 1981.

Report on the relationship between state governments and public radio, including regulations, financial support, technical requirements and state-wide organizations.

Quaal, Ward L., and Brown, James A. *Broadcast Management: Radio, Television.* 2d ed. New York: Hastings House, 1976.

Structures and processes in broadcast management covering both local and network programming for radio and for television.

Quinn, Sally. *We're Going to Make You a Star.* New York: Simon and Schuster, 1975.

Revealing tale of a network's corporate lack of interest in their news anchors.

Radio Program Department Handbook: A Basic Guide for the Program Director of a Smaller Operation. Washington, D.C.: National Association of Broadcasters, n.d.

A booklet on small-market radio programming practices.

"Radio Programming & Production for Profit." *Broadcast Management/Engineering,* monthly series, January 1977 to date.

Discussion of program formats, production and promotion, along with reports on syndicated programs and features.

Radio & Records.

Weekly trade magazine of the record industry ranking songs and albums; also, R&R Ratings Report, a twice annual comparison of formats by region and station, including a comparison of Arbitron and Birch ratings.

Read, William H. *America's Mass Media Merchants.* Baltimore: Johns Hopkins University Press, 1976.

Narrative description of American commercial film, video and print media activity overseas.

Reel, A. Frank. *The Networks: How They Stole the Show.* New York: Charles Scribner's Sons, 1979.

Critical evaluation of network programming practices and the adverse effect of advertising economics.

Regulatory Trends in the 1980's: More Owners—More Stations. New York: Station Representatives Association, 1980.

Trade association report covering the history of the Federal Communications Commission's ownership rules and policies, current practices and proposals in hand.

Religious Broadcasters. 1968 to date.

Monthly magazine emphasizing evangelical broadcasting on radio and television with informal style.

Report on Prime-Time Network Television, and Report on Daytime Network Television. New York: Batten, Barton, Durstine & Osborn, Inc., annual.

Booklet reports on the upcoming network season stressing details of interest to advertisers on upcoming trends.

Rice, Jean, ed. *Cable TV Renewals & Refranchising.* Washington, D.C.: Communications Press, 1983.

Guide to municipal options and procedures, access programming and legal considerations from the perspectives of the cable operator and the local government.

Robards, Brooks. "Situation Comedy and the Structure of Television: A Structural Analysis." Ph.D. dissertation, University of Massachusetts, 1982.

Application of four tenets of structural analysis (transformation, intelligibility, self-regulation, formalization) to television situation comedies.

Robertson Associates, Inc. *Local Station Utilization of PBS Programming: A Study for the TV Manager's Council of NAEB.* Washington, D.C.: National Association of Educational Broadcasters, 1977.

A 1977 study of public television station programming; reported in Chapter 19.

Robertson, James, and Yokom, Gerald G. "Educational Radio: The Fifty-Year-Old-Adolescent." *Educational Broadcasting Review* 7(April 1973):107–15.

Facts and opinions on the state of educational radio gathered in the course of visiting every NPR (NER) member station in 1972.

Roeh, Itzhak; Katz, Elihu; Cohen, A.; and Zeliger, Barbie. *Almost Midnight: Reforming the Late Night News.* Beverly Hills, Calif.: Sage Publications, 1980.

Construction and production of a nightly Israeli newscast, showing development, organizational framework and ultimate results from a mix of practitioner and social scientist perspectives.

Rood, Thomas R. "Cable Television: A Status Study of Services and Community Access Programming Practices in the State of Michigan." Ph.D. dissertation, Wayne State University, 1977.

Descriptive analysis of cable systems operating in Michigan, their access policies and practices.

Rosenthal, Edmond M. "Cable Culture Rush: How Much Gold Is There?" *Television/Radio Age* (9 February 1981):49–53ff.

Detailed assessment of the competing cable services offering fine arts programming.

Routt, Edd. *The Business of Radio Broadcasting.* Blue Ridge Summit, Pa.: TAB Books, 1972.

Station operations and programming from a management perspective.

Routt, Edd. *Dimensions of Broadcast Editorializing.* Blue Ridge Summit, Pa.: TAB Books, 1974.

Role, function and practical aspects of editorializing for radio and television. See also Robert Vainowski's In Our View. *Belmont, Calif.: Tresgatos Enterprises, 1976.*

Routt, Edd; McGrath, James B.; and Weiss, Frederic A. *The Radio Format Conundrum.* New York: Hastings House, 1978.

A wealth of detail on radio formats and factors affecting format decisions written from the point of view of the station manager.

Schenkkan, Robert F.; Thurston, Carol M.; and Sheldon, Alan. *Case Studies in Institutional Licensee Management.* National Association of Educational Broadcasters, 1980.

Casebook illustrating the problems and solutions or approaches in relationships between public stations and their licensees.

Scott, James D. *Bringing Premium Entertainment into the Home via Pay-Cable TV.* Michigan Business Reports, no. 61. Ann Arbor, Mich.: Graduate School of Business Administration, University of Michigan, 1977.

Program decision making by the pay cable operator.

Scott, James D. *Cable Television: Strategy for Penetrating Key Urban Markets.* Michigan Business Reports, no. 58. Ann Arbor, Mich.: Graduate School of Business Administration, University of Michigan, 1976.

Expansion of television into large cities by means of innovative programming.

Shaffer, William Drew, and Wheelwright, Richard. *Creating Original Programming for Cable TV.* Washington, D.C.: National Federation of Local Cable Programmers, 1983.

Guide for producing local origination on cable for community groups and individuals; includes a case study of the Iowa City system.

Shanks, Robert. *The Cool Fire: How to Make It in Television.* New York: Norton, 1976.

Anecdotal overview of how network television works, emphasizing producers and production but indirectly providing practical information on program decision making.

Shelby, Maurice E., Jr. "Criticism and Longevity of Television Programs." *Journal of Broadcasting* 17 (Summer 1973):277–86.

Investigation of the relationship between critical review of network programs and their long-term success rate.

Shooshan, Harry M., III, and Jackson, Charles L. *Radio Subcarrier Services.* Com/ Tech Report. Vol. 2, No. 1. Washington, D.C.: National Association of Broadcasters, May 1983.

Legal restrictions and technical potential of subcarrier services for commercial broadcasters.

Sigel, Efrem. *The Future of Videotext.* White Plains, New York: Knowledge Industries Publications, 1983.

Survey of the history and status of electronic information services, covering the legal and technical problems a new industry faces; includes summary tables.

Simkins, Tina. "Public Radio: Coming Out of Hiding." *Educational Broadcasting* 7 (May/June 1974):15–19.

Overview of changes in public radio since 1967.

Sklar, Robert. *Prime-Time America: Life On and Behind the Television Screen.* New York: Oxford University Press, 1980.

Entertaining criticism of current television as a popular art form.

Smith, V. Jackson. *Programming for Radio and Television.* Washington, D.C.: University Press of America, 1980.

Introductory text on radio and television broadcasting, emphasizing programming aspects.

Sobel, Robert. "Top 40 Revival, New Artists Rock Music Radio." *Television/Radio Age* (29 August 1983):25–27ff.

Assessment of the current trends in radio music, specific format problems and the effects of rock music on MTV.

"Special Reports: Cable." *Broadcasting* (10 May 1982):40–91; (15 November 1982):48–68; (22 November 1982):59–67; (20 June 1983):47–69.

Reports on cable networks, conventions and competitive prospects.

"Special Reports: Children's Television." *Broadcasting* (29 October 1979):39–66.

Overview of federal and industry actions and issues regarding children's television programs.

"Special Reports: Independents." *Broadcasting* (30 January 1978):41–64; (30 October 1978):25–26; (26 February 1979):43–80; (25 January 1982):47–56; (1 February 1982):36–48; (11 October 1982):43–54; (17 January 1983):55–70; (24 January 1983):66–73; (27 June 1983):49–70.

Analyses of the growth of independent television stations, including super-stations, UHFs and programming.

"Special Reports: Journalism." *Broadcasting* (16 November 1981):39–48; (26 July 1982):39–91; (27 September 1982):43–71; (25 July 1983):78–84; (19 September 1983):50–76.

Overview of broadcast news, concentrating on new field equipment.

"Special Reports: Media Corporations." *Broadcasting* (4 January 1982):39–47; (9 May 1983):37–43.

Reports on earnings of publicly owned companies with broadcasting interests.

"Special Reports: Radio." *Broadcasting* (27 September 1976):34–75; (25 July 1977):32–76; (24 July 1978):38–74; (10 September 1979):36–76; (25 August 1980):39–103; (17 August 1981):39–78; (14 December 1981):39–43; (8 February 1982):45–56, 80–88; (8 March 1982):118–28; (6 September 1982):30–40; (20 September 1982):40–51; (27 September 1982):81–82; (4 October 1982):39–47; (11 October 1982):43–54; (15 August 1983):47–52; (29 August 1983):48–104; (5 September 1983):48–66; (19 September 1983):50–56.

Analyses of all aspects of commercial radio broadcasting including programming.

"Special Reports: Reps." *Broadcasting* (4 June 1979):37–62; (2 July 1979):39–63.

Special report on the job of the television station representatives including a new role as programmer for stations; also special report on radio reps.

"Special Reports: Satellites." *Broadcasting* (March 27, 1978):62–68; (19 November 1979):36–47.

Special report on space transmission by MBS, NPR, PBS, the commercial networks and others.

"Special Reports: Sports." *Broadcasting* (13 August 1979):47–52; (1 March 1982):47–52; (9 August 1982):38–49.

Analyses of professional and college sports on television.

Spence, Michael, and Owen, Bruce M. *Television Programming, Monopolistic Competition, and Welfare.* Paper no. 9. Durham, N.C.: Center for the Study of Business Regulation, Graduate School of Business Administration, Duke University, 1977.

Analysis of the biases in program selection arising under pay television and advertiser-supported television using economic modeling.

Stedman, Raymond W. *The Serials: Suspense and Drama by Installment.* 2d ed. Norman: University of Oklahoma Press, 1977.

History of the serial dramatic form in film, radio and television; useful case study of the development of a program genre.

Steinberg, Cobbett. *TV Facts.* New York: Facts on File, Inc., 1980.

Collection of statistical and historical facts on television awards, ratings, programs, viewers, networks, stations and advertisers.

Sterling, Christopher H., and Haight, Timothy R. *The Mass Media: Aspen Institute Guide to Communication Industry Trends.* New York: Praeger, Special Studies, 1978.

Includes 50 pages of historical statistics on content trends in all media with much material on radio and television programming, both public and commercial.

Sterling, Christopher H., and Kittross, John M. *Stay Tuned: A Concise History of American Broadcasting.* Belmont, Calif.: Wadsworth, 1978.

Chronological discussion of periods of radio and television history, with detailed information on programming trends for each period, including statistical tables.

Sterman, Art. "A Look at KABC/ABC TALKRADIO." *Broadcast Engineering* (July 1982):51–59.

An insider's look at the talk format on one station.

Strong, William S. *The Copyright Book: A Practical Guide.* Cambridge, Mass.: The MIT Press, 1981.

Handbook on copyright procedures and legal considerations.

Sugar, Bert Randolph. *"The Thrill of Victory": The Inside Story of ABC Sports.* New York: Hawthorn Books, 1978.

Anecdotal narrative of the people and programming of network television's most successful sports operation.

Surlin, Stuart H. "Black-Oriented Radio: Programming to a Perceived Audience." *Journal of Broadcasting* 16(Summer 1972):289–98.

Based on a study done with an NAB research grant; discussion of the problems of identifying black audiences.

Taflinger, Richard F. "Sitcom: A Survey and Findings of Analysis of the Television Situation Comedy." Ph.D. dissertation, Washington State University, 1980.

Critical analysis of the types and plot content of situation comedies from 1950 to 1978.

The Television Audience. Northbrook, Ill.: A.C. Nielsen Company, 1959 to date, annual.

Trends in television programming and audience viewing patterns.

Television Broadcast Policies: Hearings. Serial 95-60. U.S. Senate, Committee on Commerce, Science and Transportation, May 1977.

Wide-ranging analysis of network program policies for both entertainment and journalistic material.

"Television Programming & Production for Profit." *Broadcasting Management/Engineering,* monthly series, March 1977 to date.

Discussion of programming strategies and techniques, including reports on syndicated programs and features.

Television/Radio Age. 1953 to date.

> *Biweekly trade magazine reporting on advertising and economics of television and radio.*

Television Quarterly 17(Fall 1980).

> *Issue devoted to articles on television.*

"Television: Where WE Earn Our Living!" *Facts, Figures and Film: News for Television Executives* (March 1979).

> *Sixth annual personal finance survey by the Broadcast Information Bureau, Inc., on earnings and job-related conditions of station managers, sales managers and program managers; 19 graphs and tables.*

Thompson, Lawrence D. "Trends and Issues in Commercial Prime Time Television— An Analysis of Network Programming, 1966–1976." Ph.D. dissertation, Michigan State University, 1977.

> *Analysis of the trends at the three networks in prime-time programming using an eight-program typology.*

Tims, Albert R. *Community Attitudes and Preferences Concerning Cable Television Program Services: A Survey of Cable Television Subscribers in Bloomington.* Bloomington, Indiana: Bloomington Telecommunications Council and Horizon Telecommunications, Inc., February 1982.

> *Commissioned report on a survey of subscribers on reasons for subscribing and satisfaction with services.*

Tramer, Harriet, and Jeffries, Leo W. "Talk Radio—Forum and Companion." *Journal of Broadcasting* 27(Summer 1983):297–300.

> *Report of a survey of callers to three radio talk shows investigating their motivation for calling.*

Tuchman, Gaye. *Making News: A Study in the Construction of Reality.* New York: The Free Press, 1978.

> *Sociological analysis of print and broadcast journalism process and product.*

Tuchman, Gaye, ed. *The TV Establishment: Programming for Power and Profit.* Englewood Cliffs, N.J.: Prentice-Hall, 1974.

> *Critical anthology of journalistic and research articles on news and entertainment network programming.*

Turow, Joseph. "Talk Show Radio as Interpersonal Communication." *Journal of Broadcasting* 18(Spring 1974):171–79.

> *Report of study of radio talk show callers to WCAU, Philadelphia in the spring of 1973.*

Variety. 1925 to date.

> *Weekly trade newspaper covering the stage and the film, television and recording industries, focusing on production.*

Veith, Richard. *Talk-Back TV: Two Way Cable Television.* Blue Ridge Summit, Pa.: TAB Books, 1976.

Informal assessment of pay cable and interview cable emphasizing technology and content.

View: The Magazine of Cable TV Programming. 1979 to date.

Monthly trade magazine on cable system, network and local origination programming, including economics, technology and regulation.

Virts, Paul H. "Television Entertainment Gatekeeping: A Study of Local Television Program Directors' Decision-Making." Ph.D. dissertation, University of Iowa, 1979.

Analysis of types of decision makers based on strategies used in purchase and retention of a hypothetical syndicated program series by 28 midwestern station programmers.

von Ladau, Philip F. "Ratings: An Aid to Programming and Purchase of Properties." *Broadcast Financial Journal* (March 1976):36–42.

Elementary guide to the use of ratings in programming a television station.

Wahlstrom, Fred. "Superstations' Spur Growth of Cable TV," *P.D. Cue* (January 1979):18–24.

Description of the influence of superstations, particularly WTBS-TV, on the growth in numbers of cable subscribers.

Wakshlag, Jacob J. "Programming Strategies and Television Program Popularity for Children." Ph.D. dissertation, Michigan State University, 1977.

Quantitative analysis of the characteristics that predict children's program popularity with other children.

Wakshlag, Jacob J.; Agostino, Donald E.; Terry, Herbert A.; Driscoll, Paul; and Ramsey, Bruce. "Television News Viewing and Network Affiliation Changes," *Journal of Broadcasting* 27 (Winter 1983):53–68.

Analysis of audience flow and repeat viewing of news based on ratings before and after network affiliation changes.

Wakshlag, Jacob J., and Greenberg, Bradley S. "Programming Strategies and the Popularity of Television Programs for Children." *Human Communication Research* 6(Fall 1979):58–68.

A quantitative study investigating the effects of various programming strategies commonly employed by the networks on program popularity for children.

Wald, Richard C. "Possible Courses for News and Public Affairs." *Public Telecommunications Review* 6(May/June 1978):50–57.

An abridgement of the author's report to the Programming Committee of the PBS Board.

Warren, Edward A. "Programming for a Commercial Station." In *Television Station Management*, ed. by Yale Roe. New York: Hastings House, 1964.

Collection of 17 articles by professional broadcasters emphasizing programming and sales management; this chapter covers commercial television station programming practices.

Webster, James G. *Audience Research*. Washington, D.C.: National Association of Broadcasters, 1983.

Primer on basic research methods for broadcasters.

Webster, James G., and Saxon, Judy. *Audience Research: A Workbook*. Washington, D.C.: National Association of Broadcasters, 1983.

Practice in understanding the concepts of ratings and research for broadcasters.

Webster, James G., and Wakshlag, Jacob J. "A Theory of Television Program Choice." *Communication Research,* in press, 1984.

Proposes a model of television viewing behavior combining research into the effects of scheduling.

Wells, William D. *Life Style and Psychographics*. New York: American Marketing Association, 1974.

Classic report of industry research on audience and consumer lifestyles.

Williams, Wenmouth, Jr., and Krugman, Dean M. "Innovativeness and the Public Radio Audience." *Journal of Broadcasting* 25 (Winter 1981):61–69.

Results of a mail survey that did not demonstrate a relationship between innovativeness and listening to public radio.

Wimmer, Roger D., and Dominick, Joseph R. *Mass Media Research: An Introduction*. Belmont, California: Wadsworth, 1983.

Text on research methods in mass media, emphasizing broadcasting; includes survey methods and ratings.

Wirth, Michael O., and Wollert, James A. "Public Interest Programming: FCC Standards and Station Performance." *Journalism Quarterly* 55(Autumn 1978): 554–61.

Analysis of 1975 programming data to determine the effect on network affiliates of the FCC's 5-5-10 rule (5 percent local, 5 percent informational, 10 percent nonentertainment).

Wolf, Frank. *Television Programming for News and Public Affairs: A Quantitative Analysis of Networks and Stations*. New York: Praeger, 1972.

A research study of factors affecting the quantity and proportion of news and public affairs programming on commercial television stations.

Wolper, David L., and Troupe, Quincy. *The Inside Story of TV's 'Roots.'* New York: Warner Books, 1978.

Network television's most-watched special series, showing planning, production and network decision-making stages.

Wurtzel, Alan. "Public-Access Cable TV: Programming." *Journal of Communication* 25(Summer 1975):15–21.

An analysis of public access programming on New York City cable channels.

Yellin, David G. *Special: Fred Freed and the Television Documentary*. New York: Macmillan, 1973.

Study of the late NBC executive producer's day-to-day decisions and influence.

Zoglin, Richard. "Program Testing—Support or Scapegoat?" *New York Times* (23 July 1978):D25.

Overview of the current industry program testing methods used by the networks, research firms and program consultants.

Zuckerman, Laurence, and Brown, Les. "Autumn of the Networks' Reign." *Channels* (September–October 1983):45–48.

Insiders' analysis of the effects of cable and independent television station audience shares on the power of the three commercial television networks.

Index to Program Titles

This is a guide to specific television, radio and cable **programs** and **movies** mentioned in the text. Cable, radio and television **networks** appear in the General Index.

General Index

Definitions and major text references appear in **boldface.**

WITHDRAWN